Philosophy and Salvation in Greek Religion

Religionsgeschichtliche
Versuche und Vorarbeiten

Herausgegeben von
Jörg Rüpke und Christoph Uehlinger

Band 60

De Gruyter

Philosophy and Salvation in Greek Religion

Edited by
Vishwa Adluri

De Gruyter

ISBN 978-3-11-055214-0
e-ISBN 978-3-11-027638-1
ISSN 0939-2580

Library of Congress Cataloging-in-Publication Data

A CIP catalog record for this book has been applied for at the Library of Congress.

Bibliografische Information der Deutschen Nationalbibliothek

Die Deutsche Nationalbibliothek verzeichnet diese Publikation in der Deutschen Nationalbibliografie; detaillierte bibliografische Daten sind im Internet über http://dnb.dnb.de abrufbar.

© 2017 Walter de Gruyter GmbH, Berlin/Boston
Dieser Band ist text- und seitenidentisch mit der 2013 erschienenen gebundenen Ausgabe.

Druck: Hubert & Co. GmbH & Co. KG, Göttingen
♾ Gedruckt auf säurefreiem Papier
Printed in Germany
www.degruyter.com

*Dedicated to
my teacher Seth Benardete*

Acknowledgments

This book would not have been possible without the support of many. I owe a debt of gratitude to all my collaborators on this project, who participated in rethinking the question of Greek philosophical soteriology. In particular, I thank in particular Prof. Luc Brisson for his encouragement of this idea and colleagues and co-presenters at the International Society for Neoplatonic Studies John Finamore, John Bussanich, and Svetla Slaveva-Griffin. I would further like to thank two people Joydeep Bagchee and Matt Newman, whose assistance was vital to the success of this book. Matt Newman provided the detailed word studies of terms pertaining to soteriology in Plato's *Republic* that were so crucial to making my argument in both the introduction and my contribution. Joydeep Bagchee worked tirelessly to provide an index in a short period of time for the book. I thank Joachim Eichner, Thomas Komarek, and my family for their love and endless patience as I worked on this book. At a critical time in my philosophical journey, Sara Rappe challenged me to rethink received wisdom in Greek philology. For this, I owe her a debt of gratitude. Last but not least, I thank Albrecht Döhnert, Senior Editor at Walter de Gruyter, and Series Editor Prof. Jörg Rüpke for including this volume in the RGVV series.

Vishwa Adluri

Abbreviations

A & A	Antike und Abendland: Beiträge zum Verständnis der Griechen und Römer und ihres Nachlebens
AC	L'Antiquité Classique
AE	Archaiologike Ephemeris
AGPh	Archiv für Geschichte der Philosophie
AION (filol)	Annali dell'Istituto Universitario Orientale di Napoli, Dipartimento di Studi del Mondo classico e del Mediterraneo antico, Sezione filologico-letteraria
AJPh	American Journal of Philology
AncPhil	Ancient Philosophy
AOF	Archiv für Orientforschung
AS	Anatolian Studies: Journal of the British Institute of Archaeology at Ankara
BCH	Bulletin de correspondance hellénique
BICS	Bulletin of the Institute of Classical Studies of the University of London
CCC	Civiltà classica e cristiana
CFC(G)	Cuadernos de filología clásica (Estudios griegos e indoeuropeos)
CJ	The Classical Journal
CPh	Classical Philology
CQ	Classical Quarterly
CR	Classical Review
GRBS	Greek, Roman and Byzantine Studies
HSCP	Harvard Studies in Classical Philology
Jahrb. f. class. Phil.	Jahrbücher für classische Philologie
Journ. of Cuneif. Studies	Journal of Cuneiform Studies
JHS	Journal of Hellenic Studies
MH	Museum Helveticum: revue suisse pour l'étude de l'Antiquité classique
OSAPh	Oxford Studies in Ancient Philosophy
PP	La Parola del passato: rivista di studi antichi
QUCC	Quaderni urbinati di cultura classica

REG	Revue des études grecques
RA	Revue archéologique
RhM	Rheinisches Museum
RMeta	Review of Metaphysics
RPhA	Revue de philosophie ancienne
SIFC	Studi italiani di filologia classica
SMSR	Studi e materiali di storia delle religioni
TAPhA	Transactions of the American Philological Association
TAPhS	Transactions of the American Philosophical Society
ZPE	Zeitschrift für Papyrologie und Epigraphik

Contents

Vishwa Adluri
Philosophy, Salvation, and the Mortal Condition 1

Miguel Herrero de Jáuregui
Salvation for the Wanderer: Odysseus, the Gold Leaves, and
Empedocles 29

Arbogast Schmitt
Self-Determination and Freedom: The Relationship of God and
Man in Homer. Translated by Joydeep Bagchee 59

Walter Burkert
Parmenides' Proem and Pythagoras' Descent. Translated by
Joydeep Bagchee 85

Alberto Bernabé
Ὁ Πλάτων παρωιδεῖ τὰ Ὀρφέως Plato's Transposition of Orphic
Netherworld Imagery 117

Barbara Sattler
The Eleusinian Mysteries in Pre-Platonic Thought: Metaphor,
Practice and Imagery for Plato's *Symposium* 151

Stephen Menn
Plato's Soteriology? 191

Vishwa Adluri & John Lenz
From Politics to Salvation through Philosophy: Herodotus'
Histories and Plato's *Republic* 217

John Bussanich
Rebirth Eschatology in Plato and Plotinus 243

Luc Brisson
Memory and the Soul's Destiny in Plotinus. Translated by
Michael Chase 289

Svetla Slaveva-Griffin
Between the Two Realms: Plotinus' Pure Soul 313

John Finamore
Iamblichus, Theurgy, and the Soul's Ascent 343
About the Contributors 357
Bibliography 361
Index of terms 387

Philosophy, Salvation, and the Mortal Condition
Vishwa Adluri

I. Philosophy and Theology

In 1959 Gregory Vlastos published an article titled "Theology and Philosophy in Early Greek Thought."[1] In it he wrote, "When one reads the pre-Socratics with open mind and sensitive ear one cannot help being struck by the religious note in much of what they say. Few words occur more frequently in their fragments than the term 'god'.... In Parmenides and Empedocles the whole doctrine of Being and Nature is put forth as religious revelation."[2] Vlastos was arguing against Burnet, who in his *Early Greek Philosophy* had proposed that the word "θεός" in the writings of the Ionian philosophers ought not mislead us as to the secular nature of their work. Burnet argued that "there had been a complete break with Aegean religion" by the time of the φυσικοί; and hence declared forthrightly: "It is therefore quite wrong to look for the origins of Ionian science in mythological ideas of any kind."[3]

Contra Burnet, Vlastos argued that the Presocratics believed that their concept of nature found in it "not only the principles of physical explanation, but also the key to the right ordering of human life and the answer to the problem of destiny. They began with the faith that nature itself was animated by that Wisdom and Justice which the most enlightened conscience of their race had imputed to Zeus. So long as this faith lived they could transfer to nature the reverence hitherto reserved for Zeus and could therefore call nature 'god' without indulging in an empty figure of speech."[4]

---

1 Gregory Vlastos, "Theology and Philosophy in Early Greek Thought," *The Philosophical Quarterly* 2.7 (1952): 97–123.
2 Ibid., 97.
3 John Burnet, *Early Greek Philosophy* (London: Adam and Charles Black, 1892 [with successive reprints]), 13.
4 Vlastos 1952, 100.

Vlastos' investigations into the nature and meaning of the Greeks' use of terms such as "θεός" or "θεολογία" brought to light a fundamental problem, and a puzzle. When contemporary scholars since modernity have rejected Greek eschatological concerns as a significant part of their philosophy, they were often doing so as a reaction against their own experience of Christianity. Nietzsche famously claimed Christianity was nothing but "Platonism for the masses." Much of his rejection of Plato or Platonism stems from this view. Thus, while in many ways he saw himself as committed to a recovery and revival of the Greeks, his reading of Plato remained colored by his polemics against Christianity. Likewise, one could show of a number of historically influential interpretations of Plato in contemporary thought (e.g., Heidegger or other "post-metaphysical" thinkers) that their views on ancient philosophy are rooted in theological debates implicit to Christianity.[5]

The problem becomes especially acute when speaking of Greek views of "salvation," because our tendency is immediately to interpret "salvation" on analogy with Christian ideas of the afterlife and of heaven, and hence to reject Greek eschatology. Burnet's resistance toward the idea that Ionian science might still have something in common with archaic religion is a paradigmatic example of how scholarship often projected its need for a strictly scientific worldview onto antiquity.[6] The rejection of Platonic thought as espousing a "two-world theory" is another instance of how our need to affirm certain ideas, namely, our existence here and now,[7] has shaped our reception of the ancients. But what if the two conceptions, i.e., Christian and Greek eschatology, had only the name in common? What if Greek "salvation" bespoke a radically different experience than the one we, influenced by two millennia of Christian upbringing, have come to expect and to associate with the term? The problem when speaking of "philosophy and salvation in Greek religion" is thus not simply recognizing that salvation is a necessary component of Greek philosophy, one we must grant as being

---

5   On Heidegger's theologically influenced approach to ancient philosophy, see my "Heidegger's Encounter with Aristotle: A Theological Deconstruction of Metaphysics," *Proceedings of the Forty-Fourth Annual Meeting of the Heidegger Circle*, Stony Brook University, May 2010.

6   This view still persists; see, for example, Anthony Gottlieb's popular survey *The Dream of Reason: A History of Philosophy from the Greeks to the Renaissance* (New York: W. W. Norton & Company, 2000).

7   A concept Heidegger refers to as "*Diesseitigkeit*"; Schmitt traces this interest in an immanent account to Duns Scotus, see n. 11 below.

just as legitimate as Christian salvation. Rather, the problem is that the relationship of philosophy to salvation first needs to be posed as a *question*. What *is* the relation of philosophy to salvation?

Once we set aside our aversion to talking of "salvation" (which aversion I argue is itself a residue of our Christian inheritance), a rich field of inquiry opens up. Can and ought philosophy be at all concerned with eschatology? What role does salvation play within a philosophical theory? What are the ways, historically speaking, in which salvation has been conceived of? What are the preparatory techniques (e. g., ritual initiation, learning of secret formulae, carrying of tokens, etc.) considered efficacious in its achievement? Most importantly, to what extent were these cultic practices informed by philosophical models of Being or of the cosmos? These are some of the questions the present volume attempts to address.

As scholars we are now more aware of the issues involved in our reception of ancient authors. The emphasis on the situatedness of every interpretation in the hermeneutic theories of the past century has contributed significantly to an awareness of the problems with a naïve historicism. We have learnt also to become suspicious of an Enlightenment narrative of history. In the field of classics, for example, Walter Burkert's seminal study of katabatic elements in Parmenidean and Pythagorean thought demonstrated that scholars were wrong to interpret the journey of the Parmenidean κοῦρος as an ascent to the light, allegedly a metaphor for his "Enlightenment" from ignorance to knowledge.[8] Rather, Burkert advocated relating Parmenides' journey to ritual descent, and hence to a feature of archaic religion. The work of Kingsley has also challenged the view that the presence of ritual and mythic elements in the philosophical traditions of late antiquity is evidence of degeneracy, allegedly due to "Orientalizing" influences, and of a fall away from the "rationalism" of Platonic and Aristotelian philosophy.[9] We now benefit from a wide range of theoretical approaches, including analytic, literary, aesthetic, and philological approaches.[10] Careful studies

---

8 Walter Burkert, "Das Proömium des Parmenides und die Katabasis des Pythagoras," *Phronesis* 14 (1969): 1–30.
9 See his *Ancient Philosophy, Mystery and Magic: Empedocles and Pythagorean Tradition* (Oxford: Oxford University Press, 1995) and *In the Dark Places of Wisdom* (Inverness, CA: The Golden Sufi Center, 1999).
10 The analytic approach was established by Gregory Vlastos, and relies on applying the techniques of contemporary analytic philosophy to Plato's dialogues. It is thus often opposed to a literary approach, which focuses more on dramatic

by Arbogast Schmitt and his students of the reception of Plato in late antiquity and modernity have alerted us to some of the problems with our contemporary reception.[11] Even a cursory glance at Richard Kraut's excellent companion to Plato shows how rich and multifaceted contemporary scholarship on Platonic philosophy is.[12] And yet, in spite of significant recent work on the Orphic traditions[13] and the Derveni papyrus,[14] we are yet to thematize the relationship of philosophy to the eschatological/soteriological traditions of antiquity. How does the study of the Gold Leaves, for example, contribute to an understanding of ancient man's views of soul and of its destiny? How do Presocratic cosmologies relate to their ethics? And how does the emergence of more formal philosophical accounts impact these older traditions?

---

context and literary motifs or references. Among contemporary representatives of the former are Julia Annas (see especially her studies of Plato) and Gail Fine (see her studies of Aristotle and on Aristotle's relationship to Plato). The literary approach is most often identified with the work of Leo Strauss; Stanley Rosen may be considered a contemporary representative. Christopher Janaway and Stephen Halliwell are two scholars who have focused on Plato's aesthetics. Strauss' student Benardete advocated a literary reading with attention to philological detail. Other scholars such as Kenneth Sayre, who pays attention to both the quality of arguments and the dramatic context, or Debra Nails, who combines historical, biographical, and dramatic approaches, span different schools. The recently published *Continuum Companion to Plato*, ed. Gerald A. Press (London: Continuum, 2012) provides a good overview of the different theoretical approaches in contemporary scholarship.

11 See Arbogast Schmitt, *Modernity and Plato: Two Paradigms of Rationality*, trans. Vishwa Adluri (Rochester: Camden House, 2012) with a good bibliography of his students' works.

12 Richard Kraut, ed. *The Cambridge Companion to Plato* (Cambridge: Cambridge University Press, 1992).

13 Alberto Bernabé, *Poetae Epici Graeci testimonia et fragmenta* II (fasc. 1–2, Monachii et Lipsiae: Teubner; fasc. 3, Berolini-Novi Eboraci: De Gruyter, 2004–2007); Miguel Herrero de Jaúregui et al., eds. *Tracing Orpheus: Studies of Orphic Fragments* (Berlin: De Gruyter, 2011).

14 The text and translation has recently become available in two editions: Gabor Betegh, *The Derveni Papyrus: Cosmology, Theology, and Interpretation* (Cambridge: Cambridge University Press, 2004) and Theokritos Kouremenos, George M. Parássoglou, Kyriakos Tsantsanoglou, *The Derveni Papyrus: Edited with Introduction and Commentary* (Florence: Casa Editrice Leo S. Olschki, 2006). See also the edited volume *Studies on the Derveni Papyrus*, ed. André Laks and Glenn W. Most (New York: Oxford University Press, 1997); and the *Proceedings of the Derveni Papyrus Conference*, published as *Classics@* 5 and accessible via the website of the Center for Hellenic Studies (http://chs.harvard.edu/).

Recent work by Edmonds[15] and Graf/Johnston[16] has contributed richly to our understanding of the Gold Leaves, small tablets inscribed with instructions for the initiate on what he must do in the Underworld to attain salvation. The researches of Primavesi, Janko and others have shown that Empedocles' cosmology, once thought to be independent of his religious/purificatory concerns, is closely related to the latter: the key philosophical concern that holds these two together and articulates their relation is the concern with human salvation.[17] We know from the researches of Riedweg that Plato systematically uses the language and structure of the mysteries in his dialogues.[18] Two recent studies by Luc Brisson have shown how naïve it is to assume that Plato's use of myths represents an accidental oversight, a sign of being unable to achieve sufficient conceptual clarity.[19]

The purpose of the present volume, however, is both different and much more modest. It does not aim to propound a new approach to ancient texts. Nor does it claim to overcome the perspectives and prejudices of our contemporary reception. Rather, its object is to clarify the initial ground from which we might raise the question of the relationship of Greek religion to Greek philosophy, and to do so specifically with a view to seeing what might be gained for contemporary philosophy in terms of an ontology. If eschatology is no longer approached from the perspective of Revelation, but from the perspective of the individual and his ultimate concern, how must it now be thought? Thus,

---

15 Radcliffe G. Edmonds, ed., *The "Orphic" Gold Tablets and Greek Religion: Further Along the Path* (Cambridge: Cambridge University Press, 2011).
16 Fritz Graf and Sarah Iles-Johnston, *Ritual Texts for the Afterlife: Orpheus and the Bacchic Gold Tablets* (London: Routledge, 2007).
17 Alain Martin and Oliver Primavesi, *L' Empédocle de Strasbourg* (Berlin: De Gruyter, 1999); Richard Janko "Empedocles' *On Nature* I 233–364: A New Reconstruction of *P. Strasb.* Inv. 1665–6," *PE* 150 (2005): 1–26; but see Jean Bollack, opposed, in "Empedocles: Two Theologies, Two Projects," in *The Empedoclean Kosmos: Structure, Process and the Question of Cyclicity. Proceedings of the Symposium Philosophiae Antiquae Tertium Myconense July 6th – July 13th, 2003*, part 1: Papers, ed. Apostolos L. Pierris (Patras: Institute for Philosophical Research, 2005), 45–72.
18 Christoph Riedweg, *Mysterienterminologie bei Platon, Philon und Klemens von Alexandrien* (Berlin: De Gruyter, 1987).
19 See his *Plato the Myth Maker*, trans. Gerard Naddaf (Chicago: University of Chicago Press, 1998) and *How Philosophers Saved Myths: Allegorical Interpretation and Classical Mythology*, trans. Catherine Tihanyi (Chicago: University of Chicago Press, 2004).

the task as I see it is to set aside a theological frame of reference, and to approach the question of salvation from the perspective of what we might call a "philosophical soteriology." This tradition combines initiatory ritual and near-death experience, myth and mantic insight with rational, philosophical inquiry—that is to say, with investigations into cosmology, epistemology, and ethics. In contrast to contemporary Western philosophy, it does not separate theory from praxis, and its goal is not purely propositional knowledge. Rather, it aims to bring about a philosophical transformation, leading the initiate from his mortal existence to immortal Being: "I, in your eyes a deathless god, no longer mortal, go among all," declares Empedocles (frag. B112).[20] I would like to clarify this task in two stages: first, I will develop a few key terms such as philosophy, theology, philology, religion, God, salvation, etc. below, and then I will discuss what I consider the key elements of philosophical soteriology.

II. Salvation for the Philosopher

Philosophy for us "moderns" has taken on the dimensions of an abstract conceptual science. It is systematic thinking, based on arguments, and an inquiry undertaken for its own sake. Although we do make space for its application (e.g., in political science, political theory, ethics, or aesthetics), in the main philosophy remains an abstract and theoretical activity for us. But this definition of philosophy leaves out a small but nonetheless vital area of ancient philosophy, i.e., the inquiry into what we might call man's "ultimate concern." Here, as I argued in my recent book, we find contemporary philosophy to be seriously lacking.[21] We have displaced the task of positing ultimate referents from philosophy to theology or, where we find theology to be unsatisfying, to technology.[22]

---

20 The text and translation follows Inwood, see *The Poem of Empedocles: A Text and Translation with an Introduction* (Toronto: University of Toronto Press, 2001), 211.
21 Vishwa Adluri, *Parmenides, Plato and Mortal Philosophy: Return from Transcendence* (London: Continuum, 2011).
22 I have analyzed technology as a form of metaphysics in my book on Parmenides (see previous note). Technology, by covering over φύσις and making us forget θυμός, appears as an antidote to both the fatal temporality of Becoming and to our mortality. But this antidote is merely a seduction.

But there is also a form of philosophical inquiry that is undertaken neither for the sake of constructing the ideal city nor for the sake of knowing God. This philosophy begins with the experience of being mortal, and is wholly addressed to its concerns. In ancient thought, there is no notion of philosophy as an activity undertaken for its own sake.[23] Philosophy is always tied to the mortal condition, and pursued as a cure for it: "I am afraid that other people do not realize that the one aim of those who practice philosophy in the proper manner is to practice for dying and death," Socrates tells Cebes and Simias in the *Phaedo* (64a). The philosopher lives and sleeps only with his body in the city (*Theaet.* 173e), and his entire effort is aimed at making an escape, which means to become "as like God as possible" (176b).

Likewise, in any inquiry into Greek notions of salvation, we must begin by setting apart philosophy from theology.[24] Walter Burkert in his "Platon oder Pythagoras? Zum Ursprung des Wortes 'Philosophie'"[25] remarks that "the claim of the prophet and the consciousness of the limit [Grenzbewußtsein] of the philosopher mutually exclude each other."[26] Fragments such as B112 attest to theories of self-transformation, of becoming immortal, probably through the practice of purifications.[27] And yet, here too the starting point is the mortal condition: Empedocles describes himself as an exile and a wanderer, thrust out of his heavenly home and longing to return. The longing for "salvation" expressed herein is very different from theology as we know it; its prop-

---

[23] Even Aristotle, who would seem to be an exception to this rule (cf. *Met.* A.2 982a5–983a10), would not accept the contemporary view of philosophy as an activity performed for its own sake. In Aristotle, philosophy is pursued because it is productive of εὐδαιμονία, and because it enables man to become as like the immortals as possible insofar as this is possible for him qua mortal man (see *EN* K.7–9).

[24] I am aware of how strange this must sound, since in ancient thought there was no terminological distinction between "philosophy" and what we might call "theology." Aristotle calls "θεολογία" "πρώτη φιλοσοφία" ("first philosophy"). What I mean, of course, is that we must set apart philosophy from dogmatic notions of God, of salvation, and of the doctrine of salvation.

[25] Walter Burkert, "Platon oder Pythagoras? Zum Ursprung des Wortes 'Philosophie'," *Hermes* 88.2 (1960): 159–77.

[26] Ibid., 177.

[27] As does the *Theaetetus* passage cited above. But the goal of ὁμοίωσις θεῷ does not refer to becoming like the God revealed in Revelation but "just and pious, with understanding," The means of this "becoming like" is not faith, but the pursuit of rational inquiry and self-knowledge.

er sphere appears to be what I have elsewhere called a philosophy of "mortal singularity."[28]

The term "theology" is not foreign to the Greeks. Plato in the *Republic* uses "θεολογία" (*Rep.* 379a), and Werner Jaeger considers it to have been coined by him.[29] But as Vlastos points out, the word is used in a rather disparaging sense; it is "introduced by Adeimantus (not Socrates) as a variant for 'tales about the gods'. The casualness with which [it] is used here and in *Laws* X ... suggests that it was in common use at the time."[30] Even if we accept Jaeger's suggestion, the word does not seem to acquire terminological significance until Aristotle, who speaks of θεολογική φιλοσοφία or ἐπιστήμη, and identifies this science with "first philosophy" (πρώτη φιλοσοφία, *Met.* A.1 and E.1).[31] Even then, the notion of what Aristotle means is contested. While at times his first philosophy is identified with the science that studies Being *qua* Being, this is still different from the dogmatic discipline that studies a *summum ens*. While there are unmistakable parallels at times, this is due to the fact that later Christian theologians, above all Aquinas, drew heavily on Aristotle's conceptual vocabulary, not because Aristotle himself entertained notions similar to that of the Christian monotheistic God. To speak of Greek theological salvation hence seems to be a far more problematic venture than to speak of Greek philosophical salvation.

For similar reasons, I find it preferable to eschew the use of "religious salvation." Perhaps even more so than "theology," no word is as anachronistic as "religion" in speaking of ancient beliefs about gods, soul, or the afterlife. Even though we commonly apply the word "religion" as a collective term for all forms of belief about the soul or afterlife, for worship of natural forces or divinities, and for every doctrine of divinity, the Latin "*religio*" bespeaks a specific experience. It cannot be translated unproblematically into Greek. Among terms that roughly correspond to the term in Greek, the following in

---

28 See n. 21 above.
29 Werner W. Jaeger, *The Theology of the Early Greek Philosophers* (Oxford: Clarendon, 1947).
30 Vlastos 1952, 102, n.22.
31 Debates about what exactly constitutes Aristotelian first philosophy are manifold, with many scholars arguing that Aristotle himself did not have in mind a single homogenous discipline. One scholar who defends the unity of the *Metaphysics* is Giovanni Reale, *The Concept of First Philosophy and the Unity of the Metaphysics of Aristotle*, trans. John R. Catan (Albany, NY: SUNY Press, 1980).

particular have been suggested: θεῶν τιμή, νόμος, εὐσέβια, αἰδώς, and even δεισιδαιμονία. The public and ritual aspects of Greek "religion" as we know are usually circumscribed with the terms λατρεία, θεραπεία, and (rarely) θρησκεία. If Greek gods play a role in salvation it is almost always via the salvation seeker being initiated into the cult of a specific god or goddess, and not through the mere fact of identifying with a religion.[32]

To us, conditioned by our historical experience, salvation has an intrinsic and necessary connection to God or at least to his intermediary in Christ, as is shown by the fact that the term "soteriology" or "doctrine of salvation" was for a long time used interchangeably with "Christology" (i.e., the doctrine of the person and the work of Christ).[33] In 17th century academic theology, where the term "soteriology" originated,[34] it was used to refer to the doctrine of the savior and of salvation, but no strict terminological or systematic distinction could be made from "Christology," since the term itself derived from the use of "σωτήρ" as a title for Jesus in the NT. But when speaking of Greek notions, it is best to set aside these expectations of a connection to God or his Son. The Greeks have no exact equivalent to our notion of "God" which draws on Abrahamic notions of divinity, and attempts to relate the Greek notions to ours (as has been attempted, for example by Étienne Gilson in his book *God and Philosophy*[35]) are more often than

---

32 On the esoteric character of ancient religious practice, see the useful essays by Jan M. Bremmer, "Religious Secrets and Secrecy in Classical Greece," and Walter Burkert, "Der geheime Reiz des Verborgenen. Antike Mysterienkulte," both in *Secrecy and Concealment in Ancient and Islamic History of Religions*, ed. Hans G. Kippenberg and Guy G. Stroumsa (Leiden: Brill, 1995), 61–78 and 79–100.
33 For both terms (and the related "eschatology"), see the relevant entries in *Historisches Wörterbuch der Philosophie*, ed. Joachim Ritter and Karlfried Gründer, vols. 1, 2, and 9 (Basel: Schwabe, 1971, 1972, and 1995).
34 Perhaps the earliest recorded usage (in the form σωτηροποιία) is to be found in Abraham Calov, *Theologia positiva, per definitiones causas, affectiones, et distinctiones, Locos Theologicos universos, succincte justoque ordine proponens, ceu compendium Systematis Theologici* (Wittebergae: Schrödter, 1682).
35 Étienne Gilson, *God and Philosophy*, 2nd ed. (New Haven CT: Yale University Press, 2002). Gilson resorts to a teleological or developmental account, where Greek notions are interpreted as but partial realizations of the concept of a God whose proper name is "HE WHO IS," "the God of Abraham, of Isaac, and of Jacob" and whose "very essence ... is 'to be'" (ibid., 144, capitalization in original). This concept for Gilson is properly fulfilled not even in Augustine, but only in Aquinas.

not problematic. This is not to deny that a rich synthesis between Greek philosophy and the Judaic faith took place in late antiquity and the Renaissance, above all, in the work of Augustine, producing much of what we today recognize as Christianity. But nonetheless, the question of Greek notions of salvation cannot be approached via a theological avenue. Newly arrived souls in the Underworld, to be sure, invoke Persephone, and Socrates in the *Phaedo* has Crito promise to sacrifice a cock to Asclepius (118a). And yet, both these practices must be seen against the background of the specific anthropology that gives rise to them. In Socrates' case, the body is seen as a source of ills (*Phaedo* 66b-d, *Rep.* 611b-612a), and the salvation the god provides is liberation from the body (see also *Phaedrus* 246b-249a). This is very different from the bodily resurrection promised in the Apostles' Creed and the Nicene Creed of AD 381.

Finally, what justification is there for speaking of "eschatology" in Greek thought? Like "soteriology," this term too is attributed to the Lutheran theologian Abraham Calov in his *Systematis locorum theologicorum* of 1677[36] where it denoted the final portion of Christian dogmatics dealing with death, resurrection, and the Last Judgment. We might argue that the use of both terms thus is an anachronism. Clearly, neither term can be used without the appropriate qualifications, since a doctrine of τὰ ἔσχατα, the last things or the last days,[37] has a very different meaning in the Christian context than it might have in the Greek context. At best, it might be used in the latter context as a shorthand for referring to afterlife beliefs or experiences, since a truly eschatological worldview would be foreign to Greek thought. In Empedocles, the creation of the cosmos is subject to the coming together and separation of the elements in an endless cycle under the twin impulses of Love and Strife. In Parmenides, Being and Coming-to-be are separated by a gulf; the goddess says of Being that it *is*, and neither was it in the past nor will it come to be. Likewise, Plato in the *Timaeus* makes a distinction between that

---

36 Abraham Calov, *Systematis locorum theologicorum* (Wittebergae: Excudebat Johannes Wilkius, 1677).

37 I am not clear on Calov's original reference, since I was unable to access a copy of his *Systematis locorum theologicorum*. Calov may have had in mind John 6:39, 40, and 44 ([ἐν] τῇ ἐσχάτῃ ἡμέρᾳ) or John 2:18 (ἐσχάτη ὥρα). For similar phrases, see also Peter 1:5, Jude 1:10 and 1:18, Acts 2:17, James 5:3, 2, Timothy 3:1. For ἔσχατον, ἔσχατα used as reference to the time immediately preceding Christ's return, see Hebrews 1:2, 2 Peter 3:3, 1 Peter 1:20, Jude 1:18, Matthew 12:45, Luke 11:26, 2 Peter 2:20.

which always is and has no becoming and that which becomes but never is (27d–28a). Of the universe, Timaeus says that it has come to be (28b), but Plato does not address the issue of its eternality in time or, indeed, of its end. In spite of all the objections Aristotle raises against the theory of the origination of the universe of the *Timaeus* (*Phys.* 251b14–26), he accepts that motion must be eternal (251b29–252b7).

Eschatology in the contemporary sense is thus ruled out in Greek thought. Even though Calov's term invokes the Greek ἔσχατον, its use gives complete new content to the Greek word. The Greek does have the meanings of "last," "to the end," "finally," "in the end."[38] But its use is never charged with the theological significance it later has as part of Christian dogmatics, where it not only refers to that portion of Christian dogmatics traditionally called "*De novissimis*" or "*De extremis*," but also to a very specific ideal of what constitutes the "last things," namely, death, judgment, heaven, and hell. Because the use of "eschatology" is much more laden with Christian presuppositions and hence only applicable to Greek thought in a metaphorical sense, I will set aside this term here. I propose instead "soteriology" as a possible way of speaking about the Greek understanding of the ultimate concerns of mortals, although the use of this term first needs to be justified and elaborated.

III. Soteriology in Plato's *Republic*

Can one at least justify the use of the term "soteriology" when speaking of Greek notions of salvation? In one sense, the use of this term is plainly an anachronism. In spite of its Greek morphology (deriving from σωτηρία or "deliverance, safety"[39]), the word, as we have seen, first makes its appearance in academic theology of the 17th century. It becomes widely established only by the 19th century. Nonetheless, if we set aside our expectations of soteriology as the name of a subdiscipline of Christian dogmatics, one could argue for extending the use of the term to Greek philosophy as well, since Greek authors do make use of the term σωτηρία and related terms such as σωτήρ and σῴζειν. Plato's *Republic* may serve here as an example.[40]

---

38 LSJ, s.v. "ἔσχατον."
39 LSJ, s.v. "σωτηρία."
40 One could also have examined other terms such as νόστος in Homer, but this has recently been studied in exemplary detail by Anna Bonifazi ("Inquiring into

The term σωτήρ occurs five times in the *Republic*;[41] I first list the occurrences:

> "And would not such a man be disdainful of wealth too in his youth, but the older he grew the more he would love it because of his participation in the covetous nature and because his virtue is not sincere and pure since it lacks the best guardian?" "What guardian?" said Adeimantus. "Reason," said I, "blended with culture, which is the only indwelling *preserver* [σωτήρ] of virtue throughout life in the soul that possesses it." "Well said," he replied. "This is the character," I said, "of the timocratic youth, resembling the city that bears his name." (549a–b)

> "Well, then, there are to be found in other cities rulers and the people as in it, are there not?" "There are." "Will not all these address one another as fellow-citizens?" "Of course." "But in addition to citizens, what does the people in other states call its rulers." "In most cities, masters. In democratic cities, just this, rulers." "But what of the people in our city. In addition to citizens, what do they call their rulers?" "*Saviors* [Σωτῆράς] and helpers," he said. (463a–b)

> "This difficulty disposed of, we have next to speak of what remains, in what way, namely, and as a result of what studies and pursuits, these *preservers* [σωτῆρες] of the constitution will form a part of our state, and at what ages they will severally take up each study." (502c–d)

> "That, then, would be two points in succession and two victories for the just man over the unjust. And now for the third in the Olympian fashion to the *saviour* [σωτῆρί] and to Olympian Zeus—observe that other pleasure than that of the intelligence is not altogether even real or pure, but is a kind of scene-painting, as I seem to have heard from some wise man; and yet this would be the greatest and most decisive overthrow." (583b)

Σωτηρία and forms thereof can be found at 433c8, 429c5, 6, 9 (also σώσει, διασῴζεσθαι), 346a8, 425e3, 430b2, 433b10, 453d11 (also σῴζεσθαι), 465d8, and 494a11:

> "But moreover," said I, "if we were required to decide what it is whose indwelling presence will contribute most to making our city good, it would be a difficult decision whether it was the unanimity of rulers and ruled or the *conservation* [σωτηρία] in the minds of the soldiers of the convictions produced by law as to what things are or are not to be feared, or the watchful intelligence that resides in the guardians, or whether this is the chief cause of its goodness, the principle embodied in child, woman, slave,

---

Nostos and its Cognates," *AJPh* 130.4 [2009]: 481–510). As Herrero shows in this volume, the "homecoming" of Odysseus was often understood by ancient authors as a metaphor for the soul's salvation.

41 Namely, at 549b7, 463b1, 502d1, and 583b2.

free, artisan, ruler, and ruled, that each performed his one task as one man and was not a versatile busybody." (433c–d)

"Bravery too, then, belongs to a city by virtue of a part of itself owing to its possession in that part of a quality that under all conditions will *preserve* the conviction that things to be feared are precisely those which and such as the lawgiver inculcated in their education. Is not that what you call bravery?" "I don't altogether understand what you said," he replied; "but say it again." "A kind of *conservation* [Σωτηρίαν]," I said, "is what I mean by bravery." "What sort of a *conservation* [σωτηρίαν]?" "The conservation of the conviction which the law has created by education about fearful things—what and what sort of things are to be feared. And by the phrase [*preservation*] [σωτηρίαν] 'under all conditions' I mean that the brave man *preserves* it both in pain and pleasures and in desires and fears and does not expel it from his soul." (429b–d)

And does not each art also yield us benefit that is peculiar to itself and not general, as for example medicine health, the pilot's art *safety* [σωτηρίαν] at sea, and the other arts similarly?" (346a)

"Nay, 'twould not be fitting," he said, "to dictate to good and honorable men. For most of the enactments that are needed about these things they will easily, I presume, discover." "Yes, my friend, provided God grants them the *preservation* [σωτηρίαν] of the principles of law that we have already discussed." (425d–e)

"The sole aim of our contrivance was that they should be convinced and receive our laws like a dye as it were, so that their belief and faith might be fast-colored both about the things that are to be feared and all other things because of the fitness of their nature and nurture, and that so their dyes might not be washed out by those lyes that have such dread power to scour our faiths away, pleasure more potent than any detergent or abstergent to accomplish this, and pain and fear and desire more sure than any lye. This power in the soul, then, this unfailing *conservation* [σωτηρίαν] of right and lawful belief about things to be and not to be feared is what I call and would assume to be courage, unless you have something different to say." (430a–b)

"I think that this is the remaining virtue in the state after our consideration of soberness, courage, and intelligence, a quality which made it possible for them all to grow up in the body politic and which when they have sprung up *preserves* [σωτηρίαν] them as long as it is present..." (433b)

"Then we, too, must swim and try to *escape* out of the sea of argument in the hope that either some dolphin will take us on its back or some other desperate *rescue* [σωτηρίαν]." (453d)

"The things for which those are felicitated are a small part of what is secured for these. Their victory is fairer and their public support more complete. For the prize of victory that they win is the *salvation* [σωτηρίαν] of the entire state, the fillet that binds their brows is the public support of themselves and their children—they receive honor from the city while they live and when they die a worthy burial." (465d–e)

"From this point of view do you see any *salvation* [σωτηρίαν] that will suffer the born philosopher to abide in the pursuit and persevere to the end? Consider it in the light of what we said before. We agreed that quickness in learning, memory, courage and magnificence were the traits of this nature." (494a–b)

I have cited the occurrences in detail to show the enormous range of meanings the term can take on, not just in a lexical sense (i. e., as "preservation," "conservation," "rescue"), but also being used at times in a nautical context, at others in a political context, and at still others in a psychological context. Plato also uses the term metaphorically or as a literary allusion (e. g., in the reference to the story of Arion). This makes it difficult to define Platonic "soteriology" precisely. The use of terms pertaining to a broad notion of salvation does not justify us in imputing a "soteriology" to Plato, unless of course we further clarify wherein exactly this "soteriology" lies. But the argument is purely lexical at this stage. What I wish to argue is not that salvation is present in ancient authors (and least of all that it is present in a sense analogous to Christian notions), but that it is worth considering how ancient philosophy addressed itself to the task of answering man's existential questions, and that this almost always includes some conception of the soul's ultimate fate and purpose. It is this oversight of ancient philosophers' concern with providing some form of soteriological, self-transformative, or emancipatory praxis that this volume as a whole seeks to redress.

In any case, the preceding discussion has established that terms pertaining to a broad notion of salvation do occur in the *Republic*, and their use is programmatic. The "salvation" Plato speaks of may or may not be philosophical in nature (I have argued elsewhere that it is[42]), but it certainly gives us grounds for looking to see wherein it might lie. It is in this sense of an open-ended question, supported both by lexical usage and philosophical content, that the words "salvation" and "soteriology" will be used in this volume.

---

42 See my "Plato's Saving *Mūthos*: The Language of Salvation in the *Republic*," *International Journal of the Platonic Tradition* 8.1 (forthcoming).

IV. Elements of a Philosophical Soteriology

In the following, I therefore set aside the problem of using the word "soteriology" to speak of a tradition that, strictly speaking, did not develop a "doctrine of salvation," and focus instead on a non-theological soteriology, as I see it in ancient authors. I will focus on five elements I consider central to Greek philosophical soteriology:

1. Singularity,
2. Soul,
3. Death,
4. Initiation, and
5. *Eudaimonia*.

What do I mean by "singularity"? The contrast between the singular and the particular is clarified by Reiner Schürmann as follows:

> ... death as mine temporalizes phenomena because it is absolutely *singular*. But the singular cannot be treated as the determinate negation of the universal; the contrary opposite of the universal is the particular. It takes a neglect of the persistent tie between time and the singular, a tie signified to me by my death, to append these conflicting strategies to the list, long since Antiquity, of terms that are mutually exclusive within a genus and jointly exhaustive of it.[43]

Schürmann's distinction between the singular and particular is essential to reading ancient texts, because it lets us appreciate an aspect of them that is all too often overlooked in our scientific accounts: that they are also, at one level, the accounts of living-and-dying individuals. For example, when we read Plato, we are most often interested in whether or not he held a "theory of Forms." We may wonder about how this theory relates to the Parmenidean doctrine concerning Being or the Aristotelian teaching of form in matter (ἔνυλον εἶδος). But we thereby forget that Plato's philosophy is not simply reducible to bibliography, but also embodies a specific lifespan and a trajectory, that is to say, a biography. Debra Nails has recently shown that Plato's characters all bear the names of real, existent people.[44] My work in a sense sets out from her observation "that the lives of the people of Plato, insofar as they can be reconstructed, need to be read back into the dialogues in an informed

---

43 Reiner Schürmann, "Ultimate Double Binds," *Graduate Faculty Philosophy Journal* 14.2–15.1 (1991): 224.
44 Debra Nails, *The People of Plato: A Prosopography of Plato and Other Socratics* (Indianapolis: Hackett Publishing Company, 2002).

and responsible way."[45] Likewise, in his book *The Being of the Beautiful*, Seth Benardete points out, "the longest series of dialogues, however, is connected in order of time through an external event, the trial and death of Socrates: *Theaetetus, Euthyphro, Sophist, Statesman, Apology of Socrates, Crito* and *Phaedo.*"[46] Thus, beyond and besides our textual fetishes, ancient texts were also concerned with the fates of mortals. Homer sings of Achilles to preserve his mortal voice. When Odysseus visits the dead hero in the Underworld and attempts to console him, Achilles' rebuke follows swiftly:

> O shining Odysseus, never try to console me for dying.
> I would rather follow the plow as thrall to another
> man, one with no land allotted to him and not much to live on,
> than be a king over all the perished dead. (*Od.* XI. 488–91; Lattimore trans.)

It is only when Odysseus narrates to him concerning the deeds of his son Neoptolemus that Achilles' shade is appeased and strides away happy at hearing of his son's fame (ibid., 538–40). This brief vignette illustrates something important we seem to have forgotten in contemporary academic philosophy: metaphysical λόγοι are poor consolation for mortality. In contrast, ancient authors seem to have better appreciated the mortal condition, and the need for some form of soteriological response to it.

In the Platonic context, singularity requires a further clarification. "Plato" has dominated philosophy throughout its history in a very specific way: as a metaphysician. In fact, the most recent chapter in the history of philosophy—Nietzsche, Heidegger, Derrida, to name a few—tries to overthrow this Platonic legacy. My argument here is that through the notion of singularity something essential remains in the Platonic project, an aspect that is not reducible to any metaphysics. Platonic "Forms" are important, but they are always presented in a mythic or hypothetical context, and especially as part of an explanation of the paradoxical nature of Becoming. Specifically, Plato identifies three general *topoi* of Becoming. These are:

1. The body (cf. *Phaedo*),
2. The city (cf. *Republic*), and

---

45 Nails 2002, xxxviii.
46 Seth Benardete, *The Being of the Beautiful: Plato's Theaetetus, Sophist, and Statesman* (Chicago: University of Chicago Press, 1984), xvi.

3. The cosmos (cf. *Timaeus*).

Weaving these three together (for example, the *Phaedrus* uses *eros* and writing to distinguish between what is fleeting versus what is abiding), Plato indeed does work with a broad palette of themes. But as I showed above, the notion of singularity is not reducible to the notion of particularity. Particularity, always tied to universals, requires at some level an engagement with Forms, whether immanent or otherwise. But by using narrative techniques such as the dramatic narrative which preserves Socrates' singularity, as well as the singularity of every participant, Plato creates a dialogical universe which is populated by singulars. Whether "Platonic metaphysics" can or cannot be overcome, Plato's work can never be reduced to how it appears in the history of philosophy. This aspect of Plato, beyond the body, city, and cosmos, and their ontological and epistemological referent, God, is worth philosophical rethinking. Soteriology ultimately serves to underscore the tragic condition of being a specific human, given over to death and threatened by the possibility of oblivion. With this philosophical clarification of a philosophical project, I wish to qualify the way in which "salvation" and "soteriology" are no longer simply abandoned to "religion." Philosophers can and must say something about this very important matter. In doing so, they not only follow the ancients, but also address our contemporary geo-political situation.

The notion of singularity is crucial to salvation, because it is always *qua* singular that a mortal faces death. In *The Death of Ivan Ilych*, Tolstoy brilliantly explores the puzzle that whereas language consists of general statements, it is always *qua* an individual that one must die when he shows Ilych grappling with the proposition "Caius is a man, men are mortal, therefore Caius is mortal." This proposition had always seemed correct to Ilych when applied to Caius, but not as applied to himself. Yet, as death approaches, Ilych realizes with penetrating insight that the propositional structure of reality had always blinded him to the fact of his own death, a fact no proposition seems capable of expressing. In death (and in love) the singular is revealed as ἄλογον, inexpressible by words.

Singularity, by setting aside the consolations of metaphysics, i.e., both theology and technology, provides a way to a non-theological soteriology. In the encounter between the individual and his mortality, death is revealed as inescapably mine. This singularization drives back philosophy from its textual fetishes to the urgent mortal task of addressing man in his ultimate concern.[47]

Here, one might oppose that if death reveals the utter "impossibility of possibility"[48] salvation is an illusion, and an indulgence. For, if the individual dies and there is nothing more to be done, then the only consolation is this life with its maximization of individual glory and pleasure. But this would be too hasty. As Gomperz has shown, Empedoclean and Homeric psychology possessed a two-soul theory. On the one hand, there was θυμός, which I translate as "mortal soul." Θυμός was responsible for personal identity and for the nutritive, emotional, volitional, and intellectual aspects of a person. On the other hand, there was ψυχή, which although always associated with θυμός in a body, exceeded the lifespan of the latter. Θυμός does not possess any independent existence once separated from the body; although it may be briefly scattered or even temporarily escape the body, it must, if the person is to live, return to the body immediately. Should it fail to so do, the body will perish and so will the θυμός. The ψυχή, on the other hand, purely a shade, flits underground to Hades. Thus, two "inner entities" mark the loss of consciousness (syncope), revival, and death: ψυχή and θυμός. In general, ψυχή departs at syncope, and the θυμός returns. It is the loss of ψυχή that determines a man's death and the θυμός that experiences woe at this possibility. I cite one example, quoting the anguished Achilles:

> The same fate comes to him who holds back and to him who fights, in equal *timē* (honor) are the coward and the brave man. Likewise, the man who has done nothing and the one who has accomplished much both die. Nor is there any profit for me, from the time when I suffered grief in my *thumos*, always to fight, setting my *psukhē* at hazard. (*Iliad* IX. 318–22; Caswell trans.)

---

47 See Vishwa Adluri and Joydeep Bagchee, *The Nay Science: A History of German Indology* (New York: Oxford University Press, 2013) for a discussion of the problem in a related context: 19th and 20th scholarship on the Indian epic, the Mahābhārata, and the Bhagavad Gītā.

48 The phrase is from Heidegger's *Being and Time*, trans. John Macquarrie and Edward Robinson (Oxford: Blackwell, 1962), 307. In Heidegger's work, the phrase refers to the fact that death, as something that is *"one's utmost ... non-relational, and ... not to be outstripped"* (ibid., 294, italics in original), leaves nothing over, no residual possibility of man's existence. In such a philosophy of radical immanence, salvation of course is not a meaningful notion, which is why Heidegger posits existential "resoluteness" in its place.

Greek thinkers thus seem to have wanted to have it both ways. On the one hand, Homer is committed to Achilles, Patroclus, Hector and others as mortal heroes. Their death and the woe the Achaeans or the Trojans experience at this loss are important themes to the poet; he will not quickly gloss over them or provide metaphysical redemption. The loss of a person cannot be rationalized away. In the *Odyssey*, among the many great heroes Odysseus meets in Hades, first of all he meets his companion Elpenor, who died a rather inglorious death. And yet his lament is preserved to us. On the other hand, the θυμός is not the full story. Either the ψυχή flits out (to Hades) as Odysseus' mother tells him (IX.222) or an εἰδώλων as Odysseus himself sees of Heracles (IX.602).

In my first book, I focused very strongly on θυμός and the consequences of this mortal soul for philosophy. I argued that the subsumption of θυμός under ψυχή was a problem for philosophy, and perhaps explains our present-day neglect of mortality. Thus, my book concluded by rejecting the seductions of metaphysical transcendence, and argued for a return to mortality. But this left a question open: what of the ψυχή and its fate? Does this not enable us to speak of a non-metaphysical transcendence? In the present volume, I would like to acknowledge that ψυχή presents a problem and the relation of soteriology to ψυχή needs to be still be thought through. How might the concerns of ψυχή differ from those of θυμός? In what way does the existence and endurance of ψυχή beyond the death of the body and of θυμός call for some form of philosophy addressed not just to θυμός and its mortal concerns, but also to ψυχή?[49]

These are questions that cannot be answered in an introduction such as this. The articles in this volume do a much better job of highlighting the way different traditions and different philosophers have responded to these challenges. The purpose of this introduction, however, is to highlight some issues that need to be kept in mind when reading the volume.

---

49 I was aware of the problem, but could not address it in my first book, which was on mortal philosophy. Thus, I concluded with a question, and a promise: "My analysis has taken the form of a 'return' from the transcendence of metaphysics, texts, and traditions. But, from this 'purified' state, is another form of transcendence possible for the mortal singular? But that is a subject for another work; here, I end the 'purification' portion of Parmenides, that is, our traditional reception. A philosophical investigation whereby Parmenides provides a positive response to the ultimate concerns of the mortal reader constitutes the next step." Adluri 2011, 135.

Once again, salvation has to be posed as a concern, but also as a question and a problem. The answer is not as simple as saying "one is saved," because even then the question will arise, "what is saved and how is it saved?" Mortality remains one of the basic phenomenological traits of existence, which cannot be erased even on propounding a doctrine of salvation, because it is only against the background of our mortality that soteriological doctrines make sense.

As an example of just how skillfully Greek philosophers wove mortal concerns into philosophical and cosmological doctrines, I shall take up Heraclitus' thought. Nearly 30 years after M. L. West declared in clear and unambiguous terms that there is no "Logos-Doctrine" in Heraclitus,[50] scholarship continues to focus on either λόγος or flux as the primary theme of Heraclitus' philosophy. The latter, addressed as the "flux doctrine" and first popularized by Plato, has its champions even today. On the other hand, Kahn sees in Heraclitus' doctrine of λόγος a committed monism and eschatology; in fact, he organizes the fragments in such a way that they culminate in Zeus' governance of the universe.[51] Besides these two extremes, others, either happy or unhappy with his riddling style, throw up their hands at the notion of a coherent doctrine.

To be sure, Heraclitus provides many clues to justify a variety of interpretations and attitudes. Yet, a central philosophical paradox, distinct from his enigmatic style, remains: how does he understand temporality, so that both the doctrine of transcendent λόγος and the teaching of rapid flux become possible in the first place?

A philological analysis of the texts demonstrates the significance of θάνατος to Heraclitus. "Θάνατος" (and its verbal relatives such as θνήσκω, ἀποθνήσκω, τεθνηότος) is the most frequent term of philosophical importance, occurring twelve times (fragments 21, 26, 27, 29, 36, 48, 62, 76, 77, 88). Θάνατος is not only the most frequently named theme (outnumbering ψυχή, λόγος, ἕν) in the writings of Heraclitus, but also the most philosophically significant. Heraclitus relates death to the life and decay of mortals (88), to souls (ψυχαί, 36), to fate (μοῖρα, 25), to ever-flowing fame (κλέος ἀέναον θνητῶν, 29), to religious ritual, to sleep (ὕπνος, 21), and to the immortals (62).

---

50 Martin L. West, *Early Greek Philosophy and the Orient* (Oxford: Clarendon Press, 1971).
51 Charles H. Kahn, *The Art and Thought of Heraclitus* (Cambridge: Cambridge University Press, 1979).

There is nothing morbid or otherworldly about Heraclitus' extended meditation on death: he talks of "Corpses more fit to be thrown out than dung." Even though humans cannot anticipate or comprehend what awaits them after death, death is of deep philosophical significance (frag. 27). As mortals, our temporality is defined by the paradoxical presence of death in life. Heraclitean philosophy uses death to create a complex integration of mortals and immortals: "Immortals are mortals, mortals immortal, living the others' death, dead in the others' life" (frag. 62).

Once we recognize that Heraclitean wisdom is also an understanding of the nature of death, we begin to see not a positivistic λόγος doctrine, but a thanatology spread out extensively through the extant fragments, problematizing clear and positivistic philosophical axioms. Flux and eternal λόγος reveal two forms of temporality, which Heraclitus understands in relation to θάνατος. The paradoxical relationship of θάνατος and βίος captures the simultaneity of change and stability or rather of flux and eternity. The word "αἰών" holds the key to understanding Heraclitus' view of time: rather than meaning eternity, it captures the Janus-faced temporality underlying Heraclitean thought.

Heraclitus relates θάνατος to ὕπνεος (sleep), to γένεσις, to πόλεμος (war), and finally to Dionysos. In fragments 21 and 26, preserved by Clement of Alexandria, we read:

> 21. Death is all things we see awake; all we see asleep is sleep.
> 26. A man strikes a light for himself in the night, when his sight is quenched. Living, he touched the dead in his sleep; having awakened, he touches the sleeper.

Here, Heraclitus is exploiting a classic relationship between sleep and death, which begins in Hesiod, and continues even to our day: Sleep is the brother of Death. Hesiod writes:

> And night bore hateful Doom and black Fate
> And Death, and Sleep, and the brood of Dreams. (Hesiod, *Theogony*, 211–213)

Later, Hesiod continues describing the relationship of sleep and death in his description of the house of black Night:

> There the children of black Night have their house,
> Sleep and Death, awesome gods. (Hesiod, *Theogony*, 751–764)

In Homer too, we have the episode of Hera's deception of Zeus, under the influence of Ὕπνος, allowing Θάνατος to implement part two of her plan, namely to wreak destruction on the Trojans. Parmenides was also impressed by the relationship of Night and light, as well as painful birth and hateful death. All these elements occur in Parmenides' proem as well as his cosmology. Having suggested the widespread importance of the θάνατος—ὕπνος coupling to Presocratic thought, let us return specifically to Heraclitus and the two fragments above.

The standard interpretation of these quotes is: "We are surrounded by a thicket of riddles, but a pattern begins to emerge, a sequence of psychic stages linked to one another by a thread of quenchings and lightings and ending by a cyclical return to the starting point."[52] Heraclitus links θάνατος and ὕπνος to construct a link between perception and knowing. This knowing occurs neither in the dark, nor is it foolish, as "private understanding" would imply. It is not one of pure λόγος either. It is a "lighting" which one illumines by oneself, not in terms of understanding but in terms of one's own existence. Ramfos links this dark seeing to Oedipus, and argues that one does not see with the eyes; what offers itself to sight is the invisible side of things as absent, as a blindspot.[53] The presence of death in life is never available to perception. It can only be given as a lived, experienced, personal testimony.

> 31. The reversals (*tropaí*) of fire: first sea; but of sea half is earth, half lightening storm.
> 76. Plutarch: [As Heraclitus said, the death of fire is birth for air and death of air is birth for water.]

On the level of the cosmos, θάνατος is interchangeable with τροπαί. The cyclical process of cosmogony is, in its structure, not different from the cycle of human life, in which βίος and θάνατος co-mingle. Kirk thinks the use of θάνατος is merely an idiosyncratic metaphor on Heraclitus' part.[54] I argue that this use of θάνατος inscribes mortal temporality onto the universe.

Heraclitus' use of θάνατος extends from the cycles of the cosmos to the fate of individual souls. It underlines Heraclitus' universe as one where paradox is not just a stylistic device. He speaks in riddles because our existence is a riddle. The paradoxical nature of Heraclitean sayings relate to the paradoxical experience of time. Is time stable or in flux? Heraclitus uses the word "αἰών" for time. From the Neoplatonists on,

---

52 Kahn 1979, 215.
53 Stelios Ramfos, "Héraclite. Le cercle de la mort," *Philosophia* 1 (1971): 176–194.
54 G.S. Kirk, *Heraclitus: The Cosmic Fragments* (Cambridge: Cambridge University Press, 1954), 341.

αἰών means eternity as opposed to χρόνος or "time."⁵⁵ (In Plotinus, eternity again is of two types, a good eternity αἰών in which everything is there simultaneously, while ἀιδίων designating unending duration, is a bad eternity.) In Homer, αἰών signifies something quite different, namely the marrow of a bone, and what is present in sperm. Benveniste explains that αἰών in Homer designates "the force of life, the source of vitality."⁵⁶ Someone's αἰών is his natural lifespan. The totality of one's life (seventy or eighty years) becomes the measure by which a human and vital force calibrates the entire universe. Temporality for Heraclitus is thus one that takes θάνατος into account: it is aionic, neither a flux in which λόγος is impossible, nor a λόγος in which change is relegated to unreality. In this way, we can understand fragment 52, preserved by Hippolytus and also Lucian: "Αἰών is a child at play, playing draughts; the kingship is a child's." Hippolytus reads Heraclitus correctly in the *Refutatio* (IX, 9, 1) when he says that Heraclitus says that the whole is mortal and immortal, and that λόγος is αἰών. Child's play, riddle, a dark light, these are ways in which Heraclitus is pointing to the complicated structure of αἰών. The history of philosophy dismantles this riddle, this play of αἰών. In our time, we want to focus on one aspect, and pin Heraclitus down to either a Cratylean flux or an overarching λόγος-based eternity.

In contrast to this view, Heraclitus' meditations on time unfold a pan-mortal viewpoint that includes an account of both mortals and immortals, and thus flux and transcendence. Θάνατος rather than λόγος, or rather a thanatology defines and describes time as we mortals experience it, and by extension, the κόσμος we mortals inhabit. Λόγος is just one aspect of the riddle of time. The complete understanding of the riddle results in what a recent scholar calls "temporal aporia."⁵⁷

Θάνατος thus imbues the Heraclitean universe with a surprisingly complex temporality. His is not a simple universe of eternal being nor is it one of rapid flux. Instead, Heraclitus describes a mortal temporality, with mortal life as the basic temporal phenomenon. He paradoxically unites life and death, flux and stable λόγος.

---

55 See André-Jean Festugière, "La sens philosophique du mot αἰών. Àpropos d'Aristote, *De Caelo* 1,9," in *Études de philosophie grecque* (Paris: Vrin, 1971), 254–71.
56 Émile Benveniste, "Expression indo-européen de l'éternité," *Bulletin de la Société de linguistique* 38 (1937): 107.
57 See Ned Lukacher, *Time-Fetishes: The Secret History of Eternal Recurrence* (Durham, NC: Duke University Press, 1998).

Understanding the centrality of the phenomenon of death to ancient cosmologies is an important key to interpreting the work of ancient philosophers correctly. But we must be careful to note that this concern with death was not a philosophically stylized cognition. In modern and contemporary philosophy, we have many examples of thinkers who propound the importance of death (e. g., Kierkegaard, Heidegger, Sartre). But this engagement with death differs from the ancient experience, which was mediated not by a philosophical reflection but by a form of near-death experience. The institution of ritual descent or κατάβασις in which the initiate was made to undergo an encounter with his death is well studied.[58] The researches of Burkert,[59] Kingsley,[60] and Johnston[61] have shown how significant this theme is to ancient philosophical and religious traditions. Albinus has shown its importance in the *Republic*[62] and Riedweg has recently attempted to reconstruct from the Gold Leaves the narrative recounted in the ἱερὸς λόγος told the initiate, a narrative that involves death and κατάβασις as its first two stages.[63] My own work has focused on the centrality of this theme in the Platonic dialogues, and on how the correct transmission of initiatory wisdom enables a transition for the initiate to correct knowledge of Being and, with it, to a state of εὐδαιμονία.[64] Rather than reprise these well-known researches, to which the articles by Miguel Herrero and Barbara Sattler in this volume add further material, I would merely like to emphasize the point that the presence of the descent-death-rebirth-ascent motif in ancient philosophy, whether in the form of an actual ritual descent or as a significant metaphor as in Plato's

---

58 For a useful introduction, see the chapter "The Dead" by Debbie Felton in the volume *A Companion to Greek Religion*, ed. Daniel Ogden (Malden, MA: Wiley-Blackwell, 2010), 86–99.
59 See his article "Das Proömium des Parmenides und die Katabasis des Pythagoras," reprinted in a translation as chapter 3 of this volume.
60 See n. 9 above.
61 Sarah Iles Johnston, *Restless Dead: Encounters between the Living and the Dead in Ancient Greece* (Berkeley, CA: University of California Press, 1999).
62 See Lars Albinus, "The *Katabasis* of Er. Plato's Use of Myths, exemplified by the Myth of Er," in *Essays on Plato's* Republic, ed. Erik Nis Ostenfeld (Aarhus: Aarhus University Press, 1998), 91–105.
63 Christoph Riedweg, "Poésie orphique et rituel initiatique. Éléments d'un 'Discourse sacré' dans les lamelles d'or," *RHR* 219 (2002): 459–481.
64 Vishwa Adluri, "Initiation into the Mysteries: Experience of the Irrational in Plato," *Mouseion* III.6 (2006): 407–423.

Republic,⁶⁵ gives renewed urgency to the mortal task of philosophy. It brings philosophy out of being a game, even if a very sophisticated one, and makes it existentially and ethically relevant again. Singularity rather than particularity, soul rather than subject, mortality rather than finitude, and initiation rather than anxiety—these, then, prove to be the way to a non-theological soteriology.

Finally, let me address, albeit tentatively, the nature of this proposed salvation. We have several sources that suggest that the goal of this soteriological path was εὐδαιμονία. Empedocles (frag. B114/119) recounts the state of bliss the soul in its original, divine state experiences; after wandering for thrice ten thousand years, provided it has lived intelligently, it can expect a return to the company of the blessed ones. Likewise Diotima in the *Symposium* propounds εὐδαιμονία as the final goal. When Socrates in response to her question regarding what someone who desires good things has once those things have become his own replies, "He'll have happiness" (205a), she answers, "There's no need to ask further, 'What's the point of wanting happiness?' The answer you just gave seems to be final" (205a). This concern with εὐδαιμονία is also a feature of Aristotle's philosophy. In A2 of the *Nicomachean Ethics*, Aristotle already establishes εὐδαιμονία as the goal. It alone meets the criteria of the Good, namely, that it be an end in itself, perfect, and self-sufficient (1096a11–7a14); and in K 7 and 8, it is revealed that of all the activities of man, contemplation is the most blessed and makes him most akin to the immortals (1177b21–32 and 1178b23–24).⁶⁶ Thus, one could also speak of the soteriological goal pursued by Plato and Aristotle as a noetic transcendence, an experience that involves a cognitive experience and is simultaneously rational and transformative.

---

65 Rosen puts it well: "The theme of descent plays an important role in the dramatic structure of the *Republic*. To note only the obvious, Socrates and Glaucon descend from Athens to Piraeus at the very beginning of the dialogue; Book Seven begins with a descent from the sunlight into the cave of shadows…; the dialogue closes with an account of the descent of Er into Hades. Each of these descents is described in considerably greater detail than the outstanding example of ascent to the Idea of the Good, or more properly, to its surrogate, the image of the sun." Stanley Rosen, *Plato's Republic: A Study* (New Haven: Yale University Press, 2005), 19.

66 The passage in *Met.* Λ.7 (1072b15) where Aristotle speaks of the activity of the unmoved mover does not, as one might expect, refer to εὐδαιμονία but to ἡδονή. Nonetheless, since the life of God is one of eternal (self-)contemplation (see 1072b19–30 and 1074b33), Aristotle may simply mean that the pleasure he experiences is that of εὐδαιμονία.

The concern with "salvation" thus proves not to be an irrational enterprise, but simply, as Plato and Aristotle both make amply clear, the concern with leading the best and most virtuous life possible for man *qua* man. That they simultaneously attribute an element of divinity to such a life should not lead us to dismiss the arguments with which they seek to demonstrate this claim.

V. On the Articles in this Volume

Setting out from this background, the articles in this volume adopt various approaches to the question of Greek soteriology. Miguel Herrero in his article looks at the way Homer's *Odyssey* served as a literary model for later soteriological philosophies, and suggests that Greek salvation is characterized by notions of wandering, arrival, supplication, and receiving of protection. Arbogast Schmitt's article takes up the modern prejudice against seeing genuine forms of self-determination in ancient thought. Schmitt presents numerous examples from the Homeric epics that demonstrate that the sense of existing in a reciprocal relationship with the gods need not imply that ancient Greek thought was incapable of identifying a sphere of genuinely free human activity. The third article in the volume is a translation of Walter Burkert's 1969 study, already alluded to above. Prof. Burkert has prefaced this essay with a brief comment on its status in the context of newer materials that have since come to light. Alberto Bernabé's article too shows how Plato takes up and reuses Orphic materials, albeit in service of "deeper philosophical purposes." Barbara Sattler's article continues with an examination of the parallels between the Eleusinian mysteries and the Platonic dialogues. In his article Stephen Menn examines the relation of political philosophy to soteriological concerns. He suggests that Plato remains skeptical about the possibility of rhetoric and political virtue of producing the promised σωτηρία, instead believing that "only some quite different kind of philosophy can save us." In our article, John Lenz and I take up this very point. We demonstrate how the *Republic* enters politics in Book II with the myth of Gyges, but exits it with the myth of Er in Book X. The failure of political virtue to produce salvation (underscored by the fact that even a citizen of the καλλίπολις makes a bad choice at the lot of lives in *Rep.* X) thus opens the way to a non-political understanding of salvation. The longest article in this collection, John Bussanich's piece makes a strong case for taking

Plato's salvific concerns seriously. Plato's eschatological myths, Bussanich shows, are not simply literary creations, created as adjuncts to his epistemological or political concerns. Rather, they are based on a precise and pragmatic logic: if the soul can only effect its purification bit-by-bit and over multiple lifetimes, the rebirth cycle itself needs to be "ethicized." Bussanich thus advocates seeing a notion of causality analogous to the Indian *karma* in Platonic and Plotinian philosophy. Svetla Slaveva-Griffin's following article takes up this very suggestion, although she applies it to the notion of "purification" in Plotinian philosophy. Comparisons with the Bhagavad Gītā suggest that there may be useful avenues for thinking about how Greek notions of philosophy can help us read the Indian sources too. The final two articles in this collection are concerned with the question of memory and of theurgy. Luc Brisson demonstrates how complex issues relating to memory shape Plotinus' thought. Through a virtuoso analysis of the Plotinian theory of memory, he shows that the notion of memory is essentially implied in all forms of soteriological thinking: "One cannot ... speak of the salvation of the soul without evoking memory." Finally, John Finamore's article shows how late Neoplatonic thinkers began to reshape the Plotinian system to account for perceived problems, and to make space for ritual practices. Thus, with Iamblichus' blend of theurgy with philosophy, we come full circle.

Salvation for the Wanderer:
Odysseus, the Gold Leaves, and Empedocles

Miguel Herrero de Jáuregui

I. The Wanderings of Odysseus as a Model

"Many are the wanderings and circlings of the soul: one among imaginings, one in opinions, and one before these in understanding. But only the life according to the *nous* has stability and this is the mystical harbour of the soul to which, on the one hand, the poem leads Odysseus through the great wandering of his life, and to which we too shall draw ourselves up, if we would reach salvation." These words of Proclus in the 5th century AD culminate a long tradition of interpretation of the *Odyssey* as an interior voyage which has lasted until our days.[1] In Late Antiquity, neo-Pythagoreans and neo-Platonists interpreted the wanderings of Odysseus in his return to Ithaca as an allegory for the wanderings of the exiled soul striving to reach its heavenly home. The sufferings and ordeals of the hero were taken as an image of the painful stages of the ascent of the soul through the sublunary spheres. It is probable, although the evidence is scant, that this type of exegesis of the *Odyssey* began with ancient Pythagoreanism, since the poem about the wandering hero was an obvious target for allegorical interpreters.[2] Yet whenever allegory of Homer may have started, it was

---

1 Procl. *In Plat. Parm.* 1025a, 29–37. Cf. Robert Lamberton, *Homer the Theologian* (Berkeley: University of California Press, 1986), 221–227. Cf. Piero Boitani, *The Shadow of Ulysses* (Oxford: Clarendon Press, 1994) on the interpretation of Odysseus' wandering in literature from the Middle Ages to the modern Space Odyssey.
2 Cf. Lamberton 1986, 31–43 (in favour) and Carl Huffmann, "Philolaus and the Central Fire," in *Reading Ancient Texts I: Presocratics and Plato—Essays in honour of Denis O'Brien*, ed. Suzanne Stern-Gillet and Kevin Corrigan (Leiden and Boston: Brill, 2007), 62–68 (sceptical), with earlier bibliography on the subject; also some interesting remarks in Marwan Rashed, "The Structure of the Eye and its Cosmological Function in Empedocles. Reconstruction of Fragment 84 D.-K.," in *Reading Ancient Texts I*, ed. Stern-Gillet and Corrigan (Lei-

not only through it that the *Odyssey* was intertwined with the "puritan" (to use E. R. Dodds' famous anachronism) theory of the exiled soul. New myth-makers about the soul also derived inspiration from it. Plato clearly had the *Odyssey* in mind when he composed his eschatological myths in the *Republic* and the *Phaedo*.[3] Before him, some hexametre poets made the exile of the soul their subject, and Homer was inevitably in the background of their compositions. This paper will explore the re-working of the theme of the wandering hero in epic (i.e., hexametric) poetry concerned with the soul's wanderings: the verses found in the Orphic gold leaves, and the fragments of Empedocles.[4]

When speaking of epic resonances one must be aware of the plurality of epic traditions which coexisted and competed in their oral performances well into the end of the 4th century. Neither affinities nor even close formulaic and structural parallels between epic poems are necessarily indications of dependence, as in later text-based literature. Type-scenes can be common to different epic traditions. Even relative chronology is not a secure basis for establishing dependence, since later hexametric poetry about cosmic journeys may be modelled on earlier traditions contemporary to but distinct from Homer, with which

---

den and Boston: Brill, 2007), 37 n. 51. In fact, parts of the *Odyssey*, like both *Nekyiai*, were so compatible with eschatological conceptions that they were thought by many 19th century analysts to be later Orphic-Pythagorean interpolations in the poem.

3 Amihud Gilead, *The Platonic Odyssey* (Amsterdam: Editions Rodopi B.V., 1995), 87–108 for the Platonic interpretation of the *Odyssey* as an interior voyage. Neo-Platonists carried it much further, but the specific allusions to Odysseus in *Phaed.* 94e and *Resp.* 620cd show the Homeric background in Plato's myths (Radcliffe G. Edmonds, *Myths of the Underworld Journey: Plato, Aristophanes, and the "Orphic" Gold Tablets* [Cambridge: Cambridge University Press, 2004], 202–204). On Plato's myths, cf. Adluri's chapter in this volume, and those of Sattler, Finamore, and Bussanich for the neo-Platonic methods.

4 From a narrative and literary point of view, the fact that Empedocles' *daimon* is not to be identified with the soul is irrelevant, since both are the protagonists of the tale of exile and return. This journey is not just a literary image, but a conceptual metaphor (cf. George Lakoff and Mark Johnson, *Metaphors We Live by* [Chicago: University of Chicago Press, 1980]) which shapes the whole understanding of the soul or the *daimon*. For a similar case in Parmenides, cf. Alexander Mourelatos, *The Route of Parmenides* (New Haven: Parmenides Publishing, 1970), esp. 31–34. In general, on the poetics of early Greek philosophy, cf. Glenn W. Most, "The Poetics of Early Greek Philosophy," in *The Cambridge Companion to Early Greek Philosophy*, ed. Arthur A. Long (Cambridge: Cambridge University Press, 1999), 332–662.

similar scenes in the *Odyssey* could be competing.[5] Empedocles and the poet(s) of the verses found in the gold leaves may have been familiar with other epic *nostoi* besides the Homeric *Odyssey*. Tales of the wandering hero striving to survive the wrath of the gods and the elements extend far beyond the limits of the Greek world (e.g., Gilgamesh, Sindbad), and the *Odyssey* was only the most famous version; its images and formulae need not have been exclusive to the Homeric poem. Still, the *Odyssey* is the only *nostos* poem that has been preserved, and is certainly a paradigmatic epic expression of the adventures of the wandering hero. Besides, in the 5th century when the exile of the soul is likely to have become a poetic subject, the *Odyssey* had unrivalled pre-eminence among the *nostos* poems.[6] When hexametre poets decided to sing on a new subject like the exiled soul, the Homeric model was an inevitable source of inspiration and competition for them, even if they may also have been heirs of other poetic traditions like older Orphic *katabaseis*.

Let us first recall the relevant passages in the *Odyssey*.[7] The wanderings of Odysseus are the subject of the first half of the poem. Due to its particular narrative strategy, they are not told in chronological order. On the other hand, the succession of events is determined by the succession of deities who govern Odysseus' destiny. An end to his wanderings seems possible only when Poseidon, who had been angry with him since the blinding of Polyphemus, conveniently disappears for a brief holiday in the land of the Ethiopians. Athena takes advantage of the god's absence to bring the hero home. Each god has taken turn in harassing the returning Greeks; Athena's rage against the other Achaeans, or that of the Sun and Poseidon against Odysseus and his men, is respected by all gods, and sometimes even actively helped: Zeus uses his thunderbolt to punish the transgession against Helios. Even when

---

5   Cf. Richard P. Martin, "Rhapsodizing Orpheus," *Kernos* 14 (2001): 23–33.
6   On the elements of a *nostos* tale, cf. Anna Bonifazi, "Inquiring into Nostos and Its Cognates," *AJPh* 130.4 (2009): 481–510. On the endurance of other Cyclic *nostos* poems and the progressive pre-eminence of the *Odyssey*, cf. Gregory Nagy, *Greek Mythology and Poetics* (Cornell: Cornell University Press, 1990), 70ff, and Jonathan S. Burgess, *The Tradition of the Trojan War in Homer and the Epic Cycle* (Baltimore and London: The Johns Hopkins University Press, 2001).
7   On these Odyssean passages, cf. especially Bernhard Fenik, *Studies in the Odyssey* (Wiesbaden: F. Steiner, 1974); Gilbert P. Rose, "The Unfriendly Phaeacians," *TAPhA* 100 (1969): 387–406; Charles Segal, *Singers, Heroes and Gods in the Odyssey* (Ithaca and London: Cornell University Press, 1994); Steve Reece, *The Stranger's Welcome* (Ann Arbor: University of Michigan Press, 1993).

Athena has begun to help Odysseus, she avoids revealing herself fully until he reaches his own country, for she respects her uncle's preeminence (*Od.* 6. 329–331, 13.341–343). Only when Poseidon's rage is no longer effective, after the hero's arrival in Ithaca, does Athena feel free to appear undisguised.

At the mercy of the gods' whims, Odysseus and his men strive to return home. Yet, as the proem to the poem emphatically says, only Odysseus will accomplish his *nostos*. After his men have eaten the cattle of the Sun and have been punished by Zeus' thunderbolt, Odysseus alone survives. Detained on Calypso's island, he is physically unable to face once again the rage of the sea. The narration of his wanderings starts when, after he has finally been able to leave the island, Poseidon re-asserts his anger, sending all the fury of the winds and the waves against him for a final time. From Book 5 to Book 7, we are told how Odysseus wanders helplessly through the waves, and then is helped in succession by different divinities (Ino, the river of Scheria, Athena) and human beings (Nausicaa, Queen Arete) until he is able to reach land, to be welcomed in Scheria and, finally, granted safe passage home by the Phaeacians.

I shall focus on how the poets who told of the wanderings of the exiled soul engaged with the Homeric narration. From this perspective, scholars from the Neoplatonists to the present day have usually made the *Nekyia* and the tale of Circe the focus of their attention, since the obvious link between these episodes and tales of otherworldly trips make them a natural model for a journey to Hades.[8] But, as I will show, the figure of Odysseus, who, alone and struggling against the rage of the elements, must fall back on the help of a god, provides a closer model which has not been exploited.

---

8   E.g., Fritz Graf and Sarah Johnston, *Ritual Texts for the Afterlife: Orpheus and the Bacchic Gold Tablets* (London: Routledge, 2007), 96, 112, 204 n. 21. They are particularly suitable as inspiration for any special journey: as Eric Havelock says when arguing for an Odyssean background to Parmenides' poem, in these two episodes "the *hodos* theme becomes obsessive." "Parmenides and Odysseus," *HSCP* 63 (1958): 137 f.

II. The Supplication of the Soul in the Gold Leaves

The so-called Orphic gold leaves are an ever-increasing source of excitement for scholars of ancient religion.[9] These small gold tablets which continue to appear in tombs scattered around the Greek world contain detailed instructions for the souls of initiates in Orphic/Bacchic mysteries concerning what they must do in the Underworld in order to attain salvation. The souls must drink from a specific fountain, repeat some specific words to the guardians of Hades and/or Persephone, and then they will be allowed to go to the place of the blessed. The enormous interest of the leaves lies, amongst other things, in their being the only evidence about the Underworld journey envisaged in the mysteries which comes from an internal perspective, instead of the usually partial and vague statements from external sources like Herodotus, Plato, and later authors. The evidence from this *Innenperspektive* makes it clear that around the 5th cent. BC there was a hexametrical poem (or several poems) which told the journey of the soul to the Underworld, and from which the leaves took most of their lines. I will not discuss here whether these verses were attributed to Orpheus or some other possible authors like Pythagoras, nor the hypothetical structure of the *katabasis* of the soul.[10] I will just show the presence of patterns found in Odysseus' wanderings in the scenes depicted in the leaves.

The leaves have been divided into two main types, the first of which is represented mainly by the Hipponion leaf.[11] In this leaf the soul of the initiate is given instructions for her arrival to Hades and her encounters with the guardians. These instructions show broad affinities with an epic type scene, much repeated in the *Odyssey*, in which a figure with privileged access to wisdom gives detailed instructions to the hero before a

---

9 Cf. the recent monographs on the gold leaves: Alberto Bernabé and Ana Jiménez, *Instructions for the Netherworld: The Orphic Gold Tablets* (Boston and Leiden: Brill, 2008)—; Graf and Johnston 2007; —Marisa Tortorelli, *Figli della Terra e del cielo stellato* (Naples: M. D' Auria, 2006); Yannis Tzifopoulos, *Paradise Earned: The Bacchic-Orphic Gold Lamellae of Crete* (Cambridge, MA: Harvard University Press, 2010); Edmonds 2004 and the collection of studies in Radcliffe Edmonds, ed., *The Gold Tablets and Greek Religion: Further along the Path* (Cambridge: Cambridge University Press, 2011). A new volume on them has also been announced (cf. n. 12 *infra*).
10 Bernabé and Jiménez 2008, 179–207, 227–240. Cf. also n. 13.
11 *OF* 474. I refer to the leaves with their numeration in Alberto Bernabé's *Orphicorum Fragmenta*, vol. 2 (Berlin and Leipzig: Teubner, 2005).

dangerous journey. Geographical descriptions beginning with *entha* ("there…") and preparations for future dialogues are common both to the tablets and to the instructions to Odysseus given by Athena and Nausicaa in Books 6 and 7 and by Circe in Book 10 before the visit to the Netherworld. These parallels have been recently analysed by Richard Martin,[12] so I will concentrate on the second type of leaves, those which depict a supplication of the soul to the Queen of the Underworld. Such scenes appears in several leaves from Thurii. Whether or not these two types of leaves originally belonged to the same poem is irrelevant for the purposes of the present argument.[13]

Two of the Thurii leaves (*OF* 489–490) contain an identical text:

Ἔρχομαι ἐκ καθαρῶν καθαρά, χθονίων βασίλεια,
Εὔκλε καὶ Εὐβουλεῦ καὶ θεοὶ καὶ δαίμονες ἄλλοι·
καὶ γὰρ ἐγὼν ὑμῶν γένος εὔχομαι ὄλβιον εἶναι
ποινὰν δ' ἀνταπέτεισ' ἔργων ἕνεκα οὔτι δικαίων.
εἴτε με Μοῖρα ἐδάμασσ' εἴτε ἀστεροπῆτα κεραυνῶν.
νῦν δ' ἱκέτις ἥκω παραὶ ἁγνὴν Φερσεφόνειαν,
ὥς με πρόφρων πέμψηι ἕδρας ἐς εὐαγέων.

I come pure from the pure, Queen of the chthonians,
Eucles, Eubouleus and all the gods and daimones,
for I too claim to be of your blessed lineage.
I have paid compensation in return for unjust deeds,
whether Fate overcame me or the thrower of thunderbolts.
Now I come as a suppliant to the reverend Persephone,
so that she, benevolent, may send me to the abode of the blessed.

This scene has an easy analogue in a number of well-known supplication scenes in the *Odyssey*.[14] Two of the most important for Odysseus'

---

12 In a paper delivered at the Ohio State University conference *Ritual Texts for the Afterlife* (April 2006), organized by F. Graf and S. Iles-Johnston. While awaiting publication of the papers, there is an online working version (Richard P. Martin, "Golden Verses: Voice and Authority in the Tablets," *Princeton/Stanford Working Papers*, paper no. 040701 [2007], http://ssrn.com/abstract=1426980 [accessed October 23, 2011]).

13 In my own paper in the Ohio conference (= Herrero de Jáuregui, forthcoming) I deal with the subject of the insertion of this scene in the general structure of the hypothetical *katabasis* of the soul, as reconstructed by Christoph Riedweg, "Initiation-Death-Underworld. Narrative and Ritual in the Gold Tablets," in *The Orphic Gold Tablets and Greek Religion: Further Along the Path*, ed. Radcliffe G. Edmonds (Cambridge: Cambridge University Press, 2011), 219–256.

14 On the literary form and meanings of supplication in Homer, cf. Agathe Thornton, *Homer's Iliad: Its Composition and the Motif of Supplication* (Göttingen: Vandenhoeck & Ruprecht, 1984); Reece 1993; Kevin Crotty, *The Poetics of*

wanderings are representative and brief enough to be quoted here (English translations from R. Lattimore). When Odysseus is desperately trying to reach land from the sea, he sees the mouth of a river and prays (*Od.* 5.445–450):

> κλῦθι, ἄναξ, ὅτις ἐσσί· πολύλλιστον δέ σ' ἱκάνω
> φεύγων ἐκ πόντοιο Ποσειδάωνος ἐνιπάς.
> αἰδοῖος μέν τ' ἐστὶ καὶ ἀθανάτοισι θεοῖσιν,
> ἀνδρῶν ὅς τις ἵκηται ἀλώμενος, ὡς καὶ ἐγὼ νῦν
> σόν τε ῥόον σά τε γούναθ' ἱκάνω πολλὰ μογήσας.
> ἀλλ' ἐλέαιρε, ἄναξ· ἱκέτης δέ τοι εὔχομαι εἶναι.

> Hear me, my lord, whoever you are: I come in great need
> to you, a fugitive from the sea and the curse of Poseidon;
> even for the immortal gods that man has a claim on their mercy
> who comes to them as a wandering man, in the way that I now
> come to your current and to your knees after much suffering.
> Pity me then, my lord. I call myself your suppliant.

Upon his arrival in Scheria, after some encounters and dialogues (with Nausicaa, and with Athena disguised as a child), and after traversing the imposing palace of Alcinous, Odysseus kneels down before Queen Arete and supplicates her (*Od.* 7.146–152):

> Ἀρήτη, θύγατερ Ῥηξήνορος ἀντιθέοιο,
> σόν τε πόσιν σά τε γούναθ' ἱκάνω πολλὰ μογήσας,
> τούσδε τε δαιτυμόνας, τοῖσιν θεοὶ ὄλβια δοῖεν,
> ζωέμεναι, καὶ παισὶν ἐπιτρέψειεν ἕκαστος
> κτήματ' ἐνὶ μεγάροισι γέρας θ', ὅ τι δῆμος ἔδωκεν.
> αὐτὰρ ἐμοὶ πομπὴν ὀτρύνετε πατρίδ' ἱκέσθαι
> θᾶσσον, ἐπεὶ δὴ δηθὰ φίλων ἄπο πήματα πάσχω.

Supplication: Homer's Iliad and Odyssey (Ithaca and London: Cornell University Press, 1994) and Manuela Giordano, *La supplica: rituale, istituzione sociale e tema epico in Omero* (Naples: A.I.O.N., 1999). Walter Arend, *Die typische Scenen bei Homer* (Berlin: Weidmann, 1933), 42ff studies it among the Homeric typical scenes. John Gould, "Hiketeia," *JHS* 93 (1973): 74–103 is the classic study of the ritual and historical aspects of Greek supplication (cf. the observations of Victoria Pedrick, "Supplication in the *Iliad* and in the *Odyssey*," *TAPhA* 112 [1982]: 125–140). Fred S. Naiden, *Ancient Supplication* (Oxford and New York: Oxford University Press, 2006), has undertaken an ambitious overview of supplication from Homer to Roman law, including comparison with Near Eastern sources, which distinguishes four steps in the process: the approach, the gestures, and the request of the suppliant, and the response of the addressee (the leaves allude to steps 1 and 3, but 2 and 4 are also implicit). None of these works mentions the leaves, nor does Orphic scholarship engage with the theme of supplication.

> Arete, daughter of godlike Rhexenor, after much hardship
> I have come to your knees as suppliant, and to your husband
> and to these feasters, on whom may the gods bestow prosperity
> in their own lives, and grant to each to leave to his children
> his property in his house and the rights the people have given him.
> But for me, urge that conveyance be given quickly
> to my country, since long now far from my people I suffer hardships.

These two supplication scenes play a central role in the success of Odysseus' *nostos*. Likewise, the supplication of the soul in the Thurii leaves is determinative for its salvation. We can distinguish six elements which show a parallel structure between these scenes that goes far beyond the formulaic similarities.[15]

In the first place there is an invocation. At the beginning of supplication, be it an internal prayer or a physical arrival, Odysseus utters the name (Arete) or, if he does not know it, at least the title of the addressee (ἄναξ to the river, ἄνασσα to Nausicaa). The mention of the addressee's kin is also typical: as Odysseus mentions the relatives of Arete and Nausicaa, so does the soul in the gold leaves greet the Queen of the chthonians and the other gods.

The second element is a declaration of arrival as a suppliant, a status which entitled the subject to protection and hospitality. To declare oneself expressly a suppliant (ἱκέτης) was a way to claim these rights. All suppliants in the *Odyssey* are careful to underline their status with the formula ἱκέτης δέ τοι εὔχομαι εἶναι or similar expressions. So does the soul in the leaves (ἱκέτις ἥκω).[16] Some lines earlier, the verb εὔχομαι is used to declare the familiar relationship of the soul with the gods. Relatives were even more entitled to the rights of hospitality than simple suppliants. The verb, therefore, has its old juridical nuance of "claiming" one's own rights, and at the same time, it keeps its primary meaning of "prayer," since it is addressed to the gods.[17]

---

15 Other supplication scenes in the *Odyssey* show a similar structure: 6.149–185 (to Nausicaa); 15.275–278 (a fugitive); 16.61–67 (a report in third person).
16 In Herrero de Jáuregui (forthcoming) I suggest an etymological play between the two words, as epic scenes stress the relation of ἱκητής with ἱκάνω (I come). On the other hand, Martin 2007, 10, observes that the verb ἔρχομαι is never used in epics in the sense "I come," and that it is never close to the phonetically similar εὔχομαι. As this instance shows, the relation of the tablets to Homeric epics is not subservient. They present independent elaborations of epic elements, not simple transpositions of epic models.
17 Cf. Miguel Herrero de Jáuregui, "Dialogues of Immortality from the Iliad to the Gold Leaves," in *The Orphic Gold Tablets and Greek Religion: Further*

A third element is a reference to past hardships which have put the hero in the present situation of need. In his supplications Odysseus stresses his many sufferings (πολλὰ μογήσας, πήματα πάσχω) as a way of eliciting pity from his addressee. Similarly, the soul of the initiate declares to have paid the due compensation for unjust deeds. The soul's primary aim in this declaration is to let Queen Persephone know that she has paid the price for having caused her a grief and is therefore "free of penalty" and can be saved.[18] This justification belongs to the context of the mysteries and is obviously not present in the Odyssean supplication scenes. But we should not forget that it also contains the implication of past sufferings. In place of this line another leaf from Thurii has instead: "I flew out of the circle of wearying circle of heavy grief."[19] This line refers explicitly to the wanderings of the soul as a past hardship. The supplication is envisaged as a turning point where these sufferings may come to definitive end. A frequent verbal tag of this wish is the adverb "now" (νῦν) refering to the "coming," following verbs in aorist tense which refered to past sufferings, both in the *Odyssey* (5.448, 16.65) and in the Thurii leaves.

We can point to a fourth element which does not belong to all supplications but plays an important role in some of them. In a number of contexts in which a suppliant is seeking protection from a higher power, he makes reference to the persecution which he has suffered at the hands of another, who reigns in a different sphere. We have seen Odysseus mentioning the curse of the sea-god Poseidon when asking the protection of a river.[20] All three leaves from Thurii mention the divine persecution which causes the suffering of the soul: "whether Fate overcame me or the thrower of thunderbolts [i.e., Zeus]." This statement is very

---

Along the Path, ed. Radcliffe G. Edmonds (Cambridge: Cambridge University Press, 2011), 271–290, for the dense meaning of εὔχομαι in the leaves. The mysterious tablet C from Thurii offers a parallel sentence (*OF* 492.6): "mother, answer my prayers" (ἐμὰς ἐπάκουσον εὐχάς). Cf. Bernabé and Jiménez 2008, 146 f.

18 Cf. *OF* 493 (from Pherai): ἄποινος γὰρ ὁ μύστης. This *poiné* (also in Pindar fr. 133 S-M) probably refers to the myth of Dionysus killed by the Titans, ancestors of human beings, though some scholars contest this relationship. Cf. Bernabé and Jiménez 2008, 105–115.
19 *OF* 490.5. Cf. Bernabé and Jiménez 2008, 117–132. The line probably alludes to a transmigration cycle.
20 *Od.* 5.446. In *Od.* 15.275–278 the fugitive Theoclymenos, who has killed a man, asks to be accepted by Telemachus in his ship to escape from the vengeance of his victim's relatives.

appropiate to ask the protection of another power (i. e., Persephone) in a different realm, Hades.

A fifth element is precisely a petition for protection, which can never be taken for granted. The suppliant, no matter what rights he may be entitled to, is always conscious that his fortune is in the hands of his host, and that he depends on his or her will. Odysseus is repeatedly told (6.310–315, 7.75–77) that his salvation is mainly dependent on persuading Arete and gaining her benevolence. The risk of rejection continues until she shows her acceptance after having been satisfied with the account of her guest.[21] Similarly, the soul in the gold leaves aknowledges that she depends on the benevolence of the Queen, with the formula ὥς με πρόφρων πέμψηι. The construction with ὥς followed by subjunctive leaves open the possibility that Persephone may reject the soul.[22]

The sixth and final element is the welcome and guarantee of help obtained if the host proves benevolent. The concrete form of this element may vary depending on the situation. Odysseus asks the river for help in reaching land; from Nausicaa, he asks for some clothes and di-

---

21 Queen Arete offers some striking analogies to Persephone as described in the *katabasis* of the leaves: she is announced as powerful and merciful (7.75–77); she asks directly, even abruptly, his identity and shows motherly concern lest he has harmed her child (7.238: "who are you? and who gave you these clothes?"); only when Odysseus gives a wholly satisfactory account (of his *Nekyia*!) will she show her magnificent benevolence (11.336–341). To obtain her hospitality and avoid the potential hostility of the Phaeacians, far from being an easy task, requires much skill from Odysseus (Fenik 1974, 5–133; Rose 1969, 387–406; Julian Pitt-Rivers, "Women and Sanctuary in the Mediterranean," in *Échanges et Communications: Mélanges Lévi-Strauss*, ed. Jean Pouillon and Pierre Maranda [The Hague and Paris: Mouton 1970], 869). It is possible to think that the poet of the *katabasis* of the soul modelled his Underworldly Queen on the Homeric episode. But if that *katabasis* derives from earlier poems, the parallels could be ascribed to the different epic usage of a type-scene. Transposing Wilamowitz's theory that Arete was an ancient "Totenkönigin" (Ulrich von Wilamowitz-Moellendorff, *Die Ilias und Homer* [Berlin: Weidmannsche Buchhandlung, 1916], 491 f) to neo-analytical categories, I find it probable that the character of Arete echoes the underworldly goddess in katabatic poems.
22 Cf. Parm. B 1.22 DK, whose goddess is πρόφρων and receives him cordially. Naiden 2006 rightly insists on the freedom of the addressee to accept or refuse supplication. Cf. Pitt-Rivers 1970, and Gould 1973, 95–100 on the role of women as prefered addressees of supplication. To the examples they offer, add Plut. *Vit. Sol.*12, where Cylon's people obtain salvation by supplicating to the wives of the *synarchontes* (a reference I owe to Jan Bremmer).

rections to the town; from Arete, help in reaching his homeland. In the gold leaves, the soul hopes that Persephone will send her to the abode of the purified. Other leaves and texts specify the blessings which she will enjoy there, probably a symposion in the company of other initiates.²³ Eating and drinking was also the most common gesture of hospitality for the welcome suppliant. But Odysseus' petition that Arete not include him amongst her feasting men, but send him (ἐμοὶ πομπὴν ὀτρύνετε) immediately to his own land, is particularly interesting in relation to the most recently published gold leaf from Pherai (*OF* 493 A), whose text begins "send me to the *thiasoi* of initiates" (πέμπε με πρὸς μυστῶν θιάσους). This line has allowed us to read a hitherto unreadable line from another Thurii leaf as "you must go to the *thiasos* on the right" (δεξιὸν ἐς θίασον δεῖ σ' ἰέναι).²⁴ From these sentences one can deduce that even in the Underworld envisaged by the leaves there may have been alternative happy destinies, as well as punishments and torments,²⁵ but the soul just wants to join a particular group, those which are her own kinsmen, the other *mystai* and *bacchoi* of the Hipponion leaf (*OF* 474.16). Like Odysseus, only there will she feel at home.

To sum up, the soul's supplication to Persephone shows a number of analogies between the journey to Hades and that of the wandering hero.²⁶ Not for nothing is the soul called "hero" in some leaves (*OF* 475.2, 473.13); the traditional heroic voyage is now hers. Eventual heroization of the defunct is consistent with this epic background. The similarities between the supplication in the leaves and the Odyssean scenes can be explained either as influence from the Homeric poems on the composer(s) of the *katabasis* of the soul, or as variant usages of similar type-scenes. Either way, they show how salvation was conceptualized and experienced through epic categories and images. The soul is envis-

---

23   Cf. Bernabé and Jiménez 2008, 88 ff. Cf. n. 43 *infra* for the position of the soul "over the other heroes."
24   *OF* 487.2; cf. Bernabé and Jiménez 2008, 96 (the new reading was proposed by M. A. Santamaría). Cf. also Bernabé in this volume.
25   Cf. Aristoph. *Ra.* 154, 327. Cf. Edmonds 2004, 20–27, and Graf and Johnston 2007, 104–108, on the multiplicity of paths in Hades. The soteriological function of the leaves imposes a straightforward dichotomy of right vs. wrong path, but the previous poem(s) on the *katabasis* of the soul may have presented a more complex Underworld geography.
26   The specific similarity with the arrival to Scheria is reinforced because this journey is the "principal point of crisis and transition" (Segal 1994, 17, 38), since the trip from Scheria to Ithaca will be short and safe. Likewise, the rest of the journey after Persephone does not seem to worry the soul.

aged as a wandering exiled hero who yearns to return home after much suffering—and must be brave and clever enough to manage it, doing the right things, taking the right paths, saying the right words. The image of the hero who travels and supplicates determines expectations about what one will find in the Afterlife. In all probability, the feelings involved in supplication (grief, piety, *aidos*, *philia*) also mirrored the initiate's anticipated experience before the goddess.[27] We cannot but be reminded here of a famous Christian prayer to the Virgin Mary which shows many of these elements: ...*ad te clamamus, exules filii Evae; ad te suspiramus, gementes et flentes, in hac lacrimarum valle*... But we need not travel so far in time. The most radical formulation of the exile of the soul belongs to another hexametrical poet of the 5th century BC, Empedocles.

III. The Wanderings of the *Daimon* in Empedocles

There is little doubt that Empedocles was familiar with the religious model represented by the gold leaves. His links with Pythagorean and Orphic spheres have been exhaustively studied in the last decade, and though these labels can be discussed, it is now clear that this connexion heavily determined his thought and his praxis.[28] He is sure to have known the ideas about salvation implied in the *katabasis* of the soul from which the gold leaves take their hexametres, and it is not improbable that he knew the poem itself. And it cannot be disputed that he had an intimate knowledge of the Homeric poems, whose presence in his

---

27 Although important, supplication does not need to be the only conceptual frame of the religious experience involved in the leaves. In Herrero de Jáuregui 2011, I explore the agonistic epic expressions in the leaves, which seem to indicate that the soul underwent some sort of (internal) battle.

28 Peter Kingsley, *Ancient Philosophy, Mystery and Magic: Empedocles and Pythagorean Tradition* (Oxford: Oxford University Press, 1995); Christoph Riedweg, "Orphisches bei Empedocles," *A & A* 41 (1995): 34–59; Carlos Megino Rodríguez, *Orfeo y el orfismo en la poesía de Empédocles* (Madrid: Ediciones de la Universidad Autónoma de Madrid, 2005). Beside the many parallels there are also some clear divergences: e.g., the Dionysiac element, essential to the salvation scheme of the leaves, is rejected by Empedocles, who links *mania* (a concept with obvious Dionysiac associations) with *Neikos*: B 115.14, and indirectly, also B 3.1.

work has been detected at many points.[29] To my knowledge, however, there has been no specific study of how the model of the wandering hero may have shaped the wanderings of his *daimon*. This is even more remarkable if we consider that Parmenides has been repeatedly said to shape his poem on the model of Odysseus' journey.[30] Instead, only M. Rashed has briefly but clearly pointed out in two recent sudies dedicated to fragments B 84 and B 115 that the return of the exiled *daimon* to his heavenly fatherland is explicitly mirroring Odysseus' return to Ithaca.[31] Perhaps Aristotle's statement that Empedocles had "only metre in common with Homer" is to blame partly for the fact that most modern studies of Homeric features in his poems restrict their analyses to questions of diction.[32] But it seems that Aristotle did not tell the whole story this time.

---

29 To restrict myself to a few examples from the *Odyssey*: Antonio Capizzi, "Trasposizione del lesico omerico in Parmenide ed Empedocle. Osservazioni su un problema di metodo," QUCC 54 (1987): 113 derives the opposition *Philotes / Neikos* from *Od.* 24.476, 543; Kingsley 1995, 253 relates B 146 to the apotheosis of Heracles in *Od.* 11.602; Alain Martin and Oliver Primavesi, *L'Empédocle de Strasbourg* (Berlin: De Gruyter, 1999), 302 relate the movement where the world will perish (*ensemble* d7) with the current of Charybdis in *Od.* 12.427 f (cf. Segal 1994, 46 n.13 on its resemblance to a gate of the Underworld); and Empedocles' tears (*ensemble* d7) with Odysseus' in *Od.* 8.522; more instances in nn. 51–55 *infra*.

30 Havelock 1958; Mourelatos 1970; Barbara Cassin, "Le chant des Sirènes dans le Poème de Parménide: quelques remarques sur le fr. VIII, 26–33," in *Études sur Parménide. Problèmes d'interprétation*, ed. Pierre Aubenque (Paris: Vrin, 1987), 163–170.

31 Rashed 2007, 33–37, and Marwan Rashed, "Le proème des *Catharmes* d'Empédocle. Reconstitution et commentaire," *Elenchos* 29.1 (2008): 29–30, discussed below. Jean-Claude Picot, "Empédocle pouvait-il faire de la lune le séjour des Bienheureux ?," *Organon* (Warszawa) 37 (40) (2008): 20–25 has followed Rashed's remarks, and adds that probably Lucian realized Empedocles' relation to the *Odyssey* and played with it in *Icaromenippus*. The main thesis of this paper, although using different texts, agrees with their conclusions.

32 Aristot. *Poet.* 1447b, followed by Plut. *De audiend.*, 16C-D. On Empedocles as a poet, cf. Bernhard Abraham van Groningen, "Empédocle, poète," *Mnemosyne* 24 (1971): 169–188, Jackson P Hershbell, "Empedocles' Oral Style," *CJ* 63 (1968): 352–357 and Jackson P. Hershbell, "Hesiod and Empedocles," *CJ* 65 (1970): 145–161, and Annette Rosenfeld-Löffler (in comparison to Hesiod), *La poétique d'Empédocle, Cosmologie et métaphore* (Bern and New York: Peter Lang, 2006). On Empedocles' way of alluding to Homer, cf. Kingsley 1995, 42–45, 52 f. The latest study in the usage of Homeric diction by Empedocles is Carlitria Bordigoni, "Empedocle e la dizione omerica," in *Studi sul pensiero e sulla lingua di Empedocle*, ed. Livio Rossetti and Carlo Santaniello

The study of Empedocles is largely determined by problems concerning the collocation of the extant fragments in one or two poems and their order, so it is necessary to make my position on these matters clear from the outset. Whether the exile of the *daimon* was told in an independent poem, the *Katharmoi*, or in the only work of Empedocles does not affect my argument. I take as my point of departure his greeting to the dwellers of Akragas (B 112 DK). There is no doubt that it occupied the initial position in the narrative frame of the poem to which it belonged.[33] In the following paragraphs, I will assume that fragments B 115, B 131 and B 146–147 come later in the same work, probably in this order. This is the most widely accepted collocation of these fragments.[34] It is not, however, essential to my argument that all these fragments appeared in this order within the same work, for as the *Odyssey* clearly shows, there were a number of possible narrative strategies for recounting the wanderings, and the poet may have chosen to tell the story following an order different to the chronological succession of events. In fact, Empedocles begins his poem announcing he is saved,

---

(Bari: Levante, 2004), 199–290, who offers the abundant previous bibliography on the subject, mostly by Italian scholars (cf. above all M. Laura Gemelli Marciano, *Le metamorfosi della tradizione: mutamenti di significato e neologismi nel Peri physeos di Empedocle* [Bari: Levante, 1990], and also Capizzi 1987, 107–118). Another reason for the difficulty of studying Empedocles' poetry is given by Van Groningen 1971, 176: "cent vers d'Empédocle fatiguent plus que mille vers de *l'Odyssée*."

33 Diogenes Laertius (8.61) says expressly that it is the beginning of the *Katharmoi*, and it is edited as such by Hermann Diels and Walther Kranz, *Die Fragmente der Vorsokratiker*, 6th ed. (Berlin: Weidmann, 1951) and M. R. Wright, *Empedocles: The Extant Fragments* (New Haven and London: Yale University Press, 1981). Partisans of the single poem hypothesis, i.e., Brad Inwood, *The Poem of Empedocles. A Text and Translation with an Introduction* (Toronto: University of Toronto Press, 2001), Simon Trépanier, *Empedocles. An Interpretation* (London: Routledge, 2004), also treat it as the first fragment.

34 E. g., Günther Zuntz, *Persephone: Three Essays on Religion and Thought in Magna Graecia* (Oxford: Oxford University Press, 1971) and Jean Bollack, *Empédocle. Les Purifications: Un projet de paix universelle* (Paris: Points, 2003), who follow Diels' ordering. Carlo Gavallotti, *Empedocle. Poema fisico e lustrale* (Milan: Mondadori, 1975) edits B 131 at the very beginning of the *Physika,* and Wright 1981 as her fr. 3 (*Physika*), thus separating it from the other fragments (Dirk Obbink, "The Addressees of Empedocles," *Materiali e discussioni per l'analisi dei testi classici* 31 [1993]: 51–98 [B 112] agrees with such a collocation). Cf. n. 61 *infra* for my arguments against this. Martin and Primavesi 1999 suggest that B 115 does not belong to the *Katharmoi*, since it would be the proem of the *Physika*. Cf. n. 47 *infra* against this idea.

and then tells of his previous fall and exile, from which he was able to escape, perhaps, thanks to the help of a goddess. We shall follow this sequence in tracing the motif of wandering in his extant fragments.

Ὦ φίλοι! is the beginning of Empedocles' salutation in B 112. It has been rightly pointed out that if this was the first word of the poem, the canons of epic poetry demand that it announces its subject-matter, as μῆνιν in the *Iliad* and ἄνδρα in the *Odyssey*.[35] How or why the citizens of Akragas become *philoi* to Empedocles should be linked with the contents of the poem. On the one hand, it sets him on the side of *Philotes*, in sharp contrast to his being "subject to *Neikos*" not much later (B 115.14). On the other hand, the exclamation *philoi* links him to his addressees in a way that indicates close intimacy: he feels somehow bound to them.[36] Empedocles starts with a spectacular self-characterization as a god (see below), but no less intriguing are the compliments to his addressees: he calls them αἰδοῖοι and he greets them with χαίρετε. These greetings have been sometimes taken as flattery or irony.[37] They are, however, meant very seriously. This kind of salutation at the beginning of Empedocles' poem corresponds precisely to the end

---

35 Trépanier 2004, 47 f, stresses this point, though he does not consider all its implications. The fragment not only sets the scene of the poem, but also provides its interpretative key: how to arrive at a state of blessedness.
36 The identity of these *philoi* is much debated. I believe Riedweg 1995, 35 n.12 is right that the addressees are noblemen of Akragas, living in the citadel, *pace* Wolfgang Rösler, "Der Anfang der Katharmoi des Empedokles," *Hermes* 111 (1983): 171, who prefers to interpret the address as being directed to all the inhabitants of Akragas. B 146–147 and similar texts point to an aristocratic milieu. Some of them may have shared Empedocles' beliefs; we may compare the audience of Pindar's *Odes*. Eva Stehle, "The Addressees of Empedokles, Katharmoi Fr. B 112: Performance and Moral Implications," *Anc. Phil.* 25.2 (2005): 247–72 has recently proposed that the *philoi* are the gods of Akragas, whom Empedocles greets by way of a proem, and in line 4 he turns to mortals with ὑμῖν. Gestures would help the audience to understand the change of addressee. Though she argues forcibly and gives good parallels (260), I find it hard to reconcile with another address to men as *philoi* (B 114), which I do not believe could be a periodical reminder to the audience that he was addressing the gods. Stehle's arguments, however, may serve to show that Empedocles greeted his kinsmen where gods are usually greeted, in the proem, making them close (though slightly inferior, n. 61) to his own divine status.
37 Stehle 2006, 250–253 shows the scholarly tendency to deflating these compliments, above all because they are felt to be contradictory with the insults in 2nd person plural of other fragments (B 141).

of the peregrination of the soul in the gold leaves, and of Odysseus' in Homer, when the exiled wanderer meets his kinsmen.[38]

Thus Empedocles starts his tale where other poets ended it, i.e., in the accomplishment of the journey back home. This difference in narrative strategy was probably intended to provide an element of contrast with other poetic accounts of salvation, like that of the leaves. And not only did it contrast with the soteriological journeys, but also with the Homeric wandering hero: the mention of the cities he has visited (B 112.7: ἵκωμαι ἐς ἄστεα), which has famously characterized Empedocles as a wandering priest, also appeals to the famous prologue of the *Odyssey* (1.3: ἴδεν ἄστεα, in the same *sedes metrica*) and casts him as a new Odysseus at the end of his journey.[39] It need not be the last stage of Empedocles' salvation, but at any rate he is close to it, perhaps in the penultimate stage.[40] The blessedness of Akragas' inhabitants, "caring for good works" and "far from evil" is parallel to that of the happy Phaeacians at Scheria. And their characterization as "reverend havens for the strangers" (B 112.3: ξένων αἰδοῖοι λιμένες) is clearly consistent with the image of the wanderer who arrives (ἵκωμαι) to a new land where humans are blessed, though not divine–which supports the authenticity of this disputed verse.

Reunited with his compatriots, Empedocles greets the citizens as if he were almost among his equals. Almost, because if the citizens are "reverend" and "far from evil," Empedocles' status is even higher: in

---

38 The first words of Odysseus in Ithaca when he meets a native (Athena in disguise) are ὦ φίλε... χαῖρε (*Od.* 13.228 f). The greeting χαῖρε may also have religious overtones, which in the gold leaves, as in other funerary contexts, have an eschatological meaning: Bernabé and Jiménez 2008, 96–97 (on *OF* 487, 495, 496).

39 *Od.* 1.3 was also the basis for Havelock's idea that Parmenides was alluding to the *Odyssey* in his fr. 1.3. But the reading κατὰ πάντ' ἄστη was later rejected. If the attempt of Pugliese Carratelli (Giovanni Pugliese Carratelli, "La *thea* di Parmenide," *PP* 43 [1988]: 340) to rehabilitate this reading in the light of leaf C (*OF* 492) is right (*pace* Marcel Conche, *Parménide. Le Poème. Fragments. Texte grec, traduction, présentation, et commentaire* [Paris: Presses Universitaires de France, 1996], 45 n.1), then Empedocles' proem could not only be alluding to the *Odyssey*, but also to Parmenides.

40 Stehle 2006, 270 rightly describes Empedocles' status: "It is as though he stands at the juncture of B146 and B147, highest in honor among humans and just now a new intimate of the community of gods practicing *philotes*, not yet departed to become a participant in the banquet."

B 112 he presents himself in epiphanic terms as a god amongst men.[41] He is honoured (5: τετιμένος) and revered (8: σεβίζομαι) by them, and his head is crowned, with all the associations of honour, victory, and celebration that the crown had for the Greeks.[42] Let us remember that Odysseus too wanted to join his *philoi*, amongst whom he would have the status of a king. Also, the literal translation of the line in the Petelia leaf anouncing a happy destiny, "you will reign *over* the other heroes," sounds perfectly coherent in this light.[43] In the same way, the purified *daimon* arrives among his *philoi* as their superior.

This happy destiny as a *primus inter pares* is also mentioned in fragments B 146 and B 147, which have long since been read along with Pindar's fragment 133 S-M.[44] Both establish a gradation of salvation where the wisest and noblest of men enjoy the highest possible situation before receiving a super-human status. There are some minor differences which point to different usage of the same set of beliefs. Pindar talks of heroes, while Empedocles talks of gods. Pindar talks of "kings," while Empedocles avoids that word—perhaps his democratic convictions led him to change the title—and talks of "leaders" (πρόμοι). These frag-

---

41 ἐγὼ δ'ὑμῖν θεὸς ἄμβροτος (B 112.4) recalls the revelatory formulae of *Hymn. Hom. Cer.* 120 and 268. Cf. Zuntz 1971, 191. This excludes that the *philoi* are actually gods, though Empedocles may have seen them as close to the divine status that he himself enjoys. An analogy may be found in some of the gold leaves, which speak of the divinization of the soul (Megino 2005, 68–71).

42 For the eschatological, symposiastic and victory connotations of the crown in a Thurii gold leaf (*OF* 488.6), cf. Bernabé and Jiménez 2008, 121–130. Seaford's description of the crown in this leaf (Richard Seaford, "Immortality, Salvation, and the Elements," *HSCP* 90 [1986]: 23–25) also applies to Empedocles: it is a positive circle that symbolically marks the exit from the negative one (i. e., of reincarnation). Cf. n. 76 *infra* on its appearance in Lucretius.

43 Vincenzo di Benedetto, "Fra Hipponion e Petelia," *PP* 59 (2004): 294 shows that ἀνάσσω with μετά plus dative (*OF* 476.11) expresses predominance over the other heroes. Bernabé and Jiménez 2008, 178 and Graf and Johnston 2007, 7 do not translate it in this way, but rather as an expression of co-regency "you will reign with / among the other heroes." Tortorelli 2006, 126 f follows instead Di Benedetto's translation, which is supported by the Empedoclean parallel. I do not believe Edmond's new proposal ("you will celebrate rites with the heroes") is right (Edmonds 2011, 22 f.).

44 E. g., Riedweg 1995, Megino 2005, 66 ff. On Pindar's *Olympian* 2, with famous Orphic-Pythagorean allusions, and Empedocles, cf. Nancy Demand, "Pindar's *Olympian* 2, Theron's Faith, and Empedocles' *Katharmoi*," *GRBS* 16 (1975): 347–357 and Hugh Lloyd-Jones, "Pindar and the Afterlife," *Pindar, Entretiens Fondation Hardt* 31 (1984): 245–283.

ments, like Pindar's, are widely recognized as externally linked to the Orphic eschatology of the gold leaves.[45] They are also internally linked to the beginning of the poem, for they announce Empedocles' own destiny as a *mantis*, a poet, a physician, a leader, and a god: all these elements are mentioned as well in the initial self-presentation in fr. B 112, to which we will return below. Fragments B 146–147 are generally placed at the (happy) end of the poem *Katharmoi*, which would give a neat ring composition.[46]

More important, however, than the collocation of the fragments, i.e., the narrative order of Empedocles' poem, is the logical order, i.e., the succession of events. How has Empedocles attained this blessed status? Not too long after his epiphanic entrance, he begins to tell his misfortunes in B 115.[47] He is "a wanderer, an exile from the god," like other *daimones* due to an initial fall from his divine status.[48] After breaking his oath, the *daimon* is received and rejected succesively by the four elements in a permanent and hateful peregrination from one to another.[49] Such wandering (ἀλάλεσθαι) may have brought many as-

---

45 E.g., Bernabé and Jiménez 2008, 20, 72, 75. Seaford 1986, 7 n. 22 gives another argument to think of noblemen: "the wealth of the burials containing the gold leaves may suggest that here too, as in Empedokles, return to divine status is imagined as being immediately preceded by high social status."
46 Riedweg 1995, 43; Stehle 2006, 266; Picot 2008, 11–12.
47 B 115 is cited by Plutarch as being "at the beginning of his philosophy," meaning perhaps the narration of the *daimon*'s existence in this world, after his self-presentation. Trépanier 2004, 35–38, 82 argues convincingly for keeping the traditional link between B 112 and B 115, and their contrast between the triumphant and the decadent states of Empedocles as a *daimon*. Martin and Primavesi 1998, 113 f tried to rehabilitate the 19th cent. theory that B 115 could be the proem of the *Physika*. I find Trépanier's arguments more forceful. Furthermore, Rashed 2008 unites B 112, 114, 115 and 113 as the first 30 lines of the *Katharmoi*, which is very suggestive.
48 The variant τῶν νῦν, adopted by Wright 1981, 275, is preferable to τὴν νῦν, since Empedocles' *daimon* participates in the general fall (it is adopted also in the original solution proposed by Rashed 2008). In B 115 the references to Hesiod *Theog.* 801–804 (the gods exiled from the divine banquet for having broken the oath by Styx) and Aesch. *Ag.* 1282 (Orestes exiled and wanderer) are broadly recognized. They are not incompatible with the Odyssean background.
49 It is significant that Homeric oaths are sworn by the primordial elements of the cosmos or the gods presiding over them (*Il.* 3.103–107, 3.275–280, 14.271–280, 15.36–38, 19.157–265, analysed by Giovanni Cerri in "L'ideologia dei quattro elementi da Omero ai Presocratici," *AION (filol)* 20 [1998]: 5–58): precisely these elements punish the oath-breaker *daimon* by rejecting him.

sociations to the ears of the audience, as to Empedocles' as he composed the poem. R. Seaford has suggested the mysteries as the background for this peregrination through the elements.[50] Without denying this possibility, I suggest that Odysseus' wanderings, miserably carried by the natural elements in three long scenes in the *Odyssey* (5.313–445, 7.248–283 and 12.403–444), must have sounded to Empedocles' audience as the most immediate precedent for the *daimon's* own wandering. The winds (easily identifiable with *aither*, as Seaford 1986, 10 says) and the seas are obviously hostile to Odysseus when he is at Poseidon's mercy (5.294ff). Fire is represented by Zeus' punishing thunderbolt and by the hostile Sun. These three elements pursue Odysseus constantly (e.g., 5.478, 7.248). But even the earth, usually a symbol of salvation for desperate sailors, turns hostile, as a dangerous rock which after receiving Odysseus rejects him again in the sea (5.430–435, 7.279), or as the terrifying Scylla and Charybdis (12.430–446), where Odysseus' hanging from a branch "without any place to put his feet" (12.433ff) is a powerful image of his abandonment by all the elements.[51] Only the intervention of a god makes it possible to escape this incessant whirling. But contrary to Odysseus, the *daimon* has no god to help him—not yet.

That Empedocles thinks of the erring of the *daimon* within the background of Odysseus' voyage over the seas is supported, moreover, by some fragments usually attributed to the *Physika*. In particular, fragment

---

On the primordial fault of the *daimon*, I think Renaud Gagné, "L'esthétique de la peur chez Empédocle," *RPhA* 24.3 (2006): 83–110 and Jean-Claude Picot, "Empedocles, fragment 115.3: Can One of the Blessed Pollute his Limbs with Blood?," in *Reading Ancient Texts I: Presocratics and Plato—Essays in Honour of Denis O'Brien*, ed. Suzanne Stern-Gillet and Kevin Corrigan (Leiden: Brill, 2007), 41–56, are right in defending the reading of the manuscripts φόβωι instead of the usual emendation φόνωι for B 115.3.

50 Seaford 1986, 10–12. His argument finds further support in the new readings for tablet *OF* 492). Even if this mediating instance is admitted, the relation with the passage from the *Odyssey* remains the same.

51 Segal 1994, 46. Granted, the Odyssean scenes do not show the four elements in perfect coordination as in Empedocles' poem. Although the ancient idea of the four elements is known by Homer (Cerri 1998), it is not Homer who holds a theory of wandering through them, but Empedocles who takes inspiration from the Homeric poems to express this theory, as is clear from the Homeric names which he chooses to designate them. Rashed's suggestion (2007, 36) that the ball thrown by Nausicaa and her friends at *Od*. 6.115–117 echoes the movement of the *daimon* in B 115.9–11 uncovers a purposeful Empedoclean verbal play to underline the Odyssean links.

B 20.5 says that under the bad influence of *Neikos*, some members of the body "wander on the shore of life" (πλάζεται... περὶ ῥεγμῖνι βίοιο). Empedocles not only uses the verb πλάζομαι which describes Odysseus' wanderings (i. e., in the prologue, *Od.* 1.2), but he also reelaborates the Homeric expression ῥεγμῖνι θαλάσσης substituting "sea" for "life" in the same metrical position.[52] It is pertinent to remember here that, again, the prologue of the *Odyssey* specifies that the hero suffered "in the sea" (1.4: πόντῳ). The model that Empedocles has in mind is clear: his *daimon* wanders and suffers in life as Odysseus in the seas. This basic image is supported, furthermore, by Rashed's clear demonstration (2007, 33–37) that fragment B 84, describing the eye constructed by Love to initiate the reconquest of the cosmos after Strife has retired, echoes Odysseus' construction of a boat to leave Calypso's island in *Od.* 5.247–259.

Other fragments describe the wanderings in deliberately frightening ways, raising harsh lamentations from the *daimon* (B 118: "I wept and wailed on seeing an unfamiliar place"), just as Odysseus repeatedly wept over his incessant being carried away from home.[53] There is a certain katabatic atmosphere in the description of the trip of the *daimon*, as if the terrors of the Other World were present in this world.[54] As is typical of the tradition of journey tales, there may have been descriptions of other beings, of other places, of other, happier, states of mankind (B 10–123, B 128, B 130). The *Odyssey* was probably echoed in such descriptions of places and beings, though we can only hint at such echoes due to the scarcity of preserved fragments.[55]

---

52 Bordigoni 2004, 259.
53 E. g., *Od.* 10.496 ff. The expression "unfamiliar place" (ἀσυνήθεα χῶρον) in B 18 echoes in the same metrical position the "cheerless place" (ἀτέρπεα χῶρον) of *Od.* 11.94 (Hades) and 7.279 (the rocks against which Odysseus would crash). Cf. Pablo Friedländer, "El lenguaje poético de Empédocles," *Synthesis (La Plata)* 12 (2005): 13.
54 Empedocles has since long been recognized to use the terrors of Hades to depict this world (e. g., Gagné 2006). In depicting in katabatic colours a journey that is not technically a *katabasis* (*pace* Zuntz 1971, 203ff and others who believe in a literal *katabasis*, and Wright 1981, 271 who denies it altogether), Empedocles is also following a Homeric model: cf. Priam's trip to the Aechean camp in *Il.* 24 or Odysseus' first *Nekyia* (in fact a *nekromanteia* rather than a descent) in *Od.* 9.
55 Cf., e. g., B 118 and B 121, inspired in *Od.* 11.93 (Zuntz 1971, 200 f; Rashed 2008, 30); B 77–78, which recall the ever-blooming gardens of Alcinous in

At some point, Empedocles tells of the subsequent decadence of the *daimon*, whose situation is made even worse by the institution of sacrifice and animal killing (B 136–139). This must have marked his most decadent moment in the scale of existence, the climax of his sufferings, when he wishes he had died before, as when Odysseus, left alone at the mercy of the sea, wishes he had died at Troy.[56] In the *Odyssey* this moment inaugurates the recovery of his hope, for he will be helped by Ino, Athena, Nausicaa and Arete in succession. Likewise, in the gold leaves it is after all her sufferings that the soul meets Persephone and claims to have paid the penalty. We may wonder, therefore, whether Empedocles' narration also included an explicit mention of a turning point in the logical order of events, where he comes out of his state of desperation and begins his upgrading until his current state of *theos*; a moment in which he passed from being "subject to *Neikos*" (B 115.14) to enter the realm of *Philotes*. The preserved fragments do not allow us to know with certainty how the *daimon* was rescued from his continuous falling. However, what logical link there may have been between the fragments that show Empedocles' *daimon* as a god returning home and those that tell of his fall is not a purely literary question. Important matters depend on it, like the problem of whether he received help from some deity for his ascension or he accomplished it alone by himself through personal purification and asceticism.

I think to solve this question we must look at the related question of the source of Empedocles' allegedly divine knowledge (B 23.11). Some have said that in Empedocles, in explicit opposition to Parmenides, there is no revelation from the divinity, but it is he himself who pro-

---

Od. 7.114–118, and which could well be ascribed to the *Katharmoi* (Wright 1981, 223).

56 *Od.* 5.308 ff. The lament of the *daimon* (B 139: "Alas that the pitiless day did not destroy me first") has been shown by the Strasbourg papyrus (*ensemble* d7) to belong probably to the *Physika*. The Odyssean background, however, is common to the whole theme of sacrifice as crime, treated in both poems: in that very fragment, for instance, the eating of flesh is described with the same expression as Polyphemus' cannibalism (*Od.* 9.295: σχέτλια ἔργα). Killing and immoderate eating were precisely the cause of the first misfortunes of Odysseus' men (9.45 f) and their final perverse sacrifice in Thrinakia precipitates their fatal end (12.353–419), cf. Irwin F. Cook, *The Odyssey in Athens* (Ithaca and London: Cornell University Press, 1995), 56 f, 111–127. By doing this they also break their oath (12.300ff). But the *daimon*, unlike Odysseus, also participates in the murderous transgression, which is a significant divergence from the *Odyssey*.

claims his own divine message.[57] Others, on the contrary, suppose that, as in his model-rival Parmenides, his entire doctrine is a revelation from a goddess (with Cypris, mentioned in B 128, as the likeliest candidate).[58] There is only one fragment, however, in which a goddess becomes his source of knowledge. Comparison with scenes of the *Odyssey* and the gold tablets, moreover, suggests that these lines also reflect the precise turning point where the wandering *daimon* obtains divine help. In B 131 Empedocles invokes the Muse with the following words:

εἰ γὰρ ἐφημερίων ἕνεκέν τινος, ἄμβροτε Μοῦσα,
ἡμετέρας μελέτας <ἅδε τοι>[59] διὰ φροντίδος ἐλθεῖν,
εὐχομένῳ νῦν αὖτε παρίστασο, Καλλιόπεια,
ἀμφὶ θεῶν μακάρων ἀγαθὸν λόγον ἐμφαίνοντι.

If for the sake of any one of mortal men, immortal Muse,
(it pleased you) that our cares came to your attention,
now once more, Calliope, answer my prayer,
and stand by as a worthy account of the blessed gods is being unfolded.

These verses show many features of the standard poetic invocation to the Muse which marks a transition from one theme to another.[60] Within the traditional form of invocation to the Muse, however, there are several important elements of the supplication scene which we have also seen in the gold leaves: the direct invocation; the presence of the verb εὔχομαι in the petition (in the sense of "to pray"); the mention of past hardships; the opposition between "mortal men" at the beginning and "blessed gods" at the end; the petition for help with the adverb νῦν which marks the transition, as we shall see below; the recognition of the necessity of obtaining the goddess' goodwill. This does not mean that this petition was necessarily depicted in Empedocles' poem as a for-

---

57 E. g., Trépanier 2004, 49, 57–65.
58 Bollack 1965, I, 265, 310; Zuntz 1971, 256, 404 proposed Persephone or Ananke as the revealing goddess; Tomáš Vítek, *Empedoklés* I (Prague: Herrmann & synové, 2001), argues again that the whole of Empedocles' teaching is understood as a revelation from Aphrodite. None of these goddesses, however, are attested in the fragments as sources of revelation.
59 Wilamowitz's emendation has been widely accepted (e.g., Wright 1981). The alternative is Diels' <μέλε τοι>, accepted by Bollack 2003, which would be equally compatible with my argument. Zuntz 1971, 212, held that a whole verse had dropped out, a thesis which has had no followers. Nor has the proposal of Gavallotti 1975, 322 succeeded of reading the first line (with the manuscript) as εἰκ ἀρ' in order to make it the beginning of the *Physika* (cf. n. 61).
60 Simon. fr. 11, 19–24. Cf. Obbink 1993, 64–70.

mal supplication (neither was Odysseus' supplication-like prayer to a river). It shows, however, that Empedocles blended elements from a standard invocation to the Muse begging for inspiration with an epic (and mystic) supplication for salvation.[61] The usual transition from one theme to another is turned into a transition between the fall of the *daimon* and its reascent. The invocation of the poet is at the same time the supplication of the wanderer, since Empedocles identifies himself with the fallen *daimon*. But instead of asking to be sent to a paradise amongst the blessed, Empedocles asks for help in singing a "good *logos* about the blessed gods." This is consistent with the image of his own poem as a path, which he uses in B 35.1.[62] Within the main metaphor of knowledge as a journey, salvation is envisaged as wisdom: the good *logos* is opposed to a bad *logos*,[63] as in the gold leaves the right fountain

---

61 The other invocation to the Muse in B 2 DK also has mystic expressions: "a pure stream," "what is right to hear," "send me" (cf. *OF* 493 A). I do not agree with Gavallotti 1975 and Wright 1981, who argue that both evocations to the Muse must be close to each other and belong to the same poem (*Physika*). Two invocations would be a better fit with two poems or at least two different parts of the same poem. Instead, I believe Bollack 2003 is right in setting B 131 in the middle of the *Katharmoi* as a transition, underlining that the expression "one of the mortals" is linked to "I am one of them" in B 115.14 (*pace* Zuntz 1971, 213, who refers it to Pausanias). As Picot 2008, 12 says, the *makares* are the same in B 115.6, 146.3, 147.1, 21.12, 23.8, and 131.4.
62 Havelock 1958 shows how the journey metaphor also pervades the whole of Parmenides' poem, not just his proem. Barbara Feyerabend, "Zur Wegmetaphorik beim Goldblättchen aus Hipponion und dem Proömium des Parmenides," *RhM* 127 (1984): 1–22, shows its links with the *Wegmetaphorik* in the gold leaves. Cf. also Burkert's chapter in this volume. The poetic with the image of the path in the gold leaves (*oimê*) shown by a divinity has many parallels in Hellenistic poetry and especially in Lucretius, Empedocles' imitator (Philip Hardie, "Lucretius on the Narrow Road," *HSCP* 99 [1999]: 275–87). Empedocles' image does not necessarily imply poetic immortality instead of mystic immortality, although later poets developed it in this way (Charles Segal, "Poetic Immortality and the Fear of Death: The Second Proem of the *De Rerum Natura*," *HSCP* 92 [1989]: 199 f).
63 Cf. B 132, where ὄλβιος (a typically mystic expression for blessing) is he who knows rightly about the gods, and δειλός he who has the wrong opinion, like the sacrificer who prays (B 137.2: ἐπευχόμενος) with a perverted and silly piety. Cf. Stehle 2006, 262: "it being a good discourse implies contestation with other views of the gods."

was opposed to the wrong one, and afterlife joys to punishments. The blessed are for Empedocles those who know the good *logos*.[64]

I am aware that this is not the usual way to interpret fragment B 131, but there are strong arguments to believe that this is not just a rhetorical invocation to the Muse devoid of any purpose beyond that of invoking tradition.[65] That Calliope not only inspires but also helps Empedocles to be "saved" is firmly supported by the connexion recently drawn by P. Skarsouli between this invocation and other mentions of Calliope in Hesiod, Solon and Pindar.[66] These texts show very clearly that Calliope not only grants poetic inspiration, but also justice to kings (or in the case of Solon, to a democratic leader), by giving them both the persuasive words necessary for dissolving quarrels (*neikos*) and the remembrance of just laws. As Skarsouli points out, countering *Neikos* through persuasion is fully coherent with Empedocles' philosophy, and also with some anecdotes told about his life.[67] To Skarsouli's arguments we can now add that the effects of the Muse's inspiration on kings and rulers are very similar to what Empedocles claims for himself in his initial self-presentation in B 112. He has been often said to present a dignified portrait of the wandering magician, an *Innenperspektive* of a figure much criticized in other sources.[68] That is very true, and to achieve that goal he uses the poetic framework with which he and his audience were familiar. Hesiod says that thanks to the Muses "all the people look to kings," from whose lips flow gracious words" (*Theog.* 84 f), and "when he passes through a

---

64 On the identity of philosophical knowledge and salvation in Empedocles, cf. Peter Kingsley, "Empedocles for the New Millenium," *AncPhil* 22 (2002): 348; Stehle 2006, 269.
65 The common view is exemplified by Giovanni Cerri, "Empedocle narratore di miti : la vicenda cosmica," *AION* 28 (*filol*) (2006): 56: "In Empedocle, rispetto a Parmenide, l'elemento mitico scompare perfino dai brani proemiali, riducendosi alla pura e semplice invocazione della Musa, già tradizionalmente dèa allegorica, nulla più che un'ipostasi dell'ispirazione e della competenza poetica." This matches the conception of Wright 1981; *contra*, Bollack 2003 (cf. n. 61 *supra*).
66 Penelope Skarsouli, "Calliope, a Muse Apart: Some Remarks on the Tradition of Memory as a Vehicle for Oral Justice," *Oral Tradition* 21.1 (2006): 210–228, adducing Hes. *Theog.* 80–103; Sol. 1.1–6 G-P; Pind. *Ol.*10.13–15.
67 Skarsouli 2006, 222 f; cf. D. L. 8.64, 8.67 and frags. B 114, 116 (with the association of the Muse and *Peitho* in Plut. *Quaest. Conv.* 9.5.745c)
68 Rösler 1983, 179; Riedweg 1995, 38ff; Megino 2005, 31–36. Cf. the negative portraits of wandering priests in Plat. *Resp.* 364e, Hippocr. *Morb. Sacr.* 1.22; Liv. 39.8.3 ff.

gathering, they greet him as a god with gentle reverence, and he is conspicuous among the assembled."[69] Solon asks the Muses not just that he be favoured by the gods with prosperity, but also that they grant him "a good reputation amongst men" (fr. 1.4) and "to be an object of reverence (αἰδοῖον) for them" (fr. 1.6). Empedocles, who does not claim merely to be a king, but to have an even higher, indeed divine, status, describes himself with similar words: "honoured by all, exactly as it seems,[70] while I pass through the city, crowned with fillets and flowery garlands. And when I come to the cities I am revered by all men and women" (B 112.5–8). Memory, the key to Calliope's inspiration, also determines his own power. Not only can he remember reincarnations, but also the appropiate words (εὔκεα βάξιν, B 112.11) to be uttered in specific moments, such as when healing the sick. The wandering priest, so despised by others like Plato, reaches in Empedocles' poem the highest possible status, wholly legitimized through adaptation of the traditional epic portrait of the good ruler.

It is the Muse Calliope, therefore, who helps Empedocles to attain his blessed status. It is not improbable that this begging of the Muse may also have had a cultic dimension, within the context of the Pythagorean cult of the Muses.[71] But since there is no hint of that cultic link in the

---

69 Hesiod's passage is similar to *Odyssey* 8.169–173 (and also the reference to Arete in 7.71 f). Richard P. Martin, "Hesiod, Odysseus, and the Instruction of Princes," *TAPhA* 114 (1984), 29–48 shows that this is better explained as a typical epic theme rather than influence of Homer on Hesiod or vice versa. By the 5th cent., however, it is probable that Empedocles had Hesiod and Homer in mind. Cook's suggestion (1995, 121) that legitimate kingship was incompatible with perverted sacrifice (and even more, with cannibalism) suits perfectly Empedocles' case.
70 The parallels reinforce the interpretation of the controversial ὥσπερ ἔοικεν (cf. Wright 1981, 266; Riedweg 1995, 35 n. 16) as an expression stressing the visual perception of the man inspired by the Muse.
71 Pierre Boyancé, *Le Culte des Muses chez les philosophes grecs* (Paris: De Boccard, 1937), 231–247, makes a strong case that there existed a cult of the Muses in the earliest Pythagorean circles, along with the heroization of Pythagoras (new arguments in Myrto Garani, "The Palingenesis of Empedocles' Calliope in Lucretius," in *Papers on Ancient Literatures: Greece, Rome and the Near East, (Proceedings of the "Advanced Seminar in the Humanities." Venice International University 2004–2005)*, ed. Ettore Cingano and Lucio Milano [Padova: Eisenbrauns, 2008], 231–265. If the figure alluded to in B 145 is Pythagoras, this allusion would fit nicely with a narration of an otherworldly encounter with the Muse. Boyancé 1937, 285 makes Empedocles the first testimony for the tradition, at-

extant fragments, let us pursue only the poetic dimension of Calliope's help. Was this help depicted as a physical encounter, similar to Odysseus' encounters with the goddesses and women who help him on his way home (Ino, Nausicaa, Arete, Athena), or that of the soul with the Queen of the Underworld in the gold leaves? Further parallels can be adduced, such as Parmenides' encounter with his goddess, or even the souls who must approach Lachesis in the myth of Er in the *Republic*.[72] It would, in fact, be a remarkable departure from tradition if Empedocles decided *not* to present a face-to-face interview with a deity. Perhaps B 128, in which Queen Cypris is said to be the only goddess present, might suggest an address to a goddess, given the Muse's association with Philotes.[73] But until new papyri give us new arguments, we must abandon speculation about how Empedocles' journey was similar or different to previous otherworldly trips, and whether or not he met the goddess "in person" or just figuratively.

A further narrative and philosophical problem is which lines may have followed the invocation of B 131. Was there a revelation by the Muse, or did Empedocles continue with his speech? There are different opinions about the speakers and addressees of Empedocles' poem. Some scholars attribute the whole of Empedocles' doctrine to the Muse, in a way similar to Parmenides' poem. Many others have refused to consider any of the extant fragments as words from the Muse. There is much scope for intermediate positions, since dialogues between different characters would not be strange in a revelatory journey as this one is. Again, the question cannot be solved with the preserved fragments.[74]

The question of when in the poem the invocation to Calliope may have taken place is somewhat more fruitful. Our source for B 131, Hippolytus, seems to suggest an actual physical location for the fragment

---

tested to in later funerary inscriptions, which links the Muse, immortality, and the practice of medicine.

72 *Od.* 5.339ff; 6.149ff; 7.146ff, 13.300. Parm. 1DK; Plat. *Resp.* 617d. Some of the invocations to the Muses depict a physical encounter (Hes. *Theog.* 29 ff., Sapph. fr. 1), others invoke the goddess' presence figuratively (Simon. fr. 11, 19–24).
73 Cf. Hippol. *RH* 7.31.3, who says that the Muse collaborates with Philia, identified with Cypris. Another female deity associated with Philotes is "Grace (Χάρις), who hates Necessity" (B 116). Grace is linked with the supplications whereby the supplicated is implored to feel pity and to assist the suppliant's escape from other powers (cf. n. 22 *supra*).
74 On the different addressees in the poem, cf. Obbink 1993, Trépanier 2004, 46–72.

(*RH* 7.31.3). He says that "in the middle" (μέσον) between the cosmos governed by *Neikos* and that governed by *Philotes* (which he calls *Philia*) there is a "right *logos*, through which the elements separated by Neikos are adapted to unity by Philia. This right *logos*, working together (συναγωνιζόμενον) with Philia, is called Muse by Empedocles, who exhorts her to work together (συναγωνίζεσθαι) with him, telling her: "If for the sake ..." (fr. B 131). This seems to set the invocation to the Muse in the middle of the journey, as a turning point in the *Katharmoi*, which is in consonance both with the Odyssean parallels and the tradition of the mysteries.[75] Empedocles probably invokes the Muse after he has told his entire downward wandering journey, and after the invocation he begins to sing about the blessed state that awaits him as a god. Some elements in B 131 allude to the (previous) misfortunes of B 115, others to the (later) blessings of B 112, 146, and 147. Having heard the previous hardships of "one of the mortals" ("one of them" in 115.14), now (νῦν) the Muse will inspire a "good *logos*" about the "happy gods." The contrast between Empedocles' previous song about the hardships (μελέτας) of mortals and his new, happier, song gives this νῦν the same pivotal function as the νῦν of the supplications. Salvation is equivalent, in this context, to poetic inspiration and theological knowledge. The rewards for poetic victory and the blessings of immortality are blended. Let us remember that Lucretius also has an intermediate invocation to the Muse Calliope begging for a victory crown at the end of his race, which may well be an imitation of Empedocles.[76]

The parallels with the previously quoted texts from the leaves and the *Odyssey* are clear. A female figure, in this case the Muse, has helped Empedocles to reach the status he enjoys at the moment of his recitation, i.e. a god among his *philoi*, the highest possible status envisaged

---

75 Cf. Bernabé and Jiménez 2008, 50–52 on the sacred way followed by the souls in the leaves, with parallel passages from Pindar, Plato, and Aristophanes. Gavallotti 1975, 164, 324 integrates Hippolytus words in the text of Empedocles' poem, with the sense of "putting in the middle," i.e., making public. I find this interpretation of μέσον less plausible than a more literal one like mine.
76 Lucr. 6.92–95 (cf. Segal 1989, 206 ff.; Myrto Garani, *Empedocles Redivivus: Poetry and Analogy In Lucretius* [New York and Abingdon: Taylor & Francis, 2007] and Garani 2008). If, as the Lucretian passage suggests, Empedocles also alluded to a crown in the context of his invocation to the Muse, it would fit nicely with his initial statement of being crowned (B 112.6, cf. n. 41 *supra*). Hippolytus, when quoting B 131 (*RH* 7.31.3), says that Empedocles asks the Muse for help to combat (συναγωνίζεσθαι), which means that there was some agonistic context around the fragment.

in his own poem. In other words, she helped him to achieve salvation by means of poetry and memory. In spite of their different purposes and functions this does not seem far from the conceptual universe of the gold leaves.[77] There are, however, important differences: unlike the leaves, Empedocles' poem does not present salvation as a direct consequence of his invocation, nor is it made fully dependent on the will of the goddess. Calliope is merely a "collaborator," as Hippolytus says, both with Empedocles and with Philotes.[78] The cycle of Philotes and Neikos takes precedence even over the power of the gods, and the Muse is an instrument of a higher power, Philotes. Similarly, Nausicaa was an instrument of Athena, and even Athena was working in conformity with a higher destiny that she had not determined (i.e., Odysseus' fated return). The poet of the leaves, eager to show the role of initiation in freeing the soul from destiny, does not seem to envisage a similar superior power which determined salvation. On the other hand, the leaves do seem to respect different spheres of influence of the gods, fully in the Homeric tradition, since the Underworld (Hades) is beyond the sphere of the "thrower of thunderbolts" (Zeus). So does Empedocles, whose alternation between Philotes and Neikos seems to be as precise as that between Athena and Poseidon in the *Odyssey*.[79]

Empedocles, therefore, introduces some varations while following the general pattern of the tale of the wandering hero striving to come home: his misfortunes while erring are followed by salvation and homecoming, with a female figure helping decisively in the turning point. The same structure underlies the *katabasis* of the soul in the gold leaves. These coincidences in the general epic patterns contrast with the radical divergence in the narrative ordination of a similar succession of events. Empedocles and the gold leaves take completely different paths when narrating such a tale. The narrative order of the leaves, whose aim, rather than to achieve poetic beauty, is to be a functional guide for the initiate, seems straightforward and linear, although if verses were taken

---

77 Megino 2005, 72–75.
78 The Muse as helper is also found in similar passages like Simon. 11, 20–22; Lucr. 1.24. Cf. James J. O'Hara, "Venus or the Muse as Ally (Lucr. 1.24, Simon. Frag. Eleg. 11.20–22 W)," *CP* 93.1 (1998): 69–74.
79 B 26; *Od.* 6. 329–331, 13.341–343: on the alternation of Poseidon and Athena, cf. Cook 1995; on that of *Philotes* and *Neikos*, cf. the suggestion of Capizzi 1987 in n. 29 *supra*. In B 128, the presence of Queen Cypris is explictly linked to the absence of King Zeus and other gods (Stehle 2006, 264).

from a larger poem, its structure may have been a bit more complex.[80] By contrast, the poetic art of Empedocles surpasses not only Parmenides and other theological poets like Orpheus or Pythagoras, but even vies with Homer: beginning at the end of his journey, he tells the tale of the fall of the *daimon* and his return with consummate artistry which gave him no little poetic glory. His choice of Calliope, the muse of epic, is not casual. His reception of the tale of the wanderer was partly mediated by the mystic re-working of the exiled soul found in the gold leaves, and by Parmenides, but he also went back to the Homeric paradigm.[81]

Empedocles was not only "doctrinally" influenced by Parmenides, Pythagoras or Orphic poetry. He was also in poetic competition with them, trying to lay claim to their territory in a better and more innovative way, through allusion, opposition and reworking of the resources of epic. In his poem on the exile of the *daimon* he is in rhapsodic competition with the journey of Parmenides, with the *katabaseis* of Orpheus, Heracles and Pythagoras, and with the more ancient accounts in Hesiod and Homer.[82] This context of agonistic engagement with previous poetic discourses provides the framework within which he reaches his own identity as a thinker, and it is also a key to our own understanding of his doctrines.[83]

---

80 The probable narrative structure of the katabasis of the soul underlying the leaves outlined by Riedweg 2011 follows a fairly linear pattern.
81 There is no need to postulate, as Havelock 1958 did in the case of Parmenides, that there is only one exclusive model, since the poet can engage with multiple models at the same time.
82 Riedweg 1995, 56–59 suggests that the addresses to Pausanias, and perhaps the whole composition of the *Physika*, may have echoed Orphic poems. Allusion to Pythagoras (or, less likely, Parmenides) in B 129 is a respectful allusion to a predecessor. It is perhaps no coincidence, therefore, that Orpheus is Calliope's son: invocation to Calliope would mean an emulation of Orpheus. Cf. also Kingsley 1995, 250–256 for Empedocles' identification with the Pythagorean hero Heracles.
83 I am very grateful to Sarah Burges Watson for her comments and for her help to make my English more readable, and also to Alberto Bernabé, Renaud Gagné, Ana Jiménez, Carlos Megino, and Marco Antonio Santamaría for their suggestions. This research has been funded by the Spanish Government (Project FFI2010-17047).

Self-Determination and Freedom: The Relationship of God and Man in Homer

Arbogast Schmitt

Translated by Joydeep Bagchee

I. Introduction

The life of Homeric man appears, on the one hand, to be limited entirely to his earthly existence. To be sure, Homer hints at the possibility of life after death, but this life is considered a shadowy existence. Achilles considers it to be so little worth living that he says he would rather be a slave among the living than ruler of the realm of shades. On the other hand, the reader knows that man's life is permanently subject to the will of the gods in Homer. On a superficial reading, as has been undertaken time and again, one might even think that man's life is completely and utterly delivered over to these immortal gods, who expose it to good or bad fates as they please.

Contrary to this initial impression, however, this article will argue that the life of Homeric man, although seemingly centered entirely on earthly existence, actually stands in a relationship to god and that the individual himself bears responsibility for this relationship. Indeed, an individual's happiness and salvation depend on his ability to successfully negotiate this relationship to the gods—of the mortals to the immortals. My thesis is that, for Homer, divine existence is something an individual can recognize and follow to a greater or lesser degree: the happiness or misfortune that befalls him is a consequence of his ability to live in accordance with this divine order.

Already in Homer, we find a notion, which Plato later expresses towards the conclusion of the *Republic* as follows: "virtue [*aretē*] knows no master; each will possess it to a greater or less degree, depending on whether he values it or disdains it. The responsibility lies with the one who makes the choice; the god has none" (*Republic* 617e; Grube & Reeve trans.). The Neoplatonic philosopher Proclus expressly applies this notion to Homer. Proclus does not attribute Pandarus' behavior to the divine will, but to his own willingness to accept a shameful suggestion. His universal explanation runs as follows: "everything is moved by the gods, but always in keeping with an individual's specific nature."[1] This notion, which makes man's salvation dependent on his "becoming-like" to God (*homoiōsis theōi*), was also adopted by medieval Christianity. Aquinas answers the question of whether man is responsible for his salvation, given that God, the omnipotent, steers and guides the world according to his own counsel, as follows: "omnia a deo moventur, sed secundum proprietatem uniuscuiusque."[2] As one sees, he responds with the same answer to the same question as the Neoplatonist Proclus.

An interpretation of Homer that makes the relationship of mortals to immortals (or, more precisely, the autonomous relationship of mortals to immortals) the condition for the salvation of each individual appears, of course, to founder on the problem that there does not seem to be a "genuine" form of autonomy in Homer. However, a more careful analysis of human action in Homer shows that, contrary to the widespread prejudice that Homer does not as yet possess a concept of autonomy, the "soteriological" aspect of the relationship of mortals to immortals is a function of the extent to which Homeric man is conscious of and acts in accordance with this (limited) autonomy.

II. Autonomy as a Pre-Condition for Soteriology

Man's understanding of the world and of himself in Homeric society is characterized by an especially pronounced consciousness of various forms of dependency. In many areas, where post-Enlightenment thought would consider man to be entirely dependent upon himself (or at least consider him to be autonomous in the sense of the ultimate arbiter of his fate), one has the impression that man has been deprived of the initiative to act in Homer. Thus, where we would expect a subjective decision, we find social norms and habits, formation through one's origin, natural predisposition, and, above all, the influence of divine forces of destiny. It seems as though Homer's focus in portraying the

---

[1] Proclus, *In Platonis rem publicam commentarii*, vol. 1, ed. Wilhelm Kroll (Leipzig: Teubner, 1899), 104 l. 7–16.
[2] Thomas Aquinas, *Summa Theologiae*, pars 1, q. 83 ad 1,3 and resp. ad 3.

motivations for action is virtually concentrated upon factors that do not stand at man's disposal.

On the basis of this state of affairs, scholars from the beginning of modern Homer scholarship until today have often concluded that while there are incipient signs of an understanding of the spontaneity of subjectivity, a genuine knowledge of the human subject's freedom and autonomy cannot be found in Homer. However, the question of wherein a person's moral autonomy and responsibility is "really" grounded is a highly complex question, one to which even modernity does not have a uniform answer. Indeed, there are also widespread tendencies that consider such autonomy to be impossible or even illusory.

Concerning antiquity, a certain consensus developed from the 18th century on up to contemporary scholarship, namely, that the criterion for determining whether antiquity had any knowledge of human autonomy at all (and, if so, to what extent it did so) is the reduction of all concrete choices to a final, fundamental, and universal *consciousness* of freedom. Modernity considers the discovery of such a consciousness of freedom to be one of its founding acts. It may well be true that one cannot establish—at any rate from Homer to Plato—a knowledge of this form of fundamental freedom. The question is of course whether the fact that a consciousness of freedom analogous to this modern consciousness does not exist in Homer justifies the oft-advanced conclusion that, consequently, one cannot as yet speak of "real" freedom here. Such a conclusion is indeed understandable, since the emancipation movement founded by the Enlightenment had a highly idiosyncratic attitude towards any and every form of dependence. However, this over-sensitivity misleads one into confusing partial dependence with total dependence. It thus blinds us to forms of autonomy not characterized by a radical striving for autonomy, and thereby also robs itself—apart from the insight into the historicity of our concept of autonomy—of the possibility of recognizing different, albeit equally relevant forms of autonomy in cultures that are historically alien to us. This appears to me at any rate to be the case vis-à-vis Homer, for, when we consider the nuanced, experienced, and insightful manner in which he portrays action in its various configurations, we would have to conclude that Homer's view is that only someone who knows the manifold forms of dependency to which human action is subject (and knows this in concrete situations), can at all know when and where he is really free. Simply having a basic consciousness of one's capacity for free choice cannot constitute the criterion for distinguishing when a subjective act of choice is really free from when it is only supposedly free. Indeed, one could argue that Homer's main intention in his writings is to examine the conflict between really free and supposedly free decisions with regard to the principal characters of his epic. It is only through knowing the bounds to which man is subject in general and in the particular case that one can identify the precise thread among the various factors that determine action that really lies in one's hand and through which one can influence and alter one's action. Thus, the knowledge and recognition of dependence is virtually the pre-condition for knowledge of the freedom that is still possible despite this dependence.

That Homer's portrayal of action is indeed guided by such an understanding of the human potential for action can be shown from many aspects. However, in the following I will discuss only one objection (albeit a particularly serious one) against the thesis of genuine autonomy in Homer: one concerning the relationship of humans to the gods. As long as the belief dominates that human action is controlled and guided by the gods not only with regard to external circumstances but also in its inner motivation, a genuine knowledge of one's freedom and autonomy appears impossible. Independent of the question of whether such a prejudice is at all appropriate to the Homeric understanding of god (something that cannot be appropriately examined in the following), I seek to demonstrate that a knowledge of human autonomy as conceived by Homer is possible: a knowledge of man as influenced by the divine even in his inner motivation and nevertheless the legitimate conviction that he has a genuine form of freedom of choice at his disposal. I will substantiate this thesis by initially referring in what follows to the principal interpretive approaches, out of which one attempted to understand the problem of "man–god" in Homer. Via an analysis of the Homeric portrayal of action that focuses on the Homeric distinction between what is one's own and what is alien to one, I then defend my claim that Homer's intention in this portrayal is to make visible, through a critical description of the aspects that are externally determined, the precise aspect in respect of which man becomes (through his own emotion, thought, and volition) the decisive factor that determines his action as well as the fortune or misfortune he attains through such action.

III. Previous Scholarship

At the height of the conflict between Agamemnon and Achilles in the first book of the *Iliad*, Athena tells Achilles not to draw his sword against Agamemnon. From the perspective of our understanding of human existence, these words are nothing more than a silent internal psychic process playing itself out in Achilles at this moment. In contrast, Homer appears not to see Achilles as autonomous in this self-restraint and, instead, to see him as dependent upon the gods in what is a highly individual accomplishment.

Already in Goethe's time, based upon such observations, one drew the conclusion (and scholars have even today not fully freed themselves from this prejudice) that Homeric man was as yet unacquainted with the activity of his own inner life and therefore did not distinguish between outer and inner, between self-determination and being externally determined.[3] More recently, Bruno Snell has advanced the interpretation (explicitly based upon Schelling's and Hegel's views of antiquity[4]) that human action—in Homer—does not have any real and autonomous origin; what is planned and done is the plan and deed of the gods.[5]

---

3 Hermann Fränkel, *Dichtung und Philosophie des frühen Griechentums* (Munich: C.H. Beck, 1962), 89: "[Man in the *Iliad*] does not stand before something external with an interior distinct from it, but the whole carries and pervades him." See also Georg Wilhelm Friedrich Hegel, *Ästhetik*, vol. 1, ed. V. Friedrich Bassenge (Frankfurt am Main: Europäische Verlagsanstalt, 1955), 480–1. "... the Gods are that which is immanent to man's own interior, the power of his own passion and observation or, in general, the powers of the state in which he finds himself..."

4 See Bruno Snell, *Aischylos und das Handeln im Drama*, *Philologus* Supplement, vol. 20.1 (Leipzig: Dieterich'sche Verlagsbuchhandlung, 1928), 35, fn. 55.

5 See Bruno Snell, *Die Entdeckung des Geistes* (Göttingen: Vandenhoeck & Ruprecht, 1946), 35; similar expressions, for example, in Georg Wilhelm Friedrich Hegel, *Ästhetik*, vol. 2, ed. V. Friedrich Bassenge (Frankfurt am Main: Europäische Verlagsanstalt, 1955), 563, where Hegel says of the gods: "which fantasy represents to itself externally as the circle of the disposing gods"; or, for example, in Rudolf Pfeiffer, "Gottheit und Individuum in der frühgriechischen Lyrik," *Philologus* 84 (1929): 137–52 and also in Rudolf Pfeiffer, *Ausgewählte Schriften*, ed. Winfried Bühler (Munich: C.H. Beck, 1960), 42–54: "the boulai, councils of the gods are human decisions, the gods reveal themselves in the deeds of the humans" (43). Similarly, to provide two other representative examples: Walter F. Otto, *Die Götter Griechenlands* (Frankfurt am Main: Klostermann, 1947 [1929]), 172 or Albin Lesky, *Göttliche und menschliche Motivation im homerischen Epos* (Heidelberg: Carl Winter, 1961), 44–5.

Snell's resolute denial of any capacity for real, individual decision of the Homeric individual, however, sensitized researchers to the many passages in the Homeric text which cannot be reconciled with this thesis, since they indicate a (to an extent significant) degree of autonomy of his characters. Lesky, for example, carefully collated all the passages in which human actions or decisions are portrayed as originating from humans alone, without any divine co-agency.[6] Furthermore, it has long been noted that in Homer divine influence often unfolds in the form of a drive or advice thereby granting the individual the option of either obeying or not obeying.[7] More important still is the evidence advanced above all by Gundert[8] and Heubeck[9] in a continuation of Walter F. Otto's[10] fundamental insight: divine guidance or temptation in Homer does not affect some random individual; instead, it always has a characteristic disposition as its presupposition, a "fundamental attitude and tendency within the human,"[11] as Heubeck says.

Agamemnon, for example, in his pride in his royal power allows himself to become so blind, that he imagines himself not to need Achilles' help.[12] Agamemnon can thereby invoke the agency of a divine power and say, Ate daughter of Zeus blinded him.[13] However—as Grundert has shown—"the misfortune does not therefore overtake him randomly from the outside, but is deeply founded in his own nature," since he "is, by his very nature, susceptible to blindness as no other Homeric hero."[14]

---

6 See Lesky 1961, op. cit., passim.
7 See Wolfgang Kullmann, *Das Wirken der Götter in der Ilias: Untersuchungen zur Frage der Enstehung des homerischen 'Götterapparats'* (Berlin: Akademie Verlag, 1956), see esp. 100 ff. See Hans Schwabl, "Zur Selbständigkeit des Menschen bei Homer," *Wiener Studien* 67 (1965): 46–64.
8 See Hermann Gundert, "Charakter und Schicksal," *Neue Jahrbücher* 3 (1940): 225–237.
9 See Alfred Heubeck, *Der Odyseedichter und die Ilias* (Erlangen: Palm & Enke, 1954), see esp. 72–81. Also see Alfred Heubeck, *Die homerische Frage. Ein Bericht über die Forschung der letzten Jahrzehnte.* (Darmstadt: Wissenschaftliche Buchgesellschaft, 1974), 191.
10 Otto 1947, passim, esp. 170 ff.
11 See Heubeck 1954, op. cit, 74.
12 *Iliad* 1.172–175.
13 *Iliad* 19.86 ff.
14 See Gundert 1940, op. cit., 229.

Until the end, Snell remained unconvinced by these arguments,[15] and, it seems to me, one must also acknowledge his right to his opinion. Indeed, Snell too did not mean to suggest a puppet-like dependence of Homeric characters upon their gods, but drew attention to the gods' noble and free dealings with humans "almost as though with their equals." However, he explicitly adopted the specifically modern concept of a free and autonomous self-determination founded upon man's conscious understanding of this freedom as the measure for evaluating the autonomy of Homeric man. Naturally, the evidence advanced above of a conditioned autonomy in Homer cannot satisfy this measure. Snell, closely following the philosopher Gerhard Krüger, argued that the capacity to arrive at an individual decision must allow itself to be formulated in the following terms: "that I myself, by myself, let a volition arise." According to Snell, such a consciousness is not present as yet in Homer. As Krüger wrote, "one can only say and understand all this when one is immediately by oneself, as when one is alone. The Greek, however, never thought out of this being by oneself... He even conceives human striving, which appears to come so unmistakeably from within, as something external: as a response to the being or to the divine that summoned it forth."[16]

Even though Athena permits Achilles a certain freedom, to either obey or not obey her, the fact remains that the inner process, the reflection itself, through which Achilles is led to his decision, is attributed to a goddess and thus apparently occurs without Achilles realizing that it "now depends upon him, what he is resolved to do"[17]—a view foreign to modern thought. This is also true of the proof advanced in contemporary research *contra* Snell (and even beyond Snell) that humans are generally led or misled by the gods only to do those things for which they already have a predisposition in themselves. This, too, does not show that humans act out of an understanding of their own, interior ca-

---

15 See Bruno Snell, "Göttliche und menschliche Motivation im homerischen Epos," in *Argumentationen. Festschrift Joseph König*, ed. Harald Delius and Günther Patzig (Göttingen: Vandenhoeck & Ruprecht, 1964), 249–55, also in Bruno Snell, *Gesammelte Schriften* (Göttingen: Vandenhoeck & Ruprecht, 1966), 55–61. Snell responds here to the study with the same title by Lesky, see also Snell 1946, 286–88.
16 Gerhard Krüger, *Grundfragen der Philosophie* (Frankfurt a. Main: Klostermann, 1958), 108.
17 See Bruno Snell, "Das Bewußtsein von den eigenen Entscheidungen," in Snell 1966, op. cit., 18.

pacity when they follow their own character traits albeit under the influence of a god. Heubeck and Gundert, too, do not draw this conclusion from their observation, but rather hold on to the fundamental idea that in Homer "the outer and the inner stand in an inseparable connection" and the question of whether we have to do with a personal or a god-sent decision "is raised up to a higher level of understanding and belief."[18] Gundert expressly emphasizes that Agamemnon, in spite of the fact that his misfortune is rooted in an "inner contradiction" in his nature, "had absolutely no choice," and rejects a "moral" evaluation of Agamemnon's actions. The question of personal culpability may arise, but it is promptly dismissed.[19]

Lesky arrives at an analogous result at the end of his investigation into divine and human motivation in Homeric epic in his interpretation of the evidence that besides the passages in which Homeric characters explicitly act out of themselves there are many others where human action is triggered by the gods alone. In particular, the remarkable finding that both motivations (i.e., divine and human) are often given in Homer for one and the same action (e.g., when at one time Achilles himself resolves to reenter the battle and at another time is led by a god to the very same resolve) leads Lesky to conclude that divine and human stand in a unity in Homer that refuses itself to logical analysis.[20] Following K. Latte, he writes that every form of human spontaneity presents itself from a double aspect, "it corresponds to one's own inner [nature], but is simultaneously also the work of a divine power…"[21]

In view of this judgement one will not find it astonishing that Snell could not recognize a refutation of his thesis in this explanation of the personality of Homeric man. For, if man in Homer can experience his own inner agency simultaneously as divine agency, then that means precisely that he has not yet clearly distinguished between his own agency and external agency and, furthermore, was not clearly conscious "that decisions of the will and in general any impulses and emotions have their origin in man himself."[22]

---

18 See Heubeck 1954, op. cit., 75.
19 See Gundert 1940, op. cit., 229.
20 See Lesky 1961, op. cit., 30.
21 See Lesky 1961, op. cit., 30; see esp. n. 59 with reference to Kurt Latte, "Hesiods Dichterweihe," *A&A* 2 (1946): 154.
22 See Snell 1946, op. cit., 35.

Nevertheless it cannot really be disputed that there must be something correct in these several unbiased observations (almost always made in careful interpretations) of autonomous motivations for action in Homer, and I genuinely believe that the assertion of a genuine form of autonomy of the individual in Homer can be defended against Snell's objections. However, in order to avoid a potential misunderstanding of the claim raised thereby, I would like to say in advance that what is at stake here cannot of course be evidence of the individual's autonomous self-determination founded upon pure or "philosophical" self-consciousness. Rather, what is at stake here is the fact that the radical alternative formulated ever anew from Hegel onward up to Snell that there can either be free action (action that proceeds freely from a consciousness of one's own capacity for decision) or an unfree, externally-determined action (inasmuch as it is not founded upon such a consciousness) does not measure up historically to the situation in Homer.

IV. Divine Alignment with Human Agency

From the brief outline of the state of research provided above it has already become clear that the reason why the evidence presented against Snell's thesis appears insufficient is that the different aspects of autonomous action one could demonstrate in Homer do not let themselves be clearly distinguished from those aspects under which this very action appears dependent as well.

This impression, however, only arises because, as I believe, we are insufficiently attentive to the domain in which Homer presents his characters as being autonomous. Thus, we presume of all those things which modernity considers a personal accomplishment that in Homer, too, they must be subject to man's free capacity to dispose over them if we are at all to speak of individual autonomy here. Since this is manifestly not the case, the Homeric standpoint appears to us—from this perspective—as contradictory and "antinomic" (as Lesky, for example, formulates it),[23] since he appears at times to understand that his characters bear responsibility for their actions and at other times not. In truth, there is a consistently maintained and attestable distinction in Homer between what lies in humans' own power and the domains where they obey di-

---

23 See above all Albin Lesky, *Geschichte der griechischen Literatur* (Bern and Munich: Saur, 1971), 87–95; see also Heubeck 1974, op. cit., 191.

vine powers. Even when Homer sees one and the same action at one time as being "motivated" by man and at another by "god," this motivation applies only to the same action, but not to the conditions under which it came about.

In order to bring out the precise distinction between human and divine motivation for action, I begin initially with a fundamental aspect of the relationship of god and man in Homer: with the question of whether the Homeric individual was really so unacquainted with his inner life that he could have experienced his own activity as a force that worked on him from outside. It is this faith that "divine and demonic work within a man" that, as Snell rightly says, "nullifies, so to speak, the idea" that the individual is himself the origin of his actions and his plans.[24] However, in this view, which Goethe famously formulated in the words "what man worships as god is his own inner being turned inside out," one disregards the fact that in Homer's portrayal this correspondence between inner human agency and divine agency is always produced through cooperation between gods and humans. It is produced by the gods, who adapt their overarching insights and intentions to man's limited horizon, and by the humans, who are responsible through their own effort for the divine gifts they are honored with. I will give a few examples for this, beginning with the manner in which the gods exercise influence upon humans.

When Telemachus remains in Sparta longer than planned and, as Homer portrays at the beginning of the 15th book, lies awake at night out of anxiety for his father, Athena comes to him. She urges him not to delay any longer: she presents him a vision that the suitors might in the meanwhile have divided up his property among themselves and that Penelope might still be persuaded to accept one of them as a husband, he knows after all how women are, and so on. As Homer arranges the action, Athena knows these fears to be baseless, whereas it is probably appropriate for Telemachus (who, in the meanwhile, has grown into a prudent and resolute man) to consider such possibilities and to take precautions against them. Thus, Athena speaks with Telemachus here just as Telemachus, and indeed only Telemachus, might have spoken with himself. But may one infer from this that Athena's "divine voice and the vocalization of the thought of home in Telemachus are in

---

24 See Snell 1966, op. cit., 58.

essence one and the same"[25] and that there is therefore no distinction in Homer between Telemachus' inner and Athena's outer activity?

I believe one can answer this question without hesitation in the negative. Athena does not want (as is made clear in the text through multiple references forward and backward) Telemachus to concern himself with what the suitors are doing in the palace and so on. Rather, she wants him to be back in Ithaca at the precise moment when he can meet his father again. Thus, there is a clear and clearly portrayed difference in Homer between Athena's own intentions and the intentions she suggests to Telemachus, and it is simultaneously clear that the reason why her words chime with Telemachus' own thoughts, which let her words appear to us as though Telemachus' inner wish has been projected outward, lies for Homer with Athena: she intentionally says something else to Telemachus than what she knows and wants. This means that from the perspective of Homer's portrayal she adapts herself to Telemachus' individual horizon of comprehension and to his abilities. It is not Telemachus' inner wish that Homer still portrays as though it were something divine. That Athena's words appear to give voice to nothing but Telemachus' inner wish is not due to the fact that Homer still considered this inner wish to be something external, something affecting Telemachus from the outside, but due to the fact that he credited goddess Athena with the ability to overturn this difference between herself and Telemachus' inner wish. She is so intimately familiar with this interior wish that she can speak with him as though he were speaking with himself.

Analogous adaptations of gods to men can be found—I can unfortunately only indicate this here—in many passages of the *Iliad* as well as the Odyssey: for example, when Athena incites thoughts of marriage in Nausikaa, although she herself means for Nausikaa to encounter Odysseus while washing his robes,[26] or when Penelope decides to let the suitors try themselves in vain against Odysseus' bow.[27] Here, too, there is the same difference: Penelope merely wants to be rid once for all of the suitors, whereas Athena, as is said in the text, wants to bring about the death of the suitors, i.e., wants to play the bow into Odysseus's hands. Penelope herself does not know of Odysseus' arrival.

---

25 See Otto 1947, op. cit. 182.
26 *Odyssey* 6.13 ff.
27 *Odyssey* 19.571 ff. and 21.1 ff.

Likewise, in the passage at the beginning of the *Iliad*[28] when Athena restrains Achilles from killing Agamemnon, her words only let themselves be explained as a modulation to Achilles' character and to his inner state at present. Athena's motive for restraining Achilles is her and Hera's common concern for the Greeks. Thus, while she dissuades Achilles from killing Agamemnon, she simultaneously incites him to obtain satisfaction in another form for the insult (*hybris*) he has suffered. Her suggestion no doubt represents the only possiblity Achilles is willing to accept and capable of accepting in this moment of extreme anger, but it is simultaneously advice at odds with his real desire as it gives the Trojans an advantage over the Acheans.

I cannot continue the list of examples here, but I hope that in the following it will also become clear from other aspects that we encounter a characteristic feature of the relationship of god and man in Homer in these passages. However, these examples probably already suffice to draw attention to the fact that the oft-noticed correspondence between divine gift and human effort in Homer does not at all have its ground in a mysterious and rationally indissoluble merging of the human domain into the divine. Rather, we find many instances in which Homer portrays this correspondence between individual human inner agency and divine action as something the gods produce in that they, in exercising influence upon humans, take the individual constitutions of humans (indeed, often their momentary psychic constitutions) into account.

Undoubtedly, this conclusion requires further clarification in many respects, since it renders the traditional explanation we are accustomed to untenable, namely, that Homer (still) believed in the efficacy of the gods, because living in a pre-Enlightenment age that had not yet arrived at a consciousness of itself he did not recognize man's own, spontaneous, inner activities as proper to man, but rather imagined there to be some external agency in them that worked upon man from the outside. This explanation cannot be right, for although Homer acknowledges external influences in cases where we would see man as surrendered to himself alone (e.g., when Achilles masters himself at the last minute or when Telemachus is anxious about the situation on Ithaka), he makes this assumption in spite of a concrete and detailed understanding of the distinction between what the respective god and the respective human in themselves are capable of and desire. But if Homer knows so clearly what sort of thoughts are to be credited to the young Telemachus (in-

---

28 *Iliad* 1.188 ff.

deed, Athena in her speech to Telemachus orients herself precisely to these) just ripened to manhood and growing ever more like his father Odysseus, then why does he assign these words to Athena and not to the person to whom they correspond, both actually and from the perspective of his portrayal?

The answer to this question leads, as one can see, to a nuance in the domain of what post-Enlightenment thought since the 18th century usually ascribes, uniformly and completely, to man's inner existence. This nuance becomes recognizable when one asks what degree of independence is really left Telemachus, Achilles, Nausikaa or Penelope, when one sets out from the premise that Homer lets Athena's speeches (which appear to us to belong so completely to man's own inner sphere) be addressed externally to the individual not because he is ignorant about the distinction between inner and outer, but on the basis of a demarcation between man and god that appeared meaningful to him (and to his time). The previous examples have already shown that the gods adapt themselves in exercising influence upon specific individuals. This means that they, in exercising influence upon humans (e.g., when Athena speaks with Telemachus in a way that a man like Telemachus and one in his present condition would understand her words to be intelligible and proper to him from out of himself), take into account the specific individual predispositions that humans in themselves already bring along with them. Once one takes this fact into account, however, it is clear that that an individual will must already be present, before one can consider it or show it respect, whether in a positive or a negative sense.

A particularly significant piece of evidence that the gods' modulation to humans is related to an individual will that is individually different each time is the fact that the gods also make manifold and significant distinctions concerning the intensity of the influence they exercise and thereby permit the individual a greater or lesser degree of freedom vis-à-vis this influence. For example, Apollo violently strikes Patroclus' armor from his body as he is blinded in battle-frenzy and thus in this moment leaves him almost no option of defending himself against Apollo.[29] Aphrodite, too, issues a violent threat against Helen when Helen contemplates leaving Paris (after his loss to Menelaus).[30] However, Aphrodite's threat that she will withdraw her favor from Helen and turn her into an

---

29 *Iliad* 16.787 ff.
30 *Iliad* 3.390 ff; see esp. 414 ff.

object of prey in Troy is not an absolute constraint. In the most extreme circumstance, Helen could have chosen death over dishonor. In one passage she expresses her regret to Priam (and once to herself) that she did not obey this maxim.[31] Zeus' message to Aegisthus that he should not kill Agamemnon nor marry Clytemnestra also contains a warning, since Orestes will ultimately avenge his father.[32] However, unlike Helen, Aegisthus does not let this warning influence his choices, as its fulfillment lies in the distant future. Athena carries out the plan that Pandarus should shoot Menelaus without any violence through a temptation that remains entirely within the human domain.[33] Although Athena appears before Achilles as a goddess, the means of influence she uses are merely persuasion and conviction.[34] Thetis conveys Zeus' wish that Achilles release Hector to her son without any pressure, merely in the form of a friendly, advisory request.[35] Leucothea, who wishes that Odysseus save himself by means of her veil[36] merely makes him an offer, one he moreover initially rejects. Finally, to present a last and even more delicate form of influence, Athena sits with Odysseus on Ithaka and together with him forges a plan for how he can save himself and his wealth.[37]

As these few examples already adequately show, there is a wide range of intensity when it comes to the influence the gods exercise upon humans. This range extends from mutual counsel, almost between equals, via offer, request, temptation, warning, threat up to a direct exercise of violence. This variedly powerful exercise of influence of the gods upon men leaves them distinctive degrees of freedom. That means: corresponding to this scale of the varied exercise of influence by the gods there is an analogous scale of human possibilities of freedom.

---

31 *Iliad* 3.172–75; see also 3.180; 6.344.
32 *Odyssey* 1.29–43.
33 *Iliad* 4.85 ff.
34 *Iliad* 1.194–214.
35 *Iliad* 24.120–140.
36 *Odyssey* 5.339–350.
37 *Odyssey* 13.291–310.

V. Man as Co-Origin of the Form and Degree of Divine Influence

This finding is further strengthened and complemented by an important aspect through a further peculiarity of the portrayal of the relationship between man and god in Homer, which logically results from the previous finding and which I discuss further in the following: Homer's portrayal of this relationship is manifestly guided by the conviction that humans on their part bear responsibility both for the sort of divine influences they merit and the extent to which they do so. From this follows that, for Homer, humans can to a significant degree actively contribute to the manner in which the divine presents itself to them.

Had Telemachus not already grown up into a young man like his father, Athena would not have and, indeed, could not have recited the encouraging speech by means of which she, in the form of the mind, provides him support.[38] Athena herself explains to Odysseus why she offers him aid: because you are, she says to him, among men as I am among the gods, I cannot abandon you, but must always be by your side.[39] Thus, when the gods adapt themselves to humans and make use of their divine superiority to varying degrees of intensity either for or against the humans, what is expressed therein is not divine despotism or randomness. Rather, it demonstrates the ability and the will of the gods to respond in their actions to what humans in themselves offer them. Not someone who piously looks up to heaven, but someone who in his nature and his behavior corresponds to a particular god can reckon upon support from that god, and he must reckon with harm when he does not do so. This is how Athena on her part robs the—culpably—foolish of their reason; this is how Ares gives strength only to him, who is in himself daring and capable of battle; this is how Zeus ensnares Agamemnon who is arrogantly misusing his kingdom in Ate, etc. In general, this means that each god reveals himself to the individual precisely as the individual is capable of receiving and willing to receive what is appropriate to this god, so that it ultimately lies with the individual which divine gifts he merits and whether they lead him to good or evil.

---

38 *Odyssey* 1.178–318. See on this the excellent interpretation by Ernst Siegmann, *Homer. Vorlesungen über die Odyssee* (Würzburg: Königshausen & Neumann, 1987), 179 ff.
39 *Odyssey* 13.230–33.

I believe that one could by going through all the individual cases in Homer demonstrate that this state of affairs obtains throughout, i. e., is a universal one, even though it is not equally clear and equally demonstrable in all cases. Since such an inductive approach is not possible within the framework of this essay, I would like to buttress my thesis through examining it in relation to a case that appears to conflict especially strongly with it. I refer to Athena's temptation of Pandarus, which in contemporary scholarship is cited as the paradigmatic example that shows that Homeric man, especially in the *Iliad*, is often nothing more than an instrument of the gods, who like feudal lords interfere in human affairs[40] "as the fancy takes them."[41]

By shooting at Menelaus, Pandarus breaks the solemn oath sworn by both sides that the question of victory or defeat should be settled by a duel between Paris and Menelaus. Pandarus' action has been settled upon by Zeus, triggered by Athena, and carried out by Pandarus. Scholars have therefore argued that Pandarus' decision and his action are caused by the gods alone. Nevertheless, he must and the Trojans must, in spite of "complete subjective innocence pay the full penalty for the deed."[42] Thus, the view that in Homer's world the deed alone counts, whereas the inner attitude of the individual to his deed had as yet not been discovered, found widespread acceptance.

However, in this interpretation of the Pandarus scene, the manner in which Homer portrays Pandarus' temptation through Athena is not taken into account at all. This is all the more incomprehensible, since already in antiquity Homer was famed for the proverbial pithiness of his character portrayals. Aristotle, for example, praises Homer greatly because in his character portrayals he does not hold long opening speeches (from an omniscient narrator's perspective), but presents his characters directly as they speak and act, so that one can recognize their character which underlies their actions from their forms of expression themselves.[43] The farmer indeed speaks differently from the townsman, the coward differently from the hero. Seen from this perspective, even the first step in the portrayal of Athena's actions cannot be reconciled with the view that she arbitrarily influenced one of the Trojans, for

---

40 *Iliad* 4.20–104.
41 See Lesky 1971, op. cit., 90; Martin Persson Nilsson, *Geschichte der griechischen Religion*, 2nd rev. ed. vols. 1–2 (Munich: C.H. Beck, 1955), 421 f.
42 See Lesky 1961, op. cit., 43–4.
43 Aristotle, *Poetics* 1460a5–11 und *Rhetoric* 1408a30 f.

Self-Determination and Freedom: The Relationship of God and Man in Homer 75

the lines read: "This one [Athena], a mighty man, pressed through the mass of Trojans, ... seeking Pandarus all around, the divine, whether she should find him."[44] This can only mean that Athena did not simply chose the first available person as her victim, but that she sought out Pandarus as the man most likely to fulfill her plans. The Neoplatonic philosopher Proclus already pointed out this aspect.[45] Furthermore, he points out that it is explicitly said many times in the text that Pandarus was merely tempted by Athena,[46] and not forced to perform the deed. Athena merely suggests to Pandarus that he let himself be swayed by her advice—she appeals to his intellect (fighting spirit?), to his daring spirit (τλαίης κεν, 9.94), to his ambition (she speaks of χάρις and κῦδος among all the Trojans and in particular before Paris) and in particular to his covetousness (τοῦ,— i.e., from Paris—κεν δή; πάωπρωτα πάρ ἀγλαὰ δῶρα φέροιο [4.97] she promises him) in order to influence him.[47] One certainly could not mislead just anyone to such a criminal and monstrous act with such appeals, if we along with Aristotle grant that Homer's speeches are characteristic of his personae. Indeed, one will have to agree with Proclus when he says there was probably no one quite as monstrously brazen as Pandarus in the Trojan and Greek armies.[48]

Although Pandarus, consequently, is not himself the origin of the plan to shoot at Menelaus, the fact that Athena could tempt him and that she used specific means and arguments in order to tempt him has its reasons not in the council of the gods, but in Pandarus' character and his characteristic tendencies. In fact, Pandarus' share in his action can be described still more closely: he himself is not responsible for the thought of shooting at Menelaus or the enticements of wealth and fame or the power this thought has over someone susceptible to the temptation of wealth and fame. Rather, as is said several times in the text, this is but the temptation to which he is exposed. This temptation in fact works on him from the outside—a fact Homer underscores by making Athena adapt herself not only to his way of thinking (as with Telemachus, Nausikaa, Penelope, Achilles), but also transform herself into a man and address Pandarus (who does not recognize her at all)

---

44 Iliad 4.86–88.
45 Proclus 1899, 104 l. 7–16.
46 See Proclus 1899; cf. Iliad 4.66 and 71.
47 Iliad 4.94–97.
48 Proclus 1899, op. cit., 103 l. 20–104 l. 4.

as the spear-thrower Laodocus. Pandarus therefore surrenders to the power of conviction Athena's words have for him alone and thereby makes especially manifest what his share of responsibility is: it lies in his being disposed to and open for the temptation of wealth and fame and in the spontaneous and autonomous consent he accords this temptation and with which he undertakes the deed.

In a rare and therefore especially important authorial comment, Homer calls Pandarus foolish because he let himself be convinced by Athena.[49] Proclus and Eustathius, too, take up this verdict in their discussion of this passage and say, perhaps not incorrectly, that Pandarus was not misguided by Athena at all but by his own "criminal stupidity" into performing the deed.[50] They therefore judge that Athena's actions in no way overturn Pandarus' free self-determination (τὸ ἐφ' ἡμῖν). When these ancient views are correct (and in my opinion much speaks for their correctness), then they also teach us something about the starting-point from which Homer arrives at this nuanced understanding, so strange to modernity, of the relation of man and god. Furthermore, they simultaneously show that this understanding is not naïve and uncritical, but has a rationally decipherable core.

If Pandarus' own share in his actions lies in the fact that he was focused on the riches and honor offered to him in this situation and in the fact that he was also willing, without a second thought, to grasp the chance he recognized, then this chance which was given him in this situation as a conceptual possibility is distinguished from his own willfulness. Pandarus is not subjectively responsible either for the fact that this possibility exists or that it is recognizable as such. This possibility is not his subjective construct; rather, it is present in this situation as something universally recognizable and capable of being grasped by many. Indeed, it is present as something that offers itself to someone who is attentive to it and who is capable of correctly grasping the possibilities that lie in it as something enticing or tempting. From this aspect it makes sense to portray this chance as something external, something persuasive and tempting that works upon Pandarus from without and therefore precisely does not arise from within him.

---

49 Iliad 4.104.
50 Karl Reinhardt, too, uses this expression ("Tradition und Geist im homerischen Epos," in Die Krise des Helden [Munich: dtv, 1962], 11) to characterize Pandarus' deed; cf. Proclus 1899, vol. 1, op. cit., 104 l. 11 ff.

VI. The Determination of Character and the Freedom to Decide

Against the nuance between self-determination and foreign agency attempted here, one could object that although Pandarus is only moved by Athena according to his character, he does not, for that reason, have freedom of choice. As Heubeck formulates it, "character and destiny [stand] in a deep interior and secret communication" in Homer, so that neither of these two phenomena "inner desire and capacity and divine control and guidance... can be thought independently for itself,"[51] since the individual in Homer simply has that character which predisposes him to a specific form of influence through the gods. To demonstrate that we are justified in differentiating between the inner capacity and the external influence and that the individual is not simply determined through his characteristic disposition, I would like to analyze another example more closely in which, as in Pandarus' case, the gods target an individual precisely because of his characteristic attitude and where it is nonetheless clear that the freedom of choice is not taken from him: the Ate of Agamemnon.[52]

At the beginning of the events of the *Iliad* in the battle with Achilles, Agamemnon had boasted that he did not need Achilles' help, as he was especially honored by Zeus.[53] Contrary to law and custom, he had Briseis, who had been awarded to Achilles as a prize, taken away from him.[54] Achilles had therefore ensured through his mother Thetis' mediation with Zeus that Agamemnon would pay for this insult through losses in battle against the Trojans.[55] In order to carry out this plan, Zeus decides to send Agamemnon a dream that should blind him and delude him with visions of a quick victory.[56] From this perspective, one can say that Agamemnon, who indeed lets himself be deceived by the dream, in essence only carries out Zeus' will. However, here too, there are enough signs in the text that Agamemnon is not simply robbed of his responsibility for his initiative to act.

---

51 See Heubeck 1954, op. cit., 74.
52 On this, see above all the careful analysis in Kullmann 1956, op. cit., 100 ff.
53 *Iliad* 1.175.
54 *Iliad* 1.322 ff.
55 *Iliad* 2.1 ff.
56 *Iliad* 2.1 ff.

For one thing, the dream Zeus sends works upon Agamemnon just as Athena worked upon Telemachus, Penelope, etc. in the examples discussed above: in influencing him, it orients itself to Agamemnon's individual character—indeed, to his momentary psychic condition: "I am here as messenger from Zeus, who is greatly worried about you from afar and sympathizes with you…" so begins the dream speech.[57] Thus, the dream blinds Agamemnon in a psychologically refined way by lulling him into a seductive sense of security through the hubristic conceit he had manifested in the previous fight with Achilles. Thus, as with Pandarus, one can say of Agamemnon that he fell victim not to Zeus but to his own conceit. Furthermore, this is not the only incidence of Agamemnon's hubristic confidence in the power granted him by Zeus; rather, as Gundert has convincingly shown, it constitutes a basic tendency of his nature such that one could well say that the dream from Zeus targeted a highly personal and unique internal flaw in his nature. However, that it was not necessary for Agamemnon to heed the dream in spite of his predisposition to seduction by Zeus, as Gundert thinks, is shown by Nestor's reaction to Agamemnon's report of his dream. Nestor says namely: if another of us had reported such a dream, we would have called it lies and betrayal and contemptuously turned away from him.[58] In other words, Nestor knows that one cannot blindly heed a dream even when it comes from the gods.

Moreover, Nestor not only expresses a typical caution, but rather, adopts an attitude with his reservation that is also otherwise possible in Homer. Penelope, too, calls dreams ἀκριτόμυθοι, speeches in which one cannot distinguish between true and false, and therefore does not trust the dream that suggested to her that Odysseus had returned.[59] No less important than Nestor's reaction is Homer's narrative commentary, for he calls Agamemnon—like Pandarus in a similar situation—νήπιος, stupid.[60] He, too, shares Nestor's evaluation of Agamemnon's behavior and, like him, considers it to be at the very least intellectually imprudent.

Agamemnon, however, (and this is especially informative) makes clear, through his own behavior and through the words with which he judges his behavior, how he evaluates his personal role in becoming

---

57 *Iliad* 2.23 ff.
58 *Iliad* 2.79–81.
59 *Odyssey* 19.560 f.
60 *Iliad* 2.38.

blind. To be sure, Agamemnon thereby expresses himself—at first glance—in a very contradictory manner, which is why his case has repeatedly been taken as an example of the fact that divine and human motivations for action are not clearly distinguished in Homer. However, a closer interpretation shows, as I believe, that Agamemnon knows exactly how to separate his own share and the gods' share in his failure.

In a situation of terrible distress, in which the Greeks risk losing to the Trojans and in which Agamemnon is despondent and desparate,[61] he admits freely and openly to Nestor that his unjust conduct against Achilles was his blindness and, as he straightaway adds, that it was his own fault (and he once again emphasizes his awareness of his personal guilt) which he committed against Achilles in following his harmful mind. In contrast, in the great public reconciliation scene,[62] he casts all blame upon Zeus, the Erinyes, and Moira: they deceived his mind at that time in the assembly. Indeed, Agamemnon calls upon no less a person than Zeus himself as evidence that he was powerless against Ate. Zeus, too, the first among gods and men, once let himself in his boastful pride at his regal power be deceived and blinded by Hera. I believe one should not draw the conclusion from this rhetorically talented defense of Agamemnon's that he no longer wants to acknowledge subjective responsibility for his wrongdoing, for which he is at any rate prepared to answer fully and to pay recompense in this moment. Agamemnon, so it seems to me, does not seek an acquittal from all guilt from his audience but understanding for his situation.

The parallels between his behavior and Zeus' case which Agamemnon invokes alone prove this. The suggestion that Zeus, too, once succumbed to Ate should not and indeed cannot establish that Zeus' free autonomy in acting, too, is overturned through Ate's agency, but only that it is difficult to guard oneself against Ate—so difficult, that once even Zeus' great Nous was not capable of realizing the consequences of his actions. The similarity between the mistake and the cause of the mistake that Agamemnon sees in his and Zeus' case refutes yet another common explanation of his plea. Adkins, for example, in general agreement with the interpretation of this scene that has become standard, says: "Agamemnon cannot understand how he came to do something like this, and he feels that there must have been some element there in the situation that was not under his control. Since his society

---

61 Iliad 9.115–120.
62 Iliad 19.86–138.

ascribes an extensive domain of unexpected psychological phenomena to divine influence, Agamemnon naturally speaks in these terms."[63] In contrast to this interpretation, Agamemnon does not appear to consider what occurred to him at the time in the assembly a completely unexpected and inexplicable psychological phenomenon, but rather, manifests a remarkable degree of insight into the sort of danger he succumbed to at the time. He can not only identify the god to whose power he succumbed and describe his mode of operation, but also in a detailed narration of the history of Zeus' Ate (which I unfortunately cannot interpret in detail here) says unmistakably albeit indirectly that he could not tolerate Achilles belittling his honor and, irritated by this, in his pride placed more faith in the invulnerability of his power than was prudent. This was precisely the mistake that Zeus, according to Agamemnon's speech, was supposed to have made: irritated by Hera's public doubts at his ability to realize his plans, he, the first among the gods and men (εὐξόμενος), let himself in his boastful pride be blinded and misled to imprudence. Thus, one may not attribute the fact that Agamemnon seeks to excuse his behavior by referring to the temptation of a divine agency to which he succumbed to his ignorance of the irrational forces that erupted within him. On the contrary, its reasons and justification lie therein that Agamemnon knows the opposition to which he succumbed and can describe it: it is blindness through the possession of power, a blindness to which he was not equal. Agamemnon does not attribute this power of blindness to himself, but feels a power of seduction at work in it that proceeds from Zeus himself. Further, he knows that as king and commander-in-chief, he is especially vulnerable to this power. His apology lies therein. But he also knows, as becomes clear through his reference to Zeus' identical mistake, that he has only himself to blame for not having been careful enough and for having given in to temptation.

The manner in which Agamemnon imputes blame to Zeus thus makes evident that it is not the same thing for him whether he imputes blame to the gods or to himself; indeed, it shows that he can distinguish precisely between his guilt and that which absolves him of this guilt. Agamemnon's behavior teaches us that the Homeric characters also have and are aware of a degree of free choice where a divine power works upon the weakenesses or strengths inherent to their nature. I do not believe that Homer thinks humans gain their specific character-

---

63 See A. W. H. Adkins, *From the Many to the One* (London: Constable, 1970), 27.

istic traits, their character, without their own doing. But even if one were to assume this, they are nonetheless responsible for the behavior that corresponds to their specific characteristics. Agamemnon does not consider his nature with its tendency to overestimation of his power an adequate excuse for his mistake, but merely a factor that made it difficult for him to behave correctly. He says: "I have let myself be misled," and that, as we know, means: "I have done something wrong that I could have done right." The fact that Zeus, too, once committed this mistake only means that it can be difficult to avoid this mistake, and not that it is not a mistake.

Something similar holds, to take one more example, for Helen as well. Helen is predestined by nature to be both Aphrodite's protégé and victim. It was thus especially difficult or perhaps even impossible for her to resist Aphrodite. Even Priam, who is not insensitive to the charm she radiates, recognizes this when he says to her: for me, it is not you who are responsible for this misery of war, but the gods in my eyes are the guilty ones.[64] Priam's apology, however, is no different than Agamemnon's apology for his behavior. Helen herself does not accept this apology, but says, she should have chosen death rather than given in to temptation through Aphrodite and left home and husband.[65] Indeed, she repeatedly calls herself a brazen bitch for that reason.[66] Helen thus knows that she is partly responsible for her decision to follow Paris, for she did not have to follow Aphrodite in her actions, even if it was impossible for her to resist Aphrodite's charm: she could have chosen death, as she says, and as Euripides' Phaedra actually does in a similar situation.

VII. Conclusion

Although the problem raised could not be made visible in its complete extent, I must end here and draw at least those general conclusions which can be legitimately drawn from what has been said. Our starting-point was the question of whether Homeric man's (by our standards) remarkable dependence in domains where we see the individual as autonomous (e.g., when an idea occurs to someone, when someone

---

64 *Iliad* 3.164.
65 *Iliad* 3.172–75.
66 *Iliad* 3.180; 6.344.

is filled with the spirit of battle or is swept away by passion), whether this strong external appearance in fact points to Homeric man's ignorance of the spontaneity of his own inner existence or, at the very least, to an as yet unclear understanding of the distinction between self-determination and foreign agency. I believe that the few examples analyzed here suffice to make clear that in this appearance the conspicuously other thrusts itself too far into the foreground. The difference between the modern and Homeric view of man's free autonomy is not that we possess something that either did not exist or merely existed in incipient form in Homer, but that the domain of man's autonomy is differently demarcated in Homer than the way we are used to thinking it.

The gods' adaption of themselves to humans in exercising influence that is observable in Homer and the humans' complementary responsibility for the type of divine influence upon them (through which responsibility they themselves, through their own natures, through their liking or antipathy, are the cause of the divine gifts they merit) results in a view of human autonomy in Homer that is guided implicitly but consistently by a basic idea that was probably explicitly expressed for the first time in Heraclitus' statement, ἦθος ἀνθρώπῳ δαίμων.[67] The same thought can be found in many forms in Plato[68] and in all of later Platonism,[69] but also in Aristotle[70] (e. g., at the end of the *Nicomachean Ethics*). It is the thought that it is the individual himself who discloses to himself the divinity in the world that is offered equally to everyone and who, through his own thoughts and deeds, determines in what form divinity shows itself to him—or withdraws as well.

To be sure, much that we would call the product of one's own inner life is, in this view, in fact something distinct from this inner life, something external. The illuminating power an idea may exercise upon one's thinking, the temptation that the representation of money and fame exercises upon thinking, the persuasive, tempting or even logically convincing power a thought has in itself, but also beauty's power to charm, the blindness that proceeds from power, the battle-lust or the battle-frenzy that are capable of gripping a man and many more things

---

67 Heraclitus, Fragment B 119 (Diels-Kranz).
68 See, above all, *Timaeus* 86 ff.
69 See, for example, Proclus 1899, vol. 1, op. cit., 105 l. 9 ff; see also Thomas Aquinas, *Summa Theologiae*, pars 1, q. 83 ad 1,3 and resp. ad 3.
70 Aristotle, *Nicomachean Ethics*, 1179a20 ff.

that we more or less consistently ascribe completely to man's inner life work upon a man from the outside in Homer's portrayal. However, this does not mean that Homeric characters had no knowledge of the capacity in them through which they themselves determined what they decided or planned to do. This capacity is merely not restricted to the individual's inner processes as a whole, as though the love that I feel is simply my feeling and as though the thought I think is completely my thought. Rather, this capacity is restricted to what really lies in the individual's subjective power, i.e., to the manner in which someone takes up an idea, the way in which he discloses or represents this idea to himself, what sort of idea is capable of convincing him, the extent to which he is receptive to eroticism, power, danger, etc. and how he resists or surrenders to what he has so received. That means that a knowledge of the limitations of the finite possibilities of man is constitutive for Homeric man's understanding of himself. In recognizing his dependence upon powers that are not at his disposal, Homeric man also gains an understanding of the domains in which he is truly free and autonomous.[71] It is this autonomy which is aware of its own limits that makes the human open and ready for a knowledge of the divine and thus simultaneously brings him into a "soteriological" relationship with God. For knowledge of the divine is now no longer merely a rational activity, but a "becoming-like" to God that is carried out by the individual as a whole.

---

71 For a deeper treatment, see the author's *Selbständigkeit und Abhängigkeit menschlichen Handelns bei Homer. Hermeneutische Untersuchungen zur Psychologie Homers* (Stuttgart: Steiner, 1990).

Parmenides' Proem and Pythagoras' Descent[*]

Walter Burkert

Translated by Joydeep Bagchee

I. Preface

Fragments of Parmenides—enigmatic blocks of a lost structure right at the start of what the Greeks were to call *philosophia*, with a beginning in myth and fantasy that leads to a "Goddess." Is this alluring mysticism, seclusion from the normal world for the sake of concentration on some transcendent "fullness"? Is it rather the discovery of physical reality, as it presents itself until today to natural science? Not the smallest particle will come out of nothing nor will it disappear just into nothing. Or is it just a proclamation of logic: follow the consequences of a statement with disregard for everyday variation and change? And why must this be expressed in traditional verse, with a proem about traveling to a Goddess?

It was Deichgräber's paper, "Parmenides' Auffahrt zur Göttin des Rechts" that provided the challenge for this essay, first published in 1969, as I realized that neither the claim of an "ascent" ("Auffahrt") nor the identification of the goddess ("Göttin des Rechts") were supported by the ancient evidence. The re-examination of the transmitted text in detail on the basis of Hesiod and fragments of "Orpheus" provided the impulse to collect further parallels from Greek and non-Greek sources, on the tracks of archaic theological poetry, concerning mythical traveling towards caves, sun, gods, and knowledge.

In the well-cultivated fields of classsical philology, real progress is rare; mostly the work being done is the rearrangement of known materials with the hope of bringing out some more convincing picture. One mis-spelled

---

[*] This chapter is a translation of Walter Burkert's 1969 article "Das Proömium des Parmenides und die Katabasis des Pythagoras" (*Phronesis* 14: 1–30). It includes a new preface added by Prof. Burkert, who also updated some of the citations, citing literature that has appeared since the original article. I thank Prof. Burkert for his corrections and suggestions; all errors of course are my own.

word in Parmenides' proem (line 3) has not found its definitive correction, in spite of specialists' exertions for more than a hundred years.

One further happy coincidence has occurred: The "Derveni Papyrus"[1] (4th cent. B.C.) has provided a new fundament for our knowledge of the "Theogony of Orpheus," and the fragments occurring there refer to the very scene reconstructed in this essay—Zeus entering the "sanctuary" (*adyton*) of Night to receive instructions on how to rule the world. There are further indications that Parmenides made use of this work of "Orpheus," alongside that of Hesiod. One item of Parmenides' literary background has thus been secured.

II. Parmenides' Proem and Pythagoras' Descent

The ancient historian of philosophy, who interpreted Parmenides' Proem in epistemological terms and thus occasioned Sextus to include it in the treatise περὶ κριτηρίου,[2] understood the verses as an allegory: the "path" represents *logos*, the "horses" are irrational desires, the "carriage-wheels" are the ears, and the "maidens of the sun" are the eyes. We smile at such curiosities; yet it is a challenge for even the most distinguished modern interpreters of Parmenides[3] to do without a certain level of symbolism and allegory. "Parmenides is plainly allegorizing," wrote C. M. Bowra,[4] just as Hermann Diels before him in explaining the Ἡλιάδες κοῦραι had

---

1 See Theokritos Kouremenos, George M. Parássoglou and Kyriakos Tsantsanoglou, *The Derveni Papyrus. Edited with Introduction and Commentary*. Studi e testi per il Corpus dei papiri filosofici greci e latini, vol. 13 (Florence: Casa Editrice Leo S. Olschki, 2006).
2 Sextus Emp. M. 7, 111 ff.; the source cannot be identified, cf. the discussion in Leonardo Tarán, *Parmenides* (Princeton: Princeton University Press, 1965), 19 ff.; it may belong to the historical self-reflection of philosophy in the 1st century B. C. (cf. Olof Gigon, "Die Erneuerung der Philosophie in der Zeit Ciceros,"*Entretiens Fondation Hardt* 3 [1955]: 25 ff.), i. e. to the sphere of influence of Posidonius; Sextus himself (Tarán 1965, 21) can hardly be the author of the allegory; allegorizing after all is a peculiar form of taking a text seriously, not skeptically. On the general problem of allegory, see Otto Seel, "Antike und frühchristliche Allegorik," in *Festschrift für Peter Metz*, ed. Ursula Schlegel and Claus Zoege von Manteuffel (Berlin: De Gruyter, 1965), 11–45.
3 Cf. the surveys in Mario Untersteiner, *Parmenide. Testimanoanze e frammenti* (Florence: La "Nuova Italia" Editrice, 1958); Jaap Mansfeld, *Die Offenbarung des Parmenides und die menschliche Welt* (Assen: Van Gorcum, 1964); Tarán 1965.
4 C.M. Bowra, "The Proem of Parmenides," in *Problems in Greek Poetry* (Oxford: Clarendon Press, 1953), 39.

stated that "every mythological residue" had "evaporated to become logically conceived allegory."[5] More circumspectly Hermann Fränkel speaks of "pictorial language" that is "just as impressive,… as it is transparent";[6] in Deichgräber we read: "Everything is simile."[7] The reaction did not fail to come; the two substantial dissertations recently published by Mansfeld and Tarán, notwithstanding their differences, agree in postulating a sober literal understanding of the text against all symbolic sublimation. Mansfeld demands that the revelation be taken "literally."[8] Tarán fights against the fundamental mistake of "giving to the Proem a meaning not directly expressed by the words themselves."[9]

The symbolic interpretation of course has its seductive appeal. There are two images that present, according to general opinion, the key to understanding the text: Parmenides' path to the Goddess leads from beneath upwards (Fränkel[10] and Deichgräber[11] speak of an "ascent"[12]); and: the path leads from darkness to light, "from night to day,"[13] "from error to enlightenment."[14] Allegedly, Parmenides personally ex-

---

5 Hermann Diels, *Parmenides. Lehrgedicht* (Berlin: Reimer, 1897), 50.
6 Hermann Fränkel, *Dichtung und Philosophie des frühen Griechentums* (Munich: C.H. Beck, 1962), 400,7.
7 Karl Deichgräber, *Parmenides' Auffahrt zur Göttin des Rechts* (Mainz: Akademie der Wissenschaften, 1958), 41.
8 Mansfeld 1964, 223.
9 Tarán 1965, 30.
10 Hermann Fränkel, *Wege und Formen frühgriechischen Denkens* (Munich: C.H. Beck, 1955), 158.
11 Deichgräber 1958, pass.
12 Diels 1897, 8 correctly points out: "We are not even told once, whether it goes downward or upward." Otto Gilbert, "Die Daimon des Parmenides," *AGPh* 20 (1907): 25–45, and J.S. Morrison, "Parmenides and Er," *JHS* 75 (1955): 59–68, speak of a katabasis. Cf. n. 63.
13 Bowra 1953, 39.
14 Geoffrey Stephen Kirk and John Earle Raven, *The Presocratic Philosophers* (Cambridge: Cambridge University Press, 1957), 268; Cf. also Diels 1897, 50; Walther Kranz, *Über Aufbau und Bedeutung des Parmenideischen Gedichtes* (Berlin: Verlag der Akademie der Wissenschaften, 1916), 1165 amongst others. B 8, 59 νύκτ' ἀδαῆ appears, as is often emphasized, *e contrario* to corroborate that Parmenides associated light with knowledge. C. Joachim Classen, "Licht und Dunkel in der frühgriechischen Philosophie," *Studium Generale* 18 (1965): 97–116 further points out that in Hesiod's *Theogony* (212.224.227) dreams, deceit, forgetfulness belong to the category of Night, and that in Akusilaos *FgrHist* 2 F 6 b Aether and Metis are brother and sister. Yet it is another question whether the Heliades and the "gateway of the paths of night and day" are really for that reason "purely logically conceived allegory". Cf. n. 66 as well.

perienced such a state: "He had in the act of thought an experience of ascent… he experienced a divine light in the clarity of truth";[15] "each time when he thought through his great thoughts, he felt himself borne up into a realm of light on the other side of earthly things."[16] By contrast, the literal interpretation appears to remain stuck in various aporias. Fränkel formulated it most clearly: "Thus, the one and the same, the ascent from the night to light, is symbolized in three verses (9–11) no less than four times… Each of these things refers to the breakthrough of the mind to clarity. If one takes away this meaning, in order to give the images their proper force, the entire text becomes convoluted and without hold."[17] It is different in Hesiod, for one: although even his "initiation of the poet"[18] offers possibilities of psychological interpretation ("it became clear to the young shepherd….that a spiritual realm… was accessible to him," writes Fränkel),[19] yet the portrayal of how the Muses from Helikon visit the shepherd and present the laurel-staff is consistent in itself, it makes sense. In contrast, the interpreter of Parmenides' Proem runs up against "undeniable oddities and awkwardnesses."[20] Tarán's advice, the Proem be read as "only a literary device,"[21] hardly helps against this—unless one wants to understand this as a demand not to take the details too seriously.

But perhaps the "oddities," gaps and unclarities exist only for us, because we lack the background out of which the poem arises? It would be an illusion to believe that understanding could grow out of what the "the words themselves express" alone. Even an understanding of the words is based upon previous knowledge of the language; names that are mentioned presuppose acquaintance, even narrative forms and structures of meaning have their familiar and therefore intelligible "patterns." Especially a Proem, which leads up to the subject proper, to the essential message, probably will link up in a special way with these pre-given areas. Already with the choice of the verse-form, Parmenides places himself in the tradition of ancient epic, didactic epic in particular, and

---

15 Deichgräber 1958, 42.
16 Fränkel 1962, 399.
17 Fränkel 1955, 161.
18 On this, see Kurt Latte, "Hesiods Dichterweihe," *A&A* 2 (1946): 152–163; Athanasios Kambylis, *Die Dichterweihe und ihre Symbolik* (Heidelberg: C. Winter, 1965), 31 ff.
19 Fränkel 1962, 106.
20 Diels 1897, 22.
21 Tarán 1965, 31.

with the verse, an inherited wealth of narrative patterns and images comes up; we still grasp tradition in the talk of the chariot and the path,[22] the door and the Goddess. Especially tales about gods, i.e. "myth," belong to the language of epic. It is from Hesiod and Homer that the Greeks know the names and functions of their gods (Hdt. 2,53); Parmenides' relationship to these authors has often been analyzed.

Yet, alongside Hesiod's *Theogony* there existed at least two other hexametric theogonies—those of "Epimenides" and of "Orpheus."[23] The accidental discovery of the papyrus from Derveni has brought decisive new knowledge about Orpheus' and Parmenides' links with this text. It had been assumed generally that divine creation through "thought" was an innovation of Parmenides the thinker; now the Derveni text quotes this very idea from "Orpheus."[24] Nonetheless, whatever details we may know or not know from the individual works of theogonic poetizing, this genre draws upon a broad stream of religious tradition. What level of prior agreement reigned here is most difficult for us to evaluate. A self-contented interpretation which wants to exclude the unfamiliar stands all the more in danger of falling prey to apparently convincing modern assumptions.

"Horses that carry me as far as my desire surges"—the general sentence straight away turns into the report of a past event[25]: the horses have brought Parmenides on a "path" that is important and mysterious

---

22 Especially similar is Pindar *Ol.* 6, 22 ff. (Hermann Fränkel, "Parmenidesstudien," in *Wege und Formen des frühgriechischen Denkens* [Munich: C.H. Beck, 1960], 158; Bowra 1953, 436); could Pindar be inspired by Parmenides?; Empedocles B 3,5; cf. B 35, 1; Pind. *Ol.* 9, 81 f.; *Pyth.* 10, 65; *Isthm.* 1, 6; 2,2; 8, 67; Bacch. 5, 176; Choirilos Fr. 2,5 Bernabé. On the "gate" see n. 49/50.
23 Cf. n. 53 and 67.
24 μητίσσατο (Goddess—Eros) Parmenides B 13 (see Untersteiner 1958, LXX; Tarán 1965, 249); (ἐ)μήσατο (Zeus—Okeanos) Pap. Derveni Col. 23,4 (Kouremenos 2006, 106 f., cf. Orph. Fr. 91). Cf. n. 69.
25 On the change of verb tense, cf. Hes. *Theog* 1 ff. (Kambylis 1965, l.c.); on the optative, Eduard Schwyzer and Albert Debrunner, *Griechische Grammatik,* vol. 2 (Munich: C.H. Beck, 1950), 325 f.; "that the revelation is repeated indefinitely" claims Tarán 1965, 27, with reference to φέρει (v. 3), σπερχοίατο (v. 8); but, whereas the path is naturally constantly there, v. 8 speaks of the ever renewed surging of the horses during this one journey. ὅσον τ' ἔπι θυμὸς ἱκάνοι combines stock phrases such as ὅτε θυμὸς ἀνώγοι (*Od.* 8, 70) and θυμὸν ἱκάνει (*Il.* 8,147; 15, 208; 16, 52) to new effect; the emphasis lies on the "extent" of the "surging forwards"; that the *thumos* of the horses (Mansfeld 1964, 228 ff.) is meant is completely unlikely (Tarán 1965, 10).

at the same time. It is called πολύφημος, "rich in lore";[26] it is the path "of a Daimon"—this is the unanimous transmission, which is rightly accepted in the latest editions.[27] Thus, θεῶν κέλευθος refers to the path to Olympus (*Iliad* 3, 406), ἀθανάτων ὁδός is the southern entrance to the nymphs' grotto (*Od.* 13,112), Διὸς ὁδός is the path to the Elysian fields (Pind. *Ol.* 2,70). Parmenides himself refers in another passage to πειθοῦς κέλευθος (B 2,4); above all the Goddess says of precisely the path Parmenides is following, ἥ γὰρ ἀπ' ἀνθρώπων ἐκτὸς πάτου ἐστίν (B 1,27). It is not the path on which ordinary people stray, but, rather, ὁδὸς δαίμονος. It is true we do not learn more about the "Daimon"; even his/her gender remains undecided; the relative clause ἥ ... φέρει refers to ὁδόν, as the correspondence with τῇ φερόμην shows;[28] to clear up an ambiguous expression through the immediately following words is normal in language. It is otherwise with the attempts to name the Daimon on the basis of verses that follow much later; to equate him/her for example with the "Goddess" (22) or with "Dike" (28): this is the method of a commentator. The straight-forward reader or listener cannot jump ahead, the uncertainty and tension that is aroused through the word Daimon cannot, at first, be resolved. Parmenides plays with allusions, revealing and concealing at the same time. A further obscure reference in the same verse goes with this: εἰδότα φῶτα, the "knowing man." An-

---

26 Cf. Tarán 1965, 10; Mansfeld 1964, 229.
27 Sextus 7, 111/ 112 in text and paraphrase; thus Bowra 1953; Morrison 1955; Kirk and Raven 1957; Untersteiner 1958; Deichgräber 1958; Mansfeld 1964; Tarán 1965, against Stein's conjecture δαίμονες, which Kranz accepted in the 5th edition of the *Vorsokratiker* on the authority of Wilamowitz; cf., further, Pindar Fr. 70d (Dith.) 18 δολιχὰ δ' ὁδ[ὸ]ς ἀθανάτω[ν]; Orph. Fr. 168, 15 ἀντολίη τε δύσις τε, θεῶν ὁδοὶ οὐρανιώνων; Epigram on the fallen at Coroneia SEG 10, 104 = Peek Nr. 17 ἀλλά τις ὑμᾶς ἡμιθέων θείαν εἰς ὁδὸν ἀντιάσας ἔβλαψεν. Wilamowitz' categorial pronouncement "ὁδὸς δαίμονος 'path to the Daimon' is not Greek" (U. von Wilamowitz-Moellendorf, *Der Glaube der Hellenen*, vol. 1, 1957 [Berlin: Weidmannsche Buchhandlung, 1931], 367) does not hold without exception: Philon *De post. Caini* 101 has βασιλική ὁδός = βασιλέως ὁδός = πρὸς αὐτὸν ἄγουσα ὁδός; the oldest testimonies however indicate a *genitivus subjectivus* (Vos 21) or *possesivus*.
28 Bowra 1953, 50 (following him, Mansfeld 1964, 225; 228) has objected that ὁδὸς φέρει is only attested to in the intransitive. This is not valid, cf. Hippol. *ref.* 5, 8, 43: τῆς ὁδοῦ ... φερούσης τοὺς ἀπολλυμένους ἐπὶ τὴν Περσεφόνην; (ὁδὸς) λεωφόρος = φέρουσα τὸν λεών implies an object as well. Diels 1897, 48, has, moreover, emphasized that an expression such as δαίμων φέρει φῶτα would be strange; φέρει does not mean to lead ("lead" Raven), but rather, to transport (cf. *Od.* 21,196).

other ambiguity: the "knowledge" remains without an object. Yet, before supplying the missing element, as though Parmenides knew the path or even what he is about to experience,[29] it is advisable to look at the lexical evidence. There are two cases in which εἰδώς is used without an object: either the object is defined through a corresponding *verbum dicendi*—of the type πρὸς εἰδότας λέγειν—or, alternatively, εἰδώς has a special meaning: the "initiate," the mystic.[30] Standard passages to support this are Andokides *On mysteries* 30: ἡ γὰρ βάσανος δεινὴ παρὰ τοῖς εἰδόσιν, and [Eurp.] *Rhes.* 973: σεμνὸς τοῖσιν εἰδόσιν θεός; also see the parody in Aristophanes, *Clouds* 1241: Ζεὺς γελοῖος ὀμνύμενος τοῖς εἰδόσιν. The importance of Demeter- and Dionysus-mysteries especially in southern Italy is well known. One can experience the actuality of δαίμονες most clearly in the mysteries, Plutarch attests (*Def. or.* 417 bc). Thus it is hardly accidental that the same verse of Parmenides' refers both to the Daimon and the "knowledgeable man." Indeed "knowledge" of the mysteries is the precondition for venturing onto the unfathomable path, the path into the beyond: Hercules survived the Cerberus adventure because he "had seen the ceremonies of the Eleusian initiates" (τὰ μυστῶν δ' ὄργι' εὐτύχησ' ἰδών, Eurip. *Herc.* 613).[31] The mystic does not need to fear the path under the earth, because he is someone who "knows" (οἶδε μὲν βίου τελευτάν, οἶδεν δὲ διόσδοτον ἀρχάν, Pind. Fr. 137). Thus, Parmenides presents himself as the "knower"; the exotic is already familiar: he will successfully reach the Goddess.

Unfortunately, there remains a much-discussed corruption in the middle of the verse. A. H. Coxon has established through renewed ex-

---

29 Fränkel 1955, 160; Tarán 1965, 12.
30 Diels 1897, 49, and Bowra 1953, 50, have emphasized the significance of εἰδώς in the mysteries; Mansfeld 1964, 228, 2 finds this to be "not necessary," but thereby overlooks the linguistic facts and the context, as does Tarán 1965, 12. Cf. further Eurip. *Bacch.* 73, Fr. 781; 13 (πρὸς εἰδότας λέγειν); Thuc. 3, 53, 4 cf. 2, 36, 4; Pindar *Ol.* 8, 60; Hippokr. *de arte* 1. Plato *Statesman* 300c is different.
31 Cf. a new Pindar fragment (346c Maehler), Hugh Lloyd-Jones, "Heracles at Eleusis," *Maia* 19 (1967): 208; (Plat.) Ax. 371e: καὶ τοὺς περὶ Ἡρακλέα τε καὶ Διόνυσον κατιόντας εἰς Ἅιδου πρότερον λόγος ἐνθάδε μυηθῆναι, καὶ τὸ θάρσος τῆς ἐκεῖσε πορείας παρὰ τῆς Ἐλευσινίας ἐναύσασθαι. On Hercules' initiation into the mysteries see Xen. *Hell.* 6, 3, 6; Diod. 4, 25, 1; Apollod. 2, 5, 12; Plut. *Thes.* 33; vase paintings, for example, Skyphos Brussels A 10 (ARV^2 661, 86); Pelike Brussels R 253 (ARV^2 1121, 11); Pelike Leningrad 1792 (ARV^2 1476, 1); connected with the lesser mysteries, Diod. 4, 14, 3, Schol. Aristoph. *Plut.* 1013; Relief from Ilissos, Athens Nr. 1778, Eph. Arch. 1894 T. 7.

amination of the Codex Laurentianus 85,19 that the reading ἄστη, which has been disseminated through Mutschmann's edition, is not in the text.[32] None of the many suggested emendations is convincing enough to find general acceptance.[33]

Now "maidens" (5) appear who show the way; they drive the horses on faster, so that the axle begins to glow with the spinning of the wheels. They are Ἡλιάδες κοῦραι (9). This name of theirs appears to illuminate the darkness of the Proem like a flash of lightning: are they not the "Goddesses of radiant truth,"[34] perhaps even "the thinker's own urge for knowledge, which strives for the light"?[35] And yet, Ἡλιάδες is, in contrast to ἡλιοειδεῖς, at first a name; this is not the language of allegory, but rather that of genealogical myth. Greeks, up to Parmenides' time, ask, when the conversation is about divine beings, initially not for an interpretation but for the name and lineage. Now the Heliades have their firm place in the Phaethon-myth. Aeschylus' Phaethon tragedy (Fr. 68 ff. Radt) was entitled Ἡλιάδες; the Hesiodic catalogue already

---

32 Coxon had the friendliness to communicate (Letter from 2.11.1965): "It is quite certain that ἄστη is not in this (and, so far as I know, not in any other) manuscript. What N has is substantially what the other mss. have, viz. πάντ' ἄτη (πάντἄτη L, without the second accent and apostrophe, πάντα τῇ the rest)."

33 Against ἄστη speaks V. 27 ἀπ' ἀνθρώπων ἐκτὸς πάτου ἐστίν. It was found fitting that Parmenides should outdo Odysseus (Od. 1,3: Havelock 1958: 133–43; Deichgräber 1958, 27; Mansfeld 1964, 230), yet Homer expressly mentions ἀνθρώπων ἄστεα; ἄστη never means "sites" in general (Fränkel 1955, 160, 2), "places" (Tarán 1965, 8). W. K. C. Guthrie, *A History of Greek Philosophy*, vol. 2 (Cambridge: Cambridge University Press, 1965), 7 attractively defends ἄστη by interpreting the "way" as the path of the sun: it leads "across all cities" and is yet far removed from humans. Orph. Fr. 47, 3 must remain aside, cf. n. 80. As to letters, αὐτή would be the closest (G. Hermann, thereafter Diels 1897, 48); this would mean that the path brings the knowing man to the goal "of its own accord," automatically; cf. Ulrich von Wilamowitz-Moellendorff, "Lesefrüchte," *Hermes* 34 (1899): 204, with the important objection: if the horses already know the path-marks (πολύφραστοι, v. 4, cf. Conrado Eggers Lan, "Die *odos polyphēmos* der parmenideischen Wahrheit," *Hermes* 88 [1960]: 378, Tarán 1965, 12 f.) and immortals go ahead, then ὁδὸς αὐτὴ φέρουσα is superfluous; cf. further (ὁδὸς) ἡγήσασθαι ἀρίστη Orph. Fr. 352 (*Margites?* Martin West, "A Vagina in Search of an Author," *CQ* 58 [2007]: 370–375). However, the accent in N speaks against αὐτή.

34 Deichgräber 1958, 29.
35 Fränkel 1955, 169.

knew of the amber tears they shed weeping for their brother.[36] A last reflex of a more active role is preserved in Hygin (*fab.* 152 A): *equos iniussu patris iunxerant*, for Phaethon's doomed voyage. Thus, the Heliades are associated in myth with a chariot-journey of a particular sort. Parmenides describes how the chariot-axle begins to glow, whenever the Heliades urge him on: Parmenides appears as a new Phaethon,[37] except that, in contrast to the misfortunate youth, no μοῖρα κακή drove him; Phaethon was not a "knower." Is the suggestively circumscribed ὁδὸς δαίμονος supposed, after all, to be the path of Helios, that of the φαυσίμβροτος δαίμων Ὑπεριονίδας (Pind. *Ol.* 7,39)? Yet where does the path of the sun lead?

The Heliades, it says, have left the house of Night, towards the light, they have thrust aside the veils from their heads. Without a doubt, the path from the night to light is described here; the allegorical interpretations have their origin here, from the word Ἡλιάδες. However, προλιποῦσαι is related only to Ἡλιάδες κοῦραι, not to the harnessed pair, not to the chariot and the driver. Admittedly, one tried to link at least εἰς φάος to ὅτε σπερχοίατο πέμπειν: "hastened to escort me towards the light."[38] But then, the word order employed by Parmenides would be quite strange, since the ὠσάμεναι after all takes up προλιποῦσαι right away. Even the lexical evidence shows that the specification of direction belongs to προλιπεῖν.[39] This verb, especially the *participium aoristi*, is nor-

---

36 Fr. 150, 23 Merkelbach-West, cf. Fr. 311; see Jacques Schwartz, *Pseudo-Hesiodeia. Recherches sur la composition, la diffusion et la disparition ancienne d'oeuvres attribuées à Hésiode* (Leiden: Brill, 1960), 301 ff.; 474 f.; the catalogue of names of the Heliades (Hyg. *fab.* 154; 156) most probably has its origins in a Hesiodic poem (Hes. Fr. 311 Merkelbach-West).
37 Cf. Bowra 1953, 45. Gilbert 1907, 32; Kranz 1916, 1159 too, amongst others, thought of Phaethon and the chariot of the sun; Francis M. Cornford, *Principium Sapientiae. The Origins of Greek Philosophical Thought* (Cambridge: Cambridge University Press, 1952), 118, 1 understood ὁδὸς δαίμονος as the path of the sun. Αἴθεσθαι is more than to run hot (fervidus axis Verg. georg. 3, 107; Diels 1897, 49). There existed a practice of producing fire through turning a wheel (cf. Heinrich von Wlislocki, *Aus dem Volksleben der Magyaren* [Augsburg: M. Huttler, 1893], 64), something easily associable with solar celebrations, solar sacrifices.
38 Tarán 1965, 8, following Raven and Diels.
39 Cf. e.g. Hes. *Erga* 566; Hom. *hymn. Aphr.* 66; Pind. *Pyth.* 9, 30; Aesch. *Prom.* 278 ff.; Eur. *Alk.* 124 f.; for εἰς φάος Hom. *hymn. Dem.* 337 f. ἀπὸ ζόφου ... ἐς φάος; Hes. *Theog.* 669 ὑπὸ χθονὸς ἧκε φόωσδε; see Morrison 1955, 60; H. Vos, "Die Bahnen von Nacht und Tag," *Mnemosyne* 4.16 (1963): 31 f.; Mansfeld 1964, 237 f.; Classen 1965, 99.

mally used in order to define a trajectory in terms of its two limits, beginning and end, departure and arrival; -λιπεῖν points back, προ- points forward. For example, Mimnermos (Fr. 12,3 f. West): ἐπεὶ ῥοδοδάκτυλος Ἠὼς Ὠκεανὸν προλιποῦσ' οὐρανὸν εἰσαναβῇ. In addition, there are examples that εἰς alone together with λείπειν, instead of an additional verb that means "to attain," "to arrive," may indicate the goal. And in terms of content this makes sense: "left the house of Night" and "attaining the light" are two aspects of the same process. This however appears in the perfect aspect—*participia aoristi*—, whereas the journey is described in the imperfect aspect—present-stem πέμπον, φερόμην, φέρον, ἡγεμόνευον, ἴει, σπερχοίατο. "Leaving the house" and "thrusting-back" of the veil are completed actions, whereas the journey continues. There follows, extensively described, the passage through a gateway, which, as is commonly held, likewise represents the transition to the light, indeed first represents this in the proper sense. Is this an "addendum"[40]? But in that case, Parmenides, inverting the natural sequence in an opaque fashion, should have at least helped the unsuspecting reader or listener by a clarifying, retrospective particle, a γάρ or an ἤτοι. Moreover, only someone who completely abstracts from the imagistic content can take the "house" of the Night and the "paths" of Night as simply identical. Above all, however, one would then have to assume: "The journey begins in the house of Night."[41] But how would Parmenides have gotten there? Is it creative incapacity that he "neglected to describe this"[42] or does he take it as a matter of course that all humans, βροτοὶ εἰδότες οὐδέν, are wandering about in the house of the Night? Indeed no: if the "house of Night" was at all familiar in Parmenides' time, then not as self-explanatory allegory, but rather as a name belonging in the realm of mythical geography: Νυκτὸς δ' ἐρεβεννῆς οἰκία δεινά are described in Hesiod's *Theogony* in the excursus on Tartaros, following the battle of the Titans (744).[43] It lies at the edge of the world, where Earth, Tartaros, Sea, and Heaven have their roots, where a terrible abyss, χάσμα (740), yawns, unfathomable; even the gods shrink back in fear; "the terrifying house of gloomy Night however stands there,

---

40 Kranz 1916, 1161 f.; cf. Bowra 1953, 44; Gregory Vlastos, "Parmenides' Theory of Knowledge," *TAPhA* 77 (1946): 73.
41 Gigon 1955, 246.
42 Cf. Diels 1897, 8.
43 On this passage, which has always been adduced to explain Parmenides, cf. Friedrich Solmsen, "Chaos und Apeiron," *SIFC* 24 (1950): 235 ff.; Michael C. Stokes, "Hesiodic and Milesian Cosmogonies,"*Phronesis* 7 (1962): 1 ff.

veiled by dark clouds." If one denies the relation between Parmenides and Hesiod, because Parmenides' journey purportedly leads from the house of Night to light,[44] one is moving in a circle; moreover, there are other, still closer correlations between Parmenides' Proem and this very passage of Hesiod. In consequence, the journey cannot start in the house of Night; to force one's way there or even just to come near to it would be an unheard-of, indeed, impossible undertaking. One understands Fränkel's resignation at this point; he claims that the pictures are, taken by themselves, "abstruse and without substance." And yet the aporia disappears as soon as one gives up the cherished idea that Parmenides must get from night to light. Only the Heliades have departed from the house of Night, they approach Parmenides προλιποῦσαι δώματα Νυκτός εἰς φάος.[45] In every epiphany of divine beings there is the question from whence they come, since one summons them through prayer and invocation: they should "leave" their normal residence. Thus, Hesiod commences with the dances of the Muses upon Helikon: "starting from there," ἔνθεν ἀπορνύμεναι (*Theog.* 9), they have come. Empedocles invokes the Muse: "Send, from Piety, driving, the chariot, obedient to the rein" (πέμπε παρ' Εὐσεβίης ἐλάουσ' εὐήνιον ἅρμα, B 3,5). On the other hand, it came about quite naturally that for πομπαί, which were so common in cults, one started from some meeting-place towards the god or sacred objects that were to be accompanied, in order to guide them in consequence to the destined site; cf. the Ephebic inscription IG II^2 1011.7: "in arms they went to meet the sacred objects up to the Echo-spot and guided them, and also Iakchos in a similar way" (ὑπαπήντησαν δὲ καὶ τοῖς ἱεροῖς ἐν ὅπλοις μέχρι τῆς Ἠχοῦς καὶ προεπεμψα[ν αὐ]τά, ὁμ[οίως δὲ καὶ τ]ὸν Ἴακχον). The Heliades thus have approached Parmenides and have revealed themselves to him in a sign of unusual confidence.[46] Admittedly, this is to assume that the Heliades are at home in the "house of Night." But pre-

---

44 Vlastos 1946, 73, 43.
45 Cf. Morrison 1955, 60; Vos 1963, 32; Mansfeld 1964, 237.
46 One should not downplay, through ingenious symbolical interpretation (for example, Diels 1897, 50; Gilbert 1907, 32 f.; Deichgräber 1958, 29), the unusual fact that the maidens unveil themselves to a man's glance. Nausikaa and her play-mates unveil themselves (*Od.* 6,100), because they believe to be amongst themselves. Hesiod does not see the Muses (*Theog.* 9; Latte 1946, 157). The appearance of the Libyan ἡρῷσσαι Ap. Rh. 4, 1308 ff., who remove the cloth from the head of sleeping Jason (1314; 1350 f.), is distantly comparable; Jason turns his glance away. Cf. also Aristoph. *Nub.* 287.

cisely this idea, which appears strange to us, is explicitly attested. Morrison already made reference to Stesichorus (185 Page):[47] Helios hurries at eve "in order to cross Okeanos and to arrive at the depths of holy dark Night, at his mother, his wedded wife, his dear children" (ὄφρα δι' ὠκεανοῖο περάσας ἀφίκοιϑ' ἱαρᾶς ποτὶ βένϑεα νυκτὸς ἐρεμνᾶς, ποτὶ μάτερα κουριδίαν τ' ἄλοχον παῖδας τε φίλους). Helios is at home in the "depths of holy Night," there await him mother, consort, and children. One could imagine the Heliades hurrying to meet their father in his golden bowl. Helios and the Heliades quartered in the "house of Night"—since ancient times it was self-evident to the Greeks that darkness had brought forth the light (cf. Hes. *Theog.* 123 ff.). In time-reckoning a day ends with sunset, the new count begins with the night out of which the new day then arises; yet, no matter how forcefully Helios ascends, he must return to his mother, to the house of Night.

"There is the gateway of the paths of night and day" (11): "to them Dike, the much-punishing, holds the changing keys" (14). If Parmenides' path were leading from night to light, then the gate should separate the "paths of night" and those of day, once more quite a strange idea: "a gateway that thrusts itself between two different types of ways, can hardly have existed in reality."[48] A gate is there in order to refuse or to grant passage, to gather up ways and to disperse them. As from a city-gate different roads come out to lead away through the land, so the "paths of night and day" come from a "gateway"—even if the combination πύλαι κελεύϑων seems not to occur elsewhere.[49] "Paths of night and day"—this is immediately intelligible: night and day move in alternation above the earth day by day—one hardly needs to recall the team of setting Night and the team of rising Sun

---

47 Morrison 1955, 59.
48 Fränkel 1960, 161,3: "ein Tor, das sich zwischen zweierlei 'Wege' einschiebt (11), kann es in der Wirklichkeit kaum gegeben haben." Cf. Diels 1897, 50 f.; Tarán, in his translation, goes beyond his own principles, as he feels compelled to make the insertion: "the gates [separating] the ways of day and night." 1965, 8.
49 According to Vos 1963, 29, the genitive after πύλαι can only indicate the direction, "gateway to Aether," analogous to πύλαι οὐρανοῦ, "doors to heaven." But see Empedocles B 100, 19 πύλας ἰσϑμοῖο (reading of manuscripts defended by Jean Bollack, *Empédocle I* [Paris: Minuit, 1965], 243 f.); Pindar *Ol.* 6,27 χρὴ τοίνυν πύλας ὕμνων ἀναπιτνάμεν αὐταῖς does not mean that the mules arrive "at the songs" through the gate, but rather that the song, seen in the image of a chariot-journey, should take its course unrestrictedly. But see Bacch. Fr. 5 ἀρρήτων ἐπέων πύλας ἐξευρεῖν.

in the East pediment of the Parthenon—; we experience their coming and going. It is a very old idea to represent their appearance and disappearance through the image of a gate that closes and opens.[50] Dike watches over this to ensure that it takes place in the correct order. The "lawfulness" inherent in the alternation of day and night is a basic model for the thought of the Presocratics;[51] Anaximander's famous sentence (B 1) about the "penalty" that "existing" things have to pay to each other according to the order of time finds its most impressive illustration here: the "injustice" day does to night in summer must be repaid by him to her down to the last bit in winter, down to the last cent so to speak, and vice versa. The "equality" in the alternation of day and night is the paradigm for justice *par excellence* in Euripides *Phoenissae* (535 ff.). Even Pindar's description of the afterlife presupposes the same conception: in the world beyond the chain of transgressions and penalties, the change of seasons is suspended; there is eternal equinox: "in equal nights all the time, in equal days they have sun…" (ἴσαις δὲ νύκτεσσιν αἰεί, ἴσαις δ' ἀμέραις ἅλιον ἔχοντες, *Ol.* 2, 61 f.). See also Heraclitus (B 94): "Sun will not overstep measures; or else Erinyes, helpers of Dike, will find him out" (Ἥλιος γὰρ οὐχ ὑπερβήσεται μέτρα· εἰ δὲ μή, Ἐρινύες μιν Δίκης ἐπίκουροι ἐξευρήσουσιν). Dike at the gate of the paths of day and night, this is a mythical expression for a standard element of the Presocratic understanding of nature. One also finds this "alternation" of closing and opening, of coming and going being expressed by ἀμοιβός—which does not exclude some special technical meaning of "alternating" for κληὶς ἀμοιβός.[52]

In the Greek tradition, the gateway of day and night has its first attestation once again in Hesiod, as has been seen all along, in the very passage already mentioned, the Tartarus description. In front of the

---

50 The opening of a gate, from which the sun god appears, is represented on Mesopotamian seals from the Sargonic period (3rd mill. B.C.); cf. Henri Frankfort, *Cylinder Seals* (London: Macmillan, 1939), 98 ff. esp. T. XVIIIa = Samuel Noah Kramer, *Sumerian Mythology* (Philadelphia: University of Pennsylvania Press, 1961), pl. 10, 1. That oriental cylinder seals occasionally reached Greece, has been shown by a finding at Thebes, Kadmos 3, 1964, 25 ff. See also Ernest Leslie Highbarger, *The Gates of Dreams* (Baltimore: Johns Hopkins University Press, 1940). Ἠελίοιο πύλαι *Od.* 24,12.
51 Cf. Gregory Vlastos, "Equality and Justice and Early Greek Cosmologies," *CP* 42 (1947): 156 ff. esp. 173; Olof Gigon, "Die Theologie der Vorsokratiker," *Entretiens Fondation Hardt* 1 (1952): 136 ff.
52 Cf. the discussion in Mansfeld 1964, 240 ff.; ἀμειβόμεναι μέγαν οὐδὸν Hes. *Theog.* 749; ἀμοιβαῖος Empdedocles B 30,3.

house of Night, we learn, Atlas is carrying the heavens, and it is there that Night and Day encounter each other, "alternately stepping across the great bronze threshold: the one enters within and descends, the other issues forth..." (749). Here we have the alternation of day and night, the gateway, the threshold—only Dike in her cosmic-astronomical function is missing in the early epic.[53] In Parmenides the gateway is called, in contrast to Hesiod, "ethereal"; this indicates a particular region of the cosmos, at the bright rim of the sky. This word is the only support in the entire Proem for all interpretations that speak of an "ascent," a journey to the heavens. Yet when stating that "we find ourselves in the region of heaven,"[54] one should not overlook the "stone threshold." This too is a departure from Hesiod: for Hesiod the threshold is "of bronze" (*Theog.* 750).[55] If Parmenides uses the metrically equivalent λάινος, this is done intentionally. Aether belongs to heaven, stones belong to earth. The gate looms up into all the levels of heaven; its base, however, is in the region of earth: it unites heaven and earth, just as it also collectively encloses the paths of night and day. Opposites and their unity constitutes a basic problem in Parmenidean thought. Still this interpretation remains entirely within the framework of mythical geography: we find ourselves in the region where, according to Hesiod, heaven and earth, sea and Tartarus have their sources and their limits. Nothing prevents us from associating ἔνθα with the nearest mention of a lo-

---

53 In Hesiod, the Hecatoncheires have the task of standing guard, *Theog.* 743 f. But already for Hesiod Dike is one of the Horai (*Theog.* 902), who open and close the gate of heaven in the *Iliad* (5,749 ff.; 8,393 ff.). The Δίκη πολύποινος of the Orphics (Orph. Fr. 158), already familiar to Plato (*Leg.* 715e = Orph. Fr. 21, cf. 23), appears to perform more general functions.

54 Deichgräber 1958, 33.

55 The "bronze threshold" to the underworld has its fixed place in literature (*Iliad* 8, 15) and ritual (Soph. *O.K.* 57 with Schol; 1591). That the ὑπέρθυρον should also be "of stone" (Deichgräber 1958, 31; Mansfeld 1964, 245) is not in the text; the gate "itself" (αὐταί, 13) is the side posts or columns and the lintel. Mansfeld 1964, 245 associates λάινος with the "wall-like" boundary of the cosmos in A 37; yet why is only the threshold "of stone"? It is true that in Parmenides' own cosmology there is no flat earth, no edge of the world where heaven and earth touch each other (Vos 1963, 33); in the system of the στεφάναι revolving inside each other (B 12), there can be no "gate of the paths of night and day." But not even Plato took the trouble to reconcile the "gates of heaven" (*Resp.* 614c) with the revolving "spintops" of the astronomical world-picture (616b-617c); Parmenides can all the more call upon the pre-philosophical world-picture. The Proem is leading to knowledge, the reader cannot know in advance what the Goddess is going to teach much later.

cality: δώματα Νυκτός.⁵⁶ Somewhere in this mysterious region is the massive gate. It is not directly the gate to the house of Night—one does not drive a chariot into the house—, rather the entire region is conceived as an extensive grange, on which several larger and smaller δώματα, οἰκία stand—as already in Hesiod.

Dike, "wheedled" by the Heliades, thrusts back the bolt, the gate swings open—a yawning expanse stares back at Parmenides; the revolving posts with their sockets and clasps are the only tangible, the only fixed things that remain; and the path. Nothing of heavenly brilliance; Χάσμα ἀχανές—"yawning," expressed twice, with an emphasis that is not to be overheard: the open, that which is without any foundation, without a ground, empty. This is more than to say: the door opened. And once again one is reminded of Hesiod: at the edge of the world there is that terrible χάσμα, which frightens even gods.⁵⁷ It is from Hesiod that the Parmenidean text gets its point: one could not reach the foundation of this χάσμα even in a year, Hesiod says, since storms would seize hold of the intruder and dash him this way and that (ἔνθα καὶ ἔνθα, 740). Not so Parmenides: the journey continues "straight along," since immortals guide him.

Then the "Goddess" receives him. The text, understood literally, makes it clear enough that she is not identical with Dike.⁵⁸ Dike watches the gate; as it springs open, the journey continues "straight along" past the gatekeeper. Gatekeeper and host are naturally separated in the daily life of the Greeks; the gatekeeper allows one to pass, the host or hostess receives one. If in temple-ritual the κλῃδοῦχος is a high-ranking priestess, perhaps even the highest priestess, she is still not the goddess who appears. The Goddess says to Parmenides that Themis and Dike have sent him (28). Dike is turned towards the here and now, she controls

---

56 Cf. Kranz 1916, 1160; 1163; Morrison 1955, 59 ff. It is true that the repeated ἔνθα in Hesiod's *Theogony* (729; 736; 758; 767; 775; 807) does not give us any exact topography, even the cardinal direction is at best hinted at in the word ζόφος (729); yet everything is related to the previously mentioned mysterious name: Τάρταρος (725). Similarly, ἔνθα in Parmenides too has its relations ("there is no need to identify ἔνθα," Tarán 1965, 13).
57 Morrison 1955, 60.
58 Since the force of Dike is mentioned at B 8,14, (cf. Fränkel 1960, 162 ff.), the identification of the "Goddess" with Dike (Sextus 7, 113 f.; A 37) has been defended repeatedly, cf. Deichgräber 1958, pass.; Mansfeld 1964, 62; 261 ff.; contra, Tarán 1965, 15 f.

the alternation of day and night; the goal of Parmenides' journey lies beyond that.

But how are we to name the Goddess? The most consistent is Morrison's suggestion: Nyx.[59] In that case, the connection with the Theogony of "Orpheus" would be incontestable, in which, according to Aristotle and Eudemus, Nyx was the beginning of all things.[60] The fact is, however, that Parmenides does not mention any name here. Proclus speaks of a νύμφη Ὑψιπύλη (in Parm. 640; Cousin); this is more puzzling than one tends to concede.[61] It is, however, a fixed custom of living religiosity to speak of θεός or θεά without naming names, especially among εἰδότες. For the Athenians, Athena is simply ἡ θεός, a name is superfluous. More important was the prescription of the mysteries: sometimes the names of the gods were only known to the initiates, they belonged to the ἀπόρρητα; officially, at least, only θεός, θεά, τὼ θεώ, μεγάλοι θεοί are spoken of.[62] Far from lessening the dignity of the god, θεά emphasizes the claim to being "the other one," through exclusion of all familiarity. Precisely from this the grace that is nonetheless

---

59 Morrison 1955, 60; cf. the oracle of Nyx in Megara, close to the Megaron of Demeter, Paus. 1, 40, 6; oracle of Nyx at Delphi, Orph. Fr. 294; Schol. Pind. *Pyth.* p. 2,6 Drachman; Orph. Fr. 103. It is true H. Gomperz thought he could name the goddess Hemera, "Day" (Heinrich Gomperz, "Psychologische Beobachtungen an griechischen Philosophen: Parmenides—Sokrates," *Imago* 10 [1924]: 4).

60 See n. 69.

61 Proclus is reproducing Syrian's interpretation of the Platonic *Parmenides*. It is doubtful (Cornford 1952, l.c. 120, 1) whether a commentator was capable of creating, in mythic-poetic language, a νύμφη Ὑψιπύλη through paraphrasing the passage B 1,11–15 (Tarán 1965, 16; cf. Bowra 1953, 47). On the other hand, it is clear that the Proem is preserved completely. Should we invent a concluding verse, "thus spoke the goddess, Ὑψιπύλη νύμφη"?

62 The goddesses of the Thesmophoria and the Eleusinian mysteries are officially called τὼ θεώ; θεός and θεά are separate gods in Eleusis besides these—to identify them is difficult, cf. Martin Persson Nilsson, *Geschichte der griechischen Religion*, vol. 1 (Munich: C.H. Beck, 1955), 470; Κόρης καὶ Δήμητρος καὶ αὐτῆς τῆς μεγίστης θεᾶς Procl. *Resp.* I 125,20; Kroll is enigmatic. The inscription from Andania (SIG³ 736) refers to Μεγάλοι θεοί and Ἅγνα; Paus. 4, 33, 4 f. equates Magna with Kore, he speaks of θεαὶ μεγάλαι. The Μεγάλοι θεοί of Samothrace were identified and interpreted in various ways, cf. Bengt Hemberg, *Die Kabiren* (Uppsala: Almqvist & Wiksell, 1950); dedications ταῖ θεῷ from the Persephone-sanctuary of Locri, IG XIV 630, *Not. Scav.* 1909, 321, *Rend. Acc. Linc.* 14, 1959, 227. Tarán 1965, 31: "The fact that the goddess remains anonymous shows that she represents no religious figure at all and only stands as a literary device" is wrong.

granted, the friendliness of the reception receives its contours: χαῖρε. In such a greeting some other, distant possibility is heard, some dark threat: what would happen to someone who was not dispatched by Themis and Dike but by "bad fate" (μοῖρα κακή, 26)? Parmenides is accepted. The address κοῦρε indicates his status.[63] The highpoint of life fits the presence of the Goddess.

To summarize: Parmenides' journey is neither a transition from night to light nor an ascent; it is also not a collection of heterogenous symbols, which would only be comprehensible in relation to the theoretical content, and still less a purely literary device without deeper meaning. Parmenides travels on the path of the Daimon to the edge of the world, where at the boundary between heaven and earth a towering gateway divides this world from the beyond. The Heliades approach him from the house of Night, they accompany him through the gate into the great "open," where the Goddess receives him. Everything falls into place as soon as one resolutely discards the path upward and the path to the light, those Platonic-Christian symbols. The journey might rather—with Morrison—be called a *katabasis*. More correct is to

---

63 On the concept of κοῦρος see the extensive study of Henri Jeanmaire, *Couroi et Couretes* (Lille: Bibliothèque Univ., 1939). Hermes addresses Apollo: Διὸς ἀγλαὲ κοῦρε, *hymn. Merc.* 490; Zeus is addressed ἰὼ μέγιστε κοῦρε in the hymn from Palaikastro (Nilsson 1955, I 322); Epimenides is called κούρης (νέος) (Plut. *Sol.* 12; Diog. Laert. 1, 115); and remember the Dioscuri. The explanation (Eduard Zeller, *Philosophie der Griechen in ihrer geschichtlichen Entwicklung*, vol. 1, ed. Wilhelm Nestle [Leipzig: O.R. Reisland, 1919], 728, 2; Kranz 1916, 1167; Tarán 1965, 16) that κοῦρε emphasizes the superiority of the goddess, the distance from the human realm, does not fit—that would be ὦ παῖ, cf. Heraclitus B 79. It is even less acceptable to interpret κοῦρε biographically, as though Parmenides was at the time of the composition of the poem "not much over thirty" (Kirk and Raven 1957, 268, following Karl Reinhardt, *Parmenides und die Geschichte der griechischen Philosophie* [Bonn: Cohen, 1916], 111; Francis M. Cornford, *Plato and Parmenides* [London: Routledge, 1939], 1). Vase paintings portray Hercules as he is traveling towards heaven over his funeral pyre on a chariot drawn by four horses as a youth (Pelike Munich 2630, ARV[2] 1186, 30, Furtwängler-Reichold pl. 109, 2; Henri Metzger, *Les representations dans la ceramique attique du IVe siecle* [Paris: E. de Boccard, 1951], pl. 28, 1, cf. pl. 28, 2/3). Κοῦρος is the state of perfection which is accepted among the gods—even the κοῦρος genre in Greek sculpture shows this. A. Patin, "Parmenides im Kampfe gegen Heraklit," *Jahrb. f. class. Phil. Suppl.* 25 (1899): 643 had already rightly pointed out that κοῦρε is "the brotherly counterpart to κοῦραι," that the address "in a manner of speaking, grants him identical status, an identical nature."

leave aside completely the vertical aspects, the above and below. The Beyond, in what is probably the oldest concept, is neither above nor below, but simply very, very far away. Odysseus too, in the *Neykia*, journeys neither skyward nor earthward, but simply into the distance. Something similar is true of Sumerian myth.[64] That Parmenides should link up with such ancient traditions may amaze us at first; yet, even if this appears to detract from his originality, it turns out to fit the system of Parmenidean philosophy quite well: light and night are the two "forms" of the world of *doxa*, which to have named is the basic error of the "opinions of mortals." It is not the case that "light" simply stands for being, "night" for non-being, even if Aristotle understood it in this way.[65] Non-being is neither sayable nor ascertainable (B 8,8); darkness and death, one half of the painfully real world, are not to be negated so easily. No, light and night are both only foreground aspects of the one being; the thinker must break through beyond their antagonism. Therefore, the correct κρίσις is not simply understanding the light.[66] Speaking figuratively, Parmenides has arrived on the other side of the gate, from which the paths of night and day alternately emerge. They appear in their mutual exclusivity to determine this our world. Yet he who is capable of pushing further towards the origin will grasp the unity and fullness of being; ὁ θεὸς ἡμέρη εὐφρόνη—Heraclitus (B 67) attempts, in his more mundane fashion, to grasp the same problem.

But the path into Parmenides' philosophy shall not be pursued further here. Rather, the Proem is to be placed within a broader horizon,

---

64 Cf. S. N. Kramer, "Death and Nether World according to the Sumerian Literary Texts," *Iraq* 22 (1960): 67, on the myth of *Enlil, Ninlil, and the Underworld*: "the word 'descent' is not used in this myth, only such words as 'come,' 'follow,' 'enter.'"

65 Arist. *Met.* 986b30 ff.; contra, on the relationship of Aletheia and Doxa in Parmenides, see especially Hans Schwabl, "Sein und Doxa bei Parmenides," *Wiener Studien* 66 (1953): 50 ff.; Mansfeld 1964, 254 ff.; Tarán 1965, 220 ff. Mansfeld 1964, 247 emphasizes that the meaning of the Proem is the breakthrough to "transcendence." That non-being and night are seen, to a certain extent, as analogous does not contradict this, cf. Mansfeld 1964, 132 f.; 153.

66 For the oft-discussed problem of B 16 and A 46 see Fränkel 1960, 173 ff.; Mansfeld 1964, 175 ff.; Tarán 1965, 253 ff. Even if Theophrastus' statement βελτίω δὲ καὶ καθαρωτέραν τὴν διὰ τὸ θερμόν (διάνοιαν) is supported by the fact that in the arena of the world of *doxa* positive valences are assigned to the light (B 8, 57 f.; cf. n. 34), the thinking of truth is nonetheless more than the one extremity in the swinging of νόος between light and night (cf. also Tarán 1965, 73 ff. on B 7).

through which the interpretation will be confirmed and some more precise contours will emerge. Hesiod's *Theogony* is not the only piece of tradition to which Parmenides is indebted. If his "topography" largely concurs with Hesiod's, the conviction that a chosen, a "knowing" man can find access to the realm of origin in order to receive revelation there, is more than that. Yet precisely for this we have a number of analogous statements. There is, for a start, Epimenides from Crete:[67] he claimed to have slept for many years in the Zeus-cave of the Dikte mountains; gods, among them Aletheia and Dike, appeared to him in his dream. This detail is to be found *expressis verbis* only in Maximus of Tyre; still, the situation of divine epiphany is clearly presupposed in the famous verse Κρῆτες ἀεὶ ψεῦσται, κακὰ θηρία, γαστέρες ἀργαί (3 B 1), which has for a long time been recognized as a reinforced copy of Hesiod, *Theogony* 26: ποιμένες ἄγραυλοι, κακ' ἐλέγχεα, γαστέρες οἷον. As in Hesiod, there are goddesses speaking who point out their nothingness to humans. There exists a series of fragments from a theogonical-genealogical poem that circulated under the name of Epimenides. One may suppose that Epimenides' *Theogony* was created as a kind of rival to the Hesiodic *Theogony*: it started, like Hesiod, with a Proem that described the initiation of Epimenides into seerhood, the path into a cave and the encounter with goddesses. Xenophanes (VS 21 B 20) already made fun of Epimenides, with reference to his unbelievably advanced age; this gives a *terminus ante quem* for Epimenides' *Theogony*. Other parallels to Parmenides are links to local cult-traditions besides the allusion to Hesiod. Several caves of Zeus existed as ancient cult-sites in Crete; king Minos, it is said, met his father Zeus there every eight years. Parmenides lived on as a hero in Elea.[68]

---

67 Cf. Diels 1897, on Epimenides p. 13 ff.; Diels' introduction is distinguished throughout by boldness as well as thoroughness; thereafter Morrison 1955, 60. The evidence for Epimenides is collected in VS 3 and FGrHist 457, with Jacoby's commentary; the appearance of the goddesses: Max. Tyr. 10 p. 111,3 Hobein. Jacoby assigns the verse Κρῆτες ἀεὶ ψεῦσται to the χρησμοί; the parallel in Hesiod, *Theog.* 26 speaks for the *Theogony*. Xenophanes on Epimenides: VS 21 B 20. On Cretan cult caves see Nilsson 1955, I 261 ff.; Ronald F. Willetts, *Cretan Cults and Festivals* (New York: Barnes and Noble, 1962), 141 ff.; 199 ff.; Paul Faure, *Fonctions des cavernes crétoises* (Paris: E. de Boccard, 1964); the oldest allusion to Minos and Zeus: *Od.* 19,179. Cf. the tale in the *Old Testament* of how Moses receives Yahwe's laws at Mount Sinai, Ex. 19 ff.
68 Cf. n. 83.

Another even more famous rival to Hesiod's *Theogony* was a theogony of "Orpheus," known to Aristotle.[69] He considered Kerkops, a rival of Hesiod, to be the author. In this theogony, Nyx is the beginning of all, as Aristotle and Eudemus attest. We mainly know the Orphic *Theogony* in the form that was available to the Neo-Platonists, a much later compilation. Yet, even there Nyx still has an important role, and one may suppose that old traditions are preserved in this. The cave of Night is mentioned, ἄντρον Νυκτός; at the entrance Adrasteia stands guard—here too gatekeeper and goddess are separated—; Zeus entered this cave of Nyx when he was forming the world in order to obtain oracular instructions for this task. The ruler of the world returns to the cave of the primordial mother in order to gain the wisdom he needs to rule. The resemblance to Minos-Epimenides, but to Parmenides as well is clear.

Let us turn to a monument that is not very far from the Elea of Parmenides, both in terms of chronology and distance: the cave of the Sibyll at Cumae.[70] It is best known from literature, from Virgil's *Aeneid*.

---

69 Aristotle on Kerkops: Fr. 7; 75; "Orpheus" on Nyx as origin: *Met.* 1071b26; 1091b4; Eudemus Fr. 150. Zeus in the cave of the Night: Orph. Fr. 105; 164; 165; cf. 294. For the general problem of the Orphic tradition, see Martin Persson Nilsson, *Opuscula selecta*, vol. 2 (Lund: Gleerup, 1952), 628 ff. The *Fragmenta Veteriora* are now augmented by the papyrus of Derveni, *Gnomon* 35 (1963): 222 f. See Kouremenos et al., 2006. The relationship of Parmenides' Proem to Orphism has been discussed often, cf., for example, Diels 1897, 11 ff.; Bowra 1953, 44; Deichgräber 1958, 29; 86 f.; Werner Jaeger, *Die Theologie der frühen griechischen Denker* (Stuttgart: W. Kohlhammer, 1953), 114. Guthrie 1965, II 10,3. What is remarkable is that there are links between Orphic poetry and southern Italy: on Tarentine vases depicting the netherworld, Orpheus stands before the palace of Hades and Persephone; Suda mentions besides "Zopyros of Heracles" and "Orpheus from Croton," a "Nikias of Elea" as a composer of Orphic poetry (s.v. Orpheus = VS 1 A1).

70 Since Cumae was conquered by the Oscans in 421/20 B.C., the older tradition is largely lost to us; cf. Jacoby on Hyperochos FGrHist 576. R. F. Paget believes to have found the oracle of the dead of the "Kimmerians" (Ephoros FGrHist 70 F134; Ps.-Scymn. 240) in an underground tunneling system at Baiae; R. F. Paget, *In the Footsteps of Orpheus* (London: Robert Hale, 1967); it can be associated with the journey in the netherworld as described in the gold-tablets—if it is not, as the sceptics claim, merely a water-supply system. Orpheus himself was made a "knower" by his "mother," the Muse, in the Pangaion mountains (Μοῦσα as *montja*?), according to the *Hieros Logos* of "Pythagoras", Iambl. *V. P.* 146 (cf. Eur. Rhes. 972). The cave at Cumae was discovered by A. Maiuri, see A. Maiuri, *I campi Flegrei* (Rome: Instituto Poligrafico del Stato, 1963), 125, but never officially published.

Before arriving at the site of his coronation, the future king must enter this cave to obtain instructions. A hundred doors seal the entrance, yet they spring open as Aeneas prays (*Aen.* 6,42 ff.; 81), and from the depths of the mountain the voice of the mysterious, old, divinely-possessed woman sounds. Incidentally, the man-made χάσμα in the cliff at Cumae leads neither upwards nor downwards, but rather horizontally straight into the mountain. This is the king's path towards the "Mother," to knowledge and power.

Yet it is not enough to search the world of the Greeks. A passage from the most important and best known piece of ancient Oriental literature is surprisingly similar, from *The Epic of Gilgamesh*.[71] Gilgamesh seeks immortality; he must travel to primordial Utnapistim, the man who survived the deluge, far off in the beyond. Gilgamesh arrives at a mountain named Mashu, "Twin": "When he arrived at the mountain range of Mashu, which daily keeps watch over sunrise and sunset, whose peaks reach to the vault of heaven and whose breasts reach to the nether world below—Scorpion-men guard its gate... their shimmering halo sweeps the mountains that at sunrise and sunset keep watch over the sun..." (IX, ii, 1 ff.; *ANET*, 88). After exchanging words with the guards—the text is damaged—, the scorpion-men open the gate for Gilgamesh. A tunnel leads into the mountain, twelve double-hours long in complete darkness. This is the path of the sun: "along the road of the sun he went" (IX, iv, 46); it leads northward, the northwind blows against Gilgamesh (IX, v, 38). On the other side, Siduri the ale-wife receives him. The journey continues still further, Gilgamesh has to cross the water of death as well; this too is the path of the sun (X, ii, 23; *ANET*, 91). But it is the section quoted that corresponds to Hesiod—and to Parmenides—in a remarkable way: the mountain, which reaches from the underworld to the heavens and stands guard over sunrise and sunset—in Hesiod it is Atlas, "son of Iapetos," in front of the house of Night, where day and night encounter each other in Parmenides, as a last reflex, the "aetherial" gate with the "stone" threshold, encompassing heaven and earth. Monsters guard the gate—Hekatoncheiroi, instead of scorpion men, in Hesiod; Dike has taken their place in Parmenides. For the chosen one, the gate is opened;

---

71 On the Gilgamesh-epic see James B. Pritchard, ed., *Ancient Near Eastern Texts* (ANET) *relating to the Old Testament*, 2nd ed. (Princeton: Princeton University Press, 1955), 72–99 and Wolfram von Soden, *Das Gilgamesh Epos* (Stuttgart: Reclam, 1958).

he travels along the path of the sun. The goal is to gain eternal life; if this miscarries, Gilgamesh nonetheless brings back knowledge, lore concerning Utnapistim and the flood (Proem of *Gilgamesh*, I, I, 7, *ANET*, 73); his path was a ὁδὸς πολύφημος as well.

"Northwind" indicates the direction in *Gilgamesh*. A mountain of the gods in the north is familiar from West-Semitic mythology.[72] The Greeks too told tales about a mountain massif in the North, the "Rhipaean mountains," behind which the sun disappears. "Breast of the dark night" this mountain is called in Alcman (Fr. 90 Page); in Aeschylus' *Heliades* it belongs together with Helios: ῥιπαὶ μὲν δὴ Ἡελίου (Fr. 68 Radt). Allegedly, of all the Greeks, Aristeas of Proconnesos was the one who came closest to the Rhipaean mountains; "gripped by Phoibos," he pushed forth into the farthest north; this was probably described in the Proem of his *Arimaspeia*.[73]

Enough of comparative material. The differences in detail are considerable; yet one basic theme resounds, more or less distinctly, through all the variations: the path to knowledge and power, the path to the mountain, to the cave, to the goddess. If one attempts to grasp and understand this theme more precisely, the thesis of a mythical-ritual basis will not be more than a working hypothesis, which may be tested from case to case; but one has to take the risk, else one gets completely lost in the varieties of the phenomena. As hypothetical basis the initiation rites of male groups seem to come up, whose cultic center was the sacred "maternal" cave; hence this complex of royal and solar paths towards the cave, to the Goddess. We know that initiation rites center on death and new life, around some "mystery of rebirth,"[74] which may concern the general initiation into puberty—the child dies, an adult human comes into being—, or the exceptional initiation of a chosen one, of the king, the priest, the seer, the shaman. It is evident how effectively the cave can be used in this δρώμενον of death and rebirth: the instinctive shudder on entering the dark, unfathomable space, and then the blinding and simultaneously joyous re-encounter with the light. The ancient human skill of how to master the fire could be linked to such a rite as well, so that for the "knowing" one darkness transformed itself

---

72 Jesaia 14,13; Michael C. Astour, *Hellenosemetica* (Leiden: Brill, 1965), 269.
73 Cf. *Gnomon* 35 (1963): 239; James D. P. Bolton, *Aristeas of Proconnesus* (Oxford: Clarendon Press, 1962).
74 Mircea Eliade, *Das Mysterium der Wiedergeburt* (Zürich: Rascher Verlag, 1961); originally published as *Naissances mystiques* (Paris: Gallimard, 1959).

into light. From the light to darkness and from darkness to light, from life to death and from death to life—this is the path into the cave. It may be natural for ancient thought to view, or rather to experience, the cave as a mother's womb. There is extensive literature by psychoanalysts on the symbolism of the mother, procreation, rebirth. The historian may content himself with stating that such symbolism belongs to the basic constellations of Anatolian-Mediterranean religion: the great Goddess and her dying consort. We now have a representation of the great Goddess enthroned between two panthers 5000 years before Parmenides in the Neolithic culture of Hacilar and Çatal Hüyük.[75] Its roots may reach still further back into the Palaeolithic period, as "Venus-statuettes" and cave-paintings suggest. We find similar patterns again among the Sumerians in various forms, Ninhursag "Queen of the Mountain" on the one hand, Inanna "Lady of Heaven" on the other: she presses forth into the underworld herself, to return with terrifying power, accompanied by the wild Galle, bringing ruin to Dumuzi.[76] Finally, besides manifold variations in the myths and cults of the Greeks, there is the "Phrygian goddess," the "mother of the mountain," the leader of the Korybantes or the Kuretes; how far the Demeter mysteries can be neatly separated from these is questionable.[77] The much discussed

---

75 Excavations in Hacilar (1957 ff.) and Çatal Hüyük (1961 ff.): James Mellaart, *Çatal Hüyük—A Neolithic Town in Anatolia* (London: Thames & Hudson, 1967); cf. Jürgen Thimme, "Die religiöse Bedeutung der Kykladenidole," *Antike Kunst* 8 (1965): 72–86. Goddess on panther: *AS* 11 (1961): 60 (Hacilar); goddess enthroned between two panthers: *AS* 13 (1963): 93 f., pl. 24; Thimme 1965, 74 f. (Çatal Hüyük). Men in panther-costume: *AS* 12 (1962): T. 14 f. Female figure with young boy: *AS* 11 (1961): 55 ff.; coitus p. 59, pl. 10a; Thimme 1965, 76.

76 Ninhursag "queen of the (cosmic) mountain," Kramer 1961, 41: also referred to as Nintu, "queen who gives birth"; cf. Hans Wilhelm Haussig et al., *Lexikon der Mythologie*, vol. 1 (Stuttgart: Klett-Cotta, 1961), 103 ff. On "Inanna's descent to the Nether World," in particular on the newly found concluding section, see *ANET,* 52 ff.; *Journ. of Cuneif. Studies* 5 (1951): 1 ff.; Kramer 1960, 67 f.

77 The name Kubaba/Kybebe may be of Sumerian origin (W. F. Albright "The Anatolian Goddess Kubaba," *AoF* 5 [1928/9]: 229–231; Astour 1965, 64,3; and Γάλλοι turned up in Sumerian, cf. n. 76. See also E. O. James, *The Cult of the Mother Goddess* (New York: Frederick A. Praeger, 1959), and the older comprehensive work of Henri Graillot, *Le culte de Cybèle* (Paris: Fontemoing et Cie, 1912). Euripides *Hel.* 1301 ff. already identifies Meter and Demeter. The cult in the Ida-cave had remarkable links to the Orient in the 8th century

problem of when and how the Greeks could have become acquainted with oriental traditions recedes into the background in the face of the incontrovertible fact of a common culture.

To θεά belongs her κοῦρος; the group of mortal men requires, in order to continue, the counter-image of the "Goddess." Within the framework of these initiation rites another symbol is repeatedly linked to the maternal cave: the sun—which is masculine in Egyptian, standard Semitic, and Indoeuropean. The sun is the primal image of continuous renewal; every evening its radiance wears away, every morning it returns new and undamaged. In mythical imagery this could be combined most easily with the rebirth out of the cave: every evening the sun goes to the mother, into the cave of Night, to emerge from it every morning as though born anew.[78] This lets us understand why in *Gilgamesh* the path through the cave and across the water of death is the "path of the Sun," and also the path towards eternal life. Helios, we know, has a humble role in Greek religion. Yet at least in certain mysteries Apollo was identified with Helios by the 5th century B.C.;[79] and there are indications that Helios was linked to the Demeter-cult in particular in southern Italy. Note Italian vases which represent Demeter's encounter with Helios,[80] a marginal episode in the Homeric Demeter-hymn, which must have had greater significance in another version. We have thus been led back unawares into the immediate vicinity of Parme-

---

B.C., as the bronze tympanon found there proves (Emil Kunze, *Kretische Bronzereliefs* [Stuttgart: W. Kohlhammer, 1931]).

78 The Egyptian sun-god Re enters the mouth of the sky-goddess Nut every evening, to be born from her lap in the morning, cf. Adolf Erman, *Die Religion der Ägypter* (Berlin: De Gruyter, 1934), 17 ff.; *ANET*, fig. 543 with explanation. At night, Re illuminates the dead, as does the Sumerian sun-god Utu (Kramer 1960, 62 f.; cf. Pindar Fr. 129). Utu goes every evening "to the bosom of his mother Ningal" (Kramer 1961, 42); cf. Stesichorus Fr. 185 Page.

79 Eurip. Fr. 781,11 ff.; Orpheus in Aesch. *Bassarai*, p.138 Radt; cf. Oinopides VS 41,7; Timotheos Fr. 24 Page; P. Boyancé, "L'Apollon solaire," in *Mélanges J. Carcopino*, ed. J. Heurgon (Paris, 1966), 149–170.

80 See the material in Konrad Schauenburg, "Helios: archäologisch-mythologische Studien über den antiken Sonnengott," Ph.D. Diss., Berlin, 1950, 21; 41 ff. Worth mentioning is that on the puzzling gold-leaf from Thurioi Orph. Fr. 47 (Facsimile p. 117; the text by Diels VS 1 B 21 is pure *divinatio*; cf. also G. Murray in Jane Ellen Harrison, *Prolegomena to the Study of Greek Religion*, print subsequent to the second ed. of 1907. [London: Merlin Press, 1962] 664 f.) certain names of gods are clearly readable: line. 1 ΚΥΒΕΛΕ ... ΔΗΜΗΤΡΟΣ line. 2 ΖΕΥ ... ΗΛΙΕ ΠΥΡ... line. 6 ΖΕΥ ΕΝΟΡΥΤΤΙΕ ΚΑΙ ΠΑΝΟΠΤΑ ... line. 8 ΔΗΜΗΤΕΡ ΠΥΡ ΖΕΥ ΚΟΡΗ ΧΘΟΝΙΑ.

nides. Two Greek cities in southern Italy were held to be centres of Demeter-worship: Naples, the "New-town" of Cumae, and Elea. Down to Cicero's day, the Romans made a point of appointing the priestess of Ceres from there.[81] The cliff of Cumae was presided over by Apollo (Verg. *Aen.* 6,9 f.); the lion on the oldest coins from Elea can be traced back to royal symbolism from Lydia and Asia Minor, relating to a Meter- or Apollo-cult.[82] Inscriptions from Elea, recently published, relate directly to Parmenides.[83] They make known a doctors-guild derived from Parmenides. The president has the traditional name Οὖλις; Parmenides himself is called Οὐλιάδης; this points to a cult of Apollo Οὖλιος. The leader, however, has the title φώλαρχος—a word unknown so far; it must mean "lord of the cave." What the title meant in reality is open to question; nobody will imagine Parmenides officiating as a priest of Apollo in a cult-cave. All the same, it is remarkable how Parmenides unexpectedly appears in a local Eleatic tradition; and next to Apollonian names there is a reference to a cave.

The framework has now been laid out which makes it possible to assess the testimonies about Pythagoras.[84] These appear in writings from the 4th century B.C. at the earliest, some 150 years after the death of Pythagoras. It is easy to dismiss everything as late legend; still an attempt should be made to understand the tradition. Even oral tradition can be persistent, especially when handed down in the ancient

---

81 Cic. *Balb.* 55 (thereafter Val. Max. 1, 1, 1). The temple of Ceres, Liber, Libera was consecrated in 493 B. C., cf. Kurt Latte, *Römische Religionsgeschichte* (Munich: C.H. Beck, 1960), 161 f.
82 Herbert Cahn, "Die Löwen des Apollon," *MH* 7 (1950): 185 ff.; cf. *RE* VIII A 2403; Elea takes over the coinage of the mother-city Phocaea.
83 Published by P. Ebner, "L'errore di Alalia e la colonizzazione di. Velia nel responso delfico," *Rassegna Storica Salernitana* 23 (1962): 4–6, cf. *Supplementum Epigraphicum Graecum* 38, 1988, nr.1020; Giovanni Pugliese Carratelli, "Phôlarkhos," *PP* 18 (1963): 385 f.; Marcello Gigante, "Parmenide Uliade," *PP* 19 (1964): 135–137; 450–452. These are inscriptions of names on the bases of three Herms and a statue, 1st century A.D.: three doctors with the name Οὖλις and the title φώλαρχος, and Παρμενείδης Πύρητος Οὐλιάδης φυσικός. For φώλαρχος Pugliese Carratelli refers to Pollux 6,8 ἰδίως δὲ τοὺς τῶν θιασωτῶν οἴκους φωλητήρια ὠνόμαζον and Hes. s. v. φωλεόν. The cult of Apollo Οὖλιος is attested in Miletus, Kos, Lindos, Delos, cf. Gigante 1964, 450 ff.; Pugliese Carratelli refers to underground cult-chambers of the Pythagoreans.
84 For details see Walter Burkert, *Weisheit und Wissenschaft* (Nürnberg: Carl, 1962), in particular, 98–142. In the following details I think I can make some points clearer than before.

channels of cultic religiosity. Even if all individual facts should be obscured, the overall picture nonetheless retains historical significance.

Timaios (*FGrHist* 566 F 131) reports that the Crotonians turned Pythagoras' house into a sanctuary of Demeter. This ἱερόν may still have existed in Timaios' day. In any case, the Crotonians were inclined to link Pythagoras closely to the Demeter-cult. The seemingly absurd detail, persistently reported in the legend of Pythagoras, that one of his thighs was golden (Aristotle Fr. 191) indicates precisely this connection. For an explanation, I pointed to myths of dismemberment and reanimation in shamanic initiations,[85] while E. R. Dodds thought of a tattoo.[86] Both explanations converge, inasmuch as a tattoo is, in its original function, an initiation-scar, the imprinting of an indelible mark. There is a great deal of comparable material in Greek-Oriental cults precisely for this. The "lying prophet" Alexander of Abonuteichos let his golden thigh be seen at mystic ceremonies; he presented himself as a new Pythagoras, while his rites, as Lucian reports, were modelled on the Eleusinian ones (Luc. *Alex.* 40; 38). One must take the cult founded by Alexander more seriously than Lucian does; it had a lasting influence. Here we find the golden thigh and a variation of the Demeter-cult linked. More important is a passage of Prudentius: a man who dedicates himself to the Magna Mater receives her "seal": the mark is engraved with burning needles. The body part injured in this way heals straight away. When the initiate dies, the *consecrata pars* is covered with a gold-leaf, and he is carried thus to his grave (Prud. *Peristeph.* 10, 1076 ff.). *Tegitur metallo, quod perustum est ignibus*—there we have tattooing and golden limb connected, in the cult of Meter. Certainly, the reference is late. But we have older reports about the tattooing of the Γάλλοι in the Hellenistic period;[87] something similar existed in the Dionysus-cult. The oldest instance is the golden thigh of Pythagoras. It marked him as an initiate, as a mystic or hierophant of Meter.

In Prudentius the leg is not specifically mentioned. Yet in myth, the scarring of the thigh belongs to dealings with the great Goddess. Adonis was fatally wounded by a boar on his thigh; the fate of Atys, the son of

---

85   Burkert 1962, 134.
86   E.R. Dodds, *The Greeks and the Irrational* (Berkeley: University of California Press, 1951), 163.
87   Cf. Franz Joseph Dölger, *Sphragis* (Paderborn: Schöningh, 1911), 41 ff.; *Antike und Christentum* 1 (1929): 66 ff.; Et. M. 220, 19 s. v. Γάλλος; Plut. *De adul. et am.* 56e; 3. *Makk.* 2, 29.

King Croesus, killed at a boar hunt, as narrated by Herodotus, is generally taken to be a variant of the Attis-myth.[88] Scarring of the thigh and castration appear as equivalent in the cult of the "Mother"—something that fits the ideas of psychoanalysis. Scarring the leg, tattooing, and golden thigh belong together as the "seal" of the initiate. There was a tale that the Seleucid kings bore a birthmark on their thigh; the father of Seleukos, however, was Apollo.[89]

The great goddess is the "mother of the mountain"; *katabasis*-rites belong to her cult; and initiation-scarring and *katabasis* are connected. Strabo (13, 629 f.) decribes the Plutonion in Hierapolis, a gorge from which toxic volcanic gas arose: whoever enters the holy precinct will die, "the castrated Galloi however enter without coming to harm, so that they can even approach the gorge, bend over it, indeed can dive in for a while...." How they practically achieved this is less important than the belief documented thereby: entering the world of Pluto was their privilege. Much older is the Parian version of the death of Miltiades, 489 B. C.:[90] Miltiades, so the Parians recount, attempted to steal at night into the subterranean cult-chamber of the Demeter-sanctuary, the Megaron, situated on the hill before the city of Paros. But the door did not let itself be opened—the negative door-miracle. Miltiades then climbed over the wall, but fled, struck by horror, and injured his thigh while climbing back; he is said to have died from this wound. Truly, μοῖρα κακή drove Miltiades to force his way into the realm of the goddess; in such cases a leg injury becomes fatal. It is remarkable

---

88 Hdt. 1,36–45; Eduard Meyer, *Forschungen zur Alten Geschichte*, vol. 2 (Halle: Niemeyer, 1899), 239. Psychoanalytic interpretation of initiation-rites: Moritz Zeller, *Die Knabenweihen* (Bern: Haupt, 1923). Cf. also Stephan Sas, *Der Hinkende als Symbol* (Zürich: Rascher, 1964).

89 Iustin 15, 4, 3–9.—The Ethiopians tattoo the youth on the knee, σφραγίζουσι τῷ Ἀπόλλωνι, *Lydos mens.* 4, 53 p. 110 Wuensch, just as, according to another source, Pythagoras bore Apollo's picture on his thigh, Schol. Luk. p. 124,6 Rabe.

90 Hdt. 6, 134. Cf. Ch. Picard, "La tentative sacrilege de Miltiade au sanctuaire Parien de Demeter," *RA* 36 (1950): 124 f. Something factual must underlie the Parian account, if there was an official inquiry at Delphi (Hdt. 6, 135; Herbert William Parke, and Donald Ernest Wilson Wormell, *The Delphic Oracle*, vol. 2 [Oxford: Blackwell, 1956], Nr. 91). Perhaps Miltiades could really hope to be able to enter Paros, ἔχων τὰ ἱερὰ τῶν χθονίων θεῶν, as Telines at Gela was said to have done (Hdt. 7, 153), especially since there was a cultic community that belonged to the Parian Demter-cult, the Κάβαρνοι, who certainly had political influence (references: *RE* XVIII, 4, 1842 ff.)

how a historical event could straight away take on mythic dimensions in the eyes of contemporaries. In Greek myth there are further reflexes of the same connection between *katabasis* and injury to the thigh: as Hercules forces his way into the netherworld, in order to steal Cerberus, the snake-like tail of the monster bites him in his thigh, as can be seen on vases from southern Italy.[91] The *katabasis* of Dionysos, an initiate, is different: Cerberus licks his leg, *trilingui ore pedes tetigitque crura* (Horace c. 2, 19, 3 f.). In contrast, Theseus and Peirithoos force their way without authority, nay, sacrilegeously into Persephone's dominion; punishment is prompt: both fuse with the rock, as Panyasis for example told it (Fr. 14 Bernabé); and as Hercules tore Theseus away, it was not without injury. One teased the Athenians, the Θησεῖδαι, that they lack a piece from the rump (Aristoph. *Eq.* 1368 with Schol.).

Back to Pythagoras: the material presented may suffice to establish that there is an ancient ritual connection between Meter-cult, *katabasis*, and scarring of the thigh. In fact, not only the relationship to Demeter and the golden thigh are attested for Pythagoras, but precisely his *katabasis*.[92] The main source is, admittedly, Hermippus the "Callimachean" (D. L. 8, 41), who writes with a rationalistic tendency in a mocking, parodying tone. Scholars have discarded the whole story as an impudent transfer of the Herodotean Zalmoxis story. One strange element of Hermippus' story, however, cannot be traced back to Herodotus: Pythagoras, while in his underground chamber, has messages sent him

---

91 Volute krater Naples H. 3222 = Wiener Vorlegeblätter E 2; volute krater Munich 3297 = Furtwängler-Reichhold pl. 10. Cf. Apollod 2,5,12.—According to Laconian tradition, Hercules recovered in the Demeter-sanctuary at Taygetos from the leg-injury, which he had received in the battle with Hippokoon, Paus. 3, 20, 5 cf. 19, 7.

92 Cf. Burkert 1962, 136 ff.; similar stories of a sojourn underground and the ensuing epiphany of a prophet are recounted in the Iranian-Arabic tradition, cf. Geo Widengren, *Iranisch-semitische Kulturbegegnung in parthischer Zeit* (Cologne and Opladen: Westdeutscher Verlag, 1960), 62 ff.—I also took Heraclitus' invectives of Pythagoras (B 81 and B 129) to refer to this context (Burkert 1962, 141). Miroslav Marcovich, "Pythagorica," *Philologus* 108 (1964): 41 f. is right to emphasize the relationship of B 129 and B 28b; yet, if one thinks ψευδέων τέκτονας καὶ μάρτυρας refer to Pythagoras and his students, the explanation "everything that he and his students teach, is only lies" is unsatisfactory: why are students "witnesses" (μάρτυρες)? In contrast, the stories that Hermippus tells of Pythagoras and Herodotus of Aristeas (4, 15) are graphic illustrations of κακοτεχνία and false witnesses. It is tempting as well to associate Heraclitus B 28b, in addition, with B 66 and B 14, which leads us directly to the sphere of the μύσται.

from his mother, by means of which he can amaze the Crotonians. How does Pythagoras' mother come to be in Croton? After everything that has been said in the collection of parallels here, one may surmise that μήτηρ originally meant the goddess to whom Pythagoras owed his wisdom. The "house of Pythagoras" which was a Demeter sanctuary at Croton may well have had a subterranean *megaron* which Pythagoras alone, as an initiate and hierophant, would enter: he brought the revelations of the "mother" through *katabasis*.

Alongside this we meet with an apparently contradictory tradition which claims that the Crotonians honored Pythagoras as "Hyperborean Apollo" (Arist. Fr. 191). But perhaps this is only another way of conveying the same message: Hyperborean Apollo is a god who disappears for some time, staying with a mysterious people on the other side of the cosmic mountain to the North, and returns in a new epiphany—the path of Hypborean Apollo through the northern mountain ranges has a remarkable resemblance to the path of Gilgamesh, the path of the sun.

The result would be: Pythagoras presented himself as hierophant of a Demeter-cult, influenced by traditions originating in Asia Minor. He was thus the head of a male association that gained political influence too. Meter-cult has always been a matter for male sects; we know the mythical projections—Corybantes, Curetes—as well as real associations, *orgeones*, e. g. the Kabarnoi in Paros.[93] Yet, the aboriginal pattern of male groups and initiation, of royal consecration through the great "Mother" also had an inner side, a spiritual content: the rites always revolve around the secret of death and new life. And here one can see at least one root of the famous doctrine of Pythagoras, already attested to by Xenophanes (VS 21 B 7): the transmigration of souls. To what extent other elements were at work herein, e. g., influence from India, or to what extent the separation of body and soul can be traced back to "shamanism" of northern or of Iranian origin, cannot be debated here.[94]

---

93 Cf. n. 89. Dion and his followers, who overthrew the tyrant Dionysios II, formed an association sworn to Demeter mysteries, Plat. *Ep.* VII 333e, Plut. *Dion* 56.
94 The concept of shamanism was introduced by Diels 1897, 14 ff. It has taught us at any rate to take details of the Greek tradition seriously and to understand them within a background of reality, rather than shoving them aside as a "purely literary device." This does not bring a definite solution to the problems of transmigration nor decide how the idea of a "soul" independent of the body came about. Further clarification of "shamanism" might be hoped for from Iranian studies (cf. Walter Burkert, "Iranisches bei Anaximandros," *RhM* 106

That death is not an end, but rather a stage of transition to new life—this thesis has been presented, experienced, and believed long before Pythagoras, in initiation-rites: in the path into the cave and back out of it, on the path of the sun. Therefore the tradition that Pythagoras confirmed his doctrine of death and life through a ritually executed *katabasis* may be trusted. Hermippus presents it in a mocking tone, but Herodotus (2, 121 ff.) already linked *katabasis* and the doctrine of metempsychosis much earlier as though self-evident, clearly hinting at southern Italy, where he was in a position to familiarize himself personally with indigenous traditions.[95]

But to return to Parmenides once more: Parmenides' journey—on the path of the sun?—into the beyond, to the mysterious Goddess, and the Goddess' pronouncement of the truth of being and non-being has its archetype not only in Hesiod, Epimenides, and Sibyl, but also in the *katabasis* of Pythagoras, hierophant of Demeter and herald of the doctrine of transmigration. At any rate, one can put together the frag-

---

[1963]: 110 f.), which, however, are far from attaining consensus. The majority of the Greek τελεταί and ἐνθουσιασμοί, including oriental predecessors, are practiced without an explicit *logos* of the separation of body and soul; the same is true of Parmenides' journey. Willem Jacob Verdenius, *Parmenides: Some Comments on his Poem* (Groningen: J. B. Walters, 1942), 67 f. (see also 1949, 122 ff.) and Fränkel, 1951, 417 ff. surmise that Parmenides himself was capable of ecstatic experiences. Contra, others have emphasized that the fundament of Parmenides' doctrine of being is logic, not ecstasy (Gregory Vlastos, Review of *Principium Sapientiae* by F. M. Cornford, *Gnomon* 27 [1955]: 70; Mansfeld 1964, 259 f.; Tarán 1965, 28). But it could well be that the logical proof subsequently buttresses what has been evident in the experience. Mansfeld 1964, 260, attempts to show that, for Parmenides, logic itself had the character of epiphany.

95 Hdt. 2, 123, telling the story of Rhampsinitus' *katabasis*, with a skeptical remark: ἀρχηγετεύειν δὲ τῶν κάτω Αἰγύπτιοι λέγουσι Δήμητρα καὶ Διόνυσον· πρῶτοι δὲ καὶ τόνδε τὸν λόγον Αἰγύπτιοί εἰσι οἱ εἰπόντες —there follows the doctrine of metempsychosis, in its specifically Greek form, with reference to certain Greeks (Orpheus, Pythagoras, Empedocles? Cf. Burkert 1962, 103); however, even Demeter = Isis as the ruler of the underworld is by no means a purely Egyptian notion. Rather, Demeter and Dionysos are precisely the gods of the mysteries in Italy, conveying a special piety of local type (cf. n. 81 on Ceres-Liber-Libera); as Herodotus was writing his work at Thurioi, the readers (or hearers) there would have been startled by the first sentence: "The rulers of the underworld, so say the Egyptians, are Demeter and Dionysos (oh yes, we too believe that). *But* it is the Egyptians *as well* who first articulated the following doctrine (which is familiar to us, too)... Certain Greeks have appropriated this doctrine..."

ments of tradition in a meaningful way. We know for certain that the ancients considered Parmenides to be a Pythagorean. An important detail is the information that Parmenides constructed a heroon for his teacher Ameinias, son of Diochaitas: Ameinias had led him to ἡσυχία. This reference, as specific as it is isolated, probably goes back to a monument with an epigram.⁹⁶ The heroon indicates care for a dead man that goes beyond the norm; ἡσυχία appears in the context of the mysteries, and also as something sought for by Pythagoras. The φώλαρχος in succession to Parmenides is remniscent of the "caves" of the Pythagorean tradition.⁹⁷

Parmenides' achievement stands out all the more against the background of *katabasis* and metempsychosis. In Parmenides' teachings, transmigration is at best a law of the world of *doxa*: the Daimon sends the souls now from the light into darkness, now from the darkness into light;⁹⁸ yet light and dark do not really exist. Deeper still is the one certainty: ἔστιν. Even though this certainty manifests as revelation, it is nonetheless secured through the necessity of logically consistent thinking, which Parmenides indeed has discovered. In this respect, the Proem is a prelude: Parmenides makes use of a traditional mythical style in order to highlight his claim over against predecessors such as Hesiod and "Orpheus," Epimenides and Pythagoras. Whatever was behind it in terms of external rites and inner experience, Parmenides' philosophy

---

96 Sotion D.L. 9,21; cf. Walter von Kienle, "Die Berichte über die Sukzessionen der Philosophen in der hellenistischen und spätantiken Literatur," Ph.D. Diss. Berlin, 1961, 84 f. with lit. Pythagorean ἡσυχία: D.L. 8,7; Luc. *Vit. auct.* 3 (Gomperz 1924, 3, 5); Dionysian ἡσυχία: Eur. *Bacch.* 389 f.
97 See n. 83.
98 Simpl. *Phys.* 39, 19, f. τὰς ψυχὰς πέμπειν ποτὲ μὲν ἐκ τοῦ ἐμφανοῦς εἰς τὸ ἀειδές, ποτὲ δὲ ἀνάπαλιν. This brief paraphrase is ambiguous, contrary to Deichgräber's interpretation (Deichgräber 1924, 88 ff.); see Mansfeld 1964, 169 ff., whose hypothesis that Simplicius only reproduces Theophrastus' interpretation of B 16 (174) is, however, refuted by the fact that Simplicius expressly refers to Parmenides' original text (20 f., cf. 144,25 ff.). It is significant that, in contrast to Hippocr. VI 474 L. (Diels 1897, 109) and Aeschylus *Choeph.* 127 f. (Tarán 1965, 248, 51), "passing away" is mentioned first, "becoming" afterwards: this paradox, that death is not an end, points to mysteries and metempsychosis; how Parmenides adapted this to his system is not to be found in the extant evidence. A similar problem presents itself in more acute form in Empedocles (cf. Charles H. Kahn, "Religion and Natural Philosophy in Empedocle's Doctrine of the Soul," *AGPh* 42 [1960]: 3 ff.).

went on to justify itself in terms of itself, independent of all γοητεία and κακοτεχνία.

And yet, at bottom, this is not absolutely new. The denial of non-being, οὐκ ἔστι μὴ εἶναι (B 2, 3), this unequivocally means in Greek, amongst other things: there is no death,[99] at the price, to be sure, that generation and birth are "snuffed out" too (B 8, 21). Pythagoras had taught the indestructibility of life through re-embodiment. Much earlier, Gilgamesh had sought immortality on the path of the sun. Indeed, prehistoric rites already revolve around becoming and passing away, death and life, darkness and light, attempts at knowledge that encompasse change and promise continuity. New formulations, new explanations will emerge to advance the "elucidation of existence," but the basic problems of human existence have probably not changed very much since Palaeolithic times.

---

99 Cf. Kurt von Fritz, "Der Beginn universalwissenschaftlicher Bestrebungen und der Primat der Griechen," *Studium Generale* 14 (1961): 566; the departed as οὐκ ἔτ' ἐών already in Homer, *Iliad* 22, 384, *Od.* 1, 289, in contrast to the θεοὶ αἰὲν ἐόντες; cf. the dialectically pointed text Eurip. *Alk.* 521–528.

Ὁ Πλάτων παρῳδεῖ τὰ Ὀρφέως
Plato's Transposition of Orphic Netherworld Imagery*

Alberto Bernabé

I. Foreword

The aim of this paper is to examine the descriptions of what happens in Hades to the souls of the deceased as presented by Plato in some of his dialogues, specifically the descriptions found in *Phaedo, Gorgias,* and the *Republic*. In all of these, references are made to the fact that the souls of human beings face some form of reckoning after death in Hades, either rewards or punishments depending on what have they done during their lifetimes in this world.[1] In the pseudo-Platonic dialogue *Axiochus* we find a similar description, which I shall discuss in due course. The cycle of journeys in the Netherworld as described in the *Phaedrus,* however, presents a very different pattern, which I will not deal with here.[2] Plato attributes his knowledge of what happens in the Netherworld to various sources, but in commentaries or references to these passages, the

---

* This paper is one of the results of a Consolider C Research Project, financed by the Spanish Ministry of Education and Science (FFI2010-17047). I am very grateful to Susana Torres for the translation of this paper into English and to Sarah Burges Watson for her interesting suggestions.
1 Cf. Perceval Frutiger, *Les mythes de Platon* (Paris: Librairie Felix Alcan, 1930), 61 ff., 209 ff.; Hans Werner Thomas, "ΕΠΕΚΕΙΝΑ, Untersuchungen über das Überlieferungsgut in den Jenseitsmythen Platons," Ph.D. Diss. Würzburg, 1938; John Alexander Stewart, *The Myths of Plato* (London: Macmillan, 1962), 103–162; Karin Alt, "Dieseits und Jenseits in Platons Mythen von der Seele," *Hermes* 110 (1982): 278–299 and 111 (1983): 15–33; Emilia Ruiz Yamuza, *El mito como estructura formal en Platón* (Sevilla: Servicio de Publicaciones de la Universidad de Sevilla, 1986); Luc Brisson, *Las palabras y los mitos. ¿Cómo y por qué Platón dio nombre al mito?* (Madrid: Abada, 2005a) (with bibliography on pp. 221–238).
2 Neither will I deal with *Laws* 903b–905d, which bears no distinctive Orphic features.

influence of Orphism is often adduced. The reasons for asserting Orphic influence, however, are rarely stated. I will try to explain them more precisely, by means of comparing Plato's statements to what we know of Orphic literature from other sources. As a result of the present analysis it will be seen that, whereas certain elements of these eschatologies present remarkable coincidences with Orphic eschatology, others not only do not coincide, but are even contrary to it.

On the other hand, it is clear that Plato did not create a coherent eschatology and that, despite some recurring elements in the versions of *Phaedo, Gorgias,* and the *Republic*, we could not establish a composite picture from the philosopher's various descriptions of the Beyond.[3] In the following analysis, I shall try to corroborate the idea that Plato's images of the Underworld, as presented in each of the dialogues, follow diverse literary and philosophical strategies, depending on the topics and aims of the work in which they appear.

In my view, the description of the facts as proposed by Casadesús[4] is a good starting point:

> These eschatological myths are, without a doubt, a literary creation of Plato and an excellent example of his extraordinary capacities as a narrator. Various levels are masterfully combined: firstly, the general framework, in which the image of Hades, the traditional Homeric one, as it was known by all Greeks, is evoked; and secondly, the details within this general framework, which are a combination of his own additions with brushes and nuances from other descriptions of Hades, mainly the Orphic one, which was lesser-known and more of a novelty than that of Homer. Plato uses freely all these features in order to create his own conception of the destiny of the souls.

Casadesús also underlines the fact that the Orphic elements introduced by Plato contributed to a compound image that seemed to show more Orphic influence than was really the case.[5]

---

3   The differences have been particularly highlighted by Julia Annas, "Plato's Myths of Judgement," *Phronesis* 27 (1982): 119–143.
4   Francesc Casadesús, "Orfeo y orfismo en Platón," in *Orfeo y la tradición órfica: un reencuentro*, ed. Alberto Bernabé and Francesc Casadesús (Madrid: Akal, 2008), 1239–1279.
5   Radcliffe G. Edmonds, *Myths of the Underworld Journey: Plato, Aristophanes, and the "Orphic" Gold Tablets* (Cambridge: Cambridge University Press, 2004), 20–24 and 27 offers a more radical solution; according to him, Plato's model in terms of what we call "Orphic features" shares "a common traditional mythic pattern of action," but the philosopher "seeks to co-opt the traditionally authoritative mythic discourse in service of his own philosophic projects." Al-

I will review in the following sections the descriptions of the Netherworld offered by Plato, as well as that found in the pseudo-Platonic *Axiochus*. I shall point out, in each case, the context of the tale and its purposes, the source to which Plato attributes it, the elements that are analogous to the tenets of the Orphics as regards "geography and setting," the characters, the places for rewards and punishments, and the reasons why the soul goes to one place or another, as well as the differences both in conception and details, between the Platonic version and that known from Orphic literature, insofar as it can be reconstructed.

II. Netherworld Imagery in the *Gorgias*

Socrates makes two references to the Netherworld in the *Gorgias*. The first (492e–493c) occurs in the context of an argument between Socrates and Callicles, who has been defending the position that human behaviour should not conform to any moral restraint, but rather aim at the fulfilment of desires. Socrates himself states his purpose in presenting this eschatological framework (493c):

> All this, indeed, is bordering pretty well on the absurd; but still it sets forth what I wish to impress upon you, if I somehow can, in order to induce you to make a change, and instead of a life of insatiate licentiousness to choose an orderly one.[6]

Socrates hopes that the reference to punishments in the Netherworld may eventually dissuade Callicles from his amoral attitude. This is, indeed, the simplest presentation that Plato offers, omitting, as it does, the "scientific" elements characteristic of others.[7] The cue for introducing this tale is a quote by Euripides about the possibility that life is death

---

though I support the second statement, I think it extremely unlikely that the imagery of a Netherworld with rewards and punishments follows a "traditional mythic pattern," when it clearly opposes the really traditional one, that found in Homer, in the lyric poets and in the vast majority of texts, even in Lucian, according to which the inane souls inhabit a gloomy Hades in which they are all equal. Cf. Alberto Bernabé, Review of *Myths of the Underworld Journey: Plato, Aristophanes, and the "Orphic" Gold Tablets* by Radcliffe G. Edmonds, *Aestimatio* 3 (2006): 1–13.

6   Pl. *Grg.* 493c, transl. by Walter R. M. Lamb.
7   Cf. E.R. Dodds, *Plato. Gorgias* (Oxford: Clarendon Press, 1959), 372 *ad loc.*

and death, life[8] and it is clear that Socrates is trying to be "modern" in presenting the interpretation that an anonymous "Sicilian or Italian" offers of what "the sages" used to say, instead of the Orphic tale on its own terms.[9] Some of the characteristics in this description seem to derive from Orphic images: the idea that certain souls can be punished in Hades and that such punishment would consist of taking water in a sieve to a leaky jar (πίθος).[10]

Having failed in his attempt at convincing Callicles, Socrates offers a final infernal image of the Underworld (523a-527a) at the climax of the dialogue, its purposes being identical with the first one, though undoubtedly more elaborate and harsh. He presents it as a *logos* and, furthermore, a true *logos*, although he also suggests that Callicles could take it as a *mythos* (523a). It is clear that the word *logos* has an analogue in the Orphic *hieroi logoi*; in this case, it is a tale and not an argument. On the other hand, *mythoi* would rather have the meaning of "advice," something told without the slightest endorsement of truth.[11]

Socrates begins his own, and more detailed, tale with an allusion to Homer, in which he reminds us of the distribution of powers between

---

8   Pl. *Gorg.* 492e; Eur. *Polyid.* fr. 638 Kannicht. Cf. Alberto Bernabé, "La muerte es vida. Sentido de una paradoja órfica," in *Φίλου σκιά. Studia philologiae in honorem Rosae Aguilar ab amicis et sodalibus dicata*, ed. Alberto Bernabé and Ignacio Rodríguez Alfageme (Madrid: Universidad complutense de Madrid, 2007b), 175–181; Sara Macías "Orfeo y el orfismo en la tragedia griega," in *Orfeo y la tradición órfica: un reencuentro*, ed. Alberto Bernabé and Francesc Casadesús (Madrid: Akal, 2008), 1185–1215, where is pointed out the inversion of appraisals of life and death as a characteristic feature of the Orphics.

9   I have analysed the passage in Alberto Bernabé, "Platone e l'orfismo," in *Destino e salvezza: tra culti pagani e gnosi cristiana. Itinerari storico-religiosi sulle orme di Ugo Bianchi*, ed. Giulia Sfameni Gasparro (Cosenza: L. Giordano, 1998), 37–97, pointing out the different levels of the mentioned text: ancient poetic tale, attributed to Orpheus, interpretation of the tale, and oral transmission by an "expert." Cf. also Francesc Casadesús, "*Gorgias* 493a-c: la explicación etimológica, un rasgo esencial de la doctrina órfica," *Actas del IX Congreso Español de Estudios Clásicos* II (Madrid: Sociedad Española de Estudios Clásicos 1997): 61–65.

10 The reference to the sieve is also present in *Rep.* 363d, in the context of the ideas of "Musaeus and his son," which would further support its characterization as Orphic in origin.

11 Cf. the interesting considerations in Annas 1982, 120 f., as well as Brisson 2005a, 147. On the myth in *Gorgias*, cf. Lucien Bescond, "La doctrine eschatologique dans le mythe du *Gorgias*," in *Politique dans l'Antiquité*, ed. Jean-Paul Dumont and Lucien Bescond (Lille: Un. Lille, 1986), 67–87.

Zeus, Hades, and Poseidon.[12] Subsequently, however, (without indicating that he is not quoting Homer any more), he refers to a norm from the time of Cronus that the author of the *Iliad* does not mention anywhere:

> That every man who has passed a just and holy life departs after his decease to the Isles of the Blest, and dwells in all happiness apart from ill; but whoever has lived unjustly and impiously goes to the dungeon of requital and penance which, you know, they call Tartarus.[13]

In Homer, all souls, with the exception a privileged few, obtain exactly the same destiny in the Netherworld. Therefore, this outlook in which each soul has a different destiny, according to the degree to which it has lead a just life, is not Homeric. It is, however, attributed to the Orphics in various sources.[14] Nevertheless, the two specific destinies for the souls indicated by Plato do not exactly coincide with those which appear in Orphic imagery, since the Isles of the Blest are not mentioned in any Orphic source known to us: the place to which the initiated arrive, according to the gold tablets, is clearly placed in Hades.[15] The Isles of the Blest appear in Hesiod (*Op.* 171) as the place where the lineage of the demigods went *in illo tempore,* when they disappeared from the Earth. In a passage which has very probably been interpolated, it is stated that Cronus is the king of that realm, which probably does not mean anything but the fact that their dethroned celestial king lives in the same place as the race contemporaneous with his kingdom.[16] Pindar also mentions an Isle of the Blest,[17] describing it as a place to which certain

---

12 *Il.* 15.187–192.
13 Pl. *Grg.* 523ab, transl. by Walter R. M. Lamb.
14 Cf., for example, in *OF* 340 (hereafter cited according to Alberto Bernabé, *Poetae Epici Graeci testimonia et fragmenta* II, fasc. 1–2 [Monachii et Lipsiae: Teubner]; fasc. 3 [Berolini-Novi Eboraci: De Gruyter, 2004–2007]), 340 "those who live purely beneath the rays of the sun, /as soon as they die have a smoother path /in a fair meadow beside deep-flowing Acheron, (. . .) but those who have done evil beneath the rays of the sun, /the insolent, are brought down below Kokytos /to the chilly horrors of Tartarus," transl. by William Keith C. Guthrie.
15 Alberto Bernabé and Ana Isabel Jiménez San Cristóbal, ed, *Instructions for the Netherworld: The Orphic Gold Tablets* (Leiden: Brill, 2008).
16 Martin L. West, *Hesiod. Works and Days* (Oxford: Oxford University Press, 1978), commentary on 173a.
17 Pind. *Ol.* 2.70. Cf. Marco A. Santamaría Álvarez, "Φωνάεντα συνετοῖσιν. Píndaro y los misterios: edición y comentario de la Olímpica Segunda," Ph.D. Diss., Salamanca, 2004; Marco A. Santamaría Álvarez, "Píndaro y el orfismo,"

privileged human beings go, although no longer the race of the demigods from Hesiod. The divinity with whom they are now connected is Rhadamanthys.[18] The Boeotian poet seems to have mingled Homeric and Hesiodic concepts such as Elysium with Orphic ideas. Plato assimilates this synthetic vision offered by Pindar, but adds another tale that seems to be his own; he points out that in the time of Cronus and the early days of Zeus' reign, legal disputes were not judged correctly because in old days man were judged while they yet lived, and by living judges. Zeus then decreed that henceforth souls should be judged after death and naked, stripped from everything that disguised the category of their souls during their lifetimes. In order to do so, he assigned the task to three of his children:

> Now I, knowing all this before you, have appointed sons of my own to be judges; two from Asia, Minos and Rhadamanthus, and one from Europe, Aeacus. These, when their life is ended, shall give judgement in the meadow at the dividing of the road, whence are the two ways leading, one to the Isles of the Blest, and the other to Tartarus.[19]

The character of the judges is a recurrent theme in Plato. They appear in the other descriptions of the Netherworld referred to in the present paper (even in the *Axiochus*) and, aside from these, in other noteworthy passages.

In the *Apology*,[20] Socrates mentions a series of characters that he considers it would be a privilege to see in Hades. The list starts with Minos, Rhadamanthys, Aeacus, and Triptolemus;[21] he subsequently refers to each and every demigod that was fair in life, and then he mentions the poets, beginning with Orpheus. It is likely that Triptolemus had been added by Plato to the list of those mentioned in *Gorgias* to give

---

in *Orfeo y la tradición órfica: un reencuentro*, ed. Alberto Bernabé and Francesc Casadesús (Madrid: Akal, 2008), 1168 ff.

18 On the Isle of the Blest, cf. Marcos Martínez Hernández, "Del mito a la realidad: el concepto *makaron nesoi* en Platón, Aristóteles y Plutarco," in *Plutarco, Platón y Aristóteles. Actas del V Congreso Internacional de la I. P. S.*, ed. A. Pérez Jiménez, José García López and Rosa Aguilar (Madrid: Ediciones Clásicas, 1999), 95–110.
19 Pl. *Gorg.* 523e–524a, transl. by Walter R. M. Lamb.
20 Pl. *Apol.* 41a (*OF* 1076 I).
21 In any case, as Santamaría Álvarez has suggested to me, orally, we do not have to project necessarily on the *Apology* the eschatology present in *Gorgias*; Socrates could have been thinking that Minos, Rhadamanthys, and the others exercise the administration of justice among the dead that is allocated to Minos in *Od.* 11.568.

an Eleusinian, and therefore Attic, nuance to it. The reason for mentioning the judges is obvious: Socrates opposes these real judges to the false ones who have just condemned him. In the light of this precise context, the reference in *Gorgias* becomes clearer, since it insisted on the fallibility of the judges on this earth, who could be deceived by the external look of human beings and, unlike the children of Zeus when they administer justice in Hades, were incapable of discerning the truth in bare souls.

The trial of the souls is referred to again, both in the *Seventh Letter*, where it is attributed to "ancient and sacred doctrine," and in a passage of *Laws* in which, discussing the norms on burials, there is a reminder that souls have to appear before the gods to be judged for their behaviour in this world.[22]

Therefore, the presence of the judges is an idea dear to Plato, but one that has no precedent, that we know of, in Orphic texts. The theme of the scales for weighing souls is characteristic of Egyptian religion and is not widespread in the Greek world, but resurfaces in Christianity throughout the Middle Ages. We do find the theme of scales in the Greek world in ancient times as early as Homer, there, however, it is used not in the context of weighing the actions of the soul upon death, but rather the fates (*kere*) of one hero against another, i.e., in order to determine which of the contenders is going to die.[23] Minos, too, appears in Homer, but in order to settle disputes between the dead (*Od.* 11.568). Later, we find a reference in Pindar to the trial of souls in the Netherworld.[24]

Only one testimony considered to be Orphic presents a trial of souls. It is in the remains of a codex from the second or third century CE, contained within the collection of papyri in Bologna, in which there were parts of a hexametric poem (*OF* 717). We do not know the date of the work nor its author. According to its style, it seems to be a poem from Roman times,[25] whose author some specialists place

---

22 Pl. *Epist.* 7.335a (*OF* 433 I); *Leg.* 959b.
23 Cf. *Il.* 22.208–213. A similar scene was probably narrated in a lost epic poem, the *Aithiopis*, if, as it seems, this was the source for Aeschylus' tragedy Ψυχοστασία *The Weighing of Souls*, cf. Stefan Radt, *Tragicorum Graecorum Fragmenta*, vol. 3: *Aeschylus* (Göttingen: Vandenhoeck & Ruprecht, 1985), 347 ff.
24 Pind. *Ol.* 2.59–60.
25 Hugh Lloyd-Jones and Peter J. Parsons, "Iterum de Catabasi Orphica," in *Kyklos—Griechisches und Byzantinisches. Rudolf Keydell zum 90. Geburtstag*, ed.

around the second or third century CE,[26] whereas others prefer to place him in the Judaic environment of Alexandrian Hellenism.[27] It is, without a doubt, a *katabasis* from which mythological names are absent; as such, it is closer to a theological poem, and probably Orphic.[28] Even though this matter has not been finally resolved,[29] the arguments in favour of its being an Orphic poem are quite solid.[30] It contains a description of the rewards and punishments in the Netherworld, which bears very interesting similarities with Book VI of Virgil's *Aeneid*. In a section, which, unfortunately, is in a poor state of preservation, we find the following verse-ends:

] they gave in to fatal necessity[31]
] and those without shame, but from their former Vanity
] and forget their courage   75
] and taking up its flight it stopped
] to others[32] that go in the opposite direction
] from Earth others arrived
] a tranquil path, but neither this one
] was better than the other   80
] raising the scales with his hand
] attributing the correct sentence
] she obeyed the voice of the divinity
] upon hearing words of the God.
] carrying?[33]   85

The sequence of events in the passage can be easily reconstructed. Seemingly, some souls have already been judged and condemned (v.

Hans.-G. Beck, Athanasios Kambylis and Paul Moraux (Berlin: De Gruyter, 1978), 88–108.

26 Achille Vogliano, "Il papiro bolognese Nr. 3," *Acme* 5 (1952): 394.
27 Aldo Setaioli, "Nuove osservazioni sulla 'descrizione dell'oltretomba' nel papiro di Bologna," *SIFC* 42 (1970): 179–224; Aldo Setaioli, "L'imagine delle bilance e il giudizio dei morti," *SIFC* 44 (1972): 38–54 and Aldo Setaioli, "Ancora a proposito del papiro bolognese n. 4," *SIFC* 45 (1973): 124–133.
28 Reinhold Merkelbach, "Eine orphische Unterweltsbeschreibung auf Papyrus," *MH* 8 (1951): 1–11.
29 Vogliano 1952, 385; 393.
30 Cf. Giovanni Casadio, "Adversaria Orphica et Orientalia," *SMSR* 52 (1986): 294 f.
31 It refers to the necessity that forces the soul to reincarnate under certain conditions. The idea is already present in Emped. fr. 107 Wright (= B 115 D.-K., OF 449).
32 Probably "souls."
33 *P. Bonon.* (OF 717) 73–85, cf. Alberto Bernabé, *Hieros logos. Poesía órfica sobre los dioses, el alma y el más allá* (Madrid: Akal, 2003), 281 ff.

74). It is probable that the reference to oblivion in v. 75 is due to the fact that they have drunk the water of Lethe, which makes them forget the ancient courage they used to have in life.

In verses 77 and 79 two paths are mentioned, one going downwards, the path of the deceased, and another upwards, of those to be reincarnated. There is a reference further on (v. 78) to the arrival of other souls, most likely those who have just died, and from v. 81 onwards there is a description of the trial of souls, in which a divinity uses the scales and pronounces the sentence, which the soul listens to and obeys (83–84).

Since there is an absence of judges in those texts which are firmly dated from the fifth to the third centuries BCE, we cannot help but think that the presence of the judges in the Netherworld in the poem of the *Bologna Papyrus* is a late addition to Orphic tradition, most likely from the tradition followed first by Pindar and later by Plato. The closest resemblance to a judge in the gold tablets is Persephone herself, who, according to one from Thurii (4th century BCE), decides whether or not a soul arriving before her as a suppliant will go to the dwellings of the pure.[34]

While the judges do not appear in ancient Orphic sources, the meadow and the crossroads, however, are present in the Orphic tablets; I will return to this point when analysing the eschatological myth of the *Republic*.

The most interesting question arising in reference to the eschatology of *Gorgias* is whether or not the myth, as is it is narrated by Plato, presupposes the reincarnation of the soul. Dodds considers that, despite not being explicitly mentioned, this belief is implicit in the references to mistrust and oblivion in 493c, as well as to the contemplation of the sufferings of great sinners in 525c, which could only be a lesson to souls if they were to return to our world.[35] Annas, on the contrary, maintains that the Platonic tale contradicts that idea[36] and believes, following Irwin,[37] that the passage is meaningful without having to assume that the lessons learnt by the deceased are intended be useful in this world. According to her, the myth in *Gorgias* is more meaningful if there is a definitive trial, which would be a better deterrent for wicked behaviour.

---

34 *OF* 489–490.6–7, cf. Bernabé and Jiménez San Cristóbal 2008, 115 f.
35 Dodds 1959, 303, 375, 381.
36 Annas 1982, 124 f.
37 Terence H. Irwin, *Plato. Gorgias* (Oxford: Clarendon Press, 1979), 248.

I think a compromise solution, or at least a less radical one, can be achieved in the debate. It is a fact that the dialogue only refers to what happens after the trial of a lifetime, without any references to further reincarnations, but it is also true (*pace* Annas) that nothing in the *Gorgias* contradicts the possibility that, after suffering punishments in Tartarus, the soul is given a second chance to undo its mistakes, after one or several reincarnations. It is very likely that Socrates' primary aim was to dissuade Callicles, and therefore he underlines both the primary scheme injustice-punishment, as well as the use of the eschatological tale as an incentive to be fair, rather than underlining reincarnation, which is irrelevant for the purpose of this myth and which could even weaken his argument, since it would leave room for Callicles to postpone to later lives the possibility of improving his moral condition.

III. The Beyond in *Phaedo*

Plato presents a different eschatological vision in *Phaedo*.[38] Although the myth itself starts in 107c ff., Socrates explains its *raison d'être* a while earlier:

> I am of good hope thet there is a future for those that have died, and, as indeed we have long been told, a far better future for the good than for the evil.[39]

The context justifying the myth is, therefore, Socrates' wish to explain to his disciples why he is not afraid of death and why they, too, should not be afraid for him. The ambiguous expression "as indeed we have long been told" (ὥσπερ γε καὶ πάλαι λέγεται) does not clearly express

---

38 Cf. John S. Morrison "The Shape of the Earth in Plato's *Phaedo*," *Phronesis* 4 (1959): 101–119; William M. Calder "The Spherical Earth in Plato's *Phaedo*," *Phronesis* 13 (1968): 121–125; Maria Serena Funghi "Il mito escatologico del Fedone e la forza vitale dell'αἰώρα," *PP* 35 (1980): 176–201; Peter Kingsley, *Ancient Philosophy, Mystery, and Magic. Empedocles and Pythagorean Tradition* (Oxford: Oxford University Press, 1995), 79 ff.; Jean-François Pradeau, "Le monde terrestre: le modèle cosmologique du mythe final du 'Phédon,'" *RPhilos* 186 (1996): 75–195; Stefania Mancini, "Un insegnamento segreto (Plat. *Phaed*. 62b)," *QUCC* 90 (1999): 153–168; Edmonds 2004; Bernabé 2006; Gábor Betegh, "Eschatology and Cosmology: Models and Problems," in *La costruzione del discorso filosofico nel'etá dei Presocratici*, ed. Maria Michela Sassi (Pisa: Edizioni della Normale, 2006), 27–50.
39 Pl. *Phaed*. 63c, transl. by Reginald Hackforth.

the source of this supposition, but it suggests, once again, an "ancient doctrine" (παλαιὸς λόγος).

The preparation for this final eschatology continues throughout the whole dialogue, though a bit further on it again becomes the focus of the argumentation:

> 'Well then, my friend,' said Socrates, 'if that is true, I may well hope that when I have reached the place whither I am bound I shall attain in full measure, there at last, that for which I have spent the effort of a lifetime; wherefore it is with good hope that I set upon the journey now appointed for me, as may any man who deems that his mind is made ready and purified.'[40]

Socrates is using mystical language, albeit reinterpreted in philosophical terms. Orphic mystai, upon arriving in Hades, proclaimed their purity, as a result of which they gained access to a privileged dwelling in the Netherworld, as we know from a gold tablet from Thurii dating to the 4th century BCE.

> I come from among the pure, pure, queen of the subterranean beings.[41]

Similarly, Socrates thinks that his purity guarantees him a similar privilege to that promised to the Orphic believers, although the state of purity for him is achieved otherwise: not by means of a ritual, but by practising philosophy. Instead of "soul" (ψυχή) he speaks of "mind" (διάνοια), because the cognitive conception of the soul predominates in this part of the dialogue.[42]

The philosopher even admits the possibility that the Orphics were right in their eschatological ideas, provided that they are understood in a particular manner:

> And it may well be that those persons to whom we owe the institution of mystery-rites are not to be despised, inasmuch as they have in fact long ago hinted at the truth by declaring that all such as arrive in Hades uninitiated into the rites shall lie in mud, while he that comes there purified and initiated shall dwell with the gods. For truly, as their authorities tell us, there are 'many that carry the wand, but Bacchants few are amongst them';

---

40 Pl. *Phaed.* 67b, transl. by Reginald Hackforth.
41 *OF* 489–490.1.
42 Reginald Hackforth, *Plato's* Phaedo, *translated with an introduction and commentary* (Cambridge: Cambridge University Press, 1955), 52 n. 1.

> where by 'Bacchants' I understand them to mean simply those who have pursued philosophy aright.[43]

And a bit further on he refers again to Orphic ideas, this time to transmigration:

> And we may put our question like this: do the souls of men that have departed this life exist in Hades or do they not? Now there is an ancient doctrine that comes into my mind, that souls which have come from this world exist in the other, and conversely souls come and are born into this world from the world of the dead.[44]

Thus, Socrates has been preparing throughout the dialogue for the final eschatology, that will rest upon these two pillars: the relation existing between initiation—understood as philosophy—, the rewards in the Netherworld, and the theory of transmigration of the souls.

In the eschatological tale itself, Socrates, after arguing that, since the soul is immortal, it is not freed from its wickedness at death (107c), starts describing its path to the Netherworld, introducing the tale with "it is said," hiding thus the sources once more. There is a certain agreement in considering the myth as a construction upon various materials, among which the Orphic ones are not dominant, and I am not going to enter into discussions about what is the sense of this myth in Plato.[45] I would rather focus on describing its general lines and on pinpointing the elements that could be Orphic, according to the available sources on this religious movement.

Plato refers to certain guides:

> Now this is the story: when a man has breathed his last, the spirit (δαίμων) to whom each was alloted in life proceeds to conduct him to a certain place, and all they that are gathered must abide their judgement, and thereafter journey to Hades in company with that guide whose office it is to bring them from this world unto that other.[46]

---

43 Pl. *Phaed.* 69c (*OF* 434 III, 576 I), transl. by Reginald Hackforth.
44 Pl. *Phaed.* 70c (*OF* 428), transl. by Reginald Hackforth.
45 See the recent survey, with profuse bibliography, of the state of the question in Enrique Ángel Ramos Jurado, *Platón. Apología de Sócrates. Fedón*, edición revisada, traducción, introducción y notas (Madrid: Consejo Superior de Investigaciones Científicas, 2002), 196–198.
46 Pl. *Phaed.* 107d, transl. by Reginald Hackforth.

There is no mentioning of guides in the gold tablets.[47] Until recently, the only thing related to these *daimones* was a passage in the *Derveni Papyrus*, col. III 4, in which something was read along the lines of each of us having a *daimon* as a sort of guarding angel *avant la lettre*. However, it was found out that the disposition of the fragments of the first three columns contained mistakes and now the column is read otherwise.[48] Nonetheless, three columns later, in the same papyrus, some sort of *daimones* that hinder the soul in its path to the Netherworld are also mentioned, as the object of rituals carried out by some professionals called *magoi*:

> For prayers and sacrifices placate souls. An incantation by *magoi* can dislodge *daimones* that have become a hindrance; *daimones* that are a hindrance are vengeful souls.[49]

We can attest, therefore, that at least according to some Orphic interpretations, there seemed to have been a belief in the intervention of certain intermediaries, so-called *daimones*, that hindered souls in their path to the Netherworld, though they could be placated, and eventually turned favourable. Unfortunately, the details of these beliefs are very poorly known.

The fact is that numerous non-Orphic texts mention *daimones*, often personal ones, which could have a function similar to that described by Plato. It is, therefore, a tradition that precedes Plato and that continues much longer afterwards. Heraclitus seems to know this idea already and contradicts it by considering that this *daimon* is nothing but each person's character.[50] Menander mentions a *daimon* that accompanies each person

---

47 Although William Keith C. Guthrie, *Orpheus and Greek Religion*, 2nd ed. (London: Methuen, 1952), 176 thinks that we can find them in the person who pronounces some of the words in the tablets, which is unlikely.
48 P.Derv. col. III, cf. Richard Janko, "Reconstructing (again) the Opening of the Derveni Papyrus," *ZPE* 166 (2008): 37–51.
49 P.Derv. col. VI 1–4, transl. by Richard Janko.
50 Heraclit. fr. 94 Marc. (22 B 119 D.-K.) ἦθος ἀνθρώπωι δαίμων. Cf. Kyriakos Tsantsanoglou, "The First Columns of the *Derveni Papyrus* and their Religious Significance," in *Studies on the Derveni Papyrus*, ed. André Laks and Glenn W. Most (Oxford: Oxford University Press, 1997), 105 and Kouremenos in Theokritos Kouremenos, George M. Parássoglou and Kyriakos Tsantsanoglou, *The Derveni Papyrus. Edited with Introduction and Commentary* (Florence: Casa Editrice Leo S. Olschki, 2006), 146.

from the moment of birth[51] and even Marcus Aurelius often speaks about a certain δαίμων ἵλεως, private and intimate.[52]

What is particular about this eschatological version in *Phaedo* is that the trial is somehow dimmed and there is no reference to the judges, in contrast to other versions in which each soul faces its trial alone. There is, on the contrary, a sort of "corporation of souls" that accepts or rejects those arriving, "whereupon it is borne by constraint to the dwelling-place meet for it."[53] This "corporation" bears a strong resemblance to the "thiasoi of the *mystai*" (μυστῶν θιάσους) mentioned in the gold tablet from Pherai, recently published.[54] The philosopher depersonalises the process, referring to a trial, without mentioning the judges, and states that the souls go where they are appointed to, without precisely saying who appoints them, aside from abstract references to "constraint" or "destiny."

Next, we find another novelty: a long and exhaustive description of the world, in which the Netherworld is integrated. According to the philosopher, we inhabit cavities of an immense land, thinking we are on the surface. There are many similarities between this description and the double plane described in the myth of the cavern,[55] where we also believe that we are in the real world, although, in reality, we are under it, in a different one. In the myth of *Phaedo,* communication between cavities is made through holes through which rivers also flow between them.[56]

---

51 Menand. fr. 50 K.-A.
52 Marc. Aur. 3.16, 8.45, 12.3. Also Porph. *Vit. Plotin.* 10 refers to a οἰκείου δαίμονος καλουμένου.
53 Pl. *Phaed.* 108c, transl. by Reginald Hackforth.
54 R. Parker and M. Stamatopoulou, "A New Funerary Gold Leaf from Pherai," *AE* (2004): 1–32, Franco Ferrari and Lucia Prauscello, "Demeter Chthonia and the Mountain Mater in New Gold Tablet from Magoula Mati," *ZPE* 162 (2008): 193–202, Alberto Bernabé, "Some Thoughts about the 'New' Gold Tablet from Pherai," *ZPE* 166 (2008): 53–58.
55 Pl. *Rep.* 514a ff.
56 Pl. *Phaed.* 111d. The reference to this happening in a crater has lead some scholars (Martin L. West, *The Orphic Poems* [Oxford: Oxford University Press, 1983], 10–13; Kingsley 1995, 133–147) to purport an Orphic influence. Possible as it might be, it is based on a circular argument: we hardly know anything about the Orphic *Crater* and, in order to reconstruct it, we use the evidence in Plato's texts, for which it would be necessary to claim that the philosopher's texts derive from the former. Neither instance can be proved.

One of the parts of the earth corresponds to what the poets call Tartarus, and Plato quotes Homer[57] to this effect. However, Aristotle's commentary on this passage seems to imply that the inspiration of this detail of infernal geography comes rather from an Orphic poem.[58] This point seems to be endorsed by the long passage on the infernal rivers, the Acheron, that flows into the Acherusiad lake, the Pyriphlegethon and the Kokytos.[59] The source for this fantastic and detailed description cannot be Homer, unless in its bare minimum, since the poet only makes a brief reference to the rivers upon mentioning the doors of Hades (*Od.* 10.513 f.):

> There into Acheron flow Puriphlegethon
> and Kokytos, which is a branch of the water of the Styx.

The brevity of the Homeric reference may suggest that Plato could have also found inspiration in Orphic sources, although, needless to say, the vast majority of literary ornamentation in the description is clearly his.

Indeed, Orphics were interested in the description of infernal dwellings, according to a remark in Damascius' commentary on the Platonic passage, which is itself based on a previous one by Proclus, where it was firmly asserted that Plato had found inspiration in Orphic poems:

> The four rivers here described correspond, according to the tradition by Orpheus, to the four subterranean elements and the four cardinal points in two sets of opposites: the Pyriphlegethon to fire and the east, the Kokytos to earth and the west, the Acheron to air and the south. These are arranged in this way by Orpheus, it is the commentator (i.e. Proclus) who associates the Oceanus with water and the north.[60]

In another passage, Damascius even quotes to this effect an Orphic poem (which must be the *Rhapsodies*):

> The four rivers are the four elements in Tartarus: the Oceanus, acording to commentator (i.e. Proclus), is water, the Kokytos or Stygius earth, the Pyriphlegethon fire, the Acheron air. Opposite to Pyriphlegethon is the Sty-

---

57 *Il.* 8.14.
58 Pl. *Phaed.* 111e-12a (*OF* 27 I), Aristot. *Meteor.* 355b 34 (*OF* 27 II). Cf. Kingsley's subtle argumentation in Kingsley 1995, 126 f. in order to defend the Orphic origin of this reference. Already Guthrie 1952, 168 f., noticed the Orphic vocabulary of the Platonic passage, but did not take into consideration Aristotle's words.
59 Pl. *Phaed.* 112e-113c.
60 Damasc. *in Pl. Phaed.* 1.541 (277 Westerink) (*OF* 341 IV), transl. by Leendert G. Westerink.

gius (hot against cold), opposite the Oceanus is the Acheron (water against air); hence Orpheus [*OF* 342] calls Lake Acheron Lake Aeria.[61]

From the perspective of this discussion, the most interesting aspect of Damascius' comment is his remark that Proclus used for his interpretation of infernal geography a poem attributed to Orpheus, in which there was apparently a reference to the four rivers in conjunction with the description of the destiny of souls in Netherworld. Since the poet calls the lake of Acheron *Aeria*, "nebula," it is only logical that Proclus related the Acheron to *aer* (nebulous air). The name Pyriphlegethon made its identification with fire obvious. And thus the Neoplatonic philosopher ends up identifying the other two rivers with the other two elements.

Plato tells us that the souls of most of the deceased arrive at the Acherusian Lake and that, once they have spent time there, which is apportioned more or less depending on each case, they are reincarnated again.[62] I find it particularly interesting that the philosopher relates this part of the description of infernal geography to the theory of metempsychosis, describing a sort of "Purgatory" *avant la lettre*. We do not know whether this specific point was already present in the Orphic tradition or whether it is an innovation exclusive to Plato; the latter seems more plausible to me, since there is no Orphic evidence to suggest otherwise.

The two following fragments referring to the Styx are also from Orphic infernal descriptions, though filtered through Neoplatonic interpretation:

> The theologians give evidence that Oceanus is the source of all movement, stating that it makes ten currents burst, nine out of which flow to the sea.[63]
>
> And here Numenius (fr. 36 Des Places) and the interpreters of the hidden sense of Pythagoras understand as semen the river Ameles in Plato (*Rep.* 621a) and Styx in Hesiod (*Th.* 361) and in the Orphics.[64]

---

61 Damasc. *in Pl. Phaed.* 2.145 (363 Westerink) (*OF* 341 IV and 342), transl. by Leendert G. Westerink.
62 Pl. *Phaed.* 113a.
63 Procl. *in Pl. Tim.* III 180.8 Diehl (*OF* 343). The tenth is Styx, cf. Hes. *Th.* 789–791: "A tenth part (of Oceanus) is immediately set aside, but nine around Earth and the wide side of the sea, making them twist in a silver swirl, are flown into the sea." The plural "the theologians" comprises, apparently, Orpheus and Hesiod.
64 Porphyr. *ad Gaurum* 2.2.9 (34.26 Kalbfleisch, *OF* 344).

Both passages clearly show the interpretation of Orphic texts in the hands of those who pretend they have a hidden sense, rather than their real content, about which we are very poorly informed. The second interpretation, in particular, seems to refer back to the point that, after arriving at the Styx, the soul can be reincarnated again, which leads Numenius to identify allegorically the role of the lake as seed for the growth of a new life with that of semen.

Finally, Plato states (*Phaed*. 113d) that the dead, arriving to wherever their *daimon* takes them, are put on trial, without indicating before whom, and that some are purified in the Lake of Acheron, while others, hopeless, are thrown into Tartarus, "from which they would never escape." After a certain amount of information, the philosopher refers as expected to those who have led holy lives. They are freed from those places inside Earth as from jail, and they dwell on the surface of the earth, the philosophers being those who live without bodies and "attain to habitation even fairer than those others." There are no parallels to this elaboration and we should therefore consider it Platonic. For Socrates, the conclusion is that this is the reason why one should partake of virtue and wisdom throughout life, "for the prize is glorious, and great is our hope thereof."[65]

Thus, the eschatological point of view in *Phaedo* is conditioned both by the nearness of Socrates' death and the reasons for his personal tranquility before this difficult moment.

Most likely, one of the reasons for the inclusion in the dialogue of a complex cosmology is Plato's inclination to create powerful imagery. His main purpose, however, seems to be situating the places where the soul receives rewards and punishments somewhere in the general map of the universe.[66] In order to configure it, the philosopher has partly taken inspiration from images already existing in the poetic tradition, though he has also taken advantage of new scientific ideas about the shape of the world.

The presence of a *daimon* accompanying the soul is also a novelty with respect to other eschatologies. This novelty is within a tradition I have already made references to, which, on the other hand, is not far away from "something divine and demonic" (θεῖόν τι καὶ δαιμόνιον) that seems to refer to Socrates' conscience.[67] We can see, once more,

---
65 Pl. *Phaed*. 114c, transl. by Reginald Hackforth.
66 Cf. Annas 1982, 126.
67 Pl. *Apol*. 31cd, cf. Plut. *De gen. Socr.* 10 p. 580C, 16 p. 585F.

that the whole presentation of the Netherworld is made with the destiny of the philosopher in mind.

On the other hand, Plato clearly underlines in this eschatology the transmigration of souls, while the trial as such appears undefined, with no mention even of judges. Both circumstances seem strange to Annas,[68] who considers that the philosopher has not successfully combined reincarnation and the final judgement myth, although the author herself points out that Plato is thus expressing important truths on the relation between body and soul. I think that these two characteristics, an emphasis on the transmigration and the minimum relevance of the trial, fulfil the purpose of the eschatology in the dialogue: justifying Socrates' hopes before death. The trial appears imprecise because it is obvious that his life does not deserve anything other than the best of destinies; the certainty that he is not going to be punished permeates the whole dialogue. By contrast, the idea of transmigration is pertinent in order to underline the concept that the best fortune available to the soul is to abandon the body.[69] Not only that, but the disciples who lament the prison and death of Socrates are not conscious of the paradox that he is going to be immediately really free, while they, seemingly free men, will remain prisoners of their bodies and the miseries of life.[70] Therefore, the clear addition of the idea of reincarnation provides a more optimistic message than that of *Gorgias*,[71] since even someone who is wicked and suffers punishment will have an opportunity for improvement further on. The outlook is discouraging for reprobates as well, but it brings hope in the long term.

How Orphic is this eschatology? Firstly, we should consider the insertion of cosmological elements in the description of the Underworld. The details of this cosmology coincide with those given in Orphic poems dedicated to the same topic, though Plato seems to have clearly transcended a rather simplistic schema and has elaborated a much more spectacular scenario; characters such as Adrasteia[72] could also derive from Orphic sources. Secondly, the explicit relation between transmigration and rewards or punishments. The fact of receiving punishment

---

68 Annas 1982, 127 ff.
69 Annas 1982, 127.
70 Casadesús 2008, 1268.
71 In contrast to Annas 1982, 129, who believes that "the introduction of reincarnation … blurs this message".
72 Adrasteia does not appear in Hesiod, but she does appear in Orphic sources: *OF* 77, 208–211.

in the Netherworld does not substitute, but rather complements, the punishment of reincarnation, which implies further opportunities for reprobate souls. Thirdly, the references to *daimones* that act as guides in the Beyond.

Platonic transposition is evident, not only in the impressive construction of Netherworld imagery, but also in the substitution of initiation and ritualistic perspective by a moral concept and philosophical initiation as conditions to access eternal beatitude.

IV. Eschatology in the *Republic*

Plato presents two sets of eschatological images in the *Republic*, in a rather different manner. The first set is alien to him, since it is attributed to others and even criticised by the philosopher, who only mentions it a couple of times: he attributes to "Musaeus and his son" a set up of rewards and punishments in the Beyond, the former consisting in a perpetual banquet and state of drunkenness for the pious, and the latter, for the impious, in carrying water in a sieve and lying in mud.[73] A second reference is made to the teaching of a kind of professionals who base their liberating rites on books by Musaeus and Orpheus.[74] In neither reference does Plato add a description of the place. He simply points out the difference in postmortem fortune between those who are initiated by these characters and those who are not. It is clear that Plato does not share these doctrines that, as he sees it, have the serious fault of promising expiation of guilt by means of a simple ritual and of religious purity, something that for a philosopher of deep moral convictions such as himself, who is moreover trying to define a model of city, becomes completely unacceptable.

At the end of dialogue, Plato explains his own eschatology in the myth of Er.[75] This eschatology is presented, conversely, in greater detail

---

73 Pl. *Rep.* 363cd (*OF* 431 I, 434 I).
74 Pl. *Rep.* 364be (*OF* 573 I). Cf. also the reference to those people who, upon becoming old, start fearing that some myths told about the punishments to the unfair in Hades, about which they used to laugh, were really true. Pl. *Rep.* 330d (*OF* 433 III).
75 Pl. *Rep.* 614b-621b. Cf. Hilda Richardson, "The Myth of Er (Plato, *Republic* 616b)," *CQ* 20 (1926): 115–131; Jean-Pierre Vernant, "Le fleuve Améles et la Mélétè thanatou," in *Mythe et pensée chez les grecs* (Paris: F. Maspero, 1965), 79–94; Gretchen Schils, "Plato's Myth of Er: The Light and the Spin-

and is, furthermore, the corollary to the work and the base that sustains the political system proposed in it. Since for the Greeks a completely new set of images would have been strange and scarcely convincing, Plato, albeit with modifications, models his vision upon pre-existing elements, some of which are Orphic.

The stated aim of the story (614a) is that "each one picks up from this discourse what he wants to listen to," a sentence that, within the political context of the *Republic*, indicates that the eschatology clearly follows political and moral purposes, in order to support everything he has been so far arguing for in his masterpiece about the ideal city and its perfect citizens.

The main character of Plato's tale is a Pamphylian called Er, who, after being killed in action, had the privilege of being allowed to return from the Netherworld twelve days after his own death, in order to tell what he had seen. It would seem that the philosopher wants to give his tale a veneer of truth by making his character emulate Orpheus himself in his visit to the Beyond and his return to describe what happens there; the necessity of Er's return is given even greater authority, by the fact that the gods themselves have commissioned him to do it. His tale is presented, therefore, as a direct message from the gods, aimed at correcting the false one given by Orpheus.[76] Er describes a wonderful place in which there are apertures and certain judges who send the pious up to the right and the impious down to the left. The place where Er's soul arrives is defined as a "meadow" a little bit further on,[77] when Er describes a continuous transit of souls coming and going, greeting each other and chatting vivaciously. Of these, the ones coming from underground, that is, from the place of condemnation, mention (without specifics) terrible sufferings, while the ones coming from heaven tell of visions of indescribable beauty. Er specifies that souls expiate their crimes and misdemeanours "ten times for each one and each time for a hundred years" and that those who are good receive compensation in the same proportion. After narrating the particularly violent punishments that await tyrants, personified by Ardieus, Plato provides a wonderful vision of the whole universe, turning on

---

dle," *AC* 62 (1993): 101–114; Angelica Fago, "Il mito di Er: il mondo come 'caverna' e l'Ade come 'regno luminoso' di Ananke," *SMSR* 51 (1994): 183–218.

76 Pl. *Rep.* 614b (*OF* 461).
77 Pl. *Rep.* 614e.

the spindle of Necessity (Ananke) exhaustively described, filled with traditional figures such as the Sirens and the Moirai, who are transposed into a completely new setting. All of this bears little resemblance to the Orphic universe.[78]

Lachesis announces to the souls that in their mortal condition they will begin a new temporary journey, for which each of them can choose their destiny, and lots are drawn for taking turns to choose. The first soul chooses the life of a tyrant, which it immediately regrets. It cannot but be meaningful that Orpheus appears in Er's tale precisely at this point, in a gallery of famous characters from literature and mythology. Plato humorously presents him as choosing the life of a swan due to his hatred of women.[79] It is at this point that alien eschatological imagery reappears:

> And then without a backward look it passed beneath the throne of Necessity (Ἀνάγκης). And after it had passed through that, when the others also had passed, they all journeyed to the Plain of Oblivion (Λήθης), through a terrible and stifling heat, for it was bare of trees and all plants, and there they camped at eventide by the River of Forgetfulness (Ἀμέλητα) whose waters no vessel can contain. They were all required to drink a measure of the water, and those who were not saved by their good sense drank more than the measure, and each one as he drank forgot all things.[80]

Once they have drunk the water, the souls go to rest in preparation for their new life on earth to which they return at midnight. Er, who is exempt, is told not to drink the water and finds himself "resuscitated" in his own body. The dialogue concludes with an exhortation from Socrates to practice justice in order to be compensated in the Netherworld.

In order to evaluate the possibility that Plato was using an Orphic model, I present herewith the most important document for our knowledge of Orphic eschatology of the time, the gold tablet found in Hipponium (Vibo Valentia) dated to around 400 BCE:

---

78 Ananke appears in some Orphic fragments (*OF* 77, 210, 250), but without any relation that we know of to the cycle of souls. On the other hand, Walter Burkert, "Le laminette auree: da Orfeo a Lampone," in *Orfismo in Magna Grecia*. Atti del XIV Convegno di Studi sulla Magna Grecia, Taranto 6–10 ott. 1974 (Naples: ISAMG, 1975), 98, relates the fact that those who are going to be reborn go under the throne of the goddess to the expression found in a golden tablet in Thurii (4th c. BCE): *OF* 488.7 "I went under the lap of the underground queen," which also bears clear connotations of a rite of rebirth.
79 Pl. *Rep*. 620a (*OF* 1077 I), cf. § 1.5.
80 Pl. *Rep* 620e-621a (*OF* 462), transl. by Paul Shorey.

> This is the work of Mnemosyne. When he is on the point of dying
> toward the well-built abode of Hades, on the right there is a fountain
> and near it, erect, a white cypress tree.
> There the souls, when they go down, refresh themselves.
> Don't come anywhere near this fountain!
> But further on you will find, from the lake of Mnemosyne
> water freshly flowing. On its banks there are guardians.
> They will ask you, with sagacious discernment
> why you are investigating the darkness of gloomy Hades.
> Say: "I am the son of Earth and starry Heaven;
> I am dry with thirst and dying. Give me, then, right away,
> fresh water to drink from the lake of Mnemosyne."
> And to be sure, they will consult with the subterranean queen,
> and they will give you water to drink from the lake of Mnemosyne,
> So that, once you have drunk, you too will go along the sacred way
> by which the other mystai and bacchoi advance, glorious.[81]

Guthrie, who has outlined the similarities to be found between the infernal setting described by Plato and the one presented in the Orphic gold tablets, thinks that both religious schemes can be equated[82] and, thus, he attributes to the Orphics the idea that, once the body dies, the souls go to Hades, where they are brought before infernal judges, who would determine their later destiny taking into account their conduct during their life on Earth, so the wicked ones are punished while the good ones attain happiness. The souls that have to be reincarnated must drink the water of oblivion in order to forget their previous existence; they are thus returned to body and born again.

It seems clear that Guthrie's reconstruction of Orphic version of the soul's journey is a mere transposition of the Platonic description, which takes it for granted that the Attic philosopher faithfully followed the Orphic model.

Guthrie's assessment notwithstanding, everything in fact suggests that the parallels between the Platonic description and the references in the tablets are only superficial. The "geography" coincides, but only in part: shared elements are the fountain of Lethe, the paths on both sides, the plain in which the soul experiences great thirst, and

---

81 OF 474, cf. Bernabé and Jiménez San Cristóbal 2008, 9 ff., where other similar golden tablets, slightly later, are to be found alongside a detailed commentary.
82 Guthrie 1952, 177 f., following Jane Ellen Harrison, *Prolegomena to the Study of Greek Religion* (Cambridge: Cambridge University Press, 1922), 599. Neither author could have access to the golden tablet from Hipponium, published much later, but they did know the one from Petelia (4th c. BCE), very similar to the former (OF 476), cf. Bernabé and Jiménez San Cristóbal 2008, 10 f.

the meadow, mentioned in some Orphic tablets as the place in which the blessed dwell. We may also compare a tablet from Thurii and another from Pherai (Thessaly), both dated to the 4th century BC:

> Hail, hail; take the path to the right
> towards the sacred meadows and groves of Persephone.[83]
> Enter into the sacred meadow, since the initiate is free from punishment.[84]

Yet there are profound differences. Plato tells us nothing of the deceptive cypress tree. The disposition of the paths in his account is different and has a different function, while his meadow is a mere point of transit, as contrasted with the place to which privileged souls arrive in the gold tablets. Moreover, there is no reference in the latter to any judges, but rather to guardians who wait for the soul to give them a password before allowing them to enter. Further on, moreover, Persephone herself is the one who decides whether to allow the newly arrived soul to access the blissful place or not.

Above all, however, there are two distinct eschatological schemes. In Plato, we hear of a judgment, after which the soul, completely passive, is judged, rewarded or condemned, and is taken to its allotted place. Its fate is decided, for the sins or good deeds of its past life will be its only credentials. The person who is judged and "approved" goes to Elysium for his merits. If the deceased is condemned to reincarnation, he is given water from Lethe to drink. By contrast, in the scheme described in the tablets, the soul, which is active, finds itself faced by a test which it must overcome. In the moment of its transition to the other world the soul's crucial goal must be to take the right path. Everything depends on this, and on its remembering what it must do: this is why the tablets are the work of Mnemosyne,[85] because she will help it to remember the teachings it has received. If it does what it should do, it will be successful. If it makes a mistake, it will be reincarnated. In the Platonic text, a higher authority evaluates the soul's moral

---

83 *OF* 487.5–6.
84 *OF* 493.
85 Cf. f. e. *OF* 474.1, and *Orphic Hymns* 77.9–10 μύσταις μνήμν ἐπέγειρε /εὐιέρου τελετῆς. About Mnemosyne in the tablets, cf. Bernabé and Jiménez San Cristóbal 2008, 15–19.

behavior during its terrestrial sojourn, while in the tablets a ritual declaration on the part of the deceased seems to suffice.[86]

Furthermore, Plato conceives a heavenly place for the rewarded, in complete contrast to the space for the condemned, which is the Underworld. Orphic eschatology, on the other hand, places both rewards and punishments in Hades.

It is clear, then, that Plato freely re-elaborated on Orphic motifs in the service of his own philosophical and literary interests, as, in fact, is his normal procedure in dealing with inherited material. And it is also evident that the eschatology in the *Republic*, conceived as surpassing the Orphic—partly based on it, but adapted to embody clear philosophical interests—is by far the most masterfully achieved of all of Plato's creations, as well as the culmination of his descriptions of the Netherworld.[87]

V. Eschatology in the *Axiochus*

The pseudo-Platonic *Axiochus* provides a brief but intense description of the Netherworld.[88] It occurs in the context of Socrates's arguments that Axiochus, father of Clinias, should not fear death. Firstly, he demonstrates the evils that are left behind thanks to death, a reasoning that does not seem to impress the old man. He then discusses the survival of the soul and the happiness that awaits the good in the Netherworld. Although the dialogue is not Platonic,[89] this part is clearly inspired by other descriptions of the Beyond by the Athenian philosopher, and it is thus worthwhile to include it here. The tale in the *Axiochus* is, significantly, put in the mouth of a certain Gobrias, an Iranian *magos* who, quoting as his source some bronze tablets from the land of the Hyper-

---

86 Only in the "great" tablet from Thurii (*OF* 492, 4th century BC) can we find any reference to behavior and retribution (ἀνταμοιβή) in accordance with it, but there are many obscurities in the text.

87 Even the evidence from the *Bologna Papyrus* (§ 2) seems to indicate that Plato, in a sort of return twist, influenced the Orphics themselves.

88 [Pl.] *Axioch.* 371a (*OF* 434 IX, 713 III). Cf. Jacques Chevalier, *Étude critique du dialogue pseudo-platonicien, l'Axiochos sur la mort et sur l'immortalité de l'âme* (Lyon: A. Rey, 1914); Maria Lucia Violante, "Un confronto tra *PBon.* 4 e *l'Assioco*. La valutazione delle anime nella tradizione orfica e platonica," *CCC* 5 (1981): 313–327.

89 Cf. the extremely informative state of the question in Pilar Gómez Cardó, "Axíoco," in *Platón. Diálogos* VII (Madrid: Gredos, 1992), 389–425.

boreans, says that after freeing itself from the body the soul goes to Pluto's realm. The author therefore supports the tenet of the immortality of the soul and the idea that death represents liberation from it. He adds a few "cosmological" and "geographical" references. According to him, the earth occupies the central part of the universe and is surrounded by a sphere, whose upper hemisphere is the dwelling of the heavenly gods, and its lower one the dwelling of the infernal gods, and that behind doors with iron locks are two of the Netherworld rivers, the Acheron and the Kokytos. Once these rivers are crossed, there lies the "plain of truth," where Minos and Rhadamanthys are to be found. It would seem that the author of *Axiochus* has used elements from other eschatological descriptions, but reducing them to the minimum (two hemispheres, two rivers, two judges).

The trial of the souls also takes place there:

> There are some judges sitting there, asking each one of the newly arrived what sort of life they lead and what their habits were when they inhabited their bodies. Lying is impossible.[90]

The expression "inhabit their bodies" is interesting, in that it conceives the body as a sort of dwelling for the soul, without the negative connotations of the Orphic "grave" or the Platonic "prison."[91] We should also note the relevance of the moral schema according to which the souls receive Netherworld treatment commensurate with their behaviour in this world. In contrast to his restraint in the description of infernal cosmology, the author describes in great detail the two places to which the souls may go, one paradisiacal and the other horrifying.[92]

Unlike Platonic eschatologies, in which we find very little description of paradise, the author of the *Axiochus* gives a profuse description of this locale; a *locus amoenus* in which, in addition to the stereotypical meadows, the symposium of the blessed and the ever-flowing spring, the quintessential cultural practices of the Greeks are also added: poetry, music, and philosophy. Conversely, negative images are based on *topoi* about the damned: Danaids, Tantalus, Tityus, and Sisyphus, to which the author adds the torches of the Furies. Although Eleusis is mentioned, the images are in fact typical of Southern Italy. We find them in the decoration of Apulian ceramics of the fourth century BCE

---

90 [Pl.] *Axioch.* 371c.
91 Pl. *Crat.* 400c (*OF* 430 I).
92 [Pl.] *Axioch.* 371c-372a (*OF* 434 IX, 713 III).

with motifs of the Netherworld,[93] and they have certain precedents in Pindar's descriptions in some *Threnoi* and in the second *Olympian*.[94]

The Boeotian poet, in describing the *locus amoenus* of the blessed in the Netherworld, adds athletics to the delights of paradise, in accordance with the expectations of his clientele for the *Epinikia*.[95] In sheer contrast, he also presents a horrifying description of the place of the damned,[96] and he also provides, in another passage, a brief outline of the happy destiny of certain individuals in the Netherworld.[97]

The first two Pindaric passages quoted are in *threnoi*, within the framework of a *consolatio* to the families of the deceased, which means that we do not know whether the reason for the presence of these ideas, as opposed to those developed by the poet in other works, which are closer to traditional Olympian religion, is due to the literary genre to which the fragment belongs to or, more likely, because they were part of the religious beliefs of the ode's commissioner, whom the poet is trying to please. This second possibility seems to be corroborated by the presence of the very same ideas in an *Epinikion*, *Olympian II*, most likely because Theron of Acragas, the tyrant who commissioned the work, was sympathetic to the ideas of this religious circle.[98] Pindar refers to "someone who administers justice underground, passing his judgement with ineluctable hostility," and points to the fact that some "live an existence without tears, whilst others undergo sufferings unbearable to witness."

---

93 Cf. Marina Pensa, *Rappresentazioni dell'oltretomba nella ceramica apula* (Rome: Bretschneider, 1977); Christian Aellen, *À la recherche de l'ordre cosmique* (Zürich: Akanthus, 1994); Bernabé and Jiménez San Cristóbal 2008, 195–203.

94 On religion in Pindar, in general, cf. Emilio Suárez de la Torre, "Píndaro y la religión griega," *CFC(G)* 3 (1993): 67–97; on its relation to Orphism, Hugh Lloyd-Jones, "Pindar and the Afterlife," *Pindar, Entretiens Fondation Hardt* 17 (1985): 245–283; Maria Cannatà Fera, *Pindarus. Threnorum fragmenta* (Roma: Athenaeum, 1990), 164 ff., and Santamaría Álvarez 2004; 2008. Cf. also Günther Zuntz, *Persephone: Three Essays on Religion and Thought in Magna Graecia* (Oxford: Oxford University Press, 1971), 83 ff. and Alberto Bernabé, "Una cita de Píndaro en Platón *Men*. 81b (*Fr*. 133 Sn.-M.)," in *Desde los poemas homéricos hasta la prosa griega del siglo IV d. C. Veintiséis estudios filológicos*, ed. Juan Antonio López Férez (Madrid: Ediciones Clásicas, 1999), 239–259.

95 Pind. fr. 129 Maehl. = 58 Cannatà Fera (*OF* 439).

96 Pind. fr. 130 Maehl. = 58b Cannatà Fera (*OF* 440).

97 Pind. fr. 143 Maehl. (*OF* 446).

98 Pind. *Ol*. 2.56 (*OF* 445).

Apart from the paradisiacal place, we also find here a reference to the trial of souls and a passing reference to the punishments.

Finally, returning once more to the description in *Axiochus*, it seems that the initiated continue to practice in the Netherworld the mysteries that have enabled them to reach the seat of the blessed. In this regard, Chevalier compared a fragment of Plutarch in which the τελεταί are identified with death, based upon an etymology that identifies τελετή with τελευτή "death," in which we also find interesting parallels with the outlook presented in *Axiochus*.[99]

In the *Axiochus*, the place for punishment is Tartarus, but the place for rewards is not determined by a geographic space, but rather by those who inhabit it. It is thus the "region of the pious." This expression coincides with those characteristic of the Orphic gold tablets, which refer to a path "in which the other mystai and bacchoi gloriously advance" (*OF* 474.15–16), to a place over which the souls "will reign alongside the rest of the heroes" (*OF* 476.11), to a space underground where the blessed souls go as a result of having celebrated the *teletai* ("having fulfilled the same rites as the other fortunate people [*OF* 485.7]"), to "the thiasus of the mystai" (*OF* 493a), to the "thiasus of the right" (*OF* 487.2),[100] to the "dwellings of the pure" (*OF* 489.7) or to the "sacred meadow," where the mystes is free from punishment (*OF* 493). These places are always defined by the company of the other initiated and by their happiness, not as clearly defined geographic spaces.

---

99 Plu. fr. 178 Sandbach (*OF* 594). Cf. Chevalier 1914. See also Burkert 1975, 96; Francisco Díez de Velasco, "Un problema de delimitación conceptual en Historia de las Religiones: la mística griega," in *Imágenes de la Polis*, ed. Domingo Plácido, Jaime Alvar, Juan M. Casillas and César Fornis (Madrid: Ediciones Clásicas, 1997), 407–422; Christoph Riedweg, "Initiation-Tod-Unterwelt: Beobachtungen zur Kommunikationssituation und narrativen Technik der orphisch-bakchischen Goldblättchen," in *Ansichten griechischer Rituale. Geburtstags-Symposium für W. Burkert*, ed. Fritz Graf (Stuttgart and Leipzig: Teubner, 1998), 367 n. 33; Alberto Bernabé, "La experiencia iniciática en Plutarco," in *Misticismo y religiones mistéricas en la obra de Plutarco*, Actas del VII Simposio Español sobre Plutarco, ed. Aurelio Pérez Jiménez and Francesc Casadesús (Madrid-Málaga: Ediciones Clásicas, 2001), 10 ff.; Alberto Bernabé, "Los terrores del más allá en el mundo griego. La respuesta órfica," in *Miedo y religión*, ed. Francisco Díez de Velasco (Madrid: Ediciones del Orto, 2002), 326.

100 It is a new reading provided by Marco Antonio Santamaría, included, like *OF* 493a, in the *addenda et corrigenda* to *OF* II 3 and in Bernabé and Jiménez San Cristóbal 2008, 95–98 and 151–160.

VI. Recapitulation and Comparisons

It is time to recapitulate and briefly compare the Platonic visions of the Netherworld with one other, and with what we know of Orphic images of the afterlife. In order to do so, I will unravel the different elements in which they consist. To avoid excessive repetition in the quotes, I will refer to *Gorg.* 492e-493c as Gorg.1; to *Gorg.* 523a-527a as Gorg.2; to the Orphic references to the destiny of the souls in the Netherworld in *Phaed.* 69c and 70c as Phaed.1; to the vision of the Beyond specified in *Phaed.* 107c ff. as Phaed.2; to the vision referred to in *Rep.* 363c as Rep.1; to that offered in *Rep.* 614a ff as Rep.2 and, finally, to the one referred to in *Axioch.* 371a as Ax., on the understanding that Gorg.1, Phaed.1 and Rep.1 are not Platonic, but rather reflections of Orphic doctrines.

All the images share, as a common denominator a belief in the immortality of the soul, understood as the capacity to perceive and understand also in the Underworld. The occurrence, in some cases, of physical punishment (splashing about in the mud, carrying water in a sieve, being burnt by torches), the conversations held by the souls, the enjoyment of meadows, rivers, or food, give evidence of the extreme difficulty of imagining the soul as incorporeal; instead, it still has the appearance of the body that used to carry it, or at least, a corporal appearance. Plato coincides in this point with Orphic sources, and it is, moreover, a constant throughout history, from mediaeval images to films such as *Ghost.* It seems difficult for the human being to envision anything else.

The idea of reincarnation is present in Phaed.1, Phaed.2 and Rep.2; it seems clear that it is absent from Ax., and is not expressly mentioned in the other sources, but in Gorg.1 and Rep.1 it seems to be implied, inasmuch as they reflect an Orphic point of view. Nor is it incompatible with Gorg.2. I have already explained this circumstance as a question of emphases of certain aspects over others, according to the purposes of each dialogue.

In the case of the Orphic versions, the authorship of the tale is attributed to "one of the sages" in Gorg.1; to "those who established the *teletai*" and to "an ancient tale" in Phaed.1 and to "Musaeus and his son" in Rep.1. Plato avoids mentioning the name of Orpheus, but his shadow lingers over these versions; over the unmentioned source in Phaed.2 (the expression "it is being told" refers to a former and ancient tradition) and over Gorg.2, that starts with Homer and is then followed by a tale of uncertain origin, deriving from an oral source (ἀκηκοώς in 524a). The prestige of Orpheus is also evident from a passage in the *Apology*, where the poets Orpheus and Musaeus are mentioned alongside the infernal judges. And even Er seems to be competing with Orpheus, who in his tale inhabits the Netherworld. By contrast, the author of Ax. chooses another "exotic" source, Gobrias the *magos*.

Plato's Underworld myths coincide with Orphic eschatology in the idea that in the Netherworld souls can either go to a pleasant or an unpleasant place, in contrast to the Homeric tradition, widely accepted in classical Greece, of an equally sombre Hades for all the deceased. There is a great deal of variation, however, in the specific location of the places where good and bad souls go. In Gorg.1, Phaed.1 and Rep.1 they are both in Hades. This corresponds to the idea expressed in the Orphic texts, which refer to unspecified spaces in Hades, characterised as good or evil only by the type of souls that inhabit them. Gorg.2 makes a distinction between the Isles of the Blest and Tartarus. This occurs at the end of an adaptation of an idea previously found in Hesiod and developed by Pindar (*Ol.* 2.70–82). Rep. 2 mentions "heaven" and "below." The latter could refer to Hades or Tartarus, but the reference to heaven is not compatible with any Orphic sources. Ax. mentions Tartarus as a place of punishment, while its version of paradise is characterised, as in the Orphic sources, by the people who dwell in it (the region of the pious), and not by geographical features.

There are also variations in the geography of Netherworld, which is not described at all in those versions derived directly from Orphic sources (Gorg.1, Phaed.1 and Rep.1). Such geography, however, is described in greater or lesser detail in the others, from the simple crossroads and the meadow where the judges stand in Gorg.2, which preserves a basically Orphic imagery, through the stylized account in the Ax., in which we find two infernal rivers and two spheres, celestial and infernal, and, finally, the more elaborate descriptions in Phaed.2, with bifurcations and infernal rivers, or the complex one in Rep.2, with the spindle of Necessity. Therefore, although the more elaborate eschatologies have some elements of Orphic origin, these are diluted in the grandiose Platonic creations.

The trial is present neither in Gorg.1, nor in Phaed.1 nor in Rep.1, which would support the opinion presented here that it is in fact alien to the oldest Orphic sources. Indeed, the most important point in the Orphic gold tablets is the remembering of certain passwords such as "I am the son of Earth and of the starry Sky" (*OF* 474.10, etc), "I come from among the pure, pure myself" (*OF* 488.1, etc) or "the mystes is free from punishment" (*OF* 488). The first is an indication that the newly arrived knows a tale about the origin of man that characterises him as initiated, the second refers to his ritual purity, achieved by means of the *teletai*, whilst in the third he claims the right to enjoy a privileged situation, that of avoiding punishment simply on the grounds that he is a *mystes*.

By contrast, the idea of trial is an essential element of Plato's characterisations of the Netherworld. For this, his sources are not Orphic. Minos is portrayed in Homer as administering justice among the dead (*Od.* 11.568), whilst the idea of the trial of souls is to be found in Pindar (*Ol.* 2.59–60). There are differences among the Platonic versions concerning the number and identity of the judges: four are mentioned by name in the *Apology*,[101] three in Gorg.2, two in Ax., and unnamed judges in Rep.2; the trial is undefined in Phaed.2. The only reference to a trial within an Orphic context is to be found in the *Bologna Papyrus*, and it is very likely that this reflects Platonic influence over the late Orphic tradition.

Plato's references to postmortem rewards are meagre. As regards Orphic eschatologies, there are no references to them in Gorg.1 (its main purpose being to use the punishments to scare Callicles) and Adeimantus sneers at Orphic images of drunkards in perpetual banquet in Rep.1, which has a close analogue in the phrase "you have wine, as your blessed honour" found in the tablet of Pelina (*OF* 485.6). In Phaed.1 the philosopher states that the initiated and the purified will dwell with the gods. The difference between considering the Orphic blessed as a bunch of drunkards or as cohabitants with the gods seems to run parallel with the philosopher's main focus of interest in each case. In Phaed.1 he presents a "positive eschatology," and since he is going to conclude that those initiated are the true philosophers, amongst whom is Socrates himself, he can easily accept the Orphic idea that they will dwell with the gods, but in a version a little toned down, in the sense that the souls do not turn into gods themselves. In Rep.1, however, he tries to discredit those who argue that it is possible to avoid punishment exclusively by ritual means, on the grounds that such a "comfortable" scheme would not contribute to the creation of

---

101 Pl. *Apol.* 41a (*OF* 1076 I), although their numbers grow with "other demigods, all those who were fair in life" and, moreover, it is uncertain whether these judges decided the reward or punishment of the soul, or they simply have the Homeric function of administering justice among the deceased, cf. n. 21.

good citizens. Consequently, it seems more appropriate to ridicule their proposed destiny as perpetual drunkards.

Regarding the eschatologies created by Plato himself, there is a reference in Gorg.2 to a happiness free of evil, and in Rep.2 to the fact that "they will get what they deserve." Phaed.2 contains the most important innovation, the idea that the souls of the philosophers live "free from their bodies," which avoids the imagery that tends to conceive the souls as some other form of bodies. Ax. adds to the *locus amoenus* an array of cultivated entertainments (almost aristocratic), including dance, music, and philosophical discussions; in this respect it is closer to the scenario presented by Pindar than to Orphic accounts.

In terms of punishments, Gorg.1 and Rep.1 make use of the Orphic motif of carrying water in a sieve, and both Phaed.1 and Rep.1 of lying in mud. It is clear that, according to Orphic beliefs, the condemnation of souls is not restricted to transmigration but may also entail a series of punishments in the Underworld at the end of each incarnate life.[102] Plato also refers to punishments in his visions of the Beyond: in Gorg.2 he describes Hades as a sort of jail in which souls are tormented, in Phaed.2 his emphasis shifts to the sorrowful wandering of the soul which fails to reach the realm of happiness, and in Rep.2 he mentions certain "sufferings" without specifying them. The most vivid description of postmortem suffering is to be found in the Ax., where the mythical *topoi* concerning infamous sinners are, nevertheless, also included, with the addition of the Furies with torches and the attack of some beasts.

Somewhat at odds with the main scheme is the presence, in Phaed.2 and Ax., of *daimones* who inspire or guide the souls, an idea that seems to coincide with one of the tenets of the Derveni commentator. We also find references both in Phaed.2 and Rep. 2 to meeting places where the souls hold conversations.

Aside from this, it seems worthwhile to remark upon the requirements which determine whether the soul is assiged to the dwelling place of the good or the wicked. According to the Orphics, the means to achieve a better destiny are to be found in the way of life,[103] which not only imposes taboos concerning food, such as a vegetarian diet, or clothing, such as the prohibition of wearing any woollen

---

102 Cf. Procl. *in Pl. Remp.* II 173.12 Kroll (*OF* 346), who mentions "underground places and prisons over there."
103 Mentioned in Pl. *Leg.* 782c (*OF* 625) as Ὀρφικοὶ βίοι.

cloths, but also entails ritual obligations, such as celebration of the *teletai*, and behaviour which is based upon of vague idea of justice. Hence, in Gorg.1 and Phaed.1, the precondition for obtaining a good place in the Netherworld is initiation. Plato, once more, "transposes"[104] this ritual precondition to an initiation based on moral character, and, as such, in Phaed.1 he arrives at the conclusion that the initiated is the philosopher. In Rep.1, despite alluding to the Orphics, he mentions the "good" in opposition to the "impious and unjust"; in *Meno* 81b, he proclaims the need to "live life in the holiest possible manner," as the indispensable corollary of the theory of the metempsychosis, and in his presentations of infernal eschatology, he always refers to goodness and justice as prerequisites for the souls attaining blessedness.

Finally, Plato differs from the Orphics on the subject of why to acquire knowledge about the destiny of the soul. The only aim of Orphics is salvation. As such, knowledge of the soul's destiny is only the means of getting information on the necessary procedures to achieve this aim. For this reason, the stress is put on the passwords, rights, taboos and experiences, and not on knowledge. In contrast, Plato's motivations for dealing with the destiny of the soul are various. The *ad hoc* nature of the Platonic myths allows for variation in his mythic eschatology, according to the purposes for which the myth is used: Phaed.2 is, above all, a *consolatio* to the disciples, in which Socrates considers the question of why souls, according to their degree of perfection, end up living incarcerated in a mortal body; in Rep.2, it has first and foremost a political aim; namely, to create good citizens and to challenge the belief that souls can enjoy privileges in the Netherworld exclusively on the basis of ritual, independently of their behaviour; in Gorg. 2, Plato uses the myth to denounce the dangers of Sophistic philosophy for social morals, and in the *Meno* the Orphic tale supports the theory of reminiscence. In sum, Plato, unlike the Orphics, puts religious beliefs into the service of deeper philosophical purposes. Despite the different interests that the eschatological landscapes serve in each of the works, there is no doubt that they do coincide and, even though they do not configure

---

104 The term *transposition* is coined by Auguste Diès, *Autour de Platon*, vol. 2 (Paris: Gabriel Beauchesne, 1927), 432 ff., followed by Frutiger 1930; cf. also the remarks by Alberto Bernabé, "L'âme après la mort: modèles orphiques et transposition platonicienne," in *Études platoniciennes* IV, *Les puissances de l'âme selon Platon*, ed. Jean-François Pradeau (Paris: Les Belles Lettres, 2007a), 41–44.

a coherent system, they certainly present numerous points in common within the general framework of the philosopher's theory.

The Eleusinian Mysteries in Pre-Platonic Thought: Metaphor, Practice and Imagery for Plato's Symposium*

Barbara Sattler

I. Introduction

Plato is sometimes seen as competing with the Greek mystery cults in offering a prospect of a better life, whether in this world or beyond.[1] Whatever the truth may be on that contested issue, my project in the present paper is to prepare the ground for showing that Plato also used the language, mythology, and practices of salvation employed within a well-known Greek cult to promote his own philosophical ideas. What this paper does is to give a sketch of the Eleusinian Mysteries before Plato's time in a way that shows why these Mysteries may have been attractive for Plato as a template for communicating his philosophy.

The paper forms the first part of a broader project which investigates how Plato uses the Eleusinian Mysteries in the *Symposium* for the purpose of his own philosophy.[2] The next step will be to show in detail that Plato does indeed use the imagery and metaphors of the Eleusinian Mysteries as a template for the ascent to the Form of Beauty in the *Symposium*. And the third step will finally explain why Plato may have em-

---

* I want to thank Susanne Bobzien, Justin Broackes, Corinne Pache, and Irene Peirano for helpful comments on this paper.
1 For this question cf. Stephen Menn's article in this volume.
2 While Plato's use of mystery language and metaphors in the *Phaedrus* features prominently in the literature, Riedweg is the only one, to my knowledge, who has not only noted that there are references to Mysteries in the *Symposium*, but has investigated these references further, cf. Christoph Riedweg, *Mysterienterminologie bei Platon, Philon und Klemens von Alexandrien* (Berlin: De Gruyter, 1987). However, he also looks at Plato in order to find out more about the Mysteries of Eleusis, not, as I do, in order to find out more about Plato, cf. Riedweg 1987, 1 f.

ployed Eleusinian imagery by examining what Plato may have gained for his philosophy from doing so.

In showing that Plato employs the terminology of the Mysteries I do not assume Plato's philosophy to incorporate any doctrines of the Mysteries.[3] On the question of possible "mystical" aspects in Plato's thinking I will remain agnostic in this project. However, I will show that, irrespective of whether Plato uses the imagery of the Mysteries because of their "mystical" content, a main reason for using the imagery of the Mysteries is that it enables him to overcome certain problems he faces in introducing his theory of the Forms. It helps him—or so I shall argue—make accessible a series of theoretical claims which introduce entities of a highly abstract sort: claims to the effect that there is something that is fully real but may not be perceptible with our sense-organs, something that transcends the empirical realm in some sense, that is eternal, on which everything else depends, which is rationally structured but nevertheless very hard to understand, and which is crucially connected to the possibility of leading a good life. The abstract entities these claims are intended to introduce are Plato's Forms. I will show that and how the use of the imagery of the Eleusinian Mysteries allows Plato to make intelligible his notions of Forms to the Athenian audience of his time who would hardly be familiar with his Theory of Forms. However, most of them would be acquainted with the Mysteries of Eleusis. Accordingly, imagery drawn from the Eleusinian Mysteries could make the unfamiliar Platonic theory easier to grasp for the Athenian audience of the 4th century BCE. So, for instance, the thought that the comprehension of the highest Form might be unsayable is more easily realized against this background. Why this way of expressing himself might be more helpful for Plato to establish his new philosophical ideas than other possible means is a question the third part of this project will also be addressing—a question that leads to the general problem of how a new realm or a radically different conceptualisation of an existing

---

3 As, e.g., André-Jean Festugière, *Contemplation et vie contemplative selon Platon* 4th ed. (Paris: J. Vrin, 1975 [1936]) does; cf. also Michael Bordt, *Platons Theologie* (Freiburg and Munich: Karl Alber, 2006), 30 and Robert Carter, "Plato and Mysticism," *Idealistic Studies* 5 (1975), 255–268. Kenneth R. Seekin, "Platonism, Mysticism and Madness," *Monist* 59 (1976): 574–586, on p. 580 f. wants to understand the acquisition of knowledge in the Platonic tradition as religious ecstasy. For the meaning of "mystical" cf., e.g., A.H. Armstrong, "Platonic Mysticism," *The Dublin Review* 216 (1945): 130–143. I will use the term "mystical" in the following as meaning "related to the Mysteries".

realm can in principle be integrated into a set body of knowledge, in this case into philosophy.

Given the limitations of space in the present publication, however, what I will concentrate on in this paper is setting out the first part, by reconstructing what we know about the Eleusinian Mysteries that Plato may have taken up. Or at least, I will try to do so. For it seems that we immediately run into severe problems with our sources. Mysteries—what is done, shown and said there, the δρώμενα, δεικνύμενα and λεγόμενα[4]—are only meant for people already initiated or prepared to be initiated, and are to be kept strictly secret from the general public.[5] This strictly enforced secrecy obviously leads to a problem for us moderns, since it makes it very hard to find texts or other sources describing the Mysteries at all.[6] One obvious hope in this situation might be "atheism". We are told by Aristophanes and Lysias that the "atheist"[7] and lyric poet Diagoras of Melos[8] violated the requirement of secrecy in a

---

4   Cf. Nicholas J. Richardson, ed., *The Homeric Hymn to Demeter* (Oxford: Oxford University Press, 1974), 26 and Richardson's comments on the *Homeric Hymn* lines 474–476.
5   Cf., e.g., Isocrates, *Panegyricus* 28, *Homeric Hymn* lines 478–479, Sophocles *Oedipus at Colonus*, 1050 ff., Aischylos, fr. CCCII, and George E. Mylonas, *Eleusis and the Eleusinian Mysteries* (Princeton: Princeton University Press, 1961), 224.
6   For general problems with the source material cf., e.g., Mylonas 1961, 227–229.
7   ἄθεος can mean many different things in ancient Greek. So, e.g., in the Scholia ad Aristophanem, FGrH 342 F16a, the "atheist" Diagoras is grouped with Socrates as introducing new ideas of the divine—not quite what we might call an atheist nowadays; cf. also Richard Janko, "The Derveni Papyrus ("Diagoras of Melos, Apopyrgizontes Logoi?"): A New Translation," *CP* 96.1 (2001): 1–32, especially 11. In Cicero's *De natura deorum* III, 88–89, Diagoras seems to deny all might and power of the gods, "vim omnem deorum ac potestatem", but not (necessarily) their existence. Felix Jacoby, "Diagoras ὁ ἄθεος," in *Abhandlungen der deutschen Akademie der Wissenschaften zu Berlin, Klasse für Sprachen, Literatur und Kunst*, Anh. 3 (Berlin: Akademie, 1959), however, thinks Diagoras to be an outright atheist in the sense that he denied the existence of gods. Cf. also Gábor Betegh, *The Derveni Papyrus: Cosmology, Theology and Interpretation* (Cambridge: Cambridge University Press, 2004), 380.
8   By 414 BCE he had been outlawed from Athens for impugning the Mysteries in a lyric poem, to which Aristophanes, *Clouds* 830, *Birds* 1073–74, and Lysias 6.17 refer. Cf. Diodorus Siculus, xiii.6: "[...] Diagoras who was dubbed 'the atheist' (ἄθεος) was accused of impiety and, fearing the people, fled from Attica; and the Athenians announced a reward of a talent of silver to the man who should slay Diagoras" (Loeb translation by C.H. Oldfather). Cf. also Melanthius FGrH 326 F3 and Craterus FGrH 342 F16 (= Schol. Aristoph. Av. 1073 =

poem. Unfortunately, but very understandably in view of the consequences, we are not told what our "atheist" said about the Mysteries, and the poem in question does not seem to survive.⁹ So this leak will not work for us.

The second hope, after "atheisms" in a narrow sense, might be simply later sources, authors of Christian or some other belief or with a certain distance to the traditional religion of the Greeks, authors who thus would not regard themselves as bound to any vow of secrecy. We do indeed get some information from such sources, most notably a σύν-θημα, a password, from Clement of Alexandria and a testimony from a Naassene Gnostic in the second century CE, which is preserved for us in Hippolytus. Finally, we get some references to the Mysteries from Plutarch. Among many other hints, Plutarch gives us a clear de-

---

T7 A in Marcus Winiarczyk, ed., *Diagorae Melii et Theodori Cyrenaei reliquiae* (Leipzig: Teubner, 1981).

9   Even if we assume the author of the Derveni Papyrus to be Diagoras of Melos, as Janko 2001 does, this would only give us his interpretation of some Orphic rituals for which there do not seem to be any parallels in Eleusis (cf. also Winiarczyk 1981, T7 A , T15–20 and T 69). And even if we followed Fritz Graf, *Eleusis und die orphische Dichtung Athens in vorhellenistischer Zeit* (Berlin and New York: De Gruyter, 1974) in thinking that the Orphic and Eleusinian Mysteries were intertwined, the Derveni Papyrus would still not give us any particular information on what is specific for the Eleusinian Mysteries. When col. 6 of the Derveni Papyrus mentions initiates that make sacrifices to the Eumenides, this seems to be a ritual for which there is no hint that it could have been at all relevant in Eleusis; cf. also Martin L. West, "Hocus-pocus in East and West: Theogony, Ritual and the Tradition of Esoteric Commentary," in *Studies on the Derveni Papyrus*, ed. André Laks and Glenn Most (New York: Oxford University Press, 1997), 84 and Betegh 2004, 376, n. 13. But compare Albert Henrichs, "The Eumenides and Wineless Libations in the Derveni Papyrus," in *Atti del XVII Congresso internazionale di papirologia II* (Naples: Centro internazionale per lo studio dei papiri ercolanesi, 1984), 266–268. The assumption that the Orphic and Eleusinian Mysteries were interwoven is made unlikely by Athenagoras of Athens' report on Digoras' *different* atheistic deeds: making the Orphic *logos* public on the one hand *as well as* publicizing the Eleusinian Mysteries on the other; cf. Winiarczyk 1981, T27, and also Richard Janko, "The Physicist as Hierophant: Aristophanes, Socrates, and the Authorship of the Derveni Papyrus," *ZPE* 118 (1997): 89, and Robert Parker, *Polytheism and Society at Athens* (Oxford: Oxford University Press, 2005), 368. Betegh 2004, 373–380 argues against identifying the author of the Derveni Papyrus with Diagoras. In addition, in his review of Betegh, Janko makes it clear that he has given up his earlier assumption that Diagoras is the author of the Derveni Papyrus, cf. *Bryn Mawr Classical Review* 2005.01.27.

scription of the different stages of the Mysteries, the lower ones and the higher ones.¹⁰ And he also provides us with the language that we will find in Plato's *Symposium* for the highest Mysteries, the ἐποπτικά, cf. especially his *Demetrius*, section 26, lines 2 ff. where we hear that Demetrius wrote to the Athenians:

> ὅτι βούλεται παραγενόμενος εὐθὺς μυηθῆναι καὶ τὴν τελετὴν ἅπασαν ἀπὸ τῶν μικρῶν ἄχρι τῶν ἐποπτικῶν παραλαβεῖν. τοῦτο δ' οὐ θεμιτὸν ἦν [...]
>
> that he wished to be initiated into the mysteries as soon as he arrived, and to pass through all the grades in the ceremony, from the lowest to the highest (the "epoptica"). Now, this was not lawful [...]¹¹

Clement's σύνθημα provides us with some activities performed in connection with initiation:

> ἐνήστευσα, ἔπιον τὸν κυκεῶνα, ἔλαβον ἐκ κίστης, ἐργασάμενος ἀπεθέμην εἰς κάλαθον καὶ ἐκ καλάθου εἰς κίστην.
>
> I fasted, I drank the kykeon, I took out the covered basket [*kiste*], I worked and laid back into the tall basket [*kalathos*], and from there into the other basket [*kiste*].¹²

Burkert thinks that the actions referred to by the σύνθημα are part of the preparations for the initiation, while he interprets the following two testimonies of the Naassene Gnostic as belonging to the concluding festival:

> Ἀθηναῖοι, μυοῦντες Ἐλευσίνια καὶ ἐπιδεικνύντες τοῖς ἐποπτεύουσι τὸ μέγα καὶ θαυμαστὸν καὶ τελεώτατον ἐποπτικὸν ἐκεῖ μυστήριον ἐν σιωπῇ, τεθερισμένον στάχυν.
>
> The Athenians, celebrating the Eleusinian Mysteries, show to the '*epoptai*' the great, admirable, most perfect epoptic secret, in silence, a reaped ear of grain.

---

10 Fr.178 Sandbach = Stobaeus IV,52,49 and *de aud. poet.* 47a, *de fac.* 943c, *prof. virt.* 81d. Cf. also Riedweg 1987, 5 and Walter Burkert, *Antike Mysterien: Funktionen und Gehalt* (Munich: C.H. Beck, 1994), 77.
11 Translation by Bernadotte Perrin in the Loeb edition (Cambridge, MA: 1968) with alterations.
12 Clement, *Protrepticus* II.21.2; translation from Walter Burkert, *Ancient Mystery Cults* (Cambridge, MA: Harvard University Press, 1987), 94. For a critical discussion of the authenticity of this σύνθημα cf. Martin P. Nilsson, "Die Eleusinischen Gottheiten," *Archiv für Religionswissenschaft* 32 (1935), 122–123.

And

> [ὁ ἱεροφάντης] νυκτὸς ἐν <Ἐ>λευσῖνι ὑπὸ πολλῷ πυρὶ τελῶν τὰ μεγάλα καὶ ἄρρητα μυστήρια βοᾷ καὶ κέκραγε λέγων· ἱερὸν ἔτεκε πότνια κοῦρον Βριμὼ Βριμόν.

> [The hierophant] at night at Eleusis, celebrating the great and unspeakable mysteries beneath a great fire, cries aloud, saying: The Lady has born a sacred son, Brimo has born Brimos.[13]

People predominantly interested in the Mysteries take these three sources to lay out at least some of the basics for our understanding of the Eleusinian rites. However, these sources immediately introduce a second problem: we want to show that Plato took up language and imagery from the Mysteries, but our knowledge of those Mysteries derives from sources that are in turn influenced by Platonic thought. Thus, Plato's *Phaedrus* could become one of the most important texts about mystical experiences.[14] And Plutarch and Clement seem to be strongly influenced by Plato. So not only is there a general lack of good sources due to the requirement of secrecy, but the few good sources we have date from a time later than Plato's *Symposium* and are likely to be influenced by Plato himself.[15] Hence, we seem to be stuck right at the beginning of our investigation, for apparently we cannot have access to the Mysteries independently from the philosophy for which we want to show them to be a template.

However, "εἴσ' ἔτ' ἐλπίδες", there is still hope, and indeed the hope is inspired also by the person who framed the saying like this in his *Thesmophoriazusae* (line 1009)—Aristophanes. For there are indeed some pre-Platonic sources that normally, with the possible exception of the *Hymn to Demeter*, only get briefly fed into an account of the Mysteries mostly based on later sources. What I want to do in the following is to concentrate on these pre-Platonic sources and examine in how far a careful look at them can actually provide us with some account of the Eleusinian Mysteries. This seems to be the only way to get a template for the *Symposium* that is not already influenced by Plato himself and thus to see where and how Plato took up and changed the given material for his own purpose.

---

13 Hippolytus, *Refutatio omnium haeresium*. 5.8,39–41, translations from Burkert 1987, 91, with alterations.
14 Cf. Burkert 1994, 77; and Riedweg 1987, 71 ff. for Plato's influence on Philo's discussion of the Mysteries.
15 For Clement of Alexandria's Platonism cf. Riedweg 1987, 116 and 127.

What kind of primary sources do we then have for the Mysteries that could be relevant to our investigation?[16] Since Eleusis was a Demeter cult, connected with the abduction of Persephone,[17] we get a hold of the basic mythology from the *Homeric Hymn* to Demeter. And the hymn also talks about the setting up of the Mysteries.[18] Furthermore, there are references to the Mysteries in the literature before the *Symposium*, especially in Aristophanes. Finally, there is some evidence from the material culture: we have the archaeological excavations from the old site of the ritual, several inscriptions concerning the cult, as well as some depictions of the Mysteries in portable artefacts and the visual arts, in sculptures, reliefs, terracotta, vase paintings, and *pinakes* that are pre-Platonic or contemporary with Plato.[19]

---

16 According to Burkert 1994, 78–79 and Burkert 1987, 93–94, there are at least five divergent groups of evidence for the Mysteries: 1. the topography of the sanctuary; 2. the myth of Demeter's advent as told especially in the *Homeric Hymn*; 3. a relief frieze with initiation scenes known in several replicas; 4. the σύνθημα mentioned by Clement of Alexandria quoted above; and 5. the testimonies of the Naassene Gnostic quoted above; cf. also Burkert 1987, 91. Our grouping of evidence deviates from Burkert's because of our interest in Plato rather than the Mysteries themselves. Thus, for the purposes of this paper the evidence of the Naassene Gnostic and of Clement are too late to build upon, as is the Roman relief Burkert works with (Burkert 1994, 125, n. 20). While an investigation of the *Hymn to Demeter* is taken up below as a fruitful source, the evidence from archaeology will turn out to be relatively unimportant for our inquiry.

17 For the difference between Kore and Persephone cf. Kevin Clinton, *Myth and Cult, The Iconography of the Eleusinian Mysteries* (Stockholm: Svenska Institutet i Athen, 1992), 61–63. Persephone was usually called Kore in Eleusis, cf. Parker 2005, 334, but for the sake of simplicity I will normally use her proper name. For a discussion of whether the unnamed god and goddess could be identified with Plouton and Persephone cf. Parker 2005, 335.

18 According to Graf the Mysteries are thus attested in literature since the 7th century, cf. his entry on "Mysterien" in *Der Neue Pauly*: Enzyklopädie der Antike, ed. Manfred Landfester, Hubert Cancik, and Helmuth Schneider (Stuttgart: J.B. Metzler, 2000), 615–626. Cf. also Richardson's dating 1974, 3–11. For doubts concerning the value of the hymn as a source for the Mysteries cf. below.

19 The sanctuary in Eleusis itself seems to have been emptied before complete destruction, cf. Mylonas 1961, 87. However, there were still some reliefs found in the excavations that can be of interest here. For the discussion of the artefacts from classic and pre-classical times we will use Clinton 1992, Mylonas 1961, especially 187 ff., and Nilsson 1935, 79–141. In addition, we will be working with Grossman's catalogue as it seems to be the most encompassing systematic study of the Eleusinian gods, even if not specific to the Mysteries: Betty Green-

Now this is at least something to draw on, even if a reader might think it is a rather meagre meal. In contrast to the paucity of the primary sources, there is an abundance of secondary literature. For my project the secondary literature, while rich and numerous, is problematic in ways analogous to the problems encountered when dealing with the primary sources. There is one strand of literature that gives us a vast amount of fantastic ideas about what might have happened at Eleusis during the initiation: different assumptions about the re-enactment of the whole Persephone story are on offer; the Gnostic testimonies among other things provoked various speculations about the birth of a divine child,[20] and a statement of Asterius, bishop of Amaseia around 400 CE, gave rise to ideas about the re-enactment of a holy marriage during the initiation.[21] Some of these speculations, however, seem to get much support from the imagination of the authors, thus filling in the empty space the restrictedness of our sources has left open. Lauenstein might be the most extreme example of this, but we find it to a certain extent also in Festugière.[22] The second, much more cautious group

---

field Grossman, "The Eleusian Gods and Heros in Greek Art," Ph.D. Diss., Saint Louis, Missouri, 1959.

20 Cf. also Parker 2005, 357. According to Nilsson 1935, the birth of a divine child was depicted on vases that also show Eleusinian goddesses.
21 Cf. Parker 2005, 356.
22 Festugière 1975; Diether Lauenstein, *Die Mysterien von Eleusis* (Stuttgart: Urachhaus, 1987). When Lauenstein goes through the excavation and looks at what he calls "Aussagen der Steine über den Ritus" we learn the following "Der erste Hof des inneren Heiligtums hatte eine untere und eine obere Szene. Unten stand der 'Stein ohne Lachen', Demeters Sitz, vor dem die Magd Iambe-Baubo nackt tanzte. Wahrscheinlich tanzte sie den Gestaltenwechsel, den Rückweg von Mensch und Tier hinab zur Schlange. Am Ende hielt sie ein Ei in der Hand, das sie der Göttin reichte. Dieses Geschenk gehörte in die Mitte des Rundssteines mit den vielen Kuhlen, in denen die Getreidesorten getrennt geopfert wurden. Erst dieses Ei brachte die Alte zum Lächeln." 1987, 31. His image of the initiation celebration brings in a rich array of gods, heros and other figures, so, e.g., we see that Hephaistos "schleift von den toten Zwillingen den einen über die Südseite zum Westen, den Moiren zu Füßen. Dabei geht dessen Hörnerkappe verloren, Hermes hebt sie auf, breitet einen Silberschleier darüber und reicht sie Hera als neuen Kopfschmuck. Dann legt Hermes seinen Schlangenstab dem toten Eubolus auf die Brust und ruft nach dem Heiler der Götter" (219). Lauenstein derives his wild imagery by using *Orphic Hymns* without further ado, taking them as "seelische Führer" (30), by mixing in some images from other Mythes (e.g., "Bei Thetis Hochzeit waren 'alle Götter zugegen'. Das ist eine Weihe" (239)—and thus we can

of secondary literature tries to reconstruct an image of the Eleusinian Mysteries that is mostly based on the Naassene Gnostic, Clement, and Plutarch, as we find it, for instance, in Mylonas (1961) and in Burkert (1987) and (1994). As helpful as the second group of secondary literature will be for general information on Eleusis, my project requires me to set aside the elaborate re-construction of the Mysteries we find there for the most part. Only thus can we try to derive a sketch of the Eleusinian Mysteries independent of these later sources, and attempt to reconstruct what they might have looked like in Plato's time and before Plato's own account became influential.

II. Our Knowledge of the Mysteries

Before we start our investigation of the Mysteries, we should first consider what we can reasonably expect these sources to tell us. Given the absolute secrecy of the Mysteries, we might think that whatever was written about or depicted could obviously not have been part of the secret Mysteries at Eleusis.[23] Accordingly, Mylonas thinks that the "references bearing directly on the Mysteries to be found in our ancient authors apply to the part of the celebration held in public and visible to all. We find very few references, and these descriptive rather of ritual than of substance, to the second and secret part of the celebration, of what happened in the Telesterion during the nights of the secret rites."[24] That there was a public and a strictly secretive aspect to the Mysteries is also clear from the different treatments of Aeschylus and Aristophanes, respectively. Aeschylus almost lost his life because people thought his tragedies divulge some of the Eleusinian secrets, or so Aristotle tells us.[25] Aristophanes, on the other hand, was able to play around with features of the Mysteries in his comedies without facing any accusation of impiety. As we have no reason to assume that the requirement of secrecy changed in the period that separates the work of these two poets, this difference in treatment seems to indicate that there were some features

---

bring in lots from Homer, or so Lauenstein thinks), and by "empathizing" with the happenings of the Mysteries (29–30).
23 Cf. Mylonas 1961, 210, n. 64.
24 Mylonas 1961, 227–228.
25 Cf. Aristotle's *Nicomachean Ethics* 1111a 10, and Mylonas 1961, 227. Cf. also Nilsson 1935, 79: "Die Mysterienfeier ist an sich die eigenartige Ausgestaltung eines Kultes, der nicht in allem geheim war."

that everybody could know and talk about, while others were reserved for those fully initiated. This leaves us with the suspicion pointed out by Mylonas that our sources will almost exclusively deal with the aspects of the Mysteries that could be publicly known.

While this may be a disappointment for somebody expecting to be let in on an ancient secret, it is not necessarily a problem for my project. Though one might think we are thus missing the "substance" of the secret and hence the actual Mysteries, it is not quite clear to me how much, even with much better sources, we could understand of such a "substance". This is especially the case given that we do not *perform* the Mysteries, which was supposedly a crucial feature of them.[26] And if we want to reconstruct the Eleusinian Mysteries as a template for Plato's *Symposium*, it seems to be clear that it is exactly the public aspect, or at least those features that can be hinted at without danger in a text for a public audience, that he can refer to and that we should expect to find in his text. For the purpose of my project it is less important what exactly the content of the secret rites was. More significant are the metaphors, images, and terms connected with these rites that might have been alluded to without committing a terrible crime and that evoked associations useable for Plato.

Thus I am interested in a rather broad template for the Mysteries at Eleusis, including possible popular associations that may not necessarily tell us something about the highest and most secretive part of the Mysteries. In the following we will address the different sources individually in order to investigate the language, imagery, metaphors, and practices that were most clearly associated with the Mysteries. We will ask what general pattern these elements point to. But there will not be any speculation about the way these features might have been represented and played out in the secret initiation or any reconstruction how they might have been distributed over the different days of the initiation. There will be some sketchiness in this picture of the Mysteries not only because I will have to leave out quite some details, but also because there will be hardly any space to discuss the huge secondary literature dealing with these individual sources independent of their connection with Eleusis. Besides, I will have to concentrate on some main protagonists of the Eleusinian Mysteries, leaving out for the most part figures like the divinity Eubouleus, or Eumolpos, the first hierophant and

---

26 Cf. also Richardson 1974, 29 who points out that early Greek religion is largely a matter of performance.

mythical ancestor of one of the priestly clans connected with Eleusis. Furthermore, different primary sources may represent different phases of the cult. The *Homeric Hymn* and Aristophanes' *Frogs*, for instance, may very well present different stages in the development of the cult itself, as the lack of mention of any procession from Athens to Eleusis in the former and a reference to it in the later may indicate.[27] Similarly, the fact that the *Homeric Hymn* mentions Triptolemos only as one among other nobles of Athens (lines 153 and 474), without attributing any significant role to him, while in the visual arts we get frequent depictions of him being sent out by Demeter to bring agriculture to humankind seems to indicate some development.[28] However, there will not be any space to discuss these differences suggesting a possible development in the cult. What will be dealt with is what Plato also may have had in front of him, i.e. different layers of knowledge about the Mysteries, reaching from the *Homeric Hymn* up to the then contemporary expression of the cult of Eleusis in several different media.

---

27 It seems likely that a procession was set up only once Athens got interested in Eleusis and finally included Eleusis into its territory (it might, however, still have left Eleusis in charge of the Mysteries in the beginning). Accordingly, Richardson 1974, 10 thinks that the procession was instituted in the Peisistratean period. And Anthony Snodgrass, *Archaic Greece, The Age of Experiment* (London: J.M. Dent & Sons Ltd, 1980), 117 assumes that Peisistratos "very likely established Athenian control over the Eleusinian Mysteries for the first time". John M. Camp, *The Archaeology of Athens* (New Haven: Yale University Press, 2001), 25–26 dates the takeover of Eleusis by Athens to some time in the seventh century and supports this with the claim that the "Homeric *Hymn to Demeter* contains no suggestion that Eleusis is not an independent entity; Athens does not figure in the story at all. By the sixth century, however, the town and its territory were fully integrated into the Athenian state, which administered the sanctuary and the mysteries celebrated in honor of Demeter and her daughter, Kore (Persephone)".

28 Cf. Richardson 1974, 9. It seems to be the case that this myth of Triptolemos became prominent only when the Athenians got involved in Eleusis. For an account of how the depictions of Triptolemos developed, cf. Kevin Clinton, "The Eleusinian Mysteries and Panhellenism in Democratic Athens," in *The Archaeology of Athens and Attica under the Democracy*, ed. William D.E. Coulson, Olga Palagia, T.L. Shear, H.A. Shapiro and F.J. Forst (Oxford: Oxbow Books, 1994), 161–170, and Isabelle K. and Anthony E. Raubitschek, "The Mission of Triptolemos," in *Studies in Athenian Architecture, Sculpture and Topography, presented to Homer A. Thompson* (Princeton: American School of Classical Studies at Athens, 1982), 109–117.

As the *Hymn to Demeter* is probably the most important source,[29] it will be the starting point of the investigation. From there we will go on to other pre-Platonic texts, mainly to the *Frogs*, where Aristophanes is playing around extensively with language and metaphors from the Mysteries. We will move on to what remains of the material culture, to portable artefacts first, and then to the buildings at the archeological site of Eleusis.

a) Hymn to Demeter

To deal with the entirety of this rich poem is beyond the scope of this paper. I propose to concentrate on two main strands in the myth, the rape of Persephone and the attempt to immortalize Demophon.

---

29 Clinton doubts its value as a source for the Eleusinian Mysteries, cf. especially his article, "The Author of the Homeric Hymn to Demeter," *Opuscula Atheniensia* 16 (1986): 43–49, and his modified account in Clinton 1992. I agree with Clinton that the *Homeric Hymn* obviously does leave out a lot of topological details. But leaving out topological details does not make it an unreliable source. Clinton's suggestion to see the hymn as actually referring to the Thesmophoria celebrated in Eleusis seems unlikely to me for at least two reasons: as the Thesmophoria is a widespread cult in all of Greece, why would the author bother to specify its set-up in Eleusis, if this author is indeed, as Clinton claims, neither familiar with Eleusis nor interested in it? Secondly, the Thesmophoria is a femal cult, so why would the hymn then claim that Demeter tells the rites of this cult to the highest ranking *men*? And the two aetological scenes from the hymn that Clinton claims should not belong to a cult not yet established but need to belong to a pre-existing one, like the Thesmophoria, Iambe's mockery and the nursing of Demophon, could very well be part of the set up of the cult, in case they were seen as central elements in the founding myth. The Demophon scene need not have been integrated as a nursing scene in the cult, but could have been incorporated as an important point about different kinds of immortality; and the mocking scene is normally seen as having a prominent place in the procession, as Clinton himself admits, whether or not it can thus be seen as central to the cult. Athens and some of the Athenian personage are not mentioned in the hymn, I would suggest, because at the time the hymn was written Athens did not yet play the important role in Eleusis that Clinton claims it to have played, cf. also Richardson 1974, 10 and Camp 2001, 25–26 quoted above. It might indeed have been more helpful to look at the other versions of the myth Clinton mentions, but the *Homeric Hymn* happens to be the one best preserved, and it still gives us the general frame of the story underlying the cult. Burkert in his 2nd revised edition of *Griechische Religion der archaischen und klassischen Epoche* (Stuttgart: Kohlhammer 2011), 426 thus also takes the *Hymn to Demeter* as a document for the Eleusinian Mysteries.

Though the second sequence of events can be understood in some sense as mirroring certain characteristics of the first,[30] the "logic" of both can to a certain extent be understood independently of each other. For the purposes of our analysis we will take them as two bodies of mythical thought.

The first strand of the myth as told in the hymn depicts the kidnapping of Persephone. From a meadow where she is picking flowers—indicating the blossoming of a rich vegetation[31]—she is taken to the underworld by Hades who is given permission to do so by Zeus (lines 1–39). Demeter's grief about the loss of her daughter (lines 40 ff.)[32] is driving most of the rest of the poem. As she is stopping all vegetation (especially lines 305–313), Zeus finally gives in and sends Hermes to the underworld to get Persephone back. The joy about Persephone's eventual return (especially lines 385–389 and 434–37), which prompts Demeter to bring back vegetation (lines 471–473), is interrupted by Demeter's discovery that Persephone has eaten a pomegranate seed (line 412); this forces Persephone to go back to the underworld for a third of each year.

The second train of ideas[33] is Demeter's attempt to immortalize[34] Demophon, the Eleusinian prince whose nurse Demeter in disguise

---

30   E.g., like Demeter, Metaneira is fearing for her child, cf. lines 245–250.
31   Though it is also a somewhat undifferentiated vegetation—flowers that should bloom at different seasons are all blooming at the same time. This can either be understood as a marker for a space out of the ordinary, e. g., a magic space, or as an account of vegetation before the introduction of the seasons, which the myth seems to introduce with the rape and return of Persephone. I owe this point to Corinne Pache.
32   There is plenty of vocabulary for grieving in the *Homeric Hymn*. Signs of Demeter's grief are her bitter pain, line 39; loosening her hair, lines 39–41; putting up a dark veil around her shoulders, line 42; wandering around for nine days with flaming torches without eating or drinking or washing, lines 47–50, etc. Following the σύνθημα of Clement, a lot of the secondary literature assumes that during the rituals at Eleusis the mystai had to imitate a series of Demeter's actions: fasting, drinking a barley drink, sitting down on a chair with a lambskin, putting a veil in front of one's face, being silent until being made to laugh—all actions performed by Demeter while grieving for her daughter according to the *Homeric Hymn* (cf. especially lines 192–211); cf. also Richardson 1974, 211 ff.
33   This strand might have featured less prominently than the first, cf. Mircea Eliade, *A History of Religious Ideas*, vol. 1 (Chicago and London: University of Chicago Press, 1978), 291.

had become while mourning her daughter. When Demeter's endeavour to make him immortal by anointing him with ambrosia during the day and putting him into a fire at night is brought to a stop by the boy's mother,[35] the angry goddess reveals herself suddenly to the mortals (lines 256–281). She asks for a temple, which is readily built for her (lines 270–300). In this temple she continues to grieve for her daughter (lines 302–304).

The Eleusinian Mysteries are established with the help of both story lines: first of all they are explicitly introduced when the immortalisation of Demophon is stopped and Demeter, revealing herself, not only demands a temple build for herself, but also promises to teach the people her rites (ὄργια, line 273). These, if well-performed, can win humans the νόος (the mind in the sense of heart or favour) of the goddess (line 274). Secondly, when Demeter has received back Persephone and is asked by Rhea, who acts as Zeus' messenger, not to continue her anger against Zeus, she not only brings back vegetation, but also goes to the Eleusinian leaders, to the θεμιστοπόλοι βασιλῆεσ, the kings ministering laws and right, to teach them her rites (lines 473–479).[36]

The hymn not only mentions the founding of the Mysteries, it also states the prohibition to transgress or utter the Mysteries (lines 478–479) and the well-being promised to the initiated and denied to the uninitiated (lines 480–482). Furthermore, it gives us a rough description of the temple: "all the people shall build me a great temple and an altar beneath it, below the city and the steep wall, above Callichorus on the rising hill" (lines 270–72).[37]

In order to get a clearer overview of the terrain for our project, we will flesh out a few general features from the two sequences of events depicted in the *Hymn to Demeter* that will be important for interpreting the Platonic text: the division and mediation between two realms normally held apart; the ascent of Persephone led by Hermes; the emphasis on life, the cycle of life and eternal life; and the different functions of light in the hymn.

---

34 Wisely not forgetting to combine it with eternal youth, ἀθάνατος and ἀγήραος, cf. line 242 and 260.
35 The boy now cannot escape death and κῆρας.
36 Cf. also Eliade 1978, 290.
37 Cf. Richardson 1974, 304–309, 311–15, and 326–330.

In both strands we are confronted with the division of two different realms between which some mediation or bridging takes place. Both show us someone move between two realms that are normally strictly separate: Demeter's endeavour to make the mortal Demophon immortal is an attempt to make him bridge the gap between humans and gods. And Persephone will cross the border between two separate divine realms, Olympus and Hades, every year, spending a third of the year with her husband in the underworld, and two thirds with her mother and the other gods on mount Olympus.[38]

The first time Persephone crosses the border between the two realms in a direction not often done,[39] i.e. from the underworld to the world above, this ascent is described in some detail (lines 335 ff.). Hermes is sent as a messenger in order to persuade Hades to let Persephone go; thus he mediates between the god of the heavens and the god of the underworld. Overall successful in his mediation, Hermes leads Persephone out of the underworld to the world above (lines 337–338) and steers the chariot along the long path (μακρὰ κέλευθα, line 380) back to Demeter.

Because Demeter had lost her daughter to the underworld, to what for humans would be death, she stops all vegetation. Thus she not only takes away life from all plants, but also threatens the mortals with death and, consequently, the gods with the loss of their sacrifices. The return of Persephone, now the queen of the underworld, prompts Demeter to let all vegetation germinate again and thus prevents humans from starving. But since Persephone has consumed a pomegranate kernel in Hades, she has to go back to the underworld every year. A mythos of the beginning of the seasons is thus established—Persephone's yearly return to Hades followed by her re-appearance in the world above corresponds to the never ending cycle of life and death through the seasons.

While the first strand thus tells a story about securing the continuation of natural life—natural life persists in perpetual regeneration

---

38 Lines 445–447 and also 398–400. Cf. also Parker 2005, 357–358. The gap between the underworld and the upper world is also bridged by Dionysus in Aristophanes' *Frogs*, who goes down to the underworld to get Euripides back, cf. below.

39 Ascending from the underworld to the upper world presupposes a descent in the opposite direction first, which in Persephone's case was her rape by Hades. In Plato's *Symposium*, where the focus is on the ascent to a realm likened to the divine, such a descent seems to be missing.

through the death of one and the birth of another individual[40]—, the second strand employs the idea of the eternal life of an individual. It introduces the possibility that immortal life is bestowed upon an originally mortal individual. However, this immortalization does not work. Instead, what is promised to humans—to all who undergo the initiation into the Mysteries rather than only to one single prince, Demophon—is being ὄλβιος, blissful (line 480), while those who are not initiated will be suffering hardship also in the realm of the dead (lines 481–482).

This promise of the goddess comes after Demeter's sudden disclosure of her identity in light as bright as a lightening.[41] Thus one function of light seems to be a sudden revealing of the true nature of a divinity. This revelation comes after Demeter's attempt to immortalize Demophon in fire was obstructed. Again light, here the light of fire, is connected with something divine—here it is not an insight into something divine, but a means to became divine. Moreover, Demeter, and later on also Hecate, are depicted as wandering around with torches; a second function of light in the *Homeric Hymn* seems to be orientation in a dark or obfuscated world. Finally, light is also indicating the realm of the living in contrast to the underworld, so in lines 337–338, when Hermes is sent out to bring back Persephone from the underworld to the world above (ἀπὸ ζόφου ἠερόεντος ἐς φάος, from gloomy darkness to light).

In addition to the rites of Demeter, lines 367–369 also introduce necessary sacrifices for Persephone,[42] which do not seem to be part of the rites of her mother. These sacrifices are frequently connected with the so called Lower Mysteries; we will find more about the possibility of different steps, Lower and Higher Mysteries connected with the Eleusinian Mysteries in the following Preplatonic literature.

---

40 The idea of the continuation of life within a species is a notion of eternal life that is prominently taken up in the *Symposium* by Diotima's explanation of why humans as well as animals love and have desire (207a5–208b6). For the idea that death is followed by rebirth in nature and the continuity between life and death cf. Eliade 1978, 299. Cf. also Isocrates *Panegyricus* 28.
41 Cf. lines 278–280 and also Riedweg 1987, 50.
42 These lines were sometimes taken to be aetiological or orphic and hence rejected; cf. Richardson 1974, 270–275. Richardson, however, argues that they are similar to lines 273–274, which refer explicitly to the Mysteries, and hence believes it to be "a reasonable assumption that 368–369 also refer to the Mysteries," 271.

b) Other Pre-Platonic Literature

Looking through the pre-Platonic literature for any mention of Eleusis, one might think that the historians should be able to give us some indications. And they do. However, we only get references to political events connected with Eleusis and hardly any general remarks about the rites. So in Herodotus Book VIII, 65: when the Athenian Dicaeus, who is in Attica with the army of Xerxes, explains the procession of the ghostly mystai, he refers to Eleusis as a yearly feast "for Mother and Maid". It is a feast that is connected with the cry of a Iacchos song. The Athenians are already clearly involved and all Greeks can be initiated—Isocrates in his *Panegyricus* 157 specifies that it is only barbarians and murderers who cannot participate.

Thucydides mentions the Eleusinion in Athens, Book II, 17, 1,[43] the charge against Alcibiades' alleged transgression of the Mysteries in VI, 28, 2 and VI, 53, 1, and the political motivation behind it. These accusations are also referred to by Xenophon in his *Hellenika* Book I, 4, 14 ff. And in I, 4, 20 we are told that because of the Peloponnesian War the Athenians had to undertake their procession to Eleusis via ship and could not go by land. Finally, in *Hellenika*, VI, 3, 6 we learn about the initiation of Heracles and the Dioscuri into the holy Mysteries of Demeter and Kore, and we are told that Triptolemos brought the seeds of the fruits of Demeter first to the Peloponnese.

In epic, Hesiod mentions the fathering and rape of Persephone in two lines (*Theogony* 913–914), and in lyric poetry there are a few passages in Pindar, which seem to be of interest *prima facie* but which are probably mostly Orphic. The passage that seems straightforwardly connected with Eleusis[44] is fragment 137 Snell/Maehler, which, similar to the *Homeric Hymn*, promises being blissful, ὄλβιος, to him who has seen the Mysteries and goes beneath the earth. The continuation of the fragment, however, takes an interesting turn, as it does not promise immortality or anything similar, but rather knowledge of the end of life

---

43 The amendment concerning the *epistatai* of Eleusis IG I^3 32 from ca. 432/1 BCE also attests an Eleusinion in Athens, cf. Kevin Clinton, *Eleusis, the Inscriptions on Stone: Documents of the Sanctuary of the Two Goddesses and Public Documents of the Deme* (Athens: Archaeological Society at Athens, 2005), 40–42 and Maureen B. Cavanaugh, *Eleusis and Athens, Documents in Finance, Religion and Politics in the Fifth Century B.C.* (Atlanta: Scholars Press, 1996), 19–21.

44 At least Clement of Alexandria, whom we owe its preservation, introduces it with the words "in speaking of the Eleusinian Mysteries, Pindar adds".

and "its Zeus-given beginning"—if we know the end and its divine beginning we probably know the whole of life, everything important that there is to know about it.[45]

It is really only in drama that we get more extended information on the Mysteries. Aeschylus' alleged disclosure of the secret Mysteries is unfortunately not to be found in a text that can be reconstructed. But in Sophocles' *Oedipus at Colonus* we find a short reference to Eleusis when in lines 1049–1053 the chorus refers to the "torch-lit seashore where the divine ladies nurse the august rites for mortals", and to the secrecy of these rites of the divine ladies, "on whose tongue rests the golden key of the attendant sons of Eumolpus".[46] Euripides in his *Helen* recasts Demeter's search for her daughter and the threat of her destruction of the human race when in her grief she stops all vegetation; and the description of the Charites singing and dancing in order to cheer up Demeter might refer also to some practice at Eleusis (cf. lines 1301–1352).

The text which gives us the clearest and most extensive references to the Mysteries after the *Hymn* in pre-Platonic literature, however, is Aristophanes' *Frogs*. At the time of its performance in 405 BCE the Mysteries of Eleusis were probably very much on the mind of the audience. For the Spartan fortress at Decelea, set up in 413, had forced the processions to Eleusis to be replaced by a sea journey, as we just heard from Xenophon. And Alcibiades was probably able to impress his countrymen again when, upon his return to Athens in 408, he led the traditional procession to the festival by land in spite of this danger.

Already the basic set up of the *Frogs* seems to play around with themes we saw in the *Homeric Hymn* and which are thus likely part of the imagery of the Mysteries. In the hymn as well as in the *Frogs* we have a god, Hermes and Dionysus, respectively, going down to the underworld in order to bring back somebody from there to the world above: Hermes is sent down by Zeus to get Persephone back, while Dionysus, frustrated by the current state of the theatre, wants to get back

---

45 Nilsson 1935, 119 understands what is expressed in this fragment as corresponding to the circle of the seed, which is put into the earth and germinates out of the earth again.
46 For a discussion of the ways in which Sophocles links Oedipus' death to an initiation at Eleusis cf. Claude Calame, "Mort héroïque et culte à mystère dans l'Oedipe à Colone de Sophocle: Actes rituels au service de la creation mythique," in *Ansichten griechischer Rituale: Geburtstagssymposium für Walter Burkert*, ed. Fritz Graf (Stuttgart and Leipzig: Teubner, 1998), 326–356.

Euripides, and thus undertakes himself a trip to the underworld. In order to prepare for this journey, Dionysus consults and dresses like Heracles who has done this journey before, and who is one of the most famous initiates at Eleusis.[47] We saw the *Homeric Hymn* announcing that those who are not initiated will be suffering hardship in the underworld; accordingly, it is the group of the mystai whom we see enjoying a good life in that lower region, in contrast with those apparently not initiated, who suffer.[48] Except for the scene in which Dionysus crosses

---

47 Cf. Xenophon, *Hellenika*, VI,3,6, Mylonas 1961, 240 and Richardson 1974, 22 and 211–212. If Dionysus is identified with Iacchos, then Dionysus' unfamiliarity with the mystai in the *Frogs* seems to be puzzling. And his unfamiliarity with the underworld does not square with him being a chthonic god either. Given the way Dionysus is sketched in this play, the audience might actually wonder whether this ignorant and cowardly figure did indeed become a member in the club of deities at all; cf. also Kenneth Dover, ed., Aristophanes' Frogs, with introduction and commentary (Oxford: Clarendon Press, 1993): 37–43, and compare also George Elderkin, *Mystic Allusions in the Frogs of Aristophanes* (Princeton: Princeton University Press, 1955). Etienne Lapalus, "Le Dionysus et l'Heracles des Grenouilles," *REG* 47 (1934): 1–20 reads the *Frogs* as a satire of the Eleusian Mysteries and argues that the descent of Dionysus described in the *Frogs*, with him shivering, trembling in horror, and becoming pale until he reaches the Eleusinian plains is a caricature of the experiences of the initiation in Eleusis as reported in Plutarch, fr. 178 Sandbach; cf. also Parker 2005, 352.

48 In case the Mysteries did in fact promise some kind of eternal life, as, e.g., Eliade 1978, 299 assumes, we get some additional ironic inversions in the *Frogs*: if the continuation of one's existence was thought along the lines of a possible return to life on earth, then Dionysus' attempt to bring back a certain individual human being, Euripides, to the world of the living must be quite a disappointment for the initiates, as he eventually comes back with a different person than he set out to. He brings back Aeschylus, who was accused of breaking the vow of secrecy with respect to the Mysteries. And the mere fact that it is a poet for whom Dionysus sets out to the underworld is interesting in itself, for it means trying to get back somebody who is supposed to be eternal through his works already (cf. also in the *Symposium* Diotima's evaluation of this kind of eternity as higher than the one achieved by begetting children). Aristophanes explicitly plays around with the idea of eternity achieved through literary works when in the later part of the comedy Aeschylus complains that he and Euripides would not fight on equal terms here in the underworld. For his, Aeschylus', poetry has not died with him (i.e. it is still living in the world of the living and thus immortal), while Euripides' work did pass away with him so that his rival now has it handy here in the underworld (lines 868–869). When in line 1480 Plouton announces to feed Dionysus and Aeschylus before they leave the underworld, it seems to be clear that Plouton will thus receive

the lake at the border to the underworld with Charon, the chorus of the play is formed by mystai dwelling near Plouton's palace.[49] Since the gods worshiped in their procession are Demeter[50] and Iacchos, and Persephone and Hecate are mentioned in this context, it seems to be clear that the chorus consists of mystai belonging to the Eleusinian Mysteries.[51] And Aeschylus, the poet from Eleusis, invokes Demeter before his contest with Euripides in the *Frogs*, praying to make him worthy of her mystic rites (lines 886–887).

This piece of literature is obviously a very tricky piece of evidence, as it plays around ironically with the very features of the Mysteries about which we would like to acquire evidence. For example when in 354 ff. the chorus names those who should stay away from the community of the mystai, Aristophanes brings in his own jokes related to the current

---

both of them back in his world, like he managed to bind Persephone to return by making her eat a pomegranate seed.

49 Alphonse Willems, *Aristophane: traduction avec notes et commentaires critiques* (Paris: Hachette, 1919) remarks in a note to line 316 that given the political situation, which makes the procession from Athens to Eleusis impossible on earth, the poet has it occur in Hades.

50 Cf. line 385a-b: "Δήμητερ, ἁγνῶν ὀργίων ἄνασσα", "Demeter, mistress over the holy rites". I am referring to the line numbering in the edition of Kenneth Dover (1993), rather than to the OCT text, *Aristophanis Fabulae*, recognovit brevique adnotatione critica instruixt N. G. Wilson, Tomus II (Oxford: Oxford University Press, 2007), since Dover's numbering seems to be clearer to me.

51 The fact that the Chorus consists of Eleusinian mystai together with the political context referred to above, the features we came across already in the *Hymn to Demeter*, and the fact that when Athenians referred to the Mysteries without any further qualification they normally meant the Mysteries of Eleusis indicate that Aristophanes is referring to the Mysteries of Eleusis and to no others. For the last point cf. Burkert 1994, 12, Eliade 1978, 301, and Graf 2000. For a critical discussion of the question whether these features are indeed referring to Eleusis, cf. Graf 1974, 40–41. He eventually concludes that Aristophanes used the procession to Eleusis as model and closely kept to it; cf. also Eliade 1978, 294 and Mylonas 1961, 267. Dover 1993, 61–62 is hesitant to see Eleusis directly referred to in the *Frogs*, but his hesitation seems to rest mostly on the attempt of some interpreters to read the geography of Athens passed through during the procession to Eleusis into the play. When the chorus asks Iacchos to lead their procession and to join them, this seems to be a playful inversion of the normal Eleusinian practice of the mystai joining him, which requires the connection between Iacchos and the procession to Eleusis as a basis.

political situation.[52] And when Dionysus' inquiry about the underworld touches on the subject of brothels in that place, this is very likely not an idea taken up from the Mysteries themselves. However, since Aristophanes was not accused of impiety (by contrast, he seems to have been honoured with a second performance[53]), his cheekiness and irony seem not to have distorted anything connected with the Mysteries too badly, or at least only those parts of it that were not seen as essentially tied to the secretive part. Aristophanes may also play around with the vow of secrecy required by the Mysteries when Heracles assures Dionysus that it will be the mystai, no doubt, who will φράζειν, point out to Dionysus, who is not pictured as an initiate himself,[54] everything he needs to know down there (lines 158–161). Similarly in 414ab, when Dionysus articulates his temptation to join the mystai in their activities, he is not depicted as a transgressor, but rather seems to get what one may interpret as a welcoming response.[55] However, given that at the end of the fifth century people were still banned and prosecuted for impiety towards the Mysteries, as we saw in the case of Alcibiades (415 BCE)[56] and Diagoras (414 BCE),[57] the fact that Aristophanes did not face any accusations for writing this play seems to be a clear indication that in all his jesting and joking Aristophanes is nevertheless not transgressing the vow of secrecy; he is not saying more than was permitted.

One aspect of the Mysteries that makes the seeming tension between the seriousness of the Mysteries and the joking twists natural in the genre of comedy even more interesting is the fact that there may actually have been some jesting involved in the rites. In the *Homeric Hymn*, Demeter, full of grief, is made to laugh by Iambe, and in the *Frogs* the mystai explicitly mention joking, making fun, and ridiculing during the feast for Demeter. Thus some of the irony and joking connected with

---

52 As, e.g., when the chorus mentions those who give away a ship or a fortress to the enemies as belonging to the group of people who should stay away from the community of the mystai.
53 Cf. Hans-Joachim Newiger in *Aristophanes, Sämtliche Komödien* (Munich: dtv, 1976), 467.
54 Otherwise he would have recognized the mystai when Heracles described them (lines 154—158).
55 Cf. Dover 1993, 66 for this passage.
56 Even if this accusation, according to Thucydides, might in fact have been politically motivated. For Alcibiades' condemnation, cf. also Mylonas 1961, 224.
57 Cf. also Leonard Woodbury, "The Date and Atheism of Diagoras of Melos," *Phoenix* 19.3 (1965): 178–211.

the mystai in the *Frogs* could be due not only to the genre, comedy, but also to the content, the Eleusinian Mysteries.[58]

Two passages of the *Frogs* are especially interesting for us:[59] Heracles' description of the mystai involving music, glorious (day)light, myrtle groves, and happy bands (θίασοι) of man and woman (lines 154–157); and the long encounter Dionysus has with the mystai before he knocks on Plouton's door (lines 312–459). The features which we seem to be able to derive from these two passages relatively safely as features of the Mysteries are the following:

The performance of the mystai includes flute playing, handclapping, and dancing on a flowery meadow,[60] all of which indicates some form of rejoicing. It is strengthened by the claim in line 346 that they (the old ones) will get rid of their grief, ἀποσείονται λύπας, through the ἱερά τιμή, the holy offering (line 349). Another important feature is the purity required of the initiates, which the chorus stresses (καθαρεύω, line 355, in addition to the rather mixed bag of ethical virtues required to participate in their nightly feast). This purity seems to be a feature of the rites of Demeter (ἁγνά ὄργια, line 385a).

Furthermore, the contrast between darkness and light is central: the initiates enter the scene with burning torches.[61] And the initiation is called the νύκτερος τελετή, the night-time initiation, of which Iacchos is the morning star (line 343). The meadow on which the initiates are dancing is blazing in light (lines 344). Iacchos, wearing a στέφανος of myrtles (line 330/1), is meant to lead the way to the meadows with an illuminated torch; thus he is obviously leading through the darkness

---

58 For the attempt to divide between the irony and fun due to the genre and that due to the Eleusian rites, cf. Dover 1993, 58–59. Cf. also Richardson 1974, 213–214 for the jesting or αἰσχρολογία at Eleusis and its connection to Iambe. These jests and obscenities were probably in iambic verses—as is, e.g., line 389 of the *Frogs*. According to Richardson 1974, 214, line 393 clearly suggests that we are not simply dealing with the traditional jesting of comedy as the chorus asks that they may jest in a way worthy of Demeter's festival. One may also compare the φιλοπαίγμων τιμή, the joke-loving honouring or worship (in this case of Iacchos) in line 333.

59 On possible allusions to Eleusis in the later scene of Aeschylus' and Euripides' competition cf. Elderkin 1955.

60 For the references of the chorus to flowers and vegetation, cf. also Dover 1993, 60.

61 Dionysus and Xanthias perceive the αὔρα, the breeze or steam, of the torches (lines 313–314), and in line 340 the chorus orders to stir up the φλόγεαι λαμπάδες, the burning torches.

(lines 350–351/2, cf. also lines 313 ff.). Finally, the chorus leaves Dionysus and Xanthias in front of Plouton's door with the remark that they are off to οὗ παννυχίζουσιν θεᾷ, φέγγος ἱερὸν οἴσων (line 446), they are off to where the nightlong celebration for the goddess goes on. And she (presumably the chorus-leader of the females,[62] cf. line 445) will carry the holy light. The clear contrast between the dark night in the underworld and the blazing torches of the mystai is somewhat surprisingly twisted by the reference to sunlight: not only Heracles mentions that the mystai are surrounded by glorious daylight (φῶσ κάλλιστον, line 155), also they themselves, in their last antistrophe before leaving Dionysus and Xanthias, tell us that only for them there is sun and holy/joyous light (ἥλιος καὶ φέγγος ἱερόν/ἱλαρόν[63], lines 454–455). As we are told that they are actually wandering in the dark, the reference to daylight could either be metaphorical, probably referring to a blessed life, which they are the only ones to enjoy in Hades.[64] Or we could here have a division of the functions of light along the lines of the first two roles we encountered in the *Homeric Hymn*: the light of torches for orientation, and the light that is brighter than these torches for some kind of revelation.

Roughly speaking, the celebration of the mystai has the following structure: after the *parodos*, during which they invoke Iacchos (lines 323/4–353), they give an overview of who should stay away from their rites (lines 354–371). Once all the profane people are warned, we get a series of three different songs to three different gods: the mystai start out in lines 372–382 with a song to the saviour goddess (line 378), which is probably referring to Persephone,[65] since she is the last deity named before (line 337). Then they explicitly announce a change in their tone (line 384) when switching to a hymn to Demeter, the harvest

---

62 For the different possibilities of how the chorus might have been divided, cf. Dover 1993, 66–67.
63 Manuscripts RVK have ἱερόν while A and L have ἱλαρόν; cf. Wilson 2007, 155.
64 As we saw above, daylight indicates the realm of the living in the *Homeric Hymn*. Cf. also Dover 1993, 60 who thinks that the darkness with which the unfortunate souls (those not initiated) are confronted is "naturally associated in Greek thought with the world of the dead".
65 So also Clinton 1992, 115, though for different reasons. For the possibility that this might be a hint to Athena instead cf. Dover 1993, *ad locum*. However, given what the chorus was singing before, understanding the savior goddess as a reference to Persephone seems to me more in accord with the context than a reference to Athena.

queen (lines 385a ff.). And finally they turn to a song to Iacchos (lines 394–413), asking him to accompany them along the way (ξυνέμπορον line 396). After the mockery of some contemporaries and an exchange with Dionysus and Xanthias (lines 414–439), the chorus finishes off with a song referring to three central features of their procession: joking, dancing, and being the ones exclusively lit by the sun.

For our purposes, this mystic celebration not only introduces more fully an Eleusinian deity not mentioned in the *Homeric Hymn*,[66] Iacchos.[67] It also strengthens the idea that there have been different steps to the mystic celebration: one step connected with Iacchos and the procession to Eleusis (as Iacchos is explicitly asked to accompany the mystai on their way); one connected with Persephone and the sacrifice of pigs (in lines 337–338 the tasty smell of sacrificed pigs is immediately associated by Xanthias with Persephone);[68] and finally one connected with

---

66 Herodotus VIII, 65 already connects Iacchos clearly with the cult at Eleusis, as we saw above. Both, Herodotus as well as the passage here, associate Iacchos with a procession of which we get no mention in the *Homeric Hymn*. The procession in question is normally understood as the one along the Sacred Way from Athens to Eleusis, so it is very likely that it was established only once Athens had annexed Eleusis to its territory. Richardson 1974, 8 interprets the passage from Herodotus as a clear sign that this procession had been "an established procedure by 480 BCE".

67 Richardson 1974, 8 and others explain his name as derived "from the cry (ἰαχή) of the initiates during the journey". Most people seem to take Iacchos as a different name for the god Dionysus. However, this complicates things in the *Frogs*, where this very god is for the first time making a trip to the underworld and is not identified with the Iacchos the mystai invoke. Richardson on page 27 thinks we have evidence that Iacchos, or Dionysus, was identified with the divine child born to the goddess in Eleusis from the fourth century onwards at the latest but probably already before that time. For this identification cf. also Nilsson 1935, 84.

68 This sacrifice of a pig for Persephone also seems to be alluded to in Aristophanes' *Pax*, 374–375: Trygaeus: "Then lend me three drachmas for a piglet, I've got to get initiated before I die" (translation by J. Henderson). If the sacrifice of a piglet is enough to get initiated, then surely this is not yet the full initiation into the rites of Demeter, but rather some preparatory initiation. A lot of secondary literature sees this act as part of what is called the Lower Mysteries; cf. Riedweg 1987, 10, and also Walter Burkert, *Homo Necans: Interpretationen altgriechischer Opferriten und Mythen* (Berlin and New York: De Gruyter, 1972a), 283–284. While Burkert points out on p. 284 that the sacrifice of pigs as such is not specific to Eleusis, but a common feature of all Demeter cults, he also understands the passages in Aristophanes mentioned above as referring to Eleusis where, specific for a "Mysterienopfer […] das Opfertier dem

Demeter about which we learn the least.⁶⁹ We saw that the *Homeric Hymn* explicitly mentions sacrifices to Persephone over and above the rites introduced by Demeter, and this distinction between sacrifices to Demeter and to Persephone seems to be taken up here and extended by a step connected with Iacchos. Whatever Aristophanes has told us in his comedy about the Mysteries seems to have been part of the public aspect of them so that no break of secrecy would have been risked.⁷⁰ Again, this strengthens the idea that there were different steps to the Mysteries: public ones—judging from Aristophanes, those to do with Iacchos, and probably a piglet sacrifice for Persephone—and other ones that were kept strictly secret—to judge from the *Frogs*, probably the part that dealt explicitly with Demeter's rites.⁷¹

c) Portable Artefacts

There are several inscriptions from Eleusis, concerning the cult from the time before Plato, that reveal which gods receive sacrifices and inform us about the priesthood of Eleusis.⁷² However, these inscriptions do

---

Mysten ganz individuell zugeordnet ist: jeder hat sein eigenes Opferschwein zu stellen". Burkert connects this with the idea "[d]aß er [der Myste] das Tier 'an seiner statt' dem Tod überantwortet, daß hier Leben für Leben gegeben wird" (285).

69 Different parts of the Mysteries also seem to be connected with different locations. The Mysteries connected with Persephone are normally understood to have taken place in a suburb of Athens, near Illisos. Nilsson 1935, 105–106 understands Kore as being most prominent in all of the Mysteries, since she is the main protagonist of the drama that evolves around her rape and return, while Demeter allegedly has only a passive role. However, he seems to base this assumption mainly on one fragment of Sophocles, fr. 736 Nauck (= 804 Radt), that talks about the holy mysteries of the virgin and on the Ithyphallikos to Demetrius Poliorcetes, Athenaeus VI 63, p.253 D-F (= Duris FGrHist 76 F13), which mentions holy mysteries of Kore. This, however, would still square well with different parts of the Mysteries, one in which Kore is more prominent and to which Nilsson's two sources refer, and one in which Demeter figures more prominently.

70 Cf. also Mylonas 1961, 227.

71 Apart from the *Frogs*, there might also be references to Eleusis in Aristophanes' *Clouds*; however, these could also be passages that are in fact Orphic, so we will not rely on them.

72 Cf. Clinton 2005, especially, nr. 7 (IG I³ 231 from ca 510–500 BCE), 13 (IG I³ 5 probably from ca. 500), 19 (IG I³ 6 from ca. 470–460), 23 (IG I³ 395 prob-

not concern the imagery and practice of the cult, but rather the socioeconomic role of the Mysteries and the administration of the sanctuary: the expenses for stone cutting and restoration, the perquisites of the priesthoods of the Mysteries, etc. Hence they will not be of any immediate use for our project.

What about other portable artefacts then, like vases, reliefs, or sculptures? Mylonas thinks that "art provides even less information than literature regarding the famous Mysteries."[73] However, if we look at the public depictions of the Eleusinian gods from the archaic to the classical period,[74] we get at least a few recurring motifs that will be helpful for our purposes. Even if they might not tell us anything about the most secret parts of the Mysteries,[75] they will give us some idea of what images might have been associated with Eleusis. And with the Ninnion Tablet, dated to the first half of the fourth century, we have a depiction that was found in the sacred precinct at Eleusis and thus might even tell us something about aspects that could not be depicted in other places.[76]

While there are certain tendencies for depictions to be associated with certain kinds of media (with sculpture, relief, terracotta, vase,

---

ably from ca. 450–445), 27 (IG I³ 398 probably from ca. 445–430), 28a and b (IG I³ 78a and b from ca. 440–435), and 30 (IG I³ 32 from ca. 432/1).
73 Mylonas 1961, 221.
74 According to Grossman 1959, in the transitional period, i.e., the period between the archaic and the classical time (ca. 510–450 BCE), there seems to be no clear connection of the representations of the Eleusinian gods with the cult, they mostly render stories known to the general public. However, in the classical period there seem to have been clear connections to the cult of Demeter at Eleusis. In this period we also get the first monumental statue of the goddess by Agorakritos, a student of Phidias, that became highly influential, cf. p. 216.
75 Depictions of the highest Mysteries seem to run into the same problem with secrecy as literature. Clinton 1992, 90–91, however, thinks that "vase painters had greater freedom in alluding to the myth than prose writers," probably thanks to the greater range that "could be safely expressed in the medium" and possibly because these vases might not have been accessible to non-initiates.
76 The *pinax* of Ninnion in red-figure technique, No. 11036 in the National Archeological Museum in Athens. Older sources call it "Niinnion" Tablet, but Immerwahr and Clinton have argued that "Ninnion" is the correct spelling and the museum follows them, cf. Henry Immerwahr, *Attic Script: A Survey* (Oxford: Clarendon Press, 1990), 118 n. 825 and Clinton 1992, 67 n. 26. Mylonas 1961, 213 considers the Ninnion Tablet as the only document that can be definitely associated with the Eleusinian cult. For the possibility that it could show more of the cult than objects not confined to the sacred district cf. also Nilsson 1935, 94.

masks, and pinakes), for our purposes we will arrange the findings according to general themes. Roughly put, we find 1) motifs that have to do with the rising of Persephone, her ascent; 2) images that are connected with the idea of guidance, and 3) finally a group of individual attributes specific to Demeter, Persephone, or the initiates.

1) Ascent

While the ascent of Persephone from the underworld is necessarily linked with her descent, her ascent seems to have been depicted much more often. Of her descent and her actual rape we hardly get any illustration.[77] Her depiction with Plouton, however, presupposes her descent to the underworld,[78] a descent that explains her status as a chthonic goddess. Of her ascent, her ἄνοδος, by contrast, there are frequent depictions.[79] According to Grossmann, in the Classical Period the ἄνοδος or rising of Persephone was even her most popular aspect.[80] These depictions normally show either just her head or her head and part of her upper body rising out of something like a mound; often with satyrs and Hermes present.[81] Just as Eros in Plato's *Symposium* is meant to be understood sometimes as the god of love, sometimes as love as such, so Persephone seems to have been treated as a goddess as well as a symbol for grain; accordingly, many interpreters understand Persephone's ἄνοδος as some ἄνοδος of grain. Nilsson distinguishes two

---

[77] In contrast to the 16th and 17th century CE where we find numerous depictions of the rape, e.g., by Brueghel the Younger, Rubens, G.L. Bernini and Rembrandt. However, we might think of the fleeing girl on the pediment of the old Telesterion as depicting Persephone's rape, cf. Ferdinand Noack, *Eleusis, Die Baugeschichtliche Entwicklung des Heiligtumes* (Berlin and Leipzig: De Gruyter, 1927), 219.
[78] Cf., e.g., plate VII,3 in Grossman 1959 that shows Persephone and Plouton enthroned.
[79] Cf. especially Nilsson's 1935 excursus *Die Anodos der Pherephatta auf den Vasenbildern*, 131–141.
[80] Grossmann 1959, 188.
[81] Cf., e.g., the red-figure calyx krater mentioned by Nilsson 1935 on p. 132 which shows Persephone (identified by inscription) up to her knees rising out of a mound, Hermes in front of her, and four dancing satyrs or panes on the sides (Dresden, Albertinum Museum, 5th century BCE); cf. also Jane Ellen Harrison, *Prolegomena to the Study of Greek Religion* (London: Merlin, 1962), 277–278, fig. 67. Compare also the red-figured calyx krater in Berlin with Hermes and eight dancing satyrs from the middle of the 5th century that Nilsson 1935 lists on p. 133.

ἄνοδοι, the first connected with bringing up the seed from containers underground, the second with the germination of the new shoot.[82] The second understanding of Persephone's ἄνοδος also makes intelligible one variation of her ἄνοδος that otherwise seems rather strange: representations of the rising of Persephone that show her large head hit with mallets, with a σφῦρα or βωλοκόπος.[83] The ploughing of the seed under the surface of the field seems to have left many clods, which were then smashed with hammers so as to allow the seed to come up.[84]

Persephone's ascent, as well as her descent, were connected with strong emotions, which we also find depicted on portable artefacts: the *Homeric Hymn* tells us of the deep grief of Demeter caused by Persephone's rape, grief that seems to have been expressed by showing Demeter seated in sorrow,[85] with her head covered by a veil or her hair down loose.[86] To this deep grief corresponds an abundant expression of joy when Persephone eventually returns.[87] This joy, celebrating her happy ascent back to the upper world, back to life, we find depicted on several pieces in which Persephone is greeted cheerfully by dancing figures resembling satyrs.[88] We have seen a scene of joyful dancing also

---

82 Nilsson 1935, cf. especially 140–141. And 101–102 for the fact that Persephone qua Kore could also be used metonymically for the seed of a grain (while Demeter was understood as the more mature grain).
83 Cf. Claude Bérard, *Anodoi, Essai sur l'imagerie des passages chthoniens* (Rome: Institut suisse de Rome, 1974), plates 6–7, and 10–11; Nilsson 1935, 133 ff. and Grossman 1959, 196 and 200.
84 So Nilsson 1935, 116 and in the excursus 131–141, and Grossman 1959, 103–104 following Nilsson; cf. also Aristophanes, *The Peace*, lines 566–570.
85 Cf. Grossman 1959, 159 (No. 64 in the Staatliche Museen in Berlin).
86 Cf. Grossman 1959, 166 (relief CR5 from Paris, Musée du Louvre [plate VII, 2]); Mylonas 1961, 190–1, and the *Homeric Hymn* lines 39 ff. where the undoing of Demeter's hair and putting down a veil are introduced as the first expressions of Demeter's grief; cf. also line 279 of the *Homeric Hymn*.
87 A lot of the secondary literature assumes this contrast of joy and grief to be taken up in Eleusis by ritual mourning and grieving at night which turned into rejoicing; cf. Erika Simon, *Festivals of Attica, an Archaeological Commentary* (Madison: University of Wisconsin Press, 1983), 33.
88 Cf., e.g., the kalyx crater showing Persephone greeted by three goat-horned satyrs who are dancing with joy (Dresden, Albertinum Museum No. 350). And the kalyx crater showing Persephone greeted by four dancers who wear beards, horns, and tails and four similar figures around Hermes (Berlin, Staatliche Museen No. 3275); cf. also Grossman 1959, 188 ff., and 221. Grossman

in Aristophanes' *Frogs*—though there it was the dance of the initiates rather than of satyrs—, and dancing satyrs are frequently present in the depiction of Persephone's ἄνοδος.

In the depictions of Persephone's return, Hermes is often present, since he is the messenger of the gods who guides her back from the underworld. This brings us to the second main feature relevant to us, to the idea of a guide.

2) Guidance Figures

The depictions of the Eleusinian gods include several guidance figures: Hermes with his winged boots, a πέτασος, and a κηρύκειον is leading Persephone out of the underworld—a task that Clinton sees also done by Eubouleus on 5th century scenes.[89] Furthermore, Triptolemos and Iacchos are guiding initiates or candidates for initiation,[90] and Persephone is presenting votaries to Demeter.[91]

While Hermes leading Persephone is the most prominent guidance figure depicted,[92] we find the idea of a guide leading somebody up to the realm of the gods also transferred to the realm of initiation—candidates for the Mysteries will be guided to their initiation, which is an idea that the secondary literature sees embodied in the figure of a mystago-

---

understands these satyrs as the personification of the pulsating vigour of nature at the beginning of the vegetation period.

89 Cf. Clinton 1992, 71–72 and 135. A depiction of Hermes guiding Persephone can, for instance, be found on the attic red figure bell-krater by the Persephone Painter (New York, Metropolitan Museum No. 28.57.23, ca. 440 BCE); cf. also Nilsson 1935, 137 and Grossman 1959, 362.

90 Cf. Clinton 1992, 72–73. Iacchos can be found as such a guiding figure, for instance, on the attic red figure calyx-krater by the Pourtalès Painter (London, British Museum, F68); cf. Grossman 1959, 368 and Clinton 1992, 68.

91 As does Hecate, identified by inscription, running ahead of Persephone while holding aloft two torches, cf. Grossman 1959, 191. According to Mylonas' interpretation of the Ninnion tablet, the δᾳδοῦχος too seems to have acted as a guide (1961, 213–221).

92 The presence of Hermes seems even to change the significance of the representation of Persephone and Plouton in a *quadriga*. These depictions refer normally to Persephone's κάθοδος. But when Hermes is shown together with Persephone and Plouton and the *quadriga*, this seems to represent Persephone on her return from the underworld, rather than her descent to it. For according to the *Homeric Hymn*, Hermes leads her from the lower world to her reunion with her mother. Cf. Grossman 1959, 183.

gue.⁹³ The guide depicted is himself divine, or closely connected with the divinities, but moving between two realms; either because it is his very job, as in Hermes' case, or because a certain experience has made the guide fitted to move between different realms, as is the case with Persephone.

3) Specific Attributes

Finally, there is a list of recurring central attributes with which the Eleusinian gods and initiantes are depicted, like Demeter sitting on what is identified alternatively as a κίστη, a rock, or a throne, and holding a scepter.⁹⁴ And initiates are often depicted as barefooted, carrying a piglet, and holding a myrtle staff.⁹⁵ Leaving out many of these attributes and their particular changes over time,⁹⁶ we will briefly look at five of these attributes: libation and purification tools, wreaths, pigs, torches, and ears of grain.

We find several depictions of the Eleusinian goddesses where they seem to pour some liquid either over an initiand, seemingly as a kind of purification, or as part of a libation. Both indicate some cultic context.⁹⁷ The wearing of a wreath seems to be a sign of an initiation process. Normally the wreath is worn by the mystai,⁹⁸ but we also find Demeter and Persephone wearing a rayed στεφάνη.⁹⁹ In connection with

---

93 For the notion of a μυσταγωγός see, e.g. Eliade 1978, 294–5. Parker 2005, 345, n. 78 points out that mystagogues are first attested at Eleusis by a decree of the 1ˢᵗ century BCE.
94 E.g. Grossman 1959, 165.
95 Cf. Mylonas 1961, 209, 212 and 317 and Kevin Clinton, "The Sacred Officials of the Eleusinian Mysteries," TAPhS 64.3 (1974): 103–104.
96 For these cf. Grossman's overviews on pp. 148, 220 and 314.
97 Cf. the attic red figure *hydria* by the painter of London, London, British Museum, E 183, 460 BCE, which shows Triptolemnos, Demeter, and Hecate named with Persephone and Plouton. Demeter's right holds an *oinochoe* from which she pours wine, which flows into the *phiale* of Triptolemnos; cf. Clinton 1993, 112–113 and Grossman 1959, 172, 194, 202, 345–46. Burkert 2011, 426–427 also understands the act of Demeter's sitting down on a stool covered by a fleece and covering her face in the *Homeric Hymn* as a purification ceremony (cf. lines 196 ff.).
98 Cf. the sculptures discussed by Mylonas 1961, 203 and Clinton 1974, 108.
99 Grossman 1959, 180. This feature might be already alluded to in the *Homeric Hymn* line 224 where Demeter is called εὐστέφανος. Richardson 1974, *ad locum* points out that "Demeter has a crown of corn in later representations", but thinks that "the epithet [εὐστέφανος] is probably general," as Homer uses it of Artemis, Aphrodite, the heroine Mycene, and Thebes. It is also possible

the Mysteries we also saw a sacrifice of pigs to Persephone in Aristophanes' *Frogs*. In the fine arts, we find, in addition, several depictions of pigs with people who seem to be mystai.[100] Thus it is likely that a sacrifice of pigs was part of the initiation process.[101]

Torches were already a motif in the *Homeric Hymn*: Demeter was holding one when searching for her daughter (δαίς, line 48), as is Hecate (σέλας, line 52). In the fine arts, however, it is mostly Persephone holding one in her hand, probably to look for her way (in the dark underworld?). Like in Aristophanes' *Frogs*, the holding of a torch seems to indicate that the person holding it is surrounded by darkness and thus needs the light of a torch.[102] In addition, the torches seem to get a kind of pointing function with the portable artefacts. For some torches are hold up, the way a torch would normally be held in order to illuminate the way, but some are pointing downwards. As the later position turns the torch towards the earth, Mylonas interprets it as purification and fertilization of the earth by fire when discussing the relief on the upper part of the Rhetoi inscription in the Museum of Eleusis.[103] Grossmann, commenting on the upward and downward position of a torch held by Persephone on a relief plaque from Eleusis, which is the earliest work in sculpture indisputably representing Demeter and Persephone, suggests as a hypothesis "that one torch points upward representing the world of the growing crops and the other torch points downwards

---

that this occurrence of εὐστέφανος should be better translated as well-girdled than well-crowned. However, on the Ninnion tablet the mystai as well as the deities seem to wear wreaths, a feature that thus closely connects humans and gods.

100 For instance on the relief *hydra* from Cumae known as "Regina Vasorum" (St. Petersburg, Hermitage St. 525); cf. Clinton 1992, 78–79. Grossman 1959, 166 gives a description of a depiction of Demeter and Persephone standing with votive figures of a woman, a man, a child, and a pig led by the child (Paris, Musée du Louvre [plate VII, 2]). Cf. also from Eleusis the statue of a woman bearing a piglet and a torch (Paris, Musée du Louvre MNB 1714, ca. 430–400 BCE).

101 For the sacrifice of pigs in connection with the Eleusinian Mysteries, cf. also Mylonas 1961, 201–203.

102 Cf., e.g., the Regina Vasorum; the attic red figure krater by the Pourtalès Painter (London, British Museum F68); the red figure pelike by the Eleusian Painter (St. Petersburg, Heremitage St. 1792); all of them in Clinton 1992, 134, and Simon 1983, plates 8 and 10; cf. also Simon 1983, 34. Nilsson 1935, 99 describes a *hydra* in the museum of Eleusis from the end of the 5th century showing a procession of mystai carrying torches, which he takes to be "die beste Darstellung der fackeltragenden Mysten, die wir besitzen."

103 Mylonas 1961, 193, n. 21.

towards the underworld, the resting place for the seeds."[104] In general, a torch pointing towards the earth might also be read as a symbol of death and dying, of perishing and thus becoming part of the earth, which, however, in the case of the grain is the necessary condition for new life.

Given that Demeter and Persephone were both goddesses of vegetation or agriculture,[105] that in the *Homeric Hymn* Demeter stopped all vegetation during Persephone's stay in the underworld, and that Persephone's return is often seen as alluding to the fate of a seed, it seems to be very natural to find both goddesses with the attribute of a grain in their hand. Isocrates names two gifts of Demeter to humankind: the Eleusinian Mysteries on the one hand, and the fruits of the earth (καρπός) and the handing over of seeds to Triptolemos on the other.[106] The handing-over of seeds to Triptolemos, one of the nobles at Eleusis, in order to bring agriculture and thus also civilization to humankind is a popular motive in vase painting[107] in the transitional and classical period.[108] Given that grain was a basic food source necessary for life, holding and handing over grains to human beings signifies the role of the goddesses for the continuation of human life. In the much later source of the Naassene Gnostic from the 2nd century CE mentioned above, show-

---

104 Grossmann 1959, 147.
105 Richardson 1974, 13 understands them as deities of grain and vegetation in general, while Nilsson 1935, 101 thinks of them not as deities of vegetation as such but specifically of agriculture (of "*Getreideanbau*").
106 Cf. *Panegyricus* 28.
107 Its most prominent depiction might be the Grand Relief of Eleusis in the National Archeological Museum of Athens from around 440 BCE, in which Demeter and Persephone seem to send off Triptolemos with some seeds. Clinton 1992, 50 ff. and Parker 2005, 337, however, interpret the naked boy between Demeter and Persephone not as Triptolemos but as Ploutos.
108 Cf. Mylonas 1961, 197. According to Richardson 1974, 9, the motive of Triptolemos receiving grain and agriculture from Demeter and communicating it to the rest of humankind "first appears on Attic vases of the mid-sixth century, and is particularly frequent in the first half of the fifth century. The *Hymn*, however, actually excludes this story, by presupposing that agriculture was already in existence before the Rape of Persephone," as can be taken from lines 305 ff; cf. also 450 ff. and 470 ff. and Richardson's notes *ad locum*. Nilsson 1935, 129 thinks that the spreading of this myth of Triptolemos is connected with a certain glorious image of themselves, which the Athenians wanted to bring about. As a reccurring motive in the reliefs we find wheat in Demeter's and Persephone's hands; cf., e.g., the attic red figure neck-amphora by Polygnotos (London, British Museum, E281, 450–430 BCE), and Grossman 1959, 203 and 219.

ing a reaped ear of grain is understood as an integral part of the Mysteries.

The document probably most prominent for the Eleusinian cult, the πίναξ of Ninnion, shows many of the features already mentioned: joyful dancing, candidates being guided to their initiation, lit torches pointing upwards and downwards, and wreaths worn by the mystai as well as by the deities are clearly depicted. However, not only is there no consensus about several of the details depicted—for instance whether the white semi-oval in the lower part of the πίναξ is an ὀμφαλός, a πελανός, or yet something else.[109] More importantly, it is not clear whether we are actually dealing with one or several scenes.

According to all interpretations, the tablet depicts a procession of initiands and guidance figures (priests or gods) towards the Eleusinian deities. But scholars differ on how many processions are represented, as well as on who are the initiands, the goddesses, and the guiding figures in question. Skias, who first published the tablet, understands it as one single composition depicting the πρόσοδος, the ceremonial advent of the mystai, to Demeter.[110] Nilsson interprets the tablet as two scenes, since we have Demeter seated twice on the right hand side (Nilsson, as well as Mylonas, considers the sceptre in the hand of the two female goddess on the right as a clear attribute of Demeter). In each case Demeter is approached by a procession. Persephone's absence and return is the crucial feature distinguishing the two scenes according to Nilsson: he reads the lower scene in which Persephone is missing as the advent of the mystai in Eleusis, while he understands the upper scene as the procession of the mystai being guided by Persephone to her mother. A slightly different two-scene-interpretation can be found in Svoronos,[111] who assumes the lower scene to depict the presentation of Ninnion, the dedicator of the tablet, by a δᾳδοῦχος to Persephone and thus as showing parts of the Lesser Mysteries; by contrast, he reads the upper scene as the presentation of Ninnion by Persephone to Demeter, and thus as referring to the Greater Mysteries.

---

109 Nilsson 1935 assumes it to be an ὀμφαλός while Mylonas 1961, 217–218 argues for interpreting it as a πελανός, the sacred cake of wheat and barely to be offered as a preliminary sacrifice in the Great Mysteries. Cf. also Clinton 1992, 121–123.
110 Cf. A. Skias, "Eleusiniakai keramographiai," *AE* (1901): 1–39.
111 J.N. Svoronos, "Hermêneia tou ex Eleusinos mustêriakou pinakos tês Niiniou," *Journal international d'archéologie numismatique* 4 (1901): 233–270.

Finally, Mylonas interprets the πίναξ as depicting three scenes,[112] since according to his reading we can recognize the same mortal woman that might be Ninnion—she is bearing the Eleusian κέρνος— and the same bearded man accompanying her thrice: in the lower scene, in the upper scene, as well as in the pedimental triangle. Mylonas interprets the lower scene as the public part of the Greater Mysteries with the procession approaching Demeter. Demeter is sitting next to an empty seat, which is kept for absent Persephone. Since the Lesser Mysteries were allegedly Persephone's, she cannot be absent from them. Thus, according to Mylonas, the scene cannot belong to the Lesser Mysteries, but has to belong to the Greater ones.[113] The guiding figure in this procession he assumes to be Iacchos, holding down one torch as a sign of respectfully greeting Demeter. The upper scene refers to the Lesser Mysteries in Mylonas' interpretation, since they were held in Athens, which fits the fact that here, in contrast to the lower scene, the mystai do not carry walking staffs and bags. Besides, the Ionic column could refer to the temple at the bank of Ilissos, the area where the Lesser Mysteries seem to have been held. Like Nilsson, Mylonas interprets the guiding figure of this scene as Persephone, who presents Ninnion and her bearded companion to Demeter. Finally, the scene in the pedimental triangle he reads as the παννυχίς, the night long revel that followed the arrival of the mystai at Eleusis. What is important for our purposes is that all interpretations that understand the Ninnion tablet as representing more than one scene suggest that there were different steps of initiation.

d) The Archeological Site

Although the findings of archeology are probably the oldest testimonies of the Eleusinian cult we have,[114] for our purposes they do not help very much. Among the architectural remains clearly connected with the

---

112 Cf. Mylonas 1961, 213–221.
113 Parker 2005, 344 n. 76 thinks that the "claim in Σ vet. Ar. Plut. 845b that *Greater Mysteries* belonged to Demeter, *Lesser* to Kore is pure schematism," without, however, giving any argument for this claim.
114 So Richardson 1974, 12–13 and K. Kuruniotis, "Das Eleusinische Heiligtum von den Anfängen bis zur Vorperikleischen Zeit," *Archiv für Religionswissenschaft* 32 (1935): 52–78.

Mysteries is a τελεστήριον,[115] a large hall for the celebration of the Mysteries, and a firm περίβολος on a rising hillock, below the ancient city of Eleusis and close to a cave and a well. There are some old remains from the Bronze Age on the excavation site, and Mylonas argues for the identification of the temple of Demeter with what he calls Megaron B, which he dates as reaching back to the 15th century BCE.[116] But most scholars today, as for instance Camp, Clinton, and Darque, for various reasons no longer believe that these Bronze Age remains are connected to the Mysteries of Eleusis. Rather, it seems that there is no certain evidence of cult activity at Eleusis, such as votive offerings and piles of ash, before the 8th century BCE; and the oldest Telesterion seems to date to the end of the seventh or early sixth century.[117]

The τελεστήριον Plato would have known about was the one built during the time of Pericles (and before the new work of Philon). It seems to have been erected as a kind of compromise[118] after the Persians had burnt down the older one.[119] This τελεστήριον is situated on an artificially terraced slope at the foot of the acropolis of Eleusis within a court. According to Noack's reconstruction, it was a rectangular hall with 6 times 7 columns, which contained galleries but no full second floor. There was a centrally located ἀνάκτορον, the most holy place

---

115 For a discussion of the terms "Telesterion" and "Anaktoron" cf. Clinton 1992, Appendix 7, 126–132.
116 Mylonas 1961, 36–49.
117 Cf. Camp 2001, 284; Kevin Clinton, "The Sanctuary of Demeter and Kore at Eleusis," in *Greek Sanctuaries: New Approaches*, ed. Nanno Marinatos and Robin Hagg (London: Routledge, 1993), 114; and Pascal Darcque, "Les vestiges mycéniens découverts sous le Telestérion d'Éleusis," *BCH* 105.2, (1981): 593–605. Cf. also Greg Anderson, *The Athenian Experiment: Building an Imagined Political Community in Ancient Attica 508–490B.C.* (Ann Arbor: University of Michigan Press, 2003), 188.
118 A comprehensive plan by the architect Kimon seems to have been taken up in the beginning. It was, however, never fully implemented, and finally was merged in the again only partially implemented plans of Iktinos; cf. Noack 1927, *ad locum*.
119 However, T. Leslie Shear, "The Demolished Temple at Eleusis," in *Studies in Athenian Architecture, Sculpture and Topography, presented to Homer A. Thompson* (Princeton: American School of Classical Studies at Athens, 1982), 128–140 argues that the Persian invasion came at a time when the Archaic Telesterion had already been largely dismantled on behalf of the Eleusian officials in order to give way to a new building twice its capacity, so that the Persians actually only sacked the Anaktoron.

where the ἱερόν would be kept, with an ὀπαῖον admitting air and light above, and raised tiers of steps lining the room on all four sides.[120]

According to Noack, we can negatively infer from this archeological reconstruction that the τελεστήριον would not have been equipped for a full blown staging of the journey to the underworld. For it does not have, as some people, most notably Foucart[121] assumed, two different full stories, which would be required for such a staging to take place on two different levels—descending from the higher level to the lower one. The set up of the τελεστήριον and the central arrangement of the ἀνάκτορον, which might have been only accessible to the highest priest in which case it would have been closed off from the rest of the room, would not allow for a dramatic staging in the normal Greek sense.[122] Moreover, given the limited space and the numerous columns in the τελεστήριον, Noack believes that the initiands cannot have been actively participating in any part of the ceremony that would have involved them moving, though this obviously also depends on the number of candidates for initiation in the τελεστήριον at any given time.

The only thing that we can positively infer from the archaeological remains for our purposes is that they set the scene for various light effects, especially with the help of the separate grotto and the windowless τελεστήριον with an ὀπαῖον above the centrally located ἀνάκτορον, which could be at times closed off from the rest of the room.[123] The different sources of light we saw mentioned in the primary literature might have been used here—torches could have been used in the grotto or during a nightly celebration in the τελεστήριον; and the ὀπαῖον would have allowed for some daylight effects, for instance, if the celebrations did, as many scholars believe, extend till dawn.[124] In this way, the archeological remains confirm that different kinds of light—for orientation and revelation, respectively—might have been used in Eleusis.

---

120 Noack 1927, 219–221 and 139–201.
121 Paul François Foucart, *Les Mystères d'Éleusis* (Paris: Picard, 1914).
122 Cf. Noack 1927, 235ff, and Richardson 1974, 25.
123 Noack 1927 thinks that it was closed off with the help of curtains which could be removed at least in parts.
124 For instance when, as Noack 1927 suggests, the curtains closing off the τελεστήριον were to be removed all of a sudden.

III. Conclusions—and Connections with the *Symposium*

Having gone through the pre-Platonic sources for the Eleusinian Mysteries with an eye to their attraction for Plato as a template, let us finally sum up the evidence we found and hint at some points Plato will take up in his *Symposium*: in the *Homeric Hymn* we are given the image of two realms normally kept apart, which are either "geographically" (if we want to understand the underworld and Mount Olympus in such a way) or ontologically distinct (at least the distinction between mortals and immortals could be understood like that). While bridging the gap between them is highly unusual, we are shown that it is indeed possible. It is a bridging that employs the notion of getting from somewhere lower to somewhere higher, so the bridging is an ascent (cf. the *Homeric Hymn* and the depiction of Persephone's ascent on portable artefacts). This ascent seems to be connected with different steps (the notion of different steps we might see hinted at in the *Homeric Hymn*, and we have seen it clearly indicated in the *Frogs*; depending on one's interpretation of the Ninnion tablet, there might also be a prominent example among the portable artefacts). While in principle every Greek can be initiated (as Herodotus points out, with the exception of those guilty of murder, as Isocrates specifies), some preparatory steps are required. These steps seem to include some kind of purification (which we have found in Sophocles' *Oedipus at Colonus* and the portable artefacts); the sacrifice of a pig (which we have seen represented in the *Frogs* and the portable artefacts);[125] and a certain dose of ridicule (which we have found in the *Homeric Hymn* as well as in the *Frogs*). We also find the notion of a guide leading the ascent (which we have seen represented in the figure of Hermes in the *Homeric Hymn* and the portable artefacts); and the idea that the initiands that are to be guided, as well as sometimes the deities, are wearing some kind of wreath.

The image of bridging two realms in thought by ascending, step by step, from one to the other under the leadership of a guide is a central feature of Plato's account of the ascent to the Form of Beauty in the *Symposium* —as a close reading of 209e5–211d3 shows. The two realms employed by Plato are the world of the sensible, bodily things on the one hand, and the realm of intelligible things on the other. Like a mys-

---

125 Mylonas 1961, 249 and others see a ritual of cleansing at the sea and the sacrifice of a piglet as characteristic of the so-called Lower Mysteries, the Mysteries of Persephone held near Illisos.

tagogue Diotima is introduced as guarding her charge Socrates through a series of steps, ascending in intelligibility, towards the divine knowledge of what truly and eternally is, to the knowledge of the *auto to theion kalon*.

The ascent in the *Symposium* is connected with another feature of the sources we looked at: the sudden revelation of something wonderful. After a laborious ascent something that was hidden before can all of a sudden be seen, and that means also understood. This corresponds to Demeter's sudden disclosure of herself, of her identity. Someone seemingly very mortal, an old woman, can suddenly be seen and understood as being immortal, as the goddess Demeter. In the *Hymn to Demeter* this sudden insight into the true nature of something is accompanied by light as bright as a lightening. In the sources we looked at, such a revelation was not explicitly connected with an ascent, though it may seem like a natural climax of an ascent connected with initiation. And most of the reconstructions of the Mysteries in the secondary literature join the sequence of steps of initiation together with a final revelation.[126] A light metaphor which is indeed connected with an ascent we found in the *Homeric Hymn*, where Hermes led Persephone out of misty darkness to the light of the world above, the guide for the ascent leads the guidee from darkness to the light of the living.[127]

A further dominant function connected with the rich light metaphors of our sources is that of orientation: the lit torches in the underworld allow the mystai in the *Frogs* to find their way; Demeter uses a lit torch when searching for her daughter; and on vase paintings and reliefs Persephone is normally depicted with a torch. Orientation as well as revelation through the use of light is also provided for in what we can reconstruct from the architectural remains.

With the portable artefacts, torches also seem to have a pointing function, pointing either up or down to the earth. We saw that these

---

[126] The general idea in the secondary literature seems to be that in the final ritual of the Highest Mysteries the candidates for initiation in Eleusis experienced a sudden switch from prevailing darkness to light, when the ἱεροφάντης opened the ἀνάκτορον, in which he had kindled a fire. If it is then assumed that on the background of this fire the ἱερά were shown to the initiands, the ἱερά could become a gleaming appearance of divine nature. This reconstruction seem to rest strongly on Plutarch's testimony, cf., e.g., Mylonas 1961, 228, "Plutarch's reference to the brilliant light in the midst of which the Hierophant appeared when the Anaktoron was opened," and Plutarch, *de profect. virt.* 81e.

[127] For the contrast of light and darkness, cf. also Richardson 1974, 26.

different directions of the torches are probably also referring to life and death (upwards indicating the growth of the crops, downwards referring to dying and thus to becoming part of the earth). Life and death and their connection is also alluded to by the images of the grain with the portable artefacts, perhaps taken up by the vegetation references in the *Frogs*, and clearly present when establishing a mythos of the seasons in the *Homeric Hymn*.[128]

Continuous life in spite of death and continuous life without death characterize the two kinds of immortality we came across in the *Homeric Hymn*: the first was the result of the continuation of natural life through the death of one and the birth of another individual, as we found it in the vegetation cycle established in the *Homeric Hymn*. The second was aimed at when Demeter tried to bestow eternal life to a single individual. Both kinds of immortality will be shown to be taken up prominently in Plato's *Symposium* in the next part of my project. There I will also demonstrate how the seriousness and promise of the Mysteries to improve your life here and give you hope for a life after death[129] is imported into Plato's theory with the template of the Eleusinian Mysteries.

Given that some of the features we established here as characteristic of the Eleusinian Mysteries might seem to be also general features of mystery cults and religious practices—in contrast to the later and more specific testimonies of the Naassene Gnostic, Plutarch, and Clement—, in the continuation of my project I will give some further support for the claim that this imagery, as taken up by Plato, does indeed refer to Eleusinian practices and not to any of the other mystery cults. What I hope this current paper did establish is to clarify the features of the Mysteries that could have been attractive for Plato. I tried to reconstruct these features by looking carefully only at pre-Platonic sources. And I attempted to demonstrate that these sources, which are normally neglected and only squeezed into a framework erected mostly independently of them, can in fact provide us with some evidence of the Eleusinian Mysteries. Not, of course, with such a rich account as the later sources provide, but with enough to get an idea of the features cen-

---

128 Cf. also Richardson 1974, 13–14, where he draws a connection between the different Demeter and Persephone cults and the important stages in the farming year.
129 Richardson 1974, 15 understands the Mysteries as granting "prosperity in this life, and happiness after death."

tral to the Eleusinian Mysteries that Plato could use as a template in his *Symposium*.

Plato's Soteriology?*

Stephen Menn

"Soteriology" starts as the name of a subdiscipline of Christian dogmatic theology. It is often treated immediately after Christology, but the name does not mean "doctrine of the savior" (which would presumably be soterology or the like), but "doctrine of salvation, σωτηρία." For a Christian, it seems that salvation is the main aim of religious thought and practice, and thus soteriology should be an important part of theology. Nor is a concern with salvation exclusively Christian, or exclusively Abrahamic: it seems fair to translate Sanskrit "*mukti*" or "*mokṣa*," release from the cycle of rebirth, as "salvation." Most Indian religious practice is not aimed at *mokṣa*—far more of it is directed toward success in this life, or toward gaining a good rebirth. But given the expectation of rebirth, and thus also of redeath, the question also arises whether we can somehow be released from the cycle. We might hope to attain *mokṣa* through understanding the inner meaning of ritual practices, or through devotion to a god, but perhaps also through philosophy, through making systematic inferences from sense-perception and internalizing the conclusions by meditation. So it is reasonable to speak of, say, Buddhist or Sâṃkhya soteriology. And it is natural to ask whether the concept of salvation is also important in ancient Greek religion; and, assuming that it is, whether philosophical as well as ritual practices, in Greece as in India, can be described as paths to salvation, so that we could speak of Greek philosophical soteriology.

In this paper I will focus on the case of Plato. Plato is the first Greek philosopher from whom we have a substantial corpus of texts, which we can compare with the language of Greek religion; in particular, he uses the words σωτήρ, σωτηρία, and σῴζειν often enough that we can make judgments about the range of meanings and associations that they have for him, both religious and otherwise. And Plato seems like a good candidate for a Greek philosopher who, like many Indian philosophers,

---

* I would like to thank Tad Brennan, Sarah Broadie, Renaud Gagné, Rachana Kamtekar, Kathryn Morgan, and Christian Wildberg for comments on earlier drafts of this paper.

wants philosophical argument and the internalization of philosophical doctrine to yield a salvation or release from the cycle of rebirth: he might be seen as building on religious notions of salvation as a reversal of a primal fall into the body, begun perhaps by the Orphics and introduced into the philosophical tradition perhaps by Empedocles. To anticipate my conclusions, σωτῆρες and σωτηρία are indeed an important theme in Greek religion; they are also an important theme in Plato, whose variations can be pursued across several dialogues, and in a significant number of the passages where Plato speaks of a σωτήρ or σωτηρία or σῴζειν we can see that he is exploiting religious connotations of these terms, and competing with more traditional religious saviors and practices of salvation, or with earlier philosophers who were also drawing on those same religious connotations. And to this extent we can describe Plato's concerns in these passages as religious.

But to say that these concerns are religious does not mean that they are eschatological. When a Greek god or hero is called a σωτήρ of some individual or collectivity, he is usually being asked to save us, or praised for having saved us, in this life rather than beyond it, just as when God is called the σωτήρ of Israel in the Septuagint; and when "σωτήρ" and its cognates are used with religious connotations in the philosophical tradition, in Plato and before him and after him, their application remains equally this-worldly. There are apparently just two passages in Plato where the terms are applied in an eschatological context, and, as we will see, even here the concept is not intrinsically eschatological. The context of Greek religion is helpful in understanding Plato's concept of salvation precisely because it forces us to critically reexamine the concept of salvation, and to question the assumption that if salvation is religious it must be a salvation beyond (or from) this life, and an individual rather than a public or political salvation.

I. Σωτῆρες and Σωτηρία in Greek Religion

Greek religion is not directed, like Christianity, to one single great σωτηρία. But it too speaks of salvation, and in particular makes frequent use of "σωτήρ" (more highly loaded than the verb σῴζειν, and even than σωτηρία, whose sense often comes directly from the verb rather than from σωτήρ) as an epithet for a god or hero.[1] Zeus is the σωτήρ

---

1   Much of the literature on saviors and salvation in Greek religion comes in the

par excellence (so in the set phrase τὸ τρίτον τῷ σωτῆρι, coming from offering the third drink at a symposium to Zeus; Zeus need not even be named), but this attribute is shared by many gods. Indeed, if I am exemplary in worshipping and sacrificing to a god when times are good, it is natural to hope that he would save me, would come to my rescue, in a moment of danger, and if he does so I will gratefully commemorate his saving power in a hymn of thanksgiving or a temple-dedication. Thus Croesus blames Apollo for not saving him, but in the end Apollo does save him, by extinguishing the fire that is about to consume him, and according to Bacchylides by transporting him to the land of the Hyperboreans, in recompense for his many offerings.[2]

---

form of encyclopedia articles in classical and theological encyclopedias, and articles on the background to Christianity. Typical of the older literature, and still worth consulting despite their biases, are Paul Wendland, " Σωτήρ," *Zeitschrift für die neutestamentliche Wissenschaft* v.5 (1904), 335–53, and Franz Dornseiff, "Soter," in *Pauly-Wissowa*, 2nd series, vol. 3.1 (Stuttgart: Metzler, 1921), 1211–21. (Much of the older literature follows Hermann Usener, *Götternamen: Versuch einer Lehre von der religiösen Begriffsbildung* [Bonn: Friedrich Cohen, 1896], in thinking that ὁ σωτήρ was originally a Sondergott, i. e., not a full personality but a primitive conceptual expression of the experience of salvation, so that a phrase like Ζεὺς ὁ σωτήρ must come from identifying the originally independent Sondergott σωτήρ with the later personal god Zeus. This may well reflect a Christian privileging of the concept of salvation.) For a brief survey with references to more recent literature, see Klaus Zimmermann's article "Soter," in *Der Neue Pauly*, vol. 11, ed. Hubert Cancik and Helmuth Schneider (Stuttgart: Metzler, 2003), 752–3. There is also much that is relevant in the considerable literature on Hellenistic and Roman ruler-cult, for which see references below. In being guided by Greek authors' use of "σωτήρ" and "σῴζειν" and their cognates, I am taking a different approach from much (especially Italian) scholarship which consciously uses a concept of salvation taken from comparative religious typology and not, as far as I can see, corresponding to any Greek conception: see, for instance, Dario Sabbatucci, *Saggio sul misticismo Greco*, 2nd ed. (Rome: Edizioni dell' Ateneo & Bizzarri, 1979). It would also be possible to explore Greek religious uses of "λύειν" and related words, sometimes conflated with the "σῴζειν" family in the scholarly literature (it is above all Dionysus who λύει, literally from bonds and by extension from other kinds of constraint or penalty), but in Plato this is likely to lead in a quite different direction, and probably with fewer benefits.

2   Bacchylides 3,23–62 and Herodotus I,87 and I,90–91. In Bacchylides, strictly speaking it is Zeus who puts out the fire (by bringing a cloud and raining, 53–6), and then Apollo transports Croesus to the Hyperboreans (58–62), but it is Apollo who "protects" Croesus after Zeus brings about the Persian capture of Sardis (25–9). In Herodotus I,87 it is not said what god, if any, brings

There are, in particular, many gods who save sailors from shipwreck and drowning, such as Poseidon "savior of ships" (*Homeric Hymn to Poseidon* 5), Leukothea and her son Palaimon (e.g., Orphic *Hymns* 74–5), and the gods of Samothrace (famously mocked by Diagoras of Melos, see Diogenes Laertius VI,59 and Cicero *De natura deorum* III,89). But it is above all the Dioscuri who save from shipwreck and drowning, and their broader function as saviors is an extension from this case.[3] When Simonides in a victory ode praised the Dioscuri too much and his patron Scopas too little, Scopas told him to collect half of his fee from the Dioscuri; two strangers then came to the door and asked to speak with Simonides, and after Simonides had stepped out of the banqueting-hall, the roof collapsed and all inside were killed, only Simonides having been saved.[4] Someone might also be saved, not from fire

---

the cloud, but it happens after Croesus has prayed to Apollo, and in I,91 the Pythia says that Apollo rescued (ἐπήρκεσε) Croesus when he was burning.

3   This is clear notably from Euripides *Helen*, 1495–1511 and 1658–65, where the Dioscuri are σωτῆρε of their sister Helen; so too the *Homeric Hymn to the Dioscuri* 6–7, where the Dioscuri are "saviors of men on land and of swift-traveling ships," only the latter thought being developed in detail. Likewise in the Orphic hymn to Palaimon (*Hymn* 75), he should "save the initiates both on land and on sea"—I see no reason to take this anything but literally.

4   There are several versions of the Simonides story, and there were others circulating in antiquity that are now lost to us: extant are Callimachus Fr. 64 Pfeiffer (a fictional epitaph for Simonides; see the information collected by Pfeiffer in his apparatus), Cicero *De oratore* II,351–3, Quintilian *Institutio oratoria* XI,2,11–16 (referring to many variants of the story told by different authors, none of which Quintilian believes), and, very briefly, Libanius at the end of *Oration* 5. Only Libanius uses σώζειν, but Callimachus has "you who put me outside [ἐκτὸς ἔθεσθε] a hall that was about to collapse, alone of all the banqueters," which is close, since transporting someone out of a threatening situation, sometimes (as with Croesus in Bacchylides) to the happy margins of the world, is a standard mode of salvation (and the Latin sources can't be blamed for not using the Greek word σώζειν, and Latin has no real equivalent). Quintilian XI,2,16 says that one reason he doesn't believe at least the part about the Dioscuri is that Simonides never mentions it, but at XI,2,14 he says that it appears from something by Simonides himself that the house was in Pharsalus: so apparently there was a poem by Simonides (or attributed to Simonides) around which the legend accreted. According to Cicero and Quintilian, the Dioscuri were in the myth of Simonides' victory ode, and Scopas felt that the myth eclipsed the accomplishments of the living which the ode was supposed to celebrate. Both Cicero and Quintilian tell the story as an aetiological myth of the discovery of the art of memory: the bodies of the banqueters are damaged beyond recognition, but Simonides remembers who was sitting where, and so is able to restore each corpse to its respective family for burial; and so he discovers

or from drowning or its analogue, but from disease, and Apollo and Asclepius are often called saviors in this sense.

Just as an individual or a ship can be saved, so can a city, and if a city has been saved not by a god but by a mortal, this is a good reason to worship him as a hero. To be the founder (κτίστης or οἰκιστής) of the city is the best justification for hero cult, but a savior, someone who is responsible for the continued existence of the city, is almost a second founder, and so, for instance, at Alexandria there are continuing cults both of Alexander and of Πτολεμαῖος ὁ σωτήρ; being a savior is a stronger justification for cult than being a mere benefactor of the city (εὐεργέτης). A city can be saved, most obviously, from military defeat and conquest: thus when Brasidas defended Amphipolis against the Athenians, and was fatally wounded in the battle, the Amphipolitans gave him heroic burial and a yearly heroic festival, considering him their σωτήρ and quasi-οἰκιστής and diverting to him the honors they had previously given to their original Athenian οἰκιστής (Thucydides V,11). But someone who reconciles opposing factions and so saves a city from civil war might also be called a savior, and so might someone who saves the city from a tyrant. This was the justification of the cult at Sicyon of Aratus, whom the Sicyonians buried "as οἰκιστής and σωτήρ of the city," setting up an annual sacrifice to him, the Σωτήρια, on the anniversary of the day he overthrew the tyranny (Plutarch *Aratus* 53—Σωτήρια is the standard name for any festival commemorating a σωτηρία); likewise for the cult at Athens of the "savior gods" Antigonus Monophthalmus and De-

---

the system of memorization by storing visual images in "palaces." So perhaps not only Simonides is "saved," but also the memory-images of the other banqueters, and also their corpses. There is also an epigram attributed to Simonides, "This [man] is the savior of Simonides of Ceos, [this man] who, though dead, rendered/returned χάρις" to the living" (*Greek Anthology* VII,77): several sources explain that Simonides found an unburied corpse and gave it a proper burial; in gratitude it warned him not to set sail as he was planning, he tried to persuade the sailors not to go but they set sail without him, and so they all drown and he alone is saved. (The texts are briefly cited, with references to parallels, in D.L. Page, *Epigrammata Graeca* [Oxford: Clarendon Press, 1975] and *Further Greek Epigrams* [Cambridge: Cambridge University Press, 1981], under Simonides Epigrams LXXXIV-LXXXV.) The stories are different but both illustrate the wisdom and piety of Simonides, both involve his helping to bury a corpse that would otherwise have remained without proper burial, and in both cases his piety is rewarded by a "salvation," in one case from shipwreck and drowning, in the other case from something analogous to shipwreck and by gods who typically save from shipwreck.

metrius Poliorcetes, who had saved the city from the tyranny of Demetrius of Phalerum (Plutarch *Demetrius* 9–10; what counts as tyranny, or as liberation, can naturally be contested).[5] The most obvious reason to assimilate "saving" a city from a tyrant to saving it from foreign conquest is that in either case the citizens are saved from enslavement, whether to a fellow-citizen or to a foreigner; with more sophistication, it might also be said that the continued existence of the city depends on the preservation of its πολιτεία, that if the πολιτεία were destroyed, whether through foreign conquest or through tyranny or civil war, the collectivity would not survive even if the individuals who constituted it continue to exist.

So far we have been speaking of saviors who secure the continued existence of persons or collectivities. But it is also possible to speak of the σωτηρία of someone's external possessions, his health, his knowledge (so in the *Republic* courage is the "σωτηρία ... of the opinion, generated by the law by means of education, about what things and what

---

[5] See also the Syracusan examples of Gelon and Dion, cited below. The title and sometimes the formal cult of a σωτήρ were given by various Greek cities, through gratitude or coercion in varying measures, to many Hellenistic kings and then to Roman senators, first to Titus Flamininus when he proclaimed at the Isthmian games that the Greek cities should be free and ungarrisoned and untaxed and should observe their ancestral laws (Plutarch *Titus* 10), later of course to emperors. Antiochus I and later Attalus I took the title of σωτήρ after "saving" the Greek cities and cult places by defeating the Gauls. There is a large literature on all this. There is an excellent discussion of the evidence for Greek cities' cults of Hellenistic kings (not of Roman senators or emperors) in Christian Habicht, *Gottmenschtum und Griechische Städte*, 2nd ed. (Munich: C.H. Beck, 1970); for a recent overview, with references to more recent literature, see Angelos Chaniotis, "The Divinity of Hellenistic Rulers," in *A Companion to the Hellenistic World*, ed. Andrew Erskine (Oxford: Blackwell, 2003), 431–45. If Antigonus and Demetrius at Athens, or Ptolemy I and his queen at Alexandria (and Dion at Syracuse according to Plutarch *Dion* 46), are specifically savior *gods* rather than heroes, this is in part because they have no real or notional gravesite at which to perform hero cult. They are at least potentially in competition with more traditional divine or heroic saviors, and this becomes explicit in Hermocles' notorious hymn to Demetrius (Athenaeus VI,63), which praises the addressee not only by likening him to the traditional gods, and making him the son of Poseidon and Aphrodite, but also by saying that "other gods either are far away, or do not have ears, or do not exist, or pay no attention to us, whereas you we see present, not a wooden or stone [representation], but real"; and, on the basis of this flattery, prays him to eliminate the Aitolian threat (the "Sphinx") from Greece, thus in effect to save Greece, although no form of "σῴζειν" is used.

kinds of things are to be feared," IV 429c5–8); sometimes the word should just be translated "preservation," and it does not always have religious connotations. But very often it does. It is one thing to say that Agesilaus was often responsible for rescuing his comrades from danger on military expeditions and for securing their safe return, another to say that his comrades in such ventures called him μετὰ θεοὺς σωτῆρα (Xenophon *Agesilaus* 11,13). Likewise it is one thing to say that the eyelids serve to protect the power of vision in the eyes, another to speak of "the σωτηρία which the gods contrived [ἐμηχανήσαντο] for vision, the nature of the eyelids" (*Timaeus* 45d7-e1). In both cases these authors are using the religious connotations of σωτηρία, and the mention of the gods, at least to amplify the power of the description: the phrase in Xenophon comes at the climax of a series of attributes of Agesilaus, and is intended to suggest, if not seriously to imply, that Agesilaus has the status of a hero. Even in the *Republic* IV definition of courage, "σωτηρία" means more than just a tendency to persist in some bodily or psychic condition: it is a background assumption that a city's courage is its σωτηρία, and then the distinctively Socratic contribution is that the way it saves the city is cognitive, by preserving in the military class the conviction that death and bodily suffering are not to be feared, and that vice and dishonor are.

II. Philosophers on Σωτηρία: Background to Plato

In investigating whether Greek philosophers have a philosophical soteriology, and whether they see themselves as offering a path to salvation, the obvious first step is to look at their use of "σωτήρ" and "σωτηρία" and "σῴζειν," to examine whether they are using the religious connotations of these words to persuade the reader that philosophy, or philosophical abstractions such as λόγος or virtue, or the philosophers themselves, have better title to be called saviors than the traditional objects of worship; if so, we can also ask what implications this has for their conceptions of their philosophical project. In fact it is clear that Greek philosophers did sometimes use the language of salvation in this way, and not necessary "otherworldly" philosophers: as LSJ note s.v., "σωτήρ" is said especially of Epicurus, and it is part of the justification of his cult. Salvation is here most often from something that can be compared to shipwreck or drowning. The Stoics do not often speak of σωτηρία (except as the gods' providential preservation of living things), but when they compare the person who is progressing but is not yet virtuous to someone drowning just a cubit below the surface (Plutarch *On Common Notions Against the Stoics* 1063 A-B = SVF III,539), they are implicitly comparing wisdom or virtue to salvation from drowning.[6] Lucretius speaks of watching from shore as others toss in the waves from which we are now free (II,1–2), and he says that Epicurus, who through his art brought human life out of such great waves, must be called a god (V,6–12). But Plato has the advantage, over later as well as earlier philosophers, of having left us a large enough corpus, and enough texts talking about salvation or saviors, that we can use these texts to determine the function of the concept of salvation within his philosophical project.

Not all occurrences of these words in Plato (in particular, not all uses of the verb σώζειν) have religious connotations, but in many cases it is clear that Plato is responding to earlier religious uses of the language of σωτηρία, either uses in civic religion or uses by earlier philosophers or quasi-philosophers, including those represented by characters in Plato's dialogues, who are in turn responding to uses in civic religion. And indeed there is an easy continuity between uses in civic religion and uses by 5th-century intellectuals. Polytheism is always to some degree competitive—in praising a god I will try to show that he is as worthy of praise as the other gods, or more so—and new gods were constantly being introduced, whether into official or private cult or merely into religious discourse. Abstractions such as peace or concord or δίκη or ἔρως are described as if they were gods, and there is no clear line to mark when this is mere hyperbole and when a new god has been added to the complex.[7] In the *Symposium*, near the climax of a Gorgianically excessive praise of ἔρως as a god, after a long series of attributes, Agathon says that ἔρως is "in toils, in fear, in passion, in speech the best steersman [κυβερνήτης] guard, defender and σωτήρ" (197e8-d2). But it is characteristic of the sophists to attribute to τέχναι, and thus to their human bearers, what had traditionally been attributed to the gods. Thus Euthyphro says that "if someone understands how in his prayers and sacrifices

---

6 There is explicit use of σώζειν or σωτηρία in Marcus Aurelius XII,29 and in the text of Epictetus *Discourses* IV,1 cited in a footnote below, but it is not clear whether these go back to anything in the Old Stoa.

7 On these issues see now Emma Stafford, *Worshipping Virtues* (London: Duckworth, 2000), especially the discussion of ancient and modern theories of personification in chapter 1.

to say and to do things gratifying to the gods, then these are pious things, and such things save both individual households and the common affairs of cities" (*Euthyphro* 14b2–5): it is not the gods but the master of the art of dealing with gods, and the actions dictated by his art, that can save himself and his city. Hippias in the *Hippias Major* says that the person who can produce a good λόγος in the assemblies and law-courts is able "by persuading, to depart bearing not the smallest but the greatest of prizes, σωτηρία of oneself and of one's possessions and friends" (304b1–3): the comparison is implicit that being put on trial is like facing a shipwreck that could destroy your life and those of your companions and all possessions on board, and that acquittal is like σωτηρία from shipwreck.[8]

In a similar but more elaborate way, Protagoras in the mythical portion of his "Great Speech" in the *Protagoras* says that Epimetheus gave different δυνάμεις εἰς σωτηρίαν, strength and speed and defensive armor and so on, to the different animal species, or that he himself ἔσωζεν the different kinds of animals (320d8–321a1), but that he forgot to give any σωτηρία to human beings; so Prometheus intervened and tried to find some σωτηρία for humans (321c7–8). This comes in two stages: first, Prometheus stole fire and the arts that go with it from Hephaestus and Athena (321c7–322a2). But then, because humans were still weaker than the beasts and so needed to band together in cities for protection, and because they still lacked "the political art," they were unable to live together without doing each other injustices and were scattered and destroyed, until Zeus, afraid that the race might die out, gives them αἰδώς and δίκη (322a8-d5). Many translators render "σωτηρία" minimalistically, as "means of survival" or the like, but something more is going on: it is constantly emphasized that the σωτηρία is the gift of a god, a god himself "saves" (321a1, effaced by the three English translations I have checked), and the whole story serves to exhibit the origin directly from Zeus of the "political art" which Protagoras professes to teach, and which he claims to be the savior of cities.

---

8   As Kathryn Morgan notes (*Myth and Philosophy from the Presocratics to Plato* [Cambridge: Cambridge University Press, 2000], 282 n. 69), "σῴζειν" in some contexts seems to *mean* simply "acquit" (she cites Lysias XIII,36 and XIX,6; likewise Andocides *On the Mysteries* 31). Morgan also cites *Crito* 44b9-c2, where Crito uses the verb for when he could do in getting Socrates illegally out of prison and thus saving his life.

That some such claim is likely to have been made by the historical Protagoras, or at least is not Plato's invention, is confirmed by ethical fragments of Democritus. So in Democritus B43, "repentance [μετα-μέλεια] of shameful [αἰσχρά] actions is βίου σωτηρίη," where "repentance" is something like αἰδώς, an abhorrence of shameful actions because of their intrinsic quality (so B264 says that we should αἰδεῖσθαι before ourselves more than before others, so that we will abstain from doing wrong even if no one else would know about it, cp. B181, and B179 on αἰδεῖσθαι and virtue). Likewise B280 "they are able without spending a lot of their own [wealth] to educate [παιδεῦσαι] their children and to throw a wall and a σωτηρίη around both their [sc. the children's] possessions and their bodies": the point is that genuine παιδεία is a σωτηρίη, protecting people's life and health and possessions, not by building a physical wall to keep robbers out, or by defending them in court, but by working on their soul so that they will abstain from evil and will not squander their health or possessions. Thus Democritus, like Protagoras, can advertise the importance of what he himself teaches: the care of the soul is the best way to the σωτηρίη of bodies and possessions (yours and your heirs') as well.

III. Plato's Responses to the Sophists on Σωτηρία

Plato, of course, does not endorse the claims that he represents Agathon, Euthyphro, Hippias, and Protagoras as making. But he finds it necessary to respond to claims of this type. He tries out different strategies of response in different places. The most direct confrontation is in the *Gorgias*. Callicles, as Socrates states his views for him, thinks that "I [Socrates] am unable to come to my own aid or the aid of my friends or kinsmen, or to save [ἐκσῶσαι] them from the greatest dangers" (508c5–7), and recommends instead that "a man should take care to live as long as possible, and should practice these arts which save [σώζουσιν] us on each occasion, like the one you bid me to practice, rhetoric, which saves [διασώζουσιν] in the law-courts" (511b7-c2). Socrates accepts the claim that rhetoric can produce σωτηρία, but points out that the art of piloting [κυβερνητική] also "saves not only souls but also bodies and possessions from extreme dangers, just as rhetoric does" (511d1–3); but the pilot doesn't boast, and asks only a small fee, Socrates says, because he reflects that he has not made any of his passengers better in body or soul, and that he cannot know which of them he has benefited or harmed by saving them, which of them have some grave illness of body or soul such that they can only live badly and would be better off drowning (511d3–512b2). In this speech Socrates manages to use forms of σῴζω twelve times (all in 511c7–512d8), accepting from the rhetoricians the comparison between judicial condemnation and shipwreck, and the claim that rhetoric saves, but turning the comparison against the rhetoricians: we do not greatly honor the pilot (or the military engineer, who as much as the general "saves whole cities," 512b3–7), and neither should we greatly honor the rhetorician, and for the same reason, namely that their arts only secure necessary conditions for what we should mainly be valuing, happiness or living well. Since someone with a grave illness of body or soul can only live so badly that it would be better not to live, "what is noble and good is something other than saving and being saved" (512d6–8), not living for as long a time as possible but living as well as possible for whatever time one has.

In this speech Socrates says that the soul is "more valuable than the body" (512a5–6), so that virtue as the good condition of the soul is more important for our happiness than health as the good condition of the body, and *a fortiori* than wealth as the good condition of our external possessions. So we might expect him to say that piloting and so on are unimportant because they can produce only the salvation of the body, and that we should aim instead at the salvation of our souls. But he pointedly does not do this: as we have seen, he concedes that the art of piloting saves souls as well as bodies, and he advises us not to be overfond of our souls (οὐ φιλοψυχητέον, 512e2), i.e., not to aim chiefly at prolonging our lives: he is thus implicitly assuming that the soul endures only as long as the body remains alive.[9] This refusal to speak of a salvation of souls beyond saving our earthly lives, and the assumption that the soul dies with the body, are all the more striking, given that some dozen Stephanus pages later Socrates will tell a story on which the souls of the dead are judged naked, stripped of the bodies which had disguised their good and bad qualities (523a1–525a7). But Plato refuses to aim at a salvation of souls, saying rather

---

9 Compare Thucydides I,136, where salvation of body and salvation of soul are apparently synonymous. For the use of φιλοψυχεῖν, and the apparent implication that the soul perishes with the body, compare the Anonymus Iamblichi (DK 4–5) at Iamblichus, *Protrepticus* 125,19–28 and 126,17–27 Des Places (despite the threefold contrast between soul, body, and possessions, 126,4–6, also at *Gorgias* 511c9-d3).

that we should aim at something nobler than salvation, namely being as good as possible. Indeed, this aim is connected with the thesis that the soul is more important than the body: rhetoric, which teaches us how to avoid suffering injustice, can at most ensure the good condition of our bodies or our external possessions (by helping us avoid physical punishment or confiscation), whereas philosophy, by teaching us how to avoid doing injustice, ensures the good or virtuous condition of our souls; and it is the person who does no injustice, rather than the person who suffers no injustice, who lives well and happily.

However, in other dialogues Plato gives a more positive response to the sophists' claims to produce σωτηρία, by putting forth rival claims of his own.[10] Again, he tries out different possibilities in different places. One obvious strategy turns on the *Gorgias'* comparison between courtroom trials and the elenchus, a trial in which the respondent is the witness against himself and the judge over himself (*Gorgias* 471d3–472c4). As rhetoric teaches how to avoid conviction before a jury, dialectic teaches how to avoid conviction before ourselves, and if the rhetorician or his art can be compared to those who save from drowning, so too can the dialectician. Thus Socrates, caught in a dialectical investigation ending in an infinite loop, "since I had fallen into this aporia, let out a great cry, begging the two strangers [Euthydemus and Dionysodorus], as if calling on the Dioscuri, to save us, me and the boy [the interlocutor Cleinias] from the triple wave of argument" (*Euthydemus* 292e8–293a3; although the aporia here is dialectical, "aporia" can be any condition of inability to help oneself which forces someone to appeal to a σωτήρ). So too Socrates must escape a "triple wave" in proposing the equality of women guardians, the abolition of the family among the guardians, and rule by philosophers (*Republic* V 472a1–7); already in the first of these he compares himself to someone who has fallen into the middle of a deep sea, who must "swim and try to be saved from the argument, whether hoping that a dolphin will pick us up, or some other ἄπορος σωτηρία" (453d8–10). Here Plato takes the verb "pick up [ὑπολαμβάνειν]" from Herodotus's story of Arion's rescue

---

10 One option which Plato might well have chosen to take in the *Gorgias*, but which as far as I know he never pursues in this form (perhaps closest in the Digression of the *Theaetetus*), is to say that it is the person who escapes the entanglements of this life without committing injustice, rather than the person who escapes punishment, who is truly "saved." This option is taken by Epictetus, *Discourses* IV,1,159–69, where Socrates refuses to "be saved shamefully" by escaping from prison, "but rather he is saved by dying, not by fleeing."

by the dolphin (I,23–4; note that Arion is reduced to ἀπορίη when the sailors will not accept his plea to take his money but spare his life, I,24,4). The story presumably arose, partly to glorify the power of Arion's song—Arion is saved because he has charmed the dolphin with his song and cithara-playing before leaping into the sea—but also partly because of the ἀνάθημα which Herodotus I,24,8 says Arion set up at Taenarum, presumably at the famous temple of Poseidon, showing a man riding a dolphin. So Arion, or whoever set up the ἀνάθημα, saw the rescue as a σωτηρία sent by Poseidon; and what Socrates does with words will be something like what Arion does with music.

IV. Plato on Political Σωτηρία

Elsewhere, however, the contrast is with a military σωτήρ of the city. The σωτηρία of the city, in the first instance its military σωτηρία, gives the σωτήρ a legitimacy of command going beyond, and perhaps contrary to, strictly constitutional sources of legitimacy. Thus the dubious *Eighth Letter* says that the Syracusans chose the elder Dionysius and Hipparinus as αὐτοκράτορες τύραννοι for the sake of the σωτηρία of Sicily, i.e., to prevent the island from falling under the rule of the Carthaginians, and that it was right to be grateful to these saviors (σώσαντες); if they afterward abused the city's gift of authority, then they deserve to pay the penalty (353a3-c4). Indeed it seems that σωτηρία was often used as a justification for extraconstitutional rule extending beyond the limits of wartime, perhaps especially in Sicily. Thus Diodorus Siculus says that the Syracusans proclaimed Gelon as "εὐεργέτης and σωτήρ and king" (XI,26,6), and then later that after Dion's successful defence of the city against Dionysius II the Syracusans, after sacrificing to the gods in thanks for their σωτηρία, not only "elected Dion στρατηγὸς αὐτοκράτωρ" but also "awarded him heroic honors ... honoring their εὐεργέτης as having been the only σωτήρ of the fatherland" (XVI,20,5–6, cp. Plutarch *Dion* 46,1—the point is specifically that Dion had been able to save the city from Dionysius when the pro-democratic forces under Heraclides could not). But, obviously, such authority is dangerously subject to abuse.

Plato does not mind appealing to military σωτηρία as an extra support for the authority of the philosopher (Socrates "saved" Alcibiades, both him and his armor, at Potidaea, and deserved the honors after that battle more than Alcibiades did, *Symposium* 220d5-e7), but he argues that the σωτηρία of the laws, which saves the city from civil strife or despotic abuse, is more important for the city than military σωτηρία. In the *Symposium* Lycurgus leaves his "sons," i.e., his laws personified, as σωτῆρες of Sparta (209d4–6); it is also said there that these laws have been "so to speak the saviors of Greece," which must mean that they were responsible for the Spartans' successful defense of Greece at the time of Xerxes' invasion, so Plato (or Diotima) must be connecting the laws with military σωτηρία as well, maintaining (like Xenophon in his *Constitution of the Spartans*) that Lycurgus' laws produced the civic solidarity and courage that are responsible for the Spartans' military successes. In the *Seventh Letter* Plato advises the victors in civil strife (in Syracuse, or anywhere), if they desire the city's σωτηρία from continued strife, to invite virtuous neutral advisors from all of Greece to prescribe laws which will not favor the winning over the losing party: not by one party's conquering, but by their submitting themselves to the laws, "will all things be full of σωτηρία and happiness, and will there be an escape from all evils" (337d1–2, cp. the whole text from 337b3; here, as commonly, "escape from evils [κακῶν ἀποφυγή]" is a negative synonym for σωτηρία).

Neither Lycurgus nor the pan-Hellenic legislators of the *Seventh Letter* are described as philosophers, but the *Republic* and the *Laws* argue that legislation and especially the guarding (φυλάττειν) and σωτηρία of the laws, and thus the σωτηρία of the city, require philosophers. "If the constitution is to be preserved [σῴζεσθαι]" the city needs an overseer with special training (*Republic* III 412a4–10), and only such people are "complete guardians" (414b1–6), since only they are "guardians of the laws and of the city" (this phrase IV 421a5, and cf. VI 484b9-c1) and not merely military defenders of the city. As Plato gradually reveals, these people must be philosophers in the sense described in *Republic* V, people who know eternal forms (so esp. VI 484b3-d10). The point is not that such special knowledge is needed to obey or execute the laws at ordinary times, but that without knowledge of the appropriate paradigm we cannot rightly create laws (thus philosophers are needed especially for the transition to the well-governed state), or interpret or modify them as needed in hard cases or in a crisis: people without knowledge of the forms will not be able "to lay down conventions [νόμιμα] here about what is noble and just and good, when they need to be laid down, or, by guarding [φυλάττειν] the ones that have been laid down, to preserve [σῴζειν] them" (VI 484d1–3). If some of those with a philosophical nature can themselves be "saved" (502a9, 502b2) from corruption, "the saviors of the constitution" (502c9-d2) can arise; otherwise city and citizens will have no "end to evils [κακῶν παῦλα]" (501e2–5; same phrase V 473d5, in the first introduction of the need for philosophers to rule—the phrase is equivalent to κακῶν ἀποφυγή, which as noted above is a common negative description of σωτηρία). Thus in the city we construct the people call their rulers σωτῆρες (V 463b1), and "they live a life more blessed than the blessed life which Olympic victors live ... since their victory is more noble, and their support at public expense more complete: for they win the victory of the σωτηρία of the whole city, and both they and their children are supplied with food and all the other things which life requires, and they receive honors from their cities during their lives, and when they have died partake in a worthy burial" (465d2-e2).[11]

The last book of the *Laws*, specifically the last ten Stephanus-pages after the work of legislation is finished at *Laws* XII 960b5, develop at length the theme of σωτηρία and its conditions. Making something is never really finished until we have secured σωτηρία for what we have made (960b5-c1), and "for the city and the constitution this requires that we provide not only health and σωτηρία for the bodies, but also lawfulness in the souls, or rather σωτηρία of the laws" (960d1–4). The solution is that the nocturnal (or dawn) council of the ten senior νομοφύλακες and the younger people they co-opt, "if one casts this as an anchor of the whole city ... would save [σώζειν] everything we want" (961c4–6). The soul, when reason (νοῦς) is present in it, together with the head, in which are the senses of sight and hearing, are the σωτῆρες or the σωτηρία of the animal, comparable to the captain together with his sailors who are the σωτηρία of the ship (961d1-e5), and these will be a model for the nocturnal council (so esp. 969b2-c3, almost the end of the dialogue—apparently the senior νομοφύλακες and the captain are analogous to νοῦς, while the sailors and the younger associates who bring news to the νομοφύλακες are analogous to the senses): if the personnel are selected and educated correctly and placed in the acropolis to watch over the city, they will become "guardians such as we have never seen in our previous life as regards their power [ἀρετή] of σωτηρία" (969c2–3).

---

11 See also *Republic* III 417a5-b6, where the guardians (here not especially the philosopher-rulers) "would be saved and would save the city" if they abstain from private property, but would cause its ruin otherwise.

But how must these people be educated, to be able to save the city? Although the *Laws* is much shyer than the *Republic* about calling for rule by philosophers, Plato argues that, like the general and the doctor who aim at σωτηρία, the person who would save the city must know the σκοπός at which he aims (961e7–962c3). But, as was shown in *Laws* IV, the aim of legislation is virtue as such, encompassing the standard four cardinal virtues; and Plato uses this to argue that the saving person or group must be able both to define virtue and to grasp how it is one and how it is four, i.e., that they must have the ability to collect and divide and grasp the one in the many, as described in *Philebus* 14c1–19b4 (all this argued *Laws* XII 963a1–966b3). They must thus know dialectic; and Plato argues further that they must also know physics and astronomy in order to grasp the two scientific foundations of theology, the priority of soul to body as moving cause and the rational ordering of the heavenly motions (966b4–968a4). Only then, with the training thus prescribed, can we make the nocturnal council "a guard according to law for the sake of σωτηρία" (968a4-b2). Thus the last ten pages of the *Laws* are an extended argument that only philosophers, trained in dialectic and physics and astronomy, can be the saviors of the city.

Thus far we have seen σωτηρία mainly in a political context, where the philosophers, more than the military leaders, will be saviors of the whole city, and so deserve from the city something close to herocult, at any rate honors greater than those given to Olympic victors. Even when, in these contexts, Plato says that the salvation of souls is more important than the salvation of bodies, this is just a bridge to what he thinks is most needful, the salvation or preservation of the laws and the constitution and thus of the city (so esp. *Laws* XII 960d1–4, cited above). Protagoras (as Plato represents him, see above) claimed that political virtue, added by Zeus to human nature, is the σωτηρία of cities and thus of the human race; Plato replies that while all or most of the citizens must be politically virtuous for the city to be saved, this is not sufficient, and the city needs at least a small group of leaders with a precise knowledge going far beyond political virtue (and probably also beyond the αἰδώς at shameful works in which Democritus locates virtue and thus salvation).

V. Plato on Philosophy and Individual Σωτηρία

However, less often, Plato also tries to compete with the sophists by showing that philosophy as he understands it is necessary even for the σωτηρία of the individual, in his life overall and not merely in a dialectical emergency as in the *Euthydemus*. Arguing against Protagoras in the *Theaetetus*, Socrates says that people "in the greatest dangers, in warfare or in illness or in storms at sea, attend to those who rule in such things as to the gods, expecting that they will be their saviors, although they differ from themselves in nothing other than knowledge" (170a9-b1): this includes both individual and collective σωτηρία, and Protagoras himself as educator in virtue and as legislative adviser has put himself forward as such a savior, but Socrates is arguing that Protagoras' claim cannot be justified unless he has an objective knowledge which other people lack, but that his own theory of knowledge undermines this possibility. Plato is here implicitly accepting that those who have knowledge, presumably of virtue just as much as of bodily health, can be saviors, although he is unlikely to believe that Protagoras himself has such knowledge.

But Plato's clearest positive claim that some kind of knowledge can be necessary and sufficient for saving an individual comes in the *Protagoras*, again in implicit competition with Protagoras' own claims about σωτηρία. Socrates has argued we ought to act in the way that produces the greatest pleasures and the least pains, and that in order to do this we must determine the true magnitudes of the pleasures and pains that would result from different courses of action: since pleasures and pains that are closer to us in time tend to seem larger, and more remote one tends to seem smaller, just as closer objects tend to appear larger to sight, and more remote ones tend to appear smaller, we must overcome this tendency in order to act rightly. "So if doing well [τὸ εὖ πράττειν, happiness or success] consisted for us in doing and taking long lengths, and fleeing and not doing short ones, what would appear as our σωτηρία τοῦ βίου—the art of measurement, or the power of appearance? Wouldn't [the power of appearance] make us wander and make us take and reject the same things [μεταλαμβάνειν ταὐτά] many times back and forth, and change our mind [μεταμέλειν] both in actions and in choosing long and short, while the art of measurement would make this appearance powerless, and by revealing the true would make the soul, abiding in the true, to have quietude, and would save our life?" (356c8-e2).¹² Likewise if our σωτηρία τοῦ βίου consisted in choosing among odd and even numbers, what would save our life would be arithmetic, which is also a kind of art of measurement (356e5–357a3). "But since it has become apparent that our σωτηρία τοῦ βίου consists in the right choice of pleasure and pain, the more and the fewer and the greater and the lesser and the further and the nearer, doesn't [our σωτηρία τοῦ βίου] seem to be an art of measurement, investigating their excess and deficiency and equality to each other?" (357a5-b3). Here, for the argument to work, σωτηρία τοῦ βίου must be identified with happiness [εὖ πράττειν] and also with quietude [ἡσυχία]. But what justifies calling this σωτηρία?

Some of the underlying thought, although without the word "σωτηρία," is developed in the *Euthyphro*, where disagreements about number or about greater and smaller or heavier and lighter do not give rise to anger or enmity because they are resolved by calculation or measurement or weighing (7b6-c8; as Socrates says, when we turn to measurement, παυσαίμεϑ' ἂν τῆς διαφορᾶς, 7c4–5); where humans, and according to the stories the gods, get into conflict it is about "just and unjust and noble and base and good and bad" (7d1–2), evidently because they do not have an art for measuring these things. So an art of measuring good and bad would put an end to war, or within the city to στάσις (the *Euthyphro* uses the verb στασιάζειν in this context for what the gods allegedly do, 7b2, 7e3, 8a1). So it seems justified to say that an art of measuring good and bad (and Socrates in the *Protagoras* has argued that this reduces to measuring pleasure and pain) would "save" the city from civil strife. And apparently Plato thinks that it would have an analogous effect within an individual: without a way to assess the true size of each prospective pleasure or pain, we will be unable to resolve conflicts between our different desires or aversions, as the *Protagoras* puts it we will "wander," and, especially, we will be in conflict with ourselves in pursuing and rejecting the same thing when it is present to us in different guises or at different "distances." This is something like internal στάσις (perhaps it is also something like being lost at sea, and tossed back and forth by a storm), and it seems reasonable to say that the art of measurement, by quieting this

---

12 The verb μεταμέλειν suggests that Plato is responding to Democritus B43, cited above, where μεταμέλεια is βίου σωτηρίη: for Plato μεταμέλεια, change of mind or repentance, is a sign of what we need to be saved from, and only an overall consistency of action and motivation is genuine σωτηρία.

conflict, "saves" individuals as well as cities.[13] When this passage is compared with what Protagoras has said about σωτηρία earlier in the dialogue, the implication is that political virtue is not enough to save us: to save even an individual, we need a precise knowledge going beyond what Protagoras claims to teach. And very likely, in insisting on the need for an art of measurement, Plato also intends to rebut Protagoras' claim that man is in himself a measure of all things, although Plato mentions this formula only in the *Theaetetus* and not in the *Protagoras*.[14]

VI. Eschatological Σωτηρία in Plato?

In the uses we have seen so far of σωτήρ or σωτηρία or σῴζειν, Plato is often drawing more or less clearly on the religious connotations of the terms in order to amplify the claims he is making for philosophy; but the σωτηρία he has spoken of has never been eschatological, that is, has never involved saving us from something that might happen to us after death. And this is entirely in accord with the general concerns of Greek religion, and more specifically with representations of σωτηρία in Greek religion. But there is one occurrence of σωτηρία in Plato, and another of σῴζειν, which do refer to what happens to the soul after death; and we should consider how this use of σωτηρία is related to the range of uses we have seen.

---

13 The comparison between this kind of inconsistency in our beliefs and actions and being tossed at sea seems implicit in the common philosophical use of ταραχή—from ταράσσω/ταράττω, originally applied chiefly to storms at sea—for the condition of inconsistency which we escape through philosophy. In this sense see *Republic* IX 577e1–3, where the tyrannical soul is "full of ταραχή and μεταμέλεια"; likewise the "ταραχή in the soul" of *Republic* X 602c12-d1, in a passage which develops the *Protagoras* passage on the art of measurement, consists in the fact that the same things appear to us under different circumstances as having contrary attributes. Xenocrates will say that "the motive for the discovery of philosophy is to put an end to the ταραχῶδες of things in life" (Fr. 253 Isnardi-Parente), and the idea will be taken up by many Hellenistic philosophers.

14 Compare also *Epinomis* 976e1–4, where the Athenian Stranger supposes that it is some god, rather than mere chance, that has "saved us" by giving us number, without which we would be the most foolish of animals, and which enables us to rule and be ruled justly and harmoniously (976c7-d8). The god turns out to be Ouranos, who has taught us number by showing us the succession of day and night, the regular waxing and waning of the moon, and so on.

The Socrates of the *Phaedo* concludes that

> if indeed [as Socrates has just finished arguing] the soul is immortal, it requires care not only over that time in which we speak of "living," but over all time, and the danger would now seem to be terrible, if someone neglects to care for it. For if death were the loss [ἀπαλλαγή] of everything, it would be a godsend to those who are bad, when they die, to lose their body and at the same time their vice [or badness] together with their soul; but now, since [the soul] turns out to be immortal, it would have no other escape from evils [ἀποφυγὴ κακῶν] or σωτηρία except to become as good and as wise as possible. For the soul arrives in Hades carrying nothing except its education and nurture—the things which are said most of all to benefit or harm the dead person right from the beginning of his journey thither. (*Phaedo* 107c2-d5)

This passage has close connections with passages in the *Gorgias* that we have discussed. In particular, it recalls the *Gorgias'* insistence that souls will be judged naked, having left behind the "beautiful bodies and families and wealth" (*Gorgias* 523c5–6) and the friendly witnesses who would testify on their behalf, so that the judges will not be misled by appearances: thus as the *Phaedo* passage says, "the soul arrives in Hades carrying nothing except its education and nurture," the soul's own qualities (formed by what it has done in the body) which the judges will inspect. But while the *Gorgias* argues that σωτηρία, of bodies or even of souls, is not of much value and that we should concern ourselves instead with living as well as possible (512d6-e5, discussed above), the *Phaedo* says that having our soul in as good a condition as possible, so that we will live as well as possible, *is* our only σωτηρία. This seems close to the *Theaetetus*, which although it does not speak of σωτηρία, says that we must flee (φεύγειν) from evils (cf. the ἀποφυγὴ κακῶν in the *Phaedo* passage, the negative equivalent of σωτηρία), and that this φυγή consists in "assimilation to god so far as is possible," which in turn consists in "becoming just and pious with wisdom" (176a5-b3).

But what does σωτηρία mean in the *Phaedo*? Clearly it cannot mean securing the continued existence of our body, since Plato is speaking of what happens after death; nor does it mean securing the continued existence of our soul, since the soul will automatically continue to exist whether we want it to or not, and it seems that for the vicious if the soul *did* perish with the body that would be a prospect of σωτηρία. So we might think that the desired σωτηρία is an escape from punishment by the judges of the afterlife, analogous to, but far more important than, the σωτηρία from an earthly court that rhetoric might bring about.

And indeed the *Phaedo* goes on to give a myth, like the *Gorgias'* but more elaborate, involving judgment in the afterlife.

However, Plato seems to be very cautious about identifying the desired σωτηρία with avoiding judicial punishment. In the *Phaedo* myth, while there will be a judgment, the souls must first get to the place where they will be judged, and despite the δαίμων guiding them, there are many ways to go wrong, and only "the wise and orderly soul follows and does not fail to recognize the surroundings," while "the one affected by desire for the body," reluctant to leave the body and the sensible world, resists being led and arrives only after much straying and confusion (108a6-b3): this was what Socrates was referring to, in the passage cited, when he said that education and nurture "benefit or harm the dead person right from the beginning of his journey thither," i.e., even before he has reached the place of judgment. All this is of course myth, but it seems that underlying Plato's choosing, in these eschatological myths, to attribute the outcome for each soul as much as possible to the soul itself and as little as possible to the judges, is the concern expressed in the *Republic*. In *Republic* II, Glaucon and Adeimantus express dissatisfaction with the usual grounds on which justice is praised, which seem to show the advantages of *appearing* just rather than of *being* just: if these are the only reasons to be just, then we will do better to conceal our injustice within conspiracies of like-minded friends, to use rhetoric when we are caught to avoid punishment by a human court (so 365d2–6), and to use the profits of our injustice to perform sacrifices to the gods and undergo initiations and purifications to avoid punishment in the afterlife (365d7–366b3, picking up 364b3–365a3 and 362c1–6). So Glaucon and Adeimantus challenge Socrates to show the advantages of justice independently of the advantages of *appearing* just either to human beings or to gods: so he should make no mention of rewards either from humans or from gods, but should show that justice in itself, apart from any rewards, is the best condition of the soul (366d5–367e4).

Already in the *Gorgias* and *Phaedo*, written before the *Republic*, Plato tries to avoid making the soul's welfare depend on judges who might, like human judges, be misled or corrupted, in the *Gorgias* by insisting that souls are judged naked, in the *Phaedo* likewise by insisting that the soul carries only its education and nurture. But the *Phaedo* goes a step further than the *Gorgias* by making the soul's outcome depend on the soul's own choices in the afterlife, informed by the habits that it has acquired in the body. And Plato carries this further in the myth of Er in *Republic* X. Having scrupulously avoided mentioning the afterlife in his defense of justice in *Republic* II-IX, in *Republic* X Socrates finally allows himself to say that the just person, beyond the internal benefits of justice, is also unlikely to escape the notice of the gods, and will receive rewards from them before or after death (612b6–614a8); but then, in giving a mythical narrative (on the authority of Er) of what happens to souls after death, he makes as much as possible depend on the soul's own choices, and as little as possible on any divine judge. Various things happen to souls when separated from bodies, but eventually they return for another bodily life, and while the souls are assigned lots to determine the order in which they will be able to choose their next lives, there is not much advantage in getting to choose first, or much disadvantage in having to choose last: "even for the one who comes last, there is stored up a life which is to be welcomed, a life not bad, if he chooses it with intelligence and then lives it without slack [συντόνως]. Let not the first be careless in his choice, nor let the last despair" (619b3–6). And Er reports seeing the first chooser choose the life of a tyrant, without inspecting the life carefully and not noticing that it would include eating his own children, "nor did he blame himself for the evils, but fortune and δαίμονες and everything rather than himself" (619c5–6; contrast the warning to the souls at 617e1–5, where they will choose their own δαίμονες, presumably in the sense of ἦθος ἀνθρώπῳ δαίμων); while the soul of Odysseus, which had to choose last, was able to find the life of an untroubled private person lying unwanted by the other souls, and "willingly chose it, saying that he would have done the same even had he drawn the first lot" (620d1–2). In both the *Phaedo* and the *Republic*, the fundamental point is that the soul's happiness or misery after death depends only incidentally on δαίμονες or judges or the lottery of fortune, essentially on the soul's own choices, and that these choices depend on the soul's habituation and education in this life.

Thus when the *Phaedo* says "since [the soul] turns out to be immortal, it would have no other escape from evils or σωτηρία except to become as good and as wise as possible," the point is that neither rhetoric to persuade judges in this life, nor sacrifices and initiations to persuade judges in the next life, nor simply the fact of dying, will be sufficient to save us from evils (the art of rhetoric, or money to bribe the jailers to escape, might have "saved" Socrates for a little while, but not for long), and that, since these short cuts do not work, there is unfortunately no alternative to trying to become as good and as wise as possible.[15] And Plato wants also to claim that philosophy is needed for this. In the first place, political virtue (the phrase apparently taken from Protagoras) is insufficient. In the *Phaedo*, in an earlier myth, "those who have practiced popular and political virtue, what they call temperance and justice, born of habituation and practice without philosophy or intelligence" (82a12-b3) are reincarnated in some "tame and political kind," bees or wasps or ants or humans again (b5–8), which does not sound so bad but is still contrasted with what happens to the philosophers; in *Republic* X, more sharply, the person who rashly chooses the life of the tyrant "had lived in his previous life in a well-ordered constitution, partaking by habituation without philosophical virtue" (619c7-d1). The point is that while political virtue may be sufficient for making decisions in ordinary situations, it breaks down in the extraordinary circumstances of the afterlife, and especially when given the first lot and offered a tyranny, just as it would break down when given the ring of Gyges (cf. *Republic* II 359b6–360d7).

In the *Protagoras* Plato had put forward, as a means to σωτηρία and an alternative to Protagorean political virtue, an art of measuring pleasures and pains, but in the *Phaedo* he claims that this too is insufficient: "this is not the right exchange with regard to virtue, to exchange pleasures for pleasures and pain for pain and fear for fear, greater for smaller, like coins; rather, only this is the right coin, wisdom, for which all these things should be exchanged" (69a6–10). Plato goes on to compare this wisdom to a mystery-initiation, with a grim future in the afterlife for the "uninitiated," the unphilosophically virtuous. But it would be a mistake to say that the *Protagoras* recommends living based on an art of measuring pleasure because it is concerned with salvation in this life, while the *Phaedo* rejects this as insufficient because it is concerned with salvation in the afterlife. Rather, the *Phaedo* rejects a life based on the art of measuring pleasure because it thinks that the activity of contemplating is in itself the most desirable human activity, and that wisdom should not be desired merely as a means to maximizing pleasure, or even to achieving consistency in our actions: a wisdom directed not to practical activity but to contemplation is our salvation in this life, and this is the ground for Plato's conviction that it will also be our salvation after

---

15 And thus the negative form of expression, not, e. g., "philosophy is our σωτηρία," but "there is no other σωτηρία": similar negative expressions are very common in Greek claims about σωτηρία.

death, when we will be free of the obstacles distracting us from contemplation. The *Phaedo* is willing to compare philosophical wisdom to the knowledge acquired in a mystery-initation, and to cite the evidence of cult representations of forking paths where the soul must know which fork to take after death (107e5–108a6), but Plato is demythologizing these claims, and offering philosophy as a replacement for the mysteries. He is saying not that philosophical wisdom has as its content the geography of Hades, to be of practical use after death, but that the soul habituated to bodily pleasures will try to linger in the sensible world after death, while the wise soul will go spontaneously to its proper place (108a6-b3), i.e., to where it can contemplate without distraction.

So too in *Republic* X, where something reported from the afterlife can "save" us, neither the content of the knowledge, nor the actions it leads us to take, are distinctively eschatological. Socrates has tried to show in *Republic* II-IX that the just person will be the happiest, because of the state of his soul and not because of any external rewards; where the just person is not simply someone who is just by habituation, or by calculating the external rewards, for such a person's justice will break down if offered the ring of Gyges. The truly just person will continue to act rightly even if given the ring of Gyges (or kingship in the Callipolis) because he understands the nature of the human soul, what states of it constitute its happiness and misery, and how its external actions affect its internal states, and so he refrains from unjust actions because he knows that they would make him psychically unhealthy and so unhappy (so *Republic* IV 444c1–445b4, cf. IX 591a5–592a4). That is: the philosophically just and therefore happy person will be the person who has understood and internalized the argument of the *Republic*, or of some idealized more fully worked-out version of it. Then in *Republic* X Socrates, taking a break from recounting the story of Er in order to point out its implications, says that because of what Er has told us, namely that the souls are given a choice of lives, "for this reason we should most of all take care how each of us, neglecting all other studies, shall pursue and learn this study, if he can somehow learn and discover what will make him knowing and able, discerning the good from the miserable life, always to choose the best of those possible on any occasion, reasoning through all the things that have now been said [in the *Republic*]" and assessing what external things will have what effects on a soul in this or that condition, "so that from all these things he will be able to choose on the basis of reasoning, looking to the nature of the soul and to the worse and better lives, calling 'worse' what leads to becoming more unjust, 'better' what leads to becoming more just; he will let everything else go, for we have seen that this is the best choice for him both when he is living and when he has died" (618b8-c6, 618d5–619a1). Someone who arrives in Hades with this firm conviction will avoid the temptations "both in this life, so far as possible, and in all the life hereafter: for in this way a man becomes most happy" (619a7-b1). And because Er witnessed all these things without having quite died, and returned to consciousness still lying on his funeral pyre without having drunk the water of forgetfulness, "the story was saved [ἐσώθη] and did not perish, and it would save [ἂν σώσειεν] us, if we believe it, and we will cross the river of Lethe well and will not be polluted in soul" (621b8-c2).[16] But what saves us is the conviction that the justest life is the happiest, and it will save us by guiding our choices in the next life for precisely the same reasons that it saves us by guiding our choices in this life.

VII. Conclusion

Plato has a somewhat different attitude to philosophy and how it governs individual lives in each of the dialogues we have discussed. In the *Gorgias* he distinguishes rhetoric, which aims at σωτηρία, from philosophy, which aims not at σωτηρία but at living well, but in the *Protagoras* and *Phaedo* and *Republic* he says that philosophy, in teaching us how to live well, saves the individual (as well as, in the *Republic* and *Laws*, the city).[17] In the *Phaedo* and *Republic*, and also the *Gorgias*, he fills out

---

16 See the very interesting discussion of the meanings of the (proverbial) phrase "the story was saved" in Morgan 2000, 281–9. Exploring how stories or accounts, and not just persons or cities, are saved allows Morgan to bring out different aspects of σωτηρία in Plato, complementary to those I have described.

17 Something like σωτηρία may also come up in Plato where a god is saving, not human individuals or cities, but the cosmos. Thus *Statesman* 273d4-e4: "the god who had previously ordered [the world], seeing that it was in ἀπορίαι, and being concerned lest, battered by storm and broken by the tumult [ταραχή], it should sink into the endless sea of unlikeness, takes charge once again of the steering, and, turning around what had become diseased and broken in [the world's] prior rotation under its own power, orders it and sets it right and makes it immortal and unaging." Plato doesn't here use any form of "σῴζειν," but the concept is surely implied by the comparison with sea and storms: salvation from shipwreck here fuses with salvation from disease. Likewise at *Timaeus* 32c5–33b1 the god makes the world "unaging and with-

the argument with a myth (in the *Protagoras* the mythmaking is left to Protagoras), which puts the life that the dialogue is recommending, and the thought-process that the dialogue is carrying out, in an eschatological and cosmological context. Keeping such eschatological and cosmological contexts in mind may help us to internalize the results of the argument and to keep from falling into temptation, but the myths are only likely stories, and the plausibility of their descriptions of the role of wisdom in the afterlife comes entirely from what we know about its role in the present life.

Although the notion of σωτηρία is put in an eschatological context in the *Phaedo* and *Republic*, in neither dialogue is it a distinctively eschatological notion. It is not, for instance, *mokṣa*, liberation from the cycle of rebirth. In the *Phaedo*, where Plato does apparently imply that the philosophically virtuous person will not be reincarnated (114c2–8, and maybe 82b10-c4 contrasting with 82a10-b9), he does not say anything about that in the σωτηρία passage. The point there is, negatively, that since we want to escape our vices (and not merely to escape external punishments for our vices), and since we cannot escape them simply by dying, there is "no other escape from evils or σωτηρία except to become as good and as wise as possible." In the *Republic* apparently everyone except the incurably bad is reincarnated; the study of the soul as sketched in the *Republic*, fortified by Er's story, will "save" us by helping us to make the right choices, both during and between earthly lives; but here as in the *Phaedo* the emphasis is negative, that wisdom will help us to avoid the most foolish choices, such as the tyrannical life.

What is constant in all these dialogues, except the *Gorgias*, is that rhetoric and political virtue are insufficient to save either the individual or the city. So far as we can discern the history behind Plato's dramatizations, the philosophers who first promised σωτηρία, competing with the traditional gods and heroes, were Protagoras and Gorgias or their fellows, and next perhaps Democritus. Against these earlier philosophers, Plato is saying that rhetoric and political virtue, or even Democritean moral virtue, are no more effective at producing the promised σωτηρία than are sacrifices or initiations or politicians or generals, and that only some quite different kind of philosophy can save us.

---

out disease," following precepts of the art of medicine (but again with no use of "σῴζειν"). The god orders all things "for the σωτηρία and virtue of the whole [i.e., of the cosmos]" at *Laws* X 903b4–7, although with no mention in the context of dangers from which the cosmos needs to be saved or preserved.

From Politics to Salvation through Philosophy: Herodotus' *Histories* and Plato's *Republic*

Vishwa Adluri & John Lenz

I. Introduction

Plato's *Republic* culminates with Socrates relating a story that he asserts will "save us."[1] Clearly, the myth of Er plays no small role in how we read the *Republic* as a whole. In this paper, we read it as concluding themes introduced by another myth earlier in the work, the myth of Gyges in Book II. We can see the central portions of the *Republic* as framed by these two Platonic myths: the myth of Gyges brings the discussion into politics,[2] and the myth of Er brings it out of politics and into relation with salvation. In arguing for the importance of this salvific claim for the *Republic*, we will relate it to a similar pattern discernible in the *Histories* of Herodotus.[3]

Scholars have noted that Plato drew from Herodotus, and adapted for his own purposes, the myth of Gyges.[4] Further, as Davis notes,

---

1 "And so, Glaucon, a myth was saved and not destroyed and it would save us..." (καὶ οὕτως, ὦ Γλαύκων, μῦθος ἐσώθη καὶ οὐκ ἀπώλετο, καὶ ἡμᾶς ἂν σώσειεν...; *Republic* 621b5; authors' translation).
2 The myth of Gyges can in many ways be considered the central political myth of the *Republic*: its introduction in Book II sets the stage for a renewed inquiry into justice as well as the conception of the ideal city. Cf. Michael Davis, "The Tragedy of Law: Gyges in Herodotus and Plato," *RMeta* 53 (2000): 636: "The final nine books of the *Republic* are Socrates' extended reflection on this poem invented by Glaucon [i.e. the myth of Gyges] to make visible the power and naturalness of injustice in the soul and the weakness and conventionality of justice."
3 The *Republic* is unique in its relation to Herodotus. In the entire *corpus* of Platonic texts available to us, the *Republic* contains the only direct quote from Herodotus: from the *Histories*. Cf. *Republic* VIII, 566c; the reference is to *Histories* I.55c.
4 See Andrew Laird, "Ringing the Changes on Gyges: Philosophy and the Formation of Fiction in Plato's *Republic*," *JHS* 121 (2001): 12–29; K. F. Smith, "The Literary Tradition of Gyges and Candaules," *AJP* 41.1 (1920): 1–37;

the myth of Gyges analogously structures both the *Republic* and the *Histories*. "Like Glaucon's story about the ring, it [i.e.Herodotus' account of Gyges] provides a structure for the nine books of the *History* that follow."[5] However, we can go further than these literary[6] and thematic[7] parallels by bringing the rest of Herodotus' account to bear on the comparison with Plato.

The story of Solon and Croesus, an archetypal confrontation between sage and ruler, recounts the end of the dynasty founded by Gyges. The progression from Gyges to Croesus displays a pattern we see in Plato's later myths of Gyges and Er. Both begin with the seizure of political power (by Gyges) and end with a wisdom-story involving an individual (Croesus, Er) who is saved at the point of death on the pyre.

---

see also, Mary P. Nichols, "Glaucon's Adaptation of the Story of Gyges and Its Implications for Plato's Political Teaching," Polity 17 (1984): 30–39. Andrew Laird suggests that Plato' draws directly upon the Herodotean narrative; K. F. Smith proposes an alternative view that both Plato and Herodotus draw upon a common source. Our concern in this article is not so much the literary affiliation between the two authors, but demonstrating that a comparison between Herodotus and Plato should be understood in the broadest possible context of defining and transmitting wisdom, in which both authors struggle with both form and content.

5   Davis 2000, 637.
6   Plato uses many genres in his writing; while references to poets (lyrical, comic and tragic) and philosophers are obvious, we should not underestimate the influence of historiographers. Nightingale, for example, overlooks the relationship between Plato and Herodotus in her exposition of Plato's genres; see Andrea W. Nightingale, *Genres in Dialogue: Plato and the Construct of Philosophy* (Cambridge: Cambridge University Press, 1995).
7   For a useful discussion of the Herodotean influences in the *Republic*, which extend beyond the myth of Gyges to the final myth in Book X, the myth of Er, see Stephen Halliwell, "The Life-and-Death Journey of the Soul: Interpreting the Myth of Er," in *The Cambridge Companion to Plato's* Republic, ed. G.R.F. Ferrari (Cambridge: Cambridge University Press, 2007), 448–9. Halliwell writes: "…Socrates speaks from the outset with quasi-historical immediacy, as though chronicling a factual report received from a 'messenger' (614d, 619b; cf. 619e). There are even some stylistic touches, such as the mannered verbal repetition at 614b ('he came back to life, and coming back to life…'), that remind us of Herodotus and help to create a veneer of historicity… It may be no coincidence that Herodotus' work contains the story of Aristeas of Proconnesus, a shaman-like messenger of the divine who supposedly made soul journeys while under trance and who possibly had Pythagorean connections (Herodotos 4.13–16, with a possible allusion to reincarnation, 4.15)."

Interestingly, the first known use of the word "philosophy" (in the form of the participle φιλοσοφέων) occurs in Herodotus' description of Solon's journey to Croesus' court.[8] The Lydian king says to Solon: "My Athenian guest, we have heard much [λόγος] about you because of your wisdom and of your wanderings, how as one who loves learning you have traveled much of the world for the sake of seeing it" (καὶ σοφίης εἵνεκεν τῆς σῆς καὶ πλάνης, ὡς φιλοσοφέων γῆν πολλὴν θεωρίης εἵνεκεν ἐπελήλυθας).[9] Herodotus probably uses the word in the non-technical general sense of seeking wisdom; of interest is the connection of φιλοσοφέων and θεωρίη (contemplative observation) which we discuss below. In any case, our argument relies not on the meaning of this word in the text, but on the structure of the Croesus tale. We argue that Croesus, rather than Solon, exemplifies the philosopher (or wise man) in the end. Croesus goes from being a ruler to a captive to a wise man. Solon's philosophical wisdom is implicated in the fall (the tragic "reversal of fortune," *peripeteia*) and also the subsequent saving of Croesus.

Demonstrating the existence of a pattern from political power to loss or transcendence of such power to salvation through philosophy in both Herodotus and Plato's *Republic* will have great significance for understanding the value of ancient philosophy.[10] That Plato's philosophy cannot simply be reduced to a concern with the city and with politics requires no demonstration. As Finamore notes, the philosophical com-

---

8   The use of *philosophos* by Heraclitus is not certain in a fragment from Clement (Heraclitus fragment 35 DK = 9 Kahn), as Clement is not necessarily quoting Heraclitus *verbatim* there, although Kahn argues for its authenticity. Cf. Charles H. Kahn, *The Art and Thought of Heraclitus* (Cambridge: Cambridge University Press, 1979), 105. Burkert argues Pythagorean coinage of the word; see Walter Burkert, "Platon oder Pythagoras? Zum Ursprung des Wortes 'Philosophie'," *Hermes* 88 (1960): 159–77. However, in our opinion, the stress on *love* of wisdom as something one lacks, rather than possesses, seems to be a Socratic and Platonic theme, whereas Pythagoras thought of himself as *being* a holy man or *sophos*; see Peter Kingsley, *Ancient Philosophy, Mystery, and Magic: Empedocles and the Pythagorean Tradition* (Oxford: Oxford University Press, 1995).

9   Hdt. I.30.2 (our translation). Too many translators render σοφίη as "knowledge" and ignore θεωρίη altogether.

10 Indeed, according to Benardete, the question of "what philosophy is seems to be inseparable from the question of how to read Plato." Seth Benardete, "Strauss on Plato," in *The Argument of the Action: Essays on Greek Poetry and Philosophy*, ed. Ronna Burger and Michael Davis (Chicago: University of Chicago Press, 2000), 407.

munity (*koinonia*) in Plato is neither merely that between the members of a city nor that between the philosopher and the city, but rather that between humans and the divine, as members of a rational order. In this respect, the philosophical community transcends the political community.[11] To take an example, in the *Republic*, Socrates' lengthy discussions on the nature of justice, the construction of a well-ordered city as well as the best forms of education and rule are interwoven with seemingly "religious" topics such as arguments for the immortality of the soul, descriptions of the soul's afterlife journey, and finally a cosmological vision in the myth of Er in Book X.[12] Moreover, Socrates himself underscores a disjunction between philosophical and political existence in *Hippias Major*: "But Hippias, how in the world do you explain this: in the old days people who are still famous for wisdeom—Pittacus and Bias and the school of Thales of Miletus, and later ones down to Anaxagoras—that all or most of those people, we see, kept away from affairs of state?" (281c).[13]

The disjunction between political life and the search for self-knowledge Plato invokes here would seem to be especially underscored in the *Phaedo*, a dialogue in which Socrates famously declares: "I am afraid that other people do not realize that the one aim of those who practice philosophy in the proper manner is to practice for dying and death" (64a). Socrates says to Cebes and Simmias that they "seem to have this childish fear that the wind would really dissolve and scatter the soul…" (77d-e) and suggests that they "sing a charm" to the child in them until they "have charmed away his fears" (77e). It is clear that Socrates himself is the "charmer" who charms away the fear of death, as Cebes then says, "[w]here shall we find a good charmer for these fears, Socrates… now that you are leaving us?" (78a). The theme of mortality informs the *Republic* as well: the dialogue proper begins with Socrates' question to

---

11 Cf. John Finamore and Algis Uzdavinys, *The Golden Chain: An Anthology of Pythagorean and Platonic Philosophy* (Bloomington, Indiana: World Wisdom Inc., 2004).
12 While some scholars (e.g., Annas) have argued that Plato does not succeed in harmonizing these two aspects and that the myth of Er especially is an awkward addition to an otherwise serious and rational discussion of justice and epistemology, we argue that the dialogue's integrity can be better understood if we see Socrates' central concern as the ultimate concern of mortals, which includes providing an account of death.
13 Plato, *Plato: Complete Works*, ed. John M. Cooper (Indianapolis and Cambridge: Hackett, 1997). (All references to this edition.)

the aged Cephalus, who stands on "the threshold of old age" (328e), and concludes with Er's death in battle and revival upon a pyre.

More broadly, the motif of a disjunction between the political and the philosophical, especially in its soteriological aspect, seems to be an important theme in Greek thought; echoes can be found in Sophocles' *Oedipus Tyrannus* as well as in Presocratic thinkers. Diogenes Laertius tells us that Heraclitus relinquished the title of king to his younger brother (D.L. IX.6), while Heraclitus says of himself: "I went in search of myself" (fr. 101). In the myth preserved by Heraclides of Pontus, a member of Plato's Academy, this pattern repeats in Empedocles' leap into the volcanic crater.[14]

In this article, we first examine the literary evidence for speaking of "salvation" or of a "salvific" philosophy in Plato's *Republic*. We argue that Plato's programmatic use of the term σωτηρία reveals a pervasive concern with "salvation," although how such "salvation" is to be understood remains to be defined. Although scholars have considered the *Republic's* philosophical project from the perspective of providing a therapy and of constructing the ideal city, we argue that the motif of salvation is an equally pervasive concern. In order to determine how this salvation is to be understood, we then turn to Plato's myth of Gyges. Finally, we turn to Herodotus for a fuller look at the "Gyges to Croesus" story to establish a pattern that will then help when we return to the ending of the *Republic* in the "saving" Myth of Er.

II. On Plato's "Soteriology"

The theme of salvation in Plato's dialogues in general has been addressed by several scholars, most notably by Gregory Vlastos.[15] Vlastos notes two ways in which the "sense of reverence for life" is strengthened in Greek thought, of which only the first is of relevance to us here: "The supernatural psyche could be retained and reformed, turned into an infinitely more robust affair, human and superhuman, an incarnate god or daemon, possessing in life and conserving after death all the powers of

---

14 See H.B. Gottschalk, *Heraclides of Pontus* (Oxford: Clarendon Press, 1980), and, for Empedocles as a wonder-working holy man, Kingsley 1995.
15 See his "Theology and Philosophy in Early Greek Thought," *The Philosophical Quarterly* 2.7 (1952): 97–123. See also Finamore and Uzdavinys 2004 and Stephen Menn, "Plato's Soteriology?" in this volume.

thought, will, and passion of the full-blooded man, with an extra load of divine powers thrown in for good measure. This was the way of the mystery-cults. The Orphic theogonies, Pythagoras, the Empedocles of the *Purifications*, and finally and most triumphantly Plato, adopted and justified this faith. Plato's influence made it a dominant doctrine of Hellenistic thought; thence it passed with appropriate modifications into Christian theology…"[16] Finamore, too, notes that Platonic philosophy is oriented towards a final experience of transformation, namely, from the mortality of human existence to the immortality of divine being: "Plato compares philosophy with preparing for death (*Phaedo* 67cd) and its goal with becoming like god (*Theaetetus* 176b)."[17] While one could debate the legitimacy of using terms such as "salvation" in the context of Platonic philosophy given their Christian overtones, it is clear that, at a lexical and semantic level at least, there is justification for using the term, as Plato frequently makes use of the terms σωτήρ, σωτηρία, and σῴζειν in the *Republic*.

The first occurrence of the term σωτηρία (346 a8) introduces two metaphors, that of health and navigation. Socrates says that each art produces its specific benefit (ὠφελίαν), the art of medicine (ἰατρική) health (ὑγίειαν), the art of navigation (κυβερνητική) safety at sea (σωτηρίαν ἐν τῷ πλεῖν). The nautical metaphor recurs in a passage containing both the terms σῴζεσθαι and σωτηρίαν (453 d11), in which Socrates invokes Herodotus' story of Arion's rescue from drowning (*Histories* I.23–4). Socrates says that he and his interlocutors too must try to escape (σῴζεσθαι) out of a sea of argument and hope that a dolphin provides rescue (σωτηρίαν). The concluding passage of the *Republic* once again invokes the metaphor of a "good crossing," but the emphasis now shifts from political or physical salvation to saving the soul.[18]

Other passages (425e 3 and 433c8) seem to link salvation to the city's constitution, but never to individual citizens. However, even here Socrates invokes either the gods or a guiding noetic principle in the preservation of the laws. Although we cannot make the stronger case that the word σωτηρία exclusively refers to saving the individual, the weaker point that σωτηρία and related terms have a wider applica-

---

16 Vlastos 1952, 122.
17 Finamore and Uzdavinys 2004, 1.
18 For the importance of the metaphor of sailing as a key to Socrates' entire philosophical approach, see Seth Benardete, *Socrates' Second Sailing: On Plato's Republic* (Chicago: University of Chicago Press, 1992).

tion than just to the city should be noted. Two terms (σωτηρίαν, διασῴζεσθαι) occur at 429 c5, 6, 9, and refer to the preservation of one's discrimination between what is to be feared and what not, both in desire and in pain; this preservation is in the soul (ἐν ἐπιθυμίαις). 430b2 again refers to σωτηρίαν as a power (δύναμιν) in the soul as to what is to be feared and not feared. 433b10 refers to justice as a quality that brings about and ensures the preservation (σωτηρίαν) of the remaining virtues of soberness, courage, and intelligence. At 463b1, the rulers of the democratic city are said to be σωτῆρας and ἐπικούρους (saviors and helpers). Although this appears to directly link salvation to politics, this statement must be seen against the background of the foregoing discussion of the virtues. Again, at 465d8, those who ensure the salvation of the state (τῆς πόλεως σωτηρίαν) are ensured honors and a worthy burial, but we should note that these rites do not play a role in Er's death. This suggests that "political salvation" is superseded in the final myth of Er. At 549 b7 it becomes explicit that what truly preserves is reason (λόγος); Socrates says that a certain kind of λόγος[19] itself is the φύλαξ and furthermore, that "is the only indwelling preserver (σωτήρ) of virtue throughout life in the soul that possesses it."

Socrates brings the *Republic* to a close with the words: "And so, Glaucon, a myth was saved (μῦθος ἐσώθη) and not destroyed, and it would save us (σώσειεν), if we were persuaded by it, for we would then make a good crossing of the River of Forgetfulness, and our souls wouldn't be defiled" (621b-c; our translation). Once again, the language of salvation occurs together with the metaphor of crossing or navigating a body of water, though now this image is linked specifically to not drinking from the River of Forgetfulness (cf. 621a). This passage should be read in conjunction with Socrates' words at 618b-619b where we are given a definition of what it means to be "saved": salvation is understood *both* as avoiding the greatest danger of all for a human (ὁ πᾶς κίνδυνος ἀνθρώπῳ, καὶ διὰ ταῦτα μάλιστα; 618b)[20] and as attaining the greatest happiness (εὐδαιμονέστατος γίγνεται; 619b).

---

19 Namely, λόγος blended with culture (μουσικῇ).
20 Cf. *Phaedo* 107c, 114d, *Gorg.* 526e, Eurip. *Medea* 235 ἀγὼν μέγιστος, Thucyd. i.32.5 μέγας ὁ κίνδυνος, Aristoph. *Clouds* 955 νῦν γὰρ ἅπας . . . κίνδυνος ἀνεῖται, *Frogs* 882 ἀγὼν . . . ὁ μέγας, Antiphon v. 43 ἐν ᾧ μοι ὁ πᾶς κίνδυνος ἦν. For the expression cf. *Gorg.* 470e ἐν τούτῳ ἡ πᾶσα εὐδαιμονία ἐστιν.

III. The Myth of Gyges in Plato

Given this lexical proliferation, it appears worthwhile to pursue the question of what "salvation" in a Platonic context might mean. Specifically, we shall focus on the *Republic* as framed by Plato's myths of Gyges (Book II) and of Er (Book X). The myth of Gyges poses problems which are later, it can be argued, resolved and transcended with the concluding myth of Er. Thus, while the myth of Gyges draws the work into a discussion of politics, towards the end of the dialogue Plato sets aside the political discussion of the first nine books. Indeed, in the myth of Er, he returns once more to the themes with which the entire dialogue began: the course of a human life, aging and death, and the good life (328d7 ff.).

The *Republic's* first sentence has Socrates attending a religious festival, and the opening discussion raises the question, what is true piety (331a5, b2)? Book I then introduces the lengthy analysis of justice, but we must remember that the *Republic* begins and ends with broader, generally existential and religious themes. In fact, in this light, the myth of Gyges, as Plato has Glaucon tell it, proves to pose problems that take a long time to answer.

Glaucon relates the story of a shepherd of Lydia,[21] the ancestor of Gyges, who sees a gap in the earth and descends into the chasm. "There was a violent thunderstorm, and an earthquake broke open the ground and created a chasm at the place where he was tending his sheep. Seeing this, he was filled with amazement and went down into it" (καταβῆναι καὶ ἰδεῖν... θαυμαστά; 359d). On descending into the chasm, he sees a hollow bronze horse and an oversized corpse wearing a gold ring. Finding that the gold ring had the power to make him invisible, he later uses it to seize political power after killing the king.

Glaucon offends against a sense of limits (benignly if conventionally expressed by Cephalus earlier) and against Socrates' already-stated notion of justice as more valuable than gold (336e6–7). He mounts a rigorous offense against justice by praising injustice (358e ff.), presenting the story of Gyges as the perfect example of someone who can act hubristically and get away with it. To challenge Socrates' notion that justice must be good in itself and for its possessor by itself, without regard

---

21 Thrasymachus had indeed recast the tyrant as a shepherd that fleeces his flock (343b-d). Glaucon is remaining true to his stated purpose of resurrecting the Thrasymachean argument (358b).

to its rewards or consequences (358a), Glaucon argues that those who act justly do so out of fear of punishment or out of a desire to gain a reputation for justice (359a-d). In his view, those who behave justly now would behave quite differently, were they but to find some way of carrying out their actions unnoticed. As an example, Gyges refers to the power of invisibility provided by the ring of Gyges' ancestor.

Glaucon argues that if men were in possession of such a ring which granted its wearer the power of invisibility, they would practice injustice with impunity and seek only what was to their material advantage (361c). In other words, they would seek to apply one *nomos* across the board, namely, the pursuit of their self-interest. Morever, as becomes clear from Glaucon's version of the story, nothing would be hidden to such a person any more: he could hear private conversations and look into private lives.[22] For Glaucon, Gyges' ring represents the dream of unlimited political power. Indeed, its wearer would not even need to fear retribution from the gods, being able to offer up large sacrifices to them (362b-c).[23]

Glaucon's myth offends against religious piety in another way, besides the broadly political ones just mentioned (i. e., in relation to transactions between people). His version of the myth describes a descent into the ground that can be read as a perversion of a ritual descent. A *katabasis*, or ritual descent, was a central element of mystery-cults.[24] Plato draws upon this tradition, for not only is the first word of the *Re-*

---

22 This is precisely what Candaules desired: the abolishment of the distinction between private and public. In Glaucon's version of the Gyges story, the limitless power of the ring makes the impossible possible and opens the gates to the phantasm of limitless hegemony.
23 The quasi-historical Gyges of Herodotus' *Histories* is the perfect example, for he legitimated his rule through invoking the Delphic oracle and later sent many offerings to the oracle, as did Croesus.
24 On the role of *katabasis* in ancient religion, see Walter Burkert, "Das Proömium des Parmenides und die Katabasis des Pythagoras," *Phronesis* 14 (1969): 1–30. The relation of mystery-cults to philosophical *theoria* might be explored further. See Christoph Riedweg, *Mysterienterminologie bei Platon, Philon und Klemens von Alexandrien* (Berlin: De Gruyter, 1987); Peter Kingsley, *In the Dark Places of Wisdom* (Inverness, CA: The Golden Sufi Center, 1999); Vishwa Adluri, "Initiation into the Mysteries: The Experience of the Irrational in Plato," *Mouseion* III.6 (2006): 407–423.

public κατέβην (327a),[25] but the whole dialogue is structured as a series of descents. As Rosen notes: "The theme of descent plays an important role in the dramatic structure of the *Republic*. To note only the obvious, Socrates and Glaucon descend from Athens to Piraeus at the very beginning of the dialogue; Book Seven begins with a descent from the sunlight into the cave of shadows…; the dialogue closes with an account of the descent of Er into Hades. Each of these descents is described in considerably greater detail than the outstanding example of ascent to the Idea of the Good, or more properly, to its surrogate, the image of the sun."[26]

Socrates elsewhere explicitly links the philosophical experience to initiation into the mysteries. For example, in the *Theaetetus*, he addresses the young Theaetetus, saying: "Then I dare say you will be grateful to me if I help you to discover the veiled truth in the thought of a great man… Then you have a look round and see that none of the uninitiated are listening to us—I mean the people who think that nothing exists but what they can grasp with both hands; people who refuse to admit that actions and processes and the invisible world in general have any place in reality" (155e). Unlike Theaetetus who is a mathematician, Plato's brothers are not open to the possibility of the invisible aspects of reality, whether the immortal soul or the just god.

While retaining the external appearance of a myth (such as some that Socrates makes up), Glaucon's myth is a scientifically demystifying, iconoclastic counter-account.[27] This is a natural descent with only the most superficial resonances to an initiatory *katabasis*. An earthquake

---

25 Cf. Lars Albinus, "The *Katabasis* of Er. Plato's Use of Myths, exemplified by the Myth of Er," in *Essays on Plato's* Republic, ed. Erik Nis Ostenfeld (Aarhus: Aarhus University Press, 1998), 91–105.

26 Stanley Rosen, *Plato's Republic: A Study* (New Haven, CT: Yale University Press, 2005), 19.

27 See *Phaedrus* 229c-230b for Socrates' criticism of iconoclastic rationalism; Socrates responds to Phaedrus' rationalization of the myth of Boreas and Oreithyia by saying, "Actually, it would not be out of place for me to reject it, as our intellectuals [not *sophoi* but *sophotatoi*] do. I could then tell a clever story: I could claim that a gust of the North Wind blew her over the rocks where she was playing with Pharmaceia; and once she was killed that way people said she had been carried off by Boreas… Now, Phaedrus, such explanations are amusing enough, but they are a job for a man I cannot envy at all… But I have no time for such things; and the reason, my friend, is this. I am still unable, as the Delphic inscription orders, to know myself; and it really seems to me ridiculous to look into other things before I have understood that."

and a thunderstorm, purely natural phenomena, are enough to explain the opening in the ground. Gyges' ancestor's descent is not a ritual descent into Hades but into a man-made tomb. He does not encounter something that transcends mortal life, rather, the remains of it: death and artifacts. The shepherd's descent is not only irreligious, it is a shocking profanation. He thinks nothing of looting a tomb. Although he does not dig up the corpse, he shows it little respect. He does not respect that which must remain covered. The superficial resemblance of this account to an initiatory *katabasis* only underscores the impiety of Glaucon's speech. This Thrasymachean shepherd becomes a ruler (practically a tyrant) rather than an initiate into the mysteries of being.

In this perverse *katabasis*, the wonders (the word is used twice in the span of one sentence; 359d) encountered are not those of philosophy or the mysteries.[28] Rather, the wonders the man encounters are burlesque wonders: a bronze horse, an oversized man, and a magical ring. Without philosophical piety, that is, the ability to give an account of the eternal, of the participation of divine *nous* in matter and the immortality of the soul, un-philosophical wonder is immature and laughable. The objects Gyges' ancestor encounters in the underworld belong to a world of physical materiality. They represent the inadequacy of a world of phenomena, in which historical and political relations dominate.[29] The fact that there are no consequences to unjust actions is eloquently conveyed by the corpse on which Gyges found the ring: there is no afterlife, no immortality of the soul and no judgment. Biological life is the only reality: the corpse is an oversized remainder of this biological existence. The only meaning attributable to this physical being is political power. For Glaucon and Adeimantus, trapped in this universe of phenomena where physical existence is the only reality and political power the highest end they know, Gyges' easy fortune represents the best life has to offer. In the absence of this insight into the distinction between appearance and reality, all that remains is a transactional relationship between individuals and things, a relationship that can only be one of power.

To bring them to an appreciation of justice as good in itself, Socrates must correct this view. His pedagogy takes the form of a *psychagoge*, a

---

28 Cf. *Theaetetus* 155d: "For this is an experience which is characteristic of a philosopher, this wondering: this is where philosophy begins and nowhere else."
29 The oversized horse recalls the heroic age, especially the Greek horse at Troy, while the ring provides power over the physical and political realm.

turning around of the soul, which turns the brothers' gaze away from the merely phenomenal world of becoming to eternal being. Indeed, Glaucon himself exhibits a desire for something that transcends the purely phenomenal and the changeful: he says to Socrates that he does not really believe in the story he is telling (358d) and asks him to present a robust counter-account that will establish once and for all that justice is good in itself.

The challenge to Socrates lies, therefore, in "redefining" justice so that it relates to reality rather than mere appearance. He must show the brothers that justice is linked to being rather than to either *nomos* or nature.[30] When the distinction between reality and appearance is fully explicated, Socrates will have answered the challenge posed by the myth of Gyges and provided a full demonstration of his own piety, for Socratic piety is linked to an understanding of the immortality of the soul.[31]

From the very beginning, Socrates is handicapped in three ways:

---

30 While Davis rightly sees that justice goes beyond *nomos*, because *nomos* itself is founded upon nature, Socrates goes even beyond *phusis* in the myth of Er. The ontological education in the *Republic* is meant to successively overcome phenomena (the first stage), *nomos* (the conventions founded on phenomena), *phusis* (nature which acts as a limit to *nomos*) and, finally, even *logos* (which is the articulation of the city and the cosmos). For the notion that there is a kind of "justice" operative even at the level of *phusis*, see Anaximander: "And the source of coming-to-be for existing things is that into which destruction, too, happens 'according to necessity; for they pay penalty and retribution to each other for their injustice according to the assessment of Time'" (12 A9). G. S Kirk, J. E. Raven, and M. Schofield, *The Presocratic Philosophers,* 2nd ed. (Cambridge: Cambridge University Press, 1983).

31 As Cornford notes of Plato's soteriology: "To the Orphic physical death is an escape from the bodily tomb—a rising from the dead. The idea is familiar from Euripides' famous lines, from the phrase οἱ ἄνω νεκροί applied by Aristophanes' mystics to 'living' men (*Frogs*, 420), and from many other passages. Plato adopts the same notion, but gives it a new content. To him also the body of the natural man is a sepulchre and a house of bondage; but, like S. Paul, he realizes that the escape from the prison, the resurrection from the body of this death, is not physical death (or not only that), but a 'conversion.' ... Unlike S. Paul, however, Plato conceives the process which begins with conversion—the ascent of man from flesh to spirit—as accomplished by a systematic training of the intelligence... The body with its senses and lusts hinders the clear perception of truth by the soul. The soul must be delivered from the body 'as from bonds' (67D) by philosophy, which is a 'rehearsal of death.'" Francis M. Cornford, "Plato and Orpheus," *CR* 17.9 (1903): 436.

a) He cannot appeal to the experience of *katabasis*.
b) He also cannot use the language of initiation in this context, and finally,
c) Glaucon lacks both the piety of vision (in that he figuratively lays bare what must be kept covered) and the acuity of vision (in seeing only a corpse and not the invisible soul).

Glaucon, unsurprisingly, turns Socrates' language of ritual initiation into the mysteries against him by mocking not just the ritual, but also the mystagogue. He accuses Socrates of being a snake-charmer (358b) as well as of being no better than Thrasymachus (358b3–4).

Socrates meets the brothers' challenge by presenting a new vision in the myth of Er. By turning first to the *polis* and showing its limits (in Book IX even the best state is shown to fall), he then turns in Book X to the cosmos, before finally turning to the self in the concluding myth of Er. Only by setting the cosmos aside in the myth of Er in a grand vision, can Socrates reveal to Plato's brothers the true locus of justice as harmony of the soul.

IV. The Myths of Gyges and Croesus in Herodotus

In invoking Gyges, Plato took up a story known from Herodotus. Herodotus wrote his *Histories*, in which the Lydian narrative features prominently in Book I, before 429 BCE (before Plato was born). Plato's version probably is dependent on Herodotus', as Laird argues.[32] Comparisons of Plato and Herodotus discuss Gyges' usurpation, but stop before the prophecy of the fall of the dynasty he founded; no one discusses Herodotus' ensuing philosophical "Solon and Croesus" narrative in this connection.

1. Gyges

The story begins with Gyges' usurpation and establishment of what became a rich dynasty in Lydia (just to the east of the Ionian Greek cities of Asia Minor). Indeed, it is important to note that Gyges was already a

---

32 Interestingly, Plato's family claimed descent from Solon (cf. *Charmides* 155a and *Critias*), who features prominently in Herodotus' version of the Gyges narrative.

well-known symbol of power for the Greeks before this. Gyges appears to have been the archetypal tyrant for the Greeks. The first known use of the word "tyrant" (*tyrannos*) occurs in a poem by the 7th century BCE poet Archilochus.[33] Drews writes that the word "*tyrannos*" "was unknown to the Greeks before…[Gyges'] time, and Archilochus, the first Greek writer to use the word, may have used it in reference to Gyges: I do not care for the goods of gold-rich Gyges, / Envy has not gripped me, and I do not desire / The works of gods, nor do I lust for a great tyranny."[34] Drews further notes that "the author of the *Hypothesis* to Sophocles' *Oedipus Tyrannos* noted that *tyrannos* was not an apt title for Oedipus, and that poets were inaccurate when they called kings who ruled before the Trojan War, 'tyrants'; for the word did not circulate among the Greeks until rather recently; in the time of Archilochus, as Hippias the sophist says." Hippias, the fifth century antiquarian, presumably found no use of the word in any of the Homeric or Hesiodic corpus.

While *tyrannos* probably had neutral moral connotations in early Greece—the word was borrowed from Lydian to refer to one-man, non-traditional rule—Archilochus clearly uses it negatively, to reject the weath and power of the East in favor of his own human values (as Herodotus and Plato will do in their own different ways).

Herodotus relates how Gyges unjustly seized power (I.8–12). Gyges, son of Dascylus, was the bodyguard and confidant of Candaules, the king of Lydia. Candaules, filled with conceit that his wife was the most beautiful of women, praises her immoderately to Gyges. Assuming that "people trust their ears less than their eyes" (I.8), Candaules urges Gyges to view his naked wife. Gyges protests but Candaules convinces him to hide himself and commit this voyeuristic crime.[35] The queen dis-

---

33 Of interest is the fact that Herodotus himself refers to the poem by Archilochus that mentions Gyges.
34 Robert Drews, "The First Tyrants in Greece," *Historia: Zeitschrift für Alte Geschichte* 21.2 (1972): 137; cf. also Walter Woodburn Hyde, "The Greek Tyrannies," *The Classical Weekly* 37.11 (1944): 123–125.
35 We must, however, distinguish between two types of the unseen:
   a. That which one may not see and which must remain covered over (e.g., another man's wife or a naked corpse). Oedipus in Sophocles' *Oedipus Tyrannus* exemplifies the horror of violating this type of prohibition: "He [Oedipus] tore the brooches—/ the gold chased brooches fastening her robe—/ away from her and lifting them up high / dashed them on his own eyeballs, shrieking out / such things as: they will never see the crime…" (1268–1272; transl. David

covers Gyges' crime and demands that for "seeing what you should not see" Gyges must now choose between regicide and execution. Gyges chooses the first option and through a cycle of ever-escalating injustice ascends to the throne and founds the wealthy and powerful Lydian dynasty.

For Davis, the Gyges story is emblematic of the entire *Histories*; he writes: "Now, the deepest of Herodotus' themes in the *History* is embedded in this story—the power of *nomos* or law in its relation to nature."[36] In fact, as he notes, Herodotus addresses a deeper problem, that of human mortality. "He [Herodotus] writes in order to prevent what comes to be in time from being eradicated in time.... Herodotus means somehow to overcome human temporality."[37] Davis argues that Candaules' desire is hubristic, in that he wishes to universalize his private experience of the world. "His desire for Gyges to confirm his wife's beauty is tantamount to a desire that there be no distinction between his experience of the world and the world. This is, unwittingly, but essentially, a tyrannical desire for a truly universal empire."[38] But Candaules' hegemonic desire runs up against an internal contradiction: in seeking to make the same *nomos* apply to all,[39] Candaules effectively overturns *nomos*. Davis thus interprets Candaules' wife as a symbol for nature as an autonomous, private realm that acts as a limit to political power. For Davis, the story of Gyges is of global significance to Herodotus' *History*, because it relates to the central tension at the heart of his

---

Grene). *The Complete Greek Tragedies*, vol 2. *Sophocles*, ed. David Grene and Richard Lattimore (Chicago and London: University of Chicago Press, 1992).

b. That which remains unseen owing to "mortal *doxa*" or ignorance. Here, there is no prohibition; rather, there is an urging to philosophical viewing. The Parmenidean *kouros* is invited by the goddess to lift the veil on this type of the invisible: "Gaze upon things absent nevertheless present to the mind certainly; / For you will not sever being (*to eon*) from holding fast (*echesthai*) to being (*tou eontos*), / Neither [Being] scattering everywhere in every way throughout the universe (*kata kosmon*), / Nor coming together" (Fr. 4; our translation).

While Gyges uncovers the first type of the unseen, Er discloses the second type. The former action is a transgression and leads to eventual downfall, while the latter leads to salvation.

36 Davis 2000, 637.
37 Davis 2000, 637.
38 Davis 2000, 641 ff.
39 Davis notes that Herodotus twice says that Candaules held his wife to be most beautiful, each time using the verb *nomizō* (Davis 2000, 643). The law (*nomos*) that applies to a husband who may look upon his wife is, of course, other than that which applies to a stranger such as Gyges.

main subject, the Persian wars. "Herodotus begins the *History* with the Gyges story because it points to the impossibility of this Persian project for universal dominion. For there remains something that cannot be made public itself but without which the public cannot be."[40]

The story of Gyges thus has a philosophical dimension in Herodotus, for it reveals the dependence of *nomos* upon nature. The myth underscores the temporality of *nomos* and the impossibility of overcoming human temporality, whether by positing an absolute *nomos* or by attaining universal dominion.

We need not fully agree with Davis in seeing the woman as the regenerative faculty of nature to preserve the insight that political power is essentially finite. The best empires topple. This experience of the finitude of dynastic power is radicalized in the experience of individual finitude as the experience of one's death. The mutually exclusive choice between power or death offered Gyges is further explicated in the myth of Croesus, where it becomes evident that regicide and the power it brings Gyges does not banish the specter of death. So, the true choice Candaules' wife articulates is that between death and the consolation of a seeming immortality through power. But this is not true immortality, inasmuch as death sets an ineradicable limit to political power. The mutually exclusive choice between power or death offered Gyges is further recalled when the oracle of Delphi confirms Gyges in power, but foretells that his line will fall from power in the fifth generation: with Croesus, it turns out, who learns several lessons of death and finitude.

In having Glaucon tell the story of the beginning of Gyges' dynasty (in the person of his ancestor, in that case), Plato made some changes of emphasis from his supposed model. Herodotus' version of the story underscores the dangers of *hubris*, especially of violating the boundaries of the hidden and the private and of seeking to extend one law across all subjects. Glaucon praises the limitless abilities of Gyges' ancestor and his apparent ability to bring some magical power back from the land of the dead and to violate the boundaries of *nomos*. But he is aware, perhaps uncomfortably, that Gyges is unjust, and he depicts the man as having a self-serving materialistic notion of piety.

There are good reasons why Glaucon should invoke the tyrant in his attack on justice. Gyges gets away with murder, both literally and figuratively. Moreover, Gyges' story seems to confirm Glaucon's claim that

---

40 Davis 2000, 647.

the unjust man can buy not only the approval of his fellow-men but also the sanction of the gods. According to Herodotus, Gyges was able to secure his claims to Lydian kingdom with the aid of the oracle.[41] In Glaucon's eyes, Gyges quite likely represents the archetypal example of acting unjustly while escaping detection and buying the favor of the gods. Socrates spends the next nine books of the *Republic* purifying this story of these impious charges and bringing Glaucon around to seeing that "The responsibility lies with the one who makes the choice; the god has none" (αἰτία ἑλομένου θεὸς ἀναίτιος; 617e5). And, contrary to what Glaucon believes, one cannot act without regard to the consequences of one's actions, whether in the form of rewards or retribution. Socrates concludes the *Republic* with these words: "That way we'll be friends both to ourselves and to the gods while we remain here on earth and afterwards—like victors in the games who go around collecting their prizes—we'll receive our rewards" (621b).

But before we can see how Socrates is able to turn the Gyges story to his advantage, let us first see Herodotus' continuation of the story.

2. Croesus

Although Gyges himself seems to have evaded justice and escaped execution, these themes return with full force in a *coda* concerning the fifth descendant of his line. Indeed, the same Delphic oracle that confirmed Gyges as king also foretold the eventual fall of his house after five generations (I.13).

Croesus' fall from power, and his subsequent learning of wisdom, is recounted through his memorable confrontation with the Athenian sage

---

41 For the story, see Hdt., I.13–14: "Gyges was supported in obtaining the kingdom by an oracle from Delphi. For the Lydians thought that what had happened to Kandaules was dreadful and were up in arms. However, the partisans of Gyges and the rest of the Lydians came to an agreement: if the oracle declared him king, he would be king; if not, he would return the rule to the Heraklids. The oracle did in fact declare for him, and thus Gyges became king. But the Pythia added this: retribution would come from the Heraklids to the fourth descendant of Gyges. The Lydians and their kings disregarded this part of the oracle until it actually came to pass. Thus the Mermnads obtained the kingship by taking it from the Heraklids. When Gyges became king, he sent quite a few dedications off to Delphi, and of all the silver dedications in Delphi, most are his. Besides silver, he dedicated an unbelievable amount of gold. Most worthy of mention among them are the bowls; six golden bowls are his offerings...."

Solon. Herodotus writes of their meeting in a prototype of a philosophical dialogue.[42] Solon considers the course and ends of a mortal human life, posing the question, "what is happiness?" He juxtaposes wealth and other human values that make for happiness. While this in itself is a philosophical commonplace (one with which the *Republic* itself begins in Books I [Cephalus] and II, as noted above), we wish to draw attention to the impact of his teachings on Croesus, and what Croesus gains.

Solon has come to Lydia during his travels φιλοσοφέων, as Croesus says (I.30): "My Athenian guest, we have heard much [λόγος] about you because of your wisdom and of your wanderings, how as one who loves learning you have traveled much of the world for the sake of seeing it" (καὶ σοφίης εἴνεκεν τῆς σῆς καὶ πλάνης, ὡς φιλοσοφέων γῆν πολλὴν θεωρίης εἴνεκεν ἐπελήλυθας). Significantly, Croesus says "much λόγος" has reached him. What is meant by "φιλοσοφέων" here? While we cannot assume it has its later meaning of "doing philosophy," of interest here is the connection between φιλοσοφέων and θεωρίη (contemplative observation). Herodotus probably uses both words with a non-technical general sense of seeking wisdom through observation. In any case our argument relies not on the meaning of this word in the text, which is clearly a wisdom-story, but on the structure of the Croesus narrative including the subsequent fate of Croesus.

Croesus asks Solon whom he considered the most fortunate man alive, thinking Solon would be sure to respond with his name. Solon, however, does not accord him this status. Croesus then presses him, saying, "My Athenian guest... are you disparaging my own happiness as though it were nothing? Do you think me less than even a common man?" (I.32). Solon replies with the words: "You seem to me to be very wealthy, and you rule over many people, but I cannot yet tell you the answer you asked for until I learn how you have ended your life... We must look to the end of every matter to see how it will turn out. God shows many people a hint of happiness and prosperity, only to destroy them utterly later" (ibid.).

Croesus is initially not ready to receive what Solon has to tell him about his own lack of fortune. Gyges had not seen an alternative between killing the king or being killed, but Solon, by underscoring the

---

42 Kendall Sharp, "From Solon to Socrates: Proto-Socratic Dialogues in Herodotus," in *La costruzione del discorso filosofico nell'età dei Presocratici*, ed. Maria Michela Sassi (Pisa: Edizioni della Normale, 2006), 81–102.

ephemerality of all things, provides a third alternative: happiness through philosophy.

However, Croesus rejects Solon and only recalls his words when he undergoes several bad fates because he has not understood Solon's warning regarding the limits of power and fortune. He loses his son, and when he presumes to conquer the new Persian empire, loses his kingdom and becomes a captive of the Persian conquerer Cyrus.[43] Croesus is about to be burned alive on a pyre, when he remembers the conversation he had had with Solon and calls out to him three times. Intrigued, Cyrus orders his men to question Croesus. Although he is at first reluctant to give an answer, he finally relents and explains to the king's men "how after the Athenian had seen all of the king's prosperity, he still made light of it and refused to call Croesus a fortunate man. And now everything had turned out just as Solon had said, and indeed it was clear that his words applied no more to Croesus himself than to the whole human race, and especially to all those who think themselves happy and prosperous" (I.86). Hearing this, Cyrus reflects on his actions and fears retribution, seeing how changeful human affairs are. He orders that Croesus be taken down from the pyre.

But the fires are burning high by now and Cyrus' men are unable to put them out. At this, Croesus calls out to Apollo to save him if he has ever offered him any pleasing gift. Apollo sends a shower of rain that puts out the fires and Croesus is saved. Apollo—a god of wisdom through his role at Delphi—baptises philosophy in the mortal situation of Croesus at the very threshold of death.[44] The *Republic* begins exactly here: Socrates asks Cephalos "you have reached the point in life the poets call 'the threshold of old age'. Is it a difficult time? What is your report about it?" (328e).

---

43 A frequent theme in Greek philosophy, of the body as limited and bound and even a prison, and the soul as more free, is suggested here.
44 The theme of "learning through suffering" (*Aeschylus, Agamemnon*) is powerfully portrayed in Sophocles' two Oedipus plays, *Oedipus Tyrannos* and *Oedipus at Colonos*. Oedipus falls from power in Thebes, only to become a wise and holy man, who, on the verge of death, receives an apotheosis from the gods.

V. The Myth of Er

The concluding myth[45] of the *Republic*, the myth of Er, can be seen as Socrates' answer to the problems posed in the myth of Gyges.[46] Whereas the Gyges myth introduced the political problem of the definition of justice, a problem that required the construction of the ideal city in speech, the concluding myth leads us beyond the city and, in a manner of speaking, even beyond the cosmos.

Glaucon's story arrives at a conclusion shared by a cynical interpreter of the Gyges myth, where political power is everything, death nothing and *nomos* the satisfaction of desire. His use of the story of Gyges draws exactly the opposite conclusions to that drawn in Herodotus' version of the story. Whereas Herodotus sees it as a parable of *hubris* that shows that there is a natural limit to *hubris*, Glaucon interprets the powers the ring of invisibility grants its owner as a license for *hubris*. To counter this perversion, Socrates will have to reinstate the divine, which he does in the myth of Er in Book X. Socrates will show that there is no such thing as escaping detection, for even if one remains invisible to external eyes, one's actions will determine the kind of life one chooses for oneself at the lot of lives. Socrates reinstates a limit in the form of necessity, more accurately, in the form of the goddess Necessity, in whose lap the spindle to which the cosmos is attached turns.[47]

---

45 Albinus notes: "Moreover, if the myth of Er, on a micro-level, parallels the myth of the whole of the *Republic*, on a macro-level, then the *katabasis* of Er may even correspond to the whole of the dialogue as a *katabasis* itself." Albinus 1998, 100.

46 We must distinguish between two different types of myths found in Plato: a myth in Plato and written by Plato (such as the myth of Gyges, told by Glaucon in order to pose a paradox to be refuted) and a Platonic myth (such as the myth of Er) which Socrates commends to us. Socrates himself does not shy away from using myth or from quoting the poets to make his points. But whereas Plato's brothers *begin* with myth, Socrates reveals his myths only after a great deal of elenchic preparation. Halliwell distinguishes "Myths ... that occur within an ongoing conversation" (such as, presumably, the myth of Gyges) versus "those, including *Gorgias* and *Republic*, that sound the final note of a work." Halliwell 2007, 454. Morgan also stresses "final myths" such as that of Er. Kathryn Morgan, *Myth and Philosophy from the Presocratics to Plato* (Cambridge: Cambridge University Press, 2000), 209–210.

47 Cf. 616c ff. Not only does the spindle holding together the entire cosmos turn in the lap of Necessity (617b), but its rotations are controlled by her three daughters, Lachesis, Clotho and Atropos who represent the three modes of

Two aspects of this myth stand out especially for our thesis:

1. The myth marks an explicit break with the previous political analyses in that Er is referred to as a "Pamphylian" (Παμφύλου; 614b), i.e. one who belongs to all tribes.[48] In a sense, this appellation undoes a critical moment in the creation of the second city, when the city's desires for luxury required it to go to war with its neighbours for resources (372e-373e). This transcendence of political or tribal identities suggested by the term "Pamphylian" allows the discussion to move away from politics to the self. However, our argument is not based solely upon this etymology. At the lot of lives, the speaker (προφήτην; 617d) underscores the soul's individual responsibility for its life, saying: "your daemon or guardian spirit will not be assigned to you by lot; you will choose him [οὐχ ὑμᾶς δαίμων λήξεται, ἀλλ' ὑμεῖς δαίμονα αἱρήσεσθε; 617d]." Accordingly, responsibility of blame (αἰτία) for the choice lies with the individual and not with the god (θεὸς ἀναίτιος; 617e). The nine books of the *Republic* leading up to Book X seem, in general, to articulate a move from the public realm to the individual, culminating in Er's singular journey and his resurrection upon a pyre.

2. Surprisingly, the soul of a person who had "lived his previous life under an orderly constitution, where he had participated in virtue through habit and without philosophy" (ἄνευ φιλοσοφίας; 619d)[49] chooses a life of the greatest tyranny (τὴν μεγίστην τυραννίδα; 619a). The failure of the well-ordered polity (ἐν τεταγμένῃ πολιτείᾳ; 619c) to engender a better choice at the lot of lives is extremely puzzling because Socrates thereby casts doubt upon the entire enterprise of the *Republic*: the ultimate value of the ideal city. However, this is only one among several examples where Socrates appears actively to show the limitations of the life of politics or at least show that it is not necessarily conducive to the ultimate happiness of philosophy.

---

time (617c), so that the entire universe is subject to necessity *spatially, temporally and causally*.

48 Coincidentally, Croesus the king conquered a number of peoples, whom Herodotus lists ending with Pamphylians (I.28).

49 Cf. *Phaedo* 82b, where the souls of men "who have practiced popular and social virtue ... without philosophy or understanding" are said to be reborn "a social and gentle group, either of bees or wasps or ants, and then again the same kind of human group." This passage recalls Detienne's analysis of the distinction between political philosophy and the soteriological rites of the initiates (see n. 53 below).

The seemingly arbitrary way Socrates permits the ideal city to decline at 546a-547a suggests that the construction of the city, at one level, is a diversion from the central topic: the immortality of the soul and its prospects in the afterlife.[50]

This analysis shows the three-fold function of the myth of Er:

a) It provides a response to Glaucon in leading him beyond political power as well as nature in its final manifestation as cosmos and Ananke.

b) The story also shows continuity between Herodotus and Plato in that they both link happiness to philosophy understood as contemplative observation of the vicissitudes of becoming. As a consequence, both authors demonstrate skepticism in relation to politics.

c) The myth of Er is no aberration in the otherwise epistemological and political treatise that is the *Republic*,[51] but rather completes the

---

50 Burkert notes that a blessed afterlife and transmigration of the soul were pervasive ideas in late 5th century Greece and could be found in authors as diverse as Pindar, Herodotus, Empedocles and Plato. Walter Burkert, *Greek Religion* (Cambridge, MA: Blackwell, 1985), 299. Cornford notes the Platonic conception of happiness has a religious dimension. "The words θεωρεῖν and εὐδαίμων ... are both adopted by philosophers from religion; and with them is adopted their significance, that in the beatific vision man achieves union with God." Cornford 1903, 441.

51 A view espoused by Annas, for example. For Annas, Book 10 reveals "many disturbing differences from the rest of the *Republic*," "it introduces somewhat dissimilar ideas from the central books on both knowledge and Forms (191–4, 227–32)," and "adds new and unexpected points about poetry and its role, the nature of the soul, and the kind of reward that the just person can expect." She thus concludes that it "certainly seems to have been composed at a different time (or perhaps a collection of different times) and added to a work essentially complete already." *An Introduction to Plato's Republic* (Oxford: Oxford University Press, 1981), 335. On the myth of Er, Annas writes that it is "a painful shock; its vulgarity seems to pull us right down to the level of Cephalus, where you take justice seriously when you start thinking about hell-fire. It is not only that the childishness of the myth jars; if we take it seriously, it seems to offer us an entirely consequentialist reason for being just, thus undermining Plato's sustained effort to show that justice is worth having for the agent in a non-consequentialist way." Annas 1981, 349. Although she later partially revises this judgement, Annas still maintains that "we cannot get away from the fact that book 10 is scrappy and unsatisfactory as a whole." Julia Annas, "Plato's Myths of Judgement," *Phronesis* 27.2 (1982): 131. See also Halliwell on "the myth's non-Greek affinities." Halliwell 2007, 448. Reeve's note, in his noteworthy translation, is oddly dismissive and unphilosophical. Reeve sees the word *alki-mou*, "brave," used to describe Er, as a pun that, deconstructed,

philosophical journey undertaken by Socrates and his interlocutors along the path of philosophy.

VI. Conclusion

This interpretation suggests that the philosopher and historian, each in their own way, struggle with a common problem: the destructive work of time. The motif of the ephemerality of human fortune and indeed of human life as a whole dominates the work of both Plato and Herodotus, and gives a certain tragic sense to the *Republic* itself. In the myth of Er, Plato contrasts the human life-span to the revolution of the cosmos and the enormous durations this implies. Socrates, at the conclusion of the *Republic*, speaks of a "thousand-year journey." Solon, speaking to Croesus, says, "Out of all these days in the seventy years [of a man's life-span], all twenty-six thousand, two hundred and fifty of them, not one brings anything at all like another. So, Croesus, man is entirely chance" (Hdt. I 32 4)

Herodotus' Solon and Croesus (in the end) and Plato's Socrates are all concerned with human happiness in the face of death.[52] This philosophical sense of happiness often had a religious dimension in ancient Greece, as we see from Apollo saving Croesus and Er's epoptic vision. This philosophy, further, stands in contrast to a politics of excess, and indeed, we argue, to all politics.[53]

---

seems to undermine the mindfulness of the entire tale: "Socrates would then be saying something like: it isn't a tale that shows strength of understanding [*Alkinou*] that I'm going to tell but one that shows the strength of the Muse of storytelling." *Plato: Republic*, trans. C.D.C. Reeve (Indianapolis: Hackett, 2004), 319, n. 25, at 614b2–3. (This reading also suggests that Odysseus' tales as told to Alcinous are full of *nous* in the mind of Plato the writer.)

52 Challenged by Croesus to acknowledge him the happiest man on account of his wealth, Solon declines citing the mutability of fate (I.32). The idea of the ephemerality of human existence is obviously a central philosophical concern, but what is more interesting is that Socrates adopts an almost identical view in the *Republic* at 613d-e. Cf. also *Republic* 329e, where Socrates asks Cephalus if the latter bears his old age easily not so much because of his character, but because of his wealth: "for the wealthy, they say, have many consolations." Thus, Herodotean resonances are scattered throughout the *Republic*—from Book I through Book X and, especially, in the concluding myth of Er.

53 Detienne shows as well that the meaning of ancient philosophy is not exhausted by political or practical concerns, but contains a religious and intensely individ-

Philosophy looks beyond chance and the destructive work of time. A contemplation of the human life-span provides one with a perspective that may rise to that of a sage, through a contemplative viewing that transcends one's own death and perhaps even (with Er) the very workings of time. Memory preserves this wisdom for us in their stories, as Herodotus in the first sentence of his *Histories* and Socrates in the last lines of the *Republic* emphasize. Er is able to bring back the myth that will save us through not drinking too deeply from the River of Forgetfulness. Whereas Croesus' historical recollection saves him from physical death, Er's recollection saves the soul itself from embodiment, conceived of as a kind of death for the soul. The idea that the soul must "make a good crossing of the River of Forgetfulness" (621b) is central to Plato's soteriology.

Through this philosophical understanding, as Plato says, we may rise above chance and choose better lives; responsibility for one's life lies with oneself: "The responsibility lies with the one who makes the choice; the god has none" (αἰτία ἑλομένου· θεὸς ἀναίτιος; 617e5).[54]

Finally, Herodotus underscores the inevitability of fate: the priestess says to the Lydian envoys: "Fated destiny is impossible to avoid even for a god" (I.91). Although Apollo wished that Sardis be destroyed only after Croesus' lifetime, "he was unable to deflect the Fates. Indeed, as

---

ual dimension. He writes: "Toward the end of the sixth century, certain circles in Greece witnessed the birth of a type of philosophical and religious thought absolutely opposed to that of the Sophists. The thought of the Sophists was secularized, directed toward the external world, and founded on *praxis*, while the other was religious, introverted, and concerned with individual salvation. Whereas the Sophists, as a particular type of individual and as representative of a certain form of thought, were the sons of the city, and their aim, within an essentially political framework, was to influence others, the magi and initiates lived on the periphery of the city, aspiring only to an altogether internal transformation." Marcel Detienne, *The Masters of Truth in Archaic Greece*, trans. Janet Lloyd (New York: Zone Books, 1996), 119.

54 Interestingly, the Herodotean resonances continue even here. Herodotus narrates that Croesus receives permission from Cyrus to send Lydians to the Delphic oracle bearing his chains as a remonstrance to the god. Herodotus continues: Croesus then "was able to send some Lydians to Delphi ... to ask the god if he was not at all ashamed that his oracle had encouraged Croesus to make war on the Persians with the goal of ending Cyrus' power... if the Hellenic gods were habitually ungrateful" (I.90). Croesus does precisely what the souls in the myth of Er are warned against: he blames the god for his choice (cf. θεὸς ἀναίτιος; 617e). But, as in the *Republic*, the god is blameless: the priestess says that Croesus can only blame himself (ἑωυτὸν αἴτιον; Hdt. I.91.4).

a favor to Croesus, Apollo did gain as much as the Fates would concede..." (I.91). Like Herodotus, Plato is obviously interested in the idea of μοῖρα or fate which recurs in the myth of Er. The theme of the inexorability of fate achieves what is perhaps its most stunning aesthetic representation in Er's description of the three Fates, Lachesis, Clotho, and Atropos, who control the rotation of the spindles to which the cosmos is attached (617b-d).

The Herodotean narrative provides evidence of a certain understanding that linked happiness to philosophy rather than politics. It lets us contextualize Plato's deep ambiguity regarding politics, while also illuminating his understanding of μοῖρα as a natural limit to hegemonic power. The awareness of this divine limit is perhaps what motivates Plato to a discussion of the soul in its pure condition, i.e., once it has left behind earthly embodiment.[55] The embodied, itinerant soul which is at present "beset by many ills" (διακειμένην ὑπὸ μυρίων κακῶν; 611d) is akin to the sea-god Glaucus whose body is covered over with shells and seaweeds. To discover its true nature we have to look elsewhere, "[t]o its philosophy or love of wisdom" (εἰς τὴν φιλοσοφίαν; 611e), and we must realize "what it grasps and longs to have intercourse with, because it is akin to the divine and immortal and what always is" (τῷ τε θείῳ καὶ ἀθανάτῳ καὶ τῷ ἀεὶ ὄντι; 611e).[56] The soul's earthly condition keeps it tied down and even the ideal city cannot bring about its salvation. Only philosophy, which is what is most divine in a soul and culminates in its realization of its true being, can ensure salvation.[57]

---

55 Obviously, this also implies a transcendence of the political condition.
56 Cf. *Phaedo* 79d, *Laws* 899d, and *Republic* 494d τὸ συγγενὲς τῶν λόγων.
57 We have been circumspect not to define what "salvation" in Plato may mean, which is a delicate issue, beyond showing that this "salvation" cannot be equated with salvation within or for the city. Socrates' situation in the dialogue, which takes place in the Piraeus, i.e., neither inside nor outside the city, seems to us the perfect symbol for the dialogue's careful navigation of political and soteriological questions.

Rebirth Eschatology in Plato and Plotinus

John Bussanich

I. Introduction

The theory of forms and the immortality of the soul are the familiar "twin pillars of Platonism." The transmigration of souls (μετεμψύχωσις) is an important aspect of the doctrine of immortality. However, even comprehensive lists of Platonism's essential features, which include ideas like the unity of the universe, the hierarchy of being, and becoming like god, usually ignore it.[1] Some philosophers who have examined its role in ancient thought consider it "grotesque."[2] However, scholarly bias of this sort should be set aside lest it inhibit a full examination of a theory that plays such a prominent role in the thought of the two greatest Platonists, Plato and Plotinus. Platonic soteriology involves the return of the soul to its origins, its home, in the intelligible world that transcends the cycle of births and deaths. From the practical point of view, what good are the forms unless one can experience them directly and eternally? In the Platonic perspective, to achieve that goal required purification that could not be achieved within the brief compass of a single lifetime. As a corollary, explaining the presence of good and evil in human existence depended on ethicizing the rebirth cycle more thoroughly than had been done earlier.[3] Thus, both Plato and Plotinus embrace the ideas of transmigration and rebirth in support of their belief in

---

1 In his excellent discussion of the basic features of Platonism Lloyd P. Gerson *Aristotle and Other Platonists* (Ithaca: Cornell University Press, 2005), 32 ff. doubts that reincarnation is essential, though he admits that no Platonist rejected it.
2 Julia Annas, "Plato's Myths of Judgement," *Phronesis* 27.2 (1982): 138.
3 Platonist motivations for adopting a rebirth eschatology are similar to those found in India. For Max Weber the doctrines of karma and reincarnation in ancient Hinduism comprised "the most consistent theodicy ever produced in history." *The Religion of India*, p. 121 quoted in Bimal Krishna Matilal, *The Collected Essays of B.K. Matilal* (New Delhi: Oxford University Press 2002), 52.

the moral order of the universe, the causes and purpose of suffering, and the individual's attainment of perfection.[4]

In this essay I shall delineate, first, the basic elements in Plato's rebirth eschatology, focusing briefly on its sources and then more critically on his program to ethicize the phases of the rebirth cycle.[5] In the second part, I shall examine Plotinus' reformulation of these elements. The major themes in Plato's and Plotinus' rebirth eschatology are: (1) Embodiment as punishment for previous sins. (2) Afterlife judgment followed by joyful experiences in heaven for the virtuous and punishments for wrongdoers, depending on the severity of their sins. (3) After their respective rewards and punishments, souls choose their next incarnations and are reborn. (4) The character of these new births is determined by souls' discarnate experiences and choices and also by their actions in previous lives. (5) Exceptionally good, purified philosophers are liberated from the cycle of births and deaths and achieve a divine state of ineffable bliss.

In the Platonic dialogues these elements appear primarily in the myths at the end of the *Gorgias*, *Phaedo*, and *Republic*. Important discussions of segments of the rebirth cycle appear also at the mid-point of the *Meno*, in the central myth of the *Phaedrus*, and in several passages in the *Timaeus* and *Laws*. Here I shall offer only a synoptic view of these elements in order to focus on the process of ethicization. An ethicized rebirth eschatology has these features. (1) One's status in the afterlife is determined by the ethical qualities of one's embodied existence. Thus, heavenly rewards and infernal punishments are compensation for good

---

4   See Stephen Menn's "Plato's Soteriology?" chapter above for the view that for Plato salvation does not consist in escaping the rebirth cycle.
5   At the conclusion of his still valuable study, Herbert S. Long, *A Study of the Doctrine of Metempsychosis in Greece From Pythagoras to Plato* (Princeton: Princeton University Press, 1948), 86 observes that "Plato gave to the doctrine of metempsychosis the most ethical expression of which it was capable." This judgment is correct up to Plato's time—the end point of Long's inquiry—but I hope to show that the doctrine continued to evolve in significant ways after Plato. It could be argued that the Hindu and Buddhist doctrines of karma and rebirth are even more ethically sophisticated. See K. Potter, "The Karma Theory and Its Interpretation in Some Indian Philosophical Systems," in *Karma and Rebirth in Classical Indian Traditions*, ed. W. O'Flaherty (Berkeley: University of California Press, 1980), 241–267 and Wilhelm Halbfass, *Karma und Wiedergeburt im indischen Denken* (Kreuzlingen: Diederichs, 2000).

and bad actions, respectively. (2) The character of subsequent rebirths also display ethical compensation through the agency of karma.[6]

It is important to recognize several factors that complicate understanding Plato's rebirth eschatology. (1) Its constituent elements appear in mythic narratives or symbolic passages that respond to and expand on a given dialogue's dialectical sections, which address discrete problems and engage interlocutors with various beliefs.[7] (2) The piecemeal character of these treatments is further complicated by questions about where each fits in the development of Plato's thought. When the *Apology*'s playful afterlife options proposed by Socrates (nothingness vs. unending dialectical examination of famous Greeks) are compared to the elaborate scenarios in the *Republic* and *Phaedo* myths, it appears that Plato was preoccupied with eschatological ideas from the beginning and that his reflections on the afterlife deepened throughout his life. For example, post-mortem judgment is implied at the end of *Crito* and is still endorsed in his last work, the *Laws*. Proleptic reading of successive treatments of these themes might yield insights complementary to those gleaned from examining dialogues independently.[8] (3) Especially in the middle dialogues, Plato constructs myths from motifs and elements borrowed from Orphic and Pythagorean traditions and from mystery cults like those at Eleusis, which not only differ among themselves but are also internally heterogeneous.[9] (4) Plato engaged his imagination in representing invisible realities and processes in order to explore religious truths beyond the reach of rational argument.[10] This visionary material comprises crucial evidence about the soul's moral evolution that is too often ignored by philosophers who ascribe low epis-

---

6 See Gananath Obeyesekere, *Imagining Karma* (Berkeley: University of California, 2002) for theoretical and historical elaboration.
7 See Kathryn Morgan, *Myth and Philosophy from the Presocratics to Plato* (Cambridge: Cambridge University Press, 2000) for a valuable discussion of the relationship between myth and dialectic in Plato.
8 I borrow the term from Charles H. Kahn, *Plato and the Socratic Dialogue: The Philosophical Use of a Literary Form* (Cambridge: Cambridge University Press, 1997), who applies it to what he argues is Plato's intentionally gradual presentation of the theory of forms and other positions.
9 On Orphic-Pythagorean influence on Platonic eschatology see Bernabé's "ὁ Πλάτων παρωιδεῖ τὰ Ὀρφέως: Plato's Transposition of Orphic Netherworld Imagery," above.
10 For understanding this problem I am indebted to M. Morgan's excellent 1990 study of the content and aims of Plato's mature religious thought: Michael L. Morgan, *Platonic Piety* (New Haven: Yale University Press, 1990).

temological status to myths and symbols and seek to explain paradoxes in discursive terms. (5) Inconsistencies among the various accounts of the rebirth cycle comprise intentional provocations to the reader to wrestle with puzzles and reflect on mysteries. Plato's mythic forays into the beyond can thus be seen as inducing *aporiai* about the afterlife, human identity across lifetimes, the consequences of virtue and vice, etc.

The primary eschatological themes in Plato are based on explicit or implicit treatments in pre-Platonic traditions and figures: in Orphic theogonic poems, early Pythagoreanism, Orphic-Pythagorean thinkers like Pherecydes and Empedocles, Pindar, and the Gold Leaves. Transmigration and rebirth are widely attributed to Pythagoras and the early Pythagoreans, though some scholars claim that they were imported from India.[11] In any case, they appear at the same time as do new notions of the self, a sharper distinction between soul and body, and the rise of ascetic practices and ecstatic techniques that gave initiates access to other worlds. Dodds articulates well the social-cultural framework within which these tendencies appeared:

---

11 On Pythagorean provenance of transmigration see the definitive account by Walter Burkert, *Lore and Science in Ancient Pythagoreanism* (Cambridge, MA: Harvard University Press, 1972b), 125–33. Also Hermann S. Schibli, *Pherekydes of Syros* (Oxford: Oxford University Press, 1990), 106–09. Burkert argues for shamanic experiences as the immediate source of Pythagorean teaching as do E.R. Dodds, *The Greeks and the Irrational* (Berkeley: University of California Press, 1971) and Peter Kingsley, *In the Dark Places of Wisdom* (Inverness, CA: The Golden Sufi Center, 1999) and Peter Kingsley, *Reality* (Inverness, CA: The Golden Sufi Center, 2003). Peter Kingsley, *A Story Waiting to Pierce You* (Inverness, CA: The Golden Sufi Center, 2010) identifies Central Asian shamanism as the source of Pythagorean ideas and shamanic practices. In rejecting the shamanic hypothesis, Jan N. Bremmer, *The Rise and Fall of the Afterlife* (London: Routledge, 2002) implausibly argues that "Pythagoras' loss of political power may well have been an extra stimulus for developing the doctrine of reincarnation, since it would guarantee a 'survival' beyond all previous possibilities" (25). He also suggests that the Pythagoreans promoted the idea out of a sense of their own "self-importance." It is remarkable how far scholars will go to avoid acknowledging the experiential origins of beliefs about otherworldy realms. Note also Michael Inwood, "Plato's Eschatological Myths," in *Plato's Myths*, ed. Catalin Partenie (Cambridge: Cambridge University Press, 2009), 38 who supposes that Plato embraced the idea of reincarnation in order to relieve the boredom entailed by immortality! For well-informed discussions of Indic and Greek rebirth theories see Thomas McEvilley, *The Shape of Ancient Thought. Comparative Studies in Greek and Indian Philosophies* (New York: Allworth Press, 2002) and Obeyesekere 2002.

morally, reincarnation offered a more satisfactory solution to the Late Archaic problem of divine justice than did inherited guilt or post-mortem punishment in another world. With the growing emancipation of the individual from the old family solidarity, his increasing rights as a judicial 'person', the notion of a vicarious payment for another's fault began to be unacceptable. When once human law had recognised that a man is responsible for his own acts only, divine law, must sooner or later do likewise. As for post-mortem punishment, that explained well enough why the gods appeared to tolerate the worldly success of the wicked, and the new teaching in fact exploited it to the full, using the device of the 'underworld journey' to make the horrors of Hell real and vivid to the imagination. But the post-mortem punishment did not explain why the gods tolerated so much human suffering, and in particular the unmerited suffering of the innocent: all were paying, in various degrees, for crimes of varying atrocity committed in former lives. And all that squalid mass of suffering, whether in this world or in another, was but part of the soul's long education—an education that would culminate at last in its release from the cycle of birth and return to its divine origin. Only in this way, and on this cosmic time-scale, could justice in its full archaic sense—the justice of the law that 'the Doer shall suffer'—be completely realised for every soul.[12]

The second half of Dodds's précis of the archaic and classical Greek Zeitgeist is a brilliant extrapolation beyond the available evidence. A full-blown compensatory "karmic ethics" of the sort implied in the phrase "the doer shall suffer"—in the sense of suffering in one's present life for deeds done in a past life—is not expounded in a systematic way by Plato but only later in Plotinus. I would agree, however, that, once the ideas of transmigration and reincarnation appeared on the scene, an inexorable moral logic generated a series of conceptual refinements aimed at accomodating new theories of the self, individual responsibility, and compensation for wrongdoing.

In that time of cultural change, Dodds argued, shamans like Orpheus, Zalmoxis, Epimenides, Hermotimus, Pythagoras, and Empedocles "diffused the belief in a detachable soul or self, which by suitable techniques can be withdrawn from the body even during life, a self which is older than the body and will outlast it."[13] This occult self, "the carrier of man's potential divinity"[14] and also of his guilt, was thought to be imprisoned in a physical body and bound to an empirical

---

12 Dodds 1971, 150–51. The "moral logic" and cultural factors that motivated the emergence of a complex rebirth eschatology in Vedic India is similar in many respects. Cf. Obeyesekere 2002, ch. 3.
13 Dodds 1971, 146–47.
14 Dodds 1971, 153.

personality. Ecstatic dissociation and meditative withdrawal from the body gave these Orphic-Pythagoreans experiential access to the soul's immortal nature in its passage through the rebirth cycle. Empedocles Fr. 129 confirms this in describing Pythagoras as a "man of surpassing knowledge…who had acquired the utmost wealth of understanding: for whenever he reached out with all his understanding, easily he saw each of all the things that are, in ten and even twenty generations of men."[15]

Plato invokes these religious authorities—both their ideas and the underlying experiences—in order to inject eschatological themes into the dialogues. As early as the *Meno* (81b) and *Gorgias* (493a) Socrates cites certain priests and priestesses, Pindar, and Orphic-Pythagoreans for the beliefs that the soul is immortal, that it must pay a penalty for wrongdoing, that it experiences post-mortem rewards and punishments, and that it is reborn many times. Socrates repeatedly refers to what "he has heard" or learned from the mystery teachings about otherworldly journeys.[16] Plato does not employ these phrases as gratuitous literary devices, as is often argued.[17] Nor is it likely, in my view, that he invented the otherworldy geography in the *Gorgias*, *Phaedo* and *Republic* myths, since many of its features are borrowed from the Italian Orphic-Pythagoreans.[18] Besides the experiences and teachings of these Orphic-Pytha-

---

15 G.S. Kirk, J.E. Raven, and M. Schofield, *The Presocratic Philosophers*, 2nd ed. (Cambridge: Cambridge University Press, 1983), 259, 219.

16 *Phd.* 61d6; 108a5 (paths in the underworld); 108c7, 109a6–9 (otherworldy geography); *Grg.* 493abc; *Crat.* 400c.

17 For a strong case against the orthodox view, see Peter Kingsley, *Ancient Philosophy, Mystery and Magic* (Oxford: Oxford University Press, 1995), 89–91. On "hearing" in mystery traditions, see Christoph Riedweg, *Mysterienterminologie bei Platon, Philo und Klemens von Alexandrien* (Berlin: De Gruyter, 1987), 101 n. 128.

18 For an illuminating discussion of borrowings and of Platonic innovations, see Bernabé's "ὁ Πλάτων παρωιδεῖ τὰ Ὀρφέως: Plato's Transposition of Orphic Netherworld Imagery," above. On the oral transmission of ideas and practices and on the related phenomenon of anonymity in early Pythagoreanism see Kingsley 1995, 163; Burkert 1972b, 90–91, 135. Burkert 1972b, 179 discusses Pythagorean vows not to use the Master's name. For some the anonymity of Socrates' sources marks them as fictional. C.J. Rowe, *Plato: Phaedo*, ed. with commentary (Cambridge: Cambridge University Press, 1993), ad *Phd.* 108c8, 270: "it is probably useless for us to try to identify the τις with any known person. P. in any case regularly invents sources for ideas of his own which he attributes to S. (who of course knows nothing himself); and it is safe to assume that that is what he is doing here." Similarly, Annas 1982, 126 asserts that

gorean authorities, Plato's representations of the afterlife derive also, I believe, from his own experience. I cannot defend the claim here, but the abundant evidence of mystical experiences in the dialogues demonstrates that Plato was intimately familiar with transcendent worlds. He also implies that Socrates was subject to ecstatic episodes,[19] which parallel the great ascent (*anabasis*) passages in dialogues like *Symposium*, *Phaedrus*, and *Republic*. The *Republic* itself is, of course, a descent (*katabasis*) into the Cave of the corrupt society. And the myth of Er is introduced (*Rep.* 614a ff.) as the personal report of a descent (*katabasis*) to the underworld. Plato deploys both *anabasis* and *katabasis* as symbols for movements into other worlds. The *katabasis* traditionally symbolized descent to the underworld from Homer to Parmenides.[20] In some cases Plato saw them as equivalents, as when he describes the true Hades as the world of forms (*Phd.* 79c–81a); in others, the descent to the under-

---

the *Phaedo* myth contains "fanciful cosmology." Having Socrates report these teachings is a fictional device, but that is quite a different matter than asserting that his *sources* are imaginary. For a detailed argument for Italian Pythagoreans as Plato's sources, with references to other scholars who share this view, see Kingsley 1995, 79–132. He asserts that "even the smallest details of Plato's mythical landscape, with its rivers above and below the ground, were inspired and put together as a result of intimate acquaintance with the geography and natural phenomena of Sicily. They are not figments of Plato's imagination, and they have not been fitted together from various disparate sources" (87). Halliwell is more cautious: "We need not doubt that Plato has incorporated into his myth [of Er] elements which originated in a number of different quarters, but it is now impossible to disentangle the routes by which these all reached him. It is, moreover, clear enough that Plato did not wish his myth to be taken as indicating a clear affiliation to anyone else's ideas." Stephen Halliwell, *Plato: Republic 10*, ed. with translation & commentary (Warminster: Aris & Phillips, 1988), 169–70.

19 See John Bussanich, "Socrates the Mystic," in *Traditions of Platonism: Essays Presented to John Dillon*, ed. John J. Cleary (Burlington: Ashgate, 1999), 29–51 and John Bussanich, "Socrates and Religious Experience," in *The Blackwell Companion to Socrates*, ed. Rachana Kamtekar and Sara Rappe (Oxford: Blackwell, 2006), 200–213 and William J. Prior, "The Portrait of Socrates in Plato's *Symposium*," *OSAPh* 31 (2006): 143–44 on the significance of Socrates' mystical trances.

20 On *katabasis*, see Walter Burkert, "Das Proömium des Parmenides und die Katabasis des Pythagoras," *Phronesis* 14 (1969): 1–30, translated above as "Parmenides' Proem and Pythagoras' Descent"; Adluri & Lenz, "From Politics to Salvation Through Philosophy: Herodotus' *Histories* and Plato's *Republic*," and Kingsley 1999.

world precedes the celestial ascent (e. g. Er's experiences). Or the ascent to supra-celestial forms and the Good displaces the archaic descent.[21]

The Orphic-Pythagorean afterlife symbols are invoked as a form of *paideia* or instruction for the afterlife. The fact that in some cases the ideas they contain are explored dialectically by Socrates and his interlocutors does not mean that they possess low epistemic status.[22] While we might be tempted to situate these "images" in the second segment of the divided line as "true beliefs," they do not serve the same cognitive function as the latter. The elements and features of mythic narratives exercise a transformative effect on the imagination. First, repetition of key words and symbols interrupts the normal experience of time and speech, and opens the higher cognitive and affective powers of the mind to what lies beyond it.[23] Second, becoming familiar with the otherworldly geography in *Gorgias, Phaedo,* and *Republic* assists newly disembodied souls making their way in the afterlife. At the beginning of the *Phaedo* myth Socrates reports that "the soul goes to the underworld possessing nothing but its education and upbringing, which are said to bring the greatest benefit or harm to the dead right at the beginning of the journey yonder" (107d2–5). But he does not refer only to the cultivation of virtue. Education includes also instructions for the aspirant—as in the Gold Leaves—on how to navigate the underworld, i. e., the forks in the path, the guides, the fountains, etc.[24] Third, the myths aim to per-

---

21 Cf. Guy G. Stroumsa, *Hidden Wisdom: Esoteric Traditions and the Roots of Christian Mysticism* (Leiden: Brill, 2005), 169–83; Lars Albinus, "The *Katabasis* of Er. Plato's Use of Myths, exemplified by the Myth of Er," in *Essays on Plato's Republic*, ed. Erik Nis Ostenfeld (Aarhus: Aarhus University Press, 1998), 98–99.
22 For this standard view cf. Morgan 2000, 180–210; Stephen Halliwell, "The Subjection of Muthos to Logos," *CQ* 50.1 (2000): 94–112; Annas 1982, 120–22.
23 Socrates repeats three times his conviction (πέπεισμαι) in the accuracy of the reports about the other world he has learned from Pythagoreans, *Phd.* 108c8, e4, 109a7. Cf. Walter Burkert "Craft Versus Sect: The Problem of Orphics and Pythagoreans," in *Jewish and Christian Self-Definition,* vol. 3, ed. B.F. Meyer and E.P. Sanders (London: Trinity Press, 1982), 1–22, 183–89, and M. Laura Gemelli Marciano, "Images and Experience: At the Roots of Parmenides' *Aletheia*," *AncPhil* (2008): 21–48 on repetition as a magico-religious technique among the Orphic-Pythagoreans.
24 After describing the guidance performed by allotted *daimons*, he notes that the paths are "likely to have many forks and crossroads; and I base this judgment on the sacred rites and customs here" (108a4–6). Crossroads (τρίοδοι) appear in the *Gorgias* (524a2) and *Republic* (614c) myths. Cf. Albrecht Dieterich, *Nekyia*

suade sympathetic listeners with firm beliefs about the afterlife. In the myth of Er Socrates asserts that "we must go down to Hades holding with adamantine determination to the belief" that the just life is best (618e4–619a1). This sort of belief is of a higher order than the true belief about the road to Larissa cited by Socrates at *Meno* 97b because it is not based simply on empirical fact but on imaginative participation in invisible realities. At the end of the myth Socrates informs his interlocutors that they will be saved—they will attain ultimate happiness—if they share his conviction in its truth (πεισώμεθα, *Rep.* 621c1, 3).[25] Similarly, after recounting the σῶμα-σῆμα myth, Socrates advises Callicles to be persuaded by its truth (*Grg.* 493c3-d3). Conversely, those who are *not* persuaded display their "untrustworthiness and forgetfulness" (ἀπιστίαν τε καὶ λήθην, *Grg.* 493c3; cf. *Phd.* 69e3, *Phdr.* 240c). Plato borrows this cluster of terms—persuasion, trust, memory, truth and their opposites—from the Orphic-Pythagoreans to designate mental states that are receptive to transcendent experiences.[26] Socrates alludes to the persuasive effect of myth in the *Phaedo* when he describes it as a charm or incantation (ἐπᾴδειν, *Phd.* 114d7); and also when Socra-

---

(Leipzig: Teubner, 1893), 191 ff.; James Adam, ed., *The Republic of Plato,* vol. 2 (Cambridge: Cambridge University Press, 1963), 435; S.I. Johnston, "Crossroads," *ZPE* 88 (1991): 222–23; Franz Cumont, *Lux perpetua* (Paris: P. Geuthner, 1949), 279–80. Kingsley 2003, 83 ff., 146 ff. connects the image of the crossroads to the paths of being and non-being in Parmenides B6. On the soteriological purpose of initiates familiarizing themselves with this otherworldly geography in the Gold Leaves, see Alberto Bernabé and Ana Isabel Jiménez San Cristóbal, ed., *Instructions for the Netherworld: The Orphic Gold Tablets* (Leiden: Brill, 2008), Bernabé above, and Walter Burkert, *Babylon, Memphis, Persepolis. Eastern Contexts of Greek Culture* (Cambridge, MA: Harvard University Press, 2004), 76 ff. For underworld features like fountains and meadows employed in ancient India for similar purposes, cf. Bruce Lincoln, "Waters of Memory, Waters of Forgetfulness," *Fabula* 23 (1982): 19–34.

25 On this point see Adluri and Lenz, above 223.
26 On the close linkage of transmigration and recollection in Pythagorean legend, teaching, and practice see, E. R. Dodds, *Plato. Gorgias* (Oxford: Oxford University Press, 1959), 303; Burkert 1972, 213–15, Jean-Pierre Vernant, *Mythic Thought among the Greeks* (Cambridge, MA: Zone, 2006), 115–38. On the divine power of Peitho (Persuasion), Aletheia (Truth), and Pistis (Conviction) in archaic mythopoeic thought see Marcel Detienne, *The Masters of Truth in Archaic Greece* (New York: Zone, 1996), 75–78, 120–34. On πίστις and πειθώ in Empedocles (B114) and in Parmenides see Günther Zuntz, *Persephone: Three Essays on Religion and Thought in Magna Graecia* (Oxford: Oxford University Press, 1971), 193 and Kingsley 2003, 507, 542.

tes—an ἐπῳδός—tries to assuage the fear of death through song (ἐπᾴδειν) (77e-78a).²⁷ The repetition of ἐλπίς (hope) and its verbal form ἐλπίζω is intended to awaken hope in Socrates' pupils that the mystery-teachings about the afterlife are true (*Phd.* 63c1, 5, 67b7, 68a8).²⁸ Deepening conviction through the repetition of magically potent words and phrases and through visualizing the underworld, which each soul has visited countless times but has forgotten, intensifies anticipation. The connection between being persuaded and maintaining conviction about eschatological matters is also maintained in Plato's later writings, which often refer to ancient, sacred teachings (*Laws* 904d1–4, 959b3-c2, 870d5-e1; *Ep.* vii.335a2–5).

The sequence of hearing, expectation, conviction, and vision corresponds to the progression from *mathein* to *pathein* (Aristotle, Fr. 15 Ross): "learning" about the mysteries first and then "being affected by" or "experiencing" them. This parallels the sequence of stages through which the Eleusinian initiate proceeds: *elenchos/katharmos* (purification), *paradosis* (instruction), and *epopteia* (vision).²⁹ Socratic *parado-*

---

27 Plato employs ἐπῳδός metaphorically to characterize the transformative effect of Socratic arguments on interlocutors in *Charm.* 157abc. The eschatological myth of *Laws* X is introduced with the comment that it will charm the religious sceptic (903b1–2). The philosophical use of enchantment also figures in the playful account of Hades in the *Cratylus*. Everyone purified of their desires and the agitations of the body are overcome by the enchanting words of Hades, who is likened to a philosopher because he knows everything fine and beautiful and can awaken the desire for virtue (*Crat.* 403e-404a). Incantation is employed to enhance noetic clarity homeopathically as, for example, when Socrates concludes his critique of *mimesis* with chants and incantations about the falseness of poetry (*Rep.* 608a).

28 In the Eleusinian and Bacchic mysteries the joy experienced by initiates grounds the "good hope" that present joy will be extended into an endless beatific afterlife. Cumont 1949, 240, 401–05 and Christina Schefer, *Platons unsagbare Erfahrung. Ein anderer Zugang zu Platon* (Basel: Schwabe, 2001), 105 discuss ἐλπίς as a mystery-term; contra Fritz Graf, *Eleusis und die orphische Dichtung Athens in vorhellenistischer Zeit* (Berlin: De Gruyter, 1974), 138 n. 47; cf. also *Rep.* 496e1–2: the philosopher's virtue provides good hope for the afterlife. Cf. *Laws* 898d9-e3: there is great ἐλπίς that we are part of the world soul, which though imperceptible is νοητόν.

29 Walter Burkert, *Ancient Mystery Cults* (Cambridge, MA: Harvard University Press, 1987), 153 n. 13: "Aristotle systematized the steps of Diotima's speech in Plato's *Symposium* and made the highest step of philosophy analogous to *epopteia*; this still presupposes various forms of 'teaching' and 'learning'." Cf. André-Jean Festugière, *Contemplation et vie contemplative selon Platon*, 4th ed. (Paris: Vrin 1975), 227, 231 n. 2. On the progression from initiatic instruction to vision in

sis transmits teachings about the afterlife, but also encourages dialectical examination of them to produce reliable understanding; finally, psychic transformation leads to noetic vision.³⁰

The first element in Plato's rebirth eschatology is that embodiment is itself punishment for previous sins and crimes, which requires payment of a penalty. The idea that the body (σῶμα) is the tomb (σῆμα) of the soul is identified as an Orphic teaching in *Crat.* 400c³¹ and *Grg.* 493abc. The related notion of the soul's imprisonment, a central motif in the mysteries (ἀπορρήτοις), is introduced at *Phd.* 62b2–4 (see also 67d1–2, 81e2, 92a1; cf. *Ax.* 365e6) as "an impressive doctrine and one not easy to understand fully." What the soul is being punished for, however, is not specified. *Meno* 81bc addresses Meno's paradox (how can we inquire into a subject we don't understand) by introducing the ideas of immortality, recollection, and rebirth:

> They [priests and priestesses] say that the human soul is immortal; at times it comes to an end, which they call dying, at times it is reborn, but it is never destroyed, and one must therefore live one's life as piously as possible:
>
> Persephone will return to the sun above in the ninth year
> the souls of those from whom
> she will exact punishment for old miseries,
> and from these come noble kings,
> mighty in strength and greatest in wisdom,
> and for the rest of time men will call them sacred heroes (Pindar Fr. 133 Snell)
>
> As the soul is immortal, has been born often and has seen all things here and in the underworld, there is nothing which it is has not learned; so it is in no way surprising that it can recollect the things it knew before, both about virtue and other things. (*Meno* 81b3-c9)

Empedocles, see Kingsley 1995, 230 n. 48, 367–69. On Eleusinian *epopteia*, cf. Lars Albinus, *The House of Hades. Studies in Greek Eschatology* (Aarhus: Aarhus University Press, 2000), 187–89.

30 Plato condemns superficial acquaintance with the mysteries: cf. *Ep.* vii.333e. Referring to this passage, Thomas M. Tuozzo, "Comments on Erler and Schefer," in *Plato as Author: The Rhetoric of Philosophy*, ed. Ann N. Michelini (Leiden: Brill, 2003), 202 argues unconvincingly that mystery-language in Plato should always be construed metaphorically.

31 "Some people say that the body (*sōma*) is the tomb (*sēma*) of the soul, on the grounds that it is entombed in its present life,… I think it is most likely the followers of Orpheus who gave the body its name, with the idea that the soul is being punished for something, and that the body is an enclosure or prison in which the soul is securely kept…until the penalty is paid" (*Crat.* 400c1–9).

This compressed statement of rebirth doctrine alludes to themes elaborated in later dialogues: embodiment as imprisonment, ethicization of the afterlife, expiation of wrongdoing, the duration of the rebirth cycle, immortalization, and the link between memory and wisdom. The archaic teaching is neatly epitomized in Pindar's poem and framed by Plato's ethical and epistemological inquiries.[32]

The punishment alluded to here and in related Platonic passages (*Crat.* 400c and *Laws*[33]) has usually been interpreted in terms of the Orphic anthropogony embedded in the myth of Zagreus, which is first attested in the third century BCE:

> Zeus raped his mother Rhea-Demeter and sired Persephone; he raped Persephone in the form of a snake and sired Dionysos. To the child Dionysos he hands over the rule of the world, places him on a throne, and has him guarded by Korybantes. But Hera sends the Titans who distract the child with toys, and while the child is looking into a mirror he is dragged from the throne, killed, and torn to pieces, then boiled, roasted, and eaten. Zeus thereupon hurls his thunderbolt to burn the Titans, and from the rising soot there spring men, rebels against the gods who nevertheless participate in the divine. From the remains that were rescued and collected, Dionysos rises again.[34]

The *Meno* passage contains Orphic elements, but recently it has been disputed whether Plato assigns guilt to human beings, as descendants of the Titans, for the latter's crime against Persephone. Plato may or may not have subscribed to this Orphic anthropogony. More to the point is his shift of focus from the mythical *aitia* of human embodiment to the ethical and psychological effects of the soul's imprisonment in a body.[35]

An alternative reading of the Pindar fragment takes it as an instance of the fallen-god/*daimon* motif: from its divine origin the soul falls

---

32 On Plato's use of Pindaric eschatology, see Bernabé, above pp. 118–19.

33 The impious and vicious "reveal, incarnated in themselves, the character of the ancient Titans of the story, and thanks to getting into the same position as the Titans did, they live a wretched life of endless misery" (*Laws* 701c1–4). See also Socrates' reference to our typhonic nature at *Phdr.* 230a3–6.

34 Walter Burkert, *Greek Religion* (Cambridge, MA: Harvard University Press, 1985), 297–88. Cf. Robert Parker, "Early Orphism," in *The Greek World,* ed. Anton Powell (New York: Routledge, 1995), 494–96.

35 Burkert 2004, 96–98 is cautious about identifying these as Orphic elements. Radcliffe G. Edmonds, "Tearing Apart the Zagreus Myth: A Few Disparaging Remarks on Orphism and Original Sin," *Classical Antiquity* 18.1 (1999): 35–73 argues that the anthropogony is post-Platonic.

owing to a crime committed when it dwelled with the gods.³⁶ This theme is prominent in Empedocles and the Gold Leaves. Both allude to the soul's divine origin, its fall into the cycle of birth and death, and its liberation therefrom in the return to the divine realm.³⁷ Empedocles famously proclaimed his divine status (Fr. 112.3), but also poignantly described himself as a fallen δαίμων, "a god in exile": having committed a primordial sin of violence, he had to be reborn for 30,000 seasons (= 10,000 years) owing to repeated bloodshed and meat-eating (Fr. 115).³⁸ He describes his experience: "I have already been once a boy and a girl, a bush and a bird and a leaping journeying fish" (Fr. 117). Are these incarnations ranked in any way? Is being born in one form ethically superior to another? The fragments provide no clear answer, though Fr. 127 indicates that a lion is the best form among animals and the laurel the best among trees.

The Thurian Gold Leaves also refer to the heavenly origin of the soul, the penalty it pays for wrongdoing, and its appeal to Persephone for release.³⁹ A brief passage in another Thurian Gold Leaf points to at-

---

36 Zuntz 1971, 86; Martin L. West, *The Orphic Poems* (Oxford: Oxford University Press, 1983), 110; Hugh Lloyd-Jones, "Pindar and the Afterlife," in *Greek Epic, Lyric, and Tragedy: The Academic Papers of Sir Hugh Lloyd-Jones* (Oxford: Clarendon Press, 1991), 90.
37 See the excellent discussion in Richard Seaford, "Immortality, Salvation, and the Elements," *HSCP* 90 (1986): 6–9 and in Herrero de Jáuregui above.
38 I follow the interpretation of Kingsley 2003, 358–63 who argues that the Empedoclean δαίμων has a double-fall: first, from the realm of the gods, for an unspecified primordial sin, second, into the cycle of births and deaths for the killing of living beings. For a different view, see Brad Inwood, *The Poem of Empedocles: A Text and Translation with an Introduction* (Toronto: University of Toronto Press, 1992), 55–59.
39 Phrases in the Thurian Gold Leaves: "my name is Asterius [Starry]"; "my race is heavenly"; "I too belong to your blessed race." Bernabé and San Cristóbal 2008, 187 n. 45. See further:
    "I come pure from the pure, Queen of the Chthonian Ones,
    Eucles and Eubouleus and the gods and other *daimones*. For I also claim to be of your happy race.
    I have paid the penalty for unrighteous deeds.
    Either Moira overcame me or the star-flinger of lightnings.
    Now I come as a suppliant to holy Persephone,
    so that she may kindly send me to the seats of the pure."
    Fritz Graf and Sarah Iles Johnston, *Ritual Texts for the Afterlife* (London: Routledge, 2007), 15; cp. Bernabé and San Cristóbal 2008, 100.
    On the equations Eucles = Hades or Zeus and Eubouleus = Dionysus see Bernabé and San Cristóbal 2008, 102 f. West 1983, 23 n. 57 compares this ref-

taining the pure realm of the gods and liberation from the cycle of births and deaths: "I flew forth from the painful cycle of deep sorrow."[40] The final liberation of an innately divine soul from rebirth is a soteriological innovation of the first importance that Plato appropriates for his own purpose.

Plato honors traditional sources that hint at a primordial crime as the cause of human embodiment, but he does not appear to adopt their mythic explanations literally.[41] Instead, he resymbolizes the soul's embodiment in two rather different myths, offering a positive narrative in the *Timaeus* and a negative one in the *Phaedrus*, which closely parallels the Orphic trajectory of the fallen god. I shall address only a few facets of the *Phaedrus*' complex picture of the soul's descent and re-ascent in the rebirth cycle. Discarnate souls, symbolized dynamically as chariots with a charioteer and a white and a black horse (and wings too), traverse the heavens in the train of the twelve Olympian divinities, glimpsing to varying degrees the transcendent forms that are said to lie "beyond the heaven" (247c1–3). Souls whose wings are in perfect condition rule the entire universe, but a soul that loses its wings "wanders until it lights on something solid, where it settles and takes on an earthly body" (246c1–4). Socrates cites various reasons for the descent of souls: (i) "the heaviness of the bad horse drags its charioteer towards the earth" (247b3–6); (ii) chariots of souls unable to ascend to the top of heaven, because of "incompetent drivers," struggle and crash into one another (248ab); (iii) the sort of soul that "did not see anything true because it could not keep up, and by some accident (συντυχίᾳ) takes on a burden of forgetfulness and wrongdoing…is weighed down, sheds its wings and falls to earth" (248c5-d1). The discarnate soul thus has parts, perhaps to account for the descent.[42] In other mythical passages, e.g., the myth of

---

erence to Zeus propelling the soul into embodiment to the similar event in the Myth of Er, *Rep.* 612b.

40 Bernabé and San Cristóbal 2008, 188. Cf. Radcliffe G. Edmonds, *Myths of the Underworld Journey: Plato, Aristophanes, and the "Orphic" Gold Tablets* (Cambridge: Cambridge University Press, 2004), 96; Vernant 2006, 431 n. 40; and Parker 1995, 500.

41 On the divine origin of δαίμονες, Timaeus states "we should accept on faith (πειστέον) the assertions of those figures of the past who claimed to be the offspring of gods…even though their accounts lack plausible or compelling proofs" (*Tim.* 40d6-e2).

42 In *Rep.* 611d-612a only the highest, rational part of the soul (= the driver in the *Phaedrus* myth) is immortal.

Er, the soul also has non-rational parts in order to simulate the psychology of a composite, embodied person.[43] If scholarly opinion is correct that this descent represents the first incarnation in a 10,000 year cycle, Plato is silent here on the primordial descent of soul.[44] But in other respects the teachings of Empedocles and the Gold Leaves are very much in evidence: the myth's divine banquet (i.e., feasting on the forms, 247c-e) echoes Empedocles' notion of dwelling with the gods; the contrast of the purity of the pre-natal celestial vision with the present imprisonment of the soul in a body, "locked in it like an oyster in its shell" (250c5–6), recalls the Sicilian's description of embodiment as coming "under this roofed cave" (Fr. 120) or being "clothed in an alien garment of flesh" (Fr. 126). Plato also borrows Empedocles' three times 10,000 seasons of exile, but adapts it to fit his own template of ten incarnations, one for each millenium, and the hierarchy of eight human types (from philosopher to tyrant, 248de). The philosopher is freed from the cycle after three times 1000 years.[45] The heaviness, bad luck, and forgetfulness, which initiate a new cycle of births and deaths, are caused by the driver's incompetence and the brute force of the dark horse: both are effects of incarnations in previous cycles.

Taking a different tack, the *Timaeus* presents a positive version of the soul's original embodiment, albeit mythically, but this time from the god's eye view of the Demiurge who instructs the young gods "to weave what is mortal to what is immortal" (41d1–2). Having mixed together the less pure elements left over from his earlier creation of the cosmos, the Demiurge assigns each soul to a star and then to its first birth without any karma from previous lives (41d8–42a3). After the first incarnation the virtuous soul returns "to his dwelling place in his companion star, to live a life of happiness that agreed with his character," the less virtuous fall into lesser incarnations also in accordance with their characters.[46] Does this anthropogony square with the pali-

---

43 Like *Phaedrus*, in *Laws* 897 an unembodied soul's motions include thought, belief, and various passions and emotions.
44 For defence of this view see R. S. Bluck, "The *Phaedrus* and Reincarnation," *AJPh* 79 (1958): 157–158, and R. S. Bluck, "Plato, Pindar, and Metempsychosis," *AJPh* 79 (1958): 410.
45 On this triadic symbolism, cf. Albinus 2000, 127–28.
46 "But if he failed in this, he would be born a second time, now as a woman. And if even then he still could not refrain from wickedness, he would be changed once again, this time into some wild animal that resembled the wicked character he had acquired. And he would have no rest from these toilsome transfor-

node in the *Phaedrus*? It does to the extent of employing a hierarchy of characters, albeit with different types; and, more clearly than *Phaedrus*, it alludes to liberation from the rebirth cycle. It also contains some Orphic elements, e.g., the mixing bowl[47] and the figure of time,[48] but the passage lacks the Orphic motif of a primordial crime leading to imprisonment. Three possible explanations for the omission come to mind. First, the entire narrative is authored by the Pythagoreanizing Timaeus, whose views may not reflect Plato's. Second, as early as the *Euthyphro* (6bc, 8b) and more firmly in the *Republic* (377e ff.), Socrates rejects ascribing violence or wrongdoing to the gods, on the grounds that the gods are good and engage only in good actions (380b2–6). The *Timaeus* anthropogony distinguishes the divine, immortal soul from the mortal soul, which contains the senses, passions, and emotions (*Tim.* 69cd). The former connects to the latter via our δαίμονες, which are a divine gift (90a5) and come "from heaven, the place from which our souls were originally born."[49] These, presumably, cannot sin, like the gods.[50] The mortal soul

---

mations until he had dragged that massive accretion of fire-water-air-earth into conformity with the revolution of the Same and uniform within him, and so subdued that turbulent, irrational mass by means of reason. This would return him to his original condition of excellence" (42b3-d2). The role of the elements in the cycle may also be indebted to Orphic-Pythagoreanism, as Seaford 1986 points out: "The idea of the immortal soul passing from one cosmological element to another has its origin not in philosophy but in mysteries…even the gold leaves…imply a passage of the immortal γένος οὐράνιον from the sky, by the agency of fire, to beneath the earth, and thence presumably to the ends of the earth" (12). "In Empedokles the immortal δαίμονες, of which Empedokles is one, are punished by being tossed around the cosmological elements in a circle" (22).

47 Parker 1995, 486.
48 West 1983, 189–94, 198–202.
49 In the myth of Er when disembodied souls choose their next incarnation, their guiding spirits (δαίμονες) are not allotted to them, they choose them. In the *Phaedo* myth, by contrast, the δαίμων is assigned to the soul: 107de, 108b, 113d. Cf. also *Phdr.* 249d2 and Halliwell 1988, 184.
50 "We won't allow poets to say that the punished are made wretched and that it was a god who made them so. But we will allow them to say that bad people are wretched because they are in need of punishment and that, in paying the penalty, they are benefited by the gods" (380b2–6). Another possibility is that Plato may have been sympathetic to Orphic accounts of a crime committed by souls that are divine or quasi-divine, but thought that they should only be discussed within an esoteric circle. This I take to be a possible implication of the *Republic*'s ban on telling stories about the patricidal violence of Cronus and Zeus: "But even if it were true, it should be passed over in silence, not

is created by the younger gods and encased in bodies, thus appearing to shift the responsibility, as compared to the *Phaedrus*, from human souls to divine providence. The two accounts of the soul's descent and embodiment can be reconciled if the *Timaeus* is taken as presenting the primordial descent followed by the subsequent descents recounted in *Phaedrus*.

Once a soul has entered the rebirth cycle its embodied character serves as Plato's frame for the ethicization of the afterlife in the form of post-mortem judgment, punishments, and rewards. As in *Laws* 701 cited above, Plato appropriates mystery doctrines in the *Gorgias* and *Phaedo*. Humanity's titanic nature is characterized in ethical terms: "imprisonment is…due to desires" and "the prisoner himself is contributing to his own incarceration most of all" (82e5–7). Having defined the virtues as purifications, Socrates states that "those who established the mystic rites for us were not inferior persons but were speaking in riddles[51] long ago when they said that whoever arrives in the underworld uninitiated and unsanctified will wallow in the mire, whereas he who arrives there purified and initiated will dwell with the gods. There are indeed, as those concerned with the mysteries will say, many who carry the thyrsus but the Bacchants are few" (*Phd.* 69c1-d1).[52] Wallowing in mire foreshadows the rivers of mud in the final myth (110a5–6, 111d5-e2, 113a6-b6), while the initiated, i.e., the purified, will dwell with the gods (c3–7, 81a4–6). Similarly, the uninitiated are fools without control of their desires in the Orphic myth of the water-carriers,

---

told to foolish young people. And if, for some reason, it has to be told, only a very few people—pledged to secrecy and after sacrificing not just a pig but something great and scarce—should hear it, so that their number is kept as small as possible" (378a2–6). If the true meanings of some myths must be kept secret, what can be stated publically is the sort of philosophical myth we find in the *Timaeus*.

51 On Plato's literary use of αἴνιγμα, see Peter T. Struck, *Birth of the Symbol: Ancient Readers at the Limits of Their Texts* (Princeton: Princeton University Press, 2004), 41–49.

52 Lloyd P. Gerson, *Knowing Persons* (Oxford: Oxford University Press, 2003), 62: "Philosophical purification is specifically the removal of false beliefs that are a condition of being born into and raised in a corrupt society." Such a narrow intellectualist interpretation of κάθαρσις and indeed of philosophizing in the *Phaedo* generally falls far short of the spiritual heights at which Socratic meditative practice aims. It is not surprising, therefore, that in his conclusion Gerson (98) finds Platonic "soul care," as he conceives it, inadequate to achieve the ideal cognitive state of union with the forms.

which foreshadows their post-mortem punishments at the end of *Gorgias*.⁵³

The elaborate otherwordly topography, judgment of the dead, apparatus for rewards and punishments, and mechanisms for rebirth of souls in the *Gorgias*, *Phaedo*, and *Republic* myths are unprecedented in their detail. The sources for some of these elements are well known. The earliest attested judgment of the dead occurs in Pindar's *Second Olympian*.⁵⁴ Although contemporary evidence for post-mortem judgment is scanty, Edmonds is correct to argue that "some sort of judgment is implied in the concept of different lots in the afterlife for different types of dead, since some authority must decide the fate of each deceased."⁵⁵ Certainly, Plato was committed to this doctrine throughout his life. The *Seventh Letter* maintains "we must always firmly believe the sacred and ancient words declaring to us that the soul is immortal, and when it has separated from the body will go before its judges and pay the utmost penalties" (335a2–5).⁵⁶

---

53 Burkert 1972b, 248 n. 48 suggests that the myth may have formed part of an Orphic κατάβασις. Socrates quotes his Orphic-Pythagorean source: "And fools [*anoētoi*] he named uninitiated [*amuētoi*], suggesting that that part of the souls of fools where their appetites are located is their undisciplined part, one not tightly closed, a leaking jar, as it were. He based the image on its insatiability. Now this man, Callicles, quite to the contrary of your view, shows that of the people in Hades—meaning the unseen [*aïdes*]—these, the uninitiated ones, would be the most miserable. They would carry water into the leaking jar using another leaky thing, a sieve. That's why by the sieve he means the soul (as the man who talked with me claimed). And because they leak, he likened the souls of fools to sieves; for their untrustworthiness and forgetfulness (δι' ἀπιστίαν τε καὶ λήθην) makes them unable to retain anything" (*Gorg.* 493a1-c2). Carrying water is a figure for punishment of the dead for those who remained uninitiated while alive and did not convey the water of ritual purification. On the Orphic symbols in *Gorgias* and *Phaedo*, see Albinus 2000, 131–40.
54 "Those of the dead that are lawless in mind pay the penalty straightway here, but the sins committed in this realm of Zeus are judged below the earth by one who pronounces sentence with hateful necessity" (56–60). Other pre-Platonic examples of judgment are discussed in Dodds 1959, 372–74; Edmonds 2004, 196–201; Robert Garland, *The Greek Way of Death* (Ithaca: Cornell University Press, 1985), 63–66.
55 Edmonds 2004, 196.
56 πείθεσθαι δὲ ὄντως ἀεὶ χρὴ τοῖς παλαιοῖς τε καὶ ἱεροῖς λόγοις, οἳ δὴ μηνύουσιν ἡμῖν ἀθάνατον ψυχὴν εἶναι δικαστάς τε ἴσχειν καὶ τίνειν τὰς μεγίστας τιμωρίας, ὅταν τις ἀπαλλαχθῇ τοῦ σώματος. On *hieros logos* in Plato, see Albert Henrichs, "*Hieroi Logoi* and *Hierai Bibloi*: The (Un)Written Margins of the Sacred in Ancient Greece," *HSCP* 101 (2003): 207–66 and Burkert 1987, 153 n. 15. "An-

"Our real self—our immortal soul, as it is called—departs, as the ancestral law (πάτριος νόμος) declares to the gods below to give an account of itself....To the wicked this is a terrifying doctrine...[because they can't escape] the penalty visited on evil deeds in the life to come" (*Laws* 959b3-c2).

Plato dramatizes the emotional effects of this belief when Cephalus expresses his fear about "the stories we're told about Hades, about how people who've been unjust here must pay the penalty there—stories he used to make fun of—twist his soul this way and that for fear they're true" (*Rep.* 330d).[57] However, what terrifies Cephalus are the impressions in his mind imprinted by traditional Homeric religion, by superficial acquaintance with the Eleusinian mysteries, and by the popular Orphism criticized later in the *Republic*.[58] This vulgar eschatology comprises materialistic beliefs that the virtuous are rewarded in the afterlife with feasting at endless symposia and the vicious are buried in mud or forced to carry water in a sieve (363cd). The same myth is employed by Socrates in the *Gorgias*—but in a deeper way—to distinguish the ethically pure from the impure. The door-to-door Orphics offer their services for sale in the form of sacrifices and incantations that aim to expiate the crimes of their clients (364b-e). The posthumous punishments and rewards included in Plato's myths are not avoided or won, respectively, through sacrifice, bribery, or ritual initiation. Ethical purity is efficacious where ritualist orthopraxy is not.

Pythagorean, Orphic, and Eleusinian afterlife trajectories provided Plato with a rich palette of elements and images to paint his own pictures.[59] The judges of the dead in the *Gorgias* myth are well-known

---

cient teachings" also apply to good times: *Laws* 715e7 ff. on the παλαιὸς λόγος about the just rule of Zeus; 713c ff. on the tale (μῦθος) about the "wonderfully happy life" (i.e., the βίος ὀρφικός) in the age of Cronus.

57 Injustice "sets the soul on the path to the depths of the so-called 'under'world, which men call 'Hades' and similar names, and which haunts and terrifies them both during their lives and when they have been sundered from their bodies" (*Laws* 904d1–4). The Athenian introduces the doctrine of punishment in the afterlife with the remark "we must tell the story (λόγον) which is so strongly believed by so many people when they hear it from those who have made a serious study of such matters in their mystic ceremonies (τελεταῖς). Vengeance is exacted for these crimes in the after-life" (*Laws* 870d5-e1).

58 Annas (1982, 125) argues that even Cephalus is capable of grasping the simple message that being just will benefit one in the afterlife. But this is to conflate the rewards of the vulgar afterlife scenarios with Plato's spiritualized version.

59 See the useful assessment of Parker 1995, 500–501: "Orphic poems certainly contained accounts of judgements, rewards and punishments in the under-

in the poetic tradition.[60] In the later myths (*Phd.* 113d, *Rep.* 614), they are anonymous and the judicial procedure is abbreviated. Already in *Gorgias* the judges have been thoroughly ethicized such that they examine the interior, moral character of the soul rather than the person's physical appearance and worldly reputation, or whether she was an initiate (*Grg.* 524e). Likewise in *Phaedo* "there is no escape from evil or salvation for it except by becoming as good and wise as possible, for the soul goes to the underworld possessing nothing but its education and upbringing" (*Phd.* 107d). Those attached to the body associate with ghosts and hover around the visible world (108b, 81cd), while the virtuous find divine guides (108c). Curable souls subject to punishment are benefited "both here and in Hades, by way of pain and suffering, for there is no other possible way to get rid of injustice" (525b). After being judged average souls "are purified by penalties for any wrongdoing…and suitably rewarded for their good deeds" (113e1–2), while perpetrators of great crimes are freed from their suffering only when they persuade their victims (114b). (This feature anticipates the ethicization of rebirth in the *Laws* discussed below.) The myth of Er states that wrongdoers paid penalties for each crime, ten times over, once every hundred years (615ab). These myths also feature moral incurables, who are thrown into Tartarus never to emerge (615c-616a). They may have been included as counterparts to the extreme evildoers in archaic poetry who suffered this extreme punishment or because of the political focus of *Gorgias* and *Republic* and their moral critique of tyrants. In any case, incurables are absent in the late dialogues.

With the exception of the last passage cited, in which Ardiaeus and other tyrants were flayed, the three myths of judgment provide very little graphic detail about the punishments suffered by unjust souls, and almost nothing about rewards for the virtuous. Notwithstanding Plato's reticence about infernal torments for the wicked, scholars often cite Co-

---

world; of a cycle of lives…from which escape could eventually be achieved; and that the 'purity' of the soul was doubtless defined in both moral and ritual terms. How these elements were fitted together in individual poems we can only guess. There is anyway much to be said for not worrying too much about the last details of last things. An eschatology is not a contract in law, but an imaginative picture, designed…to shape attitudes and behaviour here and now. Pindar and Plato, by changing their accounts of the afterlife from work to work, in a sense acknowledge that the details do not matter and cannot be known."

60 Cf. *Grg.* 523e-524a, 526bc with Dodds 1959, 374.

lotes the Epicurean's criticism that Plato tried to frighten people with afterlife suffering, thus contradicting his earlier condemnation (*Rep.* 386b) of poets for telling stories about "Hades full of terrors."[61] It should be noted, however, that all the passages cited by Socrates in *Republic* II-III concern the non-ethicized, Homeric Hades where all souls endure a ghostlike existence, from which there is no respite, and extraordinary punishments are inflicted only for extreme wrongdoing.[62] The simple pattern of an unending single punishment for one crime is commonly attested in the classical period. Dating from the mid-fifth century BCE, Polygnotus' famous painting of Odysseus' *Nekyia,* described in Pausanias X.28–31, depicts an afterlife that is partially ethicized. It combines, not very consistently, elements from both the Homeric and Orphic eschatologies.[63] The painter's Dantesque flare for depicting punishments contrasts sharply with Plato whose punishments are mild by comparison.[64] We listen to Er's report of what he heard from travelers in Hades who witnessed the torture of an evil tyrant, but little more. It is significant, I think, that Plato gives a restrained account of afterlife punishments. Instead, his imagination is fully engaged in representing a positive reality imbued with rationality and goodness—the dazzling vision of the Fates, the magnificent whorls, and the spindle of necessity, which are intended to induce awe in those observing the invisible order which permeates the physical universe. This inspiring picture of the inner workings of the cosmos complements a theory of punishment that is intended to be remedial and reformative, notwithstanding the presence of the incurables in the major myths.[65] The traditional Hades offered no such glorious sights or ineffable bliss for the righteous.

---

61 Cf. Halliwell 1988, 175 ad 615d4 and Annas 1982, 128–29; see also Annas 1981, 349: "The Myth of Er is a painful shock; its vulgarity seems to pull us right down to the level of Cephalus, where you take justice seriously when you start thinking about hell-fire." Hell-fire there may be, but the myth of Er is not Dante's *Inferno.*
62 Cf. Arthur W.H. Adkins, *Merit and Reponsibility: A Study in Greek Values* (Oxford: Clarendon Press, 1960), 67.
63 Cf. Albinus 2000, 133.
64 The mystery-religions and the Gold Leaves largely ignore post-mortem punishment in favor of rebirth itself as punishment. Cf. Trevor J. Saunders, *Plato's Penal Code* (Oxford: Oxford University Press, 1991), 55–61.
65 As Dodds 1959, 381 notes, the "incurables" are a feature of the *Gorgias* (525e ff.), *Phaedo* (113e), and *Republic* (615e) myths. But eternal punishment is not mentioned in the *Laws.*

Annas has urged that the *Gorgias* system of judgment, punishment, and reward possessses greater coherence than the *Phaedo* and *Republic* myths inasmuch as it promotes "the idea of a final rectification."[66] She observes: "In the *Gorgias* myth there are no roads back from Tartarus or the Isles of the Blessed. Justice, once done, stays done. Hence, the rewards and punishments after death, as in the Christian myth, form a real incentive to be just now."[67] The superiority of this myth's moral argument consists in the finality of the consequences it offers for good and evil lives. However, this Christianizing interpretation, with its absolute heaven and hell states, is based on a narrow reading of Plato's first eschatological myth; later he consistently conceives of these states as relative and temporary. Privileging the simple scheme in the *Gorgias* myth, which I take to be introductory, Annas construes the *Phaedo* as a confusing picture of the afterlife: "we do not yet see fully the moral significance of the idea of reincarnation. It does not yet suggest an alternative to the final morally rectifying judgment."[68] Alternatively, I believe that Plato never thought of judgment and subsequent punishments as final. Rather, the *Gorgias* myth, and indeed the ends of the *Apology* and *Crito*, should be read proleptically, as introducing themes and setting out problems to be dramatized later in more detail.[69] In fact, because none of the three great myths individually addresses all the elements of Plato's rebirth eschatology, it is essential that they be read together, along with passages in the *Phaedrus*, *Timaeus*, and *Laws*. The broader perspective afforded by synoptic reading enables us to see how Plato wove together disparate elements to address a host of distinct problems, combining the more popular motifs of judgment, punishment, and reward with the more esoteric doctrines of rebirth and liberation inherited from the Orphic-Pythagoreans and the mystery-religions.

Scholars have rightly raised questions about the moral purpose of post-mortem punishments and rewards when combined with rebirth. Before confronting these problems it will be useful first to note what rewards the virtuous win. The *Gorgias* employs the simplest scheme. Invoking Homer and Hesiod, Socrates recounts a "true tale" that the vir-

---

66 Annas 1982, 122.
67 Annas 1982, 123–4.
68 Annas 1982, 129.
69 Kahn 1997, 68 endorses the idea of an ingressive approach to the eschatological passages in Plato.

tuous go to the Isles of the Blessed, the abode of Hesiod's golden race (523b1, 524a3, 526c5) and the vicious to Tartarus. In the *Phaedo* the exceptionally virtuous (114b6-c2) dwell in an earthly paradise—on the surface of the earth in the myth's terms—whereas the bulk of humanity lives in the hollows—analogous to the *Republic*'s cave. Socrates paints a substantially Pythagorean picture of this true earth (110c-111c3), whose inhabitants breathe ether instead of air and live on islands, again evoking the Isles of the Blessed.[70] Fully purified philosophers have an even better fate, about which more below.

The myth of Er makes it clear for the first time in Plato's writings, assuming that *Republic* postdates *Phaedo*, that all souls are subject to a long cycle of births, deaths, and rebirths (617d). What has generated much debate is the apparent pointlessness of what happens to most souls during their post-mortem journey. The just are rewarded, the unjust punished (614c-616a), after which the majority travel until they behold the whorls, the cosmic spindle, Necessity, and her daughters the Fates (616b-617c). Informed by one of them, Lachesis, that each will choose his own δαίμων, various lots are thrown in front of the assembled souls that will determine the order in which each will choose his next birth (617d-618b). Especially puzzling is that the worst choices are made by those who have "come down from heaven" (619cd). These are the "habitually virtuous" (reborn as appealing animals in *Phd.* 82ab), who make bad choices (i) because the joy they experienced weakened their judgment, leaving them "untrained in suffering" (619d),

---

70 Cf. Hesiod *WD* 171, Pindar *Ol.* 2.68-70. Lloyd-Jones 1991, 103 adroitly characterizes Pindar's Eleusinian Orphism as holding that "the eternal bliss of the elect has a heroic colour." For details on *Phaedo*, cf. John Burnet, *Plato's Phaedo* (Oxford: Clarendon, 1911), ad 111ab. The true earth, with its perfect particulars and direct perception of divinities can be compared with the world outside the cave (*Rep.* 516a8-b1, 532a2-7) and with the celestial region in the palinode, e.g., *Phdr.* 247a4, which is inferior to the region beyond the heaven. See Morgan 1990, 76-77 on the Pythagorean background to this picture.

Platonic references to the Isles of the Blessed or to the Elysian Fields (Homer *Od.* 4.563) are compact symbolic evocations. The reason for the lack of content in visions of paradise in archaic literature is cogently explained by Bruce Lincoln, "On the Imagery of Paradise," *Indogermanische Forschungen* 85 (1980): 184: "Nothing positive is said of paradise for the reason that it is so totally unlike our own mortal sphere that our very language and normal set of images is thoroughly inadequate for the task of describing it....Of the Otherworld, all that can be said is that things there are totally other, completely opposed to all of this earth."

and (ii) because of the lottery itself. However, the most important factor in determining choices was "the character (συνήθειαν) of their former life" (620a2–3). This final point suggests that the pains and pleasures of hell and heaven, respectively, are less important in Platonic eschatology than is often assumed. They provide ethical compensation for embodied deeds but not the degree of cognitive improvement and moral maturity we might expect.

The *Phaedrus* myth expounds a paradoxical scenario for choices made by discarnate souls that parallels the myth of Er. Soul-chariots choose—before their first incarnation in the cycle—which god to follow to the divine banquet (248ab). Although Socrates does not state that the soul's character is formed in the preceding cycle, as does Er's account, this is the mostly likely explanation of the problem identified by Griswold: while the soul's selection of its leader-divinity forms its character, it must already be individuated to make the choice in the first place.[71] Thus, we are confronted with the dilemma that, despite the punishments and rewards souls experience, they choose their new lives based on who they were in a previous life,[72] but then are reborn without any memory either of their previous lives or of their prenatal choices.[73] Thus it has been argued that Plato's ascription of moral responsibility is incoherent because souls lack a continuous identity and thus the self-awareness required to make decisive choices, either between incarnations or when embodied.[74] Since afterlife rewards and

---

71 Charles L. Griswold, *Self-Knowledge in Plato's* Phaedrus (New Haven and London: Yale University Press, 1986), 100. I am indebted to this subtle analysis of the difficulties involving the soul's choices in *Phaedrus*. He points out that choices leading to subsequent incarnations are not prone to this paradox since at that stage the choosing soul has already been individuated and its character determined.

72 Halliwell 1988, 22 trenchantly states the problem: "This makes the significance of the choices hard to fathom: if they are the choices of the souls' *previous* 'selves', this would entail a harsh predestinarianism for the creatures who must live out the new lives. But if, as in fact is made quite clear (617de), the choices somehow belong to the new creatures themselves, how can they be conceived of as pre-natal and even prior to the identities to which they apply?"

73 In the myth of Er, souls drink from the river of Lethe; in *Phaedrus* 248c7, they lose their wings and descend, having been weighed down with forgetfulness.

74 So Annas: "the free choice of the souls between lives can have significance for me only if there is some way in which the free choice of my life by a soul on the cycle of rebirths implies that *within* my life I have freedom to choose and so am truly responsible for what I choose to do." Annas 1982, 133. However, it is a mistake, I think, to read the dramatis personae of the myths as ordinary embod-

punishments are temporary and only have meaning in the overall balance of good and evil in the cosmos, they have no moral significance for the self-determination and freedom of the individual agent.[75]

Mark McPherran expresses similar concerns, arguing that the myth "results in an infinite regress of states of moral responsibilty."[76] For him, the prophet's throwing of the lots determines the soul's order of life-selection (617de), which stacks the deck, leaving the gods responsible for what happens to all souls: "the order of life choice is not random, but occurs through a providence that Plato is unwilling to expose and explain."[77] This is a real concern, but we should be cautious about interpreting a myth literally, even a philosophical myth. McPherran wonders, for example, why the gathered souls don't scramble to pick up the lots. This sort of realistic approach to a symbolic narrative is anachronistic and inappropriate and thus is bound to produce insoluble paradoxes and incongruities. It is important to note first that in the *Laws* the lottery for officeholders reflects divine selection. The practice may derive from Solon, though in fifth and fourth-century Athenian democracy the lottery was often valued for its randomizing effect. In *Laws* 946b, 759c, and 690c divine providence (θεία τύχη) and divine fate (θεία μοῖρα) operate through the lottery. It might be supposed, then, that the inclusion of the lottery in the selection of one's future life in the myth of Er, in conjunction with the Fates and the prophet who dispenses the lots, is intended to remove the element of chance. To the charge that this device undermines the assignment of responsibility to souls making pre-natal choices, Plato responds that a person who does not ex-

---

ied moral agents. I note first that the notion of personal identity is fluid, even ambiguous in the myth. Stephen Halliwell, "The Life-and-Death Journey of the Soul: Interpreting the Myth of Er," in *The Cambridge Companion to Plato's Republic*, ed. G. R. F. Ferrari (Cambridge: Cambridge University Press, 2007), 462 notes two distinct ideas of soul: "that of a notionally disembodied set of capacities for ethical reasoning, desire, and emotion and that of the self-conscious identity of a person, built around memory of, and continuity with, a personal history." Even this description isn't subtle enough to encompass what we see. In each myth we are presented with varying concatenations of the parts of the soul, which include "unconscious" impressions surviving from previous lives as well as "super-conscious" impressions of the realm of forms.

75 Annas 1982, 137.
76 Mark L. McPherran, "Virtue, Luck, and Choice at the End of the Republic," in *Plato's Republic. A Critical Guide*, ed. Mark L. McPherran (Cambridge University Press, 2010), 137.
77 Ibid., 139.

amine and purify himself and seek the good damages his own capacity to choose wisely, thus making his choices unfree. These self-imposed limitations are explained by reference to the transmission of the soul's character from one birth to the next. Representing souls as constrained in these ways is of course repugnant to modern readers who assume autonomy and freedom as innate rights. Thus for some the myth of Er especially is depressing and alienating, because it seems deterministic.[78] Indeed, Necessity is invoked often in the myths,[79] but only for souls who do not remember, i.e., for those who drink too deeply from the River of Forgetfulness (Lethe) "because they weren't saved by reason" (621a). The implicit constructive message of Platonic myth is that the rebirth cycle will continue without end until one becomes detached from the desires and needs of the lower parts of the soul and seeks wisdom and virtue, even in the most constrained circumstances.[80]

In the myth of Er the benefits of wisdom and detachment are exemplified by Odysseus' prudent choice: "By chance the soul of Odysseus got to make its choice last of all and since memory of its former sufferings had relieved its love of honor, it went around for a long time looking for the life of a private individual who did his own work" (620c2–7). Despite the chance (τύχη) that deposited his lot furthest away, Odysseus' sufferings extended his memory and effaced his desire for honor—both marks of a philosophic soul. The decisive point of this episode is that Odysseus' wise choice occurs because of his internal detachment from desire. By contrast, unphilosophical

---

78 Annas 1982, 132–33.
79 *Rep.* 616c4, 617b4, b7-c1, e1–2, 618b3, 619c1, 620d6–621a; *Phdr.* 248c3 ff. I agree with Griswold 1986, 101 that it is Necessity, not Freedom, that rules the cosmos of the *Phaedrus*.
80 See Bluck's eloquent statement of this interpretation: "*despite* the conditions under which a life is lived, and *despite* even the crimes that an incarnate soul may commit through force of circumstances, and the effect that such behaviour must have on it, it is still possible to pursue wisdom and virtue (619de). Even if so doing may not be able to alter one's actions during this life, yet it may help to mould the desires of the soul in such a way as to affect its destiny hereafter." Bluck 1958b, 413, author's emphasis. Halliwell proposes a similar approach, phrased in more "existentialist" terms: "the motif of a prenatal life choice can be interpreted as a stark emblem of the inescapably self-forming consequence of ethical agency, a magnified image of how at every moment…the individual soul/person is intrinsically responsible for what matters most about its existence. Every action, we might thus say, rings with its own 'afterlife.' Every choice makes us what we are." Halliwell 2007, 469.

souls pursue harmful objects of desire, including the characters and life-conditions that will accomodate those desires, mentally identifying with and attaching themselves to them. For this reason the souls journeying through the underworld should really be seen as sleepwalkers, not as conscious, rational agents making free choices. Recall Socrates' statement in *Republic* 534cd: souls arriving in Hades without knowledge go to sleep.

Though it is beyond the scope of this essay to address such a complex problem, I concur with scholars who see Plato as a compatibilist.[81] Those who interpret the myths as incompatibilist or determinist *tout court* do not acknowledge how Plato's grounding of freedom in knowledge and goodness, instead of in unconstrained choice, complements the operation of divine providence. Moreover, the attainment of true knowledge in Plato involves a kind of self-transcendence and the activation of a synoptic cosmic vision on the part of a trans-personal soul whose life cycle extends through aeons. Er's account of the encounter with the whorls and the spindle of Necessity, and then with the three Fates, is intended as a spiritual exercise for readers to visualize the just order of the cosmos. The philosopher's aim is "to study all time and all being" (*Rep.* 486a8–9), the soul whose wings are in perfect condition governs the entire universe (*Phdr.* 246c, cf. 249c). The immortal soul should not be seriously concerned with the "short time" from childhood to old age (608cd). "If the soul is immortal, it requires our care not only for the time we call our life, but for the sake of all time" (*Phd.* 107c1–2).[82] The overriding aim of Plato's visionary meta-

---

81 See Richard F. Stalley, "Plato's Doctrine of Freedom," *Proceedings of the Aristotelian Society* 98 (1998): 145–158 and Kenneth Dorter, "Free Will, Luck, and Happiness in the Myth of Er," *Journal of Philosophical Research* 28 (2003): 129–42.

82 Contrast Annas' view: "the more my life is shown to me as being part of an unending cycle of events over which I have no control, the less I can feel that rewards for being just, or punishments for being unjust, really answer to what I have done and chosen…If the myth [of Er] is right, the proper way to view it is as being in large part the product of factors unavailable to my consciousness and beyond my control, and doomed to end in results which, whether pleasant or the opposite, are merely inevitable responses to the product in me of those factors" (133). Without casting any aspersions on the issues Annas raises, I suggest that a similar lack of awareness of relevant factors (e.g., personal memories, careful deliberation etc.) affects many choices and decisions in everyday life.

physics is to provoke humans to look beyond the narrow, individualist constraints they impose on themselves.

The apex of this universal, cosmic perspective is the philosopher's ultimate liberation from the cycle of births and death. The transitory nature of heaven and hell states and the negligible effect of inter-life rewards and punishments on the soul's choices of new lives are meant to emphasize, it seems to me, both the immense amount of time necessary for liberation and the sustained effort required to escape the rebirth cycle. It is true that Plato does not explicitly say that all souls will achieve the liberation from the cycle that is promised for philosophers. But his perfectionist ethical commitments make this likely in my view.

Though he is reticent to describe the nature of the perfect state compared to punishment, reward, and rebirth, the references to it complete the eschatological picture. Often liberation is alluded to in mythic or symbolic terms, e.g., dwelling with the gods (*Phd.* 69c, 81a4–6, 82b10) or attaining a supreme blessedness in "beautiful dwelling places" which are beyond description (114c).[83] This is the realm referred to as "the place beyond the heavens," which is ineffable like the form of the Good (*Phdr.* 247c3–4).[84] Those who have chosen philosophical

---

83 Dwelling with the gods and sharing the divine banquet recall Empedocles: "But at the end they come among men on earth as prophets, bards, doctors, princes; and thence they arise as gods highest in honour, sharing with the other immortals their hearth and their table, without part in human sorrows or weariness" (Frr. 146–147). See also Pindar *Olympian* 2.

84 Socrates asserts that "The place beyond the heaven—none of our earthly poets has ever sung or ever will sing its praises enough!" Rowe rightly says that "what is 'poetic' about his description is not so much the language which he uses about the Forms…as is his account of their location—literally speaking, they are not located anywhere." Christopher J. Rowe, *Plato: Phaedrus*, ed. with Translation and Commentary (Warminster: Aris & Phillips, 1986), 179. Cp. the remarks of Lincoln above n. 70. On the analogy between *Phdr.* and *Rep.* cf. Cumont 1949, 258, 280, 189 ff. and Halliwell 1988, 174. Philosophers tend to ignore the analogy beween the celestial experiences of purified souls in the afterlife and the noetic vision of the forms and of the Good in the ascent passages in *Symposium*, *Phaedrus*, and *Republic*, assigning the former to Plato's religious and poetic speculation, while reserving the latter for "serious" critical analysis. This is an arbitrary and unfruitful distinction. Note the similar references to vision, happiness, and blessedness: *Phd.* 81a, 111a, 114c, 115d; *Symp.* 211e, *Rep.* 516c, 615a, 619de; *Phdr.* 247cd, 249a, 250bc; *Tim.* 90c, *Laws* 660e. Riedweg 1987, 22–28, 37–67 has collected passages in the dialogues and from mystery-sources like the Gold Leaves that mention vision, happiness, and blessedness.

lives three consecutive times escape from the rebirth cycle (249a1–5), and having become completely purified and "wholly perfect and free of all troubles,…gazed in rapture at sacred revealed objects that were perfect, and simple, and unshakeable and blissful" (250b9-c5).[85] The traditional realm of the Island of the Blessed is the ultimate destination of philosophers (*Rep.* 519c, 540b), whose pursuit of the dialectical path "leads at last, it seems, towards that place which is a rest from the road, so to speak, and an end of journeying *for the one who reaches it*" (532e1–3).[86] If these *Republic* passages are compared to references to the philosopher's liberation in *Phaedo* and *Phaedrus,* the myth of Er's silence on the topic is rendered otiose.[87] As should be expected, both the timing of liberation and its content is consistently signified in mythic and symbolic terms.[88]

---

85 Scholarly opinion is divided on whether the *Phaedrus* alludes to the philosopher's final liberation from the cycle of births and deaths. Annas 1982, 136 and Reginald Hackforth, *Plato's* Phaedrus (Cambridge: Cambridge University Press, 1952), 87 accept that *Phaedo* and *Phaedrus* endorse the idea, while the myth of Er does not; Bluck 1958a, 156–57 and Griswold 1986, 264 n.41 believe, probably correctly in my view, that the perfection of a soul that has lived three successive lives devoted to philosophy (249c) is not reborn in that particular 10,000 year cycle. But it does not explicitly indicate, on the other hand, that the philosopher will be reborn in the next cycle. The various scenarios can be interpreted as complementary if the *Phaedrus* rebirth cycle is subsumed within the larger cycle that lasts through aeons.
86 *Rep.* 532e2: οἳ ἀφικομένῳ. This same phrase is found at *Phd.* 67b8, 81a6, *Gorg.* 527c5–6, and in *Rep.* 571e8–9.
87 Considering only *Republic*, G.R.F. Ferrari, "Glaucon's Reward, Philosophy's Debt: The Myth of Er," in *Plato's Myths*, ed. Catalin Partenie (Cambridge: Cambridge University Press, 2009), 129–30, supporting Annas 1982, thinks philosophers don't achieve liberation. However, he ignores the evidence of *Phaedo* and *Phaedrus*. This "siloed" method of reading the dialogues arbitrarily excludes the possibility of gaining new insights through synoptic reading. Texts that are more complex, inclusive, and comprehensive might be read as more authoritative.
88 The three successive incarnations in *Phdr.* 249a recall Pindar. Cf. Bluck 1958 for detailed analysis; also Bernabé and San Cristóbal 2008, 65–66. The end of the cycle of rebirth may be indicated in the poem's phrase "in the ninth year," though it has been construed as referring to "great years" or even cosmic cycles (see Bluck 1958, 280–83). The length of the period between incarnations and the number of incarnations within a cycle appear to be symbolic and thus opaque without the further clarification one might expect in oral discussion. This perhaps is where Platonic esotericism is to be found, not in the dry abstractions about "principles" championed by the Tübingen esotericists.

To sum up, the foundation of Plato's rebirth doctrine is that one's character at any given moment is an ever-changing bundle of impressions and processes—mysteriously conjoined to an immortal essence—which has been shaped by thoughts and actions in previous lives and by post-mortem events and which continues to form itself anew in every moment. The experiences and choices of discarnate souls, at least non-philosophical souls, should be likened, therefore, to their embodied lives as composite entities, not as free, rationally self-determining agents. Viewed *sub specie temporis* they appear as "bundle-selves" not as unified "substance-selves." Diotima's teaching in *Symposium* 207cd poignantly captures life on this level.[89] It is this Heraclitean self that is the main actor in the rebirth scenarios examined so far. A further stage of ethicization appears in the *Laws*, although hints of it appear in *Phaedo*, *Republic*, and *Timaeus*. The compensatory scheme expands to include the incarnate agent's direct experience of the effects of his previous actions. In short, the principle "as you sow, so shall you reap" appears in rudimentary form, revealing salient connections between incarnations instead of exclusively between one's incarnate and discarnate existences.

Plato's playful ethicizing of the Pythagorean doctrine of rebirth in animals is perhaps the first step in this direction. In *Phaedo* 81c-82c souls with intense corporeal attachments are drawn towards embodiment through fear of Hades: "paying the penalty for their previous bad upbringing," they wander around graveyards and eventually are reborn in various animals forms. The gluttonous and violent become donkeys etc., while those who have achieved popular virtue incarnate as bees, wasps, or ants (82c).[90] A more thoroughly ethicized version of descent into animal-forms occurs in *Timaeus* where rebirth occurs "into some wild animal that resembled the wicked character he had acquired"

---

89 "Even while each living thing is said to be alive and to be the same…even then he never consists of the same things though he is called the same, but he is always being renewed and in other respects passing away, in his hair and flesh and bones and blood and his entire body. And it's not just in his body, but in his soul, too, for none of his manners, customs, opinions, desires, pleasures, pains, or fears ever remains the same, but some are coming to be in him while others are passing away."

90 With the immediately preceding section (80c-81a) on the philosopher's final departure for the true Hades of the forms, this account of animal reincarnations as punishment comprises a rebirth scenario unto itself. It is reminiscent of Orphic-Pythagorean scenarios that lack post-mortem punishments and rewards.

(*Tim.* 42c). Clearly, Plato shared the Orphic-Pythagorean belief in the unity of living things and in cross-species sentience; he may also have adopted earlier ideas about ascribing ethical features to individual animal forms, though the evidence for this is spotty.

These are preliminary steps towards a more clearly delineated causal series, extending through multiple births, within which an agent experiences what she inflicted on others in a previous life. Perhaps the first instance of causally connecting current experience with ethical performance in an earlier life appears shortly before the myth of Er, when Socrates broaches the topic of rewards and punishments for justice and injustice, respectively. "Won't we also agree," Socrates asks Glaucon, "that everything that comes to someone who is loved by gods, insofar as it comes from the gods themselves, is the best possible, unless it is the inevitable punishment for some mistake he made in a former life" (εἰ μή τι ἀναγκαῖον αὐτῷ κακὸν ἐκ προτέρας ἁμαρτίας ὑπῆρχεν, 612e8–613a2).[91] Another instance of linkage across life-times occurs in Socrates' encomium of the philosophical life in *Republic* VI. Philosophers are the "ones who are to live happily and, in death, add a fitting destiny in that other place to the life they have lived." In response to Glaucon's objection that Thrasymachus and others won't at all be convinced by his bold claims, Socrates says that "we won't relax our efforts until we either convince him and the others or, at any rate, do something that may benefit them in a later incarnation, when, reborn, they happen upon these arguments again" (498b-d). These two passages, because of their very casualness, suggest to me that as early as the *Republic* Plato may have been thinking about this-worldly compensation and birth-to-birth continuity despite the greater emphasis placed on postmortem rewards and punishments in the myths.

For reasons that are unclear, the *Laws* intensifies the ethicization of the rebirth cycle, without rejecting afterlife compensation.[92] These are its most explicit statements of a karmic ethics of rebirth:

> Vengeance [τίσιν] is exacted for these crimes in the after-life [i.e., Hades], and when a man returns to this world again he is ineluctably obliged to pay

---

91 See Adam 1963, *ad loc.* on taking προτέρας ἁμαρτίας to refer to a previous lifetime.

92 Cf. *Laws* 870d5–7, 904d, 959bc. Contra Andrea W. Nightingale, "Plato on the Origins of Evil: the *Statesman* Myth Reconsidered," *AncPhil* 16 (1996): 73 who claims that reward and punishment now occur only within the physical universe.

the penalty [δίκην ἐκτεῖσαι] prescribed by the law of nature—to undergo the same treatment as he himself meted out to his victim, and to conclude his earthly existence by encountering a similar fate (μοίρᾳ) at the hands of someone else. (870d7-e3).

The next section includes the retributive principle that specifies the penalty for murdering relatives:

> a man who has done something of this kind is obliged to suffer precisely what he has inflicted [δράσαντί τι τοιοῦτον παθεῖν ταὐτὰ ἀναγκαίως ἅπερ ἔδρασεν]...no other purification is available when common blood has been polluted; the pollution resists cleansing until, murder for murder, the guilty soul has paid the penalty and by this appeasement has soothed the anger of the deceased's entire line. (872e-873a).[93]

These retributivist features recall the *Phaedo* myth, where the punishment of wrongdoers ceases only when they are forgiven by their victims (114b), with the notable difference that in the *Laws* the soul suffers the effects of its actions in a previous life.[94] It has been argued that Plato does not systematically ethicize rebirth in *Laws* 870–873 since he only cites examples of egregious, violent crimes.[95] The omission of re-

---

93 This principle is introduced as a "myth or account" (μῦθος ἢ λόγος) "stated clearly by ancient priests" (ἐκ παλαιῶν ἱερέων εἴρηται σαφῶς, 872e1–2.)
94 Mary Margaret Mackenzie, *Plato on Punishment* (Berkeley: University of California Press, 1981), 228–230 claims that the reformative aim of punishment enunciated in the earlier myths is supplanted in the *Laws* by a purely retributivist conception that abandons any effort to explain how punishment aids the soul to become virtuous and happy. This criticism demonstrates the need to read the myths in conjunction with each other to attain a comprehensive view of Platonic eschatology. For discussion of the retributivist features in these passages, see Richard F. Stalley, "Myth and Eschatology in Plato's and *Laws*," in *Plato's Myths*, ed. Catalin Partenie (Cambridge: Cambridge University Press, 2009), 197–98, who argues convincingly that the reformative concept of punishment, evidenced in dialogues like *Protagoras*, *Gorgias*, and *Republic* remains central to penology in the *Laws*.
95 Obeyesekere 2002, 289. He offers different reasons for Plato's "incomplete ethicization." First, relying on psychoanalytic principles, he claims that Plato had such an intense emotional reaction to violent wrongdoers that he felt compelled to punish them twice, both in the afterlife and in embodied existence (290). Second, he argues that because Plato aimed his teaching at a small intellectual elite, he did not develop a comprehensive rebirth ethics. The latter step would have required the "creation of a congregation" (274). I find this sociological criterion anachronistic. Moreover, Plato's aspirations for a just society in the *Republic* and elsewhere indicate that he hoped his ideas would be diffused throughout a community.

wards in one's current life for virtue in past lives need not lead to such a sweeping judgment. Both *Phaedo* and *Republic* refer to afterlife rewards for the virtuous, but they also stress the intra-psychic reality of the good to such an extent that Plato might well have thought it superfluous to articulate further this aspect of his rebirth ethics.

The myth in *Laws* X weaves together the elements of individual punishment and personal responsibility treated in Book IX into the perspective of cosmic providence. Everything, "down to the smallest details" of the individual parts of the universe—including punishments and rewards, births and deaths of individual souls—is under the control of "the supervisor of the universe" and various "ruling powers" (903b). The Stranger expounds the principles that the individual "exists for the sake of the universe" (903c5) not vice versa and that one's present position "contributes to the good of the whole" (d2). Thus,

> since a soul is allied with different bodies at different times, and perpetually undergoes all sorts of changes, either self-imposed or produced by some other soul, the divine checkers-player has nothing else to do except promote a soul with a promising character to a better situation, and relegate one that is deteriorating to an inferior, as is appropriate [πρέπον] in each case, so that they all meet the fate [μοίρας] they deserve ....With this grand purpose in view he has worked out what sort of position, in what regions, should be assigned to a soul to match its changes of character; but he left it to the individual's acts of will to determine the direction of these changes. You see, the way we react to particular circumstances is almost invariably determined by our desires and our psychological state...So all things that contain soul change, the cause of their change lying within themselves, and as they change they move according to the ordinance and law of destiny. Small changes in unimportant aspects of character entail small horizontal changes of position in space, while a substantial decline into injustice sets the soul on the path to the depths of the so-called underworld, which men call Hades and similar names, and which haunts and terrifies them both during their lives and when they have been sundered from their bodies. Take a soul that becomes particularly full of vice or virtue as a result of its own acts of will and the powerful influence of social intercourse. If companionship with divine virtue has made it exceptionally divine, it experiences an exceptional change of location, being conducted by a holy path to some superior place elsewhere. Alternatively, opposite characteristics will send it off to live in the opposite region (903d3-e, 904b3-e3).

Saunders and Nightingale argue that this myth differs from earlier eschatological myths in its demythologized content and lack of divine personnel. It offers, they suggest, a more scientific eschatology on which souls move "naturally"—without divine intervention and without divine judgment—to morally appropriate places within the physical universe. It is true that the myth doesn't feature as many *dramatis personae* and the otherworldly geography of earlier myths, but the all encompassing forces of fate, necessity, and the divine supervisor nevertheless represent the divine agency and teleological orientation found in the earlier myths. It even refers to judges (905a3) and to Hades (904d2, 905b1).[96] Also to be noted is the brief reference at the end to divinization and liberation from the rebirth cycle.

Problems with correlating freedom, determinism, and luck in the myth of Er noted above are taken up again in the *Laws* myth, where compatibilism is easier to discern. Each mental event and physical action adds to a soul's character, and thus to its fate; its choices set the direction it follows in accordance with cosmic necessity, which the divine supervisor manages for the good of the whole. On the individual level, personal choice and responsibility are still strongly affirmed, while on the cosmic level "he contrived a place for each constituent where it would most easily and effectively ensure the triumph of virtue and the defeat of vice throughout the universe" (904b2–4). The divine supervisor here personifies the abstract principle of necessity prominent in Er and *Phaedrus*, by expressing the Demiurge's causal efficacy within the rebirth cycle.

II. Plotinus' Rebirth Eschatology

The central elements in Plotinus' rebirth eschatology are based directly on the Platonic texts discussed in the first part of this essay, though he pressed them to serve his own philosophical agenda. Many of the issues left unresolved or unclear by Plato receive fresh attention: the relation between karma and rebirth; the nature and identity of the transmigrating agent; the scope of retribution; the mechanisms at work in karmic causality; and liberation from the cycle of births and deaths. By *karma* I simply mean deeds that produce counter-balancing effects in future births, i.e., positive and negative experiences such as pleasure and

---

96 I am indebted to the thorough analysis of this passage in Stalley 2009, 190–194. He demonstrates the operation of divine agency throughout the myth, against Nightingale 1996 and Trevor J. Saunders, "Penology and Eschatology in Plato's *Timaeus* and *Laws*," *CQ* 23 (1973): 232–44. Cf. now the valuable discussion of the passage in Robert Mayhew, *Plato* Laws 10, trans. with an Introduction and Commentary (Oxford: Oxford University Press, 2008), 179–83.

pain, the conditions of embodied existence, and dispositional tendencies. Because most of the treatises in the *Enneads* were composed in Plotinus' maturity, they offer a relatively consistent picture of the factors shaping the soul's embodiments, its post-mortem experiences, and its rebirths. Stylistically, the *Enneads* differ from the Platonic dialogues in being first-person statements by Plotinus himself in the form of lectures compiled by his pupil Porphyry into treatises addressing specific topics. Plato's reflections, on the other hand, developed over a long writing career and were embodied in symbolic and mythic narratives created by an artistic imagination without equal among ancient philosophers. Thus, Plato's thoughts, as we have seen, display notable variations and inconsistencies. Despite the abundance of inspired utterances and visionary episodes in Plotinus' writings, his accounts of the soul's journeys lack the mythical *dramatis personae* and otherworldly scene-setting characteristic of Plato's eschatological myths. Writing some six hundred years after Plato, Plotinus was influenced by philosophers who articulated their thought in the form of the scholastic commentary. Thus, his eschatological discussions distill Plato's mythopoeic accounts into more discursive form.

The metaphysical framework for Plotinus' rebirth cycle is constituted by the emanation of lower levels of being from the higher: from the One or Good proceeds the intelligible world, from which proceeds in turn the even more diversified multiplicity of the world-soul, individual souls, and the physical universe. Complementing the procession of the lower from the higher is the desire on the part of emanated entities to return in contemplation to their anterior hypostasis, the source of their being and the goal of their aspirations. The descent of individual souls into material embodiment is a major theme, to which Plotinus devotes an entire treatise as well as many passages in the *Enneads*. With Plato he accepts the Orphic-Pythagorean idea of imprisonment in the body, but he distances himself even further than Plato from the archaic theme of punishment for primordial sin, preferring the positive account expounded in the *Timaeus*. The full range of his thinking on these themes appears in the early treatise "On the descent of the soul into bodies," which begins with Plotinus "waking up" from his body and confronting this *aporia*: "I am puzzled how I ever came down, and how my soul has come to be in the body" (IV.8.1.8–10).[97] Sounding an Orphic note, he

---

97 All translations from the *Enneads* are taken from A.H. Armstrong's version in the Loeb Classical Library.

juxtaposes Empedocles' image of himself as an exile from the gods because of past wrongdoing (1.18–21, citing B115.13–14) with Plato's images of human souls held in custody (*Phd.* 62b2–5) and buried in the body (67d1)—which is "a chain and a tomb" (3.4)—and in a cave (1.30–35). The negative view of the descent is filled out with images from the *Phaedrus* (1.36–40): "the shedding of wings" is the "cause of our arriving here" (246c2, 248c9); he also refers to "judgments" (249a6) and "lots and chances and necessities" (249b2, *Rep.* 619d7). He then cites the positive teaching of the *Timaeus*, arguing that "the soul was given by the goodness of the Craftsman, so that this All might be intelligent...and the soul of each one of us was sent that the All might be perfect" (1.43–49, quoting *Tim.* 34b8).

The negative and positive reasons for the soul's descent into embodiment reflect distinct vantage-points that are more clearly articulated than in Plato. The negative take expresses the individuated view from within an agent's subjectivity, whereas the positive reason is part of the "god's-eye view" on the intelligible level. Delving deeper into the former, Plotinus translates the Platonic and Orphic-Pythagorean symbols of "moulting" and "imprisonment," respectively, into the terms of his moral psychology. Individual souls abandon the whole (i.e., the intelligible world) to become a part, desiring to "belong to themselves" (IV.8.4.13–15), "caring for things outside...[the soul] sinks deep into the individual part" (4.20–22). Their innate impulse to "belong to themselves" incites consciousness to contract from the universal to the particular.

> The souls go neither willingly nor because they are sent, nor is the voluntary element in their going like deliberate choice, but like a natural spontaneous jumping or a passionate natural desire of sexual union or as some men are moved unreasoningly to noble deeds...and the individual, which is subordinated to the universal, is sent according to law. For the universal bears heavily upon the particular, and the law does not derive from outside the strength for its accomplishment, but is given to be in those themselves who are subject to it, and they bear it about with them...it makes itself a sort of weight in them and implants a longing, a birth pang of desire to come where the law within them as it were calls them come. (IV.3.13.18–32).

Similarly, the soul "leapt out, we might say, from the whole to a part, and actualises itself as a part in it, as if a fire able to burn everything was compelled to burn some little thing although it had all its power" (VI.4.16.29–32). At the beginning of V.1, souls forget god, their father:

"The beginning of evil for them was audacity and coming to birth and the first otherness and the wishing to belong to themselves. Since they were clearly delighted with their own independence...they were ignorant even that they themselves came from that world" (4–9). Notably absent from these narratives is any sense of a primordial sin that could have been avoided. Instead, Plotinus emphasizes the naturalness and spontaneity of the soul's inchoate impulse to individuate itself. Although the result is a falling away from goodness, the beginning point is the Good itself. What results is limited self-awareness, almost a kind of unconsciousness, which is the precondition for embodiment. Once embodied, memory weakens and forgetfulness spreads. In a striking metaphor, Plotinus likens the "flowing nature of body" to the River of Lethe in the myth of Er (IV.3.26.55). Throughout the *Enneads* one encounters this psychologization of key elements in Platonic and Orphic-Pythagorean eschatology and soteriology.

In this treatise too Plotinus connects the positive and negative views, as when he draws on the Orphic myth of Zeus, Dionysus, and the Titans, appropriating again an archaic symbol to dramatize his point about self-absorption, which is extraneous to the story: "the souls of men see their images as in the mirror of Dionysus and come to be on that level with a leap from above: but even these are not cut off from their own principle and from intellect" (IV.3.12.1–4). While the soul's descent is a fall from the goodness and truth of Intellect, it never completely loses its connection with its source: "our soul does not altogether come down, but there is always something of it in the intelligible" (IV.8.8.2–3). The higher "part" remains there eternally "unaffected among the intelligibles" (ἀπαθὴς ἐν τοῖς νοητοῖς), "but that which acquires desire, which follows immediately on that intellect, goes out further in a way by its acquisition of desire" (IV.7.13.2–6). Plotinus' controversial claim that the higher part of the soul remains above (see also V.1.10.24, V.7.1) was widely criticized by the later Neoplatonists.[98] Whatever difficulties and challenges it later faced, the idea of the undescended soul afforded Plotinus much needed support for his attempt to reconcile the positive and negative views of the descent, which in Plato usually are treated

---

98 Proclus, *Elements of Theology* Prop. 211 in E.R. Dodds, *Proclus: The Elements of Theology*. (Oxford: Oxford University Press, 1963), 184, *Commentary on the Parmenides* 948.12–38; Iamblichus, *Commentary on the Parmenides* Fr. 87 in John Dillon and Lloyd P. Gerson, *Neoplatonic Philosophy. Introductory Readings* (Indianapolis: Hackett, 2004), 254–55.

separately. Whereas Plato is allusive in expression but focused on specific problems, Plotinus speaks simply and directly but with a synoptic view. In IV.8.5. he grasps both horns of the dilemma:

> There is then no contradiction between the sowing to birth and the descent for the perfection of the All, and the judgment and the cave, and necessity and free will (since necessity contains the freedom) and the being in the body as an evil (1–5)…everything which goes to the worse does so unwillingly, but, since it goes by its own motion, when it experiences the worse it is said to be punished for what it did (8–10);…and since the sin of the soul can refer to two things, either to the course of the descent or to doing evil when the soul has arrived here below, the punishment of the first is the very experience of descent, and of the lesser degree of the second the entrance…into other bodies according to the judgment passed on its deserts (17–21).

In this synthesis Plotinus encapsulates (i) the positive and negative reasons for the primordial descent of soul into embodiment, depicted separately in *Timaeus* and *Phaedrus* and (ii) the descents qua rebirths, which result from past-life actions, post-mortem experiences, and choices of new lives, derived primarily from *Republic*. Plotinus disperses the air of mystery surrounding Plato's mythical narratives. Whether his more discursive version is faithful to Plato remains an open question.

A more clearly delineated solution is proposed in the late treatise I.1. Drawing on both Platonic (*Rep.* 611d-612a) and Aristotelian theories of the soul, Plotinus distinguishes the immortal, rational part of the soul from the lower soul, which for him is an image of the higher and which forms a "compound" (τὸ σύνθετον) with the body. It is this compound that offers scope for virtue and vice (chs. 9–10), while the higher soul is impassive. The sharp metaphysical distinction between the two entities is first applied to the case of incarnation in animals (ch. 11): the higher part of the soul remains detached and inactive. Then, in ch. 12, Plotinus explicitly tries to reconcile what he considers the Platonic doctrine of the soul as eternal, good, and sinless with Plato's accounts of afterlife punishments and subsequent rebirths. He states that the "single simple soul" does not sin nor suffer punishment nor, it should be noted, does it "act rightly," rather, what acts in every case is "the compound" (τὸ σύνθετον), which is projected into the cycle of births and deaths by the higher soul: "and it is this which for Plato is punished not that other single and simple soul" (I.1.12.10–12). By means of this bifurcation of the self into higher and lower parts, Plotinus completely segregates the eternal intelligible self from the rebirth cycle.

It neither acts nor does it suffer the effects of wrongdoing nor benefit from virtuous actions. The compound self, whether incarnate or discarnate, is identified as the transmigrating agent.

The intelligible self, however, since it is a transcendent, hyper-personal being, does not seem much like a self. By definition it lacks individuation and a delimited subjectivity. Its superabundant reality, whose vital nature is to overflow, transmits via the lower soul the light and power of the higher world into the material universe. Even the latter's descent, which is called an "inclination" (νεύσις), isn't evil: "If the inclination is an illumination directed to what is below it is not a sin, just as casting a shadow is not a sin…The soul is said to go down or incline in the sense that the thing which receives light from it lives with it" (I.1.12.24–29). In these passages Plotinus adds positive spin to Plato's mythic accounts of the soul's descent, subordinating the negative effects on a soul of its descent into embodiment to the benefit of spreading the light of its inner nature into the darkness of otherness and materiality.[99]

Although he eschews the elaborate afterlife narratives of punishments, rewards, and choices of new lives in Plato's myths, Plotinus nonetheless accepts them as stages in the soul's evolution. In his clearest statement on the matter, he begins with the principle that "no one can ever evade what he ought to suffer for his unrighteous doings: for the divine law is inescapable." After death souls are conveyed to invisible places to suffer appropriate punishments (IV.3.24.9–29), recalling the myth in *Laws* X concerning the divine supervisor. The Platonic afterlife, with its otherworldy Orphic-Pythagorean topography, is demythologized but not immanentized. Yet, Plotinus gives the impression that afterlife punishments and rewards are inconsequential in the soul's new life. (This tendency is already apparent in Plato, as was noted above.) Two factors motivate this attitude. First, the boundary between embodied and disembodied existence is more transparent, if you will, in Plotinus' writings than in Plato's. The death of the body seems even less important for Plotinus, perhaps because much of his philosophizing is conducted from what would today be called the "god's-eye view"—

---

99 This permutation of the "metaphysics of light" serves as a rich source of metaphors. See especially the brilliant passages IV.3.9.23–50 and 17.19–31: the soul radiates light, casting a shadow it must fill, "the shadow is as large as the rational formative principle which comes from soul" (9.47–48). Some souls descend further into the material world "attracted by the brightness of what is illuminated" (17.20–22).

in Neoplatonic terms, from the intelligible world. The "top-down" framework of his metaphysics is prominent in many of his treatises, in contrast to the Platonic dialogues, which, though they too promote top-downism, are more often addressed to skeptics and non-philosophers.[100] Speaking from this transcendent perspective to those largely in agreement with his assumptions, Plotinus focuses on the internal character of the soul, i.e., on its level of consciousness.[101] He prefers to examine afterlife punishments and rewards as intra-psychic events. For those enmeshed in corporeal existence, wrongdoing bears its fruit both here and hereafter: "Even if there are punishments in Hades, it will be again life that is an evil for it…We must say that life in a body is an evil in itself, but the soul comes into good by its virtue, by not living the life of the compound but separating itself even now" (I.7.3.13–15, 20–22; see also I.8.13.20–26). Like Plato he devotes more attention to the wicked and their sufferings and mostly ignores afterlife rewards for the virtuous (a rare exception is III.2.9.8–10). I believe the reason for this asymmetry is that afterlife rewards for virtue are of little intrinsic significance: they offer no incentive to the philosopher who aspires to integrate the higher part of the soul first with the divine life of Intellect and then with the One. Moreover, for the acutely self-conscious philosopher, the joys of virtue are always present.

The elision of the separation between incarnate and discarnate existence also shapes Plotinus' exposition of choosing one's next birth. Commenting on the *Phaedo* myth (107d7-e4), when the δαίμων guides the soul through Hades, Plotinus remarks that "the leading to judgment means that the spirit (δαίμων) comes to the same form after the soul's departure from this life as it had before the soul's birth; then, as if from a different starting-point, it is present to the souls which are being punished during the time which intervenes before their next birth—this is not a life for them, but an expiation (δίκη)" (III.4.6.13–16). He clarifies Plato's enigmatic statements about the impact of prenatal choices on a soul's incarnation:

---

100 On hierarchy and "top-downism" in ancient Platonism, cf. Gerson 2005, ch. 1.
101 As an example of disembodied experiences not noted by Plato, see Plotinus' discussion of (i) remembering past lives while disembodied: IV.3.25.10, 33; 27.15–23; (ii) no memory when united with Intellect: IV.4.4–6; and (iii) no discursive reasoning for discarnate souls: IV.3.18.1. For discussion of memories of embodied existence while disembodied see Brisson "Memory and the Soul's Destiny in Plotinus" (section 3) below.

the choice [αἵρεσις] in the other world which Plato speaks of is really a riddling representation of the soul's universal and permanent purpose and disposition. But if the soul's purpose [προαίρεσις] is decisive, and that part of it dominates which lies ready to hand as the result of its previous lives, the body is no longer responsible for any evil which may affect the man. For if the soul's character exists before the body, and has what it chose, and, Plato says, does not change its guardian spirit, then the good man does not come into existence here below, and neither does the worthless one. (III.4.5.2–10; cf. also IV.3.8.9 ff.)

Regarding *Rep.* 620de, Plotinus insists that souls make their choices "according to their characters" (III.4.5.17–29), which depend in turn on whether they follow the direction of the δαίμων, i.e., the rational part of the soul (echoing *Tim.* 90a). Those responsive to the true self withdraw into the intelligible,[102] while those controlled by the desires of the lower, mortal self "live under destiny" (II.3.9.24–28). Every choice one makes issues from one's character, but all choices and actions "are included in the universal order, because your part is not a mere casual interlude in the All" (III.3.3.2–4).[103]

Some aspects of Plotinus' scheme of karmic causality are explicated astrologically, a science that had not yet developed in Plato's time. In its material embodiments, the soul is subject to "soft astral determinism."[104] The ascents and descents of souls are in "one harmony with [the heaven's] circuit, so that their fortunes and their lives and their choices are indicated by the figures made by the heavenly bodies and they sing, as it were, with one voice and are never out of tune" (IV.3.12.22–25). Through our emotions, desires, pains, and pleasures we are bound

> to the stars, from which we get our souls, and subject us to necessity when we come down here; from them we get our moral characters, our characteristic actions, and our emotions, coming from a disposition which is liable to emotion. So what is left which is 'we'? Surely, just that which we really

---

102 "But if a man is able to follow the spirit which is above him, he comes to be himself above, living that spirit's life, and giving the pre-eminence to that better part of himself to which he is being led; and after that spirit rises to another, until he reaches the heights" (III.4.3.17–21).

103 The passage that follows echoes the myth of the divine checkers-player in *Laws* 904bc.

104 For the phrase and for illumination on this topic see Peter Adamson, "Plotinus on Astrology," *OSAPh* 35 (2008): 267: "Hard astrology [rejected by Plotinus] is the view that the stars cause or make (*poiein*) things happen in our sublunary world. Soft astrology rejects this, but allows for the accuracy of astrology by admitting that the stars do symbolize or signify (*sēmainein*) sublunary things."

are, we to whom nature gave power to master our passions…and God gave us too… 'virtue who is no man's slave' (*Rep.* 617e3) (II.3.9.11–18).[105]

The passions are the activities of "another kind of soul" (II.3.9.9), the mortal part of soul created by the lesser gods in *Timaeus* 69cd, discussed above. This physical necessity is identified with fate from which we can extricate ourselves by identifying with the higher soul. Similarly, although he follows Plato by referring to punishment in the form of animal or plant incarnations (I.1.11, III.4.2.18), his endorsement is accompanied by the qualification that the rational part of the soul is not present in these cases.[106]

Even if Plotinus' concepts of the higher intelligible self and the embodied, composite self differ from Plato's partitioning of the self, he nevertheless agrees with his master that the situations of the philosopher and non-philosophers are substantially different as regards freedom and necessity. He makes explicit a distinction between higher providence, which arranges all events teleologically, and lower fate to which souls, who are attached to matter and the life of the composite, subordinate themselves (III.3.4.10 ff., 5.15 ff.). Like Plato, he insists that all souls are responsible for their choices (III.2.7.20 ff., with *Rep.* 617e4–5), "but when all causes are included, everything happens with complete necessity" (III.1.9.3–4). The lots made available to souls in the myth of Er he interprets as symbolizing the physical conditions and astral influences of one's imminent incarnation (II.3.15.5–8).[107] Souls subject to the passions and external causes are unfree, whereas pure souls act on their own power in freedom (III.1.9–10).

A commitment towards the type of karmic ethics that first emerges in Plato's *Laws* deepens in Plotinus. It is difficult to determine why Plotinus expands the range of his compensatory ethics beyond what we find in Plato's later writings. One likely factor is his appropriation of the Stoic theory of providence. What stands out most in his picture of the rise and fall of souls is his embrace of a universal and harmonious

---

105 The effects on body-soul composites arising from physical conditions and environment are discussed in II.3.9–12 and IV.3.15.4 ff.
106 The later Neoplatonists rejected the incarnation of human souls in animals; cf. Proclus *in Tim.* III.329de.
107 Adamson 2008, 285–86 points out that the stars operate as auxiliary causes that are subordinate to family heredity and physical conditions. Moreover, the astral influences under which souls choose their lives are causes of emotional and ethical tendencies to some extent.

order, within which each soul plays its proper and well-deserved part. By imbuing Plato's cosmic theology of *Timaeus* and *Laws* with the Stoic ideas of sympathy and providence, Plotinus conceives of the course of human lives and nature in strongly normative terms (see IV.3.15.15–23). Animating this perspective is the Hellenistic notion of human life as a play, combined with Plato's striking image of humans as "playthings of god" (*Laws* 803cd). In this perspective, since "death is a changing of body, like changing of clothes on the stage…what would there be that is terrible in a change of this kind, of living beings into each other?" (III.2.15.24–28); "battles show that all human concerns are children's games, and tell us that deaths are nothing terrible, and that those who die in wars and battles anticipate only a little the death which comes in old age—they go away and come back quicker" (II.35–40). He urges us not to concern ourselves with murders and sackings of cities since "in the events of our life it is not the soul within but the outside shadow of man which cries and moans and carries on in every sort of way on a stage" (II.48–50). At the same time, the play of opposites, of good and evil in human life, forms a cosmic dance, a magnificent play in which we all play our parts: "in this way the soul, coming on the stage in this universal poetic creation and making itself a part of the play, supplies of itself the good or the bad in its acting; it is put in its proper place…and so is given punishments or rewards" (17.49–53). And just as in the theater, life would not be a good play were there not both admirable and virtuous characters as well as inferior and vulgar ones (III.2.11.14–17). Plotinus has creatively synthesized Platonic and Stoic providence with Orphic-Pythagorean and Platonic rebirth theory.

In accord with the cosmic piety prevalent in late antiquity, Plotinus identifies the just order that supervenes on particular just and unjust actions alike. He relies on this order to explain why wrongdoers are responsible for the effects of their injustices and why bad things happen to good people:

> but as contained in the universal order it is not unjust in that order, or in relation to the sufferer, but it was ordained that he should so suffer. But if the sufferer is a good man, this will turn out for his good. For one must not think that the order is godless or unjust, but that it is accurate in the distribution of what is appropriate, but it keeps its reasons hidden and gives grounds for blame to those who do not know them. (IV.3.16.20–26; cf. III.2.4.23–27, III.2.6–7)

Plotinus issues no apologies for his assertions that the mechanisms and the evidence for this order are hidden and that they can only be understood when one has ascended to the intelligible level where a comprehensive vision of the whole is available.[108] Thus, "he who blamed the whole because of the parts would be quite unreasonable in his blame; one must consider the parts in relation to the whole, to see if they are harmonious and in concord with it; and when one considers the whole one must not look at a few little parts [*Laws* 903bc]" (III.2.3.9–13). The universal order, which can even make use of human evil to good effect (III.2.5.23–26), exerts its influence throughout cosmic cycles:

> so as to determine men's worth from these, and to change their positions, making slaves out of those who were masters before, if they were bad masters (and also because it is good for them this way); and, if men have used wealth badly, making them poor (and for the good, too, it is not without advantage to be poor); and causing those who have killed unjustly to be killed in their turn, unjustly as far as the doer of the deed is concerned, but justly as far as concerns the victim; and it brings that which is to suffer together to the same point with that which is fit and ready to execute what that unjust killer is fated to endure. There is certainly no accident in a man's becoming a slave, nor is he taken prisoner in war by chance, nor is outrage done on his body without due cause, but he was once the doer of that which he now suffers; and a man who made away with his mother will be made away with by a son when he has become a woman, and one who has raped a woman will be a woman in order to be raped. Hence comes, by divine declaration, the name Adrasteia: for this world-order is truly Adrasteia [the Inescapable] and truly Justice and wonderful wisdom. We must conclude that the universal order is for ever something of this kind from the evidence of what we see in the All, how this order extends to everything, even to the smallest, and the art is wonderful which appears, not only in the divine beings but also in the things which one might have supposed providence would have despised for their smallness, for example, the workmanship which produces wonders in rich variety in ordinary animals. (III.2.13.4–23)

This long passage offers perhaps the most comprehensive statement of karmic ethics in the *Enneads*. Rambling from one topic to another as he often does, Plotinus nevertheless expands the karmic causal nexus beyond Plato's sole reference to it in discussing punishment for matricides

---

108 Annas 1982, 136 shares Augustine's horror at the thought of reincarnation, which, she is convinced, entails cosmic indifference to an individual's attempt to live well. I note Weber's assertion (noted above) that the Indian theory of karma and rebirth is the most rational theodicy articulated in any tradition. Far more reassuring, it might be supposed, than Augustine's doctrine of original sin.

in *Laws* 872e, the passage Plotinus probably has in mind here. Though he doesn't mention rewards for the virtuous, it is implied, I think, in the statement that the cosmic law applies the ethics of karma to the smallest details, including intelligent design of animals and plants. What one was and did in a previous life shapes and determines the nature and direction of one's current life and also what one does and suffers: "One might refer the being this or that kind of man to the previous life…one must carry back the reckoning [how souls become inferior] to what happened in previous lives" (III.3.4.35–36, 53–54); "Plato says [*Rep.* 620a] that the souls' choices take place according to their previous lives" (IV.3.8.9–10). Reflection on Plato's passing references to continuity from one life to another no doubt prompted Plotinus to articulate the causal nexus with greater precision.

In his treatment of the fifth element in Platonic eschatology—the philosopher's liberation from the cycle of births and deaths—Plotinus also speaks more forthrightly than his master. While some scholars think his views on this theme are ambiguous, the *Enneads* abounds with passages indicating (i) that the higher soul comes to dwell permanently in the intelligible world and that the lower soul is merely an image and (ii) also that this higher self ultimately ascends to union with the One.[109] Concerning the soul's return to the intelligible world—and its reactivation of its awareness of what it has always been in reality—it is often said that Plotinus abolishes the distinction between the hypostases of Soul and Intellect.[110] I have addressed this concern elsewhere.[111] Suffice to say that the third hypostasis of Soul continues to exist eternally while an individual soul's awareness of and identification with the sensible world and the universal soul are negated in the mystical return. The higher soul's abandonment of its lower self is mentioned often: VI.4.16.42–44, III.4.6.30–34, IV.3.24.21–28, and III.2.4.9 ff. How the ascended soul merges with the Intellect and lives its omniscient, blissful life prompts Plotinus to write some of his most

---

109 For scholars expressing doubt on this issue, cf. Dodds 1963, 304 and McEvilley 2002, 567 n. 29.
110 Cf. Richard T. Wallis, *Neoplatonism* (London: Hackett, 1972), 82.
111 For discussion of these passages and the problem of the soul's self-transcendence, see John Bussanich "Mystical Elements in the Thought of Plotinus," *Aufstieg und Niedergang der Römischen Welt* II.36.7 (1994): 5300–5330, and John Bussanich, "Non-discursive Thought in Plotinus and Proclus," *Documenti e studi sulla tradizione filosofica medievale* 8 (1997): 191–210.

inspired passages.[112] The later Neoplatonists, with the possible exception of Porphyry,[113] maintained stricter distinctions and divisions in the hierarchy of being than did Plotinus. Later, the strong metaphysical realism of the Athenian school of Neoplatonists stipulated that one's consciousness was inextricably tied to and reflected in one's position in the hierarchy. This grounds their view that the soul descends completely into material embodiment and that it can never escape the cycle of births and deaths. A more flexible, less dogmatic attitude in this regard is evident throughout the *Enneads*. Of course, all the Neoplatonists argue that their claims are based on Plato's doctrines. I hope to have demonstrated that Plotinus follows Plato very closely on the five elements of the rebirth eschatology but that he was especially innovative in ethicizing rebirth theory more than other Platonists.[114]

---

112 Cf. I.6.9.16–25; IV.7.10.14–20; V.3.4; V.8.4.36–38, 7.31–35, 11.1–24, 12.3–7; VI.5.7 & 12; VI.7.12.22–30, 31–36.
113 Cf. Dodds 1963, 305.
114 It might be objected that Plotinus' ethicization falls short in that he did not explicitly reject reincarnation into animals as did Proclus. See n. 98 above.

Memory and the Soul's Destiny in Plotinus

Luc Brisson

Translated by Michael Chase

I. Introduction

To speak of memory in Plotinus, one cannot restrict oneself to epistemological considerations. Since the soul is and becomes what it remembers, memory has prolongations on the level of ethics. In a retributive system such as the one to which Plotinus adheres, the human soul, which can live separately from all earthly bodies, rises or descends along the scale of beings as a function of the quality of its previous lives, and therefore, in a Platonic context, of the knowledge it has acquired, knowledge which it retains in its memory and which makes it what it is. How, indeed, could a soul be rewarded or punished if it has forgotten what it has done, and therefore does not know what it is? In this context, the soul's salvation is inseparably linked to the exercise of memory.

The starting point for any investigation on memory in Plotinus is *Treatise* 41 (IV, 6),[1] to which Porphyry gave the title *On sensation and memory*. It may be considered as an introduction to the long exposition *On difficulties concerning the soul*, which Porphyry divided into three treatises, 27 (IV, 3), 28 (IV, 4) and 29 (IV, 5).[2] In these treatises, Plotinus attributes a central position to the question of memory, in a long central section that extends from the end of *Treatise* 27 (IV, 3), 25 to the beginning of *Treatise* 28 (IV, 4), 5. Plotinus' interest in memory can be explained by the two points that are at stake in this problem. Memory al-

---

1 On this subject, see Pierre Marie Morel, who has provided an introduction, translation and annotation of Plotinus' *Treatise* 41 (IV, 6) *On sensation and memory*, in *Plotin. Traités* 45–50, ed. Luc Brisson and Jean-François Pradeau (Paris: Flammarion, 2007).
2 Luc Brisson has provided an introduction, translation, and annotation of Plotinus' *Traités* 27–29, ed. Luc Brisson and Jean-François Pradeau (Paris: Flammarion, 2005b).

lows a definition of the identity of human beings, and of their relations with the higher beings.

In *Treatise* 41, Plotinus interprets and criticizes the second of Aristotle's *Short treatises on natural sciences*, entitled *On memory and reminiscence*.[3] He wants to prove the following two points:

1. Sensation is not limited to the reception of material impressions, and
2. Memory cannot be reduced to the preservation of material imprints in the soul. In addition, Plotinus does not limit his criticism to those who, like Aristotle, believe that the soul is incorporeal, for he also extends it to those for whom the soul is a body (3, 77–78), that is, to the Stoics. He thus defends a twofold position with regard to the soul: the soul is neither corporeal nor inseparable from the body, and the soul is not passive in the process of memory.

In order fully to understand the ins and outs of this polemic over memory, we must ask ourselves questions concerning the nature of soul in general for Plotinus, the place of the human soul in the continuum of living beings, the appropriate level for speaking of representation and memory, and above all concerning the wanderings of the soul, as it descends toward earth, or rises back up toward its principle.

1. Soul in General

In Plotinus, the Soul is a *hupóstasis*[4] proceeding from another *hupóstasis*, which is its cause, i.e., the Intellect, which depends on the One. Plotinus distinguishes between the total Soul (*hē hólē psukhḗ*), which always remains within the Intelligible, and particular souls. The total soul is what is traditionally called the hypostasis of Soul. All other souls, both the world soul and human souls, are attached to this soul, which is

---

3   See now Richard A. H. King, *Aristotle and Plotinus on Memory* (Berlin: De Gruyter, 2009). I had access to this book when submitting the manuscript of this article.

4   I have used the following system of transliteration. Greek letters are written in Roman letters according to the following system: eta = *ē*; omega = *ō*; zeta = *z*; theta = *th*; xi = *x*; phi = *ph*; khi = *kh*; psi = *ps*. Iota subscript is written after the letter (for example *ēi*, but if is an alpha—which in this case only is a long vowel—with a subscript iota = *āi*), rough breathings are written as h, and smooth breathings are not noted. All accents are noted. Translation of Plotinus' treatises is by Armstrong, sometimes modified. The translation of Porphyry's *Sententiae* is by Dillon.

and remains unique. These souls remain united, and form only a single soul, before being projected here and there like a light which, when it reaches the earth, is distributed without being divided. The soul of the world (*hē psukhḗ toû pantós*) produces and administers the body. In order to understand this process as a whole, we must recall the broad outlines of the constitution of the universe. The soul receives within itself the forms (*eídē*) that remain in the Intellect in the mode of rational formulas (*lógoi*).[5] The lower part of the world soul, its vegetative power, or Nature, transposes these "rational formulas" (*lógoi*) into matter (*húlē*). A body (*sôma*) may then appear, which in fact corresponds to a set of qualities (*poiótētes*) that come to attach themselves to an *ógkos*,[6] that is, to a piece of matter (*húlē*) endowed with size (*mégethos*). In short, a body is a compound made up of matter (*húlē*), with which a certain size (*mégethos*) endowed with qualities (*poiótētes*) is associated. This size and qualities are "rational formulas" (*lógoi*),[7] that is, forms engaged in matter (*énula eídē*). Of bodies, some are inert,[8] while others, which may be qualified as "alive," are moved by a soul qualified as "vegetative," which is attached to the lower part of the world soul.[9]

Human beings occupy a particular position among living beings. Their bodies are made up of the same elements as those of all other living beings, but these bodies are under the influence of several kinds of soul. They are endowed with a vegetative soul that makes them living beings; this soul depends directly on the world soul, and is responsible for the body's nutrition, growth and reproduction. The father transmits it *via* his sperm. Once inside the womb, the sperm produces the embryo. At birth, a higher soul comes to associate itself with the vegetative soul that animates the embryo. By one "part" of itself, that is, its intellect (*noûs*), this soul remains above. In short, the human soul is complex, in

---

5 Translating *lógoi* by "rational formulas."
6 On this, see Luc Brisson, "Entre physique et métaphysique. Le terme *ógkos* chez Plotin, dans ses rapports avec la matière (*húlē*) et le corps (*sôma*)," in *Études sur Plotin*, ed. Michel Fattal (Paris and Montréal: L'Harmattan, 2000), 87–111.
7 On this, see Luc Brisson, "*Logos* et *logoi* chez Plotin. Leur nature et leur rôle," *Les Cahiers Philosophiques de Strasbourg* 8, special issue on Plotinus (1999): 87–108.
8 In the strict sense, for the presence of "rational formulas" (*lógoi*) means that nothing down here below is bereft of soul, although this is hard to perceive.
9 On the general question of the soul in Plotinus, see H. J. Blumenthal, *Plotinus' Psychology* (The Hague: Martinus Nijhoff, 1971).

that one part of it remains in the intelligible, while another descends to associate with a vegetative soul.[10]

Plotinus qualifies this descended soul as "divine," for although it has fallen from the intellect, and has traversed the heavens as far as earth and Hades, it is able to return to its source. The descended soul constitutes our "self,"[11] the relative excellence of which determines our destiny, insofar as its moral dispositions explain the place it is granted within a very strict system of retribution. We cannot, therefore, separate the epistemological from the ethical aspect when it comes to memory.[12] Several types of relations are established between the human soul, when it is situated below and associated with the vegetative soul, and the same soul when it is in the intelligible, before it descends or after it has reascended. Sometimes they are united, as during a terrestrial life, and sometimes they are separated. Thus, we must envisage the various stages of the wanderings of this divine soul, either during its ascent toward the Intellect, or else during its descent. For every soul and for each of these steps, we must raise the problem of memory, a question that Plotinus discusses at length.[13]

2. Soul in Human Beings[14]

Soul in human beings is a complex entity, not in the sense that it includes parts, as the body does, for as such it is incorporeal, but in the sense in which it appears in several aspects as a function of the "place" where it is situated and the activities it then exercises.

The human soul remains attached to the Intellect, even when it is associated, on earth, with a vegetative soul that gives a body a life identical with that of the lowest part of the world soul. The descended soul

---

10 "To which soul: the one we qualify as 'divine', by which we are what we are, or that other one, the one that comes to us from the Universe?" (*Treatise* 27 [IV, 3], 27, 1–3). On this question, see Pierre-Marie Morel, "Individualité et identité de l'âme humaine chez Plotin," *Les Cahiers philosophiques de Strasbourg* 8 (1999): 53–66.
11 On this topic, see Gwenaëlle Aubry, "Un moi sans identité ? Le *hèmeis* plotinien," in *Le moi et l'intériorité*, ed. Gwenaëlle Aubry and Frédérique Ildefonse (Paris: Vrin, 2008), 107–12.
12 Everything that falls under the heading of *diáthesis* relates to this phenomenon.
13 See *Treatise* 27 (IV, 3), 28; *Treatise* 28 (IV, 4), 5.
14 On this subject, see Blumenthal 1971.

never stops oscillating between these two limits, the organism (or the living being) and the Intellect.

By one part of itself, called the "undescended soul," which corresponds to its intellect, the human soul remains in the Intelligible, which can be reached by the "descended soul" that comes to attach itself to an organism (or to a living being), that is, a body endowed with a vegetative soul. In the course of its descent, the human soul associates itself, in the heavens, with a vehicle made of fire or air, and then, in the lower world, with an earthly body. This is why two aspects must be distinguished within the human soul. There is the lower soul, which attaches itself in the course of its descent to a vehicle. On earth its vehicle is an organism, that is, a body animated by nature, that is, the lower part of the world soul; a body belongs to each human being, but this human being is not to be identified with it. And there is the higher soul, which, as it rises back up, detaches itself from what its association with the lower soul, and hence with sensation, has contributed to it.

2.1. Sensation[15]

The undescended part of the soul, that is, its intellect, maintains a permanent and direct contact with the Intelligible. Yet the descended soul has only a temporary contact with the Intelligible, mediated by sensation. In opposition to Aristotle and the Stoics, Plotinus considers that sensation (*aísthesis*) features a twofold aspect: it is not only an affection (*páthos*) of the compound made up of the descended soul and the living body, but also an act of thought. The soul is therefore active, and remains impassible, in the process of sensation. It projects itself outside itself to grasp objects located in the universe, even at a distance (*Treatise 41* [IV, 6], 1, 14–40). When the soul perceives a material object, it produces it in a way (*Treatise 41* [IV, 6], 3, 16–18) as a sensible reality, for it grasps the *lógoi* that are responsible for the production of that object by the soul of the universe, in which the human soul participates. As one can also note in *Treatise 29* (IV, 5), this doctrine of sensation is linked to the notion of general sympathy (*sumpátheia*), which ensures the unity of soul and body in the living being known as the universe. In other words, through sensation, the soul does indeed perceive impressions,

---

15 On this subject, see Eyjólfur Kjalar Emilson, *Plotinus on Sense-Perception. A Philosophical Study* (Cambridge: Cambridge University Press, 1988). This psychological analysis should be placed back into its metaphysical context.

which however must not be considered as mere material imprints, but as rational formulas deposited by the Intellect within the world soul (27 [IV, 3], 26, 29–34).

What sensation has contact with are the forms engaged in matter (*énula eíde*) by the lower part of the soul of the world; if sensible things were in the soul, the soul would not have to look out. To bridge the gap between body and soul, Plotinus calls upon the sense organs. This allows him to recall the principle that knowledge always appears in the form of an assimilation, since like is known by like. In particular, this is the reason why the soul never succeeds in knowing matter: it would then have to be in a state of complete indeterminacy,[16] since matter is bereft of all sensible quality[17]. In fact, the object of sensation is quality (*poiótes*), of which matter is completely bereft, since quality corresponds to form (*eîdos*), which appears as a "rational formula" (*lógos*) in the sensible. The soul recognizes the form of things perceived by the sense organs,[18] which allows us to understand how the soul remains unchanged in the course of this process.[19] Hence the consequence that when a soul is separated from all bodies, it cannot know sensible objects.[20] Moreover, if the soul succeeds in recognizing the forms of things in this world, not as forms (*eíde*) but as rational formulas (*lógoi*) perceived by sense organs, this means it is in contact with the world of intelligible realities.

2.2. Representation[21]

The transmission to discursive reason (*diánoia*)[22] of the rational formulas (*lógoi*) discovered in the sensible does not take place directly, but requires the intervention of a faculty, whose activities concern not only the sensible, but also the intelligible.

---

16 See *Treatise* 12 (II, 4), 10.
17 See *Treatise* 12 (II, 4), 12, 26–33.
18 "We must suppose that the perception of sense-objects is for the soul or the living being an act of apprehension, in which the soul understands the quality attaching to bodies and takes the impression of their forms. Well, then, the soul will either apprehend alone by itself or in company with something else." *Treatise* 28 (IV, 4), 23, 1–4.
19 See *Treatise* 26 (III, 6), 2, 32–41.
20 See *Treatise* 28 (IV, 4), 23, 5–35.
21 On this subject, see E. W. Warren, "Imagination in Plotinus," *Phronesis* 16 (1966): 277–285.
22 The terme *diánoia* is translated by "discursive reason."

Sense perception of an object in the universe is dispersed, insofar as it can depend on five different senses. This is why its transmission to discursive reason demands a stage of unification. Plotinus evokes a power of internal perception that becomes aware of desires, a perception that announces affections: this power is sometimes qualified as "consciousness" (*sunaísthesis*).[23] Moreover, the term *parakoloúthesis* (translated by "attention") is used to indicate a knowledge that accompanies each of the operations implicated in the mechanism of sensation. Associated with these two terms is that of *súnesis* (translated by "comprehension"), which, for its part, designates an overall vision of the process, akin to what is covered by the notion of consciousness. Indeed, by reconstituting the psychic process that has led to it, the subject can distinguish itself from the object it knows in the sensible world. The result of this activity is an image of the object perceived by sensation, its representation. In other worlds, sensation is not complete until an image (*phántasma*) of the object has been produced in and by the soul's faculty of representation (*phantasía*). In other words, perception (*antílepsis*) stops the process of sensation and fixes it in a stable image.

Yet this faculty of representation can also form an image of thoughts:

INTERLOCUTOR – But what is it that remembers thoughts (*dianoéseon*)?[24] Does the image-making power (*tò phantastikón*) remember these too?

PLOTINUS – But if an image (*phantasía*) accompanies (*parakolouthei*)[25] every intellectual act (*noései*), perhaps if this image (*phantasías*) remains, being a kind of picture (*eikónos*) of the thought (*dianoématos*), in this way there would be memory (*mnéme*) of what was known (*gnosthéntos*);[26] but if not, we must look for some other explanation.[27] Perhaps the reception into the image-making power (*tò phantastikón*) would be of the rational formula (*lógou*)[28] that accompanies (*parakolouthoúntos*) the act of intelligence

---

23 On this subject, see, E. W. Warren, "Consciousness in Plotinus," *Phronesis* 9 (1964): 83–97; F. M. Schroeder, "*Synousia, Synaisthesis* and *Synesis*. Presence and Dependence in Plotinian Philosophy of Consciousness," *Aufstieg und Niedergang der römischen Welt* II 35.1 (1987): 677–699.
24 The terms *dianóesis* and *dianóema* are translated by thoughts. They designate the activity of *diánoia* and the result of this activity. For a description, see *infra*.
25 This verb points toward consciousness, see *supra*.
26 This thesis, which is not accepted, is the one developed by Aristotle in *On memory and reminiscence* 1, 449b31.
27 The following one, which Plotinus accepts.
28 The term *lógos* is very hard to translate here. We seem to have to do with inner discourse (*lógos endiáthetos*), a Stoic notion adapted by Plotinus. This discourse

> (*noḗmati*).²⁹ The intellectual act (*nóēma*) is without parts and has not, so to speak, come out into the open, but remains unobserved within, but the rational formula (*lógos*) unfolds its content and brings it out of the intellectual act (*ek toû noḗmatos*) into the image-making power (*tò phantastikón*), and so shows the intellectual act (*nóēma*) as if in a mirror (*hoîon en katóptroi*), and this is how there is apprehension (*antílēpsis*)³⁰ and persistence (*monḗ*) and memory (*mnḗmē*) of it. Therefore, even though the soul (*psukhḗs*) is always moved (*aeì kinouménēs*) to intelligent activity (*pròs nóēsin*), it is when it comes to be in the image-making power that we apprehend it (*antílēpsis*). The intellectual act (*nóēsis*) is one thing and the apprehension (*antílēpsis*) another, and we are always intellectually active (*nooûmen mèn aeí*) but we do not always apprehend our activity (*antilambanómetha dè ouk aeí*); and this is because that which receives it does not only receive acts of the intelligence (*noḗseis*), but also, on its other side, sensations (*aisthḗseis*). (*Treatise* 27 [IV, 3], 30)³¹

Unlike Aristotle, Plotinus does not believe there is an image of every intellectual act. An intellectual act is an intuition given all at once. This intellectual act must be deployed in a rational formula (*lógos*), which expresses it and therefore unfolds it into a discourse, from which an image derives. Hence the metaphor of the mirror: there can be a rational content without an image, but not an image without rational content. It is this image, fashioned by the representational faculty, that will constitute the representation that will be retained in memory; here we are in a situation parallel to that of the sensory act. To intelligize is one thing, to know that one intelligizes is another; and this is the starting point for rational representation.

2.3. Memory³²

Memory ensures the preservation, not of material impressions, but of representations, which derive both from sensation and from discursive reason. Memory cannot belong to the intellect, for which time, and therefore the past, does not exist (*Treatise* 27 [IV, 3], 25, 10–45). It is

---

    describes the rational formula (*lógos*) that corresponds to an intelligible form (*eîdos*) within the soul.
29 The terms *noḗsis* and *nóēma* describe the intellectual act, the process and its result.
30 On the meaning of the term *antílēpsis,* see *infra*.
31 See also the annotated translation by Luc Brisson (Paris: Flammarion, 2005b).
32 E. W. Warren, "Memory in Plotinus," *Phronesis* 15 (1965): 252–260; Luc Brisson, "La place de la mémoire dans la psychologie plotinienne," *Études platoniciennes* 3 (2006): 13–27.

therefore an activity of the soul. But it has nothing to do with reminiscence according to Plato (25, 27–34). Nor does it have anything to do with the vegetative soul, which explains why a body is alive, that is, is an organism. Nor can it be reduced to the union of soul and body, for the following two reasons: the soul has memories of rational activities (16, 1–18); and the body often presents an obstacle to memory (26, 25-end). Memory therefore concerns only the descended soul. In that case, however, can we not say that each of this soul's faculties has its own memory? Plotinus' answer (*Treatise* 27 [IV, 3], 28) is negative. Each faculty preserves traces of the past, but in the form of dispositions, not of memories.

Whereas sensation demands the combined intervention of body and soul, memory, for its part, has no need of the body, at least immediately;[33] the fact that the body's state may have an influence on the quality of memory does not, in itself, constitute an argument, for this influence remains indirect.[34] Moreover, the soul may preserve the memory of activities that are proper to it and do not imply any involvement of the body.[35] Plotinus therefore rejects the idea, derived from Aristotle and the Stoics, that memory consists in storage in the soul, whether considered as incorporeal or as corporeal, conserving material impressions that are assimilated to material imprints endowed with size,[36] because he has a different idea of sensation. Moreover, in memory, the act of intellection is not preserved as such, that is, as an intuition that provides itself with everything at once. This act of intellection is revived in the mode of an image that contains distinction and division, as is the case in discursive thought. In short, for each of its memories, memory, like sensation, has a double face, one turned toward the sensible, the other toward the intelligible. This view has a strange consequence:

---

33 See *Treatise* 27 (IV, 3), 26, 1–25.
34 See *Treatise* 27 (IV, 3), 26, 50–56.
35 See *Treatise* 27 (IV, 3), 26, 34–50.
36 "But to begin with, the impressions are not magnitudes; nor are they like seal-impressions or counter-pressures or stamps, because there is no pushing and it is not like what happens in wax, but the way of it is like thinking even in the case of sense-objects. But in acts of thought what counter-pressure could there be said to be? Or what need is there of a body or bodily quality as an accompaniment?" *Treatise* 27 (IV, 3), 26, 29–34. For the followers of Chrysippus, memory is a "storing up of representations" (*thēsaurismòs phantasiôn*). See Sextus Empiricus, *Adv. Math.* VII, 372, 5—374, 5 = no 62 in the collection by Richard Dufour.

each sensation must leave behind two images, according to whether it refers to its sensible face or to its intelligible face, and memory will have to conserve both these images. Plotinus accepts this consequence, even though it is counter-intuitive.[37]

Things get complicated at this level, for a distinction must be made between the soul attached to an organism, that is, a living body, and the soul that can be detached from it, either before coming to be within a body, or afterwards. In the course of earthly life, moreover, the two images are confused to the point that they cannot be distinguished. When the descended soul frees itself from the sensible,[38] however, it makes a choice among images, retaining only those that are morally appropriate. As it frees itself, it abandons impure images. When it descends, by contrast, it reactualizes images that had subsisted only in the mode of potentiality. In short, the two types of images are not without influence upon one another: the one that is of a higher nature tries to purify the one that is of a lower nature.

2.4. Discursive Reason

Yet another activity is therefore necessary, to establish a link between the soul that has descended into a body and makes use of sensation, and the non-descended soul, or the intellect, and this is discursive reason (*diánoia*).[39] Discursive reason (*tò dianoētikón* or *tò logizómenon*) is the highest faculty that can be exercised by a human being living in the sensible world, though it remains attached to the intelligible through his intellect. Plotinus does not seem to make a significant difference between the terms *tò dianoētikón*, *logizómenon* and *logistikón* to designate the highest faculty of a soul attached to a body, and the same holds true of the terms *diánoia*, *logismós*, and *lógos*, which designate the activities carried out by this faculty.

Discursive reason (*diánoia*) is distinct from intellect (*noûs*) for the following two reasons: intellect is intuitive, while reason is discursive; intellect is inseparable from intelligible forms (*eídē*), whereas *diánoia* must be filled by the *lógoi* through intellection, intuition, and sensation, because it is empty as such:

---

37 It is justified in chapter 31 of *Treatise* 27 (IV, 3).
38 See *Treatise* 27 (IV, 3), 32.
39 This entire section is particularly indebted to the article by Laurant Lavaud, "La dianoia médiatrice entre le sensible et l'intelligible," *Études platoniciennes* 3 (2006): 29–55.

... intellect there (*noû ekeínou* = the real intellect [*noûs*]) is not the sort one might conceive on the analogy of our so-called intellects (*toùs par' hēmîn legoménous noûs* = the human discursive reason [*diánoia*]) which get their content from premises and are able to understand what is said, and reason discursively (*logizoménous*) and contemplate what follows, contemplating reality as the result of a process of reasoning since they did not have it before but were empty (*kenoús*) before they learnt (*matheîn*), though they were intellects. Intellect there is not like this, but has all things and is all things, and is with them when it is with itself and has all things without having them. (*Treatise* 51 (I, 8), 2, 9–15)

Unlike the intellect, discursive reason can turn back upon itself and know itself. Moreover, discursive reason always deals with objects that are external to it. In this sense, discursive reason may be considered the intellect of the descended soul, since genuine reason has not descended.

Whence, however, come the *lógoi* that are to fill discursive reason? Discursive reason exercises its activity symmetrically, according to whether it is turned toward the sensible or the intelligible.

2.4.1. Recognition

The activity of recognition is representation, which receives both what derives from sensation[40] and what derives from discursive reason[41] in the form of images (*phantasíai*).

2.4.1.1. *Diánoia* turned toward the sensible

By its lower part, discursive reason concerns itself with the data of sensation. Its activity is "critical," and it is the word *krísis*, or "judgment," that is used when one wishes to distinguish sensation from pure perception. We perceive things in the sensible world, because they have a quantity and qualities that are rational formulas (*lógoi*), which are related to forms (*eídē*). The common sense (*koinḕ aísthēsis*), which combines data from the various senses, can nevertheless make mistakes, as long as the relation between them it proposes has not been submitted to the critical judgment of discursive thought. Discursive thought makes a judgment (*epíkrisis*) about the data of sensation, by mobilizing the methods of division and reassembly that are proper to dialectic:

---

40 See *Treatise* 27 (IV, 3), 29.
41 See *Treatise* 27 (IV, 3), 30 and *Treatise* 49 (V, 3), 2, 7–9.

> First we must enquire about the soul, whether we should grant it knowledge of itself, and what is that which knows in it, and how. We could say at once that its sensitive part (*tò aisthetikón*) is perceptive only of what is external; for even if there is a concomitant awareness of what goes on inside the body, yet even here the apprehension is of something outside the perceptive part; for it perceives the experiences in its body by its own agency, but the reasoning power in soul (*tò d' en autêi logizómenon*) makes its judgment (*tèn epíkrisin*), derived from the mental images present to it which come from sense-perception (*parà tôn ek tês aisthéseos phantasmáton parakeiménon*), but combining (*sunágon*) and dividing (*diairoûn*) them... (*Treatise* 49 [V, 3], 2, 1–9)

In short, discursive thought recognizes the objects of sensation, and pronounces judgments about them. What discursive reason takes into account are not physical impressions, but mental images or representations (*phantásmata*) of the perceived object. It is the persistence of this image that explains memory (*mnéme*), and makes us, through a process of harmonization, aware of intellection (*noésis*), which itself is outside of time.[42] Discursive reason has as its objects the mental images that come from sense perception, that is, the representations that have been preserved in memory; and these representations preserved in memory are "rational formulas" (*lógoi*). It is with regard to these rational formulas that it pronounces judgments, develops arguments, and applies dialectic in its two moments: division and reassembly.

2.4.1.2. *Diánoia* turned toward the intelligible

But discursive thought can also take into consideration information that does not come from the senses, particularly when it deliberates on such general points as the beautiful, the just, or the good. In fact, discursive thought possesses what is in the intellect, but not in the same way. Whereas the intellect (*noûs*) enables intuition of the forms (*eíde*) that exist simultaneously, discursive thought (*diánoia*) deploys in its analyses the *lógoi*, here described as *túpoi*, that correspond to them in the soul. Here we encounter the famous image that introduces, in the case of the *lógos* and the *eîdos*, a comparison between discourse in the soul and explicitly articulated discourse. Discursive thought divides what is united in the intellect, and places in succession what was simultaneous in that realm. The "rational formula" (*lógos*) remains one, like the form (*eîdos*) to which it corresponds, and when it is reflected in the ac-

---

42 See *Treatise* 27 (IV, 3), 30, 5–15.

tivity of representation (*tò phantastikón*), which also receives sensations[43] as in a mirror, it unfolds in its multiple facets.[44]

Discursive reason also has the Intelligible as its objects, not in themselves but as imprints, that is, as "rational formulas" (*lógoi*). These rational formulas are preserved by memory in the form of images, that is, of representations.

> and, as for the things which come to it from Intellect (*ek toû noû ióntōn*), it observes what one might call their imprints (*toùs túpous*), and has the same power also in dealing with these… (*Treatise* 49 [V, 3], 2, 9–11)

Just as in the case of those that come from sensation, the impressions that come from the intellect are "rational formulas" (*lógoi*). This gives Plotinus the opportunity to propose a new conception of reminiscence, which assumes the form of a harmonization. Discursive reason places in relation the *lógoi* that come from the sensible and those that the Intelligible has left in the soul.

2.4.2. Harmonization

Discursive reason is therefore constantly filling itself with two types of objects, the origin of one of which is intelligible, and the other sensible. In both cases, discursive reason does not proceed by intuition, but provides itself with a representation (*phantasía* or *phántasma*), which it will place in relation with the *lógos*, as an imprint (*túpos*) of an intelligible form. This is possible because it is the same *lógos* which is elaborated by discursive reason on the basis of the intellect, and which representation provides on the basis of sensation.

2.4.2.1. The harmonization of the sensible with the intelligible

The *lógos* that discursive reason derives from the sensible, through the intermediary of sensation and representation, is the consequence of ever-renewed experience, whereas the *lógos* that corresponds to an intelligible form has always existed within it. Thus, the goal of discursive reason is to crown sensation by recognizing the sensible object that is perceived, that is, by relating the *lógos* recently perceived by the senses to the *lógos* that corresponds to the intelligible form in which the perceived sensible object participates. Discursive reason associates the recent imprints provided by sensation with the imprints corresponding to the in-

---

[43] See *Treatise* 27 (IV, 3), 30, 15–16.
[44] See *Treatise* 46 (I, 4), 10, 6 ff.

telligible forms perceived by the intellect. Ultimately, the recognition of sensible realities by discursive reason can only be carried out through the intermediary of a judgment, which relies on a perception of the intelligible forms. For instance, if someone sees Socrates, he recognizes in him the representation of the species man. This is a new way of considering reminiscence, which corresponds to a new way of defining memory.

> ...and it continues to acquire understanding as if by recognizing the new and recently arrived impressions (*kaì súnesin éti proslambánei hósper epiginôskon toùs néous kaì árti hḗkontas*) and fitting them to those which have long been within it (*kaì epharmózon toîs en autôi ek palaioû túpois*):[45] this process is what we should call the "recollections" of the soul (*anamnḗseis tês psukhês*). (*Treatise* 49 [V, 3], 2, 11–14)[46]

In the *Meno* and the *Phaedo*, reminiscence consists in the soul's relating the data of sensation to the corresponding intelligible form it has contemplated in the past, when the soul, separated from all bodies, followed the chorus of the gods in the heavens. For Plotinus, the goal is to establish a link between the new *lógoi* that derive from sensation, and the old *lógoi*, which the intellect has deposited within the soul. There is a considerable difference between Plotinus' approach and that of Plato, but Plotinus shows faithfulness to his master in a sense. The goal of discursive reason is to pronounce upon the *lógoi*, its proper objects, a judgment that features a moment of recognition and a moment of harmonization. This corresponds in itself with reminiscence, because it actualizes the *lógoi* by linking them to their corresponding *eídē*.

This is what Plotinus explains in *Treatise* 30 (III, 8) 6, 18–30. Porphyry comments on this text as follows in his *Sentence* 16:

> The soul contains the rational formulas of all things, but it acts on them (only) by either being provoked to actualize them by some external stimulus or through directing itself towards them inwardly. And when it is provoked by an external influence, as it were outwards, it produces sense perceptions, while when it withdraws into itself in the direction of intellect, it finds itself in the process of intelligizing. (*Sent* 16, 1–7)

---

45 According to Lloyd P. Gerson, *Plotinus* (London and New York: Routledge, 1994), 180, these ancient imprints are not those of the Forms, but those of sensible imprints. See the objections by L. Lavaud.

46 For a discussion of the meaning to be attributed to this passage, see L. Lavaud, who mentions the interpretations of B. Ham in his translation, and the position of Emilson 1988, 144.

Considered as the reactualization by the soul, in this world, of a knowledge it already possesses, reminiscence[47] can be considered as a kind of memory: "But as for its activity, the ancients seem to apply the terms 'memory' and 'recollection' to the souls which bring into act what they possessed. So this is another kind of memory; and therefore time is not involved in memory understood in this sense" (*Treatise* 27 [IV, 3], 25, 31–34). Note that *diánoia* rediscovers the Forms (*eíde̜*) not directly, but through the intermediary of the *lógoi* it contains, which are the traces (*túpoi*) of the Forms within it.[48] Yet this is not the only kind of memory. The Plotinian doctrine of the undescended soul radically modifies the notion of reminiscence Plato proposes of it in the *Meno*, the *Phaedo*, and the *Phaedrus*.[49]

2.4.2.2. The harmonization of the sensible with the intelligible

Recognition, and hence harmonization, may take place between two items of sensible data, between two individuals: someone sees Socrates and identifies him as the Socrates he has already met:

> PLOTINUS – Well, then, sense perception sees a human being and gives its impression to discursive reason.
>
> INTERLOCUTOR – What does discursive reason say?
>
> PLOTINUS – It will not say anything yet, but only knows, and stops at that; unless perhaps it asks itself "Who is this?" if it has met the person before, and says, using memory to help it, that it is Socrates. (*Treatise* 49 [V, 3], 3, 1–5)

Here, we have to do not with the reactivation of an intelligible representation on the basis of an intelligible representation, but with the reactivation of a sensible experienced in the past.

---

47 On this subject, see John McCumber, "*Anamnesis* as Memory of Intelligibles in Plotinus," *AGPh* 60 (1978): 160–167.
48 On reason's reappropriation of the intelligible through the intermediary of the *lógoi*, see the long note by J. Pépin on *Sentence* 16, 2, in Porphyre, *Sentences*, ed. Luc Brisson (Paris: Vrin, 2005), II, 457–470.
49 See, for instance, *Treatise* 2 (IV, 7), 10, 30–35.

3. Memory: A Dynamic View

In Plotinus, as was also the case for Plato, the soul is a mobile entity that travels between intelligible world and the sensible world. The question then arises of what the soul preserves of its past at each of these stages. To answer this question, we must insist on the fact that memory is ultimately not merely an act of knowledge, it is also an attachment, a commitment. We must always bear this principle in mind: "The soul is, and becomes what it remembers" (*Treatise* 28 [IV, 4], 3, 5–6).

3.1. The Soul's Descent into a Body

In chapter 3 of *Treatise* 28 (IV, 4), Plotinus, taking his inspiration from the central myth of the *Phaedrus* (246d-249b), describes the descent of a part of the soul:

> But if it comes out[50] of the intelligible world, because it cannot endure unity, but embraces with pleasure its own individuality and wants to be different and so to speak puts its head outside, it thereupon acquires memory, it seems. Its memory of what is in the intelligible world still holds it back from falling, but its memory of the things here below carries it down here; its memory of what is in heaven keeps it there, and in general it is and becomes what it remembers. For it has been told[51] that remembering is either thinking or representing; and the representation comes to the soul not because it possesses it, but as it sees, so it is disposed;[52] and if it sees sense-objects, it sinks low in proportion to the amount of them it sees. For because it possesses all things in a secondary way, and not so perfectly,[53] it becomes all things, and since it is a thing belonging to the frontier between the worlds, and occupies a corresponding position, it moves in both directions. (*Treatise* 28 [IV,4], 3)

It is the quality of this soul's contemplation of the intelligible, before a part of it falls into a terrestrial body, that guides its descent toward the sensible world. As in Plato, the soul changes places for Plotinus: it descends from the Intelligible, which it never leaves by virtue of one part of itself, establishing itself for a moment in an earthly body, and can

---

50 This chapter explains that memory returns to the soul once it departs from the intelligible. On the tragedy that individuation means for the soul, see *Treatise* 6 (IV, 8), 4, 11 ff. and *Treatise* 10 (V, 1), 1, 5 ff.
51 See *Treatise* 27 (IV, 3), 29, 31.
52 Representation finds its object outside itself, for this object is given to it by intellection or by sensation. In the following lines, we see that, even then, the disposition (*diáthesis*) takes on a moral hue.
53 Unlike the Intellect, it possesses "rational formulas" and not Forms.

consequently descend into Hades or rise back up to its source, the Intelligible. Porphyry's *Sentence* 29 provides an excellent summary of these wanderings.

The descent of the soul, which puts on several vehicles[54] as it goes down toward the sensible, is slowed by the recollection it conserves of the Intelligible whence it comes. Once on earth, the descended soul can exercise memory, on the one hand, because, unlike the intellect, it is associated with time, and hence with present, future, and past; and on the other, because, unlike bodies, which never stop changing, the soul features a genuine stability,[55] on which its identity depends. When linked to a living body, the descended soul experiences feelings of pleasure, pain, and anger, and exercises acts of sensation, representation, and especially of discursivity. Memory therefore concerns each of these levels, and thus features two faces, a sensible face and an intelligible face. After death, the soul may descend even further into Hades, or rise back up to its source, the Intelligible.

At one moment or another, it must descend once again, to return to a body in the context of the process of reincarnation. But what about the memories our soul has when it redescends? As we have said, it is memory that makes a soul what it is, and controls its descent. Memory of the intelligible prevents the soul from sinking too far down, while memories of events that have occurred in this world make it descend more surely and quickly.[56] With time, it even becomes possible for it to recall certain events of its previous life.[57] When the soul begins to separate itself from the intelligible, memories return, and in particular the memory of itself as a being distinct from the intelligible, the memory of the intelligibles of which it no longer has a vision, and that of the heavenly or earthly lives to which it draws near. Memories return as a function of this kind of fall of the soul which has been unable to keep contemplating, and which is once again taken up by the cares of

---

54 Stéphane Toulouse, "Le véhicule de l'âme chez Plotin: de la réception d'une hypothèse cosmologique à l'usage dialectique de la notion," *Études platoniciennes* 3 (2007): 103–128.
55 "And since memory is a stable condition, the body's nature, moving and flowing, must be a cause of forgetfulness, not of memory …" *Treatise* 27 (IV, 3), 26, 52–54.
56 See *Treatise* 28 (IV, 4), 4, 7–13.
57 See *Treatise* 27 (IV, 3), 27, 16–18.

the body.[58] Plotinus notes that the most dangerous memories are those that are unconscious, because, for him, it is possible to have memories without being aware of them (*mè parakolouthoûnta*).[59] If the soul has these memories again, it is because it already had them in the intelligible, but potentially.[60]

3.2. The Separation of the Soul from a Body

When separated from the body, is the soul able to conserve memories of its previous life? The answer is given as a function of this principle: the soul is or becomes the very thing it remembers. Memory is not pure contemplation and knowledge, but implies an attachment, as Plotinus explains in chapter 3 of *Treatise* 28, cited above. This answer thus depends on religious and moral considerations. Like Plato, Plotinus believes in Hades, and in metensomatosis.[61] A soul may go to Hades or be reincarnated in a specific living being as a function of its previous existence.[62] How, moreover, could a soul conserve a trace of its previous existence on the basis of which it will be judged, if it has no memory of that existence? From this perspective, memory is at the basis of an ethics that implies a retributive system. At the limit, we may say that a soul is what it is as a function of how much of its past it retains in memory. At the limit, however, to purify oneself is to lose one's identity in order to merge with one's principle.

> INTERLOCUTOR – But to which soul does memory belong? That which we shall call the more divine,[63] by which we are ourselves, or the other which comes from the universe?[64]

---

58 See *Treatise* 28 (IV, 4), 3, and Richard Dufour, "Actuality and Potentiality in Plotinus' View of the Intelligible Universe," *Journal of Neoplatonic Studies* 9 (2004): 214–215.
59 See *Treatise* 28 (IV, 4), 4, 10.
60 See *Treatise* 28 (IV, 4), 2.
61 See Jérôme Laurent, "La réincarnation chez Plotin et avant Plotin," in *L'Homme et le monde selon Plotin* (Paris: ENS éd. et Ophrys, 1999), 115–137.
62 See *Treatise* 27 (IV, 3), 8, 5–9, and *Treatise* 15 (III, 4), 2, 11–30.
63 This soul, which constitutes our identity, is the descended soul, clearly distinguished here from the vegetative soul. The descended soul remains attached to the undescended soul, that is, the intellect ; this is why the problem of identity is so complex. See *Treatise* 40 (II, 1), 5; 18–21.
64 The vegetative soul, see *Treatise* 38 (I, 5), 18–21.

PLOTINUS – Perhaps we must say that there are memories of both kinds, some proper and some common?[65] And when the two souls are together all their memories coincide; but if they become separated, if they were both to exist and persist in separation, each would have its own memories for a longer time, and the memories of the other for a shorter time. At any rate the image of Heracles in Hades—this shade too, I think, we must consider to be our self—remembers all that he did[66] in his life, for this life belonged above all to the shade. And the other souls which became the compound,[67] all the same had nothing more to talk about than the things of this life, and they themselves knew what it has experienced, and if it is something concerned with righteousness.[68] But Homer does not tell us what the real Heracles said, the Heracles without the shade.[69] What then would the other soul say when it has been freed and is alone? As long as the soul drags this "something,"[70] the soul will speak of everything which the man had done or experienced.

But as time goes on after death, memories of other things would appear from its former lives, so that it would even abandon with contempt some of these memories. For since it has become freer from bodily contamination,[71] it will go over again in its memory even what it did not have in this life;[72] but if when it goes out, it comes to exist in another body, it will speak of the events of its outward life,[73] of what it has just left and of many events of its former lives. But in time it will come to forgetfulness of many things that occurred to it from outside.[74]

INTERLOCUTOR – But when it comes to be alone what will it remember? (*Treatise* 27 [IV, 3], 27)

In this passage, Plotinus finds an expression of his own theory of the duality in the descended human soul, that is, the duality between the descended soul as such, which can live on its own, and the descended soul

---

65 Proper to each soul, but common to both.
66 From this point on, textual problems become numerous.
67 I understand *tò sunamphóteron* as designating the compound of soul and body.
68 Incarnate souls can remember only the acts they have carried out in this world, and the consequences they may entail from the viewpoint of justice.
69 The expression *áneu toû eidólou* refers, it seems to me, to the descended part of the soul, which has risen back up toward the intelligible and is no longer connected either to an earthly body or to a vehicle of air or fire.
70 The body made of earth, air, or fire.
71 By having separated itself from the body. See the passage on the purificatory virtues in *Sentence* 32.
72 The vision of the intelligible realities, even when it lacked a body. See *Philebus* 34b11.
73 This is how I understand *toû éxo bíou* following H.-S., as *toû bíou éxo sómatos*.
74 This *tôn epaktôn* seems to refer to everything that happens to the soul as a result of the body.

living in a body considered as an organism. There are two souls in us: one of them is pure, while the other is common, being attached to a body.

Plotinus illustrates this situation by giving an allegorical interpretation of Heracles.[75] In the evocation of the dead described in Book XI of the *Odyssey*, one of the shades evoked by Odysseus is that of Heracles, but Homer is careful to specify that only an image of Heracles is in Hades, while his true person is with the gods (*Od.* XI, 601–604). Heracles is a hero, a demigod, son of Zeus, the king of the gods, and the mortal Alcmene. For Plotinus, the Heracles who is in Hades is the human part of Heracles, which in his system corresponds to the descended soul, weighed down by its union with the body and the vegetative soul that animates this body, while the Heracles who is in heaven as a god is the same soul, but not contaminated by the body, and attached to the intelligible.

The descended soul can have memories of both kinds, some proper, that is to say some deriving from its intellections, and some common, coming from sensations that presuppose a union with a body animated by a vegetative soul. To know the true soul, the one that is turned toward the intelligible, it must be isolated from the additions of the sensible, just as the true figure of the sea god Glaucus (*Republic* X 611d) can only be found by ridding it of the barnacles that make it unrecognizable.

3.3. The Ascent toward the Intelligible

At death, the vegetative soul, which comes to us from the universe, returns toward its source, the world soul,[76] while the higher soul tries to rise back up to the Intellect.

If the descended soul has weighed itself down in its previous life, as a result of its contact with the body, it descends into Hades. In itself, this simple and essential soul is immaculate; it is the association of this divine soul, once it has descended into a body, with the inferior soul, which is subject to passions, that explains evil.

If, however, it has succeeded in freeing itself, it rises back up to its source, the Intelligible. When the human soul separates itself from the

---

75 On the figure of Heracles in Plotinus, see Jean Pépin, "Héraclès et son reflet dans le Néoplatonisme," in *Le Néoplatonisme*, ed. Pierre-Maxime Schuhl and Pierre Hadot (Paris: Centre National de la Recherche Scientifique, 1971), 167–192.
76 See chapter 29 of *Treatise* 28.

body it had inhabited until then, it conserves memories of its previous lives. As the soul rises and purifies itself, it becomes detached from the sensible aspect of its memories, retaining only their intelligible aspect, and the converse occurs when it goes back down. It is thus the burden of sensible memories that drags one down to Hades, like the image or the shade of Heracles, and it is the intelligible memories that enable the descended soul to find its place in the intelligible. Yet once it reaches the intelligible, it no longer has any memories of its past lives,[77] simply because there can be no memory in the intelligible.

4. Who, other than Human Beings, makes use of Memory?

This perspective enables an answer to the question of whether Zeus, understood as the demiurge and as the world soul, the celestial bodies, and the demons, can have memory.

4.1. Zeus: The Demiurge and the World

The question of whether Zeus has memory is less easy to answer, because it raises very important issues in the field of cosmology. The name Zeus simultaneously designates the two realities that Plato respectively calls the demiurge and the world soul in the *Timaeus*. To attribute memory of his acts to the demiurge would mean to deny the eternity of the world, associated with the succession of the cycles that succeed one another incessantly within it. There is no need for him to remember it, since the act by which he produces them is unique.[78]

As far as the world soul is concerned, everything depends on how its action is represented. If one considers that the soul proceeds like a human craftsman, working by reflection and proceeding part by part, then one must attribute memory to it. In the world soul, however, there is an intimate union between productive action and the variety of its products, which leaves no room for memory.[79] This implies that there is an identity between Providence and Nature in the world soul, a position Plotinus must defend[80] as he ends his exposition by a reminder that assimilates the action of the world soul to that of light on

---

77 See *Treatise* 28 (IV, 4), 1, 1–10.
78 See *Treatise* 28 (IV, 4), 10, 1–6.
79 See *Treatise* 28 (IV, 4), 10.
80 In the three following chapters of *Treatise* 28 (IV, 4): 12, 13 and 14.

the air it illuminates. The fact that Zeus, understood as the demiurge or the word soul, has no memory, entails a number of consequences: the world has no beginning, and the production of sensible things takes place in the context of a process that is permanent and, in a sense, automatic.

4.2. The Celestial Bodies

And what about celestial bodies? They have no memory, for the following two reasons.

1. Since there is memory only of things in the past, the celestial bodies cannot remember something in the past, because, since they live forever, the past means nothing to them.[81]
2. Nor do they have to remember the place they were in yesterday, since none of the points through which they pass can be distinguished in the course of their revolution.[82] The celestial bodies therefore have no memory,[83] because their knowledge has nothing to do with distinction in temporality and space. If the stars seem to exercise an action on human beings, and thus answer their prayers, it is by virtue of sympathy (*sumpátheia*), which could be defined as the interaction between a unique soul and the body of the world, which is also unique.[84] Consequently, astrology is not purely and simply denied, but it dissolves into sympathy.[85]

4.3. The Demons

The demons, who are not impassible, can have memories:

> But demons themselves, also, are not incapable of being affected in their irrational part; it is not out of place to ascribe memory and sense-perceptions to them and to grant that they are charmed by attractions appropriate to their nature and that those of them who are nearer to the things here below hear the prayers of those who call upon them according to the de-

---

81 See *Treatise* 28 (IV, 4), 7, 6–12.
82 See *Treatise* 28 (IV, 4), 8, 1–8.
83 See *Treatise* 28 (IV, 4), 8, 34–45.
84 See *Treatise* 28 (IV, 4), 42.
85 See Luc Brisson, "The Philosopher and the Magician (Porphyry, *Vita Plotini* 10, 1–13). Magic and Sympathy," in *Antike Mythen. Medien, Transformationen und Konstruktionen, Fritz Graf zum 65. Geburtstag*, ed. Ueli Dill and Christine Walde (Berlin and New York: De Gruyter, 2009), 189–202.

gree of their concern with things here below. (*Treatise* 28 [IV, 4], 43, 12–16)

Thus magic finds a certain explanation, yet its level of operation is very low: that of the vegetative soul. By his contemplation that takes place on the level of the undescended soul, and by discursive reason, the sage can defend himself against its effects.[86]

When he takes up the question of memory, Plotinus thus does not restrict himself to epistemology. His interests are much more vast. This explains why a huge portion of *Treatises* 27 and 28, that is, 27 (IV, 3), 25 to 28 (IV, 4), 17 is devoted to this question of the soul's travels up and down in the universe. Enabling the conservation of the soul's activities relative to the sensible and the intelligible, memory is at the foundation of ethics in human beings. In this world, it is associated with the mode of operation of the lower part of the world soul; hence its implications for cosmology. And its presence or absence allows one to account for the attitude and the reactions of the gods and the demons; hence the implication of memory in the fields of astrology and magic.

In conclusion, the identity and the quality of a descended soul is determined by its memory. The memories of the contemplation it has exercised of the intelligible guide it in the course of its descent, while the weight of the memories of its corporeal experiences during its previous existence in a body prevents or impedes its re-ascent toward the Intelligible whence it comes. In Plotinus, the soul's destiny, before or after it has left a body, is always associated with the exercise of memory. One cannot, therefore, speak of the salvation of the soul without evoking memory.

---

[86] See Brisson 2009, 189–202.

Between the Two Realms: Plotinus' Pure Soul[1]

Svetla Slaveva-Griffin

In *Vita Plotini* 23.3–4, Porphyry says that Plotinus kept his soul pure.[2] This remark has the air of a pupil's rhetorical embellishment of his teacher. An examination of the use of the concept of "pure soul" in the salvific literature of late Antiquity, in Plotinus' philosophy, and in the history of Greek philosophy, however, reveals the deep soteriological and ontological roots of Porphyry's statement and dispels the air of hagiographical simplicity from it. The goal of this essay is to investigate these roots and to demonstrate the confluence of philosophy and soteriology in the concept.

"Likeness to god" (ὁμοίωσις θεῷ) is Plato's prescription for the meaning of human life.[3] It is bold and unattainable, and, to some, it may even seem hybristic. Nevertheless it has not detered generations of Platonists from its theoretical elaboration and practical pursuit, especially since Plato names "purification" (κάθαρσις) as the means to achieve this goal.[4] Purification, he further specifies, "consists in separating the soul as much as possible from the body" and those who "have pu-

---

1 The idea for this article is inspired by Steven Strange who gave a paper on "Theurgy in Plotinus and Iamblichus" at the inaugural seminar of the Institute for the History of Philosophy at Emory University in 2008. I dedicate it to his memory.
2 Καθαρὰν τὴν ψυχὴν ἔχων, translated as "guarding the purity of his soul" by Mark J. Edwards, *Neoplatonic Saints. The Lives of Plotinus and Proclus By Their Students*. In *Translated Texts for Historians*, vol. 35 (Liverpool: Liverpool University Press, 2000), 44. Henceforth the Greek text of Porphyry's *Vita Plotini* (*VP*) and Plotinus' *Enneads* (*Enn.*) is from Paul Henry and Hans-Rudolf Schwyzer, *Plotini Opera*, vols. 1–3 (Oxford: Clarendon Press, 1964–1983); translations, with alterations, are from Arthur H. Armstrong, *Plotinus: Enneads*, vols. 1–2 (Cambridge, MA: Loeb Classical Library, 1969–1988).
3 *Theaet.* 176a–b.
4 *Phaedo* 67c–69d; henceforth Greek text is from E.A. Duke et al., *Platonis Opera*, vol. 1 (Oxford: Clarendon Press, 1995) and Hugh Tredennick, "*Phaedo*," in *Plato. Collected Dialogues*, ed. Edith Hamilton and Huntington Cairns (Princeton: Princeton University Press, 1996), 40–98.

rified themselves sufficiently by philosophy live thereafter altogether without bodies."[5] The determinism of his prescription seemed neither austere nor ephemeral to his successors. They all took it to heart, but, expectedly, with a very low success rate except three: Plotinus, Iamblichus, and Proclus. Proclus is said, in his biography by Marinus, to have thoroughly mastered the path Plato prescribes, to have attained "the likeness of the gods," and to have "all but departed from the body."[6] Iamblichus is also so distinguished in achieving this goal that he is bestowed, by his intellectual heirs, the constant epithet "divine" (θεῖος) which makes him equal only to Pythagoras.[7] And finally Plotinus, in whose steps both Iamblichus and Proclus follow, is described, in his biography by Porphyry, to possess "a pure soul" (καθαρὰ ψυχή), to be "a god-like man" (δαιμόνιος φώς), to raise himself "in thought to the First and Transcendent God," and four times to unite himself with this God.[8]

If one examines the use of the concept of "pure soul" in the *Enneads*, what originally seems an adoring pupil's remark about his teacher turns out to convey important philosophical meaning which itself originates in Plotinus' understanding of Soul as one of the three primary underlying principles of existence.[9] Characteristically of Plotinian thought, the expression "pure soul" has a wide range of meanings in the *Enneads*. It denotes "the first principle of the soul" that is created by the Demiurge[10] in the *Timaeus* (*Enn*. II.3.9), the existence of soul in the intelligi-

---

5 *Phaedo* 67c5–d1: Κάθαρσις δὲ εἶναι ἆρα οὐ τοῦτο συμβαίνει ... τὸ χωρίζειν ὅτι μάλιστα ἀπὸ τοῦ σώματος τὴν ψυχὴν καὶ ἐθίσαι αὐτὴν καθ' αὑτὴν πανταχόθεν ἐκ τοῦ σώματος συναγείρεσθαί τε καὶ ἀθροίζεσθαι, καὶ οἰκεῖν κατὰ τὸ δυνατὸν καὶ ... μόνην καθ' αὑτήν, ἐκλυομένην ὥσπερ [ἐκ] δεσμῶν ἐκ τοῦ σώματος; *Phaedo* 114c3–4: οἱ φιλοσοφίᾳ ἱκανῶς καθηράμενοι ἄνευ τε σωμάτων ζῶσι τὸ παράπαν εἰς τὸν ἔπειτα χρόνον.

6 Marinus, *Vit.Proc.* 515 and 607 (Masullo) respectively: ἡ τοῦ μακαρίου ἀνδρὸς ψυχὴ ἀφίστατο σχεδὸν τοῦ σώματος; ἀλλαξάμενος τὸν τῶν θεῶν· πρὸς γὰρ τούτους αὐτῷ, οὐ πρὸς ἀνθρώπους ἀγαθοὺς ἡ ὁμοίωσις.

7 The epithet is ubiquitously attested in the later philosophical tradition, to list a few: Hermias, *In Phaedr.* 113.25, 136.17; Simplicius, *In de caelo* VII.1.24, VII.169.3; Philoponus, *In analytica priora* XIII.2.26; Syrianus, *In metaph.* 103.7; and Proclus, *Theol.Plat.* I.52.3.

8 *VP* 23.3–4: ἄγρυπνος καὶ καθαρὰν τὴν ψυχὴν ἔχων; *VP* 23.7–8: τούτῳ τῷ δαιμονίῳ φωτὶ πολλάκις ἐνάγοντι ἑαυτὸν εἰς τὸν πρῶτον καὶ ἐπέκεινα θεὸν ταῖς ἐννοίαις; and *VP* 23.16: ἔτυχε δὲ τετράκις που.

9 Following the convention of Neoplatonic scholarship, Soul is capitalized in reference to the third underlying principle of existence, it is not capitalized in reference to the individual soul.

10 Referred to by Plotinus as "god" (θεός) in *Enn.* II.3.9.6.

ble realm (*Enn.* III.3.5.17–18), the soul's nature after it has separated from its compound with the body (*Enn.* I.8.4.25–28), the individual soul without body (*Enn.* IV.3.24.22–29), and above all the unifying existence of all souls before they become attached to a particular man and descend into a particular body (*Enn.* VI.4.14.18–32). In this hypercosmic state, according to Plotinus, "we were there, men who were different, and some of us even gods, pure souls (ψυχαὶ καθαραί) and intellect united with the whole of reality; we were parts of the intelligible, not marked off or cut off but belonging to the whole; and we are not cut off even now" (*Enn.* VI.4.14.18–22). This statement shares, or even overshadows, Porphyry's exaltation in describing Plotinus' soul as "pure." Plotinus conceptualizes "pure soul" in the highest ontological terms.

In the light of the extensive treatment of "pure soul" in the *Enneads*, then, Porphyry's remark does not seem to be a plain rhetorical exaggeration but an important term which raises a host of questions about Plotinus' understanding of the concept, Porphyry's adaptation of his teacher's view in the interpretation of Apollo's oracle in *VP* 22–23, the history of the concept in the pre-Plotinian tradition and last but not least its use in the salvific schools of the time. Considering the diversity of the questions, in typically Plotinian fashion, it seems reasonable to begin from the broader to the more specific ones.

I. The *Chaldean Oracles* and the *Bhagavad Gītā* on Salvation

Aside from the encomiastic praise of posterity, the accounts of the extraordinary qualities of Proclus, Iamblichus, and Plotinus objectively reflect the Neoplatonists' intensified pursuit to connect with that which is beyond sense perception and discursive thought, the metaphysical realm. Although the close relation of philosophy with sacred practices, such as the mysteries and other initiation rites, is present in the development of ancient Greek philosophy from its inception, it does not become one of its formal and, in certain cases, prevalent aspects until Neoplatonism.[11]

---

11 On the relationship between philosophy and religion in early Greek philosophy, see Peter Kingsley, *Ancient Philosophy, Mystery, and Magic: Empedocles and Pythagorean Tradition* (Oxford: Oxford University Press, 1995).

For Iamblichus and Proclus, the practice of theurgy under the influence of Eastern thought, especially that of the *Chaldean Oracles*, is a well-documented fact.[12] But this is not the case with Plotinus. We know nothing concretely about his exposure to the abundant salvific literature of his time in which Orphism, Hermetism, Gnosticism, Zoroastrianism, Hinduism, and Chaldean lore thrived by inciting withdrawal from corporeality.[13] The only certain fact we know is that Plotinus, disenchanted with the mainstream philosophers in Alexandria, was introduced to the circle of Ammonius Saccas and remained with him for "eleven complete years" (*VP* 3.20). With Ammonius, Porphyry tells us, Plotinus "acquired such a thorough instruction in philosophy that he became eager to make acquaintance with the Persian philosophical discipline and that prevailing among the Indians" (τῆς παρὰ Πέρσαις ἐπιτηδευομένης...τῆς παρ' Ἰνδοῖς, *VP* 3.15–17). In his pursuit of Eastern knowledge, Plotinus joined Gordian's expedition eastward but, after the emperor's assassination in Mesopotamia, he retreated and sought haven in Antioch (*VP* 3.21–22).

If we read between the lines of Porphyry's account of Plotinus' schooling with Ammonius, we can suppose that the latter was somehow steeped in Eastern philosophies, specifically Persian and Indian.[14] But this conjecture is all we can deduce about Ammonius' interest in the East and about some of the subjects Plotinus studied with him. We know even less whether Plotinus himself was exposed to Persian and Indian thought during his journey with Gordian, what knowledge he brought back with him, and what he thought of it all. He does not say anything about either one in the *Enneads*. But since Porphyry

---

12 Iamblichus, *De myst.* I.1.41, III.31.6, IX.4.27; Marinus, *Vit.Proc.* 24–28. Ruth Majercik, *The Chaldean Oracles. Text, Translation, and Commentary* (Leiden: Brill, 1989), 2–5. On Porphyry's relation with the Chaldaeans, see Hans Lewy, *Chaldaean Oracles and Theurgy: Mysticism, Magic, and Platonism in the Later Roman Empire* (Paris: Études Augustiniennes, 1978), 449–456.

13 Porphyry uncharitably refers to these schools as "sects" (αἱρετικοί, *VP* 16.2).

14 On Ammonius, see E.R. Dodds, "Numenius and Ammonius," in *Les Sources de Plotin* (Geneva: Vandœuvres, 1957), 3–61; John M. Dillon, *The Middle Platonists 80 B.C. To A.D. 220*, rev. ed. (Ithaca, NY: Cornell University Press, 1996), 380–383; on his tenuous relation to Indian thought, Joachim Lacrosse, "Le rêve indien de Plotin et Porphyre," *RphA* 19.1 (2001): 87; On Porphyry's attitude toward Indian philosophy, see Lewy 1978, 453 and John J. O'Meara, "Indian Wisdom and Porphyry's Search for a Universal Way," in *Neoplatonism and Indian Thought*, ed. R. Baine Harris (Albany, NY: State University of New York Press, 1982), 5–26.

deems Plotinus' interest in them important enough as to be mentioned in *VP*, we need to start our examination of the concept of "pure soul" from them.

It has been a long vexing issue for scholars that Plotinus does not directly refer to Persian and Indian thought in the *Enneads* when they contain a number of very suggestive conceptual parallels with his philosophy.[15] Among them, perhaps the idea of salvation deserves the palm of victory. Although the question of the soul's salvation is central in Greek philosophy, especially in the views of Pythagoras, Empedocles, and Plato, it is also a core principle for many Eastern schools of thought. As will be discussed later, the Greek philosophical background undeniably plays a formative role in Plotinus' understanding of "pure soul," but the salvific trends of Eastern religions make their parallel with Plotinus' views also undeniable, especially in light of his pursuits documented in *VP* 3.12–17. Recently Mazur has cogently attempted to dispel the dominant opinion that Plotinus uniquely carved his concept of soul's union with the One in some sort of conceptual vacuum, apart from possible external influences, and in particular apart from Gnosticism.[16] His arguement is favorably facilitated by Plotinus' frequent address of Gnostic views throughout his works. We are not so fortunate in uncovering his attitude towards Persian and Indian doctrines, the two Eastern disciplines he, according to Porphyry, is most interested in (*VP* 3.15–17). There are no explicit or implicit references to them in the *Enneads*. But, as Plotinus' silence on the subject of Eastern schools is an insurmountable fact, so is his soteriological interest in the soul's ascent to the intelligible realm.[17] The latter speaks up, in place of missing direct references, about the common ideological background of the concept of "pure soul."

---

15 The list is long, some of the signature views are Bréhier's assurance in the reception of Indian elements in Neoplatonic thought (Émile Bréhier, *The Philosophy of Plotinus*, trans. Joseph Thomas [Chicago: University of Chicago Press, 1958], 106–131), Armstrong's rejection of any contact between the two (Arthur H. Armstrong, "Plotinus and India," *CQ* 30.1 [1936]: 22–28), and Lacrosse's more balanced appraisal (2001).
16 Zeke Mazur, "*Unio Magica*: Part I: On the Magical Origins of Plotinus' Mysticism," *Dionysius* 21 (2003): 23–52 and Zeke Mazur, "*Unio Magica*: Part II: Plotinus, Theurgy, and the Question of Ritual," *Dionysius* 22 (2004): 29–56 copiously examines the relation between Plotinus' view of union with the One and Gnostic beliefs.
17 *Enn.* I.6.9, III.8.6.37–40, IV.8.1, V.1.11.6–12, V.8.10–11, VI.9.7–8.

Porphyry's reference to the Persian teachings in *VP* 3, although illuminating, is too broad to identify any particular school. I am inclined to agree with Bréhier's interpretation that, by Persian, Porphyry may have Mithras' cult in mind.[18] The popularity of the cult during his lifetime is ubiquitous both in the Eastern and Western Roman provinces and in Rome itself. This fact makes Bréhier's thesis certainly plausible and opens a new, promising, direction for our invesigation because the Mithraic solar theology, as suggested by Lewy, has most likely influenced the formation of certain Chaldean concepts.[19]

The *Chaldean Oracles*, a collection of late second century fragmentary texts, show explicit interest in the connection between the human and divine realms. As result, they present an intricate conceptual system of entities which regulate, oversee, and mediate this connection. The Iynges, the Connectors, the Teletarchs all mediate the relation between the two realms and facilitate the soul's ascent upward. The Iynges (ἴυγγες, fr. 76), as "thoughts" of the Father (fr. 77), are "binding" entities that act like "couriers" (fr. 78) between the two realms.[20] The Connectors (συνοχεῖς, frr. 32, 80, 81), who protect the universal harmony (fr. 82), support the descending rays of the sun upon which the soul ascends. The Teletarchs (τελετάρχαι, frr. 85 and 86), the "masters of initiation," purify "the ascending soul of material influences and guide its journey upward."[21] Closest to the material world are the angels and "the pure daemons" (δαίμονες ἁγνοί, fr. 88)[22] who directly assist the soul's ascent and guard it from the attacks of evil daemons.[23] Designed to oversee the connection between the two realms, this elaborated hierarchy of divine entities is successively mirrored in the physical world by the dis-

---

18 Bréhier's hypothesis (1958, 114) is further strengthened by Porphyry's account of the form and function of the mithraeum in *De antro nympharum* 6. On Porphyry's interpretation of the Mithraic mysteries, see Roger Beck, *The Religion of the Mithras Cult in the Roman Empire. Mysteries of the Unconquered Sun* (Oxford: Oxford University Press, 2007), 16–17, 41–63, and 85–87.
19 Lewy 1978, 409–413 although his conclusion is left unnoticed by scholars on both sides. See Majercik 1989 on the Chalden Oracles and most recently Beck 2007 on the Mithraic cult.
20 Majercik 1989, 9–10.
21 Majercik 1989, 11–12.
22 Majercik 1989, 82–83 and 175–178, against Chantraine's distinction (Pierre Chantraine, *Dictionnaire étymologique de la langue grecque, histoire des mots* [Paris: Éditions Klincksieck, 1968]) between καθαρός and ἁγνός, translates the latter as "pure."
23 Psellus, *Hypotyp.* 23; Majercik 1989, 13–14.

tinction of three types of men: the theurgists (οἱ θεουργοί), the crowd (ἡ ἀγέλη), and the "middle men" between the first two groups (οἱ μέσοι).[24] The souls of the theurgists are descendants of the angels and thus are closest to the entities, described above. This proximity with the divine is progressively diluted in "the middle men" and completely absent in "the crowd." The tripartite division resembles the triadic division of the Iynges, the Connectors, and the Teletarchs, with the difference that the divine entities are not distinguished on the basis of their ability to relate to the physical realm while the human types are grouped according to their ability to relate to the metaphysical realm.[25] This distincion elucidates that the most importance difference between the two realms is nothing else but ontological. The three divine types cannot be distinguished ontologically but only predicatively in their functions, while the three human types can be distinguished not only by their functions but also by the extent of their distance from the divine. The Chaldean system links the two ends of the ontological spectrum in a chain, which descends from the purity of the intelligible realm to the impurity of the material world, embodied in the degraded type of "the crowd."[26] It is reasonable to conclude that, by participating in this chain, each of the human types possesses a certain degree of "purity," which either brings it closer to the divine or removes it further away from it. In it, the theurgic type of men occupies the most important place as the closest, among mortals, to the purity of the intelligible. The fragments do not explain how the three types of men are determined but there is a slight notion that this is done by natural disposition.

This innate ability, however, is not the only way of reaching back to the divine. The *Chaldean Oracles* also propound the idea of actively freeing the soul from the shackles of corporeality:

Flee swiftly from earthly passions, flee far away, you who
possess the superior eye of the soul and the steadfast rays, so

---

24 Frr. 153, 154. Only the first two groups are documented in the Chaldean fragments but the third one is reported in Iamblichus, *De myst.* V.18. Majercik 1989, 20, with Friedrich W. Cremer, *Die Chaldäischen Orakel und Jamblich De Mysteriis* (Meisenheim am Glan: Anton Hain, 1969), 123–130, considers the tripartite division as originally Chaldean.
25 In addition, each of the three groups internally comprises three beings; see Majercik 1989, 12.
26 On καθαρὸς νοῦς, see Majercik 1989, 20.

that the great, heavy reins of the body might be held in check
by a pure soul [ἐκ καθαρῆς ψυχῆς] and the ethereal radiance of the Father.[27]
(fr. 213, trans. Majercik)

The fragment illustrates well the central Chaldean belief in the soul's separation from the body and introduces, from a human perspective, the concept of "pure soul" as the facilitator in the process. As Majercik has put it, "the principle means of salvation in the Chaldean system involves the purification of the soul via the techniques of theurgy."[28] It makes sense, then, that this system has developed an elaborate network of entities to procure the fulfillment of its primary soteriological premise. The "pure soul" is one of them. The fragment also hints at the slight notion that not all souls equally succeed in this process except the "pure soul."

At their heart, Indian didactic texts also pursue a soteriological goal but, unlike the *Chaldean Oracles*, they espouse it in rich literary tradition. The *Bhagavad Gītā* has long attracted the attention of Neoplatonic scholars for a number of reasons.[29] Composed in the span of the millennium from 500 B.C.E to 500 C.E.[30] as a part of the larger epic *Mahābhārata*, the *Bhagavad Gītā* offers a spiritual guide for salvation (*mokṣa*) which instructs man how to achieve *nirvāṇa*, one's union with the Supreme transcendent principle (*brahman*).[31] In the exposition of this idea, there are many compelling parallels between the *Bhagavad Gītā* and Plo-

---

27 Among the "doubtful fragments" in Majercik 1989, 130–131 and 217–218. On the authenticity of the fragment, Majercik 1989, 172, n. 403.
28 Majercik 1989, 21.
29 R. Baine Harris, ed., *Neoplatonism and Indian Thought* (Albany, NY: State University of New York Press, 1982) and Paulos M. Gregorios, ed., *Neoplatonism and Indian Philosophy* (Albany, NY: State University of New York Press, 2002); Bréhier 1958, 118–131. Against the view of Indian influence on Plotinus, see Armstrong 1936 and John M. Rist, *Plotinus: The Road to Reality* (Cambridge: Cambridge University Press, 1967), 213–230.
30 I use the dates given in Brodbeck's introduction (Simon Brodbeck, "Introduction," in *The Bhagavad Gita* [London: Penguin Books, 1962], xi) to Mascaró's translation of the *Bhagavad Gītā*.
31 J.A.B. van Buitenen, "Dharma and Mokṣa," *Philosophy East and West* 7.1 (1957): 33–40; Guy Richard Welbon, "On Understanding the Buddhist Nirvāṇa," *History of Religions* 5.2 (1966): 300–326; David White, "Human Perfection in the *Bhagavadgītā*," *Philosophy East and West* 21.1 (1971): 43–53; Gavin D. Flood, *An Introduction to Hinduism* (Cambridge: Cambridge University Press, 1996), 81; I.C. Sharma, "The Plotinian One and the Concept of *Parama puruṣa* in the *Bhagavadgītā*," in *Neoplatonism and Indian Thought*, ed. R. Baine Harris (Albany, NY: State University of New York Press, 1982), 90.

tinus' thought which have been already examined.[32] Here I will trace only the idea of "pure soul" in the *Bhagavad Gītā* in order to reconstruct its soteriological meaning.

Presented in the form of a dialogue between Arjuna and Kṛṣṇa in the field of *dharma* before the battle between the Pāṇḍavas and the Kauravas, the *Bhagavad Gītā* narrates Kṛṣṇa's instruction of Arjuna in the path of liberation and enlightment as an individual soul (*ātman*). This instruction is designed anagogically to guide Arjuna's soul on the path of its complete dissolution as individuality into the source of all, the cosmic soul (*brahman*). The means for this dissolution, Kṛṣṇa instructs, is the attainment of "purity" as a result of soul's liberation from the control of the senses, emotions, and any corporeal attachment. His main didactic points urge Arjuna's "strong soul" to rise above the appetitive world (*BhG* 2.14 and *passim*), to free himself from impetuousness through the practice of contemplation (*yoga*, *BhG* 2.48), and to detract "all his senses from the attractions of the pleasures of senses" like "a tortoise which withdraws all its limbs" (*BhG* 2.58).[33] Malinar has most recently argued for the ontological origin of these prescriptions which share some common elements with "certain contemporary philosophical schools" and are also characteristic of "the older Upaniṣads and early Sāṃkhya philosophy."[34] The indifference to life and death, prescribed by Kṛṣṇa, does not really originate in man's active pursuit of evenmindedness in the face of joy or adversity but in the deep ontological distinction between embodied soul and intelligible entity.[35] While soul's reincarnation in a new body is compared to "weaving a new cloth" (*BhG* 2.22), the intelligible entity is "unmanifest," "unthinkable," and "unchangeable" (*BhG* 2.25).[36] The goal of Kṛṣṇa's prescription is not to

---

32 Arthur H. Armstrong and R.R. Ravindra, "*Buddhi* in the *Bhagavadgītā* and the *Psyché* in Plotinus," in *Neoplatonism and Indian Thought*, ed. R. Baine Harris (Albany, NY: State University of New York Press, 1982), 63–86, Sharma 1982, and most recently Lacrosse 2001 and Joachim Lacrosse, "Un passage de Porphyre relatif au Shiva androgyne chez les Brahmanes d'Inde," *RphA* 20.2 (2002): 37–56.
33 Henceforth J. Mascaró's translation of the *Bhagavad Gītā* (1962).
34 Angelika Malinar, *The Bhagavadgītā: Doctrines and Contexts* (Cambridge: Cambridge University Press, 2007), 66.
35 White 1971, 50.
36 Malinar 2007, 66–67. The parallel between this language and Plato's analogy of the soul wearing the body as a disposable cloak (*Phaedo* 87b4-c5) is rather suggestive.

overcome life or death but to restore the soul's unity with its intelligible source.

In its essence, this prescription is metaphysical but its execution takes on physical and ethical demands. Therefore the one who succeeds in this, "is free from all bonds, his mind has found peace in wisdom, and his work is a holy sacrifice. The work of such a man is pure" (*BhG* 4.23) and the wisdom of his inner spirit has made him "pure of sin" (*BhG* 5.17 and 6.45). The Yogi who has purified his soul in this way "has inner joy, he has inner gladness, and he has found inner Light" (*BhG* 5.24). He attains the *nirvāṇa* of *brahman*. This condition, as White has pointed out, is the "ultimate goal of human existence" in the ancient Indian tradition.[37]

This ultimate goal, however, is not equally attainable by everyone. In its pursuit, Kṛṣṇa distinguishes four kinds of men (*BhG* 4.13): "the man of sorrows," who seeks Kṛṣṇa after he has been struck with unbearable grief for the loss of someone; "the seeker of knowledge;" "the seeker of something he treasures," who looks to Kṛṣṇa for wealth; and "the man of vision" or "the adept" (*jānī*) who knows Kṛṣṇa by birth (*BhG* 7.16). The latter is the greatest kind of all because in Kṛṣṇa's own words: "His whole soul is one in me, and I am his Path Supreme" (*BhG* 7.18). The emphasis on the last type suggests that the four types both pursue Kṛṣṇa and achieve union with him with a different degree of ontological success. This success can be measured by no one else but Kṛṣṇa. As the essence of existence, only he is in a position to measure how closely one has come to him: "In the manner in which they approach me, in that manner I engage with them" (*BhG* 4.11).[38] This degree of difference or manner once again is not acquired additionally. It has ontological roots. As result, only one type of man has the full potential to draw nearmost to Kṛṣṇa, "the adept."

Both the *Chaldean Oracles* and the *Bhagavad Gītā* propound the idea of a special kind of soul, "the pure soul," which is by its nature closer to the source of all and therefore has a better ability to unite with this source. Because of its natural proximity to the divine, the "pure soul" easily succeeds in separating itself completely from the body. It is reasonable to consider the theurgist's soul in the *Chaldean Oracles* as an example of this type of soul because the theurgist's soul is closest to the intelligible realm. In the *Bhagavad Gītā*, this must be the soul of "the

---

37 White 1971, 44.
38 White 1971, 50, and Malinar 2007, 101.

adept" which by birth possesses knowledge about the transcendent source of existence, i.e., Kṛṣṇa himself. But, unlike the abstract tone of the *Chaldean Oracles*, the *Bhagavad Gītā* offers a practical ethical guidance for the soul on how to achieve complete liberation from the body. The "pure soul" is free of both corporeal dictate and sin.

II. Plotinus' Pure Soul: Apollo's Oracle and Porphyry's Interpretation in *VP*

Porphyry's description of Plotinus as "pure soul" in *VP* 23.4 comes in one of the most puzzling sections in the work—Apollo's oracle about the ascent of Plotinus' soul to the intelligible realm (*VP* 22) and Porphyry's exegesis of it (*VP* 23). The two chapters (*VP* 22–23) present the journey of Plotinus' soul in the imagery of the soul's upward ascent in the *Chaldean Oracles* and in the ascetic and ethical context of the *Bhagavad Gītā*.

The oracle is prompted by an inquiry of the whereabouts of Plotinus' soul after his death (*VP* 22.8–9).[39] With encomiastic flair, it recounts how his soul has departed the body and, overcoming "the bitter wave of this blood-drinking life," it joins the company of Pythagoras and Plato, and the other most blessed spirits in their "dance of immortal love."[40] In the beginning of the poem, Plotinus is anonymously introduced as "a gentle friend" (ἀγανὸς φίλος, *VP* 22.14), next he is addressed successively as a "daemon, man once" (δαῖμον, ἄνερ τὸ πάροιθεν, *VP* 22.23), "a daemon soul" (ψυχὴ δαιμονία, *VP* 22.46), and "a blessed

---

39 The inquiry is made by Amelius Gentilianus, who was a member of Plotinus' inner circle of friends (*VP* 7.1–5). On Amelius, see Luc Brisson, "Prosopographie," in *Porphyre. La Vie de Plotin*, ed. Luc Brisson et al., vol. 1 (Paris: Vrin, 1982), 65–69. On Amelius' attitude toward traditional religion, Luc Brisson, "Plotin et la magie," in *Porphyre. La Vie de Plotin*, ed. Luc Brisson et al., vol. 2 (Paris: Vrin, 1992), 472–475.

40 Respectively *VP* 22.32–33, 54–55, and 61. For the Homeric language and imagery of the text, see Richard Goulet, "Sur quelques interprétations récentes de *L'Oracle d'Apollon*," in *Porphyry. La Vie de Plotin*, ed. Luc Brisson et al., vol. 2 (Paris: Vrin, 1992), 603–617 and Brisson, "Plotin et la magie." As the author of *De antr. nymph.* and *Hom. Quest.*, Porphyry has a lasting interest in the philosophical value of Homeric expresson. See Robert D. Lamberton, *Homer the Theologian: Neoplatonist Allegorical Reading and the Growth of the Epic Tradition*, ed. P. Brown. The Transformations of the Classical Heritage (Berkeley: University of California Press, 1986), 108–133.

one" (μάκαρ, *VP* 58). Not until the end, his name is revealed as "Plotinus, the happy" (Πλωτῖνος...πολυγηθής, *VP* 22.62). This vocabulary describes Plotinus as an extraordinary man, a man who is different from the rest. Unlike the customary riddling ambiguity of Apollo's prophecies, the oracle confirms Porphyry's earlier observation, made in relation to magic and astrology, that "Plotinus certainly possessed by birth something more than other men."[41]

The place of the oracle (*VP* 22) and Porphyry's commentary on it (*VP* 23) in the thematic composition of *VP* is perspicacious and has yielded different interpretations.[42] The two chapters follow Porphyry's elongated account of his correspondence with Longinus who took upon himself to refute the charges of plagiarism pressed against Plotinus (*VP* 19–21). They conclude the biographical section of the work by painting the last image of Plotinus in the reader's mind.

Porphyry makes an explicit attempt at associating, if not identifying, Plotinus philosophically and soteriologically with Pythagoras and Plato. In his letter, Longinus, who was in Porphyry's words "the foremost critic" of the time,[43] ascertains that Plotinus "has expounded the principles of Pythagorean and Platonic philosophy more clearly (πρὸς σαφεστέραν ... ἐξήγησιν) than anyone before him" (*VP* 20.71–73). He is directly placed in the tradition of the philosophers whose company he joins at the end of his soul's ascent as presented in Apollo's oracle. After the letter, Porphyry cites four quotations:[44] Hesiod's rhetorical question, directed at divination, of "why I should talk of oak and rock" (*Theog.* 35);[45] Herodotus' praise of god's wisdom (*Hist.* I.47);[46] and the full texts of two oracles from Apollo.[47]

---

41 *VP* 10.14–15: ἦν γὰρ καὶ κατὰ γένεσιν πλέον τι ἔχων παρὰ τοὺς ἄλλους ὁ Πλωτῖνος.

42 On the Porphyrian authenticity of the text, see Richard Goulet, "*L'Oracle d'Apollon* dans *La Vie de Plotin*," in *Porphyre. La Vie de Plotin*, ed. Luc Brisson et al., vol. 1 (Paris: Vrin, 1982), 371–412; on recent interpretations, see Goulet 1992.

43 *VP* 20.1–2: τοῦ καθ' ἡμᾶς κριτικωτάτου γενομένου καὶ τὰ τῶν ἄλλων σχεδὸν πάντα τῶν καθ' αὑτὸν διελέγξαντος.

44 While the origin of the first two references is clear, that of the oracles is unknown. Goulet 1982, 376–386 argues for Porphyrian origin.

45 The interpretation of Hesiod's expression is controversial; it is generally referred to as divination. For full discussion, see Jenny Strauss Clay, *Hesiod's Cosmos* (Cambridge: Cambridge University Press, 2003), 52, n.12; Luc Brisson and Jean-Marie Flamand, "Structure, contenu et intentions de *L'Oracle d'Apollon* (Porphyre, *VP* 22)," in *Porphyre. La Vie de Plotin*, ed. Luc Brisson et al.,

The first two invoke the authority of the ancient writers who have inspiringly praised divine wisdom, while the other two illustrate the philosophical acumen of the god of the new universal order and the arts. The first one contains the famous saying that "Socrates is the wisest of men,"[48] the second is a fifty-line hexameter poem celebrating the ascent of Plotinus' soul to the company of the gods and his intellectual predecessors.[49] The striking imbalance of the length of the two oracles places Plotinus in the limelight first as one who is of a stature similar to Socrates and second as one who has inspired the god to sing an elaborate song about his soul's journey to the divine. Apparently Plotinus' merits are so many and so great that they could not be summarized in one line even by the god of arts and poetry. The length of the poem adroitly complements Longinus' expansive letter quoted in *VP* 19–21. The message of the oracle is clear: Plotinus is above common men and he is worthy to be with the gods and to be praised by the gods as well.

The soteriological message of the oracle is clear, but its philosophical content needs further explication.[50] Thus the following chapter (*VP* 23) depicts the facts of Plotinus' character and contemplative practice which prove the pronouncement of the oracle:

> The oracle says that he was mild and kind, most gentle and attractive, and we knew ourselves that he was like this. It says that sleeplessly he kept his soul pure [ἄγρυπνος καὶ καθαρὰν τὴν ψυχὴν ἔχων] and ever strove towards the divine which he loved with all his soul [ἀεὶ σπεύδων πρὸς τὸ θεῖον, οὗ διὰ πάσης τῆς ψυχῆς ἤρα], and did everything to be delivered and "escape from the bitter wave of blood-drinking life here." So too this god-like man above all [μάλιστα τούτῳ τῷ δαιμονίῳ φωτί], who often raised himself in thought, according to the ways Plato teaches in the *Symposium*, to the First and Transcendent God. (*VP* 23.1–11)

---

vol. 2 (Paris: Vrin, 1992), 566; Goulet 1982, 389, n.2. Porphyry repeats it in *De abst.* II.5. In *VP*, it also alludes to Plato, *Apol.* 34d.
46   Brisson and Flamand 1992, 566–567.
47   Brisson and Flamand 1992, 566–602. On the oracular tradition, see Herbert William Parke, *The Oracles of Apollo in Asia Minor* (London: Croom Helm, 1985).
48   Cited by Diogenes Laertius II.5.37. Cf. Plato, *Apol.* 21a6–7; Brisson and Flamand 1992, 567.
49   It should be noted that the clarity of the meaning of the quotations increases progressively from the first to the last. Porphyry introduces the oracle in the manner in which he introduces the oracles in his *De philosophia ex oraculis haurienda*; see Brisson and Flamand 1992, 567; also Lewy 1978, 449–456.
50   By so doing, Porphyry also confirms the truth of Longinus' evaluation of Plotinus.

Porphyry translates the oracle's message in Platonic terms to mean that Plotinus is closer to the intelligible realm than anyone else. The interpretation outlines the main points of Plotinus' description in the oracle: his kindness (ἀγανός, *VP* 23.1), his "pure soul" (καθαρὰν τὴν ψυχήν, *VP* 23.4), his qualities of "a god-like man" (δαιμόνιος φώς, *VP* 23.7), his separation from the body (*VP* 23.5–8), and his union with the divine (*VP* 23.7–18). It also follows the semantic parameters of the vocabulary with which Plotinus is addressed in the oracle: the epithet ἀγανός in *VP* 22.14, the noun δαίμων in *VP* 22.23, and the expression καθαρὰ ψυχή in *VP* 22.28.

The choice of diction in Apollo's address of Plotinus as "a gentle friend" (ἀγανὸς φίλος, *VP* 22.14) is extremely suitable for an oracle delivered by Leto's son. The same epithet is used in Homer to describe the "gentleness" of the far-shooter's arrows when they bring easy death.[51] By calling Plotinus "gentle," Apollo evokes his own dual qualities of a bringer of death and health. As if with his "gentle arrows," Apollo sees to the gentle separation of Plotinus' soul from the body and, as if with his healing power, he recovers Plotinus' soul from the diseased imperfection of the body. In this context, the epithet does not only refer to Plotinus' charitable character, but also hints at the main theme of the oracle: the gentle release of Plotinus' soul from the material world. By repeating the epithet in the beginning of his interpretation, Porphyry leaves the dual Homeric meaning of the epithet to linger in the background, although he brings to the fore its ethical connotation by adding to it the synonyms of "kind," "most gentle," and "attractive" (ἤπιος, πρᾶός γε μάλιστα καὶ μείλιχος, *VP* 23.2).

The other two expressions in the oracle on which Porphyry elaborates are Apollo's reference to Plotinus as "a daemon" (δαῖμον, *VP* 22.23) and the description of the journey of Plotinus' soul as the "easy path of the pure soul" (καθαρῆς ψυχῆς εὐκαμπέα οἴμην, *VP* 22.28). Since, throughout the oracle, δαίμων is repeated six times and καθαρός three times, the two expressions must have some significance other than sheer poetic license:

> *Daemon* [my ital.], man once [δαῖμον, ἄνερ τὸ πάροιθεν], but now nearing the diviner lot of a spirit, as the bond of human necessity has been loosed for you, and strong in heart, you swam swiftly from the roaring surge of the body to that coast where the stream flows strong, far apart from the crowd

---

51 *Il.* 24.758–759: Ἀπόλλων | οἷς ἀγανοῖσι βέλεσσιν ἐποιχόμενος κατέπεφνεν. Cf. *Od.* 3.279–280, 15.410–411.

of the wicked [δήμου ἄπο νόσφιν ἀλιτρῶν], there to set your steps firm in the easy path of the pure soul [στηρίξαι καθαρῆς ψυχῆς εὐκαμπέα οἴμην], where the splendour of God shines round you and the divine law abides in purity far from lawless wickedness [ἧχι θέμιστες ἐν καθαρῷ ἀπάτερθεν ἀλιτροσύνης ἀθεμίστου]. (*VP* 22.23–30)

Porphyry has an abiding interest in the concept of "daemons" as documented in *De abst.* (II.36–43) and our passage follows this interest by introducing Plotinus as a "daemon" with a "pure soul" who has successfully overcome the necessities of the body and the desires of his human condition.[52] The thought suggests first that Plotinus has a soul which is different from that of common men ("far apart from common men"; δήμου ἄπο) and second that his soul is "apart from sinful men" (νόσφιν ἀλιτρῶν). In this context, καθαρά in "pure soul" (καθαρά ψυχή, *VP* 22.28) and καθαρός in the phrase "the divine law abides in purity far from lawless wickedness" (καθαρῷ, *VP* 22.30), respectively acquire the essential meaning of someone who is different from everybody and the ethical meaning of someone who is "pure of sin."[53]

While it is clear what it means to have a soul "pure of sin," it is not clear what it means to have a soul that is different from any one else. Perhaps it means that, since a part of soul, crudely speaking in Neoplatonic terms, belongs to the intelligible realm and thus has the same ontological constitution in everyone, when soul is characterized as being different from the other souls, the expression does not indicate a different ontological foundation, but a different degree with which the part of soul that descends into a body relates to the body. Some souls, then, retain a higher trace of their undescended counterpart. This distinction recalls the division of the types of men in the *Chaldean Oracles* and the *Bhagavad Gītā* discussed above. As the *Chaldean Oracles* create the notion of Intellect as "pure," so does, in Apollo's oracle, καθαρά ψυχή denote the highest degree of the soul's proximity to the intelligible realm and its unique ability to unite with the divine.[54] Thus the culminating point in the use of καθαρός in the oracle is the celebration of the union of Plotinus' "pure soul" with its divine origin:

---

52 On Porphyry's demonology, Lewy 1978, 497–508. On the passage as an allegory, see Lamberton 1986, 132–133.
53 Cf. the requirement for soul to be "pure of sin" in the *Bhagavad Gītā*, above 320–323.
54 Above n. 26.

> But now that you have been freed from this tabernacle and have left the tomb which held your heavenly soul [ψυχῆς δαιμονίης], you come at once to the company of heaven [μεθ' ὁμήγυριν ... δαιμονίην], where winds of delight blow, where is affection and desire that charms the sight, full of pure joy [εὐφροσύνης πλείων καθαρῆς], brimming with streams of immortality from the gods which carry the allurements of Loves, and sweet breeze and windless brightness of high heaven. (*VP* 22.45–51)

The description of Plotinus' union summarizes the main points of the oracle: Plotinus' soul is "pure;" it belongs to the intelligible realm; and the experience of his soul's union with the intelligible realm is "pure joy." If we consider the earlier meanings of "pure" in the expressions of "pure soul," as a soul withdrawn from body and the material world, and "in the pure," as in the intelligible realm, the last use of "pure" represents the culmination of the progression of the concept from the soul's ethical qualities to its union with the intelligible.[55] The "purity" of Plotinus' soul, characterized by its easy withdrawal from the body and by its high ethics, while in the body, is the medium that guides him on the ascending journey. It transforms Plotinus from "a gentle friend" (ἀγανὸς φίλος, *VP* 22.14) into someone worthy of the company of "blessed daemons" (μετὰ δαίμονας ἁγνούς, *VP* 22.59).[56] The subtle word play of the two adjectives in the oracle frames the starting and the ending point of Plotinus' ascent. Plotinus' "pure soul" mediates the transformation of Plotinus, the kind (ἀγανός), who is in the body, into Plotinus, the "blessed" (ἁγνός) whose soul joins the company of "the blessed souls" in *VP* 22.59.

Further, in *VP* 23.3–4, Porphyry makes the curious remark that Plotinus "sleeplessly kept his soul pure." Aside from the literal understanding of the statement that Plotinus preferred to stay awake, there are two other possible interpretations. The first one follows the philosophical tradition of referring to those who do not pursue any philosophical truth as "sleeping."[57] The second is Plotinus' view that the soul, while seeking its intelligible origin, is awake from its "sleep" in the physical world. The latter strongly resonates with Apollo's praise in the oracle that "sweet sleep never held your [Plotinus'] eyes" (*VP*

---

55 On the intertextual relation with *Phdr.* 250c, see Brisson and Flamand 1992, 581. There is also an intertextual play with *Enn.* III.8.11.26–33, below 335–336.
56 Cf. *Chaldean Oracles*, fr. 88.1: [ἡ φύσις] πείθει πιστεύειν εἶναι τοὺς δαίμονας ἁγνούς.
57 Heraclitus, DK B73, B75, B89.

22.40). But I think Plotinus' vigilance is also a direct expression of his possessing "a pure soul." "The pure soul" is different from the souls of men; it is divine.[58] It "stays apart from the crowd of the wicked" (*VP* 22.27) and its ascending journey leads to the place where the divine law abides "in purity" (ἐν καθαρῷ) far from the lawless depravity of earthly life (*VP* 22.29–30). Plotinus' possession of "pure soul" explains why Apollo introduces him as "a daemon, once man" (δαῖμον, ἄνερ τὸ πάροιθεν, *VP* 22.23) and as "a daemon soul" (ψυχὴ δαιμονία, *VP* 22.46). Porphyry, in his turn, translates Apollo's pronouncement by calling Plotinus "a god-like man" (δαιμόνιος φώς, *VP* 23.7). From Porphyry's anthropocentric viewpoint, Plotinus, as a man, is god-like, while, from Apollo's theocentric viewpoint, Plotinus is a "daemon" who has simply been a man previously. Both the divine and the human descriptions of Plotinus agree that he is more than just a man. They imply that there is a special group of "divine men" whose souls are "pure" and Plotinus is one of them.

Like the *Chaldean Oracles* and the *Bhagavad Gītā*, Apollo's oracle and Porphyry's interpretation of it distinguish different types of souls in regards to their kinship with the divine. In Porphyry's portrait of Plotinus in *VP*, we learn about the qualities of "pure souls."[59] But we need to look elsewhere in his works for more conceptual details. In his treatise *On Abstinence* (II.36–43), Porphyry outlines the levels of divine hierarchy as including the Supreme Being on the top, then the cosmic Soul and the planets, then the daemons.[60] The latter come from the cosmic Soul and during their descent acquire passions. Depending on how well the souls can control their passions, they are divided in two groups, the good daemons, who are in control of their passions and oversee plants, animals, climate, arts, knowledge of sciences, and the mediation between gods and men, and the bad daemons, who are overpowered by their passions and bring disease, famine, desires, and wars. It seems that Plotinus' "pure soul" belongs to the first group. But this is not certain because Porphyry does not relate these souls to the souls of mortal

---

58 In Proclus' *Hymn to the Muses* III.6–9, the Muses' souls are "pure." On the hymnic qualities of the oracle, see Brisson and Flamand 1992, 581.
59 We can only assume that the souls which are not "pure" have opposite qualities.
60 *De abst.* 37.1–8. For an exhaustive discussion of Porphyry's views on "daemons," see Lewy 1978, 497–508. For discussion of the metaphorical use of "daemon" in Greek philosophy, see Ian Kidd, "Some Philosophical Demons," *BICS* 40 (1995): 217–24. Although informative, his article fails to find any philosophically redeeming qualities of the term.

men. We find more details in Porphyry's interpretation of Plato's Atlantis story in his commentary on the *Timaeus*, fragmentarily preserved in Proclus' own commentary on the same work. Porphyry, according to Proclus, distinguishes three kinds of daemons: "a divine type of *daemon* [τὸ θείων δαιμόνων γένος], a type now in that condition [κατὰ σχέσιν] which is made up of individual souls who have received a daemonic lot [ψυχαὶ δαιμονίας], and the other corrupt kind—the soul polluters."[61] It is clear from this more systematic presentation that Plotinus' "pure soul" belongs to the second kind of soul. In fact, his soul is addressed precisely as "daemonic soul" (ψυχῆς δαιμονίης) in Apollo's oracle in *VP* 22.46. This tripartite division invokes the tripartitite hierarchical distinction in men's ability to communicate with the divine presented in the *Chaldean Oracles*. "Pure soul," then, is a particular kind of soul that is closer to the intelligible realm and further away from the material world.

III. Empedocles and Plato on "Daemons" and Purification

Porphyry's use of δαίμων and ψυχὴ δαιμονία in Apollo's oracle succeeds the long philosophical tradition of conceiving of the soul as a divine being. In *De abstinentia*, Porphyry ascribes the division of the kinds of "daemons," discussed above, to "some Platonists" (τῶν Πλατωνικῶν τινες).[62] More precisely he has in mind the Platonic definition of "daemons" as beings "between god and mortal" (πᾶν τὸν δαιμόνιον μεταξύ ἐστι θεοῦ τε καὶ θνητοῦ) which is found in Diotima's speech on the nature and power of Love in the *Symposium* (202d11–e1). In reality, "the word *daimôn* is virtually impossible to translate," as Rowe notes.[63] It is at the basis of the modern words "demon," denoting something evil, and "spirit," denoting something superhuman. The latter is also connected with the adjective "spiritual" the connotations of which have evolved even farther away from the original meaning of δαιμόνιος as something

---

61 *In Tim.* I.77.10–12: τὸ μὲν θείων δαιμόνων γένος, τὸ δὲ κατὰ σχέσιν ὃ μερικαὶ συμπληροῦσι ψυχαὶ δαιμονίας τυχοῦσαι λήξεως, τὸ δὲ πονηρὸν ἄλλο καὶ λυμαντικὸν τῶν ψυχῶν. (Tarrant's trans.).

62 *De abst.* 36.23. Lewy 1978, 497 rejects the identification of these Platonists with Numenius and Cronius. Cf. *In Tim.* I.77.22–24: "The philosopher Porphyry is of this view, and one would be surprised if he is saying anything different from the view authorized by Numenius." Porphyry. *In Tim.* Fr. 10; Tarrant, trans.

63 Christopher J. Rowe, *Plato: Symposium* (Warminster, UK: Aris & Phillips, 1998), 175.

characteristic of "divine being." "The person," Plato defines, "who is wise about [the conversation between gods and men] is a daemon-like man" (δαιμόνιος ἀνήρ, *Symp.* 203a4–5). This definition presents the "daemon-like" type of man as a mediator between the two realms. On this Platonic note, in *VP* 23.7–12, Porphyry identifies Plotinus' soul as exactly this type.

But the interest in the relation between soul and "daemon" in Greek philosophy predates Plato in the teachings of Pythagoras and Empedocles. Pythagoras is the first philosopher who, at least according to tradition, postulates the soul's immortality and lays the ground for further elaboration of this view in Empedocles, and especially in his *Purifications*. In his work, possibly under Pythagorean influence, Empedocles renounces the soul's corporeal contamination. As a fallen divine being, the soul is forced by Necessity temporarily to abide in the body. His strong conviction of the soul's otherworldliness explains his preference for calling the soul δαίμων and not ψυχή.[64] This preference highlights the divine origin of the soul and dramatizes the physical pollution of its nature, while "clothed in an alien garment of flesh."[65] To free the soul from its corporeal imprisonment, he prescribes abstinence from evil, knowledge of the divine, and most ultimately purification.[66] Although the extant fragments of the poem do not report any actual purificatory practices, they undoubtedly declare the goal of these rites to restore souls "as gods, highest in honor, sharing hearth and table with

---

64 Rowe 1998, 263. Ψυχή is attested only once in the fragments (DK B138) and with the meaning of "life." Despite the incomplete nature of the text, it is less likely that ψυχή is used more often in the lost sections considering the consistent preference of δαίμων in the extant parts. On Empedocles' "daemon" and Plotinus, see Giannis Stamatellos, *Plotinus and the Presocratics. A Philosophical Study of Presocratic Influences in Plotinus' Enneads* (Albany, NY: State University of New York Press, 2007), 119, 166–171.

65 DK B124 and 126 "clothed in an alien garment" (σαρκῶν ἀλλογνῶτι περιστέλλουσα χιτῶνι).

66 Respectively "to fast from flesh" in DK B144 and "blessed is he who has obtained the riches of divine wisdom" in DK B132 (Guthrie's trans.: W.K.C. Guthrie, *A History of Greek Philosophy: The Presocratic Tradition From Parmenides to Democritus,* vol. 2 [Cambridge: Cambridge University Press, 1965]). See R.M. Wright, *Empedocles: The Extant Fragments* (New Haven and London: Yale University Press, 1981), 70.

the other immortals."⁶⁷ Empedocles' vision strongly resonates with the final lines of Apollo's oracle (*VP* 22.45–63) which celebrate the induction of Plotinus' soul in the company of gods and blessed spirits. Empedocles' *Purifications* and Apollo's oracle in *VP* are driven by the same soteriological goal—the soul's separation from its material embodiment and the restoration of its original divine existence.⁶⁸

In this conceptual background, Plato's programmatic statement that the purpose of human existence is to achieve "likeness to god" (ὁμοίωσις θεῷ, *Theaet.* 176ab) provides the transitional link between the two accounts.⁶⁹ Like Empedocles, he envisions *katharsis* as the means for attaining this purpose (*Phaedo* 65e–70a). In constant pursuit of its appetites and needs, the body's physicality does nothing but contaminate the soul's divine nature. The primary tools for this contamination are the sense perceptions which arouse in the body experience of pleasure and pain, fear and desire, and thus detract the soul from its divine source. Juxtaposing the opposite natures of soul and body, Plato argues in the *Phaedo* 66–67 that, if sense perceptions are the body's means to fulfill its needs, intellection should be the soul's means to fulfill its divine nature. Thus, for him, the soul's separation from the body does not involve the senses but only the most pure application (τοῦτο ποιήσειεν καθαρώτατα) of thought (διάνοια) to object (ἐπ' ἕκαστον).⁷⁰ "If we're ever going to know anything purely [καθαρῶς]," Plato reasons, "we must be rid of it [the body], and must view the objects themselves with the soul by itself."⁷¹ This definition of *katharsis* relates "pure" to intellection and intellection to absolute existence.

---

67 DK B146: εἰς δὲ τέλος ... ἔνθεν ἀναβλαστοῦσι θεοὶ τιμῆσι φέριστοι; DK B147: ἀθανάτοις ἄλλοισιν ὁμέστιοι, αὐτοτράπεζοι, / εὔνιες ἀνδρείων ἀχέων, ἀπόκληροι, ἀτειρεῖς.

68 The Empedoclean motifs in Apollo's oracle are noted by Mark J. Edwards, "A Late Use of Empedocles: The *Oracle on Plotinus*," *Mnemosyne* 43 (1990): 151–155.

69 Above 313.

70 The person, pursuing intellection and the concomitant withdrawal from the material realm, "would be separated as far as possible from his eyes and ears, and virtually from his whole body, on the ground that it confuses the soul, and doesn't allow it to gain truth and wisdom when in partnership with it" (*Phaedo* 66a4–7). Henceforth Gallop's translation (David Gallop, *Plato. Phaedo* [Oxford: Clarendon Press, 1975]).

71 *Phaedo* 66e1–3: εἰ μέλλομέν ποτε καθαρῶς τι εἴσεσθαι, ἀπαλλακτέον αὐτοῦ καὶ αὐτῇ τῇ ψυχῇ θεατέον αὐτὰ τὰ πράγματα.

Predictably, due to the nature of the body, the soul's separation is not easy and attainable by anyone. It requires complete control of all corporeal needs, disregard of the senses, and possession of wisdom. According to Plato, all these characteristics can be acquired only if one is a philosopher, and more specifically a Platonic philosopher "who regards his intellect as prepared, by having been, in a manner, purified" (παρεσκευάσθαι τὴν διάνοιαν ὥσπερ κεκαθαρμένην, *Phaedo* 67c2–3). As he further elaborates,

> Then doesn't purification [κάθαρσις] turns out to be just what's been mentioned for some while in our discussion—the parting of the soul from the body as far as possible [τὸ χωρίζειν ὅτι μάλιστα ἀπὸ τοῦ σώματος τὴν ψυχήν], and the habituating of it to assemble and gather itself together, away from every part of the body [ἐκ τοῦ σώματος συναγείρεσθαι], alone by itself, and to live, so far as it can, both in the present and in the hereafter, released from the body, as from fetters? (*Phaedo* 67c5–d2)

The passage outlines the steps of the process of purification as encapsulated by certain virtues: "the true moral ideal, whether self-control or integrity or courage" (ἡ σωφροσύνη καὶ ἡ δικαιοσύνη καὶ ἡ ἀνδρεία) is "a kind of purification" (κάθαρσίς τις) and "wisdom itself" (αὐτὴ ἡ φρόνησις) is also "a sort of purification" (καθαρμός τις, *Phaedo* 69c13).[72] This ethical element, together with intellection, defines the relation of *katharsis* to philosophy. Only those who pursue philosophy correctly will succeed in purifying the soul because philosophy itself is "a release and parting of soul from body"[73] and only those who have been sufficiently purified by philosophy (οἱ φιλοσοφίᾳ ἱκανῶς καθηράμενοι, *Phaedo* 114c3) will learn the true knowledge of existence and will enjoy the company of the gods.[74] Unlike the later Neoplatonists and the Chaldeans but like Plotinus, Plato understands κάθαρσις only as an intellective process, unaccompanied by ritual practice.[75]

Like the initiates in the ancient mysteries (*Phaedo* 69a–d), philosophers who obtain this sacred knowledge do so in order to become god-like (ὁμοίωσις θεῷ). But unlike the initiates in the mysteries, the

---

72 Plotinus defines these qualities as purificatory virtues in *Enn.* I.2.3, discussed in the next section.
73 *Phaedo* 67d7–10: λύειν δέ γε αὐτήν, ὥς φαμεν, προθυμοῦνται ἀεὶ μάλιστα καὶ μόνοι οἱ φιλοσοφοῦντες ὀρθῶς, καὶ τὸ μελέτημα αὐτὸ τοῦτό ἐστιν τῶν φιλοσόφων, λύσις καὶ χωρισμὸς ψυχῆς ἀπὸ σώματος. Cf. *Phaedo* 114b6–c6.
74 *Phaedo* 69c5–7: ὃς ἂν ἀμύητος καὶ ἀτέλεστος εἰς Ἅιδου ἀφίκηται ἐν βορβόρῳ κείσεται, ὁ δὲ κεκαρθαμένος τε καὶ τετελεσμένος ἐκεῖσε ἀφικόμενος μετὰ θεῶν οἰκήσει.
75 *Phaedo* 67a2–b1.

philosophers' souls who complete the purificatory journey do not have only a glimpse of the divine reality but successfully restore their divine origin.[76] Naturally the ones who achieve this goal are very few and their souls must be exceptional.

IV. Plotinus on Pure Soul(s), Purification, and Purificatory Virtues

As discussed in the previous section, the meaning of "pure" in the philosophical tradition before Plotinus is predominantly soteriological. It conveys the goal and the result of the soul's separation from its degrading relation with corporeality. Plotinus adapts this meaning to his nuanced understanding of soul.[77] It is important to note that, throughout the *Enneads*, he consistently refers to soul in the intelligible realm as "pure." In *Enn.* II.3.9, the treatise *On Whether the Stars are Causes*, he separates the Soul which the Demiurge in the *Timaeus* creates as "the first principle of the soul" (τὴν ἀρχὴν τῆς ψυχῆς) from the soul which the lesser gods create together with passions, angers, desires, pleasures, and pains, as "the other kind of soul" (ψυχῆς ἄλλο εἶδος).[78] He sharpens this cosmogonical distinction in the concepts of descendent and undescendent soul. In *Enn.* III.3, the treatise *On Providence*, the latter is placed in the intelligible realm where "all things are rational principles … all are intellect and pure soul" (νοῦς γὰρ καὶ ψυχὴ καθαρά).[79] In this context, "pure" is used in the sense of "intelligible." This meaning is further supported by his view of Soul as an image of Intellect.[80]

---

76 Here I adapt Foley's interpretation of Demeter's failed attempt to make Demophoon immortal in the *Homeric Hymn of Demeter*. See Helene P. Foley, *The Homeric Hymn to Demeter* (Princeton: Princeton University Press, 1993), 48–52 and 84–97.
77 He distinguishes, however not without obscurity, Soul as an underlying principle of existence from the soul, which permanently abides in the intelligible realm, and from the soul which descends into corporeality. See Henry J. Blumenthal, "Soul, World-Soul and Individual Soul in Plotinus," in *Le Néoplatonisme*, ed. Pierre-Maxime Schuhl and Pierre Hadot (Paris: Centre National de la Recherche Scientifique, 1971), 56–63.
78 *Enn.* II.3.9.6–10. Cf. Plato, *Timaeus* 69c5–d3.
79 *Enn.* III.3.5.17–20.
80 *Enn.* V.1.3.6–7.

The concept of contemplation (θεωρία) is the heart of Plotinus' philosophy. Through it, everything both comes into existence and seeks to learn its source.[81] At the end of *Enn.* III.8, the treatise *On Nature and Contemplation*, Plotinus explains how Intellect substantiates itself by contemplating the One. To convey the essence of this act, he employs the traditional Platonic metaphor of sight and seeing.[82] By "seeing" the One through contemplation, Intellect, as both self-reflexive thought and thinking, comes into existence.[83] At the deepest ontological level, seeing is "knowing." As a result of this contemplation, he defines Intellect as "beautiful" and even "the most beautiful of all" and as lying "in pure light and pure radiance" (ἐν φωτὶ καθαρῷ καὶ αὐγῇ καθαρᾷ).[84] The marked use of the epithet "pure" and the nouns "light" and "radiance" has a specific ontological meaning. "Pure" denotes the non-composite homogeneous nature of Intellect, while "light" and "radiance" convey the idea of Intellect's knowledge and power to know. The two nouns do not express simple rhetorical embellishment but draw out the important distinction between the two principal aspects of Intellect: Intellect, as a self-reflexive thought and thinking, is "light," while Intellect, as "comprising the nature of all things" and thinking all beings, is "radiance." Since "pure" modifies both, it serves as a predicate to Intellect and the intelligible realm as a whole.

If Intellect is "pure," it follows that the undescendent soul must be also "pure soul," which means it is of a homogenous nature, without added corporeal elements. In viewing the undescendent soul as "pure," Plotinus ascribes an ontological meaning to "pure soul" in relation to Intellect. The same view, however, acquires soteriological meaning when considered in relation to body. *Enn.* IV.3, the first treatise in the tripartite series *On Difficulties About the Soul*, deals with the question Amelius asks Apollo's oracle about the location of soul after its departure from the body (*VP* 22.8–9).[85] Like the oracle, which pro-

---

81 In other words, contemplation, with Armstrong 1969–1988, vol. 3, 358, is "the source and goal" of every level of existence, Being, Intellect, all beings, Soul, and physical reality.
82 Cf. Plato's sun analogy in *Rep.* 507a–509c.
83 *Enn.* V.3.11, V.8.10–11.
84 *Enn.* III.8.11.26–29: τοῦ δὴ νοῦ καλοῦ ὄντος καὶ πάντων καλλίστου, ἐν φωτὶ καθαρῷ καὶ αὐγῇ καθαρᾷ κειμένου καὶ τὴν τῶν ὄντων περιλαβόντος φύσιν. Cf. *Phdr.* 250c4. Also above, pp. 328–329 and n. 55.
85 Above 323–324 and n. 39.

nounces that Plotinus' soul has joined the company of the gods and the blessed spirits, Plotinus too holds that:

> Those souls which are pure [ταῖς δὲ τῶν ψυχῶν καθαραῖς οὔσαις] and do not in any way draw anything of body to them will necessarily also have no place anywhere in body. If then they are nowhere in body—for they have no body—a soul of this kind will be where substance and reality and the divine are [οὗ ἐστιν ἡ οὐσία καὶ τὸ ὂν καὶ τὸ θεῖον]—that is in god [ἐν τῷ θεῷ]—there it will be with them and in him. (*Enn.* IV.3.24.21–26)

The above passage contains what we may consider to be Plotinus' conceptual explication of Apollo's oracle. It is in a section discussing soul's posthumous fate. It distinguishes between souls who have not lived a just life and the "pure souls." The former, he explains, are attached to their bodies and are "very aware of bodily punishments" (*Enn.* IV.3.24.20–21). The latter "do not in any way draw anything of body to them" (*Enn.* IV.3.24.22–23). It is clear that Plotinus considers "pure" the souls which are easily detachable from the body.

But what makes a soul easily detachable from the body? The answer can be found in *Enn.* I.8.4.25–26, the treatise *On What are Evils*. In it, we learn that "the perfect soul" (τελεία) which "directs itself to intellect is always *pure*" (πρὸς νοῦν νεύουσα ψυχὴ ἀεὶ καθαρά, emphasis mine) by turning away from matter. This self-turning ability is at the foundation of Plotinus' view of contemplation through which the "pure soul" remains in the intelligible realm "pure, completely defined by intellect" (καθαρὰ οὖν μένει ὁρισθεῖσα νῷ παντελῶς, *Enn.* I.8.4.27–28). In contrast, the soul, which does not remain in the intelligible, mixes itself with corporeal needs and desires and thus becomes "imperfect" (τῷ μὴ τελείῳ) and "a sort of ghost of the first soul" (οἷον ἴνδαλμα ἐκείνης, *Enn.* I.8.4.29–32).[86] Mixed *ex principio* with the needs of the body, it forms "a composite thing, the ensouled body in which the nature of body ... has the greater part."[87] To emphasize the purity of the undescendent soul, Plotinus insists that the composite kind of soul does not deteriorate the uncomposite soul.[88] This, in its turn, means that the mixed soul is ontologically "impure" (ἀκάθαρτος).[89]

---

86 This "ghostly soul" refers to "the other kind of soul" in the discussion of the creation of soul in *Enn.* II.3.9. Discussed above 334.
87 *Enn.* II.3.9.20–24.
88 Men, the heavenly bodies, every embodied thing do not "communicate evil to the other pure soul" (τῇ μὲν ἑτέρᾳ ψυχῇ τῇ καθαρᾷ οὐδὲν φαῦλον δίδωσιν, *Enn.* II.3.9.34–35).

What is then the relation between the ontological and soteriological meaning of "pure?" In regards to the intelligible realm, Plotinus' concept of "pure" has an ontological meaning, but in regards to the material world it has a soteriological meaning and it relates to the concept of purification. In purification, the original ontological distinction between "pure" and "impure" soul acquires the practical meaning of saving the soul from the material contamination of its descent. The goal of purification is to restore the original intelligible purity of soul by separating it from body. In other words, purification is the reversal of soul's embodiment, which entails soul's union with its intelligible source. Plotinus discusses the necessity of purification even at the cosmogonical level of Soul. As soon as he explains the making of the descendent soul, he is interested in the idea of separating the elements which the lesser gods added to soul from it in order to achieve the "pure" Soul which the Demiurge first creates (*Enn.* II.3.9).[90] Switching from the cosmogonical motif in the *Timaeus* to the purificatory theme in the *Theaetetus*, *Phaedo*, and the *Phaedrus*, Plotinus encourages us (as souls) to "'fly from here' and 'separate' from what has been added to us":[91]

> For, as was said in old times, self-control, and courage and every virtue, is a purification, and so is even wisdom itself. This is why the mysteries are right when they say riddlingly that the man who has not been purified [τὸν μὴ κεκαθαρμένον] will lie in mud when he goes to Hades, because the impure is fond of mud by reason of its badness [τὸ μὴ καθαρὸν βορβόρῳ διὰ κάκην φίλον]. (*Enn.* I.6.6.1–5)

The passage recalls Plato's treatment of soul's purification we earlier discussed in the *Phaedo*.[92] It transforms the ontological distinction between the composite and non-composite soul into the ethical distinction between "pure" and "impure" soul. The "pure soul," he says, does not have shape, color, or size, but possesses moderation (σωφροσύνη), all the other virtues (ἀρεταί), greatness (μέγεθος ψυχῆς), a righteous life (ἦθος δίκαιον), a pure morality (σωφροσύνη καθαρά), courage (ἀνδρία), dignity (σεμνότης), and modesty (αἰδώς, *Enn.* 1.6.9). The "impure" soul possesses all the opposite qualities.

---

89 *Enn.* I.6.5.39–43.
90 Discussed above 334.
91 *Enn.* II.3.9.20. Cf. φεύγειν ἐντεῦθεν δεῖ in *Theaet.* 176a8–b1 and χωρίζειν in *Phaedo* 67c6.
92 Cf. *Phaedo* 67c5–d1 and 69c5–6; above 332–334 and nn. 73 and 74.

In the ethical definition of "pure soul," virtue is the means of purification. The role of virtue is to annihilate the corporeal influence on the soul. In this vein, the separation of the soul from the body is not literally that the soul leaves the body, as after death, but that the soul is impermeable to the needs and desires of the body. The virtues help the soul turn its attention from that which is external to it, i.e., the material reality, toward that which is internal, i.e., its own intelligible nature and ontological "purity." These are the virtues which Plotinus defines as "purificatory" (καθάρσεις) in *Enn.* I.2.3.[93] Their goal is to achieve the Platonic ideal of "likeness to god" (ὁμοίωσις θεῷ) prescribed in the *Theaetetus* (176a–b). *Enn.* I.2.3 further divides the virtues, listed in *Enn.* I.6.9, into civic and purificatory. More important, it emphasizes that only the latter lead to "a likeness to god":[94]

> One would not be wrong in calling this state of the soul likeness to God [ὁμοίωσιν λέγοι πρὸς θεόν], in which its activity is intellectual, and it is free in this way from bodily affections. For the Divine too is pure [καθαρὸν γὰρ καὶ τὸ θεῖον], and its activity is of such a kind that that which imitates it has wisdom. (*Enn.* I.2.3.20–22)

It turns out that, at the end, the ethical meaning of "pure," contained in the civic virtues, reverts back to its original ontological meaning of "intelligible" and "divine," presented in the purificatory virtues. With this transition, Plotinus achieves the final goal he has been working towards since his explanation of the cosmogonical division of the universal soul and the individual soul in the *Timaeus* and the ontological division between undescendent and descendent soul. As Soul comes into existence

---

93 *Enn.* I.2 is the nineteenth in the chronological order of the treatises (*VP* 4) and it is written before Porphyry's arrival in Plotinus' circle. For Porphyry himself, the subject of the treatise is fundamental for understanding Plotinus' view of the material world and he places it as the second treatise in the first *Ennead*. He also summarizes the treatise in *Sententiae* 32. For the degrees of Neoplatonic virtues, see John M. Dillon, "Plotinus, Philo and Origen on the Grades of Virtue," in *Platonismus und Christentum. Festschrift für Heinrich Dörrie*, ed. Horst-Dieter Blume and Friedhelm Mann (Münster: Aschendorff, 1983), 92–105, Henri Dominique Saffrey and Alain-Philippe Segonds, *Marinus. Proclus Or Sur le Bonheur*, 2nd ed. (Paris: Les Belles Lettres, 2002), lxix–xcvii; for purificatory virtues, see Jean Trouillard, *La 'Purification Plotinienne* (Paris: Presses Universitaires de France, 1955), 167–203.
94 According to Dillon 1983, Plotinus is the first one to attempt to reconcile Plato's contradictory explanation of civic virtues (πολιτικαὶ ἀρεταί) as controlling the irrational element of the soul in *Rep.* IV. 430c–434c with his view of virtues as purifications of soul from its material attachment (καθάρσεις) in *Phaedo* 69b–c.

when it recognizes itself by contemplating Intellect and as Intellect comes into existence when it thinks itself by contemplating the One, so does the individual soul, as the object of purification (*Enn.* V.8.10–11), when united with its intelligible counterpart, recognize its true self. This self-recognition also reveals the soul's divine origin. Considering how remote this origin is from the soul embedded in us, Plotinus, almost perplexed, asks, "But we–who are we?," in *Enn.* VI.4. His answer is:

> We were there, men who were different, and some of us even gods, pure souls [ψυχαὶ καθαραί] and intellect united with the whole of reality; we were parts of the intelligible, not marked off or cut off but belonging to the whole; and we are not cut off even now. But now another man, wishing to exist, approached that man; and when he found us ... he wound himself around us and attached himself to that man who was then each one of us ... and we have come to be the pair of them, not the one which we were before–and sometimes just the other one which we added on afterwards, when that prior one is inactive and in another way not present. (*Enn.* VI.4.14.18–31)

This answer strikingly resembles Apollo's oracle in celebration of Plotinus' arrival to the company of gods, the soul's ascent in the *Chaldaean Oracles*, and the state of *nirvāṇa* in the *Bhagavad Gītā*.

V. Conclusion

A closer examination of the texts on Plotinus, Iamblichus, and Proclus surprisingly reveals that, among the three Neoplatonists, only Plotinus is called "a pure soul" (καθαρὰ ψυχή, *VP* 23.4). This appellation places him in the most exclusive group of Pythagoras and Plato, the only other philosophers who have received the same epithet.[95] At the end, it turns out that Porphyry himself composed a sophisticated proof of Longinus' praise of Plotinus, as the philosopher who has best understood "the principles of Pythagoras and Plato" (*VP* 20.71–73) by placing Plotinus in the company of their "pure souls" (*VP* 22–23).[96] This is also the

---

95 Stobaeus, *Anth.* 27.1–2: Πυθαγόρας καὶ Πλάτων καθαρὸν ἕκαστον εἶναι τῶν αἰσθητῶν ἐξ ἑκάστου στοιχείου προερχόμενον.

96 This company may also be the same as the men "of pure mind" (τοῦ καθαροῦ νοῦ) in Iamblichus' division of three types of men (*De myst.* V.18), who "employing an intellectual power which is beyond the natural, have disengaged themselves from nature, and turned towards the transcendent and pure intel-

company of the "god-like men" (γένος θείων ἀνθρώπων), the Platonic philosophers, whom Plotinus himself distinguishes as possessing "a greater power and the sharpness of their eyes ... see the glory above and are raised to it."[97]

Trouillard, in his seminal study *La purification Plotinienne*, concludes that Plotinus' philosophy is a philosophy of purification.[98] Although his opinion that such philosophy cannot establish a strict philosophical system but can present itself only in meditation would not be accepted today, his emphasis on the relation between purification and meditation in Plotinus still rings true. His general characterization that Platonism is "une doctrine et une méthode des métamorphoses du moi" also still holds true.[99] As this examination shows, Plotinus views purification not as a practical ritual of theurgic rites but as a contemplative process which transforms the self by withdrawing the soul from every external influence. This process most exactly follows Plato's prescription to become like god by shedding off the sense-corporeal garb and pursuing pure thinking and thus pure existence.[100] "Becoming like god" for Plotinus is to restore the original intelligible nature of soul. This nature is "pure" because as an image of "pure" Intellect, soul must be "pure" itself and, as an image of the pure One, Intellect is "pure" itself.[101] In Plotinus, the soteriological meaning of the concept of "pure" derives from its ontological content and both of them conflate in the understanding of "pure soul."

This is perhaps one of the reasons why theurgy does not occupy Plotinus' attention in the *Enneads*. There is no need of theurgic rites if his idea of soul's return to the intelligible is its self-directed inversed contemplation of the intelligible. The purificatory virtues are as close as Plotinus gets to the idea of a medium between the material world (controlled by the civic virtues) and the intelligible realm. Souls which have united with the One and return back to the body "remain

---

lect." Emma C. Clarke, John M. Dillon and Jackson P. Hershbell, "Iamblichus *On the Mysteries*," in *Writings from the Greco-Roman World*, vol. 4 (Atlanta: Society of Biblical Literature, 2003).

97 *Enn.* V.9.1.16–21.
98 Trouillard 1955, 207–209.
99 Trouillard 1955, 208.
100 Above 332–333.
101 Respectively, *Enn.* V.3.14.14: ὅταν νοῦν καθαρὸν ἔχωμεν and *Enn.* V.5.10.2–5: ἐννόει, τί ἂν εἴη τοῦτο, ὃ ἔστι λαβεῖν ἐφ' ἑαυτοῦ ὂν καθαρὸν οὐδενὶ μιγνύμενον μετεχόντων ἁπάντων αὐτοῦ μηδενὸς ἔχοντος αὐτό.

pure" and "stay close to god."[102] In *Enn.* V.8, the treatise on *Intelligible Beauty*, he compares the soul's vision of its union with the One to the act in which "someone possessed by a god, taken over by Phoebus or one of the Muses, could bring about the vision of the god in himself."[103]

This is precisely the vision Porphyry presents in Apollo's oracle in *VP* 22. Porphyry enacts his own teacher's vision of the soul's union with the One by using the medium which his teacher recommends— Apollo and his Muses—with one important difference, the student identifies his teacher with the soul in this vision. Porphyry understood extremely well the deep ontological roots of Plotinus' concept of "pure soul."

But he also did not understand any less that, in his time, the Plotinian concept had lost its ontological overtones in favor of stronger soteriological and theurgical motifs, as presented in his other works and in the philosophy of Iamblichus and Proclus. This shift must have also been fostered by the Neoplatonists' increased exposure to the soteriological ideas of their permanent neighbors, the Persians and the Indians.[104] Thus, if we want to study Plotinus' concept of purification in the context of the two philosophies in which we know he is particularly interested, we cannot ignore their silent parallels in Porphyry's presentation of Plotinus' soul and we need to do the best with what we have, Plotinus' ontology in the *Enneads* and Porphyry's portrayal of "pure soul" in *VP* 22–23. As Plotinus' "pure soul" is between the two realms of existence, so is the concept of it between the East and the West.

---

102 Cf. *Enn.* V.8.11.7–8: καθαρὸς μένων ἐφεξῆς ἐστιν αὐτῷ [θεῷ].
103 *Enn.* V.8.10.41–43.
104 On the concept of "daemon" as "the expression of truism" in the second century, see E.R. Dodds, *Pagan and Christian in an Age of Anxiety. Some Aspects of Religious Experience from Marcus Aurelius to Constantine* (Cambridge: Cambridge University Press, 1965), 37–68.

Iamblichus, Theurgy, and the Soul's Ascent

John Finamore

A basic doctrine of Platonic philosophy, found in Plato's *Symposium* 202b-203a, taught that gods do not mix directly with human beings but conduct their relations with mortals through the intermediate class of daemons. This doctrine had important ramifications for the history of later Platonism. Plotinus (c.204-c.270 C.E.), the first Neoplatonist, presented a doctrine whereby the philosopher on his or her own could bridge the gap between humanity and the gods, creating a salvific ascent to the gods via philosophy and searching within oneself. His disciple Porphyry (c.234-c.305 C.E.), although more sympathetic to magic and ritual than Plotinus, still believed that philosophy alone could raise the human soul to the gods. Iamblichus (c. 245-c. 325 C.E.) introduced a new turn in Neoplatonism, arguing that philosophy alone was insufficient to bring gods and mortals into contact and establishing the need for ritual. It is this change that we will examine in this paper, specifically how Iamblichus thought that human beings could ever ascend to the gods who are so far removed from them and how he conceived of the role of theurgy in the ascent.

I. The Metaphysical Hierarchy

Taking aim at Plotinus' belief that the soul can ascend without divine assistance, Iamblichus retorts (*De Myst.* 2.11, 96.13–97.2):

> It is not thinking that brings theurgists into contact with the gods, since what would hinder those who engage in contemplative philosophy from having theurgic union with the gods? As it is, the truth lies elsewhere. It is the ritual accomplishment of ineffable acts, performed divinely, surpassing any intellectual processes, and the power of unspeakable symbols known only to the gods that accomplish theurgical union.

Theurgy is the ritual activity performed by philosophical priests (theurgists) that brings the aid of the divine to human beings. Literally, "theurgy" is "god's work," and involves the human agent calling on the god, usually through intermediary divinities. The god illuminates the human being with his divine ray (separately, without descending himself, in accord with Plato's precept in the *Symposium*). The god then "works on" the human soul. We will look more at the role of illumination and theurgy shortly.[1] For now, the important point to note is that Iamblichus vehemently denies that philosophy alone can bring the soul to the gods. Instead we must look to religious ritual.

In order to understand how Iamblichus made the soul's salvation dependent on divine assistance it is essential to understand both the complex nature of the Iamblichean universe and the dual nature of the human soul itself. Iamblichus developed both doctrines in reaction to Plotinus.

Plotinus' metaphysical scheme posits four hypostases or metaphysical levels: One, Intellect, Soul, Nature. The One in its simplicity is the first principle and from its overflowing power creates the lower orders. First, Intellect separates from the One, proceeds outward, turns, and contemplates the One thereby becoming a dyad: a mind that thinks its object as other. The Hypostasis Soul proceeds from the Intellect. The human soul exists in time, making use of discursive thinking, moving from topic to topic. The soul helps order the lowest realm of Nature. The One is a unifying principle and is present to all the lower strata. The human soul, through its descent into Nature, may be unaware of the One, but its effect is still present. If the human being can look within and see the power of the One there, then ascent is possible. This knowledge of the One comes through the study of philosophy and its associated ascetic practices. Access to Intellect and the One is open to any soul through itself once it comes to know the truth about its role and place in the universe. Whether the soul ascends to those principles is dependent solely upon it.[2]

Iamblichus created a more complex, richer universe, one more in keeping with his belief that the human soul on its own is incapable of reconnecting to the higher levels.[3] In place of the single One of the Plo-

---

[1] For more on theurgy, illumination, divine *symbola*, and Iamblichus' reaction to Plotinian contemplation, see my "Plotinus and Iamblichus on Magic and Theurgy," *Dionysius* 17 New Series (1999): 83–94; for the present passage from the De Mysteriis, see 84–85.

[2] For a good introduction to the Plotinian system, see Pauliina Remes, *Neoplatonism* (Stocksfield: Acumen, 2008), 35–98 and Dominic J. O'Meara, *An Introduction to the Enneads* (Oxford: Oxford University Press, 1993), 12–78.

[3] See the comparison of the two universes at the end of this chapter.

tinian universe, Iamblichus posited three.[4] The next lower realm, The Intelligible, was made up of three moments: Being, Life, and Mind. The Intellectual Realm divided that Mind into three phases: Unparticipated Intellect, Participated Intellect, and Intellect-in-Participation. Thus Intellect itself was triple.[5] The Psychic Realm is where the human soul resides, but human souls are at the end of another triad: Hypercosmic Soul (Soul in its unparticipated aspect), the Cosmic Soul, (Soul in its participated aspect), and individual souls (Soul in participation). But even here there are different levels of individual soul. There are the "superior classes" (i.e., superior to human souls): angels, daemons, heroes, purified human souls. The human soul occupies the lowest rung of the ladder.

Each step in this chain from the highest One to human soul involves a decrease in purity and in the ability to cognize the objects above it. As

---

4   See Damascius, *On First Principles* II.1.4–8; 25.1–17; 28.1–6. Cf. John M. Dillon *Iamblichi Chalcidensis in Platonis Dialogos Commentariorum Fragmenta*, ed. with translation and commentary. Philosophia Antiqua 23 (Leiden: Brill, 1973), 29–33 and John M. Dillon, "Iamblichus of Chalcis (ca. AD 240–325)," *Aufstieg und Niedergang der römischen Welt* II, 36.2 (1987): 880–885. The concept of multiple Ones may seem odd, since a One should be unitary, but there is a philosophical principle involved for Iamblichus. Plotinus' One took on many roles. It was transcendent and uninvolved in the universe that devolved from it, but it was also the giver of unity, beauty, and goodness to that world. It was therefore both transcendent and immanent. Thus, Iamblichus determined that even the One had levels, however unified they might be. He posited a Completely Ineffable One at the top of his system. It was separate and uninvolved with entities below it. A second One acted on the Indefinite Dyad below it (a dual principle of multiplicity). Then, beneath the Dyad, there was the result of the mixing of Unity and Multiplicity, the One Being, which partakes of both unity and being and is therefore a One that is multiple: a source of multiplicity for all below it. Thus Iamblichus has isolated three phases of unity within the realm of the One.

5   For the Iamblichean principle that "an Unparticipated Monad rules every order before the Participated," see *In Tim.* Fr. 54 and Dillon's note *ad loc*. See also Dillon 1973, 33. This becomes a basic tenet of later Neoplatonism. Each realm is presided over by an entity that is unparticipated by the level below it but then the second moment of the realm transfers the essence of that moment to the third moment. Thus human souls develop from the Participated or Cosmic Soul, which in its turn is a result of procession from the Unparticipated or Hypercosmic Soul. A corollary for Iamblichus' doctrine is that the lowest moment of one realm is also the highest moment of the next below it. Thus the Intellect in Participation (i.e., the Demiurge proper) is the Unparticipated Soul under another guise. Again, the path of ascent is eased by such considerations even as the distance is increased.

in the Plotinian universe, the various levels indicate the distance between lower and higher entities. For Iamblichus the distance is greater, and human souls are far removed from the gods above. As in Plotinus again, however, the various levels border on each other and thus the ascent is possible if one takes incremental steps. Thus, although the human soul is far removed from Intellect (say), it is relatively close to the superior classes above it, and these in turn are closer to the Cosmic Soul, etc. For Iamblichus, the various levels define both the metaphysical distance to be traversed by the human soul and the means by which it can ascend. The universe is large and the human soul is not so powerful on its own, but if it can gain assistance from the souls and gods above it, it can rise.

Before we come to the soul's ascent through ritual practice, there is one more important Iamblichean doctrine that has a direct effect on that ascent. We have noted already that the human soul *qua* individual soul is the lowest category in its class, ranking below the superior classes. Iamblichus interpreted this inferiority in accordance with Plato's *Timaeus* (41d), where the Demiurge is said to have blended the human souls in the same proportion as the Cosmic Soul but with a lesser degree of purity. For Iamblichus, Plato meant that the human souls were inferior in the sense that they were flawed. In its very essence the soul partakes of both its embodied life on earth and its separated life in the Intelligible, but it can never permanently be a part of either. The soul is defined by these two essences, each of which is opposed to the other. Thus, even when the soul has ascended to Intellect and cognizes the Forms therein, it does not fully belong there and in its essence it is slipping downward. Only the aid of the Intellect itself can save it from falling away.[6] Thus, there is a sort of fault in the soul that prevents it from continual association with the higher divinities unless those divinities intervene in its favor while it is present to them. The soul is weak in its very nature, unable to ascend on its own or to remain once it has been raised above.

---

6   For the precarious position of even the ascended human soul, see the passages from Pseudo-Simplicius' *De Anima* Commentary in John F. Finamore and John M. Dillon, *Iamblichus,* De Anima: *Text, Translation, and Commentary* (Leiden: Brill, 2002), 232–239 with notes *ad loc.* For the soul's need for the Intellect when it is fully ascended and in union with the Intellect, see John F. Finamore, "Iamblichus and the Intermediate Nature of the Human Soul," in *Perspectives sur le néoplatonisme*, ed. Martin Achard and Jean-Marc Narbonne (Laval: Presses de l'Université, 2009), 129–134.

II. Iamblichus' *De Mysteriis* and Ascent

Given that the soul is in this position and that the gods do not descend into our world, Iamblichus must explain how the human soul could ever ascend to the gods. He describes this process in his *De Mysteriis*, a work written in response to Porphyry's letter to the probably fictitious Egyptian priest Anebo.[7] Porphyry's letter, which exists only in fragments mainly preserved from Iamblichus' work, presents a formidable philosophical argument against the efficacy of all manner of rites offered to the gods. Iamblichus replies in ten books of the *De Mysteriis*, whose actual title was probably *The Reply of the Master Abamon to the Letter of Porphyry to Anebo, and the Solution to the Questions it Contains*.[8] Throughout the work, Iamblichus, taking the role of Anebo's teacher Abamon,[9] refutes every point that Porphyry makes, often berating the philosopher as if he were a mere tyro.

Since the gods cannot come to us, we must ascend to them. How can we deficient souls do so? Iamblichus offers two separate but related solutions in the *De Mysteriis*, and we shall consider each in turn. The first is the obvious one: the intermediate divinities can help with our ascent. But how is this possible? Iamblichus' doctrine of these intermediary classes and their roles is derived from Plato. In the famous myth of the *Phaedrus* 246a-250c, human souls (each pictured as a charioteer driving two white horses, one good and one recalcitrant) endeavor to follow the chariots of the gods as they rise to the world of the Forms (for Iamblichus, the Intelligible and the Intellectual Realms) and strive to glimpse the Forms there. Plato imagines this ride occurring in the time between the earthly lives of the soul, when the soul is disembodied. It thus can follow the gods to that "place above the heavens" (*Phdr.* 247c3), where bodies would be inappropriate. Plato imagines the gods as the twelve Olympians (minus Hestia, who remains home, 247a1–2). The souls follows in their train, but they are not alone, for daemons follow the gods as well (246e6). It is clear that Iamblichus in-

---

7 But see Emma C. Clark, John M. Dillon and Jackson P. Hershbell, *Iamblichus, On the Mysteries* (Atlanta: Society of Biblical Literature, 2003), xxix n. 54 for the possibility that Anebo was a member of "Iamblichus' circle."
8 Édouard Des Places, *Jamblique, Les Mystères D'Égypte* (Paris: Les Belles Lettres 1966), 6.
9 On the significance of the name (or lack thereof), see Clark, Dillon and Hershbell 2003, xxxiv-xxxvii. I accept their arguments that the name "Abamon" is not to be associated with the Egyptian god Ammon.

terpreted this myth broadly, taking the gods as (probably) the invisible gods above the cosmos[10] and the daemons as including all the superior classes. These groups view the Forms without problem (247de), but human souls see them (if at all) with difficulty and unclearly.

Following another hint in Plato (*Phdr.* 252c3-d2), Iamblichus believes that each human soul follows in the train of a single god (Zeus or Ares or another). These trains or "chains" (*seirai*) serve to connect the invisible gods above the cosmos to their visible counterparts and to their following of superior classes. Thus, each human soul was originally connected to a chain of divinities who may help him in his ascent, a chain that he had followed before birth in a body. Thus, appropriate sacrifice must be made to these divinities.[11]

In the first two books of the *De Mysteriis*, Iamblichus introduces and differentiates the superior classes.[12] Angels (including a separate and higher sub-group of archangels), like the visible gods (the planets and stars), do not descend to our realm. They remain with the gods above. The daemons, heroes, and purified human souls can descend to aid us. Thus, human beings could begin with sacrifices to these lower three superior classes who are closer to us in this realm. These in turn (as Plato stated of the daemons in the *Symposium*) would carry our prayers to the gods—for Iamblichus, these would be the gods in our and the superior classes' chain.

At this point one might assume as Porphyry had (*De Myst.* 5.1) that the smoke from animal sacrifices entices the gods and superior classes. Iamblichus chides Porphyry for this view, arguing that the gods are

---

10   We possess no record of Iamblichus' opinion on this point, but we know that Proclus conceived these gods as the Intelligible-and-Intellectual gods in his *Platonic Theology* 4.4. On this topic, see my "Proclus on Ritual Practice in Neoplatonic Religious Philosophy," in *Being or Good? Metamorphosis of Neoplatonism*, ed. Agnieszka Kijewska (Lublin: KUL, 2004), 125–127. It seems likely that Iamblichus would have chosen Hypercosmic gods as well, for the visible gods cannot easily be imagined leaving the cosmos.

11   For the role of daemons in theurgy and the differences between Iamblichus' and Porphyry's views about daemons, see Gregory Shaw, *Theurgy and the Soul* (University Park, PA: Pennsylvania State University Press, 1995), 130–131.

12   For this arrangement of the superior classes into those that do not descend and those that do—a purely Iamblichean view that differs from that of both Proclus and Damascius—see John F. Finamore, "Iamblichus's Interpretation of Parmenides' Third Hypothesis," in *Plato's Parmenides and Its Heritage*, vol. 2., ed. John D. Turner and Kevin Corrigan (Atlanta: Society of Biblical Literature, 2010), 122–131.

far removed from anything material and antithetical to it (5.3) and that the smoke could not rise more than five stades off the ground let alone reach the gods in the cosmos (5.4). Iamblichus argues that the reasons that Porphyry had listed for sacrificing to the gods (giving honor to them, thanking them for gifts they have bestowed, or offering greater gifts than the gifts they bestowed) are incorrect (5.4). Rather, we sacrifice to the gods to effect the separation of the soul from body and its ascent to the gods (5.5). Neither the gods nor the superior classes are interested in our material offerings *qua* matter. The sacrificial objects have a special association with them, as we will see shortly.

To understand sacrifices, or indeed any ritual act between human beings and divinity, we must understand ascent ritual. Thus, Iamblichus places sacrifice and ritual on a firm footing with philosophy. All ritual is about the soul's ascent, and Iamblichean philosophy is aimed at the same goal. The two, philosophy and ritual, work hand in hand, and philosophy alone is insufficient because it cannot raise us to the gods.

Although we might begin our initiation to ascent with the lower groups of the superior classes, Iamblichus makes it clear that the power they have is derived from the gods themselves. In book III of the *De Mysteriis*, Iamblichus considers different sorts of exchange between human beings and the gods via ritual practice. In the first chapter, he speaks of divination, although what he says is soon seen to be applicable to all rituals. Divination, he says, is not obtained through material means or by human endeavor alone. "All its authority comes from the gods, is received from the gods, and is accomplished through divine works or signs" (3.1, 100.13–101.1). Thus, false divinations are caused by human error or malfeasance. The gods provide only truth, if we know how to obtain it from them.

This leads us to the second way in which human souls may ascend to the gods. It works in tandem with the first, *viz.* beginning our ascents with the lower superior classes, since the gods in fact are the principles behind those divine intermediaries. In order to rise to the gods, we must be adapted to receiving their aid directly. This might seem impossible, since the gods cannot descend to us, but there is a way for the gods to affect those in this realm: divine illumination.[13]

---

13 For the importance of divine illumination in Iamblichean philosophy and the way it works, see John F. Finamore, *Iamblichus and the Theory of the Vehicle of the Soul* (Chico, CA: Scholars Press, 1985), 125–155 and John F. Finamore, "Iamblichus on Light and the Transparent," in *The Divine Iamblichus: Philosopher*

The concept of divine illumination plays an important role in book 3 of the *De Mysteriis*, where Iamblichus discusses various forms of ritual practice. In chapter 14, Iamblichus responds to Porphyry's concern about the various means by which we seem to gain foreknowledge by saying that all divination occurs by illumination (132.7–9). The gods shine their light from above and "illuminate the ethereal and luminous vehicle with divine light" (132.8–9). This vehicle is a spiritual body, made from aether (the fifth element, the substance of the planets and stars) and attached to the rational soul. It provides a body for the soul's sojourn in the heavens, and it is to this body that the material body attaches in our earthly existence. Its role, besides housing the rational and irrational souls, is as the seat of human imagination. It is thus critical for receiving images from the gods.[14] The gods direct their ethereal light to the soul's ethereal vehicle, and (like to like) imbue the vehicle with divine images, which in the case of divination provide evidence for future events. Iamblichus emphasizes often (as he does in 3.14, 134.10–11)[15] that the gods remain external to our world. Thus the gods do not descend but are able to reach out to us, if we are prepared to receive their luminous message.

Divine illumination explains another principle of ritual practice. In *De Mysteriis* 5, where Iamblichus (as we have seen) corrects Porphyry's mistaken view of animal sacrifices, the gods illuminate not only human beings but also plants and animals. Iamblichus writes (5.9, 11–14):

> … when we grasp that some animal or plant in the earth preserves inviolately and purely the will of its maker, then through such we appropriately set in motion the demiurgic cause that rests in it purely.

The chain that exists from the gods to us is here developed further to extend from the Intellect (and presumably ultimately from the One) to the sacrificial animal itself or to sacred plants. Thus, in 3.17, Iamblichus includes "pebbles, staffs, wood, stones, fire, barley" in his list of illuminated objects (141.11–12),[16] and then a few lines later (142.3–7)

---

    and Man of Gods, ed. H. J. Blumenthal and E. Gillian Clark (Bristol: Bristol Classical Press, 1993), 55–61.

14 See Finamore 1985, 11–27.

15 Cf. *De Myst.* 1.9, 30.9–31.8; 3.12, 128.4–13; 3.14, 143.10–15; 3.17, 140.10–18.

16 See also *De Myst.* 5.23, 233.9–13. Cf. Shaw (1995) 48. These illuminated objects can be used in various rituals, including the animation of statues (5.23,

he brings in human beings with feeble minds. In this way, Iamblichus can explain the use of ritual objects and even of young witless boys in sacred rites.[17] They themselves are illuminated by the gods and receive from them special powers that a philosopher-theurgist can exploit in rituals. Again, the god is separate, existing above and apart from the material world in which the ritual animal, object, or boy resides.

This notion of the gods illuminating something or someone in the material world leads us to another important feature of Iamblichus' doctrine: receptability. For animals, plants, and inanimate objects, the method of participation in the divine light is obvious. The gods have selected these, and so they are prepared in advance for the reception of the gods' rays. The trained theurgist will be able to recognize them and use them in rituals, whether the rituals operate through the superior classes or begin immediately with the gods themselves. In the case of human beings, the question of receptivity is not so simple. We have a will of our own, and we have an irrational soul that interferes with the processes of the rational one. How do we make ourselves capable of receiving the god's light?

Iamblichus tackles this issue in *De Myst.* 3.11, while he is discussing how certain oracles operate. Porphyry had (mistakenly, Iamblichus thinks) associated the prophetic ability of priests and priestesses with matter: the priest of Apollo at Colophon with water, the priestess at Delphi with fumes emitted from the earth, and the priest at Didyma with inhaling vapors from the water.[18] Iamblichus argues instead that divination arises because of divine illumination.

Let's consider his discussion of the oracle at Colophon (3.11, 124.8–126.3). Iamblichus grants that the water that the priest imbibes provokes the priest to prophecy. It is the way it does so that requires explanation. He denies that the water houses a "prophetic pneuma" (124.13–14), for this would indicate that the god was present to the water, which Iamblichus must deny (124.14–125.3):

> For the divine does not permeate what participates in it in an extended or fragmented way, but when providing from without and illuminating the spring, it fills it from itself with its prophetic power.

234.1–4). For whole geographical regions participating in illumination, see 5.24.
17 For the use of boys in magical rites, see Apuleius, *Apology* 42–43.
18 On these three oracles of Apollo, see the notes of Des Places 1966, 112–113, and of Clarke, Dillon and Hershbell 2003, 145.

Thus, again, the god illuminates from above and separately, not being physically present to the water, but its ethereal light does enter the water and provides the potential for divination through it. The illumination, however, is not sufficient. The priest's psychic vehicle must be prepared to accept the god's gift. Iamblichus writes that the priest prepares himself in advance (125.11–126.3):

> Before he drinks he abstains from food during the whole day and night, and as he embarks on his frenzy, he withdraws alone to certain sacred precincts inaccessible to the crowd, and through separation and freedom from human affairs he makes himself pure for receiving the god. From this he possesses the inspiration of the god as it illuminates the pure seat of his soul, and he offers it no hindrance to its possession and perfect, unimpeded presence.

The divine illumination is only part of the ritual. The priest must be prepared, through fasting and physical withdrawal to an appropriate place, to receive the light. There are therefore two aspects to any rite: divine illumination and someone or something appropriately prepared to receive the illumination. Proper preparation is therefore crucial to the successful accomplishment of any ritual involving a human subject. This suggests a third necessary feature: a trained individual who knows how the sacrifice works, i.e., the theurgist.

If we return briefly to the sacred stones used in some rites, we can see that although the stones have been illuminated by the gods and are adapted to receive the divine light, not anyone can use the stone effectively. The theurgist in this case must himself or herself be prepared to use the stone. This would again be a matter of ascetic purificatory actions, of course, but it should be clear now that proper philosophical education is also necessary so that the theurgist will know how to be prepared. In order to use the stone properly, the theurgist must be receptive to the god as well, and it is Iamblichean philosophy that teaches how this state can be achieved. The same would be true in the case of simple-minded children. They are chosen for such rites because they can be manipulated as inanimate objects are: the theurgist prepares the boy for the rite so that the boy may be illuminated by and filled with the god. This also explains why the boy does not understand the messages of the gods any more than the frenzied priest at Colophon does. His rational soul is not operating in harmony with the divine message. It is the theurgist who makes use of the boy as a medium (much as he or she would make use of a stone or plant) and interprets the divine message. Thus, it is the theurgist in these cases who must be purified and trained.

A badly trained or false theurgist cannot bring about a successful rite. In *De Myst.* 3.13, Iamblichus discusses such charlatans who try to use shortcuts in their rites, such as standing on characters.[19] They do sometimes succeed in drawing down "a weak phantasmal appearance" (130.3–4) which evil daemons can manipulate. These evil daemons are not in the chain of any god but rather are free agents dedicated to causing trouble to would-be theurgists and to humanity generally. Iamblichus complains (131.1–132.2) that such pseudo-theurgists circumvent the correct practice of theurgy, and so fail to contact the gods at all. This is not surprising since they have aligned themselves with renegade evil daemons who have no connection to those higher powers. The failure is caused ultimately by laziness and a lack of philosophical knowledge.

Just as theurgists must be properly trained and pure in order to effect rites involving sacred objects or witless boys, they must also have the same training when they work a rite involving their own souls. In *De Myst.* 3.14, Porphyry raises the case of those who "are conscious of themselves in other ways but are frenzied in their imaginative faculty" (132.3–4). As we have seen above, Iamblichus associates such rites with divine illumination in which the divine rays strike the soul's vehicle, its seat of imagination. The gods, as it were, take over the vehicle and replace the theurgist's own images with their own. As Iamblichus goes on to say (133.3–7):

> … the divine presence and illumination are separate. Thus, the soul's attention and rational functioning follow what is happening since the divine light does not touch them. But the imaginative faculty is frenzied because, being alert to these sorts of images, it is roused not from itself but from the gods, since its customary human activity has been completely suppressed.

Thus, in cases in which the theurgist or medium is conscious of the images and can report them after the rite is completed, the gods' illumination affects only the ethereal vehicle and not the rational soul itself. This requires rigorous philosophical training so that the rational soul stays alert and "tuned in" as the rite is underway. Nonetheless, all three aspects of the ritual practice are present: the divine illumination, the illu-

---

19 These characters are inscriptions of letters or drawing on papyrus or other materials. We have evidence of some in the *Greek Magical Papyri*, but not specifically one that the practitioner stands on. For an example of incising characters on tin and throwing it into a river to make a magic rite effective, see *PGM* 7.417–422.

minated object (in this case, the psychic vehicle), and the trained theurgist (here his or her rational soul), who is receptive of the god and trained to endure the god's illuminative presence.

How then does the ascent work? It is caused by the divine illumination. The ethereal rays irradiate the ethereal vehicle, in which the rational soul is housed. The soul (housed in the vehicle) is drawn upward via these rays. If the rays originate from a daemon, the soul rises to that daemon's ethereal vehicle; if from an angel, to its vehicle; if from a planetary god, to that god's ethereal body. If the illumination originates higher, from gods or principles without ethereal bodies, then the soul ascends to the ethereal body of its leader god, leaves its ethereal vehicle behind with that god's ethereal body, and ascends higher as pure rational soul to the elevating divinity. The vehicle waits below for the soul's return. The higher, immaterial gods therefore work through the subordinate gods and divinities in its chain. There is a single great chain stretching (ultimately) from the One to the soul.[20] The type of ritual used depends on the divinity to which we offer it, but every ritual is aimed in an appropriate manner to some divinity in the chain. The goal is separation of the soul (in its vehicle) from the body and union with the gods.

III. Conclusion

We can now see how Iamblichus bridged the gap between mortal and god in a new and innovative way. The human soul is separated from the gods and cannot ascend to them alone since the distance is too great and the soul itself is flawed. Human beings are not left abandoned on the face of the earth, however. The gods have provided a means of access through their intermediaries and through divine illumination. The gods have left as well tokens of their power on the earth, irradiated with their ethereal light. Men and women trained in Iamblichean philosophy act as intermediaries, being able to explain and perform ritual practice for others less enlightened. Thus, human souls are not trapped below but can, if they study philosophy *and* use the correct rituals, ascend again to the gods.

---

20 For a more detailed explanation of the ritual ascent, see Finamore 1985, 125–155.

Comparison of the Plotinian and Iamblichean Universes:

Plotinus	Iamblichus
The One	Completely Ineffable One
	|
	Simply One
	/\
	Limit — The Unlimited
	\/
	The One Existent
	|||
Intellect	Being
	|
	Life
	|
	Mind
	|||
	Unparticipated Intellect
	|
	Participated Intellect
	|
	Intellect-in-Participation
	|||
Soul	Hypercosmic (Unparticipated Soul)
	|
	World (Participated Soul)
	|
	Individual Souls (in Participation)
	(1) Superior classes:
	angels, daemons, heroes,
	purified human souls
	(2) Human souls
	|||
Nature	Nature

About the Contributors

VISHWA ADLURI received his Ph.D. in Philosophy from the New School for Social Research in 2002. His research focuses mainly on Plato, the Greek and Indian epics, and the tradition of rational soteriology in ancient philosophy from the Pre-Socratics to the Neo-Platonists. He is the author of *Parmenides, Plato and Mortal Philosophy: Return from Transcendence* (London: Continuum Publishing, 2011) and has also written on Plato, Plotinus, and interpretations of ancient philosophy in 20th century Continental thought. He also recently published a translation of Arbogast Schmitt's *Die Moderne und Platon: Zwei Grundformen Europäischer Rationalität* (*Modernity and Plato: Two Paradigms of Rationality* [Rochester, NY: Camden House, 2012]).

ALBERTO BERNABÉ is Professor of Greek Philology at Universidad Complutense de Madrid, Spain. His research focuses on Greek religion and philosophy, especially mystery religions and their relationship to the Presocratics and to Platonism. He has published an edition of the Orphic Fragments in Bibliotheca Teubneriana and the book *Instructions for the Netherworld: The Orphic Gold Tablets* (Leiden: Brill, 2008) in collaboration with Ana I. Jiménez San Cristobal.

LUC BRISSON, researcher at the National Center for Scientific Research in Paris, France, has published widely on both Plato and Plotinus, including bibliographies, translations, and commentaries. He has also published numerous works on the history of philosophy and religions in antiquity.

WALTER BURKERT is Emeritus Professor of Classical Philology at the University of Zürich. He has been working on Greek religion from an anthropological perspective, on Greek philosophy and on Greek-Oriental interrelations. His books include *Lore and Science in Ancient Pythagoreanism* (Cambridge, MA: Harvard University Press, 1972), *Homo Necans: The Anthropology of Ancient Greek Sacrificial Ritual and Myth* (Berkeley, CA: University of California Press, 1983), *Greek Religion: Archaic and Classical* (Malden, MA: Blackwell Publishing, 1985), *Creation of the Sacred: Tracks of Biology in Early Religions* (Cambridge, MA: Harvard

University Press, 1996), *The Orientalizing Revolution: Near Eastern Influence on Greek Culture in the Early Archaic Age* (Cambridge, MA: Harvard University Press, 1992), *Babylon Memphis Persepolis: Eastern Contexts of Greek Culture* (Cambridge, MA: Harvard University Press, 2004).

JOHN BUSSANICH is Professor and Chair of the Department of Philosophy at the University of New Mexico. He is also the co-editor of *Ancient Philosophy*. His research interests include wisdom, ethics, and mystical themes in ancient Greek philosophy, especially Pythagoreanism, Socrates, Plato, and the Neoplatonists. Other interests include comparative philosophy and mysticism in South Asia.

JOHN F. FINAMORE is Professor at the University of Iowa. He has published two books on the Neoplatonic philosopher Iamblichus, including (with John Dillon) an edition with commentary of the fragments of Iamblichus' *De Anima*. He has also written numerous papers on Iamblichus and other ancient philosophers, especially on the topic of the soul.

MIGUEL HERRERO DE JÁUREGUI is Assistant Professor of Greek Language and Literature at Universidad Complutense de Madrid, Spain. He is the author of *Orphism and Christianity in Late Antiquity* (Berlin: de Gruyter, 2010) and of several papers on Greek literature and religion and its Christian reception. He is currently preparing a book on early Greek religious poetry and a commentary on the *Protrepticus* of Clement of Alexandria.

JOHN LENZ is Associate Professor and Chair of the Department of Classics at Drew University in Madison, NJ, USA. A former Fulbright Fellow in Greece, he received his Ph.D. in Classical Studies from Columbia University. He was President of the Bertrand Russell Society from 1994–98. Publications include "Bertrand Russell and the Greeks," "Deification of the Philosopher in Classical Greece," and "How Epicurean Science Saves Humanity in Lucretius."

STEPHEN MENN is Associate Professor of Philosophy at McGill University and Professor für Philosophie der Antike und Gegenwart at the Humboldt-Universität zu Berlin. He works on ancient Greek and medieval Arabic and Latin philosophy, theology, and mathematical science. He is the author of *Plato on God as Nous* (Carbondale, IL: Southern Illinois University Press, 1995), *Descartes and Augustine* (Cambridge:

Cambridge University Press, 2002), and the forthcoming *The Aim and the Argument of Aristotle's Metaphysics*.

BARBARA SATTLER is Assistant Professor at Yale University. She works mainly on ancient metaphysics and philosophy of science in the period from the Presocratics to Plato and Aristotle. She recently published articles on time and space in Plato's *Timaeus* as well as on Parmenides' logical operators and criteria for philosophy. She is currently finishing a book manuscript on how motion and change came to be established as a proper object of scientific endeavour in ancient Greece.

ARBOGAST SCHMITT is Emeritus Professor of Classical Philology at Philipps University, Marburg. He is the author of *Die Moderne und Platon: Zwei Grundformen europäischer Rationalität* (Stuttgart: J. B. Metzler, 2003 and 2008) and of a translation and commentary of Aristotle's *Poetics* (Berlin: Akademie Verlag, 2008). His main research area is the relationship of Platonic-Aristotelian epistemology to modern epistemology. Other research areas are Homeric epic, Attic tragedy, and literary theory in antiquity as well as its reception in early modernity and modernity.

SVETLA SLAVEVA-GRIFFIN is Associate Professor of Classics at the Florida State University. She is the author of *Plotinus on Number* (Oxford: Oxford University Press, 2009) and articles on Plato, Plotinus, and the Platonic tradition. Her main research specialization is the history of Platonism, especially the dialogue between literary form and philosophical content, the relationship of ancient philosophy to disciplines such as poetry, myth, religion, and medicine, and Neoplatonism and its interaction with Eastern thought. Along with Pauliina Remes, she is currently editing the forthcoming *Handbook of Neoplatonism* (Durham, NC: Acumen).

Bibliography

Adam, James, ed. *The Republic of Plato*. Cambridge: Cambridge University Press, 1963.
Adamson, Peter. "Plotinus on Astrology." *OSAPh* 35 (2008): 265–91.
Adkins, Arthur W.H. *Merit and Reponsibility: A Study in Greek Values*. Oxford: Clarendon Press, 1960.
—. *From the Many to the One*. London: Constable, 1970.
Adluri, Vishwa. "Initiation into the Mysteries: The Experience of the Irrational in Plato." *Mouseion* III.6 (2006): 407–423.
—. "Plato's Saving *Mūthos*: The Language of Salvation in the *Republic*." *International Journal of the Platonic Tradition* 8.1 (forthcoming).
—. *Parmenides, Plato and Mortal Philosophy: Return from Transcendence*. London: Continuum, 2011.
Adluri, Vishwa, and Joydeep Bagchee. *The Nay Science: A History of German Indology*. New York: Oxford University Press, 2013.
Aellen, Christian. *À la recherche de l'ordre cosmique*. Zürich: Akanthus, 1994.
Albinus, Lars. "The *Katabasis* of Er. Plato's Use of Myths, exemplified by the Myth of Er." In *Essays on Plato's* Republic, edited by Erik Nis Ostenfeld, 91–105. Aarhus: Aarhus University Press, 1998.
—. *The House of Hades. Studies in Greek Eschatology*. Aarhus: Aarhus University Press, 2000.
Albright, W. F. "The Anatolian Goddess Kubaba" *AOF* 5 (1928/9): 229–231.
Alt, Karin. "Dieseits und Jenseits in Platons Mythen von der Seele." *Hermes* 110 (1982): 278–299.
—. "Dieseits und Jenseits in Platons Mythen von der Seele." *Hermes* 111 (1983): 15–33.
Anderson, Greg. *The Athenian Experiment: Building an Imagined Political Community in Ancient Attica 508–490B.C.* Ann Arbor: University of Michigan Press, 2003.
Annas, Julia. *An Introduction to Plato's* Republic. Oxford: Oxford University Press, 1981.
—. "Plato's Myths of Judgement." *Phronesis* 27.2 (1982): 119–43.
Arend, Walter. *Die typischen Scenen bei Homer*. Berlin: Weidmann, 1933.
Armstrong, Arthur H. "Plotinus and India." *CQ* 30.1 (1936): 22–28.
—. "Platonic Mysticism." *The Dublin Review* 216 (1945): 130–143.
Armstrong, Arthur H., and R.R. Ravindra. "*Buddhi* in the *Bhagavadgītā* and the *Psyché* in Plotinus." In *Neoplatonism and Indian Thought*, edited by R. Baine Harris, 63–86. Albany, NY: State University of New York Press, 1982.
Astour, Michael C. *Hellenosemetica*. Leiden: Brill, 1965.
Aubry, Gwenaëlle. "Un moi sans identité ? Le *hèmeis* plotinien." In *Le moi et l'intériorité*, edited by Gwenaëlle Aubry and Frédérique Ildefonse, 107–12. Paris: Vrin, 2008.

Beck, Roger. *The Religion of the Mithras Cult in the Roman Empire. Mysteries of the Unconquered Sun*. Oxford: Oxford University Press, 2007.
Benardete, Seth. *The Being of the Beautiful: Plato's Theaetetus, Sophist, and Statesman*. Chicago: University of Chicago Press, 1984.
Benveniste, Émile. "Expression indo-européen de l'éternité." *Bulletin de la Société de linguistique* 38 (1937): 103–139.
Bérard, Claude. *Anodoi, Essai sur l'imagerie des passages chthoniens*. Rome: Institut suisse de Rome, 1974.
Bernabé, Alberto. "Platone e l'orfismo." In *Destino e salvezza: tra culti pagani e gnosi cristiana. Itinerari storico-religiosi sulle orme di Ugo Bianchi*, edited by Giulia Sfameni Gasparro, 37–97. Cosenza: L. Giordano, 1998.
—. "Una cita de Píndaro en Platón *Men*. 81b (*Fr.* 133 Sn.-M.)." In *Desde los poemas homéricos hasta la prosa griega del siglo IV d. C. Veintiséis estudios filológicos*, edited by Juan Antonio López Férez, 239–259. Madrid: Ediciones Clásicas, 1999.
—. "La experiencia iniciática en Plutarco." In *Misticismo y religiones mistéricas en la obra de Plutarco*, Actas del VII Simposio Español sobre Plutarco, edited by Aurelio Pérez Jiménez and Francesc Casadesús, 5–22. Madrid-Málaga: Ediciones Clásicas, 2001.
—. "Los terrores del más allá en el mundo griego. La respuesta órfica." In *Miedo y religión*, edited by Francisco Díez de Velasco, 321–329. Madrid: Ediciones del Orto, 2002.
—. *Hieros logos. Poesía órfica sobre los dioses, el alma y el más allá*. Madrid: Akal, 2003.
—. *Poetae Epici Graeci testimonia et fragmenta* II, fasc. 1–2. Monachii et Lipsiae: Teubner. Fasc. 3. Berolini-Novi Eboraci: De Gruyter, 2004–2007.
—. Review of *Myths of the Underworld Journey: Plato, Aristophanes, and the "Orphic" Gold Tablets* by Radcliffe G. Edmondso. *Aestimatio* 3 (2006): 1–13.
—. "L'âme après la mort : modèles orphiques et transposition platonicienne." In *Études platoniciennes* IV, *Les puissances de l'âme selon Platon*, edited by J. François Pradeau, 25–44. Paris: Les Belles Lettres, 2007a.
—. "La muerte es vida. Sentido de una paradoja órfica." In Φίλου σκιά. *Studia philologiae in honorem Rosae Aguilar ab amicis et sodalibus dicata*, edited by Alberto Bernabé and Ignacio Rodríguez Alfageme, 175–181. Madrid, 2007b.
—. "Some Thoughts about the 'New' Gold Tablet from Pherai." *ZPE* 166 (2008): 53–58.
Bernabé, Alberto, and Francesc Casadesús, ed. *Orfeo y la tradición órfica: un reencuentro*. Madrid: Akal, 2008.
Bernabé, Alberto, and Ana Isabel Jiménez San Cristóbal, ed. *Instructions for the Netherworld: The Orphic Gold Tablets*. Leiden: Brill, 2008.
Bescond, Lucien. "La doctrine eschatologique dans le mythe du *Gorgias*." In *Politique dans l'Antiquité*, edited by Jean-Paul Dumont and Lucien Bescond, 67–87. Lille: Un. Lille, 1986.
Betegh, Gábor. *The Derveni Papyrus: Cosmology, Theology and Interpretation*. Cambridge: Cambridge University Press, 2004.

—. "Eschatology and Cosmology: Models and Problems." In *La costruzione del discorso filosofico nel'etá dei Presocratici*, edited by Maria Michela Sassi, 27–50. Pisa: Edizioni della Normale, 2006.
Blank, D. "The Fate of the Ignorant in Plato's *Gorgias*." *Hermes* 119 (1991): 22–36.
Bluck, Richard Stanley. "The *Phaedrus* and Reincarnation." *AJPh* 79 (1958): 156–64.
—. "Plato, Pindar, and Metempsychosis." *AJPh* 79 (1958): 405–14.
Blumenthal, Henry J. *Plotinus' Psychology*. The Hague: Martinus Nijhoff, 1971.
—. "Soul, World-Soul and Individual Soul in Plotinus." In *Le Néoplatonisme*, edited by Pierre-Maxime Schuhl and Pierre Hadot, 56–63. Paris: Centre National de la Recherche Scientifique, 1971.
Boitani, Piero. *The Shadow of Ulysses*. Oxford: Clarendon Press, 1994.
Bollack, Jean. *Empédocle*, 3 vols. Paris: Minuit, 1965–1969.
—. *Empédocle. Les Purifications: Un projet de paix universelle*. Paris: Points, 2003.
—. "Empedocles: Two Theologies, Two Projects." In *The Empedoclean Kosmos: Structure, Process and the Question of Cyclicity. Proceedings of the Symposium Philosophiae Antiquae Tertium Myconense July 6th – July 13th, 2003*, part 1: Papers, edited by Apostolos L. Pierris, 45–72. Patras: Institute for Philosophical Research, 2005.
Bolton, James D. P. *Aristeas of Proconnesus*. Oxford: Clarendon Press, 1962.
Bonifazi, Anna. "Inquiring into Nostos and Its Cognates." *AJPh* 130.4 (2009): 481–510.
Bordigoni, Carlitria. "Empedocle e la dizione omerica." In *Studi sul pensiero e sulla lingua di Empedocle*, edited by Livio Rossetti and Carlo Santaniello, 199–290. Bari: Levante, 2004.
Bordt, Michael. *Platons Theologie*. Freiburg and Munich: Karl Alber, 2006.
Bowra, C.M. "The Proem of Parmenides." In *Problems in Greek Poetry*, 38–53. Oxford: Clarendon Press, 1953.
Boyancé, Pierre. *Le Culte des Muses chez les philosophes grecs*. Paris: De Boccard, 1937.
—. "L'Apollon solaire." in *Mélanges J. Carcopino*, edited by J. Heurgon, 149–170. Paris: Librairie Hachette, 1966.
Brann, Eva. *The Music of the Republic*. Philadelphia: Paul Dry Books, 2004.
Bréhier, Émile. *The Philosophy of Plotinus*. Translated by Joseph Thomas. Chicago: University of Chicago Press, 1958.
Bremmer, Jan M. "Religious Secrets and Secrecy in Classical Greece." In *Secrecy and Concealment in Ancient and Islamic History of Religions*, edited by Hans G. Kippenberg and Guy G. Stroumsa, 61–78. Leiden: Brill, 1995.
—. *The Rise and Fall of the Afterlife*. London: Routledge, 2002.
Brisson, Luc. "Prosopographie." In *Porphyre. La Vie de Plotin*, edited by Luc Brisson et al., vol. 1, 49–114. Paris: Vrin, 1982.
—. "Plotin et la magie." In *Porphyre. La Vie de Plotin*, edited by Luc Brisson et al., vol. 2, 465–475. Paris: Vrin, 1992.
—. "*Logos* et *logoi* chez Plotin. Leur nature et leur rôle." *Les Cahiers Philosophiques de Strasbourg* 8 (1999): 87–108.

—. *Plato the Myth Maker*. Translated by Gerard Naddaf. Chicago: University of Chicago Press, 1998.
—. "Entre physique et métaphysique. Le terme *ógkos* chez Plotin, dans ses rapports avec la matière (*húlē*) et le corps (*sôma*)." in *Études sur Plotin*, edited by Michel Fattal, 87–111. Paris and Montréal: L'Harmattan, 2000.
—. *How Philosophers Saved Myths: Allegorical Interpretation and Classical Mythology*. Translated by Catherine Tihanyi. Chicago: University of Chicago Press, 2004.
—. *Las palabras y los mitos. ¿Cómo y por qué Platón dio nombre al mito?*. Madrid: Abada, 2005a.
—. *Plotinus' Traités 27–29*. Edited by Luc Brisson and Jean-François Pradeau. Paris: Flammarion, 2005b.
—. "La place de la mémoire dans la psychologie plotinienne." *Études platoniciennes* 3 (2006): 13–27.
—. "The Philosopher and the Magician (Porphyry, *Vita Plotini* 10, 1–13). Magic and Sympathy." In *Antike Mythen. Medien, Transformationen und Konstruktionen, Fritz Graf zum 65. Geburtstag*, edited by Ueli Dill and Christine Walde, 189–202. Berlin and New York: De Gruyter, 2009.
Brisson, Luc, and Jean-Marie Flamand. "Structure, contenu et intentions de *L'Oracle d'Apollon* (Porphyre, *VP* 22)." In *Porphyre. La Vie de Plotin*, edited by Luc Brisson et al., vol. 2, 565–602. Paris: Vrin, 1992.
Brodbeck, Simon. "Introduction." In *The Bhagavad Gita*, translated by Juan Mascaró, xi–xxix. London: Penguin Books, 1962.
Burgess, Jonathan S. *The Tradition of the Trojan War in Homer and the Epic Cycle*. Baltimore and London: The Johns Hopkins University Press, 2001.
Burkert, Walter. "Platon oder Pythagoras? Zum Ursprung des Wortes 'Philosophie'." *Hermes* 88 (1960): 159–77.
—. *Weisheit und Wissenschaft*. Nürnberg: Carl, 1962.
—. "Iranisches bei Anaximandros." *RhM* 106 (1963): 97–134.
—. "Das Proömium des Parmenides und die Katabasis des Pythagoras." *Phronesis* 14 (1969): 1–30.
—. *Homo Necans: Interpretationen altgriechischer Opferriten und Mythen*. Berlin and New York: De Gruyter, 1972a.
—. *Lore and Science in Ancient Pythagoreanism*. Cambridge, MA: Harvard University Press, 1972b.
—. "Le laminette auree: da Orfeo a Lampone." In *Orfismo in Magna Grecia*. Atti del XIV Convegno di Studi sulla Magna Grecia, Taranto 6–10 ott. 1974, 81–104. Naples: ISAMG, 1975.
—. *Griechische Religion der archaischen und klassischen Epoche*, 2nd rev. ed. Stuttgart: Kohlhammer, 2011.
—. "Craft Versus Sect: The Problem of Orphics and Pythagoreans." In *Jewish and Christian Self-Definition*, vol. 3, edited by B.F. Meyer and E.P. Sanders, 1–22, 183–89. London: Trinity Press, 1982.
—. *Greek Religion*. Cambridge, MA: Harvard University Press, 1985.
—. *Ancient Mystery Cults*. Cambridge, MA: Harvard University Press, 1987.
—. *Antike Mysterien: Funktionen und Gehalt*. Munich: C.H. Beck, 1994.

—. *Babylon, Memphis, Persepolis. Eastern Contexts of Greek Culture*. Cambridge, MA: Harvard University Press, 2004.
—. "Der geheime Reiz des Verborgenen. Antike Mysterienkulte." In *Secrecy and Concealment in Ancient and Islamic History of Religions*, edited by Hans G. Kippenberg and Guy G. Stroumsa, 79–100. Leiden: Brill, 1995.
Burnet, John. *Early Greek Philosophy*. London: Adam and Charles Black, 1892.
—. *Plato's Phaedo*. Oxford: Clarendon, 1911.
Bussanich, John. "Mystical Elements in the Thought of Plotinus." *Aufstieg und Niedergang der Römischen Welt* II.36.7 (1994): 5300–5330.
—. "Non-discursive Thought in Plotinus and Proclus." *Documenti e studi sulla tradizione filosofica medievale* 8 (1997): 191–210.
—. "Socrates the Mystic." In *Traditions of Platonism: Essays Presented to John Dillon*, edited by John J. Cleary, 29–51. Burlington: Ashgate, 1999.
—. "Socrates and Religious Experience." In *The Blackwell Companion to Socrates*, edited by Rachana Kamtekar and Sara Rappe, 200–213. Oxford: Blackwell, 2006.
Cahn, Herbert. "Die Löwen des Apollon." *MH* 7 (1950): 185–199.
Calame, Claude. "Mort héroïque et culte à mystère dans l'Oedipe à Colone de Sophocle: Actes rituels au service de la creation mythique." In *Ansichten griechischer Rituale: Geburtstagssymposium für Walter Burkert*, edited by Fritz Graf, 326–356. Stuttgart and Leipzig: Teubner, 1998.
Calder, William M. "The Spherical Earth in Plato's *Phaedo*." *Phronesis* 13 (1968): 121–125.
Calov, Abraham. *Systematis locorum theologicorum*. Wittebergae: Excudebat Johannes Wilkius, 1677.
—. *Theologia positiva, per definitiones causas, affectiones, et distinctiones, Locos Theologicos universos, succincte justoque ordine proponens, ceu compendium Systematis Theologici*. Wittebergae: Schrödter, 1682.
Camp, John M. *The Archaeology of Athens*. New Haven: Yale University Press, 2001.
Cannatà Fera, Maria. *Pindarus. Threnorum fragmenta*. Roma: Athenaeum, 1990.
Capizzi, Antonio. "Trasposizione del lesico omerico in Parmenide ed Empedocle. Osservazioni su un problema di metodo." *QUCC* 54 (1987): 107–118.
Carter, Robert. "Plato and Mysticism." *Idealistic Studies* 5 (1975): 255–268.
Casadesús, Francesc. "*Gorgias* 493a-c: la explicación etimológica, un rasgo esencial de la doctrina órfica." *Actas del IX Congreso Español de Estudios Clásicos* II (Madrid: Sociedad Española de Estudios Clásicos, 1997): 61–65.
—. "Orfeo y orfismo en Platón." In *Orfeo y la tradición órfica: un reencuentro*, edited by Alberto Bernabé and Francesc Casadesús, 1239–1279. Madrid: Akal, 2008.
Casadio, Giovanni. "Adversaria Orphica et Orientalia." *SMSR* 52 (1986): 291–322.
Cassin, Barbara. "Le chant des Sirènes dans le Poème de Parménide: quelques remarques sur le fr. VIII, 26–33." In *Études sur Parménide. Problèmes d'interprétation* edited by Pierre Aubenque, 163–170. Paris: Vrin, 1987.
Cavanaugh, Maureen B. *Eleusis and Athens, Documents in Finance, Religion and Politics in the Fifth Century B.C.* Atlanta: Scholars Press, 1996.

Cerri, Giovanni. "L'ideologia dei quattro elementi da Omero ai Presocratici." *AION (filol)* 20 (1998): 5–58.
—. "Empedocle narratore di miti : la vicenda cosmica." *AION (filol)* 28 (2006): 49–63.
Chaniotis, Angelos. "The Divinity of Hellenistic Rulers." In *A Companion to the Hellenistic World*, edited by Andrew Erskine, 431–45. Oxford: Blackwell, 2003.
Chantraine, Pierre. *Dictionnaire étymologique de la langue grecque, histoire des mots.* Paris: Éditions Klincksieck, 1968.
Chevalier, Jacques. *Étude critique du dialogue pseudo-platonicien, l'Axiochos sur la mort et sur l'immortalité de l'âme.* Lyon: A. Rey, 1914.
Clarke, Emma C., John M. Dillon and Jackson P. Hershbell. *Iamblichus, On the Mysteries*. Writings from the Greco-Roman World, vol. 4. Atlanta: Society of Biblical Literature, 2003.
Classen, C. Joachim. "Licht und Dunkel in der frühgriechischen Philosophie." *Studium Generale* 18 (1965): 97–116.
Clay, Jenny Strauss. *Hesiod's Cosmos*. Cambridge: Cambridge University Press, 2003.
Clinton, Kevin. "The Sacred Officials of the Eleusinian Mysteries." *TAPhS* NS 64.3 (1974).
—. "The Author of the Homeric Hymn to Demeter." *Opuscula Atheniensia* 16 (1986): 43–49.
—. *Myth and Cult, The Iconography of the Eleusinian Mysteries*. Stockholm: Svenska Institutet i Athen, 1992.
—. "The Sanctuary of Demeter and Kore at Eleusis." In *Greek Sanctuaries: New Approaches*, edited by Nanno Marinatos and Robin Hägg, 110–124. London: Routledge, 1993.
—. "The Eleusinian Mysteries and Panhellenism in Democratic Athens." In *The Archaeology of Athens and Attica under the Democracy*, edited by William D.E. Coulson, Olga Palagia, T.L. Shear, H.A. Shapiro and F.J. Forst, 161–170. Oxford: Oxbow Books, 1994.
—. *Eleusis, the Inscriptions on Stone: Documents of the Sanctuary of the Two Goddesses and Public Documents of the Deme*. Athens: Archaeological Society at Athens, 2005.
Conche, Marcel. *Parménide. Le Poème. Fragments. Texte grec, traduction, présentation, et commentaire*. Paris: Presses Universitaires de France, 1996.
Cook, Irwin. F. *The Odyssey in Athens*. Ithaca and London: Cornell University Press, 1995.
Cornford, Francis M. "Plato and Orpheus." *CR* 17.9 (1903): 433–445.
—. *Plato and Parmenides*. London: Routledge, 1939.
—. *Principium Sapientiae. The Origins of Greek Philosophical Thought*. Cambridge: Cambridge University Press, 1952.
Cremer, Friedrich W. *Die Chaldäischen Orakel und Jamblich De Mysteriis*. Meisenheim am Glan: Anton Hain, 1969.
Crotty, Kevin. *The Poetics of Supplication: Homer's Iliad and Odyssey*. Ithaca and London: Cornell University Press, 1994.
Cumont, Franz. *Lux perpetua*. Paris: P. Geuthner, 1949.

Darcque, Pascal. "Les vestiges mycéniens découverts sous le Telestérion d'Éleusis." *BCH* 105.2 (1981): 593–605.
Davis, Michael. "The Tragedy of Law: Gyges in Herodotus and Plato." *RMeta* 53 (2000): 635–655.
Deichgräber, Karl. *Parmenides' Auffahrt zur Göttin des Rechts*. Mainz: Akademie der Wissenschaften, 1958.
Demand, Nancy. "Pindar's *Olympian 2*, Theron's Faith, and Empedocles' *Katharmoi*." *GRBS* 16 (1975): 347–357.
Des Places, Édouard. *Jamblique, Les Mystères D'Égypte*. Paris: Les Belles Lettres, 1966.
Detienne, Marcel. *La Notion de Daïmôn dan le Pythagorisme ancien*. Paris: Les Belles Lettres, 1963.
—. *The Masters of Truth in Archaic Greece*. Translated by Janet Lloyd. New York: Zone Books, 1996.
Di Benedetto, Vincenzo. "Fra Hipponion e Petelia." *PP* 59 (2004): 293–306.
Diels, Hermann. *Parmenides. Lehrgedicht*. Berlin: Reimer 1897.
Diels, Hermann, and Walther Kranz. *Die Fragmente der Vorsokratiker*. 6th ed. Berlin: Weidmann, 1951.
Diès, Auguste. *Autour de Platon*, vol. 2. Paris: Gabriel Beauchesne, 1927.
Dieterich, Albrecht. *Nekyia*. Leipzig: Teubner, 1893.
Díez de Velasco, Francisco. "Un problema de delimitación conceptual en Historia de las Religiones: la mística griega." In *Imágenes de la Polis*, edited by Domingo Plácido, Jaime Alvar, Juan M. Casillas and César Fornis, 407–422. Madrid: Ediciones Clásicas, 1997.
Dillon, John M. *Iamblichi Chalcidensis in Platonis Dialogos Commentariorum Fragmenta*. Edited with translation and commentary. Philosophia Antiqua 23. Leiden: Brill, 1973.
—. "Plotinus, Philo and Origen on the Grades of Virtue." In *Platonismus und Christentum. Festschrift für Heinrich Dörrie*, edited by Horst-Dieter Blume and Friedhelm Mann, 92–105. Münster: Aschendorff, 1983.
—. "Iamblichus of Chalcis (ca. AD 240–325)." *Aufstieg und Niedergang der römischen Welt* II, 36.2 (1987): 880–885.
—. *The Middle Platonists 80 B.C. To A.D. 220*, rev. edition. Ithaca, NY: Cornell University Press, 1996.
—. *The Heirs of Plato: A Study of the Old Academy (347–274 BC)*. Oxford: Oxford University Press, 2003.
Dillon, John M., and Lloyd P. Gerson. *Neoplatonic Philosophy. Introductory Readings*. Indianapolis: Hackett, 2004.
Dodds, E. R. "Numenius and Ammonius." In *Les Sources de Plotin*, 3–61. Geneva: Vandœuvres, 1957.
—. *Plato. Gorgias*. Oxford: Oxford University Press, 1959.
—. *Proclus: The Elements of Theology*. Oxford: Oxford University Press, 1963.
—. *Pagan and Christian in an Age of Anxiety. Some Aspects of Religious Experience from Marcus Aurelius to Constantine*. Cambridge: Cambridge University Press, 1965.
—. *The Greeks and the Irrational*. Berkeley: University of California Press, 1971 [1st ed. 1951].

Dolin, Edwin F. "Parmenides and Hesiod." *HSCP* 66 (1962): 93–98.
Dölger, Franz Joseph. *Sphragis*. Paderborn: Schöningh, 1911.
Dornseiff, Franz. "Soter." In *Paulys Realencyclopädie der classischen Altertumswissenschaft* 2nd series, vol. III A1, 1211–21. Stuttgart: Metzler, 1927.
Dorter, Kenneth. "Free Will, Luck, and Happiness in the Myth of Er." *Journal of Philosophical Research* 28 (2003): 129–42.
Dover, Kenneth, ed. *Aristophanes' Frogs*, with Introduction and Commentary. Oxford: Clarendon Press, 1993.
Drews, Robert. "The First Tyrants in Greece." *Historia: Zeitschrift für Alte Geschichte* 21.2 (1972): 129–144.
Dufour, Richard. "Actuality and Potentiality in Plotinus' View of the Intelligible Universe." *Journal of Neoplatonic Studies* 9 (2004): 214–215.
Duke, E.A., et al. *Platonis Opera*, vol. 1. Oxford: Clarendon Press, 1995.
Ebner, P. "L'errore di Alalia e la colonizzazione di. Velia nel responso delfico." *Rassegna Storica Salernitana* 23 (1962): 4–6.
Edmonds, Radcliffe G. "Tearing Apart the Zagreus Myth: A Few Disparaging Remarks on Orphism and Original Sin." *Classical Antiquity* 18.1 (1999): 35–73.
—. *Myths of the Underworld Journey: Plato, Aristophanes, and the "Orphic" Gold Tablets*. Cambridge: Cambridge University Press, 2004.
—. ed. *The "Orphic" Gold Tablets and Greek Religion: Further Along the Path*. Cambridge: Cambridge University Press, 2011.
Edwards, Mark J. "A Late Use of Empedocles: The *Oracle on Plotinus*." *Mnemosyne* 43 (1990): 151–155.
—. *Neoplatonic Saints. The Lives of Plotinus and Proclus By Their Students*. In *Translated Texts for Historians*, vol. 35. Liverpool: Liverpool University Press, 2000.
Eggers Lan, Conrado. "Die *odos polyphēmos* der parmenideischen Wahrheit." *Hermes* 88 (1960): 376–379.
Elderkin, George. *Mystic Allusions in the Frogs of Aristophanes*. Princeton: Princeton University Press, 1955.
Eliade, Mircea. *Das Mysterium der Wiedergeburt*. Zürich: Rascher Verlag, 1961. Originally published as *Naissances mystiques*. Paris: Gallimard, 1959.
—. *A History of Religious Ideas*, vol. 1. Chicago and London: University of Chicago Press, 1978.
Emilson, Eyjólfur Kjalar. *Plotinus on Sense-Perception. A Philosophical Study*. Cambridge: Cambridge University Press, 1988.
Erman, Adolf. *Die Religion der Ägypter*. Berlin: De Gruyter, 1934.
Fago, Angelica. "Il mito di Er: il mondo come 'caverna' e l'Ade come 'regno luminoso' di Ananke." *SMSR* 51 (1994): 183–218.
Faure, Paul. *Fonctions des cavernes crétoises*. Paris: E. de Boccard, 1964.
Felton, Debbie. "The Dead." In *A Companion to Greek Religion*, edited by Daniel Ogden, 86–99. Malden, MA: Wiley-Blackwell, 2010.
Fenik, Bernhard. *Studies in the Odyssey*. Wiesbaden: F. Steiner, 1974.
Ferrari, G. R. F., ed. *The Cambridge Companion to Plato's* Republic. Cambridge: Cambridge University Press, 2007.

—. "Glaucon's Reward, Philosophy's Debt: The Myth of Er." In *Plato's Myths*, edited by Catalin Partenie, 116–33. Cambridge: Cambridge University Press, 2009.
Ferrari, Franco, and Lucia Prauscello. "Demeter Chthonia and the Mountain Mater in New Gold Tablet from Magoula Mati." *ZPE* 162 (2008): 193–202.
Festugière, André-Jean "La sens philosophique du mot αἰών. Àpropos d'Aristote, *De Caelo* 1,9." In *Études de philosophie grecque*, 254–271. Paris: Vrin, 1971.
—. *Contemplation et vie contemplative selon Platon*. 4th edition. Paris: Vrin 1975.
Feyerabend, Barbara. "Zur Wegmetaphorik beim Goldblättchen aus Hipponion und dem Proömium des Parmenides." *RhM* 127 (1984): 1–22.
Finamore, John F. *Iamblichus and the Theory of the Vehicle of the Soul*. Chico, CA: Scholars Press, 1985.
—. "Iamblichus on Light and the Transparent." In *The Divine Iamblichus: Philosopher and Man of Gods*, edited by H. J. Blumenthal and E. Gillian Clark, 55–64. Bristol: Bristol Classical Press, 1993.
—. "Plotinus and Iamblichus on Magic and Theurgy." *Dionysius* 17 NS (1999): 83–94.
—. "Proclus on Ritual Practice in Neoplatonic Religious Philosophy." In *Being or Good? Metamorphosis of Neoplatonism*, edited by Agnieszka Kijewska, 123–137. Lublin: KUL, 2004.
—. "Iamblichus and the Intermediate Nature of the Human Soul." In *Perspectives sur le néoplatonisme*, edited by Martin Achard and Jean-Marc Narbonne, 123–136. Laval: Presses de l'Université, 2009.
—. "Iamblichus's Interpretation of Parmenides' Third Hypothesis." In *Plato's Parmenides and Its Heritage*, vol. 2, edited by John D. Turner and Kevin Corrigan, 119–132. Atlanta: Society of Biblical Literature, 2010.
Finamore, John F., and John M. Dillon. *Iamblichus*, De Anima: *Text, Translation, and Commentary*. Leiden: Brill, 2002.
Finamore, John F., and Algis Uzdavinys. *The Golden Chain: An Anthology of Pythagorean and Platonic Philosophy*. Bloomington, Indiana: World Wisdom Inc., 2004.
Flood, Gavin D. *An Introduction to Hinduism*. Cambridge: Cambridge University Press, 1996.
Foley, Helene P. *The Homeric Hymn to Demeter*. Princeton: Princeton University Press, 1993.
Foucart, Paul François. *Les Mystères d'Éleusis*. Paris: Picard, 1914.
Fränkel, Hermann. *Wege und Formen frühgriechischen Denkens*. Munich: C.H. Beck, 1955.
—. "Parmenidesstudien." In *Wege und Formen des frühgriechischen Denkens*, 159–197. Munich: C.H. Beck, 1960.
—. *Dichtung und Philosophie des frühen Griechentums*. Munich: C.H. Beck, 1962.
Frankfort, Henri. *Cylinder Seals*. London: Macmillan, 1939.
Friedländer, Pablo. "El lenguaje poético de Empédocles." *Synthesis (La Plata)* 12 (2005): 59–77.
Frutiger, Perceval. *Les mythes de Platon*. Paris: Librairie Felix Alcan, 1930.

Funghi, Maria Serena. "Il mito escatologico del Fedone e la forza vitale dell'αἰώρα." *PP* 35 (1980): 176–201.
Gagné, Renaud. "L'esthétique de la peur chez Empédocle." *RPhA* 24.3 (2006): 83–110.
Gallop, David. *Plato. Phaedo.* Oxford: Clarendon Press, 1975.
Garani, Myrto. *Empedocles Redivivus: Poetry and Analogy In Lucretius.* New York and Abingdon: Taylor & Francis, 2007.
—. "The Palingenesis of Empedocles' Calliope in Lucretius." In *Papers on Ancient Literatures: Greece, Rome and the Near East, Proceedings of the "Advanced Seminar in the Humanities" – Venice International University 2004–2005*, edited by Ettore Cingano and Lucio Milano, 231–265. Padova: Eisenbrauns, 2008.
Garland, Robert. *The Greek Way of Death.* Ithaca: Cornell University Press, 1985.
Gavallotti, Carlo. *Empedocle. Poema fisico e lustrale.* Milan: Mondadori, 1975.
Gemelli Marciano, M. Laura. *Le metamorfosi della tradizione: mutamenti di significato e neologismi nel* Peri physeos *di Empedocle.* Bari: Levante, 1990.
—. "Images and Experience: At the Roots of Parmenides' *Aletheia*." *AncPhil* (2008): 21–48.
Gernet, Louis. *The Anthropology of Ancient Greece.* Baltimore and London: Johns Hopkins University Press, 1981.
Gerson, Lloyd P. *Plotinus.* London and New York: Routledge, 1994.
—. *Knowing Persons.* Oxford: Oxford University Press, 2003.
—. *Aristotle and Other Platonists.* Ithaca: Cornell University Press, 2005.
Gigante, Marcello. "Parmenide Uliade." *PP* 19 (1964): 135–137; 450–452.
Gigon, Olof. *Der Ursprung der griechischen Philosophie.* Basel: Schwabe & Co., 1945.
—. "Die Theologie der Vorsokratiker." *Entretiens Fondation Hardt* 1 (1952) 127–155.
—. "Die Erneuerung der Philosophie in der Zeit Ciceros." *Entretiens Fondation Hardt* 3 (1955) 25–61.
Gilbert, Otto. "Die Daimon des Parmenides." *AGPh* 20 (1907): 25–45.
Gilead, Amihud. *The Platonic Odyssey.* Amsterdam: Editions Rodopi B.V., 1995.
Gilson, Étienne. *God and Philosophy.* 2nd ed. New Haven, CT: Yale University Press, 2002.
Giordano, Manuela. *La supplica: rituale, istituzione sociale e tema epico in Omero.* Naples: A.I.O.N., 1999.
Gómez, Cardó, Pilar. "Axíoco." In *Platón. Diálogos* VII, 389–425. Madrid: Gredos, 1992.
Gomperz, Heinrich. "Psychologische Beobachtungen an griechischen Philosophen (Parmenides—Sokrates)." *Imago* 10 (1924): 1–92.
Gottlieb, Anthony. *The Dream of Reason: A History of Philosophy from the Greeks to the Renaissance.* New York: W.W. Norton & Company, 2000.
Gottschalk, H.B. *Heraclides of Pontus.* Oxford: Clarendon Press, 1980.
Gould, John. "Hiketeia." *JHS* 93 (1973): 74–103.

Goulet, Richard. "*L'Oracle d'Apollon* dans *La Vie de Plotin*." In *Porphyre. La Vie de Plotin*, edited by Luc Brisson et al., vol. 1, 371–412. Paris: Vrin, 1982.

—. "Sur quelques interprétations récentes de *L'Oracle d'Apollon*." In *Porphyry. La Vie de Plotin*, edited by Luc Brisson et al., vol. 2, 603–617. Paris: Vrin, 1992.

Graf, Fritz. *Eleusis und die orphische Dichtung Athens in vorhellenistischer Zeit*. Berlin and New York: De Gruyter, 1974.

—. "Mysterien." In *Der neue Pauly: Enzyklopädie der Antike*, edited by Manfred Landfester, Hubert Cancik, and Helmuth Schneider, 615–626. Stuttgart: J.B. Metzler, 2000.

Graf, Fritz, and Sarah Iles Johnston. *Ritual Texts for the Afterlife: Orpheus and the Bacchic Gold Tablets*. London: Routledge, 2007.

Graillot, Henri. *Le culte de Cybèle*. Paris: Fontemoing et Cie, 1912.

Gregorios, Paulos M., ed. *Neoplatonism and Indian Philosophy*. Albany, NY: State University of New York Press, 2002.

Griswold, Charles L. *Self-Knowledge in Plato's* Phaedrus. New Haven and London: Yale University Press, 1986.

Grossman, Betty Greenfield. "The Eleusian Gods and Heros in Greek Art." Ph.D. Diss., Saint Louis, Missouri, 1959.

Gundert, Herrmann. "Charakter und Schicksal." *Neue Jahrbücher* 3 (1940): 225–237.

Guthrie, William Keith C. *Orpheus and Greek Religion*, 2nd ed. London: Methuen, 1952.

—. *A History of Greek Philosophy: The Presocratic Tradition From Parmenides to Democritus*, vol. 2. Cambridge: Cambridge University Press, 1965.

—. *A History of Greek Philosophy*, vol. 5. Cambridge: Cambridge University Press, 1978.

Habicht, Christian. *Gottmenschtum und Griechische Städte*, 2nd ed. Munich: C.H. Beck, 1970.

Hackforth, Reginald. *Plato's* Phaedo. Cambridge: Cambridge University Press, 1952.

—. *Plato's Phaedo*. Translated with an Introduction and Commentary. Cambridge: Cambridge University Press, 1955.

Halbfass, Wilhelm. *Karma und Wiedergeburt im indischen Denken*. Kreuzlingen: Diederichs, 2000.

Halliwell, Stephen. *Plato: Republic 10*. Edited with Translation and Commentary. Warminster: Aris & Phillips, 1988.

—. "The Subjection of Muthos to Logos." *CQ* 50.1 (2000): 94–112.

—. "The Life-and-Death Journey of the Soul: Interpreting the Myth of Er." In *The Cambridge Companion to Plato's Republic*, edited by G.R.F. Ferrari, 445–473. Cambridge: Cambridge University Press, 2007.

Hardie, Philip. "Lucretius on the Narrow Road." *HSCP* 99 (1999): 275–87.

Harris, R. Baine, ed. *Neoplatonism and Indian Thought*. Albany, NY: State University of New York Press, 1982.

Harrison, Jane Ellen. *Prolegomena to the Study of Greek Religion*. Cambridge: Cambridge University Press, 1922 and London: Merlin Press, 1962.

Haussig, Hans Wilhelm, et al. *Lexikon der Mythologie*, vol. 1. Stuttgart: Klett-Cotta, 1961.
Havelock, Eric. "Parmenides and Odysseus." *HSCP* 63 (1958): 133–43.
Hegel, Georg Wilhelm Friedrich. *Ästhetik*, vol. 1. Edited by V. Friedrich Bassenge. Frankfurt am Main: Europäische Verlagsanstalt, 1955.
Heidegger, Martin. *Being and Time*. Translated by John Macquarrie and Edward Robinson. Oxford: Blackwell, 1962.
Hemberg, Bengt. *Die Kabiren*. Uppsala: Almqvist & Wiksell, 1950.
Henrichs, Albert. "The Eumenides and Wineless Libations in the Derveni Papyrus." In *Atti del XVII Congresso internazionale di papirologia*, II, 255–268. Naples: Centro internazionale per lo studio dei papiri ercolanesi, 1984.
—. "*Hieroi Logoi* and *Hierai Bibloi*: The (Un)Written Margins of the Sacred in Ancient Greece." *HSCP* 101 (2003): 207–66.
Henry, Paul, and Hans-Rudolf Schwyzer. *Plotini Opera*, vol. 1–3. Oxford: Clarendon Press, 1964.
Herodotus. *The Landmark Herodotus: The Histories*. Translated by Andrea L. Purvis. New York: Pantheon, 2007.
Herrero de Jáuregui, Miguel. "Dialogues of Immortality from the Iliad to the Gold Leaves." In *The Orphic Gold Tablets and Greek Religion: Further Along the Path*, edited by Radcliffe G. Edmonds, 271–290. Cambridge: Cambridge University Press, 2011.
—. "Poetics of Supplication and the Katabasis of the Soul." In *Proceedings of the OSU Conference: Ritual Texts for the Afterlife (April 2006)*, edited by Fritz Graf (forthcoming).
Herrero de Jáuregui, Miguel et al., eds. *Tracing Orpheus: Studies of Orphic Fragments*. Berlin: De Gruyter, 2011.
Hershbell, Jackson P. "Empedocles' Oral Style." *CJ* 63 (1968): 352–357.
—. "Hesiod and Empedocles." *CJ* 65 (1970): 145–161.
Heubeck, Alfred. *Der Odyseedichter und die Ilias*. Erlangen: Palm & Enke, 1954.
—. *Die homerische Frage. Ein Bericht über die Forschung der letzten Jahrzehnte*. Darmstadt: Wissenschaftliche Buchgesellschaft, 1974.
Highbarger, Ernest Leslie. *The Gates of Dreams*. Baltimore: Johns Hopkins University Press, 1940.
Horn, Christoph. *Plotin über Sein, Zahl und Einheit: Eine Studie zu den systematischen Grundlagen der Enneaden*. Stuttgart and Leipzig: Teubner, 1995.
Huffmann, Carl. "Philolaus and the Central Fire." In *Reading Ancient Texts I: Presocratics and Plato—Essays in Honour of Denis O'Brien*, edited by Suzanne Stern-Gillet and Kevin Corrigan, 57–96. Leiden and Boston: Brill, 2007.
Hyde, Walter Woodburn. "The Greek Tyrannies." *The Classical Weekly* 37.11 (1944): 123–125.
Immerwahr, Henry. *Attic Script: A Survey*. Oxford: Clarendon Press, 1990.
Inwood, Brad. *The Poem of Empedocles: A Text and Translation with an Introduction*, rev. 2nd ed. Toronto: University of Toronto Press, 2001.
Inwood, Michael. "Plato's Eschatological Myths." In *Plato's Myths*, edited by Catalin Partenie, 28–50. Cambridge: Cambridge University Press, 2009.
Irwin, Terence H. *Plato. Gorgias*. Oxford: Clarendon Press, 1979.

Jacoby, Felix. "Diagoras ὁ ἄθεος." In *Abhandlungen der deutschen Akademie der Wissenschaften zu Berlin, Klasse für Sprachen, Literatur und Kunst*, Anh. 3. Berlin, 1959.
Jaeger, Werner W. *The Theology of the Early Greek Philosophers*. Oxford: Clarendon, 1947.
—. *Die Theologie der frühen griechischen Denker*. Stuttgart: W. Kohlhammer, 1953.
James, E. O. *The Cult of the Mother Goddess*. New York: Frederick A. Praeger, 1959.
Janko, Richard. "The Physicist as Hierophant: Aristophanes, Socrates, and the Authorship of the Derveni Papyrus." *ZPE* 118 (1997): 61–94.
—. "The Derveni Papyrus ("Diagoras of Melos, Apopyrgizontes Logoi?"): A New Translation." *CPh* 96.1 (2001): 1–32.
—. "Empedocles' *On Nature* I 233–364: A New Reconstruction of *P. Strasb*. Inv. 1665–6." *ZPE* 150 (2005): 1–26.
—. Review of *The Derveni Papyrus: Cosmology, Theology and Interpretation* by Gabor Betegh. *Bryn Mawr Classical Review* 2005.01.27.
—. "Reconstructing (again) the Opening of the Derveni Papyrus." *ZPE* 166 (2008): 37–51.
Jeanmaire, Henri. *Couroi et Couretes*. Lille: Bibliothèque Univ., 1939.
Johnston, Sarah Iles. "Crossroads." *ZPE* 88 (1991): 217–24.
Kahn, Charles H. "Religion and Natural Philosophy in Empedocles' Doctrine of the Soul." *AGPh* 42 (1960): 3–35.
—. *The Art and Thought of Heraclitus*. Cambridge: Cambridge University Press, 1979.
—. *Plato and the Socratic Dialogue: The Philosophical Use of a Literary Form*. Cambridge: Cambridge University Press, 1997.
—. *Restless Dead: Encounters between the Living and the Dead in Ancient Greece*. Berkeley, CA: University of California Press, 1999.
Kambylis, Athanasios. *Die Dichterweihe und ihre Symbolik*. Heidelberg: C. Winter, 1965.
Kamtekar, Rachana, and Sara Ahbel-Rappe, ed. *The Blackwell Companion to Socrates*. Oxford: Wiley-Blackwell, 2006.
Kidd, Ian. "Some Philosophical Demons." *BICS* 40 (1995): 217–24.
King, Richard A. H. *Aristotle and Plotinus on Memory*. Berlin: De Gruyter, 2009.
Kingsley, Peter. *Ancient Philosophy, Mystery and Magic: Empedocles and Pythagorean Tradition*. Oxford: Oxford University Press, 1995.
—. *In the Dark Places of Wisdom*. Inverness, CA: The Golden Sufi Center, 1999.
—. "Empedocles for the New Millenium." *AncPhil* 22 (2002): 333–413.
—. *Reality*. Inverness, CA: The Golden Sufi Center, 2003.
—. *A Story Waiting to Pierce You*. Inverness, CA: The Golden Sufi Center, 2010.
Kirk, G.S. *Heraclitus: The Cosmic Fragments*. Cambridge: Cambridge University Press, 1954.
Kirk, G.S., and J.E. Raven. *The Presocratic Philosophers*. Cambridge: Cambridge University Press, 1957.

Kirk, G.S., J.E. Raven and M. Schofield. *The Presocratic Philosophers*, 2nd ed. Cambridge: Cambridge University Press, 1983.
Kouremenos, Theokritos, George M. Parássoglou and Kyriakos Tsantsanoglou. *The Derveni Papyrus: Edited with Introduction and Commentary*. Florence: Casa Editrice Leo S. Olschki, 2006.
Kramer, Samuel Noah. "Death and Nether World According to the Sumerian Literary Texts." *Iraq* 22 (1960): 59–68.
—. *Sumerian Mythology*. Philadelphia: University of Pennsylvania Press, 1961.
Krämer, Hans Joachim. *Plato and the Foundations of Metaphysics*. Edited and translated by John R. Catan. Albany: State University of New York Press, 1990.
Kranz, Walther. *Über Aufbau und Bedeutung des Parmenideischen Gedichtes*. Berlin: Verlag der Akademie der Wissenschaften, 1916.
Kraut, Richard, ed. *The Cambridge Companion to Plato*. Cambridge: Cambridge University Press, 1992.
Krüger, Gerhard. *Grundfragen der Philosophie*. Frankfurt am Main: Klostermann, 1958.
Kullmann, Wolfgang. *Das Wirken der Götter in der Ilias: Untersuchungen zur Frage der Entstehung des homerischen 'Götterapparats'*. Berlin: Akademie Verlag, 1956.
Kunze, Emil. *Kretische Bronzereliefs*. Stuttgart: W. Kohlhammer, 1931.
Kuruniotis, K. "Das Eleusinische Heiligtum von den Anfängen bis zur Vorperikleischen Zeit." *Archiv für Religionswissenschaft* 32 (1935): 52–78.
Lacrosse, Joachim. "Le rêve indien de Plotin et Porphyre." *RPhA* 19.1 (2001): 79–97.
—. "Un passage de Porphyre relatif au Shiva androgyne chez les Brahmanes d'Inde." *RPhA* 20.2 (2002): 37–56.
Laird, Andrew. "Ringing the Changes on Gyges: Philosophy and the Formation of Fiction in Plato's *Republic*." *JHS* 121 (2001): 12–29.
Lakoff, George, and Mark Johnson. *Metaphors We Live by*. Chicago: University of Chicago Press, 1980.
Laks, André, and Glenn W. Most, eds. *Studies on the Derveni Papyrus*. New York: Oxford University Press, 1997.
Lamberton, Robert D. *Homer the Theologian: Neoplatonist Allegorical Reading and the Growth of the Epic Tradition*. Edited by P. Brown. The Transformations of the Classical Heritage. Berkeley: University of California Press, 1986.
Lapalus, Etienne. "Le Dionysus et l'Heracles des Grenouilles." *REG* 47 (1934): 1–20.
Latte, Kurt. "Hesiods Dichterweihe." *A&A* 2 (1946): 152–163.
—. *Römische Religionsgeschichte*. Munich: C.H. Beck, 1960.
Lauenstein, Diether. *Die Mysterien von Eleusis*. Stuttgart: Urachhaus, 1987.
Laurent, Jérôme. "La réincarnation chez Plotin et avant Plotin." In *L'Homme et le monde selon Plotin*, 115–137. Paris: ENS éd. et Ophrys, 1999.
Lavaud, Laurant. "La *dianoia* médiatrice entre le sensible et l'intelligible." *Études platoniciennes* 3 (2006): 29–55.
Lesky, Albin. *Göttliche und menschliche Motivation im homerischen Epos*. Heidelberg: Carl Winter, 1961.

—. *Geschichte der griechischen Literatur*. Bern and Munich: Saur, 1971.
Lewy, Hans. *Chaldaean Oracles and Theurgy: Mysticism, Magic, and Platonism in the Later Roman Empire*. Paris: Études Augustiniennes, 1978.
Lincoln, Bruce. "On the Imagery of Paradise." *Indogermanische Forschungen* 85 (1980): 151–64.
—. "Waters of Memory, Waters of Forgetfulness." *Fabula* 23 (1982): 19–34.
Lloyd-Jones, Hugh. "Heracles at Eleusis." *Maia* 19 (1967): 206–229.
—. "Pindar and the Afterlife." *Pindar, Entretiens Fondation Hardt* 17 (1985): 245–283.
—. "Pindar and the Afterlife." In *Greek Epic, Lyric, and Tragedy: The Academic Papers of Sir Hugh Lloyd-Jones*, 80–109. Oxford: Clarendon Press, 1991.
Lloyd-Jones, Hugh, and Peter J. Parsons. "Iterum de Catabasi Orphica." In *Kyklos—Griechisches und Byzantinisches. Rudolf Keydell zum 90. Geburtstag*, edited by Hans-G. Beck, Athanasios Kambylis and Paul Moraux, 88–108. Berlin: De Gruyter, 1978.
Long, Herbert S. *A. Study of the Doctrine of Metempsychosis in Greece From Pythagoras to Plato*. Princeton: Princeton University Press, 1948.
Long, Herbert S. *Diogenes Laertius: Lives of the Philosophers*. Oxford: Oxford University Press, 1964.
Lukacher, Ned. *Time-Fetishes: The Secret History of Eternal Recurrence*. Durham, NC: Duke University Press, 1998.
Macías, Sara. "Orfeo y el orfismo en la tragedia griega." In *Orfeo y la tradición órfica: un reencuentro*, edited by Alberto Bernabé and Francesc Casadesús, 1185–1215. Madrid: Akal, 2008.
Mackenzie, Mary Margaret. *Plato on Punishment*. Berkeley: University of California Press, 1981.
Maiuri, Amadeo. *I campi Flegrei*. Rome: Instituto Poligrafico del Stato, 1963.
Majercik, Ruth. *The Chaldean Oracles. Text, Translation, and Commentary*. In *Studies in Greek and Roman Religion*, vol. 5. Leiden: Brill, 1989.
Malinar, Angelika. *The Bhagavadgītā: Doctrines and Contexts*. Cambridge: Cambridge University Press, 2007.
Mancini, Stefania. "Un insegnamento segreto (Plat. Phaed. 62b)." *QUCC* 90 (1999): 153–168.
Mansfeld, Jaap. *Die Offenbarung des Parmenides und die menschliche Welt*. Assen: Van Gorcum, 1964.
Marcovich, Miroslav. "Pythagorica." *Philologus* 108 (1964): 29–44.
Martin, Alain, and Oliver Primavesi. *L'Empédocle de Strasbourg*. Berlin: De Gruyter, 1999.
Martin, Richard P. "Hesiod, Odysseus, and the Instruction of Princes." *TAPhA* 114 (1984): 29–48.
—. "Rhapsodizing Orpheus." *Kernos* 14 (2001): 23–33.
—. "Golden Verses: Voice and Authority in the Tablets." *Princeton / Stanford Working Papers* Paper No. 040701 (2007), http://ssrn.com/abstract=1426980 (accessed October 23, 2011).
Martínez Hernández, Marcos. "Del mito a la realidad: el concepto *makaron nesoi* en Platón, Aristóteles y Plutarco." In *Plutarco, Platón y Aristóteles. Actas del V*

Congreso Internacional de la I. P. S., edited by A. Pérez Jiménez, José García López and Rosa Aguilar, 95–110. Madrid: Ediciones Clásicas, 1999.

Mascaró, Juan. *The Bhagavad Gita*. London: Penguin Books, 1962.

Masullo, Rita. *Marino di Napoli. Vita di Proclo*. Naples: D'Auria, 1985.

Matilal, Bimal Krishna. *The Collected Essays of B.K. Matilal*. New Delhi: Oxford University Press, 2002.

Mayhew, Robert. *Plato* Laws 10: *Translated with an Introduction and Commentary*. Oxford: Oxford University Press, 2008.

Mazur, Zeke. "*Unio Magica:* Part I: On the Magical Origins of Plotinus' Mysticism." *Dionysius* 21 (2003): 23–52.

—. "*Unio Magica:* Part II: Plotinus, Theurgy, and the Question of Ritual." *Dionysius* 22 (2004): 29–56.

McCumber, John. "*Anamnesis* as Memory of Intelligibles in Plotinus." *AgPh* 60 (1978): 160–167.

McEvilley, Thomas. *The Shape of Indian Thought: Comparative Studies in Greek and Indian Philosophies*. New York: Allworth Press, 2002.

McPherran, Mark L. "Virtue, Luck, and Choice at the End of the *Republic*." In *Plato's Republic. A Critical Guide*, edited by Mark L. McPherran, 132–146. Cambridge University Press, 2010.

Megino Rodríguez, Carlos. *Orfeo y el orfismo en la poesía de Empédocles*. Madrid: Ediciones de la Universidad Autónoma de Madrid, 2005.

Mellaart, James. *Çatal Hüyük —A Neolithic Town in Anatolia*. London. Thames & Hudson, 1967.

Merkelbach, Reinhold. "Eine orphische Unterweltsbeschreibung auf Papyrus." *MH* 8 (1951): 1–11.

Metzger, Henri. *Les representations dans la ceramique attique du IVe siecle*. Paris: E. de Boccard, 1951.

Meyer, Eduard. *Forschungen zur Alten Geschichte*, vol. 2. Halle: Niemeyer, 1899.

Michelini, Ann N., ed. *Plato as Author: The Rhetoric of Philosophy*. Leiden: Brill, 2003.

Morel, Pierre Marie. "Individualité et identité de l'âme humaine chez Plotin." *Les Cahiers philosophiques de Strasbourg* 8 (1999): 53–66.

—. Plotinus. Treatise 41 (IV, 6) *On Sensation and Memory*, in *Plotin. Traités* 45–50. Edited by Luc Brisson and Jean-François Pradeau. Paris: Flammarion, 2007.

Morgan, Kathryn. *Myth and Philosophy from the Presocratics to Plato*. Cambridge: Cambridge University Press, 2000.

Morgan, Michael L. *Platonic Piety*. New Haven: Yale University Press, 1990.

Morrison, John S. "Parmenides and Er." *JHS* 75 (1955): 59–68.

—. "The Shape of the Earth in Plato's *Phaedo*." *Phronesis* 4 (1959): 101–119.

Most, Glenn W. "The Poetics of Early Greek Philosophy." In *The Cambridge Companion to Early Greek Philosophy*, edited by Arthur A. Long, 332–362. Cambridge: Cambridge University Press, 1999.

Mourelatos, Alexander. *The Route of Parmenides*. New Haven: Yale University Press, 1970.

Mylonas, George E. *Eleusis and the Eleusinian Mysteries*. Princeton: Princeton University Press, 1961.

Nagy, Gregory. *Greek Mythology and Poetics*. Cornell: Cornell University Press, 1990.
Naiden, Fred S. *Ancient Supplication*. Oxford and New York: Oxford University Press, 2006.
Nails, Debra. *The People of Plato: A Prosopography of Plato and Other Socratics*. Indianapolis: Hackett Publishing Company, 2002.
Newiger, Hans-Joachim. *Aristophanes, Sämtliche Komödien*. Munich: dtv, 1976.
Nichols, Mary P. "Glaucon's Adaptation of the Story of Gyges and Its Implications for Plato's Political Teaching." *Polity* 17 (1984): 30–39.
Nightingale, Andrea W. *Genres in Dialogue: Plato and the Construct of Philosophy*. Cambridge: Cambridge University Press, 1995.
—. "Plato on the Origins of Evil: the *Statesman* Myth Reconsidered." *AncPhil* 16 (1996): 65–91.
Nilsson, Martin Persson. "Die Eleusinischen Gottheiten." *Archiv für Religionswissenschaft* 32 (1935): 79–141.
—. *Opuscula selecta*, vol. 2. Lund: Gleerup, 1952.
—. *Geschichte der griechischen Religion*, 2nd rev. ed. 2 vols. Munich: C.H. Beck, 1955.
Noack, Ferdinand. *Eleusis, Die Baugeschichtliche Entwicklung des Heiligtumes*. Berlin and Leipzig: De Gruyter, 1927.
O'Hara, James J. "Venus or the Muse as Ally (Lucr. 1.24, Simon. Frag. Eleg. 11.20–22 W)." *CPh* 93.1 (1998): 69–74.
O'Flaherty, Wendy Doniger. *Karma and Rebirth in Classical Indian Traditions*. Berkeley: University of California Press, 1980.
O'Meara, Dominic J. *An Introduction to the Enneads*. Oxford: Oxford University Press, 1993.
O'Meara, John J. "Indian Wisdom and Porphyry's Search for a Universal Way." In *Neoplatonism and Indian Thought*, edited by R. Baine Harris, 5–26. Albany, NY: State University of New York Press, 1982.
Obbink, Dirk. "The Addressees of Empedocles." *Materiali e discussioni per l'analisi dei testi classici* 31 (1993): 51–98.
Obeyesekere, Gananath. *Imagining Karma*. Berkeley: University of California Press, 2002.
Ostenfeld, Erik Nis, ed. *Essays on Plato's Republic*. Aarhus: Aarhus University Press, 1998.
Otto, Walter F. *Die Götter Griechenlands*. Frankfurt am Main: Klostermann, 1947 [1st ed. 1929].
Page, Denys Lionel. *Epigrammata Graeca*. Oxford: Clarendon Press, 1975.
—. *Further Greek Epigrams*. Cambridge: Cambridge University Press, 1981.
Paget, R. F. *In the Footsteps of Orpheus*. London: Robert Hale, 1967.
Parke, Herbert William. *The Oracles of Apollo in Asia Minor*. London: Croom Helm, 1985.
Parke, Herbert William, and Donald Ernest Wilson Wormell. *The Delphic Oracle*, vol. 2. Oxford: Blackwell, 1956.
Parker, Robert. "Early Orphism." In *The Greek World*, edited by Anton Powell, 483–510. New York: Routledge, 1995.
—. *Polytheism and Society at Athens*. Oxford: Oxford University Press, 2005.

Parker, Robert, and Maria Stamatopoulou. "A New Funerary Gold Leaf from Pherai." *AE* (2004): 1–32.
Partenie, Catalin, ed. *Plato's Myths*. Cambridge: Cambridge University Press, 2009.
Patin, A. "Parmenides im Kampfe gegen Heraklit." *Jahrb. f. class. Phil. Suppl.* 25 (1899): 489–660.
Pedrick, Victoria. "Supplication in the *Iliad* and in the *Odyssey*." *TAPhA* 112 (1982): 125–140.
Pensa, Marina. *Rappresentazioni dell'oltretomba nella ceramica apula*. Rome: Bretschneider, 1977.
Pépin, Jean. "Héraclès et son reflet dans le Néoplatonisme." In *Le Néoplatonisme*, edited by Pierre-Maxime Schuhl and Pierre Hadot, 167–192. Paris: Centre National de la Recherche Scientifique, 1971.
Pfeiffer, Rudolf. "Gottheit und Individuum in der frühgriechischen Lyrik." *Philologus* 84 (1929): 137–52.
—. *Ausgewählte Schriften*. Edited by Winfried Bühler. Munich: C.H. Beck, 1960.
Picard, Charles. "La tentative sacrilege de Miltiade au sanctuaire Parien de Demeter." *RA* 36 (1950): 124–125.
Picot, Jean-Claude. "Empedocles, fragment 115.3: Can One of the Blessed Pollute his Limbs with Blood?" In *Reading Ancient Texts I: Presocratics and Plato—Essays in Honour of Denis O'Brien*, edited by Suzanne Stern-Gillet and Kevin Corrigan, 41–56. Leiden: Brill, 2007.
—. "Empédocle pouvait-il faire de la lune le séjour des Bienheureux ?" *Organon* (Warszawa) 37(40) (2008): 9–38.
Pitt-Rivers, Julian. "Women and Sanctuary in the Mediterranean." In *Échanges et Communications: Mélanges Lévi-Strauss*, edited by Jean Pouillon and Pierre Maranda, 862–875. The Hague and Paris: Mouton, 1970.
Plato. *Plato: Complete Works*. Edited by John M. Cooper. Indianapolis and Cambridge: Hackett, 1997.
—. *Republic*. Translated by C.D.C. Reeve. Indianapolis: Hackett, 2004.
Plotinus. *Enneads*, with an English Translation by Arthur H. Armstrong, 7 vols. Cambridge, MA: Harvard University Press, 1966–1988.
—. *The Enneads*. Edited by John Dillon and translated by Stephen McKenna. London: Penguin Books, 1991.
Plutarch. *Plutarch's Lives*. Translated by Bernadotte Perrin. Cambridge, MA. Harvard University Press, 1968.
Porphyry. *Sentences*. Edited by Luc Brisson. Paris: Vrin, 2005.
Potter, K. "The Karma Theory and Its Interpretation in Some Indian Philosophical Systems." In *Karma and Rebirth in Classical Indian Traditions*, edited by W. O'Flaherty, 241–267. Berkeley: University of California Press, 1980.
Pradeau, Jean-François. "Le monde terrestre: le modèle cosmologique du mythe final du 'Phédon.'" *RPhilos* 186 (1996): 75–195.
Press, Gerald A., ed. *Continuum Companion to Plato*. London: Continuum, 2012.

Prior, William J. "The Portrait of Socrates in Plato's *Symposium*." *OSAPh* 31 (2006): 137–66.
Pritchard, James B. ed. *The Ancient Near East in Pictures*. Princeton: Princeton University Press, 1954.
—, ed. *Ancient Near Eastern Texts* (ANET) *relating to the Old Testament*. Princeton: Princeton University Press, 1955.
Proclus. *In Platonis rem publicam commentarii*, vol. 1. Edited by Wilhelm Kroll. Leipzig: Teubner, 1899.
Pugliese Carratelli, Giovanni. "Phôlarkhos." *PP* 18 (1963): 385–386.
—. "La *thea* di Parmenide." *PP* 43 (1988): 336–346.
Radt, Stefan. *Tragicorum Graecorum Fragmenta*, vol. 3: *Aeschylus*. Göttingen: Vandenhoeck & Ruprecht, 1985.
Ramfos, Stelios, "Héraclite. Le cercle de la mort." *Philosophia* 1 (1971): 176–194.
Ramos Jurado, Enrique Ángel. *Platón. Apología de Sócrates. Fedón*, edición revisada, traducción, introducción y notas. Madrid: Consejo Superior de Investigaciones Científicas, 2002.
Rashed, Marwan. "The Structure of the Eye and its Cosmological Function in Empedocles. Reconstruction of Fragment 84 D.-K." In *Reading Ancient Texts I: Presocratics and Plato—Essays in Honour of Denis O'Brien*, edited by Suzanne Stern-Gillet and Kevin Corrigan, 21–39. Leiden and Boston: Brill, 2007.
—. "Le proème des *Catharmes* d'Empédocle. Reconstitution et commentaire." *Elenchos* 29.1 (2008): 7–37.
Raubitschek, Isabelle K. and Anthony E. "The Mission of Triptolemos." In *Studies in Athenian Architecture, Sculpture and Topography, presented to Homer A. Thompson*, 109–117. Princeton: American School of Classical Studies at Athens, 1982.
Reale, Giovanni. *The Concept of First Philosophy and the Unity of the Metaphysics of Aristotle*. Translated by John R. Catan. Albany, NY: SUNY Press, 1980.
Reece, Steve. *The Stranger's Welcome*. Ann Arbor, MI: University of Michigan Press, 1993.
Reinhardt, Karl. *Parmenides und die Geschichte der griechischen Philosophie*. Bonn: Cohen, 1916.
—. "Tradition und Geist im homerischen Epos." In *Die Krise des Helden*. Munich: dtv, 1962.
Remes, Pauliina. *Neoplatonism*. Stocksfield: Acumen, 2008.
Richardson, Nicholas J., ed. *The Homeric Hymn to Demeter*. Oxford: Oxford University Press, 1974.
Richardson, Hilda. "The Myth of Er (Plato, *Republic* 616b)." *CQ* 20 (1926): 115–131.
Riedweg, Christoph. *Mysterienterminologie bei Platon, Philon und Klemens von Alexandrien*. Berlin: De Gruyter, 1987.
—. "Orphisches bei Empedocles." *A & A* 41 (1995): 34–59.
—. "Initiation-Tod-Unterwelt: Beobachtungen zur Kommunikationssituation und narrativen Technik der orphisch-bakchischen Goldblättchen." In *An-

sichten griechischer Rituale. Geburtstags-Symposium für W. Burkert, edited by Fritz Graf, 359–398. Stuttgart and Leipzig: Teubner, 1998.

—. "Poésie orphique et rituel initiatique: Éléments d'un 'Discourse sacré' dans les lamelles d'or." *RHR* 219 (2002): 459–481.

—. "Initiation-Death-Underworld. Narrative and Ritual in the Gold Tablets." In *The Orphic Gold Tablets and Greek Religion: Further Along the Path*, edited by Radcliffe G. Edmonds, 219–256. Cambridge: Cambridge University Press, 2011.

Rist, John M. "Theos and the One in Some Texts of Plotinus." *Medieval Studies* 24 (1962): 169–180.

—. "Monism: Plotinus and Some Predecessors." *HSCP* 69 (1965): 329–344.

—. *Plotinus: The Road to Reality*. Cambridge: Cambridge University Press, 1967.

—. "The One of Plotinus and the God of Aristotle." *RMeta* 27.1 (Sep., 1973): 75–87.

Ritter, Joachim, and Karlfried Gründer, eds. *Historisches Wörterbuch der Philosophie*, 12 vols. Basel: Schwabe, 1971–2007.

Rösler, Wolfgang. "Der Anfang der Katharmoi des Empedokles." *Hermes* 111 (1983): 170–179.

Rose, Gilbert P. "The Unfriendly Phaeacians." *TAPhA* 100 (1969): 387–406.

Rosen, Stanley. *Plato's Republic: A Study*. New Haven, CT: Yale University Press, 2005.

Rosenfeld-Löffler, Annette. *La poétique d'Empédocle, Cosmologie et métaphore*. Bern and New York: Peter Lang, 2006.

Rowe, Christopher J. *Plato: Phaedrus*. Edited with Translation and Commentary. Warminster: Aris & Phillips, 1986.

—. *Plato: Phaedo*. Edited with Commentary. Cambridge: Cambridge University Press, 1993.

—. *Plato: Symposium*. Warminster, UK: Aris & Phillips, 1998.

Ruiz Yamuza, Emilia. *El mito como estructura formal en Platón*. Sevilla: Servicio de Publicaciones de la Universidad de Sevilla, 1986.

Sabbatucci, Dario. *Saggio sul misticismo Greco*, 2nd ed. Rome: Edizioni dell' Ateneo & Bizzarri, 1979.

Saffrey, Henri Dominique, and Alain-Philippe Segonds. *Marinus. Proclus Or Sur le Bonheur*, 2nd ed. Paris: Les Belles Lettres, 2002.

Santamaría Álvarez, Marco A. "Φωνάεντα συνετοῖσιν. Píndaro y los misterios: edición y comentario de la Olímpica Segunda." Ph.D. Diss., Salamanca, 2004.

—. "Píndaro y el orfismo." In *Orfeo y la tradición órfica: un reencuentro*, edited by Alberto Bernabé and Francesc Casadesús, 1161–1184. Madrid: Akal, 2008.

Sas, Stephan. *Der Hinkende als Symbol*. Zürich: Rascher, 1964.

Saunders, Trevor J. "Penology and Eschatology in Plato's *Timaeus* and *Laws*." *CQ* 23 (1973): 232–44.

—. *Plato's Penal Code*. Oxford: Oxford University Press, 1991.

Schauenburg, Konrad. "Helios: archäologisch-mythologische Studien über den antiken Sonnengott." Ph.D. Diss., Berlin, 1950.

Schefer, Christina. *Platons unsagbare Erfahrung. Ein anderer Zugang zu Platon*. Basel: Schwabe, 2001.
Schibli, Hermann S. *Pherekydes of Syros*. Oxford: Oxford University Press, 1990.
Schils, Gretchen. "Plato's Myth of Er: The Light and the Spindle." *AC* 62 (1993): 101–114.
Schmitt, Arbogast. *Selbständigkeit und Abhängigkeit menschlichen Handelns bei Homer. Hermeneutische Untersuchungen zur Psychologie Homers*. Stuttgart: Steiner, 1990.
—. *Modernity and Plato: Two Paradigms of Rationality*. Translated by Vishwa Adluri. Rochester: Camden House, 2012.
Schroeder, F. M. "*Synousia, Synaisthesis* and *Synesis*. Presence and Dependence in Plotinian Philosophy of Consciousness." *Aufstieg und Niedergang der römischen Welt* II 35.1 (1987): 677–699.
Schürmann, Reiner. "Ultimate Double Binds." *Graduate Faculty Philosophy Journal* 14.2–15.1 (1991): 224.
Schwabl, Hans. "Sein und Doxa bei Parmenides." *Wiener Studien* 66 (1953): 50–75.
—. "Hesiod und Parmenides." *RhM* 106 (1963): 59–68.
—. "Zur Selbständigkeit des Menschen bei Homer." *Wiener Studien* 67 (1965): 46–64.
Schwartz, Jacques. *Pseudo-Hesiodeia. Recherches sur la composition, la diffusion et la disparition ancienne d'oeuvres attribuées à Hésiode*. Leiden: Brill, 1960.
Schwyzer, Eduard, and Albert Debrunner. *Griechische Grammatik*, vol. 2. Munich: C.H. Beck, 1950.
Seaford, Richard. "Immortality, Salvation, and the Elements." *HSCP* 90 (1986): 1–26.
Seekin, Kenneth R. "Platonism, Mysticism and Madness." *Monist* 59 (1976): 574–586.
Seel, Otto. "Antike und frühchristliche Allegorik." In *Festschrift für Peter Metz*, edited by Ursula Schlegel and Claus Zoege von Manteuffel, 11–45. Berlin: De Gruyter, 1965.
Segal, Charles. "Poetic Immortality and the Fear of Death: The Second Proem of the *De Rerum Natura*." *HSCP* 92 (1989): 193–212.
—. *Singers, Heroes and Gods in the Odyssey*. Ithaca and London: Cornell University Press, 1994.
Setaioli, Aldo. "Nuove osservazioni sulla 'descrizione dell'oltretomba' nel papiro di Bologna." *SIFC* 42 (1970): 179–224.
—. "L'imagine delle bilance e il giudizio dei morti." *SIFC* 44 (1972): 38–54.
—. "Ancora a proposito del papiro bolognese n. 4." *SIFC* 45 (1973): 124–133.
Seth, Benardete. *Socrates' Second Sailing: On Plato's Republic*. Chicago: University of Chicago Press, 1992.
—. "Strauss on Plato." In *The Argument of the Action: Essays on Greek Poetry and Philosophy*, edited by Ronna Burger and Michael Davis, 407–418. Chicago: University of Chicago Press, 2000.

Sharma, I. C. "The Plotinian One and the Concept of *Paramapuruṣa* in the *Bhagavadgītā*." In *Neoplatonism and Indian Thought*, edited by R. Baine Harris, 87–100. Albany, NY: State University of New York Press, 1982.
Sharp, Kendall. "From Solon to Socrates: Proto-Socratic Dialogues in Herodotus." In *La costruzione del discorso filosofico nell'età dei Presocratici*, edited by Maria Michela Sassi, 81–102. Pisa: Edizioni della Normale, 2006.
Shaw, Gregory. *Theurgy and the Soul*. University Park, PA: Pennsylvania State University Press, 1995.
Shear, T. Leslie. "The Demolished Temple at Eleusis." In *Studies in Athenian Architecture, Sculpture and Topography, presented to Homer A. Thompson*, 128–140. Princeton: American School of Classical Studies at Athens, 1982.
Siegmann, Ernst. *Homer. Vorlesungen über die Odyssee*. Würzburg: Königshausen & Neumann, 1987.
Simon, Erika. *Festivals of Attica, an Archaeological Commentary*. Madison: University of Wisconsin Press, 1983.
Skarsouli, Penelope. "Calliope, a Muse Apart: Some Remarks on the Tradition of Memory as a Vehicle for Oral Justice." *Oral Tradition* 21.1 (2006): 210–228.
Skias, A. "Eleusiniakai keramographiai." *EA* (1901): 1–39.
Slaveva-Griffin, Svetla. *Plotinus on Number*. Oxford: Oxford University Press, 2009.
Smith, K. F. "The Literary Tradition of Gyges and Candaules." *AJPh* 41.1 (1920): 1–37.
Snell, Bruno. "Das Bewußtsein von den eigenen Entscheidungen." In *Gesammelte Schriften*, 18–31. Göttingen: Vandenhoeck & Ruprecht, 1966.
—. *Aischylos und das Handeln im Drama*. Leipzig: Dieterich'sche Verlagsbuchhandlung, 1928.
—. *Die Entdeckung des Geistes*. Göttingen: Vandenhoeck & Ruprecht, 1946.
—. "Göttliche und menschliche Motivation im homerischen Epos." In *Argumentationen. Festschrift Joseph König*, edited by Harald Delius and Günther Patzig, 249–55. Göttingen: Vandenhoeck & Ruprecht, 1964.
—. *Gesammelte Schriften*. Göttingen: Vandenhoeck & Ruprecht, 1966.
Snodgrass, Anthony. *Archaic Greece, The Age of Experiment*. London: J. M. Dent & Sons Ltd, 1980.
Solmsen, Friedrich. "Chaos und Apeiron." *SIFC* 24 (1950): 235–248.
Sophocles. *The Complete Greek Tragedies*, vol. 2: *Sophocles*. Edited by David Grene and Richard Lattimore. Chicago and London: University of Chicago Press, 1992.
Stafford, Emma. *Worshipping Virtues*. London: Duckworth, 2000.
Stalley, Richard F. "Plato's Doctrine of Freedom." *Proceedings of the Aristotelian Society* 98 (1998): 145–158.
—. "Myth and Eschatology in the *Laws*." In *Plato's Myths*, edited by Catalin Partenie, 187–205. Cambridge: Cambridge University Press, 2009.
Stamatellos, Giannis. *Plotinus and the Presocratics. A Philosophical Study of Presocratic Influences in Plotinus' Enneads*. Albany, NY: State University of New York Press, 2007.

Stehle, Eva. "The Addressees of Empedokles, *Katharmoi* Fr. B 112: Performance and Moral Implications." *AncPhil* 25.2 (2005): 247–72.
Stewart, John Alexander. *The Myths of Plato*. London: Macmillan, 1962.
Stokes, Michael C. "Hesiodic and Milesian Cosmogonies." *Phronesis* 7 (1962): 1–37.
Stroumsa, Guy G. *Hidden Wisdom: Esoteric Traditions and the Roots of Christian Mysticism*. Leiden: Brill, 2005.
Struck, Peter T. *Birth of the Symbol: Ancient Readers at the Limits of Their Texts*. Princeton: Princeton University Press, 2004.
Suárez de la Torre, Emilio. "Píndaro y la religión griega." *CFC(G)* 3 (1993): 67–97.
Svoronos, J.N. "Hermêneia tou ex Eleusinos mustêriakou pinakos tês Niiniou." *Journal international d'archéologie numismatique* 4 (1901): 233–270.
Tarán, Leonardo. *Parmenides*. Princeton: Princeton University Press, 1965.
Tarrant, Harold. *Proclus. Commentary on Plato's Timaeus*, vol. 1. Cambridge: Cambridge University Press, 2007.
Thimme, Jürgen. "Die religiöse Bedeutung der Kykladenidole." *Antike Kunst* 8 (1965): 72–86.
Thomas, Hans Werner. "ΕΠΕΚΕΙΝΑ, Untersuchungen über das Überlieferungsgut in den Jenseitsmythen Platons." Ph.D. Diss., Würzburg, 1938.
Thornton, Agathe. *Homer's Iliad: Its Composition and the Motif of Supplication*. Göttingen: Vandenhoeck & Ruprecht, 1984.
Tortorelli, Marisa. *Figli della Terra e del cielo stellato*. Naples: M. D' Auria, 2006.
Toulouse, Stéphane. "Le véhicule de l'âme chez Plotin: de la réception d'une hypothèse cosmologique à l'usage dialectique de la notion." *Études platoniciennes* 3 (2007): 103–128.
Tredennick, Hugh. "*Phaedo*." In *Plato. Collected Dialogues*. Edited by Edith Hamilton and Huntington Cairns, 40–98. Princeton: Princeton University Press, 1996.
Trépanier, Simon. *Empedocles. An Interpretation*. London: Routledge, 2004.
Trouillard, Jean. *La Purification Plotinienne*. Paris: Presses Universitaires de France, 1955.
Tsantsanoglou, Kyriakos. "The First Columns of the *Derveni Papyrus* and their Religious Significance." In *Studies on the Derveni Papyrus*, edited by André Laks and Glenn W. Most, 93–128. Oxford: Oxford University Press, 1997.
Tuozzo, Thomas M. "Comments on Erler and Schefer." In *Plato as Author: The Rhetoric of Philosophy*, edited by Ann N. Michelini, 197–202. Leiden: Brill, 2003.
Tzifopoulos, Yannis. *Paradise Earned: The Bacchic-Orphic Gold Lamellae of Crete*. Cambridge, MA: Harvard University Press, 2010.
Untersteiner, Mario. *Parmenide. Testimonianze e frammenti*. Florence: La "Nuova Italia" Editrice, 1958.
Usener, Hermann. *Götternamen: Versuch einer Lehre der religiösen Begriffsbildung*. Bonn: Cohen, 1896.
Van Buitenen, J.A.B. "Dharma and Mokṣa." *Philosophy East and West* 7.1 (1957): 33–40.

Van Groningen, Bernhard Abraham. "Empédocle, poète." *Mnemosyne* 24 (1971): 169–188.
Verdenius, Willem Jacob. *Parmenides*. Groningen: J. B. Walters, 1942.
—. "Parmenides' Conception of Light." *Mnemosyne* 4.2 (1949): 116–131.
Vernant, Jean-Pierre. "Le fleuve Améles et la Mélétè thanatou." In *Mythe et pensée chez les grecs*, 79–94. Paris: F. Maspero, 1965.
—. *Mythic Thought among the Greeks*. Cambridge, MA: Zone, 2006.
Violante, Maria Lucia. "Un confronto tra *PBon*. 4 e *l'Assioco*. La valutazione delle anime nella tradizione orfica e platonica." *CCC* 5 (1981): 313–327.
Vítek, Tomáš. *Empedoklés* I. Prague: Herrmann & synové, 2001.
Vlastos, Gregory. "Parmenides' Theory of Knowledge." *TAPhA* 77 (1946): 66–77.
—. "Equality and Justice and Early Greek Cosmologies." *CP* 42 (1947): 156–178.
—. "Theology and Philosophy in Early Greek." *The Philosophical Quarterly* 2.7 (1952): 97–123.
—. Review of *Principium Sapientiae* by F. M. Cornford. *Gnomon* 27 (1955): 65–76.
Vogliano, Achille. "Il papiro bolognese Nr. 3." *Acme* 5 (1952): 385–417.
Von Fritz, Kurt. "Der Beginn universalwissenschaftlicher Bestrebungen und der Primat der Griechen." *Studium Generale* 14 (1961): 601–636.
Von Kienle, Walter. "Die Berichte über die Sukzessionen der Philosophen in der hellenistischen und spätantiken Literatur." Ph.D. Diss., Berlin, 1961.
Von Soden, Wolfram. *Das Gilgamesh Epos*. Stuttgart: Reclam, 1958.
Von Wilamowitz-Moellendorff, Ulrich. "Lesefrüchte." *Hermes* 34 (1899): 203–230.
—. *Platon* I. Berlin: Weidmannsche Buchhandlung, 1909.
—. *Die Ilias und Homer*. Berlin: Weidmannsche Buchhandlung, 1916.
Von Wlislocki, Heinrich. *Aus dem Volksleben der Magyaren*. Augsburg: M. Huttler, 1893.
Vos, H. "Die Bahnen von Nacht und Tag." *Mnemosyne* 4.16 (1963): 18–34.
Wallis, Richard T. *Neoplatonism*. London: Hackett, 1972.
Warren, E. W. "Consciousness in Plotinus." *Phronesis* 9 (1964): 83–97.
—. "Memory in Plotinus." *Phronesis* 15 (1965): 252–260.
—. "Imagination in Plotinus." *Phronesis* 16 (1966): 277–285.
Welbon, Guy Richard. "On Understanding the Buddhist Nirvāṇa." *History of Religions* 5.2 (1966): 300–326.
Wendland, Paul. "Σωτήρ." *Zeitschrift für die neutestamentliche Wissenschaft* v.5 (1904): 335–53.
West, Martin L. *Early Greek Philosophy and the Orient*. Oxford: Clarendon Press, 1971.
—. "Hocus-pocus in East and West: Theogony, Ritual and the Tradition of Esoteric Commentary." In *Studies on the Derveni Papyrus*, edited by André Laks and Glenn Most, 81–90. New York: Oxford University Press, 1997.
—. *Hesiod. Works and Days*. Oxford: Oxford University Press, 1978.
—. *The Orphic Poems*. Oxford: Oxford University Press, 1983.

—. *Iambi et Elegi Graeci*, editio altera. Oxford: Oxford University Press, 1989.
—. "A Vagina in Search of an Author." *CQ* 58 (2007): 370–375.
White, David. "Human Perfection in the *Bhagavadgītā*." *Philosophy East and West* 21.1 (1971): 43–53.
Widengren, Geo. *Iranisch-semitische Kulturbegegnung in parthischer Zeit*. Cologne and Opladen: Westdeutscher Verlag, 1960.
von Wilamowitz-Moellendorf, Ulrich. *Der Glaube der Hellenen*, vol. 1. Berlin: Weidmannsche Buchhandlung, 1931.
Willems, Alphonse. *Aristophane: traduction avec notes et commentaires critiques*. Paris: Hachette, 1919.
Willetts, Ronald F. *Cretan Cults and Festivals*. New York: Barnes and Noble, 1962.
Wilson, Nigel G. *Aristophanis Fabulae*, recognovit breveque adnotatione critica instruixt, Tomus II. Oxford: Oxford University Press, 2007.
Winiarczyk, Marcus, ed. *Diagorae Melii et Theodori Cyrenaei reliquiae*. Leipzig: Teubner, 1981.
Woodbury, Leonard. "The Date and Atheism of Diagoras of Melos." *Phoenix* 19.3 (1965): 178–211.
Wright, M. Rosemary. *Empedocles: The Extant Fragments*. New Haven and London: Yale University Press, 1981.
Zeller, Eduard. *Philosophie der Griechen in ihrer geschichtlichen Entwicklung*, vol. 1. Edited by Wilhelm Nestle. Leipzig: O.R. Reisland, 1929.
Zeller, Moritz. *Die Knabenweihen*. Bern: Haupt, 1923.
Zimmermann, Klaus. Article "Soter." In *Der Neue Pauly*, vol. II, edited by Hubert Cancik and Helmuth Schneider, 752–753. Stuttgart: Metzler, 2003.
Zuntz, Günther. *Persephone: Three Essays on Religion and Thought in Magna Graecia*. Oxford: Oxford University Press, 1971.

Index of terms

Acheron   131–3, 141
Achilles   16, 19, 59, 63–5, 70–2, 75, 77–9
Adkins, Arther W.H.   70
Aeschylus   92, 106, 159, 168, 170
afterlife   2, 8, 40, 97, 144, 210–14, 216, 227, 238, 244–6, 249–54, 259–61, 263–4
– punishments   263, 280–2
– rewards   266, 275, 282
Agamemnon   63–4, 66, 72, 77–81
air   22, 131–2, 186, 265, 293, 310
Akragas   42–4
Alcibiades   167–8, 171, 204
allegory   29, 86–7, 92, 94
alternation   56, 96–8, 100
ancient Greek philosophy   315
Ancient Near Eastern Texts see ANET
ancient philosophy   2, 6, 14, 24, 219
ANET (Ancient Near Eastern Texts)   105–6
angel   129, 318–19, 345, 348, 354–5
Annas, Julia   125, 134, 264
antílepsis see apprehension
antiquity   2–4, 10, 15, 29, 61, 63, 74, 285, 313, 357–9
Apollo   71, 109, 111, 193–5, 235, 240–1, 324, 326, 329, 341
Apollo's oracle   315, 323–4, 327, 330, 332, 335–6, 339
Apology   122, 145–6, 245, 264
aporia   95, 202, 277
appearance   97, 144, 207, 210, 227–8
apprehension   295–6, 300
Arete   32, 35–6, 39, 49, 54
Aristophanes   91, 153, 156–7, 159, 162, 170–1, 175

Aristophanes' Frogs (*also* Frogs)   162, 168, 170–2, 175, 179, 181, 187–9
Aristotle   8, 11, 25–6, 41, 74–5, 82, 100, 102, 104, 110, 131, 159, 252, 290, 293, 296–7, 359
art   13, 176, 181, 198–202, 208, 212–13, 222, 286, 325, 329
ascent   3, 29, 85, 87–8, 98, 101, 151, 165, 177–8, 187–8, 226, 250, 283, 292, 328, 343–4, 346–9
astrology   310–11, 324
atheist   153–4
Athena   31–2, 34–5, 49, 54, 56, 63, 65, 68–9, 70–8, 100, 199
Athenians   100, 112, 155, 167, 195, 235
Athens   161, 167–8, 184, 195, 226
audience   47, 52, 79, 168
autonomy   60–2, 64–5, 67, 82–3, 144, 268
Axiochus   122, 140–1, 143–4
– father of Clinias   140
– pseudo-Platonic   117, 119, 140

Bacchylides   193
behavior   60, 73, 78–81, 112, 140
beings   48, 289, 330, 335
beliefs   8, 13, 45, 62, 66, 111, 125, 129, 144, 148, 154, 243, 247–8, 251, 261, 343–4
Bernabé, Alberto   26
Bhagavad Gītā   27, 320–3, 327, 329, 339
birth   22, 116, 130, 158, 166, 189, 243–4, 247, 255–7, 265, 268, 270, 273, 275–6, 278–80, 282, 287–8, 291, 322–4, 348
– cycle of   243–4, 247, 255–6, 270, 276, 280, 287–8

blessedness   44, 148
blindness   64, 79–80, 82
body   10, 16–19, 133–4, 137–8, 141, 200–2, 205–6, 210–12, 246–8, 253–4, 259–60, 275, 277–8, 280–3, 285–6, 290–4, 297–8, 300, 304–11, 313–15, 322–3, 326–8, 331–3, 335–8, 347–50
– celestial   309–10
– earthly   256, 289, 293, 304
– ethereal   354
– grave illness of   201
– living   3, 7, 26, 293, 298, 305
Bowra, C. M.   86
Brisson, Luc   5, 27
Burkert, Walter   3, 7, 24, 26, 155, 159
Bussanich, John   26, 27

Calliope   50, 52, 54, 56–7
Candaules   230–1
cave   85, 103–9, 114–15, 185, 249, 278, 280
celebration   45, 148, 159, 173, 185–6, 327, 339
chain (of beings or of divinities)   97, 319, 345, 348, 350, 353–4
Chaldean Oracles   316, 318–20, 322–3, 327, 329
chance   239–40, 267–8, 286
change   21, 23, 85, 97, 275, 285
chariot   89, 93, 95, 99, 165, 256, 266, 347
charm   81–2, 220, 251, 328
choice   26, 61, 66, 72, 208, 212, 215–6, 232, 244, 265–9, 272, 276, 278, 282–3, 287, 298
– free   61, 80, 269,
– freedom of   62, 77
– soul's own   211–2
– of lives/ new lives   214, 270, 280–1
– responsibility for   59, 233, 237, 240, 284
chorus   168, 170, 173, 302
Christian dogmatics   10–11
Christianity   2, 10, 123, 192

Cicero   194
citizens   12, 26, 43–4, 196, 205–6
city   7, 12–14, 16–17, 44, 53, 111, 135, 164, 195–7, 199, 203–6, 208–9, 215–16, 219–20, 223, 236–8, 285
– ideal   7, 136, 221, 236–8, 241
classical period   176–7, 182, 263
Clement   21, 154–6, 159, 189
Clinton, Kevin   179, 185
Colophon   351–2
columns   185–6
comedy   159, 171–2, 175
commentary   117, 131, 330
conflict   62–3, 74, 208–9
Connectors   318–19
consciousness   7, 18, 65, 67, 70, 215, 282, 288, 295
constitution   12, 204–6, 291
contemplation   25, 125, 213–14, 240, 277, 311, 321, 335–6
continuation of natural life   165, 189
conviction   12–13, 72–3, 103, 197, 202, 215, 251–2
corpse   21, 227, 229
Cosmic Soul   321, 329, 345–6
cosmology   5–6, 22, 134, 309, 311
cosmos   3, 10, 17, 22, 48, 55, 98, 229, 236, 238–9, 241, 257, 267, 269, 348–9
courage   13–14, 124, 197, 204, 223, 333, 337
Coxon, A.H.   91
crime   136, 160, 230–1, 247, 253–6, 258, 261–3, 273–4
Croesus   193–4, 218–19, 232–5, 239–41
Cronus   121–2
crossroads   125, 145
Crotonians   110, 113
cult   9, 53, 95, 107, 109, 110–11, 151, 157, 161, 175–6, 195, 197–8, 318
– hero   105, 206
mystery   183–4, 189, 222, 224–5, 245
Cumae   104–5, 109

daemon (*also* daemons) 221, 237, 318, 323, 326–8, 329–31, 343, 345, 347–8, 353–5
daimon (*also* daimones) 34, 41–2, 46–9, 51, 57, 90–1, 101, 115, 129, 133, 135, 147, 281
demon (*also* demons) 309–11, 330
Damascius 131–2
darkness 87, 92, 96, 102, 106–7, 115–16, 138, 172, 181, 188, 281
daughter 163–5, 168, 181, 188
Davis, Michael 217, 231–2
death 10–11, 15, 17–24, 81, 105–9, 113–14, 116–17, 119–20, 122–3, 133–4, 140–1, 143, 165–6, 189, 209–10, 212, 214, 220–4, 232, 239–40, 243–4, 255–7, 264–5, 285, 321–3
Deichgräber, Karl 85, 87
Delphi 232, 235, 351
Demeter 91, 108, 110, 112, 114, 156, 161–8, 170–1, 173, 175, 177–85, 188–9, 334
Demeter-cult (*also* Demeter cult) 108, 110, 113, 157
Demetrius 155, 196
demigods 121–2, 308
demiurge 257, 276, 309–10, 334, 337, 346
Derveni Papyrus 4, 86, 129
descent 177–8, 225–6, 249, 256–7, 259, 272, 277–81, 283, 292–3, 304–5, 311, 329, 337, 344
– soul's 256, 259, 278–9, 281, 304
destiny 1, 4, 31, 39, 45–6, 56, 60, 77, 118, 121, 130, 132, 134, 137–8, 142, 144, 147–8, 275, 292
Diagoras 171
dialectic 202, 206, 299–300
Dike 90, 96–9, 101, 103, 105
Dionysus 168–9, 171–4, 279
Dioscuri 167, 194, 202
discourse 136, 296, 300
discursive reason 294, 296, 298–303, 311
divination 324, 349–52

divine agency 66, 68, 80, 276
divine illumination 349–54
divine law 247, 281, 327, 329
divine light 88, 350–3
divine message 50, 352
divine nature, soul's 332
divine origin, soul's 255, 339
divine power 64, 66, 222
divine soul 256, 292, 308
divine status 46, 255
divine supervisor 276, 281
divinities 8–9, 26, 32, 49, 82, 122, 124, 166, 180, 346, 348–9, 354
Dodds, E.R. 30, 125, 247
dolphin 13, 202–3, 222
doxa, world of 102, 115
dream 21, 77–8, 103, 225

earth 22, 47, 91, 94, 98, 101, 105, 121, 123–4, 131, 133, 137–8, 167, 181–2, 188–9, 224, 233, 256, 258, 265, 290–3, 305, 346, 350–1, 354
edge of the world 94, 99, 101
Edmonds, Radcliffe G. 5, 260
Eleusinian cult 183–4
Eleusinian gods 176, 179–80
Eleusinian Mysteries (*also* Mysteries of Eleusis) 26, 151–3, 155–6, 159–60, 164, 166, 168, 170, 172, 182, 185, 187, 189–90, 261
Eleusinion 167
Eleusis 141, 156–62, 167–70, 174–6, 181–6, 245
embodiment 240, 244, 253–4, 257, 259, 272, 278–81
emotion 62, 66, 178, 258, 267, 283, 321
Empedocles 1, 5–7, 10, 25, 30–1, 40–57, 95, 192, 221–2, 246–7, 255, 257, 314–15, 317, 331–2, 334–9, 341
Enlightenment 3, 61
Enneads (*also* Enn.) 277, 279, 286–8, 314–17, 334–9, 340–1
Epimenides 89, 103, 114–15, 247

Er 136–7, 212, 214–16, 218, 221, 223–4, 236–7, 239–41, 250, 257, 263, 266–7, 269, 271, 276
– myth of 26, 54, 135, 217, 220–1, 223–4, 229, 236, 238–9, 241, 249, 251, 262, 265–8, 271, 273, 276, 279, 284
escape 7, 13, 18, 43, 47, 133, 202, 204, 210, 212, 216, 222, 261–2, 270, 288, 325
eschatology 2, 3, 5, 10–11, 20, 46, 118, 125, 127–8, 134–7, 140, 145–6, 148, 243–5, 253, 261, 264, 266, 275–6, 279, 287–8
eternity 21, 23, 309
ethereal vehicle 353–4
ethics 4, 6, 287, 289, 306, 311
Euripides 119, 168–70
evil daemons 318, 353
evils 73, 126, 140, 145, 147, 200, 204, 210, 212, 216, 243, 262, 264, 267, 279–83, 285, 308, 330–1, 336
exile 7, 30–1, 40, 42–3, 46, 57, 257, 278
existence
– earthly 59, 274, 350
– previous 138, 306, 311
experiences, near-death 6, 24

fate 16, 18–20, 22, 60, 110, 123, 139, 182, 234, 240–1, 260, 275–6, 284
Fates 240–1, 263, 265, 267, 269
Finamore, John 27, 219, 222
flux 20–3
forgetfulness 137, 215, 223, 240, 251, 256–7, 268, 279, 307
forms, intelligible 298, 301–2
fountains 33, 138, 250
fragments 1, 7, 20–3, 30, 41–2, 45–50, 52, 54, 85–6, 103, 129, 142–3, 167, 255, 319–20, 347
– extant 21, 42–3, 54, 331
Fränkel, Hermann 87–8, 95,
freedom 61–2, 65, 72, 267–9, 280, 284, 352

– and autonomy 61–2
– consciousness of 61

gate 96–7, 99, 101–2, 105
gatekeeper 99, 104
gateway 94, 96–8
geography 138, 145, 214, 250, 276
– infernal 131–2
– otherworldy 248
Gilgamesh 31, 105–6, 108, 113, 116
Glaucon 211, 223–9, 232–3, 236, 238, 273
God 6, 9, 17, 60, 83, 124, 192, 234, 284, 314, 338
goddess 9–10, 40, 43, 50, 54, 56, 65, 72, 85, 87, 89–91, 99–101, 103–4, 106, 108, 111, 113–14, 164, 166, 173, 177, 182–3
– great 107, 110–11
gods 31–2, 36, 56, 59–60, 62–3, 65–6, 68–75, 77–82, 89, 136, 146, 165, 179, 193–4, 197–9, 207–8, 211–12, 233, 247, 254–9, 273, 308, 325, 343–4, 346–54
– blessed 50–1
– company of 332, 339
– immortal 35, 59
– invisible 348
– lesser 144–8, 284, 334, 337
– traditional 216
Gold Leaves (*also* gold leaves) 4, 5, 24, 30–1, 33–4, 36, 38–9, 40, 44, 46, 49, 50–1, 54, 56–7, 246, 250, 255, 257,
gold tablets (*see also* Gold Leaves) 33, 50, 121, 125, 127, 129–30, 137–9, 141, 143, 145,
Gorgias (*also* Gorg.) 117–19, 122–3, 125–6, 134, 144–8, 200, 202, 210–11, 215–16, 244, 248, 250, 259–62, 264
grain 177, 180, 182, 189
Greek philosophical salvation 8
Greek philosophical soteriology 15, 191

Greek philosophy 2, 5, 10–11, 313, 317
Greek religion 2, 5, 9, 108, 191–2, 209
guardians 12, 33, 138–9, 202, 204–5
guidance figures 179, 183
guide 56, 60, 95, 128–9, 135, 147, 179–80, 187–8, 250, 262, 304, 318, 328
guilt 79–80, 135, 247, 254
Gundert, Hermann 64, 66, 78
Gyges 213–14, 218, 221, 224–5, 227, 229–34, 236
– myth of 26, 217–18, 221 224, 228, 236

Hades 18–19, 32–3, 38–9, 56, 117–18, 120–3, 127–8, 131, 138, 140, 145, 147, 163, 165, 173, 210, 214–15, 226–7, 251, 261–3, 269, 272–3, 275–6, 282, 305–9
happiness 25, 59, 121, 138, 140, 143, 147, 201, 204, 207–8, 214, 234–5, 239, 257
health 196, 200–1, 205, 222, 326
heaven 2, 11, 73, 94, 98, 101, 105, 136, 145, 165, 244, 256, 258, 266, 270, 283, 292–3, 302, 304, 308, 328, 350
Hecate 166, 170, 181
Helen 71–2, 81, 168
Heliades 92–3, 95–6, 99
Helios 31, 93, 96, 106, 108
Heracles 19, 57, 167, 169, 171, 173, 307–9
Heraclitus 20–3, 82, 97, 102, 129, 221
Hermes 163–6, 168, 177, 179–80, 187–8
Hermippus 112, 114
Herodotus 33, 111–12, 114, 187, 203, 217–19, 221–2, 229–34, 236, 238–40, 324
Herrero, Miguel 24, 26

Hesiod 21, 52, 57, 85–6, 88–9, 95, 97–9, 103–5, 114–15, 121–2, 132, 145, 167, 264
Hesiod's Theogony (also Theogony, Theog.) 21, 52, 89, 94–6, 98, 103–4, 167, 324
Heubeck, Alfred 64, 66, 77
hierarchy 243, 257–8, 288
hierophant 110, 113–14, 156
Hippias 199–200, 220, 230
Hippolytus 23, 54, 56, 154
Histories 217–8, 222, 229, 240
history 16, 80, 144, 216, 315, 343
– Enlightenment narrative of 3
– of philosophy 17, 23
– of Greek philosophy 313
– Herodotus' 218, 231–2
Homer 16, 19, 21, 23, 29–30, 44, 57, 59–71, 73–80, 82, 89, 118, 120–1, 123, 131, 144, 146, 249, 264, 307–8, 326
Homeric characters 65–6, 80, 83, 157, 334
Homeric man (also Homeric individual) 59, 60, 63–6, 68, 74, 81–3
Homeric Hymn 161, 166–9, 171, 173–5, 178, 181–2, 187–9
– to Demeter 156–7, 162, 164, 188
– to Poseidon 194
Homeric poems 31, 39–40
honor 14, 18, 76, 80, 195, 201, 203, 205, 268, 331, 349
House of Night 93–6, 98–9, 101, 105
hubris 232, 236
human life 1, 22, 182, 198, 224, 234, 239, 285, 313
human life-span 239–40
human souls 214, 253, 259, 278, 289–93, 308, 343–9, 354–5
– descended 307
– purified 345, 348, 355
hymn 157, 164, 168, 173, 193
Hypercosmic Soul 345

Iacchos 170, 172–5, 179, 184
Iamblichean philosophy 349, 352

Iamblichus   27, 314–16, 339, 341, 343–55
Iliad   18, 43, 63, 69–70, 74, 77, 90, 121
illumination   281, 344, 350, 352–4
immortality   55, 105, 116, 141, 144, 189, 220, 222, 227–8, 232, 238, 243, 253, 328
immortals   7, 20–1, 23, 25, 59–60, 128, 164, 187–8, 210, 212, 241, 248, 253, 257–8, 260, 269, 280, 332
incantation   129, 251, 261
incarnation   244, 255, 257, 266, 272–3, 280, 284
individual souls   22, 275, 277–8, 315, 321, 330, 334, 338–9, 345–6, 355
initiands   180, 183, 186–7
initiation   15, 25, 56, 103, 113, 128, 135, 148, 155, 158, 160, 166–7, 172, 179, 183, 186, 188, 211–12, 216, 226, 229, 349
injustice   199, 202, 211, 262, 273, 285
inscription   95, 109, 157, 175, 181
intellect   75, 279, 282, 287, 290–4, 296, 298–302, 305, 308, 315, 327, 333–6, 339–40, 344–6, 350, 355
intellection   298, 300, 308, 332–3
– act of   297
intellectual act   295–6
intelligence   12–13, 212–13, 223, 295–6
Intelligible   290, 293, 301, 304–5, 308, 311, 334, 338, 345–7
intermediaries   9, 129, 301–3, 354
intuition   296–8, 300–1
invocation   36, 50–2, 54–6, 95
Island of the Blessed   271
Isles of the Blest (*also* Blessed)   121–2, 145, 264–5
Ithaca   29, 32, 41, 69
Iynges *see* Connectors

journey   3, 32–3, 39, 41, 44, 51, 54–5, 57, 94–5, 98–102, 105, 114, 117, 127–8, 169, 186, 248, 316, 318
– ascending   328–9
– philosophical   239
– soul's   138, 325
judgment   11, 139, 191, 211, 227, 260, 262, 264–5, 275–6, 278, 280, 282, 299–300, 302
justice   1, 52, 97, 123, 146, 148, 211–13, 220, 223–5, 227–9, 232, 236, 247, 264, 273, 286

karma   245, 257, 276, 287
katabasis   33, 39–40, 56, 101, 111–15, 124, 225, 229, 249
Katharmoi   42, 55
Kingsley, Peter   3, 24
Kirk, G.S.   22
Kokytos   131, 141
Kore   167

Lauenstein, Diether   158
Lenz, John   26
Lesky, Albin   64, 66–7
Lewy, Hans   318
liberation   10, 141, 196, 216, 255–6, 258, 264, 270–1, 276, 321
life
– cycle of   164–5, 269
– earthly   298, 329
– eternal   106, 108, 164, 166, 189
– inner   63, 68, 82
– new   106, 113–14, 133, 137, 182, 281
– previous   205, 213, 237, 266, 273–4, 287, 305–6, 308
lifetime   27, 117, 122, 126–7, 240, 243, 246, 318
light   2–3, 14, 21–2, 26, 45, 87–8, 92–6, 101–2, 106–7, 115–16, 123, 166, 172–3, 181, 186, 188, 224, 235, 256, 281, 291, 309, 315, 335, 350–2
– ethereal   350, 352, 354
Longinus   324, 339
lottery   212, 266–7
Lydians   229–30

Majercik, Ruth   320
Malinar, Angelika   321
Mansfeld, Jaap   87
meadows   122, 125, 136, 139, 144–5, 163, 172
measurement, art of   207–9
mediation   77, 164–5, 329
memory   14, 27, 53, 56, 148, 240, 251, 254, 266–8, 279, 289–90, 292, 295–8, 300–11
Menelaus   71, 74–5
Menn, Stephen   26
Meno   148, 244, 248, 251, 253, 302–3
messenger   78, 164–5, 179
metaphysics   16–17, 282
Miltiades   111
Minos   122–3, 141, 146
Mnemosyne   138–9
modernity   2, 4, 61, 67, 76
Morrison, J.S.   96, 100–1
mortal condition   7, 16, 137
mortality   16–17, 19–20, 25, 220, 222
mortals   6–7, 11, 16–17, 19–21, 23, 50, 55, 59–60, 108, 164–6, 168, 187, 195, 234, 257, 319, 329, 343, 354
Muses   50, 52–7, 88, 95, 341
Mylonas, George E.   159–60, 176, 181, 183–5
mystai   39, 138, 143, 167, 169–74, 180–1, 183–4, 188
mysteries   5, 33, 37, 47, 55, 91, 100, 108, 115, 143, 155, 214, 226–7, 229, 246, 252–3, 259, 315, 333, 337
– greater   184
– lesser   183–4
– lower and higher   166
– highest   155
– of Demter   107
– of Demeter or Dionysus   91
– of Demeter and Kore   167
myth   5–6, 85, 89, 93, 107, 110, 125–6, 128, 130, 148, 162–3, 211, 216–18, 221, 223, 225–6, 232, 236–7, 240, 250–1, 256, 261–4, 267–9, 275–6, 347–8

Naassene Gnostic   154–5, 159, 182, 189
nature   1–2, 13–14, 21, 25, 60, 64, 66, 73, 78, 80–2, 97, 179, 197, 214, 220, 228, 231–2, 238, 284–5, 290–1, 309–10, 330–1, 335–6, 344, 355
Nausicaa (also Nausikaa)   32, 34–6, 38, 49, 54, 56, 69, 71, 75
necessity   50, 115, 136–7, 236–7, 265, 268, 276, 280, 283–4, 327, 331, 337
Neikos   48, 55–6
Neoplatonism   343
Neoplatonists (also Neo-Platonists)   22, 29, 32, 104, 279, 288, 315, 333, 339, 341
Nestor   78–9
Netherworld   34, 112, 117, 119, 121–5, 127–30, 132, 134–7, 140, 141–6, 148
Nilsson, Martin P.   177, 183–4
Ninnion   183–4
Ninnion Tablet   176, 181, 184, 187
nomos   225, 228, 231–2, 236
non-being   102, 114, 116
nostos   32, 36
nostos poems   31
Numenius   132–3

oblivion   17, 125, 137–8
Oceanus   131–2
Odysseus   16, 19, 29, 31–9, 41, 44–5, 47–9, 51, 54, 56, 69, 72–3, 78, 102, 239, 268, 308
soul of   212, 268
Odyssey   19, 29–31, 33–4, 36–7, 42–4, 47–50, 55–6, 69, 308
Oedipus   22, 230
oracle   232–3, 323–8, 335, 351
organism   293, 297–8, 308
Orpheus   33, 57, 85–6, 89, 100, 104, 115, 122, 131–2, 135–7, 144–5, 247

Orphic eschatologies   46, 118, 137, 140, 145–6
Orphic Poems   124, 131, 134
Orphic poetry   57
Orphic-Pythagoreans   248, 251, 264
Orphic sources   121, 131, 134, 144–5
Orphics   118–21, 123–4, 127–8, 131–2, 134, 136, 138, 140–1, 144, 146–8, 167, 192, 261, 277

pain   13, 207–8, 213, 223, 262, 266, 277, 283, 305, 332, 334
Pamphylian   136, 237
Pandarus   72, 74–8
paradise   51, 141–2, 145
Parmenides   1, 3, 10, 21–2, 41, 49, 54, 57, 85–7, 89–96, 98–105, 107, 109, 114–15, 249
passion   82, 198, 222, 258, 284, 308, 319, 329, 334
path   25, 40, 51, 56, 86–7, 89–91, 93–4, 96, 99, 101–3, 105–8, 113–14, 116, 124, 125, 128–9, 138–9, 143, 165, 191, 197, 214, 239, 250, 275, 321–2, 326–7
paths of night and day (*also* day and night)   96–8, 102
penalty   49, 74, 97, 203, 248, 253, 255, 260–2, 272, 274
Penelope   68–9, 71, 75, 78
perception   22, 295, 300, 302–3, 315, 332
Persephone   10, 33, 38–9, 49, 125, 139, 157, 163–6, 168, 170, 173–5, 177–84, 188, 253–5
– return of   165
Persephone's rape   178
Persians   185, 316, 318, 341
Phaedo (*also* Phd.)   7, 10, 16, 30, 117–18, 126, 130, 133, 144–8, 210–16, 220, 222, 244–5, 248–9, 250–3, 259–60, 262, 264–5, 269, 270–2, 274–5, 278, 282, 302–3, 332–3, 337
Phaedrus (*also* Phdr.)   10, 17, 117, 156, 244, 249, 251, 256, 258–9, 264, 266, 269–71, 276, 278, 280, 303–4, 337, 347–8
Pherai   39, 130, 139
philosopher   1, 6–7, 14, 17, 19–20, 24, 59, 65, 75, 118, 127, 130, 132–6, 138, 140, 146–9, 191–2, 197–8, 202–6, 213, 216, 219–20, 239, 257, 269–71, 273, 282, 284, 324, 333–4, 339, 343, 347
philosophical soteriology   6, 197
philosophy   1–3, 6–9, 18–20, 25–7, 52, 86, 102, 115, 128, 141, 151–3, 156, 191, 197, 202, 207, 209, 213–16, 219, 237–41, 313–17, 333, 340–1, 343–4, 349
Philotes   43, 49, 54–6
Physika   47
piety   40, 95, 228–9, 232
pigs   180–1, 187, 259
– sacrifice of   174, 181
Pindar (*also* Pind.)   45–6, 52, 90–1, 93, 97, 121–3, 125, 142, 145–7, 167, 246, 248, 253–4, 260
Plato   2, 4–5, 14–17, 24–6, 117–19, 121–3, 128–9, 131–2, 134–40, 147–8, 151–3, 156–7, 187, 189–92, 200–4, 206–11, 213–18, 229–30, 238–41, 243–9, 263–5, 272–88, 323–5, 331–3, 346–8
Platonic dialogues (*also* Plato's dialogues)   24, 26, 198, 221, 244, 277, 282
Platonic eschatology   141, 266, 287
Platonic myths   148, 217, 268
Platonic philosophy   4, 222, 324, 343
Platonism   2, 82, 243, 340, 343
Plato's eschatological myths   27, 277
Plotinus   23, 27, 243–4, 247, 276–90, 292–8, 301–4, 306–8, 311, 313–17, 323–41, 343–4, 346, 355
Plouton   172–3, 177
Plutarch   22, 143, 154, 156, 159, 189, 198
politics   26, 217, 219, 223–4, 237–9, 241

Index of terms

Porphyry   288–9, 302, 313–18, 324–31, 339, 341, 347–51, 353
Poseidon   31, 35, 56, 121, 194, 203
power   13, 38, 53, 56, 67, 75–6, 78, 80–3, 105–6, 120, 197, 203, 205, 219, 221, 223–4, 227, 230–3, 235–6, 278, 281, 284, 295, 301, 343–4
– image-making   295–6
power of appearance   207
power of invisibility   225
prayer   36, 40, 50–1, 95, 129, 198, 310, 348
preservation   13–14, 124, 196–7, 206, 222–3, 290, 296
Presocratics   1, 22, 97
priestess   99, 109, 240, 248, 253, 351
priest   44, 53, 106, 109, 183, 186, 248, 253, 343, 347, 351–2
procession   161, 167–8, 170, 174, 183–4, 277
Proclus   29, 59–60, 75–6, 100, 131–2, 314–16, 330, 339, 341
proem   22, 32, 85–8, 92, 98, 102–3, 106, 115
Protagoras   199–200, 206–9, 213, 215–16
punishments   39, 52, 112, 117, 119–20, 124, 126, 133–5, 139–40, 143, 145–7, 210–11, 225, 244, 248, 253–4, 259–60, 262–4, 266–7, 270, 273–5, 277, 280–2, 284, 286
– post-mortem   247, 260, 264
pure soul   313–15, 317, 320–3, 326–30, 334–41
purification   7, 27, 180–1, 187, 211, 222, 252, 259, 274, 313, 320, 331, 333–4, 337–41
purity   127, 172, 257, 319, 321, 327–8, 336, 338, 345–6
pyre   218, 221, 235, 237
Pythagoras   7, 33, 57, 109–10, 112–16, 132, 222, 246–8, 314, 317, 323–4, 331, 339

Rashed, Marwan   41, 48

rational formulas   291, 294–6, 299–302
rational soul   350, 352–4
rebirth   106–8, 191–2, 216, 243, 245–6, 253, 256, 260, 262, 264–5, 270, 272–3, 276–7, 280
rebirth cycle   27, 191–2, 216, 243–4, 246, 248, 254, 256, 258–9, 268, 270–1, 273, 276–7, 280
rebirth eschatology   244, 247, 249, 251, 253, 255, 257, 259, 261, 263, 265, 267, 269, 271, 273, 275–7, 279, 281, 283, 285, 287
recognition   50, 62, 299, 302
recollection   240, 253, 302–3, 305
reincarnation   53, 125–6, 134–5, 139, 144, 247, 264, 305
religion   1–3, 5–6, 8–9, 17, 33, 107–8, 123, 142, 154, 191–2, 198, 209, 261, 264, 317
reminiscence *see* memory
representations   290, 295–6, 299–302, 304–5
Republic (*also* Rep.)   8, 10, 12, 14, 16, 24–6, 30, 54, 59, 117–18, 125, 132, 135–6, 140, 144–8, 202, 204, 206, 211–18, 220–4, 226, 233–40, 244, 249–51, 258, 261–3, 269, 271–2, 275, 278, 280, 283–4, 287
– Republic, Plato's   11, 217, 221
responsibility   59, 61, 67, 73, 76–7, 82, 233, 237, 240, 259, 267, 276
return, soul's   287, 340, 354
revelation   1, 5, 49–50, 54, 87, 103, 113, 115, 166, 173, 186, 188
reward   55, 117, 119, 124, 128, 133–5, 140, 143, 146, 211–12, 214, 225, 233, 244, 259–62, 264, 266, 270, 273, 275, 281–2, 285, 287
Rhadamanthys   122, 141
rhetoric   26, 200–2, 210, 212, 215–16
Riedweg, Christoph   5, 24
rite   106, 108, 110–1, 113, 115–6, 127, 135, 143, 156, 159–60, 164,

166–8, 170–73, 173, 175, 223, 259, 315, 331, 340, 347, 352–3
ritual   3, 9, 127, 129, 135, 146, 148, 157, 159, 229, 340, 343, 349, 351–2, 354
ritual descent   3, 24, 225, 227
ritual practice   27, 191, 333, 346, 349–50, 353–4
River of Forgetfulness   137, 223, 240, 268
river   32, 35–8, 51, 130–2, 137, 141, 144–5, 215, 223, 240, 259, 268, 279
ruler   12–13, 52–3, 59, 104, 205, 218–19, 223, 227

sacrifice   10, 49, 129, 165–6, 174–5, 181, 187, 195, 198, 211–12, 216, 225, 261, 322, 348–9, 352
salvation   2–3, 5–7, 9–11, 13–15, 17–18, 20, 25–7, 29, 33, 36, 38–40, 44–5, 47, 51, 55–6, 59–60, 148, 191–2, 197–8, 201–2, 206, 213, 221–4, 241, 320
– doctrine of   9, 15, 20, 191
salvation of souls   201, 206
Sattler, Barbara   24, 26
satyrs   177–9
savior   9, 12, 191–2, 194–9, 203–7, 223
scales   123–5
Scheria   32, 35, 44
Schmitt, Arbogast   26
Seaford, Richard   47, 258
secrecy   153, 156, 159, 168, 175, 259
– vow of   154, 171
sensation   289–90, 293–302, 305, 308
– data of   299, 302
senses   205, 258, 295, 300–1, 321, 332–3
separation   10, 113, 307, 320, 326, 332–4, 338, 349, 352, 354
– from the body   320, 326, 332, 338, 349, 354
– of body and soul   113
– of the elements   10

shade   16, 18, 59, 307–9
shipwreck   194, 197, 199, 201
sieve   120, 135, 144, 147, 261
sight   21–2, 205, 207, 328, 335
Simonides   194
singularity   15–17, 25
sins   139, 244, 258, 280–1, 323
– pure of   322, 327
Skarsouli, Penelope   52
Skias, A.   382
Slaveva-Griffin, Svetla   27
sleep   20–1, 269, 328
Snell, Bruno   63–8
Socrates   7–8, 10, 17, 25, 119–20, 122–3, 126–8, 133, 137, 146, 148, 200–3, 207–8, 210–12, 214, 217, 220, 222–4, 226–9, 233, 235–40, 248–52, 258–9, 273, 302–3
– death of   16, 134
Solon   52–3, 218–19, 234–5, 239, 267
sophist   16, 198, 200, 202, 207, 230
soteriology   9–11, 14–15, 17, 19, 191, 279, 313
soul   29–31, 33–4, 36–40, 117–30, 132–4, 136–41, 143–8, 200–2, 205–7, 209–12, 214–16, 240–1, 243–8, 252–62, 267–70, 274–5, 277–85, 287–94, 296–8, 300–9, 313–15, 322–3, 325–41, 343–7, 352–5
– arrived   10, 139
– descended   292–3, 297, 299, 305, 307–9, 311
– descendent   337–8
– discarnate   256, 266, 272
– disembodied   250
– exiled   29–32, 57
– first   137, 336
– the first principle of the   314, 334
– higher   280, 284, 287, 291, 293, 308
– hypostasis of   287, 290
– immortal   226, 258, 261, 269
– impure   337
– irrational   350–1
– non-philosophical   272

- lower 280–1, 287, 293
- mortal 18–19, 258
- the other kind of 334
- philosophic 268
- primordial descent of 257, 280
- theurgist's 322
- total 290
- undescended 279, 293, 303, 311
- undescendent 334–6
- universal 287, 338

soul's afterlife journey 220
soul's ascent 317–18, 324, 339, 346, 349
soul's character 266, 268, 276, 283
soul's destiny 4, 118, 121, 132, 144, 148, 311
soul's embodiments 256, 277, 337
soul's faculties 295, 297
soul's imprisonment 253–4
soul's otherworldliness 331
stars 257, 283, 310, 334, 348, 350
Stoics 197–8, 290, 293, 297
Styx 131–3
substance 159–60, 336, 350
sufferings 29, 37, 49, 125, 142, 147, 268, 282
sun 31–2, 85, 93, 96–7, 105–6, 108, 113–14, 116, 173–4, 226, 253, 318
sunset 96, 105
superior classes 345–6, 348–9, 351, 355
suppliant 34–8, 125
supplication 26, 34, 36–7, 39–40, 51, 55
sympathy 285, 310
Symposium (also Symp.) 151, 155–7, 160, 187–9, 190, 198, 204, 249, 325, 330–1, 343–4, 348

tablets see Gold Leaves
Tarán, Leonardo 87–8
Tartarus 98, 121–2, 126, 131, 133, 143, 145, 262, 264–5
tattooing 110–11
Telemachus 68–71, 73, 75, 78
teletai 143–4, 146, 148

Teletarchs 318–19
temple 164, 184–5, 203
temporality 20–1, 23, 232, 310
Theaetetus 16, 207, 209–10, 222, 226, 337–8
theology 6–8, 17, 191, 206
Theogony see Hesiod's Theogony
- of Orpheus 86, 89, 100, 104
- of Epimenedes 89, 103
theurgist 319, 322, 343, 351–4
theurgy 27, 316, 320, 340, 343–4, 353
thigh, golden 110–12
thought, discursive 297, 299–300, 315
throne 137, 180, 231, 254
Thurii 34, 36–7, 125, 127, 139
Timaeus 10–11, 17, 197, 244, 256–7, 259, 264, 272, 277–8, 280, 284–5, 309, 314, 330, 334, 337–8
Titans 94, 254, 279
torch 141, 144, 147, 166, 168, 172–3, 180–4, 186, 188–9
transmigration 113, 114–15, 128, 134, 147, 243, 246, 247
- and rebirth 243, 246
- doctrine of or theory of or idea of 114, 128, 134
- of souls 113, 134, 243
trial 126, 130, 133–4, 145–6, 199, 202
- of Socrates 16
- of souls 123, 125, 141, 143, 146
Triptolemos 161, 167, 179, 182
Trojan 19, 21, 70, 74–5, 77, 79
Trouillard, Jean 340
tyranny 195–6, 213
tyrant 136–7, 142, 195–6, 212–13, 227, 230, 232, 257, 262–3

underworld 5, 10, 16, 33–4, 39, 54, 56, 105, 107, 118, 120, 134, 140, 144, 147, 163, 165–6, 168–71, 173, 177, 179, 182, 186–8, 249–50, 252–3
Underworld Journey 33

union   287, 297, 308, 320, 322, 326–8, 341, 354
– soul's   317, 328, 337, 341
universe   11, 20, 22–3, 133, 136, 141, 227, 237, 243–4, 256, 269, 275–6, 291, 293, 295, 306, 308, 311, 344, 346
Unparticipated Soul   355

vegetation   163–5, 168, 182
vegetative soul   291–3, 297, 308, 311
vehicle   293, 305, 350, 353–4
victory   12–13, 45, 74, 77, 205, 317
virtue   12–13, 59, 133, 197–8, 200–1, 206–7, 213, 223, 237, 246, 250, 253, 259, 268, 275–6, 280, 282, 284, 304, 310, 333, 337–8
– civic   338, 340
– political   26, 206, 209, 213, 216
– purificatory   334, 338, 340
vision   68, 77, 136, 144, 147, 197, 229, 252, 263, 295, 305, 332, 341
Vita Plotini *see* VP
Vlastos, Gregory   1–2, 8, 221
VP (Vita Plotini)   313, 315–17, 323–9, 331–2, 335, 339, 341

wanderer   7, 44, 46, 51, 57

wandering hero   29–31, 39, 41, 56
wanderings   25–6, 29, 31–3, 35, 37, 40–3, 46–8, 94, 166, 173, 219, 234, 290, 292, 305
water   22, 120, 125, 131–2, 135, 137–8, 144, 147, 215, 223, 261, 351–2
wisdom   1, 33, 51, 104, 113, 133, 198, 210, 213, 216, 219, 233–5, 240–1, 253–4, 268, 322, 324, 333, 338
world
– intelligible   243, 277–8, 282, 287, 304
– material   277, 318–19, 326, 328, 330, 337, 340, 351
– sensible   211, 214, 287, 295, 298–9, 304
world soul (*also* world-soul)   277, 290–4, 308–9, 311

Xanthias   173–4
Xenophon   167–8, 197, 204

Zagreus myth   254
Zeus   1, 20–1, 32, 37, 47, 56, 64, 72, 74, 77–81, 86, 103–4, 121–3, 163–4, 168, 192–3, 199, 206, 254, 308–10, 348

www.ingramcontent.com/pod-product-compliance
Lightning Source LLC
Chambersburg PA
CBHW071809230426
43670CB00013B/2408